A Student's Guide to Unix

A Student's Guide to Unix

Harley Hahn

McGraw-Hill, Inc.
New York St. Louis San Francisco Auckland Bogotá
Caracas Lisbon London Madrid Mexico City Milan
Montreal New Delhi San Juan Singapore
Sydney Tokyo Toronto

A Student's Guide to Unix

4567890 DOC DOC 90987654

ISBN 0-07-025511-3

Executive Editor: Eric M. Munson
Production Supervisors: Denise L. Puryear and Michele Armstrong
Cover Design: Caliber/Phoenix Color Corporation
Copy Editor: Lunaea Hougland
Produced by Print Producers, Los Angeles
Printed and bound by R. R. Donnelly & Sons Company

Library of Congress Catalog Card Number: 92-63095

About the Author

Harley Hahn is an internationally recognized author, analyst and consultant, specializing in Unix and other operating systems. He is the author of many highly regarded books, including the popular *Peter Norton's Guide to Unix*.

Hahn has an undergraduate degree in mathematics and computer science from the University of Waterloo, Canada, and a graduate degree in computer science from the University of California at San Diego.

Hahn has written ten books and over fifty technical articles and papers. He is an active participant in the Unix community and is widely regarded as a master explainer whose writing is known for its clarity and insight.

To my lovely wife, Kimberlyn,
and to my parents, Murray and Marilyn Hahn.

List of Chapters

Appendixes

Table of Contents

List of Figures and Tables

Introduction

This book will change your life.

That's a strange thing to say about a computer book, but, as sure as you are reading this introduction, your life will be different by the time you finish the book.

You will think differently, and you will approach problems differently. No matter what you think of computers now, you will like them better.

You see, computers aren't really lifeless, mechanical pieces of machinery. They are tools. Tools that change and interact with your very thought processes. The magic is not in the box itself, but what happens inside the box when you turn it on and run a program.

What is Unix? Unix is a system that makes the computer behave in a certain way. Unix provides a set of tools for solving problems, talking with other people and having fun. Unix runs on virtually every computer that is made. Although there are many variations, Unix works pretty much the same no matter what computer you happen to use (which is one reason why it is so popular).

The key point to understand is that the computer only does what it is programmed to do. This means that when you work with Unix, you are not working with a computer. You are working with the people who designed Unix. Every line you read on your display screen was put there by a person. Every tool you use was invented by a person. Every new word that you learn was spoken by a person. When you use Unix, you are interacting with these people, just as you are interacting with me as you read this book.

What makes Unix so wonderful is that the people who invented it were bright, creative and had a good sense of humor. They were very, very smart, and they knew what they were doing.

So, it really doesn't matter why you want to learn Unix or why you picked up this book. Don't worry if someone is forcing you to learn Unix against your will. Don't worry if you know nothing about computers. You might even hate computers. It doesn't matter.

The title of this book is *A Student's Guide to Unix*. Although the book is oriented toward the university/college environment, that is not what the word "student" refers to in the title. This book is for *anyone* who wants to learn Unix. Do you work for a company that uses Unix? Are you part of a school (student, staff member, teacher, professor)? Do you have your own Unix computer? Do you have access to any type of Unix system? Then you are a student, and I wrote this book for you.

This is not your average computer book. (I'm sure you realize that by now.) Aside from a large amount of technical material, there are hints, jokes and a lot of plain-spoken advice. I did the very best I could to show what you really need to know. This is not a computer manual. This is not a compendium of impersonal details. This is one person (me) talking to another person (you).

Buy this book. I am on your side.

Acknowledgments

A lot of people help with a book like this. Let's start with the six most important. First, we have Cathy Eichlin, the typesetter and project manager, and Lunaea Hougland, the copy editor. These two fine people spent many long hours slaving over a hot computer (and a hot manuscript) to make sure that everything you read is correct and looks perfect. If you like the way this book looks, thank Cathy the typesetting goddess.

If you like the fact that all the commas are correct, thank Lunaea. (If you ever happen to meet Lunaea, be sure to ask her about quotation marks. There is something about the unstudied majesty of her discourse upon so prosaic a subject that can make even the lowly quotation mark shine forth with the brilliance of a semicolon. "Age cannot wither her," you will find yourself saying, "nor custom stale her infinite variety.")

The other four people whose help was essential are all accomplished Unix experts. Each of these people read and reviewed every chapter of this book, line by line. Their effort was immense, and they deserve great thanks. (If any of you four are reading this, be sure to drop by some time and we'll do lunch.)

First, there is Mark Schildhauer, system manager of the Social Science Computing Facility at the University of California, Santa Barbara. One of the best system managers in the business, Mark is a true gentleman. His insight into what users need is profound and greatly contributed to the success of this book.

Second, I would like to thank John Navarra at Northwestern University in Evanston, Illinois. John, also known as The MaD ScIenTIst, is a respected participant in the Unix question-and-answer newsgroup on Usenet (see Chapter 23). There might be some technical aspect of Unix that John doesn't know about, but if there is I have yet to find it.

Next comes Michael Peirce from Trinity College at the University of Dublin in Ireland. Michael is currently the holder of the Northern European record for finding mistakes in Unix book manuscripts. If you are ever thinking of writing a computer book, let me give you a hint: think twice before sending your manuscript to Michael. He is so thorough and so clever that his changes and suggestions will keep you busy for weeks.

Finally, we have Michael Schuster at the Technical University of Vienna in Austria. Michael gave generously of his time and energy during many late-night conversations over the Internet. (See the `talk` command in Chapter 12.) He is a wonderful fellow whose help made a significant difference to this book.

(Michael, by the way, holds the Southern European record for finding mistakes in Unix book manuscripts. It is certainly a humbling experience to have your grammar corrected by someone who learned English as a second language.)

The next group of people contributed by reading the original plan for this book and sharing generously of their comments and suggestions.

Ajay Shah:	University of Southern California
Bruce Varney:	Purdue University
Herb Lam:	Unocal Corporation
Howard C. Huang:	Harvard University
Jerry Whelan:	Bradley University
Jim Davis:	National Optical Astronomy Observatories
Lup-Houh Ng:	University of Michigan, Ann Arbor
Malachy Devlin:	Strathclyde University, Glasgow, Scotland
Meg Grice:	University of Missouri, Kansas City
Michael Charlton:	University of Manitoba, Winnipeg, Canada
Michaela Harlander:	Technical University of Munich, Germany
Paul Joslin:	GE Aircraft Engines, Ohio
Peter Deutsch:	McGill University, Montreal, Canada
Sam Sampath:	IBM Research Division, Yorktown Heights
Sathis Menon:	Georgia Tech University
Simona Nass:	Yeshiva University, New York
Stephane Bortzmeyer:	Conservatoire National des Arts et Metiers, Paris
Tom Millis:	Birmingham, Michigan
Tristram Mabbs:	Canterbury, Kent, England

During the writing of the book, the following people provided technical expertise and assistance:

Bart Miller:	University of Wisconsin
Gene Spafford:	Purdue University
Heidi Stettner:	BASIS Incorporated, Berkeley
Jeremy ☺ Smith:	ManTech Environmental Services
John December:	Rensselaer Polytechnic Institute
Jonathan Kamens:	Aktis Incorporated, Massachusetts
Mark McCahill:	University of Minnesota
Mike Ramey:	University of Washington
Milt Epstein:	University of Illinois
Mitchell Porter:	Brisbane, Australia
Paul Lindner:	University of Minnesota
Scott Yanoff:	University of Wisconsin, Milwaukee
Steven Foster:	University of Nevada at Reno
Todd C. Tibbetts:	3M Health Information Systems, Connecticut

At McGraw-Hill College Division, I would like to thank Eric Munson, the executive editor who initiated the project, Holly Stark, his editorial assistant, and Joe Murphy, the senior editing manager who managed the production.

For professional, courteous delivery service – more important than most people realize – I thank Ruben Solis Campo of the Santa Barbara Federal Express office. For driving to the Los Angeles airport in a fierce rainstorm to deliver a crucial part of the manuscript, I thank Jonathan Eichlin.

And, finally, for her enthusiasm and encouragement, I thank my wife, Kimberlyn Hahn.

Harley Hahn

A Student's Guide to Unix

Introduction to Unix

What This Book Is About

This book is about Unix: a computer system that is used throughout the world and runs on virtually all types of computers.

The first Unix system was developed in 1969 by a programmer so he could run a "Space Travel" program. Unix today is nothing less than a worldwide culture, comprising many tools, ideas and customs.

The full details of Unix – which long ago ceased to be a single computer system – are well beyond human understanding. In other words, there is no single person who knows everything about Unix. In fact, there is no single person who knows even most of Unix.

The Unix culture – which you are about to enter – contains an enormous number of tools for you to use. You can create and manipulate information in more ways than you can imagine; you can send messages and talk with people almost anywhere in the world; you can play games, create documents, and write your own computer programs; and you can participate in ongoing discussions on hundreds of different subjects with people all over the world.

To use Unix, all you need is access to a Unix computer. For most people in a university environment, such access is available for free. This means that the facilities of Unix – the tools, the electronic mail system, the games, the discussion groups – are all waiting for you. All you need to do is learn how to use the system and how to participate in the culture.

This book will teach you what you need to know to get started and a lot more.

Although Unix may be free to you (in the sense that it does not cost you money out of your pocket), you should realize that someone, somewhere, is paying a lot of money and devoting a lot of time to maintain the system. Part of learning Unix is understanding what it means to be a responsible, honest and polite user – after all, we are sharing limited resources. In this book, we will discuss not only how to use Unix, but what it means to be a member of the Unix community.

The Unix Language

Around the world, the first language of Unix is American English. Nevertheless, Unix systems and documentation have been translated into many other languages, and it is not necessary to know English, as long as your system works in your language. However, as you explore the worldwide Unix-based network, you will probably find that much of the information and many of the discussion groups are in English.

In addition, the Unix community has introduced many new words of its own. In this book, we will pay particular attention to these terms. Each new word is explained and defined as it is introduced. For easy reference, all the definitions are collected into a glossary at the end of the book.

When we come to a name with a particularly colorful history, we will give a special explanation inside a box like this:

WHAT'S IN A NAME?

Unix   In the 1960s, a number of researchers at Bell Labs (a part of AT&T) worked at MIT on a project called Multics. The name was an acronym for "Multiplexed Information and Computing Service". (The word "multiplex" refers to combining multiple electronic signals into a single signal.)

By the late 1960s, the management at Bell Labs decided not to pursue Multics and moved their researchers back into the lab. In 1969, one of these researchers, Ken Thompson, developed a simple, small operating system for a PDP-7 minicomputer. In searching for a name, Thompson compared his new system to Multics.

The goal of Multics was to offer many features to multiple users at the same time. Multics was large and unwieldy and had many problems.

Thompson's system was smaller, less ambitious and (at least at the beginning) was used by one person at a time. Moreover, each part of the system was designed to do only one thing and to do it well. Thompson decided to name his system Unics (the "Uni" meaning "one", as in unicycle), which was soon changed to Unix.

In other words, the name Unix is a pun on the name Multics.

Throughout the book, we print certain names in boldface, usually the names of commands. This allows you to see immediately that a word is a special Unix term. Here is an example:

"To copy a file, you use the Unix **cp** command. To remove (erase) a file, you use the **rm** command."

Hints for Learning Unix

As you read, you will notice many hints for learning Unix. These are ideas and shortcuts that we have found to be important, for newcomers and experienced users alike. To emphasize these hints, we present them in a special format that looks like this:

 HINT Unix is fun.

Getting the Most from this Book

We have designed this book to make it easy for you to find what you need quickly. Before you start, take a moment to examine the various parts of the book.

First, look at the Quick Index on the inside back cover. This is a list of every command covered in this book and where to look for the discussion and examples.

Second, take a glance at the Quick Index for **vi** (the principal Unix text editing program). Once you learn how to use **vi**, you will find this index especially helpful.

Of course, there is also the standard general index. Spend a few minutes now to skim through it (always a good idea with a new book). This will give a rough idea of the new ideas that you will be meeting and what we will be emphasizing.

Aside from the glossary and the indexes, there are two summaries of Unix commands, also at the back of the book. These summaries contain one-line descriptions of each Unix command.

One summary lists the commands in alphabetical order; the other summary groups the commands by category. These summaries are a good place to check if you want to do something and are not sure what command to use. Once you have found your command, check with the Quick Index to see what page to read.

If you want to find the discussion of a particular topic, you can, of course, use the general index. Alternately, you can look up the appropriate term in the glossary. Along with each definition, you will find a reference to the chapter in which that term is explained. Once you know the chapter you want, a quick look at the table of contents will show you what section to read.

What We Assume in this Book

In this book, we make two important assumptions as to what type of Unix system you are using.

First, as you will see in Chapter 2, there are many versions of Unix, based on two principal variations: Berkeley Unix and System V Unix. Modern Unix systems combine the most important elements from both of these types. Thus, for the most part, it doesn't matter what type of Unix you are using.

We have oriented this book toward the needs of people who work in the academic and research communities, not toward a particular type of Unix. Nevertheless, for some aspects of your work, there is a choice between the Berkeley or System V functionality. In such cases, we will lean toward the Berkeley conventions as these are the more popular.

Second, as you will see in Chapter 4, the program that reads and interprets the commands you type is called the "shell". In Chapter 10, we will explain that there are various shells that you might choose to use. Almost all of the time, it doesn't really matter what shell you use. However, in those few places where it does matter, we will use the C-Shell. If you want to use another shell, that is fine. A few details may be different, but you won't have any real problems.

Since you are just starting, such distinctions may not be all that meaning-ful. Not to worry: if you are using Unix in an academic or research environment, you are most likely using the C-Shell along with some form of Berkeley Unix. In fact, the newest versions of System V contains most of Berkeley Unix.

What We Do Not Assume in this Book

If you are an experienced computer user who wants to learn about Unix, this book will get you started and provide you with a firm background in all the important areas.

However, we do not assume that you have any prior experience. It's okay if you have never really used a computer. You do not need to know anything about Unix. You do not need to be a programmer, nor do you need to know anything about electronics or mathematics.

We will explain everything you need to know. Work at your own speed and enjoy yourself.

How to Use this Book

Before we start, it is important to realize that the world of Unix is bursting with information. As we mentioned earlier, it is impossible to learn everything about Unix, so don't even try. Concentrate on what you need and what you think you will enjoy. To get started, you should probably read the first six chapters. They will introduce you to Unix and teach you the basic skills.

 HINT   It is impossible to learn everything about Unix. Concentrate on what you need and what you think you will enjoy.

After you are oriented to Unix, and you know how to start and stop a work session, enter commands and use the keyboard, you can read the rest of the book in any order you want.

Although every effort has been made to make each chapter as independent as possible, you should realize that each topic is dependent on other topics. There is no perfect place to start learning Unix and no perfect order in which to study the various topics.

For example, say that the main reason you want to learn Unix is to send and receive electronic mail. Naturally, it makes sense to read the chapter on the Unix mail program (Chapter 14) as soon as possible.

However, before you study this chapter, you may want to read the chapter that explains how the Unix mail system is organized (Chapter 13). In order to compose messages, it is handy to already know how to use the Unix text editing program (Chapter 19). And since you may want to save your messages, you should know how to store data in files. This means that you should already understand the file system (Chapter 20), the commands to display your files (Chapter 17), as well as the commands to manipulate your files (Chapters 19 and 20). And, of course, before you can type in messages, you need to understand how to start a work session (Chapters 4 and 5) and how to use the Unix keyboard (Chapter 6).

Obviously, this sort of approach leads nowhere fast, but it does underscore the most important principle that you need to understand at the outset: Unix was not designed to be learned; Unix was designed to be used. In other words, it can be confusing and time-consuming to learn Unix. However, once you have mastered the skills that you need, for whatever work you want to do, working with Unix is fast and easy.

If you think back to when you learned how to drive a car, you will remember that it was anything but easy. Once you had some experience, though, your actions became smooth and automatic. By now, you can probably drive all day with one hand on the wheel as you listen to the radio and talk to other people.

Let us embody this idea as the following hint:

 HINT   Unix is easy to use, but difficult to learn.

Remember, once you have read the first few chapters of this book, you can teach yourself any topic in any order. If you come across an idea or skill that you do not yet understand, you can either pause for a quick look at another chapter, or skip the part that confuses you and learn it later. This is how people learn Unix in real life: a bit at a time, depending on what they need at the moment.

Don't worry about memorizing every detail. In some chapters, we treat topics in depth. Learn what seems interesting and useful to you and just skim the rest. If you know the basics and you have an idea as to what is available, you can always return to the details when you need them.

 HINT   Start by learning the basics. Then learn whatever you want, in whatever order you want.

What Is Unix?

In this chapter, we will orient ourselves to the world of Unix: what it does, where we find it, the variations, and the culture that has grown up around it. To lay the groundwork, we start with a discussion of the fundamental component of any computer system: the operating system.

What Is an Operating System?

Computers perform tasks automatically by following instructions. A list of instructions is called a PROGRAM. As the computer follows the instructions, we say that it RUNS or EXECUTES the program. In general, programs are referred to as SOFTWARE, while the physical components of the computer are referred to as HARDWARE. The hardware includes the keyboard, mouse, display screen, printers, disk drives and so on.

An OPERATING SYSTEM (which is software) is a complex master control program whose principal function is to make efficient use of the hardware. To do so, the operating system acts as the primary interface to the hardware. The operating system helps you (to do your work) and helps programs (as they execute).

For example, when you type a command to display the names of your data files, the operating system does the actual work of finding the names and displaying them on your screen. When you run a program that needs to open a new data file, the operating system sets aside storage space for the data and takes care of all the details.

As you work, the operating system is always there, waiting to serve you and to manage the resources of your computer. The most important jobs are: controlling how the computer's memory is used, maintaining a file storage

7

system, scheduling work to be done, and providing accounting and security services.

Most operating systems come with a variety of programs for you to use. For example, there will be a program to display the names of your data files. A Unix operating system comes with literally hundreds of such programs, each of which is a tool to perform one specific job.

"Unix" Can Refer to One Specific Operating System

In Chapter 1, we described how the first Unix system – in fact, a primitive operating system – was developed in 1969 by a single programmer. The work was done at Bell Labs, the research arm of AT&T. Since then, a large number of people have developed Unix into a modern family of operating systems.

For many years, Bell Labs remained one of the centers of Unix development. In 1990, AT&T formed a new organization, called Unix Systems Laboratory or USL, to take over the work. In June 1993, AT&T sold USL to Novell Corporation. In October 1993, Novell transferred rights to the name "Unix" to X/Open, an international standards organization. At one time, the name "UNIX" referred to the product from AT&T. Now, we use the more generic "Unix" to describe any operating system that meets certain specific standards.

The most modern direct descendent of the original AT&T UNIX is System V version 4, often referred to as System V.4. The "V" is the Roman numeral 5, and the name is usually pronounced as "System five-dot-four". You may also see SVR4, which means System V Release 4. SVR4 is pronounced "System five-R-four".

"Unix" Can Refer to a Family of Operating Systems

Since the 1970s, many other Unix operating systems have been developed. As a family, Unix operating systems all share two important characteristics: they are multitasking and multiuser timesharing systems. MULTITASKING means that a Unix system can run more than one program at a time. MULTIUSER means that Unix can support more than one user at a time.

When people talk about Unix as an operating system, they mean any operating system that is Unix-like. In this sense, the word "Unix" refers to any member of the family of Unix-like operating systems. For example, somebody might say, "I am thinking of buying my own personal computer. What types of Unix will run on it?"

One of the most important Unixes comes from the University of California at Berkeley. At first, Berkeley Unix was based on AT&T UNIX. However, the newest version was designed to be as free as possible of AT&T System V UNIX programming.

The official name of Berkeley Unix is BSD, an acronym standing for Berkeley Software Distribution. Thus, although it seems strange, "BSD", like "UNIX", is the name of an operating system. The most recent version of this operating system is BSD 4.4. The name is usually pronounced as "BSD four-point-four".

WHAT'S IN A NAME?

BSD   Berkeley Unix did not start off with a typical name. The original release – a variation of AT&T UNIX – came to be known as "the first Berkeley software distribution", which was abbreviated to 1BSD. The next major release was known as 2BSD and so on.

Today, Berkeley Unix has taken on a life of its own and, as an operating system, is known as BSD. Thus, a purist might say that the newest version of Berkeley Unix should really be called 4.4BSD, not BSD 4.4.

Although there are many types of Unix, virtually all of them are based on either BSD, System V, or both. In the academic and research communities, most people use a Unix that is based on both, with an emphasis on Berkeley Unix.

Figure 2-1 shows the names of the Unixes that you are likely to use at a university. The most common is probably Solaris or SunOS (the old name), running on a computer from Sun Microsystems. All of these Unixes are derived – at least in part – from Berkeley Unix and System V.

Name of Unix	Company
AIX	IBM
Dynix	Sequent
HP/UX	Hewlett-Packard (HP)
Nextstep	Next
Solaris	Sun Microsystems
SunOS	Sun Microsystems
System V UNIX	Some type of personal computer
Ultrix	Digital Equipment Corp. (DEC)

Figure 2-1
Types of Unix Commonly Used at Universities

Name of Unix	Company or Organization
386-BSD	free on the Internet
A/UX	Apple
BSD/386	Berkeley Software Design (BSDI)
Coherent	Mark Williams Company
Hurd (GNU)	Free Software Foundation
Linux	free on the Internet
Mach	Carnegie-Mellon University
MKS Toolkit	Mortice Kern Systems
Minix	included with book by Andy Tanenbaum
Nextstep 486	Next
SCO Unix	Santa Cruz Operation
Unixware	Novell

Figure 2-2
Other Unix or Unix-like Systems that You May Hear About

Figure 2-2 shows the names of other Unix or Unix-like systems that you may hear about within the Unix community. This, of course, is not a complete listing. There are many variations of Unix.

People often ask, how do you tell if a particular operating system is Unix? Although there is no universal agreement, the best answer is: If an operating system looks like Unix to you as you work, and if it looks like Unix to your programs as they execute, then it's Unix. In other words, Unix is whatever people call Unix.

"Unix" Is the Name of a Culture

Realistically, Unix means much more than a family of operating systems: Unix means computer networks, electronic mail, a great many programs (including games) and a very real culture based on these tools. The third and most important way to use the word "Unix" is as a name for the global community that we described in Chapter 1: the community that encompasses the Unix culture.

Some thoughtful people go further and consider Unix to be an abstract idea: an actual applied philosophy that dictates a particular approach to problem solving. This will make more sense to you as you learn more. In using Unix, you will learn to approach and solve problems by combining simple programs, like building blocks, into elegant structures. (You will learn about this in detail in Chapters 15 and 16.)

Perhaps the best definition of Unix – and the one that we would like you to remember as you read this book – is the following:

Unix is a set of tools for smart people.

 HINT   Unix is a set of tools for smart people.

What Is It Like to Use Unix?

Using Unix means interacting with a computer by using a keyboard and possibly a mouse. As you type (or move and click the mouse), you watch the screen on your display. From time to time, you may want to print something on paper.

To start a work session, you "log in". When you are finished working, you "log out". We will explain how all of this works in Chapter 4. Basically, you log in by typing your name and your password. After Unix verifies that you are allowed to use that particular computer system, you can start work. When you log out, it tells Unix that you are finished working and you are ready to stop.

The Unix Connection

The reason why Unix is so important is that any Unix computer can connect with any other Unix computer. As a result, we have countless computer networks and a worldwide Unix community. In this chapter, we will take a look at the connections that make this all possible. We start with the most basic connection of all: the one between you and the computer.

Hosts and Terminals

As we explained in Chapter 2, Unix is a multiuser timesharing system. That means that Unix computers can support more than one user at the same time. The main computer – the piece of hardware that actually does most of the work – is called the HOST. One of the jobs of the operating system is to make sure that the resources of the host are shared among all the users.

To work with Unix you use a TERMINAL. A basic Unix terminal consists of a display screen, a keyboard and not much more. (However, as we will see later, some terminals are more complex. In particular, X terminals, which we will discuss in Chapter 5, allow you to use a mouse to manipulate graphical images.)

Your terminal is connected to the host. As you type, or move the mouse, signals are sent to the host. A program running on the host interprets these signals and reacts appropriately.

When a host program needs to display output, it sends signals to your terminal, which then displays the appropriate information on your screen. Figure 3-1 shows the relationship between the host and the terminals. All Unix systems use this host-terminal relationship.

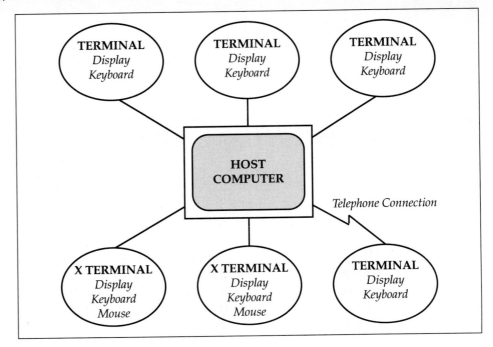

Figure 3-1
The Host-Terminal Relationship

What Happens When You Press a Key?

Each time you press a key, a signal is sent to the host. The host responds by sending its own signal back to your terminal telling it to display the appropriate character on the screen. For example, as you type the **date** command (to display the current time and date), your display shows the letters "date". However, your terminal does not display each letter until the host tells it to do so.

At first, this may seem strange. When you press the <d> key, it does not cause the symbol "d" to be displayed on your screen. Rather, the "d" signal is sent to the host, which then sends a signal to your terminal, which then displays the letter "d". We say that the host ECHOES the character to your display. In most cases, it happens so fast that it looks as if your keyboard is connected directly to your screen.

When you learn more about Unix, you will see that it is possible to use a host computer that is many miles away. In such cases, there will be times when the characters you type will not be echoed for a few seconds. In other words, you will press keys, but you will not see the letters appear on the screen immediately. This can happen if the host computer is far away and the communication line you are using happens to be slow.

As you type, your position on the screen is marked by the CURSOR. On most terminals, the cursor is an underscore character (_), or a small box, that blinks. The cursor shows you where the next character you type will be displayed. As you type, the cursor advances, one position at a time.

How Multiuser Systems Are Connected

Many Unix hosts are connected directly to terminals. All you have to do is turn on the terminal and you are ready to work. Some universities have rooms full of such terminals. If you look at the back of the terminal, you will see a wire that leads, ultimately, to the host computer. You may never see the actual host, which might be locked away in an office somewhere.

This system is adequate when all the terminals are used with only a single host computer. However, many computing facilities offer a variety of hosts. In such cases, your terminal will be connected to a special computer, called a TERMINAL SERVER, that acts as a switch.

After you turn on your terminal, you may need to type a command to the terminal server, telling it which host you want to use. For example, you might type:

```
connect compsci
```

to connect to a host named **compsci**. The terminal server then makes the connection for you. The advantage of using such a system is that any terminal can work with any of the host computers.

This configuration is illustrated in Figure 3-2.

The Console

Almost all host computers have a keyboard and display that are a part of the computer itself. As far as Unix is concerned, this keyboard and display are just another terminal. However, they are given a special name, the CONSOLE. In some sense, the console is built into the computer; all other terminals are separate and have to be connected.

A typical Unix system might use a host computer that sits in the office of the system manager. This computer could be connected to a room full of terminals down the hall or on another floor. The system manager uses the console – the built-in keyboard and display – to do his or her work, because it is more convenient. Everyone else uses a regular terminal.

However, as far as Unix is concerned, there is really nothing special about the console. The system manager could just as easily use any terminal to do whatever he or she needs to do.

You might ask, is it necessary for a Unix system to have a console? Not at all. Some computers do not come with a keyboard and display. The

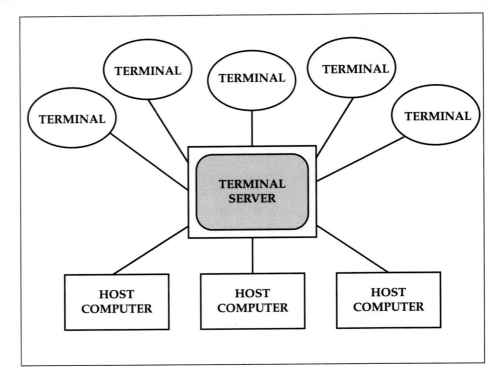

Figure 3-2
Connections Made by a Terminal Server

system manager uses a regular terminal, just like everybody else. The host computer, which is just a box, can be locked in a closet somewhere.

Workstations

In principle, all Unix systems can support multiple users. However, some Unix computers are used by only one person at a time. Such computers are called WORKSTATIONS.

When we refer to a computer as a workstation, we mean that there is only one terminal, the console. When you use a workstation, you have the entire computer to yourself. This will be the case, say, if you have your own personal computer at home running Unix.

If someone were to give you a choice, would it be better to have a workstation or a terminal? You might think that it is always better to have your own computer. That way, you don't have to share, and the system won't slow down when a lot of people use it at the same time. If you are a knowledgeable user who demands a lot of resources – for example, if you are writing large programs – having your own workstation is a good idea.

However, there are three important advantages to using a terminal. First, if you are paying for the equipment yourself, a terminal is a lot less expensive. Second, a host computer that is shared by many users may offer more facilities than an isolated workstation. The host may be more powerful, have more data storage space, and offer a larger variety of programs.

Finally, if you use a terminal to access a host, it is likely that someone else is maintaining the system for you. If you have a workstation, you (or somebody) will have to install and maintain an entire Unix system. You will find, quite quickly, that administering a Unix system is not for the faint at heart or for those pressed for time. In the world of Unix, system administration is euphemistically referred to as a "nontrivial task". In other words, running your own Unix system is a great deal of work.

Moreover, when a system is administered by an experienced manager, it means that backups (extra copies of your data files, usually stored on tape) will be made regularly. If you have to administer your own computer, you may have to do your own backups.

Realistically, you will never have the time nor the inclination to organize and maintain a proper backup system. This puts you at risk of losing all your data when your disk fails (as it surely will one day).

As we will see in a moment, many workstations are connected to a network. Some network administrators make sure that all the workstations are backed up automatically over the network. For example, every night at 2 AM, a computer on the network may check each workstation for new files and copy those files to a tape.

Such a system may solve your backup problems, but someone will still have to manage your Unix system.

Network Connections on Your Campus

A NETWORK refers to two or more computers connected together. We connect computers into networks in order to share resources. For example, it is often convenient to allow all the users on a particular network to share a pool of printers.

Moreover, network users can share data files, send electronic mail, and even use one another's computers remotely. For example, say that you are using a workstation that is connected to another workstation over a network. You can run a program that allows your keyboard and display to act as a terminal for the other computer. As you work, signals are passed back and forth, over the network, between your keyboard/display and the remote host.

When computers are connected directly (using some type of cable), we call it a LOCAL AREA NETWORK or LAN. A typical LAN is contained within a single building, often on a single floor.

Connectivity, however, doesn't have to stop with a local network. Many LANs are connected to other networks, forming what is called a WIDE AREA NETWORK.

In most universities, just about every Unix computer is connected to some local area network. These LANs are usually connected to a high-speed link (called a BACKBONE) that ties together the entire campus into one large wide area network. Large campuses may have more than one backbone.

This means, for example, that it is possible to send electronic mail from any computer on the campus to any other computer (as long as they are connected by the network). In fact, it is as easy to send a message across the campus as it is to send a message across the hall.

One mistake that beginners often make is thinking that they have to be near the computer they want to work with. If your campus is well connected, you can use a terminal in, say, the Psychology building, to work with a computer in the Math building. This is especially important if you are using the X Window system, which we will explain in Chapter 5. Figure 3-3 shows the variety of connections that you might find on a campus.

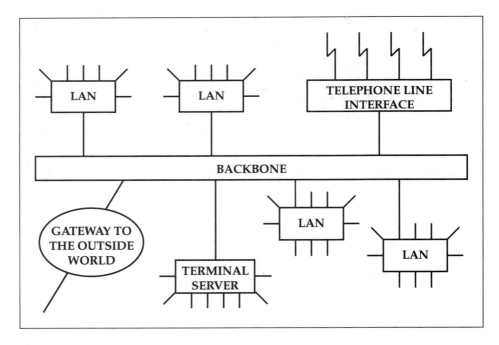

Figure 3-3
Network Backbone Connections on a Campus

The Client-Server Relationship

One of the principal reasons to create a network is to share resources. For instance, one computer may have a large amount of disk space to store files. This space can be shared throughout the network. It may well be that you will store your personal files not on the computer you are using, but on another computer. When your programs need to access a file, the data is sent to your computer over the network.

Such a system is common in large organizations. If all the data files are kept in one or two locations, it is easy for the system manager to make backup copies of the data.

In network terminology, any program that offers a resource is called a SERVER. A program that uses a resource is called a CLIENT. This terminology, of course, is taken from the business world. If you go to see a lawyer or an accountant, you are the client while they serve you.

If a program provides access to files over the network, it is called a FILE SERVER; a program that coordinates the printing of data using various printers is called a PRINT SERVER; and so on.

Sometimes the name "server" is used to refer to the actual computer, rather than a program. For example, you might hear someone say, "Our main file server sits in a closet in the system manager's office."

Here are two other common examples. On many campuses, one computer on the network transmits electronic mail between campus computers and the outside world. This computer is called the MAIL SERVER.

Another computer (or perhaps the same computer) will provide users with access to the worldwide Usenet news service (see Chapter 23). This machine is called the NEWS SERVER.

Unix system programmers will often talk about the connection between a client program and a server as the CLIENT-SERVER RELATIONSHIP. (Indeed, for many programmers, this is the most enduring relationship they have ever had.)

Large Scale Network Connections

Many campus-wide networks are connected to very large regional and national networks. On your campus, designated computers, called GATEWAYS, will act as the links between the campus network and the outside world. For example, all electronic mail that is sent in and out of the campus will pass through one specific gateway computer. This computer will look at the address and route the message to the appropriate network.

Around the world (and especially in the United States), the major wide area networks that serve the academic and research communities are connected together into a system known as the INTERNET. Any computer on the Internet – including, probably, the system that you use, if you are at a university – can connect to any other computer on the Internet.

For example, from your computer, you can log into and use a computer across the continent. Even better, if you are working with someone in a remote location, you can use a simple command (called `talk`) to connect your two computers and have a conversation (as long as they are both on the Internet).

What is amazing is that the computers you connect to do not have to be the same type as your computer. As long as the remote computer uses Unix and communicates in the standard way, everything will work just fine.

When you are using a program that seems to react instantly, we say that the program is working in REAL TIME. Using an Internet connection, it is possible to use the `talk` command to type messages back and forth in real time. That is, as you type a message, it echoes, not only on your screen, but on your friend's screen, which may be hundreds or even thousands of miles away.

As an example, while working on this book in California, we used `talk` to have long distance conversations with a Unix expert in Europe (Michael Schuster, who can now consider himself to be famous).

Most other countries have large national networks that, through gateways, are connected to one another. Effectively, this connects many hundreds of thousands of computers into an enormous, worldwide network. This means that you can, with little trouble, send electronic mail and data files all over the world. There are even gateways to commercial computer networks. For example, you can exchange messages with someone who uses CompuServe, MCI Mail or AT&T Mail.

Connecting Over a Phone Line

The network connections we have discussed so far are all set up and administered by experts. These connections usually use cables or leased telephone lines. The very large-scale connections may use satellite links.

However, what if you have a personal computer (or Macintosh) at home and you want to connect to the campus network, say, to work on an assignment or send a message? You can use a regular phone line and have your PC call a campus computer and make the connection. To do so, you will need a special device to convert computer signals back and forth to phone signals.

Technically speaking, converting computer signals to telephone signals is called MODULATION. The reverse process is called DEMODULATION. Thus, the device that you need is called a MODEM (modulator/demodulator). You connect the phone line to your modem and the modem to your PC.

To run the whole show, you need to use a PC communication program. This program will dial the remote computer and establish the connection.

Now, remember that we said that the only way to work with a Unix host computer is by using a terminal. Since your PC is not a terminal, your communication program must make your computer act like a terminal. We say that your program EMULATES a terminal. In a sense, this forces your PC – a full-fledged computer – to act like a much less powerful device. (After all, a terminal is not much more than a keyboard and display.) The whole scheme is shown in Figure 3-4.

Unix systems can work with many different brands and types of terminals. However, there is one specific terminal that, by custom, is the one that is emulated when you need to work over a telephone line. This is the VT-100 terminal.

In other words, when you are using your PC to work with a remote Unix system, the remote system thinks it is working with a VT-100 terminal. The job of your PC communication program is to make sure that your computer acts like a VT-100. (Ironically, the VT-100, which was made by the Digital Equipment Corporation, is quite old and has not been sold for years.)

A detailed discussion of communication programs is beyond the scope of this book. However, we will mention that most such programs offer a multitude of features, aside from the basic modem dialing and terminal emulation. Two of the most useful features are maintaining a directory of frequently dialed numbers and being able to transfer data files from one computer to another.

Character Terminals and Graphics Terminals

As we explained earlier, you use a terminal to work with Unix. The terminal has a keyboard and a display screen. You type on the keyboard and read the characters on the display.

There are two classes of terminals that you can use with Unix. How you use Unix will vary somewhat, depending on which type of terminal you are using.

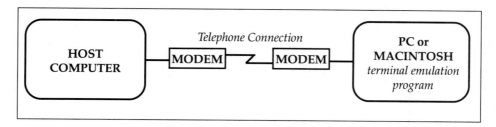

Figure 3-4
Using a Personal Computer to Access a Unix Host

The basic terminal furnishes not much more than a keyboard and a screen. This type of terminal, called a CHARACTER TERMINAL, displays only characters – such as letters, numerals, punctuation – and not pictures. Character terminals are inexpensive and are usually monochrome (for example, green characters on a black background). When you watch people access the computer in a bank or at an airport counter, you are looking at a character terminal.

If you use a personal computer to emulate a terminal, you will be using a character terminal.

The other type of terminal is called a GRAPHICS TERMINAL. It can display not only characters, but just about anything that can be drawn on a screen using small dots: pictures, geometric shapes, shading, and so on. Graphics terminals are more expensive than character terminals. Typically, a graphics terminal will have a large screen. The screens are often monochrome, but you may see full color.

Most graphics terminals have a mouse and are designed to be used with a so-called graphical user interface. The most popular interfaces are based on a system called X Window. Terminals that are designed for X Window are known as X terminals.

Most of the time, using X Window calls for the same Unix skills as using a regular character terminal. However, there are a few special considerations. In this chapter, we discussed what everyone needs to know to start using Unix. In Chapter 5, we will go over the extra details that apply only to X Window users.

One last point: If you use a personal computer as a terminal (say, over a telephone line), you use a communication program that emulates a terminal. Such programs always emulate character terminals. Graphics terminals need a high-speed link between the terminal and the host because communicating in pictures requires a lot more data transmission than communicating in characters. The speed of a phone line is not fast enough to support graphics.

Thus, an X terminal must be connected to the host either by a direct cable link or over a high-speed network. (Although, with very fast modems, it is possible to make X Window work over a telephone line if you fuss with it enough.)

## CHAPTER 4

Starting to Use Unix

In this chapter, we'll take a look at what you need to know to start using Unix. You will learn how to start and how to stop a work session. To begin, let's talk about how Unix keeps track of who is allowed to use the system.

Userids and Passwords

All Unix systems require administration and maintenance. The person who performs these duties is called the SYSTEM MANAGER or SYSTEM ADMINISTRATOR. (Most people use the terms interchangeably.)

If you have your own Unix computer and are the only one who uses it, you will have to act as the system manager. In a university or business, the system manager is usually a paid employee. With a large Unix computer, system administration is a full-time job that calls for a great deal of specialized knowledge. Indeed, some system managers have a staff of assistants.

When you register to use a Unix system, the system manager will give you a name that identifies you to the system. This name is the USERID (pronounced "user-eye-dee"). Along with the userid, you will get a PASSWORD. The password is a secret code that you must type in each time you use the system.

Once you have permission to use a system, we say that you have a Unix ACCOUNT on that computer. Even if you don't pay real money for your account, your Unix system will probably keep track of how much you use the computer. (Unix comes with a lot of built-in accounting, which your system manager may use to keep track of who is doing what.) In addition, your account will probably come with certain predefined limits, such as how much disk storage space you are allowed for your files.

One limit you are likely to encounter is an expiration date. For instance, your account may automatically be deactivated five days after the end of the semester.

What will your userid be? Usually, your system administrator will choose a userid for you. One common method is to base the userid on the person's real name. For example, for the name Harley Q. Hahn, the userid might be **harley**, **hahn**, **hhahn**, **harleyh** or **hqh**. Alternatively, your userid may reflect some completely objective criteria. For example, if you are the 25th student in the CS110 class to ask for a Unix account, you might be assigned the userid **cs11025**.

Each time you start a Unix session, you must enter your userid. This name is used by Unix to identify you. For example, any data files that you create will be "owned" by your userid.

It is important to realize that userids are not secret. In fact, as you will see in Chapter 13, your userid is part of the address that people use when they send you electronic mail and messages. However, to make sure that access to Unix is controlled, you will also be assigned a password which is secret.

Your password will probably be a meaningless group of characters, such as **gtY%12x**, which is difficult for someone else to guess. Later in the chapter, we will explain how to change your password if you don't like it.

Logging In: Starting Work with Unix

When you sit down in front of your terminal, the process you go through to start work is called LOGGING IN. When we express this idea as a noun or adjective, we use a single word, LOGIN. For example, "In order to log in, you need to learn the login procedure." Logging in consists of typing your userid and your password. Here is how it works:

When your Unix terminal is ready to use, it will display the following:

```
login:
```

This is an invitation to log in. Type your userid and press the <Return> key.

(We will talk about the Unix keyboard in Chapter 6. For now, all you need to know is that after you type a line you need to press the <Return> key. On some terminals, this key will be called <Enter>. If you are using a personal computer to emulate a terminal, you will press <Enter>.)

If you make an error while you are logging in, some systems allow you to press the <Backspace> key, to erase one character at a time, and correct your mistake. Other systems require that you press <Return>, wait for the message that tells you the login was incorrect and try again.

Once you have entered your userid, Unix will display:

```
Password:
```

Type your password and press <Return>. As you type, Unix will not echo your password – that is, the letters will not appear on your screen. This helps keep your password secret.

Once your userid and password are accepted, Unix will start a work session for you. If either your userid or password were incorrect, Unix will display:

`Login incorrect`

and let you try again. If you are connecting over a phone line or a network, some systems will disconnect you if you log in incorrectly a certain number of times.

Whenever you type a userid, Unix always asks for a password, even if the userid was invalid. This is to make it more difficult for people to break into the system by guessing userids.

What Happens After You Log In?

After you log in successfully, Unix will display an informative message describing the system. Here is an example:

`Last login: Mon Apr 27 16:16:33 from lscftrmsrv.lscf`
`SunOS Release 4.1.2 (LIFESCI) #2: Tue Apr 21 12:09:08 PDT 1992`

This message is from a Unix system run by the Life Sciences Computing Facility at the University of California at Santa Barbara.

The first line tells us the last time we logged in. Take a minute to check this line. If the time is more recent than you remember, someone else may be using your account without your permission. If so, change your password immediately. (This is explained later in the chapter.) At the end of the first line, we see the name of the terminal server from which the last login occurred.

The second line shows that we are using the SunOS operating system on a computer named LIFESCI. We are using version 4.1.2 of the operating system, which was last updated on April 21, 1992.

What happens next depends on how your system was set up by your system manager. As part of the login process, Unix executes a list of predefined commands that are kept in a special file.

Each person has his or her own file of login commands. The first time you log in, your file will contain whatever your system manager put in it. As you become more experienced, you can modify this file to suit your preferences. For example, you might have Unix execute a certain program automatically each time you log in.

One thing that you may notice is the MESSAGE OF THE DAY. This is a message that the system manager will update from time to time, showing important information. Some systems also have their own news facilities.

News items are entered by the system manager and you can display them as you wish, usually by using a command named **news**. You may see the newest items displayed automatically each time you log in.

Another message you may see is one that looks like this:

TERM = (*terminaltype*)

at which point everything will stop.

What is happening is that one of the startup commands (named **tset**) is asking you what type of terminal you are using. The name inside the parentheses is a guess. For example, if **tset** thinks you might be using a VT-100 terminal, you will see:

TERM = (vt100)

We will discuss terminal types in detail in Chapter 6. For now, all you need to do is type the name of your terminal and press the <Return> key. If the name that is displayed is correct, or if you are not sure what to do, just press <Return>.

Getting Down to Work: The Shell Prompt

Once your startup commands have finished executing, you are ready to start work. For the most part, your work will consist of entering one command after another until you are finished working. You then log out to end the session.

The program that reads and interprets your commands is called a "shell". When the shell is ready for you to type the next command, it will display a "prompt". We will talk more about the shell in Chapter 10.

For now, we will say that there are various choices of shells. Each allows you to interact with Unix in a somewhat different way. When you first log in, the shell you use will be chosen by your system manager. Once you become more knowledgeable, you can opt to use a different shell. Your prompt will vary depending on what shell you are using. In this book, we assume that you are using the C-Shell.

When you use the C-Shell, your prompt will be a **%** (percent sign). That is, when Unix is ready for you to enter a command you will see:

%

If your system manager has customized your environment, the prompt may be somewhat different. For instance, it may show the name of the machine that you are logged into:

nipper%

In this case, the prompt shows us that we are logged into the machine called **nipper**. The important thing is that the **%** means the shell is telling you that you can type in a command.

With some shells, your prompt may be different. In particular, if you are using the Bourne shell or the Korn shell, you may see a **$** (dollar sign) instead of **%**. (We will discuss the various shells in Chapter 10.)

Whatever your shell, once you see the prompt, you can type any command you want and press the <Return> key. If you are logging in for the first time and you want to practice, try the **date** command (to display the time and date) or the **who** command (to display the userids of all the people who are currently logged in).

Logging Out, Stopping Work with Unix: `logout`, `exit`, `login`

When you are finished working with Unix, you must end your session by LOGGING OUT. (When we refer to this idea as a noun or adjective, we use a single word, LOGOUT.) You log out to tell Unix that you are finished working under the current userid. Unix will stop your work session.

It is important to make sure that you log out when you are finished. If you were to just pick up and leave with your terminal logged in, anyone could come by and use it under the auspices of your userid. At the very least, you run the risk of someone fooling around under your userid. At the other extreme, some mischievous person might erase files (including yours) and cause all types of trouble. If this happens, you will bear some responsibility: leaving a terminal logged in is like parking your car unlocked with the keys in the ignition.

There are several ways to log out. The first way is to press <Ctrl-D>. This means you hold down the <Ctrl> key and press the <D> key at the same time. (We will discuss the Unix keyboard in detail later, in Chapter 6.)

When you press <Ctrl-D>, it sends a signal called "end of file". Essentially, this tells the shell (the program that interprets your commands) that there is no more data coming. The shell terminates, and Unix logs you out.

However, as you will find out, the end-of-file signal has other uses. It is altogether possible that you might press <Ctrl-D> once too often and inadvertently log yourself out. Thus, as a safeguard, most shells have a way for you to specify that you do not want to log out by pressing <Ctrl-D>. Rather, you must enter a special command; in this way, it is impossible to log out accidentally.

It may be that your system manager has set up your system so that, by default, you cannot log out by pressing <Ctrl-D>. If this is the case, you must use one of the logout commands. They are **logout** and **exit**.

To find out how to log out with your system, first try pressing <Ctrl-D>. If it works, fine. If not, you may see a message like this:

```
Use "logout" to logout.
```

In this case, use the **logout** command. (Type "logout" and press the <Return> key.) If, instead, you see a message like this:

`Use "exit" to logout`

you will need to use the **exit** command.

One final way to log out is to use the **login** command. This tells Unix to log you out and then get ready for a new person to log in. After you are logged out, Unix will display the

`login:`

message, asking for a new userid. This command is handy if you want to leave your terminal ready for someone else to use.

It is important to end your session with Unix by logging out. Do not simply turn off your terminal. You may not be logged out automatically. Someone else may come along, turn on the terminal, and take over your session (under the auspices of your userid).

How do you know for sure you have logged out successfully? The shell prompt will stop and, if you press <Return>, you may see the next **login:** prompt. On some systems, you may also see a message like "Session disconnected" or "Connection closed".

To summarize: to log out, press <Ctrl-D>. If that doesn't work, use the **logout** or **exit** command. Alternatively, you can use the **login** command to allow someone else to log in right away. Do not, under any circumstances, walk away from your terminal and leave it logged in.

Upper- and Lowercase

As you might have noticed, Unix distinguishes between small letters and capital letters. For example, when we discussed possible userids, we used the examples **harley** and **hahn**, both of which start with a small "h". At the same time, we suggested a possible password, **gtY%12x**, that contains three small letters and one capital letter.

Some computer systems are designed to ignore the differences between small and capital letters, a notable example being a personal computer using DOS. Unix, however, was written to be more specific.

For convenience, we refer to small letters as LOWERCASE and capital letters as UPPERCASE. The names come from typewriter terminology. When you use an old-fashioned typewriter, pressing the <Shift> key moves the "upper" case into position to print capital letters.

The idea of upper- and lowercase applies only to the letters of the alphabet, not to punctuation, numbers or any special characters.

When you type names or commands, you must be sure to be exact. For example, if your userid is **harley**, you must type all lowercase letters when you log in. If you type **Harley**, Unix considers it to be an entirely different userid. Similarly, when you log out, you must type **logout**, not **Logout**. When a program or system distinguishes between upper- and lowercase, we say that it is CASE SENSITIVE.

 HINT Unlike some other computer systems (such as DOS), Unix is case sensitive.

Since Unix considers uppercase letters to be different from lowercase letters, it is possible for a system manager to assign two different userids, such as **harley** and **Harley**. However, in practice, you would never see this because it would be too confusing; lowercase userids are used exclusively.

To maintain scrupulous accuracy in this book, we will not capitalize command names, even when they come at the beginning of a sentence – for instance: "**logout**, **exit** and **login** are three commands that you can use to log out."

Please appreciate that the distinction between upper- and lowercase applies only when you are logging in and entering Unix commands. When you use a program that works with regular textual data – for example, when you use a word processor to create a document – you type in the regular manner.

Remembering When to Use Upper- or Lowercase

You might ask, how will I ever remember which words use what types of letters? The answer is that, by convention, almost all Unix names (including userids and command names) use only lowercase.

There are only four common situations in which you will see uppercase letters:

- Passwords often have both upper- and lowercase letters. This makes them harder to guess, especially if someone is watching over your shoulder as you log in.

- When you send electronic mail, most systems allow you to write the address in upper- or lowercase (or mixed).

- Within Unix, there are certain quantities called "environment variables" that hold important information. The names of these variables are, by convention, all uppercase letters. For example, the **TERM** variable describes the type of terminal you are using.

- When you write programs (especially in the C programming language), you will find some words are all uppercase and some words are mixed upper- and lowercase.

Don't let these few exceptions confuse you. In practice, all you have to do is make sure that you get your password right. Virtually everything else will be lowercase.

A Sample Session with Unix

Figure 4-1 shows a short work session with Unix. This session used a computer that serves the life sciences departments at the University of California at Santa Barbara.

The session starts by logging in, using userid **harley**. Notice that Unix does not echo the password. After the userid and password are accepted, the Unix system tells us when we last logged in and then identifies itself. We see that we are using the SunOS 4.1.2 operating system.

Next, we see the message of the day. We are welcomed to the system and told how to send messages to the system manager. We are also told that we can use the **news** command to look at other information (presumably local news).

Finally, the preliminaries are over, and we are presented with the **%** character. This is a prompt telling us that the shell (command interpreter)

```
login: harley
Password:

Last login: Wed Apr 29 10:46:48 from lscftrmsrv.lscf
SunOS Release 4.1.2 (LIFESCI): Tue Apr 21 12:09:08 PDT 1992

Welcome to the Life Sciences Computing Facility.
In the event of system problems, please send mail
to the system administrator using the command
"mail sysadmin".  Information through 1/2/91 available
using the command "news".

% date
Wed Apr 29 10:49:43 PDT 1992

% who
addie      ttyp0    Apr 29 10:41(nipper.lscf.ucsb)
kim        ttyp1    Apr 29 10:48(nipper.lscf.ucsb)
murdock    ttyp2    Apr 25 13:33(macfly.psych.ucs)
harley     ttyp3    Apr 29 10:49(lscftrmsrv.lscf)


murdock    ttyp5    Apr 27 08:54(macfly.psych.ucs)

% logout
Connection with LIFESCI closed.
```

Figure 4-1

Sample Unix Work Session #1

is ready for us to type in a command. In this case, we type the **date** command. The system responds by displaying the current time and date.

Once the **date** command finishes, the shell displays another prompt. This time we type the **who** command. This command shows us what userids are currently logged in.

After the **who** command finishes, we see another shell prompt. We type the **logout** command, ending the session.

Notice that userid **murdock** is logged in twice at different terminals. Unix allows you to log in as many times as you want without logging out. However, you would normally use only one terminal at a time. In our example, **murdock** is the system manager, who has more than one terminal in his office.

If you ever enter the **who** command and see yourself logged in to more than one terminal, you should find out what is happening. You may have inadvertently finished a previous work session without logging out. Alternately, someone may be using your userid without your permission.

Figure 4-2 shows a second sample session. In this case, we used the **login** command to log out. Notice that the connection is not dropped. Instead, Unix (after logging us out) displays the **login:** prompt, asking for the userid of the next user.

```
login: harley
Password:

Last login: Wed Apr 29 10:46:48 from lscftrmsrv.lscf
SunOS Release 4.1.2 (LIFESCI): Tue Apr 21 12:09:08 PDT 1992

Welcome to the Life Sciences Computing Facility.
In the event of system problems, please send mail
to the system administrator using the command
"mail sysadmin".  Information through 1/2/91 available
using the command "news".

% date
Wed Apr 29 10:49:43 PDT 1992

% login
login:
```

Figure 4-2
Sample Unix Work Session #2

Changing Your Password: `passwd`

When your Unix account is set up, the system manager will assign you a userid and a password. System managers usually have their own ways of organizing things, and you may not be able to get the userid you want.

For example, you may want to use your first name as a userid, but the system manager may tell you that he or she has decided that all userids should be last names. Don't fight with your system manager. He or she has a great deal of responsibility – Unix systems are hard to manage – and is probably massively overworked.

You can, however, change your password whenever you want. Indeed, some Unix systems require you to change your password regularly for security reasons. As you change your password, the characters you type will not be echoed. This prevents anyone from reading your new password over your shoulder.

To change your password, use the **`passwd`** command. Unix will first ask you to enter your old password. This proves that you are authorized to make the change. Otherwise, anyone who walks by a terminal that was left logged in could change that person's password.

Next, **`passwd`** will ask you to type in the new password. Some systems require all passwords to meet certain specifications. For example, your password may need to be at least six characters. If your new password does not meet the local criteria, you will be so informed and asked to enter a new choice.

Finally, **`passwd`** will ask you to retype the new password. Remember, the characters are not echoed as you type. Entering your new password a second time ensures that you did not make a mistake.

Choosing a Password

The reason we use passwords is to make sure that only authorized people use Unix accounts. This security is not mean-spirited. Many people depend on the computer to store their data and to run their programs. Moreover, computer resources, such as disk storage space, are limited and must be allotted deliberately.

As you might imagine, there are always a number of bright people who take pleasure in trying to break into a system. Such people are called CRACKERS or HACKERS. Some crackers want only to match wits against the Unix security system to see if they can log in on the sly. Other crackers enjoy causing real damage.

(Sometimes, though, the word HACK is used as a verb to indicate a massive amount of nerd-like effort. For example, "Randall spent all week-end hacking at his Space War program." Thus, the term hacker is often used in a positive sense, to describe someone who is capable of massive amounts of nerd-like effort.)

It behooves you to (1) never tell your password to anyone, and (2) choose a password that cannot be guessed easily. Remember: if you give your password to someone who damages the computer system, you are responsible.

When you first get your Unix account, the system manager will choose a password for you. Whenever you want, you can use the **passwd** command to change your password.

The rules for choosing a password are actually guidelines for what *not* to choose:

- Do not choose your userid. (This is like hiding the key to your house under the mat.)
- Do not choose your first or last name, or any combination of names.
- Do not choose the name of a loved one or friend.
- Do not choose a word that is in the dictionary.
- Do not choose a number that is meaningful to you, such as a phone number, important date (such as a birthday), social security number and so on.

In addition, there are several routine precautions that you should practice:

- Never write down your password on a piece of paper. (Someone is bound to find it after you lose it.)
- Change your password regularly.

Within the hacker community, there are programs that exist to guess passwords. Such programs are surprisingly successful. Protect yourself (and your files) by choosing wisely.

The best idea is to make up a pattern of meaningless characters. For good measure, mix in uppercase, lowercase, numbers and punctuation. As an example, consider the password **gtY%12x** that we used earlier in the chapter. If you suspect that someone knows your password, change it right away.

If you should forget your password, all you need to do is tell your system manager. He or she can assign you a new password without knowing the old one.

Userids and Users

A USER is a person who utilizes a Unix system in some way. However, Unix itself does not know about users: Unix only knows about userids.

The distinction is an important one. If someone logs in using your userid, Unix has no way of knowing whether or not it is really you. That is why you need to protect your password.

Later in the book, we will describe how you can create files to hold your data. Such files are said to be "owned" by your userid. Thus, anyone who knows your password can log in with your userid and access (or even destroy) your files.

In the world of Unix, only userids have a real identity. It is userids, and not users, who own files, send electronic mail, and log in and out.

Earlier in this chapter, we saw a sample session in which we used the **who** command to find out who was logged in. Here is the result of that command:

```
% who
addie     ttyp0     Apr 29 10:41(nipper.lscf.ucsb)
tln       ttyp1     Apr 29 10:48(nipper.lscf.ucsb)
murdock   ttyp2     Apr 25 13:33(macfly.psych.ucs)
harley    ttyp3     Apr 29 10:49(lscftrmsrv.lscf)
murdock   ttyp5     Apr 27 08:54(macfly.psych.ucs)
```

Notice that you see only userids, not people's names.

In Chapter 12, we will explain how you can use the **finger** command to display information about the person to whom a particular userid is registered. This is handy, for example, when you receive a message from, say, userid **tln**, and you would like to know the name of the person behind the userid.

The Superuser Userid: `root`

Within Unix, all userids are considered equal, with one notable exception.

From time to time, it becomes necessary for the system manager to have special privileges. For example, he or she may need to add a new user to the system, or change somebody's password.

Toward this end, Unix supports a special userid, called **root**, that has extraordinary privileges. A person who has logged in using the **root** userid can do anything he or she wants. (Obviously, the **root** password is a closely guarded secret.) When someone logs in as **root**, we refer to him or her as the SUPERUSER.

At first, the name **root** may not make any sense. However, in Chapter 20, we will see that the basis of the entire Unix file system is called the "root directory". Thus, the name **root** refers to a very important part of Unix.

Most of the time, a good system administrator will use his or her regular userid. He or she will change to superuser only to do work that requires special privileges. Once the work is done, the system administrator will change back to a regular userid. This prevents the power of the superuser from causing inadvertent damage.

For example, if you make a mistake entering the **rm** (remove) command, it is possible to erase data files accidentally. If you are logged in under your own userid, the worst that you can do is erase your own files. If you are logged in under **root**, you might erase everybody's files.

If you ever get a message from userid **root**, make sure that you are polite. You are talking to someone who can wipe you out of the system with a single command.

Having Fun While Practicing Safe Computing

From its early days, Unix was designed for people working together who needed to share programs and documents. The basic design of the system assumes that everybody is honest and of good will. Even modern Unix, with its passwords and security measures, is not bulletproof, nor is it meant to be. People who use Unix are supposed to respect the other users and to share.

Since Unix is so complex, there are always a few crackers who get a kick out of trying to beat the system. In some environments, young programmers who figure out how to break into a system and perform clandestine acts are tolerated, perhaps even admired for their ingenuity.

Not so in the Unix community (which, as we described in Chapter 1, extends all over the world). Crackers and troublemakers are tracked down and punished. For example, we mentioned earlier that there exist programs that guess people's passwords. In some universities, just being caught running such a program is grounds for immediate expulsion.

However, the wonderful thing about Unix is that there are so many challenging and pleasant diversions. For example, in Chapter 23, we will discuss the worldwide Usenet network which consists of hundreds of different discussion groups.

It is unlikely that you will ever become bored enough to get into mischief. Nevertheless, if you are ever so tempted, please remember that system managers are always overworked, and they have little patience with willful people who create unnecessary trouble.

If you find that you like Unix, you can get a great deal of pleasure out of helping other people. Two of the most important Unix traditions are to share and to help others.

Starting with X Window

In Chapter 4, we discussed how to get started with Unix. In particular, we explained how to log in and log out.

If you have a regular (character) terminal, the process is pretty much as we have described it, regardless of what type of terminal you are using. However, if you are using a graphics terminal with X Window, the procedures vary. Moreover, where users of regular terminals need only know how to use the keyboard, X Window users need some extra skills.

In this chapter, we'll examine X Window: a graphical system that lets you work within windows and run programs on any computer in your network. We will discuss the X Window system itself, what you can do with it, and how you log in and log out. If you do not use X Window, you can skip this chapter.

Before we can talk about X Window, though, we need to lay a foundation. Let's start with the idea of a graphical user interface.

GUI: Graphical User Interface

If you have ever used a Macintosh, or a PC with Microsoft Windows or OS/2, you know what a GRAPHICAL USER INTERFACE is. It is a system in which you use not only the keyboard, but also a mouse. Your screen contains not only characters, but boxes (windows) and pictures as well. You work by manipulating the boxes and pictures as objects. Sometimes a graphical user interface is called a GUI (pronounced "gooey").

There are several basic ideas you need to understand to work with a GUI. First, you need to learn to use two input devices: the keyboard and a POINTING DEVICE. As the name implies, you use the pointing device, from time to time, to point to a part of the screen. The most common pointing device is a mouse, but you may also see trackballs and joysticks. In this chapter, we will assume that you are using a mouse.

Typically, you will move the mouse around on your desktop. As you do, a pointer on the screen follows the motion. This pointer is a small picture, often an arrow. To point to a particular picture, you would move the mouse until the pointer on the screen rests within that picture. With some GUIs, you may find that the pointer changes as you move from one region of the screen to another.

Pointing devices usually have buttons that you can press. The X Window system uses three buttons, although it is possible to use fewer. By convention, these buttons are numbered from left to right. Button number 1 is on the left, number 2 is in the middle, and number 3 is on the right. When you use a GUI, you will find that you will use button 1, the leftmost button, most often. (If you are lefthanded, it is possible to change the order of the buttons.)

The next important idea about GUIs is that they divide the screen into a number of bounded regions called WINDOWS. As with real windows, the boundary is usually, but not always, a rectangle. The windows can overlap like pieces of paper on a desk. Moreover, you can change the size and position of the windows as you see fit.

Within each window, you can have a different activity. For example, you might use a number of different windows, each of which contains a different program. As you work, it is easy to switch from one window to another. This allows you to use each program whenever you want. On a regular character terminal, you can see only one program at a time (unless you have special software). In fact, one of the prime motivations behind the development of X Window – and of windowing systems in general – has been to allow a user to work with multiple programs.

There are other important ideas and skills that you need to understand in order to work with a GUI, but before we get to them, let's talk about X Window.

What Is X Window?

X Window is a system designed to support graphical user interfaces. For convenience, we usually refer to X Window as X. Thus, you might ask a friend, "Does your computer run X?"

WHAT'S IN A NAME?

X Window The roots of X lie in a particular operating system that was developed at Stanford University. This system was called V (the single letter "V"). When a windowing interface was developed for V, it was called W. Some time later, the W program was given to someone at MIT who used it as a basis for a new windowing system he called X.

Since then, the name has stuck, perhaps for two reasons. First, names of Unix systems often end in "x" or "ix", and X Window is used mostly with Unix. Second, if they kept changing the name, they would reach the end of the alphabet in just two more letters.

The idea behind X is to provide standard services to programs that display graphical data. You can, for example, run programs on one computer whose output is displayed on a screen attached to another computer. X stays behinds the scenes, orchestrating all the details, providing the supporting structure.

X was developed at MIT as part of Project Athena. Currently, X is maintained by an independent organization called the X Consortium. In 1987, MIT released X version 11, referred to as X11. Various versions of X11 are known as X11.4, X11.5 and so on. Notice, by the way, that the proper name is X Window, not "X Windows".

The Window Manager: `mwm`, `olwm`, `twm`

The actual graphical user interface is provided not by X itself, but by a program called the WINDOW MANAGER. The window manager controls the appearance and characteristics of the windows and the pictures.

There are several window managers that work with X. On your system there may be just one, or you may have a choice. As you work, you don't really interact with X, you interact with the window manager. Thus, the look and feel of your system depends on which window manager you use.

The three most common window managers are **mwm** (the Motif window manager), **olwm** (the Open Look window manager) and **twm** (the Tab window manager), although there are others. Motif is a product of the Open Software Foundation and is found on a variety of systems. Open Look was developed by AT&T and Sun, and is found on many Sun systems. The Tab window manager comes with the basic X system. If you have a choice, you will probably opt for Motif or Open Look, which are easier to use and look nicer than Tab.

Using a graphical user interface is like using a car; if you know how to use one, it is easy to use another. We might carry the analogy one step further and say that **twm** is like a car with a manual transmission, while **mwm** and **olwm** are easier to use, like cars with automatic transmissions.

If you have ever used a Macintosh, or a PC with Microsoft Windows or OS/2, you have used a graphical user interface. You will have no trouble learning how to use one of the X-based GUIs. Indeed, if you have used OS/2 and are familiar with the Presentation Manager GUI, you will find **mwm** especially easy. Motif was designed to look and work like Presentation Manager.

X Servers and X Clients

Imagine yourself writing a computer program that offers a graphical user interface. You would find that it is a lot of work to attend to all the details of drawing windows, moving pictures around, keeping track of the mouse, and so on. Moreover, your program would have to know the exact hardware specifications of the screen, the keyboard and the mouse.

What would happen if your program became popular? People would want to use it on various types of computers. You would have to modify the program to work with all kinds of different screens, keyboards and mice. It wouldn't be long before most of the program was taken up with the details of maintaining the graphical user interface!

The X Window system was designed to make it easy to create and use graphical programs. To do this, X offers a standard service: a program called a DISPLAY SERVER. The display server takes care of all the details of interfacing with a graphical user interface.

Let's take a moment to review the terminology. As we explained in Chapter 3, a program or a computer that offers a resource over a network is called a server. A program that uses such a resource is called a client.

For example, say that you run a program that uses a file stored on another computer. Your program is the client. The file is sent over the network to your program by a file server. Similarly, you might send a file to another computer to be printed. The other computer acts as a print server.

In the world of X, the word "display" refers to more than just your screen display; DISPLAY is a technical term that refers to your screen, keyboard and mouse. That is, your display consists of all the equipment that you use to interact with your programs.

The display server is a program that manages the screen, keyboard and mouse for other programs. When you write an X program, you do not need to worry about the input/output details. Your program can call on the display server to do the job.

For instance, if an X program needs to draw a window on the screen, it just tells the display server to draw a window of a certain size at a certain location. The display server takes care of the details. In particular, the X program does not need to know what type of screen is being used.

This means that X programs are highly portable. They can interact with any graphical user interface on any computer, using any screen, keyboard and mouse, as long as there is an X-based display server to perform the actual input and output.

Borrowing from the terminology of networks, the display server is usually referred to as an X SERVER. Similarly, any program that uses the display server is called an X CLIENT. In other words, an X client is a program that runs under X, using the resources of the X server to handle the input and output.

The X system comes with over fifty utility programs that run under X. In X terminology, we would say that the system comes with over fifty X clients. For example, there is an X client that displays a picture of a clock to tell you what time it is.

When you use X, your computer executes a single X server program. This X server interfaces for all the X clients that you want to use.

For instance, you may decide to run five X programs (X clients) at the same time, switching back and forth from one to the other as you see fit. On your screen, each program is displayed within its own window. The input and output from all of these X clients is handled by a single X server program, which executes on your computer. The relationship between X clients and an X server is shown in Figure 5-1.

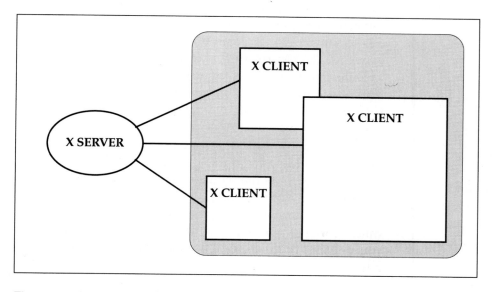

Figure 5-1
X Clients and an X Server

(You will remember – as we explained in Chapter 2 – that Unix is a multitasking operating system that can run more than one program at the same time.)

Using X to Run Programs Remotely

You might ask, all these details are nice (and even mildly interesting), but do I really need to understand them just to use a graphical user interface? After all, there is no need to get so involved to learn how to use a Macintosh or Microsoft Windows or OS/2.

The reason that you must understand the X client-server relationship is that it provides a wonderful service. Since the display (screen + keyboard + mouse) is handled by a single X server for all X clients, we have effectively separated the input/output from the processing. Thus, the X server program that runs on your computer can service any X client no matter where it is executing.

Of course, your X server program serves X clients that execute on your computer. However, your X server can also interface for X clients that run on another computer – as long as there is a network connection between the two machines.

This is the beauty of the X system: using a graphical user interface, you can work with several windows at the same time, each of which contains a separate program. Although the X server runs on your computer, the programs in the window can be running on any computer on the network.

For instance, you might be running three programs on your own computer, one program on a friend's computer down the hall, and one program on the supercomputer in another building. Each program will run its own window. You control the whole thing by using a graphical user interface.

Thus, from a single computer, you can use any X-based graphical user interface to run any X client programs you want, on any computers in the network. This idea is shown in Figure 5-2.

One last point: since X can work with various window managers, your screen may look somewhat different depending on what graphical user interface you are using.

For example, say that you and a friend are working, side by side, on two identical graphics terminals. You decide to use the **mwm** (Motif) window manager, while she is using the **twm** (Tab) window manager. You are both running the same set of five programs we just described. However, since you are using different GUIs, your screen display and interactions are different.

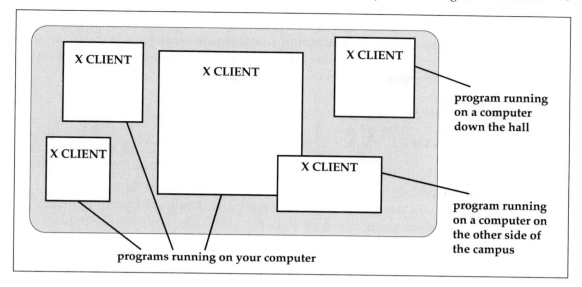

Figure 5-2
X Window Connection Over a Network

The Most Important X Client: `xterm`

As we explained in the last section, an X client is a program that runs under the X Window system. X, being a graphical system, is designed to support only graphics displays. However, much of the time you will want to enter Unix commands, one after the other, at the shell prompt (see Chapter 4). For such work, you need a plain vanilla character terminal.

Since this is a fundamental requirement, the X Window system comes with an X client whose sole purpose is to run within a window and emulate a terminal. This program is called **xterm**. When you start **xterm**, it sets up a window that acts like a small version of a terminal.

Thus, if you have four different **xterm** clients, each running in its own window, it's like having four different terminals, all logged in. You can move from one to the other whenever you want.

xterm is capable of emulating two types of terminals: the ubiquitous VT-100 (see Chapter 3), to act as a character terminal, and the Tektronix 4014, for graphics work. Most of the time you will use **xterm** as a VT-100 (which is the default).

We mentioned earlier that X does not offer a full-featured graphical user interface. This is provided by whatever window manager you decide to use. The window manager, though, is itself an X client; that is, it is a program that runs under X. As we will see in a moment, the window manager may need to be started from within an **xterm** window.

In other words, out of all the X clients that come with the system, **xterm** is indispensable. You need it not only to act as a terminal, so you can enter Unix commands; you may also need it to start the window manager that provides your graphical user interface.

Starting Work with X Window

In Chapter 4, we explained how you start work at a regular terminal. Essentially, all you need to do is wait for the login prompt and enter your userid and password. You will then see the shell prompt. You can now enter one Unix command after another. When you are finished, you log out, either by entering the **logout** or **exit** command, or by pressing <Ctrl-D>.

If you are using X, getting started is more complex. How much work you have to do depends on whether or not your system manager has set up your system to start X and a window manager automatically. If not, you will have to enter the appropriate commands yourself.

There are three basic possibilities. Let's start with the most automated and work our way down. Before we start, realize that you can only use X if your terminal supports it. That is, you need to be using a workstation with a graphics display screen, or a special purpose terminal, called an X TERMINAL, designed just for running X. Moreover, the X Window software must already be installed and accessible on whatever host computer you are using.

To make starting X easy, some systems use a program called a DISPLAY MANAGER. The display manager moderates your login procedure. When you start work, you will see a message, such as "Welcome to the X Window System", as well as a login window in which you can enter your userid and password.

Once you log in, the display manager will start everything automatically. This involves starting X itself and then starting the window manager. Thus, if your system has a display manager, there is really nothing more for you to do than log in.

Without a display manager, Unix will present you with the standard login prompt that we discussed in Chapter 4. Log in by entering your userid and password. At this point, one of two things will happen.

First, your system manager may have set up your account so that, once you log in, X will start and the window manager will begin. As with the display manager, you are ready to start work without much trouble.

If, however, you are working at a terminal capable of using X, but nothing has been automated, you will have to start the system manually. You can tell this is the case because, after you log in, X will not start. Instead, you will find yourself at the regular shell prompt (see Chapter 4). You will have to enter two commands: one to start X Window, the other to start the window manager.

At the shell prompt, enter the command:

`xinit`

and wait for a few moments. **xinit** will start the X Window system and create the first **xterm**, which will be in a window. (On some systems, there may be another command that works better than **xinit**.)

Once X has started and you see the **xterm** window, you must indicate that you want to work with that particular window. Simply move the mouse so that the mouse pointer lies within the window.

Now that you are within the **xterm** window, enter the command to start your window manager. The command you use is the name of the window manager program followed by an **&** (ampersand) character. You will have to ask around to see what window managers are available on your system. You can always use **twm** (Tab), the window manager that comes with X. However, if your system has either **mwm** (Motif) or **olwm** (Open Look), you are better off using those.

So, for example, if you are using Motif, enter the following command within the **xterm** window:

`mwm &`

After a few moments, your window manager will start. You are now ready for work.

To summarize: From the shell prompt, enter the **xinit** command. Once X has started, move to the **xterm** window and enter the name of your window manager, followed by an ampersand, for example, **mwm &**.

Why do we append the **&** character to the end of the command? The **&** tells Unix that the program we are starting should run by itself, in the "background". In other words, the window manager should have a life of its own.

If you forget the **&**, Unix will start the window manager, but will not release the keyboard and screen. If this happens, terminate the program by pressing the **intr** key (usually <Ctrl-C>). You can then reenter the command properly. (Note: Terminating programs by using the **intr** key is discussed in Chapter 6.)

One last point: As you work with X, you will create and delete windows as you see fit. When you delete a window, any program that is running in the window will be terminated. Thus, if you were to delete the original **xterm** window, the program that is running in it – the window manager – will terminate and your graphical user interface will vanish!

To avoid this, it is a good idea to leave the original **xterm** window alone. If you want to enter Unix commands, you can create another **xterm**. In fact, you can create as many as you want. Some people like to minimize the original **xterm** window and move it out of the way. We will discuss how to perform such manipulations later in the chapter.

 HINT If you started your window manager manually from the original **xterm** window, iconize this window and move it out of the way. ("Iconize" means to turn a window into a small picture so as to take up less space on the screen. We discuss this later in the chapter.)

Learning to Use a Graphical User Interface

Learning to use a graphical user interface is easy, but the way to learn is by practicing and experimenting on your system, not by reading.

Because GUIs are mostly visual, the best way to learn is to have someone show you in person. Although it is possible to read about how to use a GUI, words do not convey the visual ideas well. You will find yourself reading and rereading instructions when what you really need is someone to take a few seconds and show you what to do. Using a GUI is so simple that once you see someone perform the basic operations, you will have no problems.

Although the various window managers offer GUIs that have a lot in common, there are small but important differences. It is difficult to write down a single set of instructions that will work for all the different interfaces. In addition, virtually every part of X Window can be customized. Your system manager may have set up your particular system to look and act in a certain way. Once you become a veteran X user, you can customize your system according to your own needs and preferences.

In the following sections, we will discuss the basic ideas that you must understand to use a GUI. However, make sure that, after reading this chapter, you take some time to practice with your particular window manager.

We have already covered the first few important ideas: A graphical user interface allows you to work with windows. A window is a bounded area of the screen, usually a rectangle. Windows can overlap. As the need arises, you can change the size of a window, or move it from one part of the screen to another.

Of Mice and Menus

On your screen will be a pointer. You use a pointing device, usually a mouse, to move the pointer around the screen. The shape of the pointer may change, depending on what you are doing and where you are on the screen.

You can indicate an action by moving the mouse to a particular position and pressing a button. Your mouse may have either one, two or three buttons. X Window is designed to use a three-button pointer, but a two-button device will also work.

There are only two things that you can do with a mouse button: First, you can press it and let go. When you do so, we say that you CLICK the button. If you press the button twice in rapid succession, we say that you DOUBLE-CLICK. On some occasions, you may also have to TRIPLE-CLICK: that is, press a button three times quickly.

The other thing you can do with a button is press it and hold it down.

Much of the time, you will make choices by selecting them from a list called a MENU. There are two types of menus. POP-UP menus appear out of nowhere after some action has occurred. For example, if you move the pointer to an empty area of the screen and hold down a button, a menu will pop up.

The other type of menu is a PULL-DOWN menu. With some X programs, there will be a horizontal list of words near the top of a window. If you move the pointer to one of these words and hold down the left button, a menu of related items will appear below the word.

One of the most common actions within a graphical user interface is to move the pointer to an object and click a mouse button. We call this POINT AND CLICK. For example, to change the size of a window, you may need to point and click on a particular part of that window.

Another common action is to move the pointer to an object, hold down the mouse button, move the pointer some more, and then let go of the mouse button.

For example, to move a window, you move the pointer to the title bar of the window (the place where the name is displayed near the top of the window). Hold down the left button and move the pointer to wherever you want the window to be. When you release the button, the window manager will redraw the window at the new location.

When we move something in this way, we say that we DRAG it. So we can say that, to move a window, you drag the title bar to the new location.

Icons

It is possible to change the size of windows. We won't go into the details here; they vary depending on your graphical user interface. It may be that you move the pointer to one of the borders of the window, hold down a button, and drag the border to a new location. Or you may click or hold down a button to bring up a menu and select a "size" option from the menu.

However, there will be times when you want to make a window as small as possible. For instance, you may have a window that contains a word processing program that you are not currently using. It is nice to be able to shrink the window and move it out of the way. Later, when you want to return to the word processor, you can enlarge the window.

All GUIs have a facility for transforming a window into a small picture, called an ICON. How you do this depends on your GUI. You may click or double-click on a particular part of the window; you may select an item from a menu. However you do it, we say that you ICONIZE or MINIMIZE the window.

Later, when you expand the window, either by clicking or by menu selection, we say that you MAXIMIZE the window.

It is often convenient to iconize a number of windows and drag them out of the way, to a remote corner of the screen. Some GUIs have a special window to hold all your icons.

Controlling Your Focus

With a graphical user interface, you can have multiple windows, each of which contains its own program. However, when you type on the keyboard, the input will go to one specific window.

To choose a window to work with, you use the mouse to move the pointer to that window and then press the left button. When you select a window in this way, we say that you are changing the keyboard FOCUS. (With some GUIs, you do not have to press a button to change the focus; merely moving the pointer into the window is enough.)

Once you focus on a window, everything you type goes to the program that is running in that window. That is, to start working with a window, you need only move to it and click. The keyboard is now connected to that window.

When you focus on a window, it will be highlighted in some way to show that it is now the active window. In addition, if the window is partially obscured by another window, the window with the focus will be redrawn to be on top and will become completely visible.

Starting a Program: `xcalc`, `xclock`

There are two ways to start a program. First, when you move the pointer to a blank area of the screen and press a button, you will pop up the MAIN MENU, sometimes called the ROOT MENU. (Which button you press, left or right, will depend on your window manager.) This menu may have a selection to allow you to start or "open" a new program. When you make such a selection, the program will start in its own window.

As we mentioned earlier, nearly every part of X can be customized. In particular, the items on your main menu can be modified. If the person who set up your system is an ambitious enthusiast, there may be all kinds of wonderful items on this menu, including a long list of programs.

The second way to start a program is to change your focus to an **xterm** window and type in a command at the shell prompt. Of course, you can type in any regular Unix command or program name.

If you are starting an X program that needs to reside in its own window – that is, an X client – you must type an **&** (ampersand) character at the end of the command. This tells Unix to let the program execute in the "background". In other words, this program has a life of its own; you do not want to wait for it to finish before you can enter the next command. We saw this earlier when we talked about starting the window manager from within an **xterm** window.

Here is an example. If you want to display the time and date, change your focus to an **xterm** window. At the shell prompt, enter:

```
date
```

Since **date** is a regular program, it will execute, display its output and end. Once the **date** program finishes, the shell prompt will be redisplayed.

On the other hand, let's say you want to start another **xterm** window. At the shell prompt, enter the command:

```
xterm &
```

A new **xterm** will start in its own window. Once it starts, the shell prompt will be redisplayed in the original window.

If you want to experiment with these ideas, try starting **xclock** and **xcalc**, two X clients that come with the X Window system. **xclock** displays a picture of a clock that shows the current time. **xcalc** provides a scientific calculator.

Starting a Program on a Remote System

As we described earlier, one of the most powerful features of X is that it allows you to work with an X client that is executing on a remote computer. Just make sure that there is a network connection between the remote computer and your computer, and that you have authorization to log in to the remote computer.

To run a program on a remote computer, you must tell your system what computer you plan to use, log in to that system, tell the remote system to work with the X server on your computer, then start the program. Follow these five steps:

1. Move the focus to an **xterm** window.

2. Use the **xhost** command to tell your X server that the remote computer is allowed to access your machine. After the command name, type the

name of the remote computer. For example, if you will be accessing a supercomputer named **super**, enter the command:

```
xhost super
```

3. Log in to the remote computer. Normally you will use the **telnet** command (see Chapter 25). For example, to log in to the computer named **super**, you might enter:

```
telnet super
```

Enter your userid and password in the regular manner. You are now working on the remote system from within the **xterm** window on your screen.

4. Tell the remote system that any X clients you start should interact with the X server on your computer. To do this, use the **setenv** command to define a global variable named **DISPLAY** to point to your system. (We won't explain the details here.) Type **setenv**, followed by the word **DISPLAY**, followed by the name of your system, a colon, and the number **0**.

For example, if your system is named **nipper**, enter the command:

```
setenv DISPLAY nipper:0
```

This tells any X client you run on the remote computer to use the X server on computer **nipper**. The **0** refers to display number 0. This is a default that you don't need to worry about; just put it in.

Note: The command we just described assumes that you are using a C-Shell on the remote system (see Chapter 4). If you are using a Bourne or Korn shell, you will need to use the following two commands:

```
set DISPLAY nipper:0
export DISPLAY
```

These commands can be combined onto a single line by separating them with a semicolon:

```
set DISPLAY nipper:0; export DISPLAY
```

5. Start the X client. Remember to end the command with an **&** (ampersand) character so that the program will run in the background in its own window. For example, if you want to run a program named **statistics**, enter:

```
statistics &
```

To summarize, let's say that you want to run an X client named **statistics**, on a remote system called **super**, from your computer named **nipper**.

From within an **xterm** window, enter the commands:

```
xhost super
telnet super
```

After logging in, enter:

```
setenv DISPLAY nipper:0
statistics &
```

When you are finished, terminate the program and log off the remote system in the usual manner.

Stopping Your Work with X Window

When you work with a regular character terminal, logging out is simple. At the shell prompt, you enter either the **logout** or **exit** command, or press <Ctrl-D>, whichever is appropriate for your shell. (This is all explained in Chapter 4.)

If you are using X, you must go through a few more steps. The details that we discuss in this section may seem a trifle involved and may not all be necessary for your computer. Ask around and find out what works best on your system. What you read in this section are general guidelines.

Before you log out, it is a good idea to terminate all your programs. Go to each window in turn and stop the program. If a window is an **xterm** in which you are logged into a remote system, you should log out of that system.

Once all your programs are stopped, close each window. You usually do this by selecting an item from a pop-up or pull-down menu associated with the window. You may also be able to double-click on part of the title bar. The details will depend on your window manager. With an **xterm** window, there is usually a menu with a "quit" selection.

Note: Closing a window terminates it. Do not confuse this with minimizing or iconizing a window. Minimizing a window simply shrinks it into a small icon. When you log out, you want to actually get rid of the window.

Finally, stop your window manager. With most window managers, all you need to do is pop up the main menu and select some type of "quit" operation.

With some systems, stopping the window manager will terminate X and log you out automatically. With other systems, you will be left at a shell prompt. If so, you can log out in the regular manner (using **logout**, **exit**, or <Ctrl-D>, as appropriate).

If you had to start X and your window manager manually (by using the **xinit** command and so on, as we explained above), you may have to close the original **xterm** window in order to stop X.

HINT   To learn more about X on your system, check the Unix online manual (explained in Chapter 8). Try looking under **x** and **xterm**. Your system may or may not have such manual pages.

Using the Keyboard with Unix

As we explained in Chapter 4, Unix works with many different types of terminals. Of course, what you are probably most interested in is, how does Unix work with your terminal?

In this chapter, we will discuss how Unix uses the keyboard, and, in particular, we will show you how to find out which keys have special meanings for you. To start, let's consider the problem of how Unix is able to work with any type of terminal.

TTYs: The First Terminals

When Unix was first developed, the programmers used Teletype ASR33 terminals: electromechanical devices that printed output on paper. The terminals had the letters of the alphabet, numbers, punctuation, and a special "Control" key. (In fact, to this day, it is possible to use Unix using only these keys.) Many of the conventions used with modern terminals are based on these terminals.

For instance, the name Teletype was abbreviated as TTY. This quickly became a way to refer to any terminal. For example, the command to display the name of your terminal is **tty**, and one of the commands to set up your terminal is **stty**.

WHAT'S IN A NAME?

TTY   In Unix, TTY means a terminal. The name comes from the abbreviation for the old Teletype terminals.

Another convention derived from Teletypes is how we use the word PRINT. As we mentioned, Teletypes printed output on paper. Now, of course, the same information would be displayed on a screen. However, the custom is still to refer to such operations as "printing".

For example, the **tty** command displays the name of the terminal you are currently using. However, the official description of the purpose of this command is "print current terminal name".

Similarly, the command to display the name of your working directory (see Chapter 21) is **pwd**, or "print working directory".

You might ask, if "print" means "display", what term do we use when we really mean print? Sometimes we can use the word "print" and it is clear by context that we mean real printing. Other times, we use the term "line printer" (an anachronism itself) to refer to a real printer. For example, the command to print a file is **lpr**.

Since the time of the Teletypes, many different types of terminals have been developed. Most terminals do more than display a series of characters. They can also recognize and carry out certain commands. For example, there is a command to clear the screen.

The problem is that each type of terminal has its own characteristics and uses its own set of commands. What would you do if you were writing a program that, at a certain point, needed to clear the screen of the terminal? The signal your program must send depends on what type of terminal is being used.

Every program would need to know about every different type of terminal – an enormous burden to place upon software developers. Moreover, what happens when a new terminal is introduced? If it uses different commands, it would not work properly with existing programs.

The solution used with Berkeley Unix is to collect descriptions of all the different types of terminals into a single file. This collection is called the TERMCAP DATABASE (terminal capabilities). This database is stored in the file **/etc/termcap**. (The name will make sense after we discuss the Unix file system.)

When you write a program that needs to send commands to the terminal, you use a standard programming interface called **curses**. (The name comes from the idea of controlling the cursor.) A program will tell **curses** what it wants to display on the screen. **curses** checks what type of terminal is being used and, referring to the termcap database, sends the appropriate commands. This allows programs to be compatible with a wide variety of terminals.

The question is: How does Unix know what terminal you are using?

How Does Unix Know What Terminal You Are Using?

The part of the host computer to which a terminal is connected is called a PORT. Data moves in and out of the computer through the port. (Think of planes flying in and out of an airport.)

When the system manager sets up a system, he or she tells Unix what type of terminal will be attached to each port. This works well for terminals that are connected directly. For such ports, the terminal type will always be the same. If the system manager changes the terminal, he or she changes the setup.

However, a port might not always connect to the same type of terminal. It may be attached to a terminal server or a network that services different types of terminals. Or the port may be attached to a modem that supports a dial-in connection.

When you log in, Unix looks at the port you are using and guesses what type of terminal you have, based on how the system manager set up that port. However, if you log in using a network, terminal server or modem, guessing is not enough. You must make sure that Unix knows exactly which terminal you are using.

As you use Unix, there are a number of quantities called ENVIRONMENT VARIABLES that are always available to the shell and to any programs you may run. An environment variable has a name and a value. At any time, a program can ask what is the value of the environment variable with such-and-such name.

In particular, there is an environment variable named **TERM** whose value is the type of terminal you are using. (You may remember that, in Chapter 4, we mentioned that the names of environment variables are one of the few instances in Unix where we use uppercase letters.) You can display the value of any environment variable by using the command **echo** *$name*. For example, if you enter:

```
echo $TERM
```

Unix will show you the value of the **TERM** variable.

How Is the TERM Variable Set?

It is up to you to make sure that the **TERM** variable is set properly. In other words, it is up to you to make sure that Unix knows what type of terminal you are using.

Usually, this is done automatically in one of two ways: First, if your terminal is directly connected to the port, the system manager will have set it up so that Unix knows what terminal you are using.

Second, every time you log in, your shell executes a list of predefined startup commands. One of these commands will set the **TERM** variable appropriately. As we mentioned in Chapter 4, one of your startup commands (**tset**) may guess at the terminal type you are using and ask you for confirmation.

For example, say that you are connecting via a phone line. The system manager knows that many communication programs will emulate a VT-100 terminal. He or she will set up the port to expect such a terminal. The specific **tset** command in your startup file will display the message:

```
TERM = (vt100)
```

whenever you log in using that port. You can either specify an alternate terminal type or simply press the <Return> key to continue.

What Happens If the TERM Variable Is Set Incorrectly?

If **TERM** is set incorrectly, you may not notice it when you use simple commands that display one line of output at a time. However, when you run programs that use the entire screen, such as the **vi** text editor which we will meet in Chapter 19, your terminal may not work properly.

To check that your setup is okay, enter the command:

```
echo $TERM
```

If Unix displays the correct terminal name, everything is okay. Otherwise, you will need to change your startup commands. Unfortunately, this requires advanced skills. Until you are more experienced, you will need to find someone to help you.

Understanding Your Keyboard: The <Ctrl> Key

There are two aspects to using your terminal well. One is making sure that Unix knows what type of terminal you have, by making sure the **TERM** variable is set properly. We discussed this topic in the last three sections. The other aspect of using your terminal is learning about the various keys on your keyboard and how they are used.

Since Unix must work with any terminal, there is no such thing as a standard keyboard. Instead, Unix defines standard codes that are mapped onto different keyboards. Before we discuss the various codes, let's take a quick look at the keyboard.

Note: When we refer to an actual key, we will put the name in angled brackets. For example, the key for the letter "A" is <A>.

The first thing you will notice is that most of your keyboard looks like the standard typewriter layout. There are keys for the letters of the alphabet, the numbers 0 through 9, and punctuation. There is also a <Shift> key for typing uppercase letters.

Among the miscellaneous keys are <Esc>, <Backspace>, <Delete> and <Ctrl>. The first three have special uses that we will discuss later. However, let's spend a moment talking about <Ctrl>.

The <Ctrl> key (the name stands for "Control") was a feature on the early Teletype terminals we mentioned at the beginning of the chapter. The use of this key was adopted by the Unix developers and integrated into the system in several important ways.

To use the <Ctrl> key, you hold it down (like the <Shift> key) while you press one of the other keys, usually a letter. For example, you might hold down <Ctrl> and press the <A> key.

There are 26 such combinations based on the alphabet – <Ctrl>+<A> through <Ctrl>+<Z> – as well as a couple of others that you might run into. Because it is awkward to write "Ctrl" over and over again, the Unix community uses a shorthand notation: the character ^ means "hold down the control key". For example, **^A** means hold down <Ctrl> and press the <A> key. (You might also see the notation <Ctrl-A>, which means the same thing.)

By convention, we always write a <Ctrl> combination using a capital letter. For instance, we write **^A**, never **^a**. Using capital letters makes such combinations easier to read (compare **^L** to **^l**).

To get used to this notation, take a look at the following example. This is part of the output from an **stty** command that we will meet later in the chapter.

```
erase kill werase rprnt flush lnext susp  intr quit stop  eof
^H    ^U   ^W     ^R    ^O    ^V    ^Z/^Y ^C   ^\   ^S/^Q ^D
```

This output tells us what keys to press to send certain codes. The details aren't important for now. What we want you to notice is the notation. In this example, we see that to send the **erase** code, you use **^H**. That is, you hold down <Ctrl> and press <H>. For the **kill** code, you use **^U**; for **werase**, you use **^W**, and so on.

The Unix Keyboard Codes

In order to be able to work with any terminal, Unix defines a number of keyboard codes for standard operations. These codes are then mapped onto the keys of each particular keyboard.

For example, there is a code, called **intr** (interrupt), that tells Unix to abort the program that is currently running. Thus, to stop a program instantly, you can press the key that sends the **intr** code.

The idea of the **intr** code is standard: it is built into the definition of how Unix processes its input. What is not standard is the actual key that you need to press to send this code.

Because the input codes are not mapped to a standard set of keys, there is flexibility in the definition of what each key does. For instance, on some terminals, you press **^C** (Ctrl-C) to send the **intr** code. However, if you want, you can change this so that you can press another key, say, <Delete>, instead.

In the next few sections, we will describe the important keyboard codes and how you use them. We will then show you how to find out exactly what keys are used on your terminal and how you can change them if you want.

Special Keys to Use While Typing: **erase**, **werase**, **kill**

There are three keyboard codes that you can use to help you while you are typing. They are: **erase**, **werase** and **kill**.

erase tells Unix to erase the last character that you typed. The **erase** key is usually **^H** (Ctrl-H). On most terminals, the <Backspace> key will send a **^H** character. Thus, you can correct typing mistakes by pressing either <Backspace> or **^H**.

Although you will almost always press <Backspace>, it is handy to remember **^H**. If, for some reason, your <Backspace> key does not work properly, you can use **^H** to correct typing mistakes.

For example, say that you want to enter the **date** command (to display the time and date), but you spell it wrong, **datx**. Before you press the <Return> key, press <Backspace> or **^H** to erase the last letter and make your correction:

datx<Backspace>**e**

On your screen, the **x** will disappear when you press <Backspace>.

The next code, **werase**, tells Unix to erase the last word you typed. The **werase** key is usually **^W**. This key is useful when you want to correct one or more words that you have just typed. Of course, you can always press **^H** repeatedly, but **^W** is faster when you want to erase whole words.

Here is an example. You type the command to send mail to three friends whose userids are **curly**, **larry** and **moe**. The command to use is **mail curly larry moe**.

However, after you type the command (and before you press the <Return> key), you decide that you really only want to send mail to **curly**. Press **^W** twice to erase the last two words:

mail curly larry moe^W^W

On your screen, first the word **moe** and then the word **larry** will disappear.

The third code to use while typing is **kill**. The **kill** key is usually **^U** or **^X**. This code tells Unix to erase the whole line.

For example, let's say that you are just about to send mail to your three friends. You type the command, but, before you press <Return>, someone runs in the room and tells you that they are giving away free money at the Student Union building. Thinking quickly, you press **^U**:

```
mail curly larry moe^U
```

to cancel the command. On your screen, the entire line will disappear. Now you can log out. (Of course, you would never leave your terminal logged in, even to rush out to get free money.)

Note: The **kill** code does not stop programs. It only erases the line you are typing. To stop a program, use the **intr** code.

For reference, Figure 6-1 summarize the keyboard codes to use when typing.

Code	Usual Key to Use	Purpose
erase	**^H** or <Backspace>	erase the last character typed
werase	**^W**	erase the last word typed
kill	**^U** (sometimes **^X**)	erase the entire line

Figure 6-1
Keyboard Codes to Use While Typing

Stopping a Program: `intr`

There are several keyboard codes that you can use to stop or pause a program. These codes are **intr**, **quit**, **stop** and **susp**. When you press a key that generates one of these codes, we say that you send a SIGNAL to the program. Either the program or Unix itself will notice the signal and take appropriate action.

The **intr** (interrupt) code actually has two uses. First, it stops a program dead in its tracks. The **intr** key is usually **^C**. You may also see this key referred to as the "break" key. (If you use a personal computer, you may know that **^C** acts as a break key under DOS. As you can see, this idea – along with many others – was taken from Unix.)

Say that you enter a command to log in remotely to another system. Nothing happens, and you decide to stop waiting. Just press **^C**. The remote login program will abort, and you will be back at the shell prompt.

Some programs will ignore the **intr** signal. In such cases, there will always be a well-defined way to end the program. By ignoring the **intr** signal, the program keeps you from accidentally causing damage by pressing **^C** inadvertently. We say that the program TRAPS the signal.

For example, consider what happens if you are using, say, a word processor, and you press **^C**. The word processor traps the **intr** signal and does not stop. In order to terminate the program, you need to use the word processor's own quit command (whatever that is). If the word processor had not trapped the **intr** signal, pressing **^C** would abort the program and lose all the data that you had not yet saved.

The second use for the **intr** key arises when you are typing a Unix command at the shell prompt. If you press **^C** before you press <Return>, it cancels the command completely. Thus, if you are typing a command and you change your mind, press **^C** instead of <Return>.

Be sure that you do not confuse the **intr** key (**^C**) with the **kill** key (usually **^U** or **^X**). When you are typing a command, **intr** cancels the command, while **kill** erases all the characters on the line. Effectively, this has the same result: what you were typing is discarded, and you can enter a new command.

However, only **intr** will stop a program. In spite of its name, **kill** will not "kill" a program.

Another Way to Stop a Program: `quit`

Aside from **intr**, there is another keyboard code, **quit**, that will stop a program. The **quit** key is usually **^** (Ctrl-Backslash).

What is the difference between **intr** (**^C**) and **quit**? **quit** is designed for advanced programmers who may need to abort a test program. When you press **^**, it not only sends a **quit** signal (to stop the program), it tells Unix to make a copy of the contents of memory at that instant.

On some Unix systems, this information is stored automatically in a file named **core** (the old name for computer memory). A programmer can use special tools to analyze a **core** file.

The reason we mention this is that if a file named **core** mysteriously appears in one of your directories, it may mean that you have pressed **^**. Unless you really want the file, you can erase it. In fact, you should erase it because **core** files are rather large and there is no reason to waste the space.

Pausing the Display: `stop`, `start`

When a program writes a line of output to the bottom of your screen, all the other lines move up one position. We say that they SCROLL upwards. If a program produces output too fast, data will scroll off the top of the screen before you can read it.

In such cases, you have three choices. First, if the lost data is not important, you can ignore it. Second, you can restart the program that generates the data and have it send the output to one of the so-called paging programs that will display the data nicely, one screenful at a time. (The names of the paging programs are **more, pg** and **less**. We will discuss them in Chapter 17.)

Finally, you can press a key to send the **stop** code. This tells Unix to temporarily pause the screen display. The **stop** key is usually **^S**. Once the display is paused, you can restart it by sending the **start** code. The **start** key is usually **^Q**.

Thus, when data is scrolling by too fast, press **^S** to pause, **^Q** to continue. (Think of "S" for Stop and "Q" for Qontinue.)

Using **^S** and **^Q** can be quite useful. However, you should understand that **^S** only tells Unix to stop displaying output. It does not stop the program that is executing. The program will keep going and will not stop generating output. However, Unix will store the output so that none will be lost. As soon as you press **^Q**, Unix will display what output remains. If a great many lines of new data were generated while the screen display was paused, they will probably whiz by rapidly once you press **^Q**.

Although it is handy to be able to pause and restart using **^S** and **^Q**, you may find that it is just too difficult to press the keys fast enough. If this is the case, you should use the **more** program to control your output.

 HINT   If your terminal ever locks up mysteriously, try pressing **^Q**. You may have pressed **^S** inadvertently and paused the display. When everything seems to have stopped, you will never cause any harm by pressing **^Q**.

The End of File Code: eof

From time to time, you will work with programs that expect you to enter data from the keyboard. When you get to the point where there is no more data, you indicate this by pressing **^D**, which sends the **eof** (end of file) code.

Here is an example: In Chapter 14, we will discuss the **mail** program that you can use to send electronic mail. As you compose your message, you type one line after another. When you are finished, you press **^D**. This indicates that there is no more data. **mail** knows the message is complete and sends it to the recipient.

Here is another example: The **bc** program provides the services of a built-in calculator. After you start **bc**, you enter one calculation after another. After each calculation, **bc** displays the answer. When you are finished, you press **^D** to tell **bc** that there is no more data. The program terminates.

The Shell and the `eof` Code

In Chapter 4, we explained that the shell is the program that reads your Unix commands and interprets them. When the shell is ready to read a command, it displays a prompt (usually a `%`). You type a command and press <Return>. The shell processes the command and then displays a new prompt. Thus, your session with Unix consists of entering one command after another.

Although the shell may seem mysterious, it is really just a program. And, from the point of view of the shell, the commands that you type are just data that needs to be processed. So, you can stop the shell by indicating that there is no more data. Just press `^D`, the `eof` key.

But what does stopping the shell really mean? It means that you have finished your work. Thus, when the shell stops, Unix logs you out automatically. This is why you can log out by pressing `^D`. You are really telling the shell (and Unix) that there is no more work to be done.

Of course, there is a potential problem. What if you press `^D` by accident? You will be logged out immediately. The solution is to tell the shell to trap the `eof` code. You do this by entering the command:

`set ignoreeof`

This tells the shell to trap and ignore the `^D` signal. Now, if you press `^D`, the shell displays:

`Use "logout" to logout.`

You must deliberately enter the `logout` command. It is impossible for you to log out inadvertently by pressing `^D`.

It would be difficult to remember to enter the `set ignoreeof` command every time you start work with Unix. Most people put the command in their startup file so that the command will be executed automatically each time they log in. (The name of the startup file is `.login`. Yes, the "`.`" is part of the name. We will discuss this file in Chapter 11.)

It is likely that, when the system manager set up your account, he or she gave you a startup file that already contains this command. That is why, in Chapter 4, we said that you should try logging out by pressing `^D` and, if that didn't work, to use the `logout` command.

Note: What we have described here works for the C-Shell and most other shells. If you are using the Bourne shell, however, there is no way to prevent `^D` from logging you out. You will just have to be careful.

Checking the Special Keys for Your Terminal: `stty`

So far, we have mentioned a number of keyboard codes, each of which corresponds to some key on your keyboard. These are shown in Figure 6-2.

Code	Usual Key Assignment	Purpose
intr	^C	stop a program that is running
erase	^H, <Backspace>	erase the last character typed
werase,	^W	erase the last word typed
kill	^U	erase the entire line
quit	^\	stop a program and save core file
stop	^S	pause the screen display
start	^Q	restart the screen display
eof	^D	indicate that there is no more data

Figure 6-2
Summary of Keyboard Codes

The key assignments we have shown are the most common ones, but they are changeable. It may be that, on your system, some of these keys are different. For example, on some systems, the **kill** key is **^X**.

To check how your Unix system uses your particular terminal, you can use the **stty** (set terminal) command. Enter:

```
stty all
```

You will see several lines of information about your terminal. Here is a sample:

```
new tty, speed 38400 baud , 0 rows, 0 columns; tabs
crt
erase kill werase rprnt flush lnext susp  intr quit stop  eof
^H    ^U   ^W     ^R    ^O    ^V    ^Z/^Y ^C   ^\   ^S/^Q ^D
```

We can ignore the first two lines. The last two lines show the keyboard codes and the keys to which they correspond. Notice that there are several codes that we did not cover (**rprnt**, **flush**, **lnext**, **susp**). These are not so important, and we can ignore then for now.

If you would like to change a key assignment, the **stty** command will do that for you. Just type **stty**, followed by the name of the code, followed by the new key assignment. For example, to change the **kill** key to **^U**, enter:

```
stty kill ^U
```

Now, we have said that the abbreviation **^U** stands for <Ctrl-U>; that is, a single character. However, when we type the name of such a key for the

stty command (and only for this command), we literally type two characters: ^ followed by a letter; the **stty** command knows what we mean.

Strictly speaking, we can assign a code to any key we want. For example, we could set the **kill** code to the letter "k":

```
stty kill k
```

Of course, such a command will only lead to problems. Every time we press the <k> key, Unix will erase the line we are typing! Normally, we use only <Ctrl> keys and, actually, it is best to stay with the standard assignments.

If your keyboard has a <Delete> or <Del> key, you may wish to assign it to a code. When you use **stty**, you can refer to this key as ^?. However, with the C-Shell, the "?" character has a special meaning. To tell the shell that, in this case, the character is to be taken literally, you need to enclose it in single quote marks.

For example, say that you decide it would be easier for you if you could press <Delete> instead of ^C to stop a program (the **intr** code). Enter:

```
stty intr '^?'
```

You can now verify your change by entering **stty all**. If you enter the **stty** command by itself:

```
stty
```

it will display an abbreviated report, showing only those values that are non-standard. If you want to see everything that **stty** knows about (which is much more than you really need), enter:

```
stty everything
```

Teletype Control Signals

Note: The material covered in the rest of this chapter is not essential. It is included only for your interest. If you are getting bored, feel free to start skimming. However, if you still have patience, by all means push on. The following sections really are interesting (to certain strange types of people, anyway). In any event, be sure not to skip the story at the end of the chapter.

There are a number of control characters that Unix uses in a special way. To understand how they are used, it is necessary to revisit the early Unix developers.

As we mentioned earlier in the chapter, the developers of Unix used Teletype ASR33 machines for terminals. A Teletype is an electromechanical device that was developed to send messages from place to place. A message would be typed on one Teletype and sent over a connection to another Teletype, where it would print on paper. The operator at the destination could rip off the paper and deliver the message.

The Teletype keyboard had the standard alphabet, some punctuation and a <Ctrl> key. Holding down <Ctrl> while pressing one of the letters of the alphabet gave 26 auxiliary signals. These signals were used to control the operation of the Teletype.

A few of the <Ctrl> signals affected the printing of the message. <Ctrl-H>, or Backspace, caused the print carriage to back up a single space before printing the next character.

For example, if you wanted to underline a word, you could type the word, followed by a number of <Ctrl-H>s (which would move the print carriage backward), followed by some underscore characters.

<Ctrl-M>, or Carriage Return, caused the print carriage to return to the beginning of the line. <Ctrl-J>, or Line Feed, moved the paper vertically, up one position, so as to be ready to print on the next line. Thus, when a line had completed printing, the sequence <Ctrl-M> <Ctrl-J> – Carriage Return, Linefeed – would position the carriage and the paper at the beginning of the next line.

Another signal, <Ctrl-I>, used tab settings. These were predefined positions along the width of the print line. If you had a message that needed to print in columns – say, at positions 10, 15 and 30 – you could physically set the tabs at those positions. When a <Ctrl-I> was encountered during printing, the carriage would move horizontally to the right to the next tab setting.

Finally, the <Ctrl-G> was called the Bell signal. The Bell signal literally rang a bell on the destination Teletype. This sound could be used to signal the operator. For example, you might send the following message:

```
NEXT REPORT REQUIRES YOU TO SET TABS AT 10 15 AND 30
Carriage Return
Linefeed
Bell
Bell
```

This message prints some instructions, moves the print carriage to the beginning of the next line, and rings the bell twice.

How Teletype Control Signals Are Used by Unix: ^H, ^I, ^G

Since the early Unix developers used Teletype machines for terminals, it was only natural that they should make use of some of the Control signals when they began to use display terminals.

<Ctrl-H>, or ^**H** as we write it now, is used to send the **erase** code. Thus, when you are typing a command, you can make corrections by using ^**H** to erase the most recently typed character.

As a convenience, when you press the <Backspace> key, Unix interprets the signal as being a ^**H**. Thus, you can correct mistakes using <Backspace> or ^**H**, whichever is more convenient.

<Ctrl-I>, or `^I`, is used as a horizontal tab code. It is possible to set your Unix terminal to specific tab positions. However, this is a lot of trouble, and it is rare that anyone bothers. Left to its own, Unix assumes that tabs are set every 8 positions, starting with position 1. In other words, Unix assumes that tabs are set at positions 1, 9, 17, 25 and so on.

For convenience, when you press the <Tab> key, Unix interprets it as a `^I`. Thus, if you need to use tabs, you can press either <Tab> or `^I`.

As an experiment, press <Tab> or `^I` as you type. Notice how the cursor moves to the right. Realize, though, that no matter how many positions the cursor moves, `^I` is still considered a single character. For instance, if you type 3 letters, press <Tab>, and type another letter,

ABC<Tab>**D**

Unix counts it as 5 characters.

As you remember, <Ctrl-G>, or `^G`, rang the bell on a Teletype. Of course, modern terminals do not have a bell, but they can beep. A Unix terminal will beep when it is asked to display a `^G` character. For instance, say that you are using a program and you press the wrong key by mistake. The program may beep at you. It does this by "displaying" a `^G` character.

If you would like to try this for yourself, type the following **echo** command. (**echo** simply displays whatever you type after the name of the command.) Type **echo**, then a space, then press `^G` three times, then press <Return>:

echo ^G^G^G

You will hear three beeps.

So, as you can see, three of the Unix control characters, `^H`, `^I` and `^G`, owe their existence to the early Teletype machines. The manner in which Unix has adopted the last two control characters, <Ctrl-M> and <Ctrl-J>, is more complex, and will be discussed in the next section.

What Unix Does at the End of a Line: `linefeed, newline`

As we explained earlier, the old Teletype terminals used the `^M` (Carriage Return) character to move the print carriage to the beginning of the line, and the `^J` (Linefeed) character to move the paper vertically up one line.

Unix borrows the Linefeed character as follows:

Within a data file, it is sometimes convenient to divide the data into lines. To do this, Unix will use a `^J` character to mark the end of each line. When it is used in this way, `^J` is called **newline** rather than Linefeed. When a program reads a data file, it knows it has reached the end of a line when it encounters a **newline**.

Unix borrows the Carriage Return character as well:

When you are typing, you send the Carriage Return code (**^M**) to signal that you have reached the end of a line. To make life simple, Unix lets you press either the <Return> key or **^M**. Of course, we use the <Return> key most of the time because it is more convenient, but **^M** will work just as well. When used in this way, **^M** is called **return** rather than Carriage Return.

Now, one of the most elegant features of Unix is that data typed at the keyboard is treated the same as data read from a file. For example, say that you have a program that reads a series of names, one per line, and prints them. The program can read the names either from a disk file or from the keyboard.

The program does not need to be written in any special way to achieve this flexibility; this feature is called "standard input" and is built into Unix. (We will discuss standard input in Chapter 15.)

In order for standard input to work properly, each line must end with a **newline** (**^J**). But, when you enter a line at the terminal, you are actually sending a **return** (by pressing <Return> or **^M**).

To make things more confusing, Unix must make sure that when it displays data each line ends with a **^M^J** sequence – the old Carriage Return, Linefeed characters (which we now call **return** and **newline**). This tells the terminal to move the cursor to the beginning of the next line.

How is this all reconciled?

As you type, every time you press <Return>, Unix changes the **return** code (**^M**) into a **newline** (**^J**). When you display data, each **newline** code (**^J**), is changed by Unix into a **return newline** (**^M^J**) combination.

At first, this may seem hopelessly confusing. Eventually, you will come to see that it all makes perfect sense, at which time you will know that you have finally started to think in Unix.

☑ **HINT**   If you use DOS with a PC, your files will be stored with a Carriage Return + Linefeed (**^M^J**) at the end of each line. Unix uses only a solitary linefeed (**^J**). Thus, when you copy files from DOS to Unix, each **^M^J** must be converted into **^J**. Conversely, when you copy files from Unix to DOS, each **^J** must be replaced by **^M^J**.

On PCs that run both Unix and DOS, there are special Unix commands that will do the conversion automatically. (See your documentation for details.) Similarly, if you are using a PC communication program to access a Unix host computer, there is usually a way to specify that the DOS-Unix conversion should be performed whenever data is transferred between the two systems.

An Important Use for ^J: `stty sane`

As you might imagine, it is not really necessary to know all of this just to work with Unix (unless you want to be a programmer). Just remember to press <Return> at the end of each line and let Unix do the work.

However, there is one case where understanding these ideas is helpful. On rare occasions, the settings for your terminal may become so screwed up that the terminal does not work properly. There is a command you can use, **`stty sane`**, that will reset your terminal settings to reasonable values.

However, it may be that when you try to enter the command by pressing <Return>, the **`return`** to **`newline`** conversion does not work and Unix will not accept the command. Pressing **^M** instead of <Return> is no help because it is essentially the same key.

The solution is to press **^J**, the **`newline`**, which is all Unix wants anyway. Thus,

`stty sane^J`

may rejuvenate your terminal when all else fails.

You might ask, if that is the case, can you press **^J** instead of <Return> to enter a command at any time? Of course – try it.

The Fable of the Programmer and the Princess

A long time ago, there lived a young, handsome, charming programmer (you can tell this is a fable) who won the love of a beautiful princess. However, the night before their wedding, the princess was kidnapped.

The programmer followed the trail to a remote corner of the lawless Silicon Valley, where he discovered that his love was being held captive in an abandoned tech support center by an evil Vice President of Marketing.

Thinking quickly, the programmer took a powerful magnet and entered the building. He tracked down the princess and broke into the room where the VP of Marketing stood gloating over the terrified girl.

"Release that girl immediately," roared the programmer, "or I will use this magnet and scramble all your disks."

The VP pressed a secret button, and in the blinking of an eye, four more ugly, hulking vice presidents entered the room.

"On the other hand," said the programmer, "perhaps we can make a deal."

"What did you have in mind?"

"You set me any Unix task you want," said the programmer. "If I do it, you let the princess and me go free. If I fail, I will leave and never return."

"Agreed," said the VP, his eyes gleaming like two toady red nuggets encased in suet. "Sit down at this terminal. The task has two parts. First, using a single command, display the time and date."

"Child's play," said the programmer, as he typed **date** and pressed the <Return> key.

"Now," said the VP, "do it again." However, as the programmer once again typed **date**, the VP added, "But this time you are not allowed to use either the <Return> key or **^M**!"

"RTFM, you ignorant buffoon!" cried the programmer, whereupon he pressed **^J**, grabbed the princess and led her to his waiting Ferrari and a life of freedom.

## CHAPTER 7

Programs to Use Right Away (Including Games)

When you enter a command, you are telling Unix to run the program by that name. For example, when you enter the **date** command, Unix runs the **date** program.

Unix has literally hundreds of different programs, which means that there are hundreds of different commands that you can enter. Many of these commands require that you understand some theory. For instance, before you can use the file system commands you need to learn about the file system.

On the other hand, there are commands that you can use right away which require no special knowledge. In this chapter, we'll take a look at some of these commands. You will see that they can be useful, interesting and even fun.

Your system may not have all the programs we discuss in this chapter (or in this book). The fundamental programs – such as the **date** command we will meet in the next section – are on every Unix system. However, some of the more esoteric programs (especially the games) may not be available.

If you enter a non-existent command, don't worry, it won't cause any problems. Unix will just tell you that it could not find that command.

Displaying the Time and Date: `date`

The **date** command is one of the most useful. Simply enter:

```
date
```

and Unix will display the current time and date. Here is some sample output:

`Thu Jun  4 20:39:42 PDT 1992`

If you live in a place that uses daylight savings time, Unix knows how to spring forward and fall back at the appropriate times. The example here shows Pacific Daylight Time.

Notice that **`date`** gives both the time and date. There is a Unix **`time`** command, but it does not display the time; **`time`** measures how long it takes to run a program.

Internally, Unix does not really run on local time. All Unix systems really use Greenwich Mean Time (GMT). Unix silently converts between GMT and your local time zone as necessary. (The details about your local time are specified by the system manager when he or she installs Unix.)

Sometimes it is handy to see what time it is in GMT. To display the time in GMT (universal time), enter:

`date -u`

You will see a time and date like this:

`Fri Jun  5 03:39:42 GMT 1992`

This time, by the way, is the GMT equivalent of the time in the previous example.

Displaying a Calendar: `cal`

One of the nice things about Unix is that it was not designed by a committee. When the programmers decided that they wanted a new tool, they just added it to the system. A good example of this is the **`cal`** command, which displays a calendar.

To display the calendar for the current year, enter:

`cal`

To display a calendar for a particular year, just specify the year. For example:

`cal 1952`

When you specify a year, make sure to type all four numbers. If you enter **`cal 52`**, you will get the calendar for 52 A.D. You can use any year between 1 and 9999.

 HINT When you display the calendar for a full year, the output is long enough so that it may not fit entirely on your screen. If the top part of the calendar scrolls out of sight before you get a chance to read it, there are two things you can do:

- press ^S to pause the screen display; then press ^Q to continue (Chapter 6)
- send the output to a paging program such as **more** (Chapter 17)

To display a calendar for only one month, specify that month as a number between 1 and 12 (1 = January), as well as the year. For example, to display the calendar for December 1952, enter:

```
cal 12 1952
```

You will see:

```
    December  1952
   S   M Tu   W Th   F   S
       1   2   3   4   5   6
   7   8   9  10  11  12  13
  14  15  16  17  18  19  20
  21  22  23  24  25  26  27
  28  29  30  31
```

If you want a specific month, you must always specify both the month and the year. For instance, if it is currently June of 1993, and you want a calendar for that month, you must enter:

```
cal 6 1993
```

If you enter:

```
cal 6
```

you will get the whole year for 6 A.D.

Note: Unix does have a **calendar** command, but it is completely different. **calendar** offers a reminder service based on a file of important days and messages that you can create. The **calendar** command will check that file and display any messages for the current day. We won't go into the details here.

For extra credit

Our modern calendar – with regular years of 365 days and leap years of 366 days – is derived from the Julian calendar. This calendar was introduced by Julius Caesar in 46 B.C. (Actually, the calendar was developed by a grad student, but Caesar put his name on the paper.)

However, assuming that a year is exactly 365.25 days is too long by a matter of 11 minutes 10 seconds. By the sixteenth century, this small error had accumulated into about 10 days, which meant that the calendar everyone was using did not match the sun and the stars.

continued

> To solve this problem, Pope Gregory XIII decreed in 1582 that the world should modify its calendar so that not all centenary years (1600, 1700, and so on) should be leap years. Only the centenary years that are divisible by 400 (such as 2000) would be leap years. This scheme is called the Gregorian or New Style calendar.
>
> To calibrate the current calendar, Gregory further decreed that 10 days should vanish mysteriously.
>
> The Gregorian calendar was not adopted in Great Britain until 1752, by which time the error had increased to 11 days. Thus, if you enter the command:
>
> `cal 9 1752`
>
> you will see that between September 2 and September 14, 1752, there is a gap of 11 days. This gap is necessary for the sun and stars to work properly (at least in Great Britain).

How Long Has the System Been Up? `uptime`, `ruptime`

If you want to check how long your particular computer has been up (running continuously), enter:

`uptime`

You will see something like this:

`8:44pm up 4 days, 7:56, 3 users, load average: 0.13, 0.05, 0.00`

In this case, the system has been up for 4 days, 7 hours and 56 minutes, and there are 3 userids currently logged in. The last three numbers show the number of programs that have been waiting to execute, averaged over the last 1, 5 and 15 minutes respectively. These numbers give you an idea of the load on the system. The higher the load, the more the system is doing.

If you want to see similar information about all the machines on your local network, enter the "remote" version of this command:

`ruptime`

Here is some typical output:

```
ccse       up       4:27,   0 users,   load 0.42, 0.08, 0.02
engrhub    up  4+07:56,   2 users,   load 0.16, 0.07, 0.00
hub        up 33+06:25,   0 users,   load 2.64, 3.97, 3.90
mondas     up       3:31,   0 users,   load 0.00, 0.00, 0.00
nowhere    up 37+05:58,   0 users,   load 0.41, 0.26, 0.00
topgun     up  2+04:42,   0 users,   load 0.45, 0.48, 0.01
```

This example was generated at night (when the best computer book authors tend to work). Notice that the only computer that has anyone logged in is **engrhub**. You will also notice that the computer with the highest loads is **hub**. It happens that, in this network, **hub** is the computer that provides the link to the Internet (Chapters 13 and 25) and to the Usenet network (Chapter 23).

Which computer has been up the longest? The prize goes to **nowhere** which has been up for 37 days, 5 hours and 58 minutes. **mondas**, which has been up for only 3 hours and 31 minutes, gets the James Dean live-fast-die-young-and-leave-a-good-looking-corpse award.

Finding Out What's New in Your Neighborhood: `msgs`, `news`

Many Unix systems provide some type of news service to keep users abreast of the local current events. The news items at a university might concern job opportunities, special lectures, course changes, scheduled downtime for a computer, and so on.

If your system has a local news service, it will probably be accessed by either the **msgs** (messages) command or the **news** command. Just type in the command name; the program will do the rest. If you are not sure which command to use, try both.

msgs is actually a system that allows anyone to post a message to the local user community. To post a message, you simply mail it to userid **msgs**. (We will discuss sending mail in Chapter 14. In the meantime, you can read the messages mailed in by other users.)

When you start **msgs**, it describes the oldest message you have not yet seen. For instance:

```
Message 4356:
From harley@nipper.ucsb.edu Sun May 17 16:57:11 1992
Subject: Free money
(22 lines) More? [ynq]
```

In this example, we see a message from a userid named **harley**. The subject looks interesting, and the message is 22 lines long.

If you would like to see the entire message, enter **y** (for yes) or press the <Return> key. If you do not want to see the message, enter **n** (for no). Once you have disposed of this message, one way or the other, **msgs** will display information about the next message.

Aside from **y** and **n**, you can enter – (the minus sign) to display the previous message.

When you are ready to quit, enter **q**. **msgs** will make a note of where you were. Next time you run the program, it will continue from where you left off.

If you see a particularly interesting message, you can enter **s** to save it to a file named **Messages**. Entering **s-** will save the previous message. If you want to specify an alternate file name, you can do so. Just make sure to leave a space after the **s** or **s-**. For example, you can enter **s money** to save the current message to a file named **money**.

The **news** program differs from **msgs** in that the system administrator controls what messages are posted. If you have a **news** command on your system, it will display news items, from newest to oldest, one after the other. Each item will be displayed in full, one screenful at a time.

At the bottom of each screen, you will see something like:

`--More--[Press space to continue, 'q' to quit.]`

There are a number of responses, only two of which are really important. If you want to continue, press the <Space> bar. If you want to quit, type **q**. If you feel ambitious and you want to see all possible responses to this message, press **h** (for help).

If you keep pressing <Space>, **news** will display screen after screen of news items. Unlike **msgs**, the **news** program does not remember what you have already read. It always starts with the newest item and works its way backwards. If you have the patience, **news** will be glad to take you back through months or even years of local announcements. Most people press <Space> until they see stuff that looks familiar, and then type **q**.

Note: In Chapter 23, we will talk about the worldwide Usenet news network. This has nothing to do with the local news we just described. Usenet is actually a collection of global discussion groups, although it is often called "The News".

Information About You and Your System: `hostname`, `whoami`, `quota`

Here are a few quick commands to display information about you and your system.

The **hostname** command will display the name of the system you are using. This can come in handy if you are in the habit of logging in to more than one computer. If you forget what system you are using, all you need to do is enter **hostname**.

The **whoami** command displays the name of your userid. This command is handy when you come upon a terminal that someone has left logged in. Enter **whoami** to see the current userid. (This command is also useful if you are suddenly struck by amnesia and forget your name. Looking at your userid may give you a clue.)

On many computers, the system manager will impose a limit as to how much disk storage space each user is allowed to use. If you want to check your limit, enter the **quota** command. Note: Unix measures disk space in KB or kilobytes; 1 KB = 1024 bytes (characters).

Locking Your Terminal: `lock`

As we mentioned in Chapter 4, it is a bad idea to leave your terminal logged in. Someone can come along and, under the auspices of your userid, cause a lot of trouble. For example, they may delete all your files, send rude messages to the system manager in your name, and so on. However, if you do need to step away from your terminal for a moment, it is irritating to have to log out and in again.

Instead, you can use the **lock** command. This tells Unix that you want to lock your terminal temporarily. The terminal will remain locked until you enter a special password.

To use this command, just enter:

```
lock
```

Unix will display:

Key:

Enter the password that you want to use to unlock the terminal. This password can be anything you want; it has nothing to do with your login password. Unix will not echo the password as you type, just in case someone else is looking at your screen.

After you enter the password, Unix will display:

Again:

This is asking you to retype the password, to ensure that you did not make a mistake.

As soon as you have entered and re-entered the special password, Unix will freeze your terminal. Nothing will happen, no matter what anyone types on the terminal, until you enter the password. (Don't forget to press the <Return> key.) As soon as you enter the password, Unix will reactivate your terminal and you can return to your work.

If you are working in a place where you must share terminals and there are people waiting, it is considered bad form to lock your terminal and leave for a long time – say, to eat dinner. Since Unix was developed in such an environment, the **lock** command has a built-in limitation: the terminal will unlock automatically after 15 minutes.

By default, **lock** will freeze a terminal for 15 minutes. However, if you want to override this default, some versions of **lock** will let you specify an alternate time limit when you enter the command. After the name of the command, leave a space, and then type – (a minus sign), followed by a number. For example, to lock your terminal for 5 minutes, enter:

```
lock -5
```

You might ask, what happens if someone locks a terminal and then leaves for good? Eventually, the command will time out and unlock. If the terminal needs to be reactivated right away, the system manager can enter the **root** (superuser) password. **lock** will always accept the **root** password (sort of like a master key).

Remember though, if you lock your terminal and don't come back, someone will come along eventually and find your terminal reactivated and logged in under your userid. Whatever trouble they cause under your userid will be your responsibility.

Asking Unix to Remind You When to Leave: `leave`

As you know, working on a computer can be engrossing, and it is easy to lose track of the time. To help you fulfill your worldly obligations, Unix has a command that reminds you when it is time to leave.

The name of the command is **leave**. When you enter this command, Unix will ask you:

`When do you have to leave?`

Enter the time that you want to leave in the form *hhmm*. For example, if you want to leave at 10:33, enter **1033**.

You can enter times using either a 12-hour or 24-hour system. For instance, **1344** means 1:44 PM. If you enter a number of hours that is 12 or less, Unix assumes that it is within the next 12 hours. For instance, if it is 8:00 PM and you enter **855**, Unix assumes you mean 8:55 PM, not 8:55 AM.

If you need to leave after a certain time interval, type a **+** (plus sign) followed by the number of minutes. For example, if you need to leave after 5 minutes, type **+5**. (Be sure not to leave a space after the **+** character.)

An alternate way to start the program is to enter the time right on the command line. After the name of the command, leave a space and type the time. For example, to leave at 10:30, enter:

`leave 1030`

To leave in 45 minutes, enter:

`leave +45`

 HINT   When you log out, Unix discards a pending **leave** command. Thus, if you use **leave**, but then log out and in again, you will have to enter a new command.

Once you have entered the **leave** command, Unix checks periodically to see how much time is left. When it is five minutes before the time you specified, Unix will display:

`You have to leave in 5 minutes`

When there is one minute left, you will see:

Just one more minute!

When the time is up, Unix displays:

Time to leave!

From that point on, Unix will keep nagging you with reminders, once a minute:

You're going to be late!

until you log off. Finally, after ten such reminders, you will see:

You're going to be late!
That was the last time I'll tell you. Bye.

Perhaps this program should have been named **mother**.

A Built-in Calculator: bc

One of the most useful (and least appreciated) Unix programs is **bc**, which implements a full-fledged, programmable scientific calculator. Many people do not bother learning how to use **bc**. "I spit on **bc**," they sneer, "nobody uses it." Don't be misled. Once you learn how to use **bc**, you will find it invaluable for quick calculations.

If you use X Window (see Chapter 5), there is a program named **xcalc** that you can use. **xcalc** looks nice – it actually draws a picture of a calculator on your screen – but, for minute-to-minute work or for extensive calculation, **bc** is better. Moreover, **bc** does not require X Window and will work with any terminal.

To explain **bc**, we will start with a short technical summary. If you don't understand all the mathematical and computer terms, don't worry. In the next few sections, we will explain how to use **bc** for basic calculations (which is easy) along with a few examples. If after reading the summary, you are not interested, you can skip right to the games.

A technical summary of **bc**: **bc** is a fully programmable mathematical interpreter. **bc** offers extended precision; each number is stored automatically with as many digits as necessary. In addition, you can specify a scale of up to 100 digits to the right of the decimal point. Numeric values can be manipulated in any base from 2 to 16. It is easy to convert from one base to another.

You can use **bc** either by entering calculations from the keyboard, which are interpreted immediately, or by running programs stored in files.

The programming syntax of **bc** is similar to the C programming language. You can define functions and use recursion. There are arrays, and local and global variables. You can write your own functions, store them in a file, and have **bc** load and interpret them automatically. **bc** comes with a library that contains the following functions: sin, cos, arctan, ln, exponential and Bessel function. (Everybody who knows what a Bessel function is, raise your hand...)

For more information, see the online manual description of the **bc** command. (We will explain the online Unix manual in Chapter 8.)

Using bc for Calculations

Most of the time, you will use **bc** for routine calculations, which is simple. To start the program, enter:

```
bc
```

If you want to use the built-in library of mathematical functions (see below), start the program using:

```
bc -l
```

Once you start **bc**, there is no specific prompt; just enter one calculation after another. Each time you press <Return>, **bc** evaluates what you have typed and displays the answer. For example, if you enter:

```
122152 + 70867 + 122190
```

bc will display:

```
315209
```

You can now enter a new calculation. If you want to enter more than one calculation on the same line, separate them with semicolons (just like Unix commands). **bc** will display each result on a separate line. For example, if you enter:

```
10+10; 20+20
```

you will see:

```
20
40
```

When you are finished working with **bc**, stop the program by telling it there is no more data. To do this, press **^D**, the **eof** key (see Chapter 6). Alternatively, you can enter **quit**.

Within a calculation you can use the following operations:

addition:	**+**
subtraction:	**–**
multiplication:	*****
division:	**/**
modulo:	**%**
exponentiation:	**^**
square root:	**sqrt** (x)

Modulo finds the remainder after a division. For example, **53%10** is 3. Exponentiation refers to taking a number to a power. For example, **3^2** means "3 to the power of 2", which is 9. The power must be a whole number, but can be negative. If you use a negative power, enclose it in parentheses; for example, **3^(-1)**.

bc follows the general rules of algebra: multiplication, division and modulo have precedence over addition and subtraction; exponentiation has precedence over everything. Just like algebra, you can change the order of evaluation by using parentheses. So, **1+2*3** is 7, where **(1+2)*3** is 9.

Aside from the standard operations, there are a number of useful functions in a special library. These functions are:

sin:	**s** (x)
cos:	**c** (x)
arctan:	**a** (x)
ln:	**l** (x)
exponential:	**e** (x)
Bessel function:	**j** (n, x)

If you want to use the functions in this library, you need to start **bc** using the command:

bc -l

When you use this command, **bc** automatically sets the scale factor to 20 (see below).

As we mentioned earlier, **bc** can compute to arbitrary precision. That is, it will use as many digits as necessary to perform a calculation. For instance, you can ask it to add two 100-digit numbers. (We tested this.)

However, by default, **bc** will assume you are working with whole numbers. That is, **bc** will not keep any digits to the right of the decimal point. If you want to use fractional values, you need to set a scale factor to tell **bc** how many digits you want to keep to the right of the decimal point. To do this, set the value of **scale** to the scale factor you want.

For example, to ask for 3 digits to the right of the decimal point, enter:

scale=3

From now on, all work will be done to three decimal places. Any extra digits will be truncated.

If, at any point, you want to check what the scale factor is, simply enter:

scale

bc will display the current value.

When you start **bc**, **scale** is set automatically to 0. One of the most common mistakes is to start calculations without setting a scale factor. For instance, let's say that you have just started **bc**. You enter:

150/60

bc displays:

2

You now enter:

35/60

bc displays:

0

Finally, you figure out what the problem is and set an appropriate scale factor:

`scale=3`

Now, **bc** will display what you want to see. (Try it.)

Remember, when you use the mathematical library, **bc** automatically starts with a scale factor of 20.

Using Variables with bc

Like all programming languages, **bc** allows you to set and use variables.

A variable is a quantity with a name and a value. Variable names consist of a single lowercase letter; that is, there are 26 variables, from **a** to **z**. (Make sure that you do not use uppercase letters; these are used when working with bases – see below.)

You set the value of a variable by using an = (equals sign) character. For example, to set the value of the variable **x** to 100, enter:

`x=100`

To display the value of a variable, just enter its name. For example:

`x`

bc will respond with the current value. By definition, all variables are assumed to be zero unless you set them otherwise.

You will find that using variables is straightforward and adds a lot of power to your work with **bc**. Here is an example that illustrates the basic principles:

The Maharaja of Gaipajama has been impressed with your facility in Unix. As a token of his esteem, he offers you twice your weight in rubies, worth $1000 a pound, and one third of your weight in diamonds, worth $2000 a pound. (The Maharaja of Gaipajama buys his gems wholesale.)

You weigh 160 pounds. How much is the Maharaja's present worth? To solve this problem, start **bc** and enter:

```
w=160
r=(w*2)*1000
d=(w/3)*2000
r+d
```

The answer is displayed:

```
426000
```

Thus, your gift is worth $426,000.

But wait: Once the Maharaja realizes how much his promise will cost him, he says, "Did I say I would give you gems based on your weight in pounds? I should have said kilograms."

Since 1 kilogram is 2.2 pounds, you quickly convert the **w** variable to kilograms:

```
w=w/2.2
```

Now you re-enter the calculations for the value of rubies and diamonds:

```
r=(w*2)*1000
d=(w/3)*2000
r+d
```

The new answer is displayed:

```
192000
```

Thus, by adhering to the metric system, the Maharaja has saved $234,000 (and has allowed you to demonstrate how to set a new value for a variable, based on its old value; in this case, **w=w/2.2**).

Using bc with Different Bases

As you would assume, **bc** normally uses base 10 arithmetic. However, there will be times when you may want to calculate using another base. For example, in computer science, it is sometimes necessary to use base 16 (hexadecimal), base 8 (octal) or base 2 (binary). If you are not a computer science student, you may want to skip this section.

bc allows you to specify different bases for input and for output. To do so, there are two special variables that you can set: **ibase** is the base that will be used for input; **obase** is the base that will be used for output.

For example, if you want to display answers in base 16, enter:

```
obase=16
```

If you want to enter numbers in base 8, use:

```
ibase=8
```

In the last section, we said that, by default, variables have a value of 0 until you set them. **ibase** and **obase** are exceptions: they are automatically initialized to 10 so you can work in base 10. If you want to work in another base, you can set either of the variables to any value from 2 to 16.

You should appreciate that the values of **ibase** and **obase** do not affect how **bc** manipulates numbers internally. Their only effect is to specify how numbers should be translated during input or output.

To work with bases larger than 10, **bc** represents the values of 10, 11, 12, 13, 14 and 15 as the uppercase letters A, B, C, D, E and F, respectively. Always remember to use uppercase; if you use lowercase, **bc** will think you are referring to variables, and the result will be wrong.

For convenience, you can use these uppercase letters regardless of what input base you have set. For instance, even if you are working in base 10, the expression **A+1** will have the value 11.

As with all variables, you can find out the current values of **ibase** and **obase** by entering the names by themselves:

```
ibase
obase
```

However, you must be careful. Once you set **obase**, all output will be displayed in that base, and you may have trouble interpreting what you see.

For instance, if you enter:

```
obase=16
obase
```

you will see:

```
10
```

This is because all output is to be displayed in base 16, and – in base 16 – the value of "16" is expressed as 10.

Similarly, once you change **ibase**, you must be careful what you type as input. For example, say that you set:

```
ibase=16
```

You now want to set **obase** to base 10, so you enter:

```
obase=10
```

However, you have forgotten that input is now in base 16, and 10 in base 16 is really "16". Thus, you have set **obase**, as well, to base 16.

To avoid such errors, use the letters A though F, which retain the same value regardless of the **ibase** value. Thus, if things become confused, you can always reset the bases by entering:

```
obase=A
ibase=A
```

Here are two examples of changing bases. In the first, you want to add two hexadecimal (base 16) numbers, F03E and 3BAC. Enter:

```
obase=16
ibase=16
F03E + 3BAC
```

bc displays the answer:

```
12BEA
```

In the second example, you want to convert the hexadecimal number FFC1 to binary (base 2). Reset the bases:

obase=A
ibase=A

then enter:

obase=2
ibase=16
FFC1

bc displays the answer:

1111111111000001

Using the Unix Games

Almost since its inception, Unix has come with a number of games and curiosities. Although some commercial Unix vendors have removed the games, Berkeley Unix still retains them.

Virtually all of the standard games are old; indeed, some of them date way back to ancient versions of Unix that were developed at Bell Labs. However, as Shakespeare once put it (while playing Hunt the Wumpus), "Age cannot wither her, nor custom stale her infinite variety."

Your system may have a variety of new games. If you use X Window (see Chapter 5), there may be X games. There may also be games specially written for your computer. For instance, Next computers come with their own games.

Before we get into a description of the games, there are two points that you should understand.

We said earlier that when you enter a command, Unix looks for a program by that name to execute. Where does Unix look? We won't go into the details here, but programs are stored in files, and files are collected into directories. Unix has a list, called the "search path", that describes which directories should be searched for programs. If you want to see the search path, enter:

echo $PATH

Whenever you enter a command, Unix looks in each directory in the search path, one after another, until it finds the program you want. If Unix can't find the program, it will tell you so. (This may happen if you misspell the name of the command.)

To start a game, you enter the name of the appropriate command. For example, to start Hunt the Wumpus, you enter:

wump

Now, the name of the directory in which all the games are kept is **/usr/games**. (This name will make sense after we discuss directories in

Chapter 21.) When you enter the **wump** command, Unix must look in this directory to find a program named **wump**.

But, on some systems, the "games" directory is not in the search path. Unix will not be able to find the program and you will see:

wump: Command not found.

If this is the case on your system, you must tell Unix explicitly which directory to search. You do this by specifying the directory name, followed by a **/** (slash), before the name of the command:

/usr/games/wump

Now Unix will be able to find the program, and the game will start.

In the following sections, we will give you the names of all the Unix games. You may find that, on your system, you will have to preface each name with **/usr/games/** when you enter the command. (Try it and find out.) For instance, to start the **fortune** program, you may have to enter:

/usr/games/fortune

When you enter such a command, be sure that you do not put any spaces before or after one of the slashes. Also, make sure that you do not spell **usr** with an "e".

The second point we want you to realize is that, although the games can provide pleasant diversions, they are not the main reason that someone is spending a lot of money to provide you with a Unix system.

The games, of course, are Unix programs, just like many of the tools that you will use. You will find that in learning how to start, stop and use a few games, you are also learning a great deal about how to use Unix programs in general. In other words, using the Unix games is, arguably, an educational experience.

Still, it behooves you to respect the wishes of your system manager. Do not tie up a terminal or workstation playing games when other people need to get more serious (and boring) work done.

Some system managers restrict game playing to certain off hours. Other system managers remove the games completely. (You may find, though, that even if all the other games are gone, **fortune** will be retained, simply because it is so amusing.)

How Do You Stop a Game?

It is always a good idea to know how to stop a program. The hints that we give in this section apply to all Unix programs, and not just to games.

Some programs are complex enough to have a whole list of commands that you can use. For example, the **adventure** game allows you to enter commands as you explore a large cave. With such programs, there will be some type of prompt to let you know when you can enter a command.

If you need help, wait for the prompt and enter **help**. If that doesn't work, try **h** or **?** (a question mark).

When you are working with a program that reads commands, entering **quit** will often stop the program. If that doesn't work, try **q**, **Q** or **bye**. If none of these work, read the instructions.

Once you enter the quit command – whatever it is for that game – you may be asked if you really want to quit. This prevents you from accidentally losing hours of work (!) by typing the wrong word.

Since most games read input from your terminal, you can often end them by indicating that there is no more data. To do this, press **^D**, the **eof** key (see Chapter 6). If all else fails, you may be able to stop a program by pressing **^C**, the **intr** key (also Chapter 6).

Learning How to Play a Game

In the next section, we will give brief descriptions of each Unix game. Most of the complicated games are able to provide you with instructions as you play. However, for extra help, you can look in the online Unix manual.

We will discuss the online manual in detail in Chapter 8. For now, we will mention that to learn about a command – any command, not just a game – you use the **man** command. Enter **man** followed by the name of the program you want to learn about.

For example, to learn about the **fortune** program, enter:

man fortune

(To learn about the **man** command itself, enter **man man**.)

man will display information about the command you specify, one screenful at a time. At the bottom of the screen, you will see:

--More--

This tells you that there is more information. To display the next screen, press the <Space> bar. To quit, press the **q** key.

Before you start playing a new game, always check the description in the online manual. This will tell you how to start the game and, generally, how it works.

When you use a game for the first time, answer **y** (for yes) if it asks if you want instructions. Even if you think you know how to play – for example, the backgammon game – it will be different when played on a computer.

A Description of the Unix Games

When we refer to the Unix "games", we are really talking about two types of programs, all of which reside in the **/usr/games** directory.

First, there are a good many real games: blackjack, Monopoly, Hunt the Wumpus and so on. Second, there are diversions and curiosities (such as weird math programs and fortune telling programs) that are also part of Unix. In this section, we will describe the actual games. In the next section, we will discuss the other programs.

We can divide the standard Unix games into several categories. First, there are the games that you will find familiar. Several programs are based on well-known board games: **chess**, **mille** (Mille Bournes) and **monop** (Monopoly). There are also programs based on cards and gambling: **backgammon**, **btlgammon** (another backgammon), **bj** (blackjack), **canfield** (a form of solitaire), **craps**, **cribbage**, and the old standby, **fish**. In addition, there is a quiz program, **quiz**, as well as a guessing game called **moo**. Finally, there are two word games, **boggle** and **hangman**.

Next, there are games that will take you into some type of strange new world. All the information is textual; the program describes what you are looking at, what you are carrying with you, and so on. These games are habit-forming and are perfectly capable of occupying all your time for the foreseeable future.

The granddaddy of such games is **adventure**. In this game, you explore a large, labyrinth-like cave. Part of the charm of the game is that you have to figure out not only how everything works, but what it is exactly that you are supposed to do (just like real life). Indeed, before you can even start your explorations, you have to discover how to get into the cave. If you decide to play **adventure**, we have a hint for you: make yourself a map as you go. Another, more modern, game in this genre – with a completely different scenario – is **battlestar**.

The third category consists of visual games that draw pictures on your terminal. First, there is **snake**, in which you try to make as much money as possible without getting eaten by the snake (another allegory for real life.) Second, there is **worm**, in which you see how long you can keep a growing worm alive.

There are also visual games in which you shoot at something: **robots** (where you shoot at tiny robots), **trek** (based on Star Trek-like concepts) and **wump** (where you go after the cave-dwelling Wumpus with your bow and arrow).

The last two shooting games are **hunt** and **sail**. Both are multi-user, designed to be played by more than one person on the same network. Unlike **wump**, where you are restricted to the isolated pleasure of hunting an imaginary animal, **hunt** and **sail** afford the much more satisfying experience of tracking down and destroying your friends.

The final fantasy game is **rogue**, a popular visually oriented Dungeons and Dragons game, in which you evade the attacks of various monsters as you search for the Amulet of Yendor. If your system does not have **rogue**, it may have **hack**, a replacement for **rogue**. **hack** offers twice as many monster types (but requires three times the memory).

Diversions and Curiosities

Along with the games that we described in the previous section, Unix also contains a number of miscellaneous programs under the "games" heading.

For the mathematically inclined, there are **factor** (which decomposes any number into its prime factors) and **primes** (which generates all the prime numbers larger than a specified value).

For the non-mathematically inclined, we have **arithmetic** (to practice simple computation) and **number** (which reads any integer and converts it to English words).

To create signs and notices, you can use **banner**, which takes any series of characters and displays them enlarged.

There are two versions of the **banner** program. The first displays letters that are just the right size for your screen. For example:

```
#       #
#       #  # # # # # #   #         #         # # # #
#       #  #            #         #       #       #
# # # # # #  # # # # #     #         #       #       #
#       #  #            #         #       #       #
#       #  #            #         #       #       #
#       #  # # # # # #   # # # # # #   # # # # # #   # # # #
```

The other version of **banner** displays extremely large characters suitable for printing. These characters come out sideways and, when printed on continuous paper, make a nice sign. You will have to experiment to see which type of **banner** program is on your computer. In Chapter 18, we give an example of the commands you can use to print a sign using **banner**.

If you are a real old-timer, you may remember paper tape and punch cards. Well, Unix does, too. The **ppt** program reads a string of characters and shows how it would look encoded on paper tape. For example, the words "Harley Hahn" look like this:

```
| o   o.     |
| oo    .   o|
| ooo  . o  |
| oo o.o    |
| oo   .o o|
| oooo.   o|
| o    .    |
| o   o.    |
| oo   .   o|
| oo o.     |
| oo o.oo  |
|     o. o  |
```

The **bcd** program makes a similar translation to a punch card:

```
/HARLEY HAHN                                                        |
|]]   ]  ]]]                                                        |
|  ]]        ]                                                      |
|     ]                                                             |
|1]111111]1111111111111111111111111111111111111111|
|22222222222222222222222222222222222222222222222|
|333]333333333333333333333333333333333333333333|
|44444444444444444444444444444444444444444444444|
|5555]55555]5555555555555555555555555555555555|
|66666666666666666666666666666666666666666666666|
|77777777777777777777777777777777777777777777777|
|]8]88]8]8]88888888888888888888888888888888888|
|99999999999999999999999999999999999999999999999|
|  _____|
```

(If you are not sure what "bcd" stands for, ask an old person.)

If you have very little imagination and nothing to do, you might try **rain** or **worms**, which display moving shapes on the screen of your terminal. (Do not confuse **worms** with **worm**, the game we mentioned in the previous section.)

If you have a moderate imagination and nothing to do, you will love **fortune**. This program draws on a large database of pithy, humorous and offensive items. Every time you run **fortune**, it randomly selects and displays an item from the database.

To run **fortune**, simply enter its name:

fortune

Here is some sample output:

Any small object that is accidentally dropped
will hide under a larger object.

The idea is to simulate the type of fortune you might find inside a bizarre type of fortune cookie. Left to its own, **fortune** selects an item from the entire database, including the obscene entries. If you want to request an obscene fortune specifically, enter:

fortune -o

Here is one of the few examples that we can print in a family-oriented book like this one:

There was a young lady from Maine
Who claimed she had men on her brain.
**   But you knew from the view,**
**   As her abdomen grew,**
It was not on her brain that he'd lain.

Be aware that some Unix companies remove the obscene fortunes from the database. When you ask for such a fortune, you may see a message like this:

```
Sorry, no obscene fortunes.  Don't want to offend anyone.
(Now that's obscene!)
```

As you will see in Chapter 11, there is a way to specify commands for Unix to run each time you log out. Some people add **fortune** to this list. Indeed, your system manager may have already set up your account in this way. If so, you will have noticed a different fortune every time you log out. Now you know where it comes from.

Finally, if you are one of those unusual people with an enormous imagination and nothing to do, try **ching**. This program draws on the I Ching, a Chinese book that has been a source of wisdom and advice for centuries. (Many calculus teachers use it to set final exams.) Enter:

```
ching
```

Now type a question, as many lines as you want. (If you are not sure what to ask, try "Is it time for me to get back to work?") When you are finished, press **^D**, the **eof** key (see Chapter 6).

ching will display the same type of cryptic analysis as the real I Ching. You now have many happy hours ahead of you, interpreting the results and deciding how they apply to your life. Perhaps, with a little practice, you may even be able to start your own religion. If so, be sure to mention Unix.

The Online Unix Manual

When it comes to learning, there are two important parts of the Unix tradition that you should understand: first, you are expected to teach your-self; second, if you have tried your best and you still have a problem, a more advanced user will be glad to help you. (The converse of this, of course, is that once you are experienced you are expected to help anyone who knows less than you.)

Unix comes with a large, built-in manual that is accessible at any time from your terminal. Before you ask for help, it is expected that you will have looked in the manual. After all, it is available to everybody at all times.

In this chapter, we will discuss the Unix online manual: What is it? How do you use it? And what are the best strategies for finding information?

What Is the Online Manual? man

The ONLINE MANUAL is a collection of files, stored on disk, each of which contains the documentation about one Unix command or topic. You can access the online manual at any time by using the **man** command. Type the word **man**, followed by the name of the command you want to know about. Unix will display the documentation for that command.

For example, to display the documentation about the **cp** command, enter:

```
man cp
```

To learn about the **man** command itself, enter:

```
man man
```

HINT The **man** command is the single most important Unix command, because you can use it to learn about any command you want.

If you want, you can specify more than one command name. For example:

```
man cp mv ln
```

Unix will display the documentation for each command in turn.

WHAT'S IN A NAME?

The Manual

The online Unix manual has always been important. Indeed, at one time, when Unix was primarily a product of AT&T's Bell Labs, versions of Unix were named after the current edition of the manual: Unix Sixth Edition, Unix Seventh Edition, and so on.

Although there are many Unix books and references, there is only one online manual. When someone says, look it up in "the manual", he or she means to use the **man** command and check with the online manual. There is never any doubt as to which manual is The Manual.

Displaying the Online Manual on Your Terminal

Virtually all the entries in the online manual are longer than the number of lines on your screen. If an entry were displayed all at once, most of it would scroll off the screen so fast that you would not be able to read the text.

This is a common situation for which Unix has a good solution: send the output to a program that will display the output more carefully, one screenful at a time. There are three such programs, called paging programs, that are commonly used on Unix systems. Their names are **more**, **pg** and **less**.

In Chapter 17, we will talk about each of the paging programs. For now, we will give you a brief overview so that you will know enough to be able to read the online manual.

A paging program displays data one screenful at a time. After each screenful, the program pauses and displays a prompt at the bottom left-hand corner of the screen. The prompt differs depending on what paging program is being used.

The **more** program displays a prompt that contains the word "More". For example, you might see:

```
--More--(25%)
```

This means that there is more to come and you have read 25% of the data. (You can see where the name of the program comes from.) The **pg** program displays a prompt that is a simple colon:

:

The **less** program also displays a colon, possibly followed by some other information.

Once you have read what is on the screen, you can display more data by pressing the <Space> bar (for **more** and **less**) or the <Return> key (for **pg**). If you are not sure which paging program you are using, just experiment. Nothing bad will happen.

The idea is that by pressing <Space> (or possibly <Return>) repeatedly, you can page through the entire manual entry, one screen at a time. At any time, you can enter **q** to quit. (With **pg**, you will have to press <Return> after the **q**.)

When all the data has been displayed, the paging program will either stop by itself (**more**), stop when you press <Return> (**pg**), or stop when you enter the **q** command (**less**).

As you are reading, there are many commands that you can enter when the program is paused at a prompt. We will mention two of those commands here.

First, if you are looking for a specific pattern, press the **/** (slash), type the pattern, and then press <Return>. For example:

/output

In this case, the paging program will skip to the next line that contains the word "output".

Second, for instant assistance, you can enter the **h** (help) command at any time. (With **pg**, you will have to press <Return> after the **h**.) This command will display a summary of commands.

In Chapter 17, we will discuss the three paging programs in detail. If you want some extra information, look at the manual entries for these programs. You can use the commands:

man more
man pg
man less

Note: Not all systems have the **less** program.

 HINT   If you are using X Window, there is an X client named **xman** that provides a graphical version of the **man** command. If you prefer to use the regular **man** command, you will need to execute it from within an **xterm** window.

How Is the Online Manual Organized?

The best way to think about the online manual is to imagine a gargantuan reference book that lives somewhere inside your Unix system. The book is like an encyclopedia in that it contains many entries, in alphabetical order, each of which covers a single topic.

You can't turn the pages of this book; hence, there are no page numbers, no table of contents and no index. However, there are several layers of organization that are appropriate to an electronic book.

Traditionally, the entire manual is divided into eight main sections. These classic divisions are shown in Figure 8-1.

As you might imagine from looking at the names, the most important sections are 1, 6 and possibly 7.

Section 1 contains the descriptions of the bulk of the Unix commands. Most users can get by just fine with only this section of the manual.

 HINT The most important section of the online Unix manual is Section 1, which contains descriptions of most of the commands. It may be the only section you will ever need.

Section 6 contains descriptions of the Unix games (see Chapter 7). If the system manager has not installed the games on your system, you will probably find that Section 6 of the manual will also be missing. Otherwise, the system manager risks having complaints from users who can read about

Section	Topic
(1)	Commands
(2)	System Calls
(3)	Library Functions
(4)	Special Files
(5)	File Formats
(6)	Games
(7)	Miscellaneous Information
(8)	Maintenance Commands

Figure 8-1
The Eight Main Sections of the Online Unix Manual

the games, but can't use them (sort of like Moses standing on Mount Pisgah and gazing down at the Promised Land).

Section 7 contains a grab-bag of information, much of which pertains to using the Unix typesetting facilities.

If you are a programmer, Sections 2, 3, 4 and 5 may be important. Section 2 describes the system calls – ways in which your programs may call on Unix to perform certain tasks. Section 3 explains the built-in libraries of functions and subroutines that you can use in your programs. Section 4 describes the interfaces to various hardware devices, while Section 5 shows the formats of the important files that are used by the system.

Section 8 contains descriptions of the special commands that system managers use to carry out their work.

☑ HINT

Sections 2, 3, 4 and 5 of the Unix manual are of interest only to programmers; Section 8 is only for system administrators.

Before we move on, we would like to mention that the eight-section organization, derived from the earliest Unix implementations, has pretty much remained intact.

However, the modern Unix online manual covers much more material than its venerable ancestor. Thus, you may see different, more comprehensive section names.

For example, on one Unix system, Section 4, Special Files, is called "Devices and Network Interfaces", while Section 7, Miscellaneous Information, is called "Environments, Tables and Troff Macros". (**troff** is the name of the Unix typesetting program.)

You may also see sections broken down into sub-sections. For instance, Section 1 is always the main command reference. However, you may see Section 1c (for communication commands), Section 1g (graphics commands), Section 1X (X window commands), and so on.

Within a section, a single piece of documentation is called a PAGE or an ENTRY.

WHAT'S IN A NAME?

Page   In the beginning, Unix users had slow terminals, many of which printed on paper. Thus, it was convenient to print out pages of the manual, rather than access them on a terminal. At the time, most of the manual entries fit on a single page. To this day, each entry is still referred to as a "page", even though it may be hundreds of lines.

For example, you might overhear two Unix experts talking. One says, "I can't decide what to get my girlfriend for her birthday." The other replies, "Why not print her a copy of the manual page for the C-Shell?"

The word "page" is used in this manner even though, in this case, the actual entry might take up many printed pages.

In informal conversation or writing, the word "manual" is often abbreviated to "man". For example, "Last Mother's Day, I gave my mother a copy of the Korn shell man page."

Specifying the Section Number When Using the man Command

So far, we have seen how to use **man** by typing the name of the command you want to learn about. For example, to learn about the **kill** command (which can stop a runaway program), you can enter:

```
man kill
```

You will see the description of **kill** that resides in Section 1 of the manual.

However, it happens that there is also an entry for **kill** in Section 2 (System Calls). If this is what you are really interested in, you can specify the section number before the name of the command:

```
man 2 kill
```

This tells Unix that you are only interested in a particular section of the manual. If the section you are referencing is divided into sub-sections, you can be as specific as you want. For example, there is an entry for **kill** in Section 3f, the part of the manual that documents Fortran subroutines. To display this description, enter:

```
man 3f kill
```

As we mentioned earlier, you can ask for more than one part of the manual at a time. For instance, if you want to see all three entries for **kill**, you can enter:

```
man 1 kill 2 kill 3f kill
```

When you do not specify a section number, Unix starts at the beginning of the manual (Section 1) and works its way through until it finds the first match. Thus, the following two commands will have the same result:

```
man kill
man 1 kill
```

Most of the time, you will be interested in the basic commands (Section 1), so it will not be necessary to specify a section number.

To orient you to the various parts of the manual, each section and sub-section contains a page called **intro** that acts as a brief introduction. A good way to become familiar with the contents of a section is to display its **intro** page.

Here are some examples of commands that display such pages:

```
man intro
man 1 intro
man 1c intro
man 6 intro
```

As you know, **man** will assume Section 1 by default; thus, the first two examples are equivalent.

 HINT To learn more about using the online manual, use the following two commands:

```
man man
man intro
```

How Manual Pages Are Referenced

When you read about Unix, you will frequently see a name followed by a number in parenthesis. This number tells you what section of the manual to look in for information about this item.

For example, here is part of a sentence taken from the Berkeley version of the man page for the **chmod** command (which we will meet in Chapter 22). For now, don't worry about what the sentence means, just look at the reference:

```
"...but the setting of the file creation mask,
    see umask(2), is taken into account..."
```

This reference tells us that we can enter the command:

```
man 2 umask
```

for more information. However, since we know that Section 2 describes system calls, we can guess that we would only care about this reference if we were writing a program.

At the end of the **chmod** man page are the following two lines:

```
SEE ALSO
    ls(1), chmod(2), stat(2), umask(2), chown(8)
```

These references tell us that there are five other man pages related to this one. As you can see, three of the references are in Section 2 and are for programmers. The last reference is in Section 8 (Maintenance Commands) and is for system administrators.

On the other hand, the first reference suggests that we look at the man page for **ls** in Section 1 of the manual. Since Section 1 describes general commands, there is a good chance that this reference will be of interest.

 HINT   If you see a reference to a command that is in Section 1 of the online manual – for example, **ls(1)** – it is usually worth looking at. References to other sections can be ignored unless the Section 1 information is not adequate.

The Format of a Manual Page

Each man page explains a single topic. Some pages are short, while others are quite long. (For example, **csh(1)** – the man page that describes the C-Shell – is a reference manual in its own right.)

For convenience, each man page is organized according to a standard format using the headings shown in Figure 8-2. Not all man pages will have each of these headings. Moreover, some Unix systems use different headings. However, if you understand the standard headings, you should be able to figure out whatever your system uses.

Let's take a quick look at each of these headings. To show you how it all works, Figure 8-3 contains a typical man page. As you read Figure 8-3, remember that, in Unix, the word "print" usually refers to displaying text on your terminal, not actual printing (see Chapter 6).

Name:

In one line, this is what the command is all about. Be aware that some of the descriptions are vague.

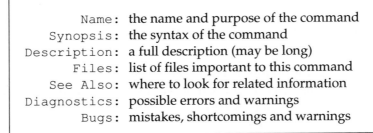

```
      Name:  the name and purpose of the command
  Synopsis:  the syntax of the command
Description:  a full description (may be long)
     Files:  list of files important to this command
  See Also:  where to look for related information
Diagnostics:  possible errors and warnings
      Bugs:  mistakes, shortcomings and warnings
```

Figure 8-2
The Standard Headings Used in the Online Unix Manual

```
MAN(1)                    USER COMMANDS                      MAN(1)
NAME
     man - display reference manual pages; find reference pages
     by keyword
SYNOPSIS
     man [-] [section] title ...
     man -k keyword ...
     man -f filename ...
DESCRIPTION
     Man is a program which gives information from the programmers manual.
     It can be asked for one-line descriptions of commands specified by
     name, or for all commands whose description contains any of a set of
     keywords. It can also provide on-line access to the sections of the
     printed manual.

     When given the option -k and a set of keywords, man prints out a one
     line synopsis of each manual section whose listing in the table of
     contents contains one of those keywords.

     When given the option -f and a list of names, man attempts to locate
     manual sections related to those files, printing out the table of
     contents lines for those sections.

     When neither -k or -f is specified, man formats a specified set of
     manual pages. If a section specifier is given man looks in that
     section of the manual for the given titles. Section is either an
     Arabic section number (3 for instance), or one of the words "new",
     "local", "old" or "public". A section number may be followed by a
     single letter classifier (for instance, 1g, indicating a graphics
     program in section 1). If section is omitted, man searches all
     sections of the manual, giving preference to commands over
     subroutines in system libraries, and printing the first section it
     finds, if any.

     If the standard output is a teletype, or if the flag - is given, man
     pipes its output through more(1) with the option -s to crush out
     useless blank lines and to stop after each page on the screen. Hit a
     space to continue, a control-D to scroll 11 more lines when the
     output stops.
FILES
     /usr/man            standard manual area
     /usr/man/man?/*     directories containing source for manuals
     /usr/man/cat?/*     directories containing preformatted pages
     /usr/man/whatis     keyword database
SEE ALSO
     apropos(1), more(1), whatis(1), whereis (1) catman(8)
BUGS
     The manual is supposed to be reproducible either on a
     photo-typesetter  or on an ASCII terminal.  However, on a terminal
     some information (indicated by font changes, for  instance) is
     necessarily lost.
```

Figure 8-3

A Sample Manual Page (the Output of the Command **man man***)*

Synopsis:

This section shows the syntax of the command. This is the official explanation of how to enter the command. We describe command syntax in detail in Chapter 9.

Description:

This section is the largest and usually takes up the bulk of the man page. On some systems, the full explanation is divided into two separate sections: Description and Options. Options allow you to control just how a command will execute. We discuss options in detail in Chapter 9.

Remember that this is a reference manual. Be prepared to find that many descriptions are not understandable until you know what you are doing. If you have trouble, keep reading until you run out of patience – some of what you read will stick – and when you learn more, you can try again.

There are some descriptions (like **csh(1)**) that you will probably never understand completely. If you become frustrated, remind yourself that the people who do understand everything are less attractive and less socially proficient than you.

Files:

This section shows the names of the files that are used by this command. (File names are explained in Chapter 21.) If the information in this section makes no sense to you, you can ignore it.

See Also:

This is an important section. It shows you other places to look in the manual for more information. In particular, you will see commands that are related in some way to the command under discussion. Following up these references is a good way to learn. Concentrate on the references to Section 1 man pages.

Diagnostics:

This section can contain two types of information: First, there may be an explanation of possible error messages. Second, there may be a list of error codes that a command can return upon completion.

Error codes are important for programmers who can use a command in a program or shell script and then test if the command completed successfully. (A shell script is a file containing a list of commands to be executed automatically.) If the command was successful, the error code will have a value of zero. Otherwise, the error code will be non-zero.

When a command returns an error code, its value is stored in the variable named **status**. You can display its value by entering:

```
echo $status
```

(This is if you are using the C-Shell or the Tcsh. If you are using the Bourne shell, the Korn Shell, Bash or the Zsh, use **echo $?**. The various shells are described in Chapter 10.)

Bugs:

All programs have two kinds of bugs: the ones you know about and the ones you don't know about. The original developers of Unix recognized that no program is perfect and users deserve to know about the imperfections. Unfortunately, some vendors have decided that a section named Bugs gives the paying customers the wrong idea. Thus, you may see this section renamed to be more politically correct (for example, Limitations).

A Quick Way to Find Out What a Command Does: `whatis`

When you enter the basic **man** command, Unix will display the full manual page. However, sometimes you are interested in just a quick description.

As we explained above, the Name section of each man page contains a one-line description. If all you want to see is this single line, use the **man** command as follows: Type **man**, followed by **-f**, followed by the names of one or more commands. For example:

```
man -f time date
```

In this form of the **man** command, the **-f** is called an option. (We will discuss options in Chapter 9.) The letter "f" was chosen to stand for the word "files". Each man page is stored in a separate file; when you use the **-f** option, you are telling **man** which files to look at.

As a convenience, you can type a single word **whatis**, instead of **man -f**. For instance, if you want to display the time, but you are not sure whether to use the **time** or **date** command, enter:

```
whatis time date
```

You will see something like this:

```
date (1)          - print date and time
time (1)          - time a command
time (7)          - time a command
time, ftime (3)   - get date and time
```

You can ignore the last two lines as they do not refer to Section 1 of the manual. Looking at the first two lines, you see that the command you want is **date**. The **time** command actually measures how long it takes for a program or command to execute.

When you enter the regular **man** command, you can specify a particular section number (such as **man 1 date**). With **man -f** or **whatis**, you cannot be so specific. Unix will always search the entire manual.

Thus, a good way to find out what your manual contains is to enter:

```
whatis intro
```

You will see quick summaries of each **intro** page.

Note: For the **whatis** command to work properly, the man pages must be preprocessed in a certain way. All the one-line descriptions are collected and stored in certain files. It is these files that the **whatis** command searches, not the actual manual. (That would be far too slow.) Unless the preprocessing has been carried out, the **whatis** command will not be able to return useful information. If this is the case on your system, talk to your system manager.

Searching for a Command: `apropos`

When you want to learn about a command, you can use **man** to display the appropriate manual page. But what if you know what you want to do, but you are not sure which command to use?

The solution is to use **man** with the **-k** option to search for commands whose descriptions contain specified keywords. For example, say that you want to find all the entries in the online manual that have something to do with the manual itself. Enter:

```
man -k manual
```

As a convenience, you can use the single word **apropos** instead of **man -k**:

```
apropos manual
```

("Apropos of" is an elegant expression meaning "concerning" or "with reference to".)

When you use the **apropos** command, Unix searches through all the one-line command descriptions, looking for those that contain the same string of characters that you specified. To make the command more powerful, Unix does not distinguish between upper- and lowercase.

Here is some sample output from the previous example.

```
catman (8)    - create the cat files for the manual
man (1)       - displays manual pages online
man (5)       - macros for formatting entries in REFERENCE manual
man (7)       - macros to typeset manual
route (8c)    - manually manipulate the routing tables
whereis (1)   - locate source, binary, and or manual for program
```

Notice that there are only two commands of interest, **man** and **whereis** (the ones in Section 1). Notice also that the **route** command was cited because the characters "manual" happen to appear in its description.

You might ask, why don't **apropos** and **whatis** appear in this list? After all, they are important commands to help you access the online manual. To answer this question, enter:

```
whatis apropos whatis
```

You will see:

```
apropos (1) - locate commands by keyword lookup
whatis (1)  - display command description
```

The word "manual" does not appear in these descriptions.

The **apropos** command is not magic – all it can do is search for character strings. So if you can't find what you want, try asking in a different way.

☑ **HINT**

Most commands are actually programs. For example, the **man** command is really a program named "man". However, some of the most basic commands are carried out by the shell (the command processor) itself. These commands will be documented within the man page for the shell. They will not have their own separate entries in the manual.

If you are looking for a command that you know exists, but you cannot find it under its own name, check the man page for the shell that you are using. If you are using the C-Shell, check the man page for **csh**; for the Korn shell, check under **ksh**; for the Bourne shell, check **sh**; for the Zsh, check **zsh**.

Command Syntax

Much of your work with Unix will be entering commands, one after another. As long as you work with Unix, you will never stop learning new commands – there are literally hundreds of them.

As you know, a command must be used just so, according to well-defined rules. Putting a comma in the wrong place, or spelling a word incorrectly, will invalidate the entire command. In the worst case, a mis-typed command may execute incorrectly and cause problems.

The formal description of how a command must be entered is called the COMMAND SYNTAX. In this chapter, we will explain the conventions and how they are used. Once you finish this chapter, you will be able to understand how to use any command just by reading its syntax in the online manual (see Chapter 8).

The Unix Command Line

When you enter a command, the entire line that you type is called the COMMAND LINE. Most of the time, you will type one command at a time. However, the command line can contain multiple commands. Simply separate them with semicolons. For example:

```
date; cd; ls -l -F file1
```

You do not need a semicolon at the end of the command line.

When you enter a command, you type the name of the command, possibly followed by other information. The items that follow the name are called ARGUMENTS. For example, consider the following **ls** command. (**ls** lists information about files.)

```
ls -l -F file1
```

This particular command has three arguments, **-l**, **-F** and **file1**.

In order to process a command, Unix searches for, and then executes, a program with the name of the command. If you were to enter the previous **ls** command, Unix would find and start the **ls** program.

When Unix starts a program, it passes along the arguments. It is up to the program to figure out what to do with them.

Options and Parameters

There are two types of arguments, OPTIONS and PARAMETERS. Options come right after the command name and consist of a – (minus sign character) followed by a letter. Parameters come after the options. The example:

```
ls -l -F file1 file2 file3
```

has two options, **-l** and **-F**, and three parameters, **file1**, **file2** and **file3**. Occasionally, you will see an option that is a number, such as:

```
ls -1 file1 file2 file3
```

You will have to be careful not to confuse **-l** (the letter "l") with **-1** (the number 1).

You use options to tell the command exactly how you want it to work. In our example, the **-l** option tells the **ls** command to display the "long" listing. Normally, the **ls** command lists the names of files. When you use the **-l** option, **ls** lists extra information about each file, along with the names.

You use parameters to pass information to the program. In this case, we want **ls** to display information about three files named "file1", "file2" and "file3".

When we talk about a command, the tradition is to pronounce the – character as "minus", even though the – has nothing to do with arithmetic and acts more like a hyphen than anything else. For instance, if someone asks you how to make the **ls** command display a long file listing, you would say out loud, "Use the minus L option."

When a command has more than one option, you can combine them using a single – character. Moreover, you can specify options in any order. Thus, all of the following commands are equivalent:

```
ls -l -F file1
ls -F -l file1
ls -lF file1
ls -Fl file1
```

As with all Unix commands, you must make sure that you use the exact upper- or lowercase. For example, the **ls** command has both **-F** and **-f** options, and they are different. As a general rule, most commands have only lowercase options. (As we explained in Chapter 4, almost everything in Unix is lowercase.)

Whitespace

When you enter a command, you must make sure to separate each option and parameter. The rule is: Between each word you must use one or more spaces or tabs. For example, here are several ways of entering the same command (we have indicated where we pressed the <Space> bar and <Tab> key):

```
ls<Space>-l<Space>-F<Space>file1
ls<Tab>-l<Tab>-F<Tab>file1
ls<Space><Tab>-l<Space>-F<Tab><Tab><Tab>file1
```

Normally, of course, you would just put a single space between each part of the command. However, the idea of using spaces and tabs as separators is important enough to have its own name: WHITESPACE. Whitespace means one or more consecutive spaces or tabs.

Thus, we can summarize the format of a Unix command as follows. Unix commands are of the form:

```
COMMAND-NAME   OPTIONS   PARAMETERS
```

the various options and parameters being separated by whitespace.

WHAT'S IN A NAME?

Whitespace   The term "whitespace" refers to consecutive spaces and tabs that are used to separate two items. The name derives from the earliest Unix terminals that printed on paper. As you typed a command, there was real white space between each word.

The Unix command processor was designed to be flexible; it didn't care how much space there was, as long as the words were separated. Thus, the term "whitespace" came to mean any amount of spaces and tabs.

One or More; Zero or More

In the next section, we will discuss the formal method for describing commands. Before we do, however, we need to define two important expressions: "one or more" and "zero or more".

When you see the expression ONE OR MORE, it means that you must use at least one of something. Here is an example:

In Chapter 8, we discussed how you can use **whatis** to display a short description of a command, based on its entry in the online manual. When you use **whatis**, you must specify one or more command names as parameters. For instance:

```
whatis man cp
whatis man cp rm mv
```

The first example has two parameters; the second example has four parameters. Because the specifications of this command calls for "one or more" names, we must include at least one – it is not optional.

The expression ZERO OR MORE, on the other hand, means that you can use one or more of something, but it is also okay to leave it out.

For instance, we said earlier that the **ls** command, along with the **-l** option, lists information about the files you specify. The exact format of the command requires you to specify zero or more file names. Here are three examples:

```
ls -l
ls -l file1
ls -l file1 file2 data1 data2
```

Whenever you see a specification that requires zero or more of something, you should ask, "What happens if I don't use any?" Frequently, there is a DEFAULT – an assumed value – that will be used.

With **ls**, the default is the set of files in your "working directory" (explained in Chapter 21). Thus, if you do not specify any file names – as in the first example – **ls** lists information on all the files in your working directory.

 HINT   Whenever you can specify zero or more of something, ask: "What is the default?"

The Formal Description of a Command: Syntax

A good approach to learning a new command is to answer the following three questions:

- What does the command do?
- How do I use the options?
- How do I use the parameters?

You can learn what a command does by using the **man** command to look up the command in the online manual (see Chapter 7).

When you check the man page, you will see the exact, formal specification for using the command. This specification is called the COMMAND SYNTAX. Informally, we can say that the syntax for a command is its "official" description.

The syntax that is used to describe Unix commands follows five simple rules:

1. Items in square brackets are optional.

2. Items not in square brackets are obligatory and must be entered as part of the command.

3. Anything in boldface must be typed exactly as written.

4. Anything in italics must be replaced by an appropriate value.

5. Any parameter that is followed by an ellipsis (. . .) may be repeated any number of times.

Here is an example to show how it all works.

The following is the syntax for the **ls** command on one particular Unix system:

ls [**-aAcCdfFgilLqrRstul**] [*filename...*]

From looking at the syntax, what can we say about this command?

- The command has 18 different options. You can use **-a**, **-A**, **-c**, **-C**, and so on. Since the options are optional, they are enclosed in square brackets.

- There is one parameter, *filename*. This parameter is optional, so it too is enclosed in square brackets.

- The name of the command and the options are printed in boldface. This means that they must be typed exactly as they appear.

- The parameter is in italics. This means that you must replace it with an appropriate value. (In this case, the name of a file or a directory of files.)

- The parameter is followed by " . . ."; this means that you can use more than one parameter (to specify the name of more than one file). Since the parameter is itself optional, we can be precise and say that you specify zero or more file names.

Based on this syntax, here are some valid **ls** commands. Remember, options can be typed separately or grouped together with a single – (minus) character.

```
ls
ls -l
ls file1
ls file1 file2 file3 file4 file5
ls -Fl file1 file2
ls -F -l file1 file2
```

Here are some invalid **ls** commands:

```
ls -lz file1 file2      (There is no -z option)
ls file1 -l file2       (All options must precede the parameters)
```

This last example is tricky and shows why you must follow the syntax exactly.

Unix expects the options first. Since the second argument (**file1**) does not begin with a – character, Unix assumes that this argument, and all the other arguments, are parameters. Thus, the **ls** program thinks you are specifying the names of three files: **file1**, **-lz** and **file2**. Of course, there is no file named **-lz**, so the results of this command will not be what you wanted.

Learning Command Syntax from the Unix Manual

When you read a printed manual, you will see boldface and italics as we described. However, when you use **man** to display the online manual on your terminal, you will not see any special typefaces. On some systems, the boldface and italics may be highlighted in some way. On other systems, you will have to be careful and deduce, from the context, which of the arguments are parameters. Usually, this is not difficult.

All man pages explain each option and parameter. However, some manuals use a simplified form of syntax in which all the options are represented by the word "options". Here is an example. Earlier we showed the syntax for the **ls** command:

ls [**-aAcCdfFgilLqrRstu1**] [*filename...*]

Using the simplified system, the syntax would be:

ls [**options**] [*filename...*]

In either case, each option would be explained separately as part of the description of the command.

How Can You Learn So Many Options?

You will have noticed that the example we have been using, the **ls** command, has 18 different options. How can you ever learn so many options? The answer is, you don't.

Nobody remembers all the options for every command that they use. The best idea is to memorize only the most important options. When you need to use other options, look them up – that is what the online manual is for.

One of the characteristics of Unix programmers is that they tend to write programs with many options, most of which you can safely ignore. Moreover, it is not uncommon to find that different versions of Unix have different options for the same command.

The **ls** command that we have been using is from one particular type of Unix. Other systems will have **ls** commands that have a different number of options. However, the most important options – the ones you will use most of the time – do not vary much from system to system.

In this book, we explain many Unix commands. We will make a point to describe only the most important options and parameters. When you feel a need to learn more about a command, check with the manual on your system. You will see the exact syntax and description that pertains to you.

As an example, here is the syntax for the **man** command that we described in Chapter 8:

man [*section*] *title...*
man **-f** *command-name...*
man **-k** *keyword...*

Since this command can be used in three different ways, it is easiest to show three different syntax descriptions.

The first way to use **man** is with an optional *section* name and one or more *title* values. The second way uses the **-f** option and one or more *command-name* values. The third way uses the **-k** option and one or more *keyword* values.

These are not the only options that **man** uses, just the most important ones. On some systems, **man** has a large number of options. However, for most day-to-day work, **-f** and **-k** are the only ones you will need.

To conclude this chapter, here are two final examples. As we explained in Chapter 8, you can use the **whatis** command instead of **man -f**, and the **apropos** command instead of **man -k**. The syntax for these two commands is:

```
whatis command-name...
apropos keyword...
```

The syntax shows us that, to use either of these commands, you enter the command name followed by one or more parameters.

The Shell

The program that reads and interprets your commands is called the "shell". From the beginning, Unix was designed so that the shell is an actual program (albeit a complex one), separate from the main part of the operating system. Today there are a number of shells in use. If your system has more than one shell, you can use the one you want.

In this chapter, we will answer the questions: What is a shell and why is it important? What shells are there, and which shell should you use? In Chapter 11, we will show you what you need to know to use the shell well.

What Is a Shell?

Once you start using Unix, you will hear a lot of talk about the SHELL. Just what is this "shell" thing anyway?

There are several answers.

The simplest answer is that the shell is a COMMAND PROCESSOR – a program that reads and interprets the commands that you enter. Some shells offer facilities to make your minute-to-minute work more convenient. For instance, a shell may let you recall, edit and re-enter previous commands. You may also be able to execute and control more than one program at a time.

Aside from being a command interpreter, the shell is also a programming language. You can write programs, called "scripts", for the shell to interpret. These scripts can contain regular Unix commands, as well as special shell programming commands. Each shell has its own programming language and rules. We will discuss shell scripts in Chapter 11.

However, neither of these explanations really captures the aura of *je ne sais quoi* – that certain something – that surrounds the idea of the shell. You see, the shell is the main interface into your Unix system. Using the facilities that are built into your shell, you can create a highly customized environment for yourself (although most people have no need to do so).

Moreover, since there are several shells, you may have a choice as to which interface you want to use. As you can imagine, there are all kinds of arguments among the cognoscenti as to which shells are best and which shells should be avoided at all costs.

 HINT　Until you are an experienced Unix user, it does not really matter what shell you use.

Once you get used to Unix, you will understand the mysterious feeling that people have for the shell. You can't taste it or touch it, but it is always there, ready to serve you by interpreting your commands and running your programs and scripts. (If you are a pantheist, all of this will make perfect sense.)

WHAT'S IN A NAME?

The Shell　There are three ways to think of the name "shell". First, the shell provides a well-defined interface to protect the internals of the operating system. In this sense, a Unix shell acts like the shell of an oyster, shielding its vulnerable parts from the harsh realities of the outside world.

Second, you can imagine the cross section of one of those sea shells that wind around and around in a spiral. With the Unix shell, you can pause what you are doing and start another shell or another program. Thus, you can put as many programs as you want on hold, each one "inside" its predecessor, just like the layers of the spiral.

However, the best way to think of the name "shell" is as a brand new word. Let the meaning come solely from your experience with Unix. The analogies to sea shells are somewhat far-fetched and can only lead to disillusionment and disappointment.

The Bourne Shell Family: Bourne Shell, Korn Shell, Bash, Zsh

The earliest Unix shell that is still in use is the BOURNE SHELL. This shell is named after its primary developer, Steven Bourne of AT&T Bell Labs. A modern version of the Bourne shell – the original dates from the late 1970s – is available on every Unix system in the world. The Bourne shell is a command interpreter with its own programming language.

As we mentioned, shells are themselves programs. The name of the Bourne shell program is `sh`.

In the mid-1980s, another Bell Labs scientist, David Korn, created a replacement for the Bourne shell, called the KORN SHELL. The name of the Korn shell program is `ksh`.

The Korn shell is an upwards compatible extension to the Bourne shell. That is, anything that works with the Bourne shell will work with the Korn shell. In addition, the Korn shell provides three important features: a history mechanism, job control and aliasing. (We discuss the history mechanism and aliasing, as they apply to the C-Shell, in Chapter 11.)

The next member of the Bourne shell family is BASH, which stands for "the Bourne Again Shell". This shell was first released in 1989 and is the product of the Free Software Foundation. The primary authors were Brian Fox and Chet Ramey.

The Free Software Foundation is an organization dedicated to the proposition that all software should be free (at least to individuals). They have developed many widely used tools. Their project to develop an entire Unix system is called GNU. (GNU is a recursive acronym that stands for "GNU's Not Unix". GNU is pronounced, "guh-new", to rhyme with "canoe".)

Bash extends the capabilities of the basic Bourne shell in a manner similar to the Korn shell. The name of the Bash program is `bash`.

The final member of the Bourne shell family is the ZSH (pronounced "zee-shell"). This shell offers all of the important features of the other Unix shells as well as new capabilities, not widely available. For example, you can tell the Zsh to notify you when a particular userid has logged in.

The Zsh was developed by Paul Falstad in 1990. His philosophy was to "take everything interesting that I could get my hands on from every other shell". As he explains, "I wanted a shell that can do anything you want."

Within a short time of being released, the Zsh developed a cult following around the world and became popular among programmers and advanced Unix users. The name of the Zsh program is `zsh`.

Falstad created the shell when he was an undergraduate at Princeton University. Today, he works as a programmer and is developing a commercial version of the Zsh. The Zsh program is currently maintained by various members of the worldwide Unix community.

The C-Shell Family: C-Shell, Tcsh

There are two members of the C-SHELL family. The first is the C-Shell itself, written by Bill Joy (who was a student at the University of California at Berkeley). The C-Shell was designed to be the Berkeley Unix alternative to the Bourne shell, which, at the time, was the standard shell. The name of the C-Shell program is **csh**.

Like all shells, the C-Shell is a command interpreter that offers a programming language. In addition, the C-Shell offers many advantages over the Bourne shell. We will describe the most important features in Chapter 11.

The C-Shell is the most popular shell among experienced Unix users, especially at universities and research organizations, where it is often the default shell. In this book, we assume that you are using the C-Shell (which is most likely the case).

The other member of the C-Shell family is the TCSH (pronounced "Tee See Shell"). The development of the Tcsh was started in the late 1970s by Ken Greer at Carnegie-Mellon University and carried on in the 1980s by Paul Placeway at Ohio State. Since then, many people have contributed to the shell, which is distributed over the worldwide Internet network. The Tcsh is maintained primarily by a group at Cornell University.

This shell is an enhanced C-Shell that offers a constellation of advanced features. We won't describe all the details here, but if you are an experienced user, you may want to check out the Tcsh manual page. The name of the Tcsh program is **tcsh**.

WHAT'S IN A NAME?

C-Shell, Tcsh

The developer of the C-Shell designed its programming facilities to work like the C programming language. Thus, the name C-Shell (which is also a pun on "sea shell").

The "T" in the name Tcsh stands for Tenex, an operating system used on the old PDP-10 computers. The original work that led to the Tcsh was done on a Tenex system.

For reference, the table in Figure 10-1 shows each shell along with the name of its program. To display the reference manual for a shell, use the **man** command with the name of the appropriate program. For example, **man csh**.

Shell	Name of the Program
Bash	`bash`
Bourne Shell	`sh`
C-Shell	`csh`
Korn Shell	`ksh`
Tcsh	`tcsh`
Zsh	`zsh`

Figure 10-1
The Unix Shells

WHAT'S IN A NAME?

C Both the C-Shell and the Tcsh are named after the C programming language. But how did such an odd name arise for a language?

In 1963, a language called CPL was developed in England during a project involving researchers from Cambridge and the University of London. CPL stood for "Combined Programming Language" and was based on Algol 60, one of the first well-designed modern programming languages.

Four years later, in 1967, a programmer at Cambridge named Martin Richards created BCPL, "Basic CPL". BCPL itself gave rise to yet another language, known by a single letter, B.

The B language was taken to Bell Labs, where Ken Thompson and Dennis Ritchie made modifications and renamed it NB. In the early 1970s, Thompson (the original Unix developer) used NB to rewrite the basic part of Unix for its second edition. Up to then, all of Unix had been written in assembly language.

Not long afterwards, the NB language was extended and renamed C. C soon became the language of choice for writing new utilities, applications and even the operating system itself.

You might ask, where did the name C come from? Was it the next letter in the alphabet after "B", or was it the second letter of "BCPL"? This has philological implications of cosmic importance. Would the successor to C be named D or P?

continued

The question proved to be moot when, in the early 1980s, Bjarne Stroustrup (also of Bell Labs) designed the most popular extension of C, which he called C++ (pronounced "C-plus-plus").

In the C language, **++** is an operator that adds 1 to a variable. For instance, to add 1 to the variable **total** you can use the command **total++**. Thus, the name C++ is one of those wonderful programming puns that make people scratch their heads and wonder if Man is really Nature's last word.

What Shell Should You Use?

We have described six different shells, all of which are in widespread use: the Bourne shell, the Korn shell, Bash, the Zsh, the C-Shell and the Tcsh.

Worldwide, the most widely used shells are the Bourne shell and its replacement, the Korn shell. However, in the academic, research and programming communities, the C-Shell is the most popular shell. (Although there are significant numbers of people who use Bash, the Zsh and the Tcsh). In a university environment, it is likely that your default shell will be the C-Shell, which is just fine.

The Tcsh is designed to be upwards compatible with the C-Shell. This means that if you ignore the extra features, everything works just the same as the C-Shell.

Similarly, both the Korn shell and Bash are upwards compatible with the Bourne shell. On many systems, the Korn shell is the default and veteran Bourne shell users don't even notice a difference.

Remember, though, a shell has two main purposes: to act as a command processor and to provide a programming language for shell scripts. As a command processor, the C-Shell family provides a good all-around working environment. However, the programming language used by the Bourne shell family is easier and more pleasant to use than the C-Shell language.

Thus, many people use the C-Shell as a command processor, for minute-to-minute work, but write their shell scripts for the Bourne shell. So, here is our advice:

Use the C-Shell as your principal shell, but use the Bourne shell to execute your scripts. (On many systems, these choices are the default.) Once you become an experienced Unix user, look at the online manual pages for Bash, the Zsh and the Tcsh, and see if the extra features appeal to you.

In this book, we assume that you are using the C-Shell.

☑ **HINT** Use the C-Shell as your principal shell, but use the Bourne shell to execute your scripts.

An interesting question to ask is: How complex are each of the shells? A complicated program will have extra features and capabilities, but it will also demand more of your time to master. Moreover, like a lot of Unix programs, the shells have many esoteric features and options that you will never really need. These extra facilities are often a distraction.

One crude way to measure the complexity of a program is by looking at the length of the documentation. The table in Figure 10-2 shows the number of bytes (characters) in the manual pages for each of the shells. For comparison, we have also normalized the numbers, assigning the smallest a value of 1.0. (Of course, these numbers change from time to time as new versions of the documentation are released.)

From these numbers, it is easy to see why the C-Shell provides a nice middle ground between the older, less capable Bourne shell and the other more complex shells.

Of course, someone may argue that the more complicated shells are all upwards compatible, either with the Bourne shell or the C-Shell. If you don't want the added features, you can ignore them and they won't bother you.

Name of Shell	Size of Man Page (Bytes)	Relative Complexity
Bourne Shell	44,500	1.00
C-Shell	76,816	1.73
Bash	127,361	2.86
Zsh	133,565	3.00
Korn Shell	141,391	3.18
Tcsh	199,834	4.49

Note: All the manual pages are self-contained except for Tcsh. This page is actually a large addendum, describing only those extra features that are not part of the C-Shell. In this table, the number for Tcsh includes the C-Shell documentation. The Tcsh manual page on its own is 123,018.

Figure 10-2

The Relative Complexity of the Different Shells

However, you must remember that documentation is important. The manual pages for the more complex shells take a long time to read and are much more difficult to understand. Even the shortest manual page (for the Bourne shell) is too large to peruse comfortably.

Changing Your Shell Temporarily

By default, you will be assigned a shell to start automatically whenever you log in. If you want to change your shell, you can do so in two ways.

When you log in, the shell that Unix starts automatically is called your LOGIN SHELL. From the shell prompt, you can start a new shell any time you want simply by entering the name of that shell (see Figure 10-1). For example, say that you are using the C-Shell and you want to try out the Korn shell. Enter:

```
ksh
```

(Of course, the new shell must be available on your system.)

The original login shell will put itself on hold and execute the Korn shell. This is exactly the same as when you enter a command to run a program. After all, a shell is just a program.

When you are finished with the new shell, you can stop it. Either enter the **exit** command or press **^D**, the **eof** key (see Chapter 6). When the new shell is finished, the old shell will restart and wait for a new command.

One point to remember is that you can only log out from the original shell. If you have started one or more new shells, you must back out to the login shell before you can end your work session.

Changing Your Default Shell

Unix maintains a password file of userids to keep track of who is allowed to log in to the system. Each userid has one entry in the password file. Within this entry, Unix keeps the name of the shell to start when that userid logs in.

If you want to change your default shell, use the **chsh** command. The syntax is:

```
chsh userid name-of-shell
```

When you specify the shell, you are really telling Unix what program to run. As part of this specification, you must include the name of the directory that contains the shell program. (We will discuss directories in Chapter 21.) This is called the "pathname" of the program.

On most systems, the shells are contained in the **/bin** directory. For reference, the table in Figure 10-3 shows the pathname of each shell program, assuming that they are in this directory. On your system, though, one or

Shell	Full Name
Bash	`/bin/bash`
Bourne Shell	`/bin/sh`
C-Shell	`/bin/csh`
Korn Shell	`/bin/ksh`
Tcsh	`/bin/tcsh`
Zsh	`/bin/zsh`

Figure 10-3
The Full Pathname of Each Shell

more of the shells may be in a different directory and you will have to modify the specification accordingly.

Here is a quick example. You want to change your default shell to the Korn shell, which, on your system, is in the **/bin** directory. Your userid is **harley**. Enter the following command:

```
chsh harley /bin/ksh
```

On some systems, you can enter the command name by itself:

```
chsh
```

and Unix will prompt you to enter the name of the new shell.

When you use **chsh**, you are making a change to your password file. Thus, the change will not take effect until the next time you log in (just like when you change your password).

Note: On some systems, the **chsh** command will not be enabled and you may have to ask your system manager to help you.

Using the C-Shell

This chapter describes the most important features of the C-Shell. If you are using a different shell, the principles will be more or less the same although the exact particulars may differ.

Many people do not take much time to learn how to use the shell well. This is a mistake. To be sure, the shell has many features that you really do not need to understand. However, there are a handful of fundamental ideas that are of great practical value.

The time you spend reading this chapter will repay you well. You will find that the skills you learn here will save you a lot of time in your day-to-day work. There are many topics in this chapter, and you don't need to understand them all immediately. Just read the chapter once so you know what is available. As you become more experienced, you can reread parts of the chapter as you need them.

If, after reading this chapter, you decide that you want to know more details, check the C-Shell manual page (**man csh**). This is the ultimate reference as to how the shell works on your particular system.

Shell Variables That Act as Switches: set, unset

One of the ways the shell lets you customize your working environment is by using SHELL VARIABLES. A shell variable is an item, known by a name, that represents a value of some type. As the term "variable" implies, the value of a shell variable can be changed.

There are two types of shell variables. First, there are variables that act as off/on switches. Second, there are variables that store a particular value as a string of characters.

You can create your own shell variables, but, unless you write programs, you will usually make do with the ones that are built in. Figure 11-1 shows the predefined shell variables that act as switches. (Your list of variables may vary slightly, depending on the version of your C-Shell.) Don't worry if you don't understand what all these variables do; this list is for reference. By the time you learn enough to care about using a variable, you will understand its purpose.

To turn on switch variables, use the **set** command. The syntax is:

set [*variable-name*]

For example, to turn on the **ignoreeof** switch, enter:

set ignoreeof

To turn off a switch, use **unset**. For example:

unset ignoreeof

To display all the shell variables and their current settings, enter the command with no arguments:

set

If a variable is set, its name will appear in the list. If a variable is unset, its name will not appear.

Variable Name	Purpose
echo	display each command before execution
filec	enable filename completion
ignoreeof	must log out with **logout** rather than **eof** key (**^D**)
nobeep	no beep, command completion has ambiguous file name
noclobber	do not allow redirected output to replace a file
noglob	inhibit expansion of filenames
nonomatch	no error if filename expansion matches nothing
notify	notify about job completions at any time
verbose	display full command after history substitution

Note: The name **nonomatch** is spelled correctly.

Figure 11-1
Built-in Shell Variables: Switches

Shell Variables That Store Values: `set`, `echo`

Aside from shell variables that act as off/on switches, there are variables that store values. Some of these values can be set by you to modify the shell's behavior. Other values are set by the shell to pass information to you.

Figure 11-2 shows the predefined shell variables that store values, along with their uses; don't worry if you don't understand them all. (Your list of variables may vary slightly, depending on the version of your C-Shell.) Whenever you log in, the shell automatically initializes the **argv**, **cwd**, **home**, **path**, **prompt**, **shell** and **status** variables.

To set a variable of this type, use the **set** command with the following syntax:

set [*variable-name* **=** *value*]

Variable Name	Purpose
argv	list of arguments for current command
cdpath	directories to search to find a subdirectory
cwd	pathname of current working directory
fignore	suffixes to ignore during file name completion
hardpath	no symbolic link pathnames in directory stack
histchars	the two characters used for history substitution
history	size of the history list
home	pathname of your home directory
mail	pathnames where shell should check for mail
path	list of directories to search for programs
prompt	string of characters to use for command prompt
savehist	number of history lines to save upon logout
shell	pathname of the shell program
status	return status of last command
term	type of terminal you are using
time	threshold value for reporting of command timing
user	name of the userid currently logged in

Figure 11-2
Built-in Shell Variables That Store Values

For example, to set the **history** variable to the value "50", use:

```
set history = 50
```

To display all the variables and their values, use:

```
set
```

To display the value of a single variable, use the **echo** command with the following syntax:

```
echo $variable-name
```

For instance, to display the value of **history**, use:

```
echo $history
```

On occasion, you may want to give a variable a value that contains spaces, punctuation or other special characters. In that case, you must put single quotes around the value. For example:

```
set prompt = 'nipper% '
```

Another alternative is to assign a value of a variable that is a list of words, by enclosing the list in parentheses. The most important example of this occurs when you are setting the **path** variable (discussed in detail later in the chapter).

As an example, here is a **set** command that defines the value of the **path** variable to be a list of four words: **/usr/local/bin**, **/bin**, **/usr/bin** and **~/bin**.

```
set path = ( /usr/local/bin /bin /usr/bin ~/bin )
```

Environment Variables: `setenv, printenv`

The shell variables that we have just described are used only within the shell to control preferences and settings. However, there is a whole other set of variables that the shell maintains for passing values between programs. These are called ENVIRONMENT VARIABLES or GLOBAL VARIABLES.

By convention, environment variables have uppercase names. Figure 11-3 shows the most common environment variables; don't worry if you don't understand them all. (The variables on your system may differ slightly.)

The value of a global variable is available to any program or shell. For example, many programs look at the **TERM** variable to see what type of terminal you are using. If this variable is not set correctly, the output may not be displayed properly.

 HINT Some programs cannot display their output properly unless they know exactly what type of terminal you are using. If a program that uses the full screen for output - such as the **vi** editor or **more** - displays its output in a strange manner, make sure that your **TERM** variable is set correctly.

Variable Name	Purpose
EDITOR	pathname of your text editor
HOME	pathname of your home directory
LOGNAME	name of the userid currently logged in
MAIL	pathname of your mail program
MANPATH	list of directories to search for manual pages
PAGER	name of paging program you prefer (Chapter 17)
PATH	list of directories to search for programs
SHELL	pathname of the shell program
TERM	type of terminal you are using
USER	name of the userid currently logged in

Note: Some versions of the C-Shell use only **USER** and not **LOGNAME**.

Figure 11-3
Common Environment Variables

To set the value of an environment variable, use the **setenv** command. The syntax is:

setenv [*variable-name value*]

Notice that, unlike the **set** command, you do not use an equals sign. For example, to set the name of your terminal to **vt100**, use:

setenv TERM vt100

To display the value of one or more environment variables, use the **printenv** command. The syntax is:

printenv [*variable-name*]

If you enter the command with no parameters:

printenv

it will display all the environment variables. To display the value of a single variable, there are two choices. You can use **printenv** with the name of the variable, such as:

printenv TERM

or you can use **echo** with the syntax:

echo $*variable-name*

such as:

echo $TERM

Another way to display all the environment variables is to use **setenv** with no parameters:

```
setenv
```

However, do not try to display a single variable with **setenv**. If you were to enter, say:

```
setenv TERM
```

it would not display the value of **TERM**. Rather, it would set **TERM** to a null value.

How Environment and Shell Variables Are Connected

There are six common shell variables that have the same names as environment variables (except that environment variables have uppercase names). The shell variables are **home**, **mail**, **path**, **shell**, **term** and **user**. We can divide these variables into three groups.

First, **home** and **shell** contain information that is stored as part of your userid profile. **home** contains the pathname of your home directory; **shell** contains the pathname of the shell program you use.

(A pathname is an exact description of the location of a file or directory. The home directory is where you store your personal files. We will discuss these ideas in detail in Chapter 21.)

Whenever you log in, Unix automatically sets the values of **home** and **shell** (and **HOME** and **SHELL**). Your programs will examine these variables from time to time, but you will probably never need to change them yourself.

The next group of shell variables – **term**, **path** and **user** – also have global variable analogs. The difference is that these local variables are tied to the corresponding global variables. Whenever you change the shell variable, the shell will automatically update the global variable.

Later in the chapter, we will explain how you specify initialization commands in two special files, named **.cshrc** and **.login**. Within these files you will set the values of **term** and **path**. You will not have to set **TERM** and **PATH** because they are updated automatically.

Try this. Display the value of **term** and **TERM** by entering:

```
echo $term; echo $TERM
```

Now, change the value of **term**:

```
set term=hello
```

Re-display both variables:

```
echo $term; echo $TERM
```

Notice that the value of **TERM** has been updated automatically. (When you are finished, don't forget to set **term** back to its original value.)

Note: The bond between **HOME**, **TERM** and **USER**, and **home**, **term** and **user**, only works in one direction. Changing the environment variable does *not* change the shell variable. So changing **TERM** does not change **term**.

The final shell variable we need to look at is **mail**. There is a global variable name **MAIL**, but they have different meanings. (See Figures 11-2 and 11-3).

Commands That Are Built In to the Shell

When you enter a command, the shell breaks the command line into parts that it analyzes. We say that the shell PARSES the command. The first part of each command is the name, the other parts are options or parameters (see Chapter 9).

After parsing the command, the shell decides what to do with it. There are two possibilities. Some commands are internal to the shell; this means that the shell can interpret the command directly. The table in Figure 11-4 shows the various shells and the number of commands that are built in.

Name of Shell	Internal Commands
Bourne Shell	32
Korn Shell	43
Bash	50
C-Shell	52
Tcsh	56
Zsh	73

Figure 11-4
The Number of Internal Commands in Each Shell

 HINT   If you want to see which commands are internal, look at the manual page for the shell you are using. All other commands will be separate programs and will have their own separate manual pages.

If you can't find the manual page for a particular command, check with the documentation for your shell: the command may be internal.

The Search Path

If a command is not built in to the shell - and most of them are not - the shell must find the appropriate program to execute.

For example, when you enter the **date** command, the shell must find the **date** program. The shell then starts the program and puts itself on hold. When the program finishes, the shell regains control. It is now ready for you to enter another command.

The **path** variable tells the shell where to look for programs. The value of **path** is a series of directory names called the SEARCH PATH. (We will discuss directories in Chapter 21. Basically, a directory holds a collection of files.)

When the shell is looking for a program to execute, it checks each directory in the search path in the order they are specified. As soon as the shell finds the program, it stops the search and executes the program. Thus, you should specify the directory names in the order you want them to be searched.

Here is a typical **set** command to define a search path:

```
set path = ( /usr/local/bin /usr/ucb /bin /usr/bin ~/bin )
```

The command sets the **path** shell variable's value to be a list of directories. Each of these directories is a place where programs are kept.

The names will make more sense after we cover directories in Chapter 21. For now, all we will say is that "**bin**" is often used to indicate a directory that holds programs, and the tilde (**~**) character is an abbreviation for the name of your home directory. In other words, **~/bin** indicates a directory that holds programs that lies within your home directory. The **/usr/ucb** directory holds programs specific to Berkeley Unix. ("**ucb**" stands for University of California at Berkeley.)

If you are a programmer, you may find it convenient to have the shell also check the current directory (the one you are currently working in) when it looks for a program. To do this, add the dot (**.**) character to the search path:

```
set path = ( . /usr/local/bin /usr/ucb /bin /usr/bin ~/bin )
```

Remember, you can place the entries in any order you want. In this case, Unix will search the current directory before it searches any other directories. For example, say that you create a program and name it **date**. You are working in the directory that holds this program, and you enter:

```
date
```

What happens?

First, the shell checks, is this an internal command? The answer is no, so the shell starts searching for a program named **date**. Since the search path tells the shell to check your current directory first, it finds and executes your program named **date**, not the Unix **date** command (which is in the **/bin** directory).

Now, suppose you had defined the search path with the current directory after **/bin**:

```
set path = ( /usr/local/bin /usr/ucb /bin /usr/bin . ~/bin )
```

In this case, the shell will find the Unix **date** command first (in **/bin**).

A detailed discussion of search paths is beyond the scope of this book (and not all that necessary). Normally, you can accept the search path that is set up for you by default. The only thing you must remember is that if you modify the search path, order is important.

One final note: As we mentioned earlier, the shell automatically copies the value of **path** to the environment variable **PATH**. This allows any program to look at your search path. (Remember, programs can only examine environment variables, not shell variables.) However, if you display the value of **PATH**, you will see that its format is slightly different from **path**. This is to maintain compatibility with the older Bourne shell.

The value of **PATH** is not a word list; rather, it is one long string of characters in which the various directory names are separated by colons. The current directory is specified by an empty directory name, not by a dot (.).

For example, if you wanted to explicitly set **PATH** to have the value of **path** in our last example, you would use:

```
setenv PATH /usr/local/bin:/usr/ucb:/bin:/usr/bin::~/bin
```

The empty directory name (the current directory) is specified by the two colons in a row. If the current directory were at the end of the list, the character string would end in a colon:

```
setenv PATH /usr/local/bin:/usr/ucb:/bin:/usr/bin:~/bin:
```

The Shell Prompt

As we explained in Chapter 4, the shell displays a prompt whenever it is ready for you to enter a command. By default, the C-Shell displays a percent character:

```
%
```

while the Tcsh uses a greater-than character:

```
>
```

The Bourne shell and the Korn shell display a dollar sign:

```
$
```

Bash displays:

```
bash$
```

The Zsh displays the name of your computer followed by **%**. For example, if your computer is named **nipper**, your prompt will be:

```
nipper%
```

The C-Shell uses the value of the shell variable **prompt** as its command prompt. Thus, you can change your prompt to whatever you want by setting the value of this variable. (This is also true for the other shells.)

Here is an example. You are in the habit of logging in remotely to various computers on your network, and you want to use a different, unique prompt with each system to remind you where you are.

Say that one of the systems is named **nipper**. On that system, you can set your prompt as follows:

```
set prompt = 'nipper% '
```

(Remember, if you assign a value that contains spaces or punctuation, you must enclose it in single quotes.) For a system named **princess**, you can use:

```
set prompt = 'princess% '
```

Later in the chapter, we will discuss the history substitution. When we do, you will see that it is useful to have a value called the "event number" as part of the prompt. (The event number is a value that is increased by 1 every time you enter a new command. This value is used to identify specific commands that you have already entered.)

To display the event number within a prompt, use an exclamation point (**!**). Whenever the shell displays the prompt, it will replace the **!** with the current event number.

When you use an **!** in a **set** command, there is one point you need to remember. As you will see later, the **!** has a special meaning on the command line. When you set the prompt, you must take precautions to make sure the **!** is interpreted correctly.

Let's say that you want your prompt to be the name **nipper**, followed by a space, followed by the event number in square brackets, followed by a percent sign, followed by a space. If you were to enter the command:

```
set prompt = 'nipper [!]% '
```

the **!** would retain its special meaning and the command would fail. You need to precede the **!** with a backslash (****). A backslash tells the shell, "Interpret the next character literally"; the backslash itself is ignored. So, the correct command would be:

```
set prompt = 'nipper [\!]% '
```

If, as an example, the value of the event number happens to be 21, the prompt will be:

```
nipper [21]%
```

When the event number changes to 22, the prompt changes to:

```
nipper [22]%
```

Setting Up History Substitution: `history`

After you use Unix for awhile, you will know the frustration of having to type a command over and over because of spelling mistakes. There are two mechanisms that the C-Shell provides to make it easier to enter commands: history substitution and aliasing. These features are one reason why many people prefer to use the C-Shell over the older Bourne shell. We will discuss each feature in turn briefly. For more information, see the manual page for the C-Shell (**man csh**).

HISTORY SUBSTITUTION is a feature that lets you change and re-enter a previous command without having to re-type it. History substitution in the C-Shell has many esoteric rules and features. If you know them all, that's great; you will have enormous facility in recycling your commands. However, most people just use a few of the simpler features: the ones we will describe in this section.

At all times, the shell saves your commands in a list called the HISTORY LIST. Each command is given an identification number. Whenever you log in, the shell starts numbering the commands at 1.

You determine how long the history list should be - that is, how many commands the shell should save - by setting the shell variable named **history**. For example, to tell the shell to save the last 5 commands, enter:

```
set history = 5
```

If the **history** variable is not set, the shell, by default, will save only the last command. For many people, this may be enough.

To display the history list, use the **history** command. The syntax is:

```
history [-r] [number]
```

If you enter the command with no arguments:

```
history
```

the shell will display the entire history list. Here is some sample output:

```
21   ls
22   datq
23   datw
24   date
25   history
```

If you specify a number, the shell will display only that many commands. For example:

```
history 3
```

might display:

```
24   date
25   history
26   history 3
```

If you use the **-r** option, the shell will display the commands in reverse order (most recent first). For example:

```
history -r
```

might display:

```
27   history -r
26   history 3
25   history
24   date
23   datw
```

Notice that every command you enter is added to the history list, including commands with mistakes as well as the **history** commands themselves.

Displaying the history list is important for two reasons. First, as we will describe in a moment, you can edit and recall previous commands. Second, you can check back and see what commands you have already entered. ("Did I really delete all those files?") If you think that you may want to keep a long record of your work, you should set the **history** variable to a large number, say, 100.

In the world of the C-Shell, past commands are referred to as EVENTS. (That should make you feel important every time you enter a command.) The number that identifies each command is called an EVENT NUMBER. If you decide to use history substitution, you will find it handy to display the current event number as part of your prompt. We explained how to do this in the section on the shell prompt. Here is an example:

```
set prompt = 'nipper [\!]% '
```

This prompt displays a reminder that you are using a system named **nipper**, followed by the current event number (in square brackets) and a percent sign. A sample prompt might be:

```
nipper [24]%
```

Using History Substitution

The C-Shell supports a large variety of complex substitutions. In this section, we will discuss the simplest, most useful substitutions. For more details, see the C-Shell manual page (**man csh**).

The two most useful substitutions are **!!** and **^^**. To re-use the previous command, exactly as you typed it, enter:

```
!!
```

The shell will re-display and then execute this command.

To replace a string of characters in the previous command, type **^**, followed by the characters you want to replace, followed by another **^**, followed by the new characters. Here is an example: You want to use the **date** command to display the time and date, but you accidentally enter:

```
datxq
```

You can correct the command by entering:

```
^xq^e
```

☑ **HINT** If you remember nothing else about history substitution, make sure to memorize how to use ! ! and ^^.

To re-use an older command, use an **!** followed by the event number for that command. For example, say that the history list is:

```
21   ls
22   datq
23   datw
24   date
25   history
```

If you enter:

```
!24
```

the shell will re-execute the **date** command.

It is also possible to add characters to the end of a command. For example, event #21 is the **ls** command, which lists the names of files. As we will see in Chapter 21, **ls** with no arguments displays the names of all the files in your current directory. However, if you want to display only those names that begin with the letters "temp", you can use **ls temp***. We can re-use event #21 to create this new command by entering:

```
!21 temp*
```

To re-use a command that begins with a particular pattern, enter **!** followed by that pattern. For example, to re-use that last command that began with **ls**, enter:

```
!ls
```

If you need to use certain commands repeatedly, this facility can really come in handy. For example, say that you are working on a C program named **summary.c**. You use the **vi** text editor to modify the program. After each modification, you use the **cc** command to recompile the program. The two commands you will be using are:

```
vi summary.c
cc summary.c
```

Once you enter the commands for the first time, you can refer to them as `!v` and `!c` respectively. This makes it easy to go back and forth from one command to the other.

You can also reference a command by specifying a pattern within question marks (?). The shell will execute the last command that contained this pattern. For example, you can re-use the command `ls temp*` by entering:

```
!?temp?
```

As you can see, most history substitutions begin with an `!` character. Whenever the shell sees such a character in a command line, it assumes you are referring to some type of event. If you want to use a command that contains a real `!`, you must put a backslash (\) in front of it. This tells the shell that the `!` is not part of a history substitution. (The shell will ignore the backslash itself.) We saw this earlier when we used the `set` command to redefine the command prompt:

```
set prompt = 'nipper [\!]% '
```

History Substitution Example: Avoid Deleting the Wrong Files

The final substitution that we will explain uses an exclamation point followed by an asterisk (`!*`). This combination stands for everything on the command line after the name of the command.

For example, say that you have just entered:

```
ls temp* extra?
```

You can enter a new command and use `!*` to stand for `temp* extra?`.

Most of the time, such substitutions are complicated and not worth the effort. However, there is one case in which using `!*` is invaluable.

As we will discuss in Chapter 22, the `rm` (remove) command will delete files. When you use `rm`, you can specify patterns to stand for lists of files. For example, the pattern `temp*` stands for any filename that begins with `temp` followed by zero or more characters; the pattern `extra?` refers to any filename that starts with `extra` followed by a single character.

The danger with `rm` is that once you delete a file it is gone for good. If you discover that you have made a mistake and erased the wrong file - even the instant after you press the <Return> key - there is no way to get back the file.

Now, let's say that you want to delete a set of files with the names `temp`, `temp_backup`, `extra1` and `extra2`. You are thinking about entering the command:

```
rm temp* extra?
```

However, you have forgotten that you also have an important file called **temp.important**. If you enter the preceding command, this file will also be deleted.

A better strategy is to first enter the **ls** command using the patterns that you propose to use with **rm**:

```
ls temp* extra?
```

This will list the names of all the files that match these patterns. If this list contains a file that you have forgotten, such as **temp.important**, you will not enter the **rm** command as planned. If, however, the list of files is what you expected, you can go ahead and remove the files by entering:

```
rm !*
```

You may ask, why do I need to use **!***? Now that I have confirmed that the patterns match the files I want, couldn't I just type the **rm** command using those patterns?

The answer is, when you use **!*** you are guaranteed to get what you want. If you retype the patterns, you may make a typing mistake and, in spite of all your precautions, end up deleting the wrong files.

To make the whole process easier, you can use an alias, as you will see later in the chapter.

Command Aliasing: `alias`, `unalias`

An ALIAS is a name that you give to a command or list of commands. You can then type the name of the alias instead of the commands.

For example, say that you enter the following command all the time:

```
ls -l temp*
```

If you give it an alias of **lt**, you can enter the command more simply by typing:

```
lt
```

To create an alias, use the **alias** command. The syntax is:

```
alias [name [command]]
```

Here is an example in which we create the alias we just mentioned:

```
alias lt 'ls -l temp*'
```

As you can see, we enclosed the command in single quotes. Certain punctuation characters (such as *****) have special meanings to the shell. The single quotes tell the shell to treat the characters literally. This is a good idea when you specify an alias for any command that has punctuation.

Here is an example that creates an alias for a list of two commands:

```
alias info 'date; who'
```

You can now enter **info** to first find out the time and date, and then check who is logged in to the system. One of the most useful aliases is:

alias a alias

This allows you to use **a** instead of typing the whole word "alias". For example, once you define this alias, you can enter:

a info 'date; who'

Another useful alias, along the same lines, is to define **h** to stand for the **history** command:

alias h history

If you want to check the current value of an alias, enter the **alias** command with a name only. For example:

alias info

If you want to display all the aliases, enter the command name by itself, with no arguments:

alias

To remove an alias, use the **unalias** command. The syntax is:

unalias *alias-name*

For example, to remove the alias that we just defined, use:

unalias info

Using Arguments with an Alias

When you use an alias, you can add arguments (options and parameters) to the end of the command line. (These terms are explained in Chapter 9.) Here is an example.

The **ls** command lists the names of files. When you use the **-l** option, **ls** displays a "long" listing with extra information. Many people use the following alias to make it easy to use **ls   -l** (which is easy to mis-type):

alias ll ls -l

By default, **ls** lists all the files in your current directory (explained in Chapter 21). Thus, you can display a long listing of all such files by entering:

ll

If you want information only on certain files, you specify their names as parameters. For example:

ls -l myfile yourfile

Using our alias, you can enter:

ll myfile yourfile

The shell replaces the **ll** alias and then tacks the parameters onto the end of the command.

If you want to insert arguments into the middle of an alias, you can refer to them as **!***, just as we did with history substitution. (In fact, many of the history substitutions work with aliases. See the C-Shell manual page for details.) However, you must remember to put a backslash (\) before the **!** so the shell does not interpret it as an event specification. This is true even if you use single quotes.

The following example shows how this works. The alias **lld** displays long listings for the files you specify, and then displays the time and date.

```
alias lld 'ls -l \!*; date'
```

So now, if you enter:

```
lld myfile yourfile
```

the shell replaces it with:

```
ls -l myfile yourfile; date
```

Alias Example: Keeping Track of Your Working Directory

Here is an example that uses the concepts from the previous section to produce a particularly useful alias.

In Chapter 21, we will explain the idea of a working directory. Briefly, directories contain files and, at any time, you are working within a particular directory called your "working directory". To change your working directory, you use the **cd** (change directory) command. (This is also discussed in Chapter 21.)

To use the **cd** command, you specify the name of the directory to which you want to change. For example, to change to a directory named **bin**, you would use:

```
cd bin
```

To display the name of your working directory, you use the **pwd** (print working directory) command. (Don't worry about the details right now.)

If you change directories a lot, you will find that it is easy to lose track of where you are. However, it is a bother to type **pwd** repeatedly. As an alternative, we will develop an alias to display an automatic reminder whenever you use **cd** to change your working directory.

If you refer to Figure 11-2, the table of built-in shell variables, you will see a variable named **cwd**. At all times, this variable contains the name of your current working directory. You can display the contents of **cwd** by using:

```
echo $cwd
```

What we want to do is issue this **echo** command every time we change directories. To do so, we will alias the **cd** command to two separate commands: a **cd** command followed by the **echo** command:

```
alias cd 'cd \!*; echo $cwd'
```

Now, whenever we change directories, we will know exactly where we are.

Alias Example: Avoid Deleting the Wrong Files

In this section, we will show you how to combine an alias with a history substitution to produce an exceptionally handy tool. Earlier in the chapter, we showed how to use the **ls** command to check what file names would be matched by a particular set of patterns. We did this before using those patterns with the **rm** (remove) command to delete files. This is important because once Unix deletes a file it is gone forever.

The example we used was deleting the files that match the patterns **temp*** and **extra?**. First, we checked what files these patterns match by entering:

```
ls temp* extra?
```

If the results were what we expected, we entered:

```
rm !*
```

to delete using the exact same pattern.

It would be nice to define an alias for this exact command. Unfortunately, for technical reasons, we cannot. (In an alias, the **!*** would refer to the current command, not to the previous command. For details, see the C-Shell manual page.)

However, it is possible to define an alias that does the job:

```
alias del 'rm \!ls:*'
```

(Again, we won't go into the details here. Basically, we are extracting the arguments from the last command that contained "**ls**".)

Once this alias is defined, you can use the following procedure to delete files that match a particular pattern:

First, enter the **ls** command with the pattern that describes the files you wish to delete. For example:

```
ls temp* extra?
```

If the pattern displays the names that you expect, enter:

```
del
```

If not, re-enter the **ls** command with a different pattern until you get what you want, then use **del**.

If you make a habit of using **ls** with a **del** alias in this way, we promise that, one day, you will save yourself from a catastrophe. (In fact, we have a mathematical proof - using Bessel functions - that this one trick alone is worth the price of this book.)

Initialization and Termination Files: .cshrc, .login, .logout

So far, we have met several types of commands that are useful for setting up your working environment. In addition, we have discussed variables that must be set before you can start work. How can you be sure that everything is set up properly? Certainly you don't want to enter a long sequence of commands each time you log in. In addition, there may be certain commands that you want to run each time you log out.

The shell provides a way for you to specify such commands once and have them executed at the appropriate time. Here is how it works.

The C-Shell recognizes three special files, named `.cshrc`, `.login` and `.logout`, in which you can store commands to be run automatically.

Every time a new shell is started, the commands in the `.cshrc` file are executed. This happens, of course, whenever you log in and your initial shell is started. It also happens whenever you run a shell script. (We discuss shell scripts later in the chapter.) The commands in the `.login` file are executed only once: when you log in, right after the `.cshrc` file is processed. As you might imagine, the `.logout` commands are also executed only once, just after you log out.

Commands whose names start with a period are called "dot files". We discuss dot files in Chapter 21.

WHAT'S IN A NAME?

The `.cshrc` File

Although few people know it, the "`rc`" stands for "run commands" - that is, initialization commands that are run automatically.

The name derives from the CTSS operating system (Compatible Time Sharing System), developed at MIT in 1963. CTSS had a facility called "runcom" that would execute a list of commands stored in a file.

Aside from the C-Shell itself, other programs look for "rc" initialization files in your home directory. Three examples are `.exrc` for the `ex` and `vi` text editors, `.mailrc` for the mail program, and `.newsrc` for the Usenet news program.

There is an important reason why these three filenames start with a dot. When you use the `ls` command to list your files, the names that begin with a dot are normally not displayed. This means that you do not have to look at these names each time you list your files. On those rare occasions when you want to display the names of all your files, including the names that begin with a dot, you can use `ls` with the `-a` (list all) option.

Most system managers set up their systems so that all new users have `.cshrc` and `.login` files in their home directories. (There may or may not be a `.logout` file.) In most cases, you will not have to make any changes to these files. Your shell and environment variables will be set up for you. You may also have some useful aliases.

If you want to take a look at these files, use the **more** command. For example:

more .cshrc

From time to time, you may decide to modify these files. For example, you might want the system to display the message:

HELLO, GOOD LOOKING!

each time you log in. Or you may wish to start the mail program automatically if there are messages for you.

To make such changes, you will have to know how to use a text editor: either **vi** or **emacs**, which are discussed later in the book.

☑ **HINT**   Which commands should go in the `.cshrc` file and which should go in the `.login` file? Here's what works best:

Your `.cshrc` file should contain commands to:

- set your shell variables
- define your aliases

Your `.login` file should contain commands to:

- set up your terminal
- define environment variables
- set the user mask for default file permissions (Chapter 22)
- perform initialization tasks each time you log in

The `.logout` file is less essential than `.cshrc` and `.login` and may be omitted if you want. This file holds commands that are executed whenever you log out. A nice command to put in your `.logout` file is **fortune** (see Chapter 7). Every time you log out you will see a funny remark. Some system managers (the ones with a good sense of humor) put this command in everybody's `.logout` file.

Shell Scripts

As we explained in Chapter 10, the shell is more than a command processor. The shell also supports a full programming language. In addition to regular Unix commands, you can also use special shell programming commands.

A file of such commands is called a SHELL SCRIPT. As the shell processes a script, it reads one command at a time. (Think of an actor reading a movie script, one line at a time.) To describe the processing, we say that the shell INTERPRETS each command.

In general, any program that reads and processes SCRIPTS - lists of sequential commands - can be called an INTERPRETER. Unix has a number of interpreters. For example, some of the text editors can interpret predefined scripts.

The details of programming the shell are beyond the scope of this book. However, for your interest, we have included two sample scripts: one in the Bourne shell programming language and one in the C-Shell programming language. Within the scripts, lines that begin with a number sign (**#**) are comments that are ignored by the shell.

Many C-Shell users feel that the Bourne shell language is better for writing scripts than the C-Shell language. Thus, it is common to find people who use the C-Shell (or Tcsh) as a command interpreter, but write Bourne shell scripts.

In the sample Bourne shell script, you will notice that the first line is:

#! /bin/sh

This tells the C-Shell to run the script under a Bourne shell. On many systems, this is the default.

Some people feel that the design of any shell programming facility is necessarily compromised because the shell must do double duty: as a command interpreter and as a programming language. Such people prefer to use an alternate interpreter designed only for scripts.

```
#! /bin/sh
# SHOWINFO: Bourne shell script to display an information file

# If the information file exists, display its contents.
# Otherwise, if the file does not exist, but if an older
#   version exists, display the older version.
# If neither file exists, display an error message
    if [ -f info ]
    then
        echo "The information file has been found.";
        more info
    elif [ -f info.old ]
    then
        echo "Only the old information file was found.";
        more info.old
    else
        echo "The information file was not found."
    fi
```

Figure 11-5

A Sample Bourne Shell Script

```
#! /bin/csh
# SHOWINFO: C-Shell script to display an information file

# If the information file exists, display its contents.
# Otherwise, if the file does not exist, but if an older
#   version exists, display the older version.
# If neither file exists, display an error message
    if (-f info ) then
        echo "The information file has been found.";
        more info
    else if (-f info.old) then
        echo "Only the old information file was found.";
        more info.old
    else
        echo "The information file was not found."
    endif
```

Figure 11-6
A Sample C-Shell Script

The most popular such interpreter is Perl, the Practical Extraction and Report Language. Perl was designed by Larry Wall, one of the Unix folk heroes. Perl provides a much more powerful scripting facility than the shell and is widely used by system managers. However, Perl programming is more difficult than shell programming and is not for the faint at heart.

Communicating with Other People

One of the wonderful things about Unix is that every time you log in you become a member of a global electronic community. In this chapter, we will show you how you can find out about members of this community. You will learn how to see who is doing what on your computer and how to display the public information that Unix keeps about each userid.

We will then show you how to hold a "conversation" with anyone: on your own computer or anywhere in the world. With a simple command, you can connect your computer to another and type messages back and forth in real time.

To start, let's take a look around your own local system.

Displaying Userids Who Are Logged In: `users`

Unix is not a world of secrets. For example, to find out who is currently logged in to your system, simply enter the command:

```
users
```

Unix will display the name of each userid that is logged in. If a userid is logged in more than once, it will be displayed more than once. For example, say that in response to a **users** command you see:

```
addie addie harley tln kim
```

This means that there are four different userids currently logged in. One of them, **addie**, is logged in twice. Usually this means either (1) the same person is logged in at two different terminals or (2) the person is using X Window and is logged in within two different windows.

Information About Logged-in Userids: who

The **users** command only shows the names of the userids that are currently logged in to your system. For more information, use the **who** command.

Here are some examples. You enter:

```
who
```

and you see:

```
addie      console Jul  8 10:30
addie      ttyp0   Jul 12 16:45
harley     ttyp1   Jul 12 17:46
tln        ttyp4   Jul 12 21:22    (cat)
kim        ttyp3   Jul 12 17:41    (tintin.ucsb.edu)
```

The first column shows the userids that are logged in to your computer (the same information as the **users** command). The next column shows the name of the terminal at which the userid is logged in. Most terminal names start with "tty" (which, as we pointed out in Chapter 6, is often used as an abbreviation for "terminal").

Following the terminal name is the date and time at which the userid logged in. In this example, you can see that userid **addie** has been logged in to terminal **console** for a long time. This userid may represent a system manager who has a terminal in her office that is permanently logged in.

Finally, if a userid has logged in from another computer, the name of this computer will be shown following the time. In our example, **addie** and **harley** have logged in to the host directly from a terminal. **tln** and **kim**, on the other hand, have logged in via network connections. In other words, they have first logged in to their own computers and, from there, logged in remotely to our computer.

When a userid has logged in remotely from a computer on the local network, you will see only a simple name. For example, **tln** has logged in from the computer named **cat** which is on our local network.

When a userid has logged in remotely from a computer on a different network, you will see the full network address. For example, **kim** has logged in from the computer **tintin.ucsb.edu** which is on a totally different network. (We will discuss addresses when we talk about sending mail in Chapter 13.)

Information About Local Network Logged-in Userids: rwho

The **users** and **who** commands display information about your computer. However, there may be times when you want to see who is logged in to the computers that are on the same local campus network as your computer. The **rwho** (remote **who**) command will display this information. The syntax is:

```
rwho [-a]
```

Here is some typical output:

```
addie     nipper:ttyp0    Jul 12 16:45
harley    nipper:ttyp1    Jul 12 17:46
kim       nipper:ttyp3    Jul 12 17:41  :10
melissa   princess:ttyp1  Jul 12 20:01
randy     law:ttyp3       Jul 12 20:35
```

We see some of the userids from the **who** example above, all of which are logged in to our system (**nipper**). We also see two other userids: **melissa**, who is logged in to **princess**, and **randy**, who is logged in to **law**.

Like the **who** command, **rwho** also shows the date and time at which the userid logged in. To the right of this information, **rwho** displays information about users who have been idle – have not pressed a key – for at least a minute. In this example, we see the user logged in as **kim** has not pressed a key for 10 minutes.

Notice, however, that two userids seem to be missing. When we entered the **who** command above, we saw that userid **addie** was logged in twice. What happened to the second session? Furthermore, userid **tln** has disappeared completely.

The answer is that **rwho**, unlike **users** or **who**, does not display the names of userids that have been idle for more than an hour. If you want **rwho** to list all the userids, use the **-a** option:

```
rwho -a
```

Here is some sample output:

```
addie     nipper:console  Jul  8 10:30 99:59
addie     nipper:ttyp0    Jul 12 16:45
harley    nipper:ttyp1    Jul 12 17:46
tln       nipper:ttyp4    Jul 12 21:22   1:40
kim       nipper:ttyp3    Jul 12 17:41    :10
melissa   princess:ttyp1  Jul 12 20:01
murray    princess:ttyp3  Jul 12 10:11   3:09
randy     law:ttyp3       Jul 12 20:35
```

Now we see userid **tln** as well as the other session for **addie**. We also see another userid named **murray** who is logged in to **princess** and is idle.

To the right of the login time and date, we see the idle time in hours and minutes. In our example, **tln** has been idle for 1 hour, 40 minutes, **kim** has been idle for 10 minutes, and **murray** has been idle for 3 hours, 9 minutes. The maximum time that **rwho -a** will display is 99 hours and 59 minutes (about 4 days, 4 hours). Thus, we know that **addie** has been idle at the console for at least that long.

HINT To find out who is logged in to your computer, use **users** or **who**. To find out who is logged in to any computer on your local network, use **rwho** or **rwho -a**.

Finding Out What Someone Is Doing: w

The commands we have discussed so far merely tell you who is logged in to your computer or to a computer on your network. If you want to find out what somebody is doing, use the **w** command. The syntax is:

w [**-hsu**] [*userid*]

Think of the name **w** as meaning "Who is doing what?"

Note: The **w** command, like the **who** command, displays information only about users on your computer, not about all the users within the network.

The output of **w** consists of two parts: First, there is a one-line summary showing overall system statistics. This summary is the same as the output of the **uptime** command that we discussed in Chapter 7. Next, there is information describing the activities of each userid that is logged in.

You can control what output you get by using the options. With no options, you get all the output. For example, if you enter:

w

you will see output like this:

```
8:44pm up 9 days, 7:02, 5 users, load average: 0.11, 0.02, 0.00
User      tty       login@  idle   JCPU    PCPU   what
addie     console   Wed10am 4days  42:41   37:56  -csh
addie     ttyp0     4:45pm         1:40    0:36   vi existential
harley    ttyp1     5:47pm         15:11          w
tln       ttyp4     9:22pm  1:40   20      1      -rn rec.pets.cats
kim       ttyp3     5:41pm  10     2:16    13     -csh
```

The first line shows the system statistics which we explained in Chapter 7. In this case, the system has been up for 9 days, 7 hours and 2 minutes, and there are 5 userids currently logged in. The last three numbers show the number of programs that have been waiting to execute, averaged over the last 1, 5 and 15 minutes respectively. These numbers give you an idea of the load on the system.

The next line shows the headings for the information that is to follow. For each userid, we see:

   User: userid
     tty: terminal name
 login@: time of login
    idle: time since the user last pressed a key (idle time)
   JCPU: processor time used by all processes (jobs) since login

PCPU: processor time used by the current process
what: the command (and its arguments) that is currently running

Note the term IDLE TIME. This refers to the elapsed time since the user has typed anything. Thus, if you are waiting for a time consuming job to finish and you are not typing while you are waiting, the **w** will show you being "idle".

WHAT'S IN A NAME?

CPU

In the days of mainframes, the "brain" of the computer – what we would now call the processor – was a large box. This box was referred to as the central processing unit or CPU (and still is for large computers). In Unix, we sometimes use the term "CPU" to mean processor.

Thus, we use the term "CPU time" to refer to processor time. You may hear someone say, "Ron's program slows down the system because it takes up too much CPU time." This means that Ron's program is so demanding that, when it runs, it makes all the other programs wait.

In our example above, we can see that userid **addie** is logged in to more than one terminal. First, **addie** is logged in to the console, although there has been no activity for about 4 days. A C-Shell (**csh**) is running, probably waiting for input. At another terminal, **ttyp0**, userid **addie** is active, editing a file named **existential** with the **vi** editor (which we will meet in Chapter 19).

Userid **harley** is logged in to terminal **ttyp1** and is running the **w** program. The processing time used by this program is so small (less then 1/100th of a second) that it is not even displayed.

(Note: Whenever you run the **w** command, you will see yourself running the **w** command. However, you won't really see yourself, you will see your userid, just like **harley** in our example. This situation is fraught with important philosophical implications which we do not understand in the least.)

Finally, you can see that userids **tln** and **kim** are both idle. **tln** is reading the Usenet news group about cats (see Chapter 23) and has not pressed a key for 1 minute and 40 seconds. **kim** is running a C-Shell that is probably waiting for a command and has not pressed a key for 10 seconds.

By default, the **w** command will display all of this information. You can use the options to specify that you want less information.

If you specify a userid, **w** will display information about that userid only. Using the previous example, if you enter:

```
w addie
```

you would see:

```
8:44pm up 9 days, 7:02, 5 users, load average: 0.11, 0.02, 0.00
User      tty          login@ idle   JCPU    PCPU   what
addie     console   Wed10am 4days  42:41   37:56  -csh
addie     ttyp0        4:45pm         1:40    0:36  vi existential
```

The **-s** option displays a short report. For example, if you enter **w -s** the report looks like this:

```
8:44pm up 9 days, 7:02, 5 users, load average: 0.11, 0.02, 0.00
User      tty     idle   what
addie     co     4days  csh
addie     p0            vi
harley    p1            w
tln       p4     1:40   rn
kim       p3       10   csh
```

This report is a lot simpler. The name of the terminal has been abbreviated. The processing times have been omitted. Finally, only the name of the current command is displayed; the arguments are omitted.

If you use **w -h**, you will get the long report, but without the headings:

```
addie     console   Wed10am 4days  42:41   37:56  -csh
addie     ttyp0        4:45pm         1:40    0:36  vi existential
harley    ttyp1        5:47pm        15:11           w
tln       ttyp4        9:22pm 1:40      20       1  -rn
rec.pets.cats
kim       ttyp3        5:41pm    10   2:16      13  -csh
```

This is handy if you are going to send the output of **w** to another program for further processing, since each line represents a single userid. (Sending the output of one program to another program is called "piping" and is explained in Chapter 15.)

Perhaps the most useful form of this command is to combine these two options: **w -sh**. The output looks like this:

```
addie     co       4days   csh
addie     p0               vi
harley    p1               w
tln       p4       1:40    rn
kim       p3         10    csh
```

This is an easy way to have a quick look at what is happening in the system. You might even want to put the following alias in your **.cshrc** file:

alias snoop w -sh

You can now check out the system whenever you want by entering:

snoop

(Aliases and the **.cshrc** file are explained in Chapter 11.)

Finally, if you use **w -u**, the command will display only the first line of the heading. For example:

```
8:44pm up 9 days, 7:02, 5 users, load average: 0.11, 0.02, 0.00
```
This is the same as the **uptime** command (see Chapter 7).

Note: The **w** command will not display system information about other computers in your network. You will have to use **ruptime** (also Chapter 7).

Public Information About a Userid: the Password File

Unix maintains information about userids that is available to anyone. This information is kept in your computer's PASSWORD FILE. On many systems, this file is named **/etc/passwd** and you can display it by entering the command:

```
more /etc/passwd
```

(We will discuss the **more** command in detail in Chapter 17.)

The name **/etc/passwd** refers to a file named **passwd** that lies in the **/etc** directory. We will discuss directories and file names in Chapters 21 and 22.

The standard password file holds the information that the system needs to identify you and to help you log in: your userid, your real name, what shell you use, your home directory (discussed in Chapter 21) and other information. Actually, the name of this file is a misnomer. It might better be called the "userid information file".

Note: In some networks, all the userid/password information is gathered into one or more central network files. This may allow you to use any computer on the network. In such cases, the **/etc/passwd** file will contain only a few basic entries; the bulk of the userid information will be elsewhere. You may have to ask around to find out where this information is kept on your system.

Knowing that all sorts of information, including userids, is kept in the password file, it is natural to ask: What about passwords? Are they kept in the password file? The answer is, maybe.

On some systems the passwords are kept right in the password file. On other systems the passwords are kept, along with special password data, in what is called a SHADOW FILE. In either case, the actual password is encoded.

Thus, it is safe to let anyone read the password file, which allows the basic information about each userid to be public. This method of organization is a long-standing Unix tradition.

Understanding What's in the Password File

One way to find out all the public information about a particular userid is to display the line of the password file that pertains to that userid. For example, the following command searches the password file for a line that contains "harley":

```
grep harley /etc/passwd
```

(We won't explain the details here. See Chapter 16. Briefly, **grep** displays all the lines in a file that contain a specified pattern.)

Here is some typical output: the entry for userid **harley** within a password file.

```
harley:62VvAhkOJI:101:90:&Hahn,,,2024561414:/usr/harley:/bin/csh
```

The standard Berkeley Unix password file (which may be modified on your system) contains seven fields, separated by colons.

- The first field is the userid, in this case, **harley**.
- The second field is the password (encoded, of course).

  By the way, it is impossible to figure out the actual password from the encoded pattern. It is also impossible to guess the encoding algorithm by using **passwd** to feed Unix different passwords and seeing what patterns are created. Don't waste your time trying to beat the system. Even the system manager, who can log in as superuser, has no way to find out your password.

- The next two fields contain the numeric value for the userid and the groupid.

As you know, all users have a login name, or userid. As we will discuss later, each userid belongs to a group, and each group has its own name, called a groupid.

For example, if someone gives you a complimentary account on their computer, just for fun, your userid might be put into a group named **guests**. Groups and groupids are important when you use file permissions, which we will discuss in Chapter 22.

Internally, Unix assigns each userid and groupid a unique number. In this example, the userid is number **101** and the groupid is number **90**. We know that the userid is **harley**, but we don't know the actual groupid (the name of the group). This information is stored in the file **/etc/group**, which you can display by using the command:

```
more /etc/group
```

- The fifth part of a password file entry is called the GECOS FIELD. (We will explain why in a minute.) Traditionally, this entry has four components, separated by commas:
  - your full name
  - the room number of your office
  - the phone number of your office
  - your home phone number

Some systems maintain this structure; others have modified it somewhat. However, at the very least, the GECOS field should contain your real name. In the example above, the GECOS field contains:

`&Hahn,,,2024561414`

The `&` character means that the first name is the same as the userid (which, in this case, is `harley`). Although there is no room number or phone number, there is a home phone number: (202) 456-1414.

- The sixth field shows the userid's home directory: the place where that user keeps his or her files. (We will discuss home directories in Chapter 21.)

- The last field contains the name of the shell that is started automatically for the userid upon login. In this case, the userid will be using the C-Shell (`/bin/csh`)

WHAT'S IN A NAME?

The GECOS Field

The fifth field within each entry in the Unix password file is called the GECOS field. Typically, this field contains the user's real name and, perhaps, other information such as the phone number.

Where does the name come from?

Around 1970, programmers at General Electric (then in the computer business) developed a clone of IBM's System/360 low-end DOS operating system. The GE system was called GECOS: General Electric Comprehensive Operating System.

Some years later, Honeywell bought out GE's computer division and changed the name of the system to GCOS: General Comprehensive Operating System.

It happened that some early Bell Labs Unix systems used GCOS machines for printing and other services. (Bell Labs is where Unix was first developed.) For this reason, someone at Bell Labs added a field to the password file to hold the GCOS identification information.

It has been a long time, of course, since this field has actually held real GCOS information; the space is now used to hold personal data. However, for the sake of historical obscurity, the entry is still known as the GECOS field (or, occasionally, the GCOS field).

Displaying Public Information About a Userid: `finger`

In the last section, we explained how you can look at your system's password file to display public information about a particular userid.

However, the information that is displayed in this manner is not all that easy to read. In addition, some networked systems keep the password information in central files that are not directly accessible to most users.

In this section, we will show you how to use the **finger** command to get at all this information easily. Moreover, as we will see later, **finger** has a reach that goes far beyond your local computer.

The syntax for the **finger** command is:

`finger` [`-ls`] [`name...`]

The most common way to use this command is to specify the name of a particular userid, such as:

`finger harley`

The command will display the public information about this userid:

```
Login name: harley                 In real life: Harley Hahn
Phone: 202-456-1414
Directory: /usr/harley             Shell: /bin/csh
On since Aug  9 21:01:56 on ttyp3 from nipper.ucsb.edu
```

Aside from the information that can be found in the password file, **finger** will let you know if the userid happens to be logged in at the time. In this case, userid **harley** was logged in from the remote computer **nipper.ucsb.edu** using terminal **ttyp3**.

If you are not sure of someone's userid, try using their name. For example:

`finger Hahn`

On some systems, **finger** will check in the GECOS fields of the password file, looking for names. Other systems are less sophisticated and you can use only userids. If you specify more than one userid, for example,

`finger harley addie tln`

finger will display information about each one in turn. Alternatively, you can use the command without any names at all:

`finger`

You will get a short report that contains one line for each userid that is currently logged in. For example:

```
Login         Name              TTY  Idle     When
harley        Harley Hahn       p1    1:   Wed 17:45
kenn          Kenn Nesbitt      p0         Wed 17:46
ron           Ron Dragushan     p6         Mon 09:17
rick          Rick Stout        p4   10:   Mon 09:17
```

Some systems may show you extra information, such as the computer from which the userid has logged in, or the information in the userid's GECOS field.

To control the output, you can use the **-s** and **-l** options to force **finger** to display a short or long report. For example, to display a short report on several specific userids, you can use:

```
finger -s harley addie tln
```

To display a long report on all the userids who are logged in, use:

```
finger -l
```

Your system may have other options. Check the man page (use the **man finger**).

Note: We sometimes use the word FINGER as a verb, meaning to use the **finger** program to check out someone. For example, you might say to someone that you meet at a dance, "If you forget my home phone number, just finger me." (Yes, Unix people really do talk like this.)

Changing Your Publicly Accessible Information: chfn

As we explained earlier in the chapter, your entry in the password file contains public information about your userid. Some of this can be changed only by your system manager: for example, your userid and your home directory.

However, you can change some of the information. First, as we explained in Chapter 10, you can use the **chsh** command to change your default shell. Second, you can use the **chfn** (change finger information) command to modify whatever is in the GECOS field. Just enter:

```
chfn
```

and follow the instructions.

The GECOS field contains information about you: your name, and possibly your office number, office phone number and home phone number. The **chfn** allows you to modify or remove this information whenever you want by making the appropriate changes to the system password file.

In fact, the **chfn** command is really just the **passwd** command with a **-f** option. This makes sense because what you are doing is changing the system password file, just like when you use the **passwd** command to change your password.

Note: Some systems will not allow you to use **chfn**. On such systems, all changes must be performed by the system manager.

The `finger` Command and the `.plan` and `.project` Files

Aside from the public information in the password file, `finger` will display information from two other files: files that you can control directly. Their names are `.plan` and `.project`. If one or both of these files exists in your home directory, `finger` will read them.

(Why do these file names begin with a period? You list the names of your files by using the `ls` command. The `ls` command will not list file names that begin with a period unless you use the `-a` [all] option. Many system files have names that begin with a period so that you don't have to look at the names each time you list your files. This is discussed in Chapter 21.)

(What is your home directory? It is the directory that has been created for you to store your own personal files. We will discuss the home directory in Chapter 21.)

It is up to you to create the `.plan` and `.project` files; they are purely optional. To create these files, you will need to know how to use a text editor like `vi` (which we will discuss in Chapter 19). Make sure that the files have the appropriate permissions for other people to read them. (File permissions are explained in Chapter 22.)

Here is how the `.plan` and `.project` files are used: If you have a `.plan` file, `finger` will display its contents. If you have a `.project` file, `finger` will display the first line.

Remember, Unix was designed in academic and research environments where just about everybody had a project to work on (and a few people even had plans). You would describe your project in your `.project` file, and everyone who fingered you would know what you were doing.

The `.plan` file was intended to be a description of your current location and upcoming plans. The idea was that you could change your `.plan` file whenever necessary to let people know where you were.

Nowadays, people use these files to hold all types of information. For example, if you are giving a party, you can put the directions for getting to your house in your `.plan` file. You can then mail people invitations, telling them to finger you if they need directions. One common use of the `.plan` file is for professors and teaching assistants to list their office hours.

If you finger a variety of people, you will see a variety of `.plan` files: jokes, poems, drawings, quips, and, very occasionally, an actual plan.

Here is one example so you can see what it looks like. You enter:

```
finger harley
```

and you see:

```
Login name: harley                      In real life: Harley Hahn
 Phone: 202-456-1414
Directory: /usr/harley                      Shell: /bin/csh
On since Aug  9 21:01:56 on ttyp3 from nipper.ucsb.edu
```

```
Project: writing a Unix text book for students
Plan:
      To live forever, or die in the attempt.
```

If you finger someone who does not have a `.project` file, `finger` will silently omit it. However, if the person does not have a `.plan` file, you will see:

No Plan.

(which is usually appropriate).

Displaying Mail Status with `finger`

Some versions of **finger** will display information about a userid's mail box. (We will discuss mail in Chapter 13.)

If the user has read and disposed of all the mail in his or her mail box, **finger** will display the message:

No unread mail

along with the regular information.

If the user has read all the mail, but has not disposed of it, you will see a message like this:

Mail last read Mon Aug 10 17:06:10 1992

Finally, if there is mail that is waiting to be read, the message will look like this:

New mail received Mon Aug 10 17:22:26 1992;

unread since Mon Aug 10 17:06:10 1992

Some systems may also show the amount of unread mail in kilobytes (1 kilobyte = 1K = 1024 characters).

You might think that this will come in handy when you need to know if someone has read the mail you sent. However, looks are deceiving. **finger** actually has no way to know if someone has read his or her mail. All it can find out is the last time that the mail file was accessed.

Isn't this the same thing as knowing if someone has read his or her mail? Not at all.

In Chapter 14, we will learn that you can use the **from** command to display a summary of the mail that is waiting for you. When you use **from**, you do not actually read the mail, you just see a summary.

Many people put the **from** command in their `.login` file so that they can see a summary of their mail each time they log in. Since the **from** command accesses the mail file, it fools **finger** into thinking that the mail has already been read by a person.

Here is a common scenario: You have sent someone an urgent mail message and you want to know if he has read it yet. You use a **finger** command, which reports that the mail was last read on such and such a date.

Since your message was urgent, you are annoyed that, after having read your message, the recipient did not even bother to reply. (We won't say that you are disgruntled, but you are certainly far from gruntled.)

So, you send him a nasty note in which you tell him exactly what you think of people who do not respond to important messages in a timely fashion.

Meanwhile, unbeknownst to you, the recipient has never actually read your message. All that happened is that a **from** command in his `.login` file has looked at the mail file once.

When he gets your second note, the recipient gets so mad that he sends over two plug-uglies named Erb and Vito to break both your legs.

Imagine your embarrassment!

Fingering the World

If **finger** could only display information about the userids on your own computer, that would be useful enough. But **finger** can do a lot more: it can tell you about any userid on any Unix computer that is connected to yours.

We are referring to more computers than the ones in your local or campus network. If your computer is connected to the Internet – the global collection of networks – you can finger anyone on any other Internet computer, anywhere in the world. All you need is his or her electronic address.

In Chapter 13, we will discuss addresses. For now, we will explain briefly that standard Internet addresses, are of the form:

userid@domain

where *domain* is the official name of the person's computer. Here is an example:

harley@nipper.ucsb.edu

So, you could enter the command:

finger harley@nipper.ucsb.edu

Your computer will send a request to the remote computer. Its **finger** program will service the request and send the response back to your computer.

If you leave out the userid, **finger** will ask for information regarding which userids are currently logged in to the computer whose name you specify. For example, to see a short report about all the userids who are logged in to the computer named **nipper.ucsb.edu**, enter:

finger @nipper.ucsb.edu

Be sure not to leave out the @ character, or **finger** will think you are specifying a userid, not a computer name.

On your own network, you can usually refer to a computer using only the first part of its full name. For example, if there is a computer in your network named **misty**, you can display a short report about all the userids currently logged in by entering:

```
finger @misty
```

Systems that support remote fingering have a finger daemon (see below) that receives and processes finger requests. Some system managers do not like the idea of their userids and computers being fingered from anywhere in the world. They will specify that their finger daemon should not service remote requests. If you ask **finger** to connect to such a system, you will get a message like:

```
connect: Connection refused
```

Note: A "daemon" (yes, that is how you spell it) is a program that executes in the background and provides a useful service. We will discuss such programs in Chapter 18 when we meet the daemon that handles the Unix printing services.

Checking to See If a Computer Is Alive and Well: `ping`

If your computer has trouble contacting another computer that you think is on the Internet, you may see a message like:

```
unknown host: nipper.ucsb.edu
```

This can mean one of three things.

First, you may have entered a bad name (check your spelling). Second, one of the links between your computer and the remote computer may be down temporarily. The third possibility is that the destination computer may exist, but it may not be connected to the Internet.

This can be confusing because there are many computers that have names that look like official Internet addresses but that are not really connected to the Internet.

If you want to check if a computer is actually connected, you can use the **ping** command. The syntax is:

```
ping computer-name
```

For example, you might enter:

```
ping nipper.ucsb.edu
```

You will get one of three responses. If the computer is on the Internet and is responding, you will see a message like this:

```
nipper.ucsb.edu is alive
```

If the computer is on the Internet, but is not responding, you will see a message (after a while) like this:

```
no answer from nipper.ucsb.edu
```

Finally, if the computer is not connected to the Internet, you will see a message like this:

```
ping: unknown host nipper.ucsb.edu
```

The **ping** command is useful if you are trying to connect to someone using the **talk** command (explained below) and you are having trouble making the connection.

Note: There are various versions of the **ping** command. The one on your system may work differently, but the main idea will be the same.

WHAT'S IN A NAME?

Ping   On a ship, a single sonar pulse that is sent out to reflect off another ship is called a "ping". You can see the analogy to a computer command that sends out an electronic query to check the status of another system. Thus, we have the **ping** command. Officially, the name stands for "Packet Internet Groper". (On the Internet, data is sent in packets.)

In conversation, the word ping is used as a verb: "I couldn't connect to the other computer, so I pinged it to see if it was alive." If you ever telephone someone who answers by saying "ping", you know you have reached a Unix expert (or a sonar operator).

Communicating with Someone Directly: `talk`

If you need to send a message to someone, you can always use the Unix mail system (see Chapter 13). However, there will be times when what you really want to do is talk with someone directly, back and forth, like a telephone call.

If that person is logged in to a computer that is connected to yours, you can use the **talk** command. The syntax is:

talk *user-name* [*terminal-name*]

If the person you want to talk to is logged in to your computer, all you need to do is specify their userid. For example:

```
talk harley
```

If the person is logged into another computer, specify the full address (as we described for the **finger** command). For example:

```
talk harley@nipper.ucsb.edu
```

(How do you tell if a particular userid is logged in? For your own computer, use the **users** or **who** commands; for remote computers use the **rwho** or

finger commands. To see what computers are connected to your local network, use **ruptime**.)

When you use **who** or **rwho**, you may see that the userid you want to talk to is logged in to more than one terminal. If so, you will want to connect to the terminal that is active. The output of **who** and **rwho** shows you what is happening on each terminal. Pick the one that looks the best. You can then specify that terminal name as part of the **talk** command.

For example, say that you want to talk to a userid named **addie**. The **who** command shows you:

```
User       tty          login@  idle   JCPU   PCPU  what
addie      console     Wed10am 4days  42:41  37:56  -csh
addie      ttyp0        4:45pm         1:40   0:36  vi existential
```

In this case, it is best to talk to the **ttyp0** terminal. Enter:

```
talk addie ttyp0
```

Once you enter the **talk** command, you will see the message:

```
[Waiting for your party to respond]
```

At the other end, the **talk** daemon is displaying a message for the recipient:

```
Message from Talk_Daemon@nipper at 13:19 ...
talk: connection requested by harley@nipper.
talk: respond with:  talk harley@nipper
```

The message means: Someone with the userid of **harley**, on a computer named **nipper**, is trying to talk with you. To establish the connection, you must enter your own **talk** command, in this case:

```
talk harley@nipper
```

You will then see a message telling you that the connection has been established.

If you enter a **talk** command and the other userid is not logged in, you will see:

```
[Your party is not logged on]
```

If the other person is logged in, but is not responding, **talk** will display:

```
[Ringing your party again]
```

If you see this last message repeatedly, you should probably give up. Abort the **talk** command by pressing the **intr** key (usually **^C**, see Chapter 6).

Once you make a connection, **talk** will take control of your screen and divide it into two parts. From now on, everything you or the other person types will be echoed on both screens. The top half of the screen shows what you type. The bottom half of the screen shows what the other person types.

If the data is not being displayed properly – for example, if the characters are dribbling down the left-hand side of the screen – make sure that you have set the global **TERM** variable correctly (see Chapters 4 and 11).

The nice thing about `talk` is that both people can type at the same time, just like talking over the telephone. However, to keep from getting confused there are two conventions that you should follow.

First, when you are finished typing something, press <Return> twice to put in a blank line. This tells the person, who may have been waiting patiently, that you are finished for the moment. Second, it is polite to say goodbye (type **bye**) before terminating a conversation.

As you are typing, you can use any of the regular correction keys that we discussed in Chapter 6. These keys are shown in Figure 12-1. In addition, if the screen becomes garbled, you can tell `talk` to redisplay it by pressing `^L`.

To quit talking, you can either press `^D` (the **eof** key) to tell `talk` that there is no more data, or you can press `^C` (or whatever your **intr** key is) to abort the command. Either person can sever the connection by pressing one of these two keys.

Communicating with Someone Directly: `write`

Aside from `talk`, there is another, older program named `write` that you can use to talk with someone directly. The syntax is:

`write` *userid* [*terminal-name*]

Unlike `talk`, `write` does not divide the screen into two parts. Once you establish a connection, all `write` does is copy data from your terminal directly to the other person's terminal, and vice versa. This has two immediate disadvantages:

- If you both type at the same time, the characters will be mixed together. You will have to take turns.

- You can only use `write` to connect to a terminal on your own computer. You cannot connect to someone who is using a different computer.

Key	Purpose
`^H` or <Backspace>	erase the last character typed (**erase**)
`^W`	erase the last word typed (**werase**)
`^U` (sometimes `^X`)	erase the entire line (**kill**)
`^L`	redisplay the entire screen

Figure 12-1
Special Keys to Use with `talk`

However, there are advantages to **write**:

- Some systems do not have a **talk** command, but **write** is almost always available. You will at least be able to communicate with people on your computer.

- When you are using **write**, it is possible to enter a regular Unix command without severing the connection. With **talk**, there is no easy way to do this.

To write to someone, specify his or her userid. For example:

```
write harley
```

If he or she are logged in to more than one terminal, you can specify the one to which you want to connect. (See the discussion for the **talk** command above.) For example:

```
write harley ttyp0
```

If you mistakenly enter an Internet-style remote address, such as:

```
write harley@nipper.ucsb.edu
```

write will try to interpret it as a userid and you will see a message telling you that the userid is not logged in:

```
harley@nipper.ucsb.edu not logged in
```

This message is misleading, as it implies that **write** could connect to the remote computer if only the userid were logged in. (If you want to see who is logged in to your computer, use the **users** command.)

☑ **HINT**   You can use the **talk** command to communicate with anyone who is logged in to any Unix computer that is connected to yours.

You can use the **write** command only with userids that are logged in to your own computer.

When you enter a **write** command, the other person will see a message. Here is an example:

```
Message from addie@nipper on ttyp1 at 16:56 ...
```

In this example, someone with the userid of **addie** is trying to connect to you. To make the connection, you must enter your own **write** command. In this case:

```
write addie
```

The connection will now be completed.

Note: When you enter a **write** command, you will not see anything until the other person responds. Thus, if you have entered a **write** command

and nothing happens for a while, you should probably give up. Abort the **write** command by pressing the **intr** key (usually **^C**, see Chapter 6).

Once you have established a connection, each line that is typed by either person is echoed on both screens. Thus, you need to take turns. By convention, the person who initiated the connection goes first.

To keep things straight, there are two simple rules that you should follow. First, don't type until the other person is finished. Second, when you are finished, let the other person know by typing a lowercase **o** in parentheses. For example:

```
blah blah blah blah blah
blah blah blah blah blah
(o)
```

This stands for "over". When the other person sees this signal, he will type as long as he wants, again finishing with **(o)**. It is now your turn. When you want to stop the conversation, you tell the other person by typing:

```
(oo)
```

which stands for "over and out".

At any time, you can enter a regular Unix command by starting the line with an **!** (exclamation mark) character. For example, say that you are talking with someone who asks if you have a particular file. Tell him to hold on for a moment and then type:

```
!ls
```

This will run the **ls** command to list the names of your files. After the output of the command is displayed, you will see a second **!** character. You can now continue your conversation.

As you are typing, you can use any of the regular correction keys that we discussed in Chapter 6. These keys are shown in Figure 12-2.

To quit talking, you can either press **^D** (the **eof** key) to tell **write** that there is no more data, or you can press **^C** (or whatever your **intr** key is) to abort the command. Either person can sever the connection by pressing one of these two keys.

Key	Purpose
^H or \<Backspace\>	erase the last character typed (**erase**)
^W	erase the last word typed (**werase**)
^U (sometimes **^X**)	erase the entire line (**kill**)

Figure 12-2
Special Keys to Use with **write**

Keeping Others from Sending You Messages: `mesg`

You can use the **mesg** command to keep other people from connecting to your terminal with **talk** or **write**. This is handy if you are using the full screen and unsolicited messages would mess up what you are doing. The syntax is:

```
mesg [n] [y]
```

To indicate that you do not want interruptions, enter:

```
mesg n
```

To indicate that you will accept messages, enter:

```
mesg y
```

To check the current status, enter the command with no parameters:

```
mesg
```

The response will be either **y** or **n**.

Some system managers put a **mesg n** command in everyone's `.login` file (see Chapter 11). Check the **mesg** status next time you log in. If it is set to **n** and you want to talk with people, you will have to change your `.login` file.

Note: The **mesg** command does not affect the sending and receiving of mail.

 HINT You cannot use **talk** or **write** if **mesg** is set to **n**. If people are having trouble connecting to your terminal, check to see if your `.login` file contains a **mesg n** command.

Being Courteous and Conventional While Talking

When you talk in person or over the telephone, there are various verbal and visual cues that you use.

For example, imagine you are a male freshman talking (in person) to your roommate. He is wondering if he should ask out the girl who sits beside him in his Political Commitment in Twentieth Century American Literature class.

You look at him, raise your eyebrows and, with a mocking lilt to your voice, say, "Do you really think she would go out with someone like you?" All in good fun, of course.

Now, imagine that, instead of talking in person, you are communicating over a computer connection using the **talk** program. You type:

```
Do you really think she would go out with someone like you?
```

But this time there is no look, no raised eyebrows and no actual voice. What would have been subtle irony has become gross sarcasm.

This phenomenon – the ease with which you can insult someone over a computer connection – was noticed years ago. The solution used in the Unix community is to tell people explicitly whenever there may be any doubt that you are making a joke. You do this by typing what is called a SMILEY FACE or SMILEY. It looks like this:

```
:-)
```

(Turn your head to the left and look at it sideways.)

You should type a smiley every time you write something that may be offensive. (Another way to look at it is that you should type a smiley every time you want to point out to someone that you are being subtly ironic.) For example:

```
Do you really think she would go out with someone like you? :-)
```

We will talk more about smileys in Chapter 24.

There is one alternative that you might run into. If someone is used to using commercial networks – such as Compuserve – where the proletariat gathers, he or she might type **<g>** instead of a smiley face:

```
Do you really think she would go out with someone like
you? <g>
```

The **<g>** stands for "grin".

 HINT Communicating with **talk** or **write** is a lot slower than speaking, and it is easy to get bored if someone is typing too slowly.

Don't worry about simple mistakes in grammar or spelling. Instead of stopping to backspace and correct, plunge on with abandon. Your recipient will figure out what you mean.

The Importance of Universal Addressing

As we explained earlier, when you use **talk** or **finger** with a userid from a remote system, you must specify the full electronic address. In the Internet, this address takes the form:

userid@domain

for example:

```
harley@nipper.ucsb.edu
```

(We will explain more about addresses in Chapter 13.)

In the world of Unix, you use the same address for everything: mail, fingering, talking, and so on. In addition, you can also receive mail at this address from most of the public commercial mail systems, such as Compuserve and MCI Mail.

Compared to a postal address, your electronic address is much easier to understand and remember. Moreover, you will find computer communication to be more reliable and a lot faster. We happen to think that this is an amazing achievement, and we would like you to take a moment to think about it.

☑ **HINT** A single electronic address allows you to receive any type of computer communication from anywhere in the world (as long as the connection is there).

Networks and Addresses

Once you are a part of the Unix community, you can communicate with people and transfer data all over the world. All you need is an electronic address and a knowledge of how to use the networking programs.

In this chapter, we will explain the fundamental ideas. We start by giving you an overview of the Unix mail system. We then discuss the large Internet network and what it offers. Finally, we explain how electronic addressing works.

Later in the book, you will learn how to send and receive mail (Chapter 14), log in remotely (Chapter 25), transfer files (Chapter 25), read the news (Chapter 24), share software (Chapter 25), and search for information (Chapter 25). However, this chapter explains the basic principles, so read it first.

An Overview of the Unix Mail System

MAIL or EMAIL (electronic mail) refers to the sending and receiving of messages or files. When a Unix person uses the word "mail", you can take it for granted they mean electronic mail, not regular post office mail. Similarly, when you see the word ADDRESS, it refers to an electronic mailing address, not a postal address.

Mail is an important part of Unix, and all Unix systems come with a built-in mail system. Even if your computer is not connected to other computers, you can still send mail to other people on your system and even to yourself.

You can exchange mail with anyone whose computer is connected to yours, as long as the systems are configured properly. The recipient's system does not necessarily have to run Unix. Mail system configuration is not easy, but it is a job for the system manager and there is no reason for you to care about the details. All you need to know is what capabilities are available and how to use them.

Most university computers are connected to a campus network and just about all campuses are connected to the outside world. (A network is a group of computers connected together in order to share resources. See Chapter 3 for more details.) You will find that sending mail across the world is as easy as sending mail across the hall. Moreover, mail travels fast. If the network is not too busy, sending messages over long distances may take only seconds. Even on slow days, electronic mail on the Internet is always faster than the regular postal service.

WHAT'S IN A NAME?

Snail Mail   When Unix people talk about "mail", they always mean electronic mail. When they refer to regular post office mail, they will always make it clear by context.

One term that is often used to refer to post office mail is SNAIL MAIL. This name describes the relative pace of mailing through the post office compared to mailing via an electronic network.

Working with mail is easy. Here is a quick overview of how it works. In Chapter 14, we will describe everything in detail.

To send mail you enter:

mail *address*

where *address* is the address of the person to whom you want to send a message. For example:

mail harley@nipper.ucsb.edu

If the recipient is on your own system, you only need to specify a userid:

mail harley

Note: It is not necessary for someone to be logged in to receive mail. The remote Unix system will receive and store the message. The next time the person logs in, Unix will display a message saying that mail is waiting.

After entering the **mail** command, you type the message, one line at a time. At the end of each line, you press <Return>. When you are finished, you press **^D** (the **eof** key) to tell the **mail** program there is no more data. The message will be sent automatically and you will see:

EOT

This stands for "end of transmission".

To read mail, just enter:

```
mail
```

The **mail** program will show you a list of all the messages that are waiting for you. Using simple commands, you can read one message at a time. When you have read it, you can save it, delete it, reply to it, or forward it to someone else. You can even have Unix tell you when mail arrives so you don't have to keep checking for yourself.

Of course, there are some particulars you need to learn (there always are with Unix programs). We will discuss the **mail** program in detail in Chapter 14.

Where can you send mail? It makes sense that you should be able to send mail to anyone on your own computer, your own network, and even to any computer on your campus. However, if your campus is connected to the Internet – and it probably is – you can send mail to computers in every part of the world. All you need to know is the address of the recipient.

However, before we get into addressing, we need to talk about the Internet, the mysterious network that holds together the worldwide electronic community. The best place to start is with TCP/IP, the glue that holds together the Internet.

TCP/IP

The Internet is a collection of networks, all over the world, that contain many different types of systems. Something must hold it all together. That something is TCP/IP (plus a lot of volunteer labor).

The details of TCP/IP are highly technical and well beyond the interest of almost everybody. However, there will be many times when you see or hear the term "TCP/IP", so we might as well spend a few minutes talking about it.

TCP/IP is the common name for a collection of more than 100 different protocols. (A PROTOCOL is a set of rules that allow different machines and programs to communicate with one another.) The TCP/IP protocols are used within the Internet (and other networks) to connect computers, communications equipment and programs. Not all computers on the Internet run Unix, but they all use TCP/IP.

WHAT'S IN A NAME?

TCP/IP   The name TCP/IP is derived from two of the basic protocols: TCP is an acronym for Transmission Control Protocol; IP is an acronym for Internet Protocol.

Within a TCP/IP system, data that is to be transmitted is divided into small packets. Each packet has the address of the recipient computer along with a sequence number. For example, the system may divide a mail message into 10 different packets; each of those packets will have its own sequence number.

The various packets are sent out over the network, and each packet is transported, on its own, to the destination. When the packets are all received, the destination system uses the sequence numbers to put them back together. If, for some reason, a packet has arrived in garbled condition, the destination system will transmit a message to the sender asking for that particular packet to be resent.

Breaking data into packets has several important benefits. First, communication lines can be shared among many users. All kinds of packets can be transmitted at the same time, and they will be sorted and recombined when they arrive at their respective destinations. Compare this to how a telephone conversation is transmitted. Once you make a connection, the circuits are reserved for you and cannot be used for another call, even if you put the other person on hold for twenty minutes.

The second advantage of the TCP/IP system is that data does not have to be sent directly between two computers. Each packet is passed from computer to computer until it reaches its destination. This, of course, is the secret of how you can send messages and data between any two computers, even if they are not directly connected to one another.

What is amazing is that it may take only a few seconds to send a large file from one machine to another, even when they are thousands of miles apart and the data must pass through multiple computers. One of the reasons for this speed is that, when something goes wrong, only a single packet may need to be retransmitted and not the whole message.

Another benefit of this system is that every packet does not need to follow the same path. This allows the network to route each packet from place to place, using the best connection that is available at that instant. Thus, your message packets do not necessarily all travel over the same route, nor do they necessarily all arrive at the same time.

Finally, the flexibility of the system makes for high reliability. If one particular link goes down, the system will use a different one.

When you send a message, it is TCP that breaks the data into packets, sequences the packets, adds some error control information and then sends packets out to be delivered. At the other end, TCP receives the packets, checks for errors, and combines all of the packets back into the original data. If there is an error somewhere, the destination TCP program will send a message asking for the required packets to be resent. (TCP would have done a lot better at putting Humpty Dumpty back together than did all the King's men.)

The job of IP is to get the raw data – the packets – from one place to another. The computers that direct data from one network to another – called ROUTERS – use IP to move the data.

In other words, IP moves the raw data packets, while TCP manages the flow and ensures that the data is correct.

Historical aside: During the Persian Gulf war of 1991, the Allies had trouble destroying the Iraqi command network even when some of the computers were damaged. Why? The Iraqis were using commercial IP routers that were able to find alternative routes quickly whenever a link went down.

 HINT   Do not sell IP routers to hostile governments.

Thus, when someone asks you what is TCP/IP, you can give three different answers. First, you can say that TCP and IP are two protocols that manage and perform data transmission between networks. Second, you can say that the term "TCP/IP" is often used to refer to a collection of more than 100 different protocols that are used to organize computers and communication devices into a network.

Or you can simply wave your hands and say that TCP/IP is the glue that holds the Internet together.

 HINT   If you are interested in seeing the route from your computer to another, you can use the **traceroute** command.

This command is not available on all systems. If your system does have **traceroute**, just enter the command name followed by the address of another computer on the Internet. (We will discuss addresses below.)

For example, to see the route from your computer to the computer whose address is **nic.ddn.mil**, enter:

```
traceroute nic.ddn.mil
```

The output will show you each step in the path between the two computers. From time to time, you may see a different path as conditions change in the network.

The **traceroute** command has many technical options and is really meant for people who maintain network connections. However, you may find it fun to check a connection path once in a while.

What Is the Internet?

There are two ways to think of the Internet.

First, we can define it in a technical sense. We can say that the Internet is a worldwide collection of networks that transmit data using the IP protocol.

This is a good definition in the sense that it is accurate. However, it is not satisfying. What we really want to know is, what can we do with the Internet?

There are six main services that the Internet has to offer you. We will talk about these services in detail later in the book. For now, here is a short description so you can orient yourself.

- Mail: You can send and receive messages.
- File Transfer: You can copy files from one computer to another.
- Remote Login: You can log in to another computer and work with it, just as if your terminal were attached directly.
- News: You can read and post articles to the hundreds of discussion groups that comprise the Usenet news network.
- Sharing Software: You can get free copies of all kinds of software, and you can share your own programs with others.
- Accessing Information: You can search for and retrieve any kind of information. If you are not sure where to look, there are special programs that will look for you.

These are not all the resources offered over the Internet (for example, there is also the `talk` command that we discussed in Chapter 12). However, they are the services you are most likely to use.

Thus, here is a good, practical definition of the Internet: The Internet is a worldwide network that offers the services of mail, file transfer, remote login, news, sharing software and accessing information. (We will talk more about the Internet services in Chapter 25.)

Are You Really Part of the Internet?

As we will see later in this chapter, there are other large networks that have mail connections to the Internet. However, just being able to exchange mail with the Internet does not mean that a computer is actually part of the Internet. For example, people using Compuserve or MCI Mail can send mail to Internet addresses. However, they do not have file transfer, remote login and all the rest.

Similarly, there are many people who use non-Internet systems to partici-pate in the Usenet news network. Most of these people can send mail to

Internet addresses, but they do not have access to the resources that require a direct connection.

Some people are confused about all of this and think they are connected to the Internet when they are not. Usually, this means that they have some sort of mail or news service, but not a full connection.

A good test is: If you can log on to a remote Internet computer, you are probably on the Internet. In a university, you will find that almost every computer will afford you access to the Internet, either directly or via another local system.

Some people ask: All I want to do is send mail. Do I really need an Internet connection? The answer is, no, you don't *need* an Internet connection, as long as your computer has some way to route mail to the outside world.

However, if you send mail regularly to people on Internet computers, you will find that an Internet connection is a lot faster. It is not uncommon for Internet mail to be transmitted in minutes or even seconds. This is because the Internet uses permanent, high-speed connections. When mail is sent from the outside, the transmission is slower and all the data must be routed through whatever computer provides the mail connection to the Internet.

Moreover, if you have a chance to use an Internet connection, there are many wonderful services available that go well beyond simple mail delivery.

Standard Internet Addresses

The key to using the Internet (and the mail system) is to understand the addresses. The amazing thing about the Internet addressing scheme is that each userid and each computer need only a single address no matter what service is being used. For instance, when you send mail to someone, you use the same address as when you connect via the **talk** command (see Chapter 12).

As you will come to appreciate, this system really is remarkable. Imagine being able to use the same address or identification number to mail someone a postcard, call them on the telephone, or send them a fax. Yet with a single Internet address, you can do much more.

An Internet address consists of a userid, followed by an @ character (the "at" sign), followed by the name of a computer. The part of the address that contains the computer name is called the DOMAIN. Thus, the standard Internet address looks like this:

userid@*domain*

Here is an example:

harley@nipper.ucsb.edu

In this example, the userid is **harley**, and the domain – the name, or address, of the computer – is **nipper.ucsb.edu**. (All Unix computers have a name.) To send mail to this userid, you would enter:

```
mail harley@nipper.ucsb.edu
```

The notation using the **@** character is appropriate. As you enter this command, you can say to yourself, "I am sending mail to Harley, who is at the computer named **nipper.ucsb.edu**."

The parts of the domain that are separated by periods are called SUB-DOMAINS. The address above has three sub-domains: **nipper**, **ucsb** and **edu**. The rightmost sub-domain (in this case, **edu**) is referred to as the TOP-LEVEL DOMAIN.

To read an address, look at the sub-domains from right to left. This will take you from the most general name to the most specific name. The leftmost sub-domain will usually refer to a specific computer.

When you type an Internet address, you can mix upper- and lowercase letters. For example, the following addresses are equivalent:

```
mail harley@nipper.ucsb.edu
mail harley@NIPPER.UCSB.EDU
```

As a general rule, it is a good habit to stick with lowercase, especially for userids, although some people do mix upper- and lowercase. Here are two common variations:

```
mail harley@nipper.Ucsb.Edu
mail harley@nipper.ucsb.EDU
```

The first address emphasizes the name of the main computer at the site; the second emphasizes the name of the top-level domain. In either case, the uppercase letters are optional.

 HINT   If you are using an Internet address in which some of the letters are uppercase, it is safe to change the letters to lowercase.

Internet Addresses: the Old Format

There are two types of top-level domains: the old format and the newer, international format. The old format is used mainly in the United States and Canada, and has seven different top-level domains. These domain names are shown in Figure 13-1.

The address:

```
harley@nipper.ucsb.edu
```

Domain	Meaning
`com`	commercial organization
`edu`	educational institution
`gov`	government
`int`	international organization
`mil`	military
`net`	networking organization
`org`	non-profit organizations

Figure 13-1

Top-Level Domains for United States and Canada

has a top-level domain of **edu**, which shows it to be an educational institution (in this case, a university). Within the United States, most of the addresses that you will encounter will use either the **edu** or **com** domains.

After you look at the top-level domain, look at the other sub-domains, from right to left. They will become progressively more specific. In our example, the domain refers to a computer named **nipper** at the University of California at Santa Barbara.

Variations on the Standard Internet Address

Sometimes you will see addresses that use extra sub-domains to be more specific. A common sub-domain is **cs**, referring to a Computer Science department. For example, the address:

`samuel@emmenthaler.cs.wisc.edu`

refers to userid **samuel** at a computer named **emmenthaler**, within the Computer Science department at the University of Wisconsin.

Once you see enough addresses, you will start to notice patterns among computer names. For example, at the University of Wisconsin – which is in a state that is well known for its dairy products – many computers are named after a type of cheese.

Sometimes you will see Internet addresses that are as simple as can be, having just the name of the organization and a top-level domain. For example:

`melissa@ucsd.edu`

This address refers to userid **melissa** at the University of California at San Diego.

Whenever you see such an address, it means that the organization uses one main computer to receive and distribute mail. In this case, the computer named **ucsd.edu** has a directory of many of the userids in the university. When you mail a message to one of these userids, for example, **melissa**, this computer knows which of the campus computers is used by **melissa**.

The nice thing about this system is that the addresses are simple. Of course, someone has to maintain the central mail service and keep the list of userids up to date.

A final variation that you may see is an address that uses a **%** (percent) character. This is used occasionally to specify a more complex recipient name. Here is an example:

randy%anaconda@ucsd.edu

The idea is that the computer that receives the message (in this case, **ucsd.edu**) will look at everything to the left of the **@** character (in this case, **randy%anaconda**) and make sense out of it.

Typically, the **%** separates a userid from a local computer name. In this case, it may be that mail for **randy** should go to the computer named **anaconda**. However, there may be several local paths to that computer, and the main computer (**ucsd.edu**) will figure out the best path at the time.

Don't worry too much about the details: just use whatever address your recipient gives you. A lot of people know what their address is, but they don't understand it. Many sites have more than one way to address mail, and the system managers will usually tell their users which address works best.

Standard Internet Addresses: the International Format

We said earlier that there are two types of top-level domain names. The old-style uses abbreviations that describe the type of organization: **edu**, **com** and so on. This type of address was developed for the Arpanet network, an ancestor of the Internet, and was meant to be used only in the United States.

As the Internet expanded, it became clear that a better system was needed. The solution was to use top-level domains that represented countries. For most countries, the top-level domain is the two-letter international abbreviation. Table 13-2 shows some of these abbreviations:

Here are two typical addresses that use an international top-level domain:

sean@unix1.tcd.ie
hans@physik.tu-muenchen.de

The first address is for a computer named **unix1** at Trinity College in Dublin, Ireland. The second address is for a computer in the physics department (physik) at the Technical University in Munich (Muenchen) in Germany (Deutschland).

Some countries use a sub-domain, just to the left of the top-level domain, to divide the top-level domain into categories. Thus, you may see **ac**, for

Domain	Meaning
at	Austria
au	Australia
ca	Canada
ch	Switzerland ("Cantons of Helvetia")
de	Germany ("Deutschland")
dk	Denmark
es	Spain ("España")
fr	France
gr	Greece
ie	Republic of Ireland
jp	Japan
nz	New Zealand
uk	United Kingdom (England, Scotland, Wales, N. Ireland)

Figure 13-2

Some of the International Top-Level Domains

academic sites, and **co**, for commercial sites. For example, the following address:

`otto@spam.tuwien.ac.at`

refers to a computer named **spam** at the Technical University Vienna (Wien) Austria.

✓ HINT The British and New Zealanders may reverse the order of the sub-domains in their addresses. For example, you may see an address like:

`victoria@uk.ac.cambridge.history`

If you need to use such an address (outside of that country) be sure to reverse the order of the sub-domains:

`victoria@history.cambridge.ac.uk`

so that they form a standard address.

Outside of the United States, virtually all Internet sites use the newer international-style of addressing, in which the top-level domain shows the country code. However, within the United States (and to some extent in Canada), most Internet computers still use the old-style addresses: the ones with top-level domains of **edu**, **com** and so on.

Of course, there are international-style addresses for the United States (using the country code **us**). It's just that most American sites have not yet moved away from the old system. There is no problem, though. Regardless of what type of address your location uses, you can communicate with any computer on the Internet.

Pseudo-Internet Addresses

There are many system managers who would like their computers to be on the Internet, but who do not have the time or money to maintain a permanent Internet connection. As an alternative, they arrange to connect regularly with an Internet site and then register their address as if it were an Internet address. (We won't go into the details here.)

For example, a small company named Sigma Star Research might have an address of **sigstar.com**. From time to time, their computer calls another computer (which is on the Internet) to exchange mail. From your point of view, you can send mail to **sigstar** in the usual way. For instance, to send mail to userid **ron** at this company, you would enter:

```
mail ron@sigstar.com
```

However, you do need to remember that mail to such an address will not be as fast as mail to a real Internet address.

When you see an Internet-like address, there is often no way to tell, just from the address, whether or not that computer is really on the Internet. If you see an address like **small-company-name.com**, you might have your suspicions. However, even some large, well-known companies do not have a full Internet connection.

☑ **HINT** The best way to find out if a computer is on the Internet is to use the **ping** command (Chapter 12).

On the Internet, it is not enough just to look like a duck and feel like a duck. You must also **ping** like a duck!

UUCP Addresses and Bang Paths

All Unix systems have a built-in networking system, called UUCP, that allows any Unix machine to exchange messages with any other Unix machine. With UUCP, messages are passed from one computer to another until they reach their final destination. However, unlike the Internet, the address you use must specify every step along the way.

UUCP   The UUCP system is implemented as a family of commands. The most well-known command is **uucp**. It is this command that gives its name to the system as a whole.

The **uucp** command copies files from one computer to another. Thus, the name, which stands for "Unix to Unix copy".

Using UUCP, it is possible to form a network in which the computers do not have to be connected at all times. They can use modems to call one another over the phone line. This makes for an inexpensive system in which messages can be passed from computer to computer over vast distances.

Here is an example: You are working on a computer that, from time to time, connects over the phone to another computer named **beta**. You have sent messages to two different userids, one on your local system, the other on computer **beta**.

After you send the messages, the mail daemon examines the addresses. (Daemons are explained in Chapter 18.) Since the first message is going to a local userid, the message is delivered immediately. However, the daemon recognizes the second address as being a UUCP address. Thus, it puts the second message in a queue of messages waiting for a UUCP connection.

Later, when your computer connects to computer **beta**, this message, along with any others that have been waiting, are sent on their way. Conversely, any messages that **beta** is holding for your machine are passed over to your computer at the same time.

The format of UUCP addresses is conceptually simple. All you need to do is specify exactly what path you want your mail to take. Separate each computer name with an **!** character (exclamation mark). At the end of the path, put a final **!** followed by the userid of the recipient.

For example, to send mail via UUCP to a userid named **arthur**, who uses computer **beta**, use:

```
mail beta!arthur
```

Here is another example. You want to send a message to a userid named **chance** who uses a computer named **evers**. This computer does not have a UUCP connection with your machine. However, your computer connects to a machine named **tinker** that does have a UUCP connection to **evers**. You can have UUCP pass the mail along for you by using:

```
mail tinker!evers!chance
```

A list of names separated by **!** characters in this way is called a BANG PATH (because one of the slang names for the **!** character is "bang").

Each time mail is passed from one computer to another, we call it a HOP. Thus, the address above contains two hops. The UUCP address:

```
alpha!beta!gamma!delta!epsilon!username
```

contains five hops. It is not at all unusual to encounter addresses that have more than ten hops.

When we refer to the UUCP NETWORK (or, sometimes, just plain "UUCP"), we mean the thousands of computers that are reachable using a UUCP-style bang path address. Some of these machines are on the Internet, but most are not.

Note: If you are using the C-Shell, you must make sure that the ! characters are not interpreted as event indicators. (See Chapter 11.) To do so, you must put a \ (backslash) in front of each ! character. This tells the shell to take the ! literally. For example:

```
mail beta\!arthur
mail tinker\!evans\!chance
alpha\!beta\!gamma\!delta\!epsilon\!username
```

If you forget the \ characters, you will see a message like this:

```
Event not found.
```

Simplified UUCP Addressing

Using UUCP and bang path addresses, it is possible to send messages for vast distances as long as (1) you know the exact path to use, and (2) the connections are made properly.

The nice thing about UUCP is that it is cheap and accessible to anyone who has a Unix system and a modem. All that is needed is a connection to one other computer in the UUCP network.

(In fact, no one really knows how many UUCP machines there are. Suffice it to say that, in sheer numbers, the worldwide UUCP network is much larger than the Internet.)

The downside, however, is that to send messages via UUCP you must use exact path names for addresses (which can become quite long) and that mail delivery is slow and, at times, unreliable.

Moreover, it can be difficult to give someone a correct UUCP address, because how mail should travel to a recipient depends very much on where the mail originates. For example, the route that someone in New York uses to send mail to a computer in Los Angeles may not be the same route used by someone in San Francisco to send mail to Los Angeles.

With Internet addresses, you specify only the name and location of the recipient. The routing software decides what is the best path to follow. Thus, Internet addresses are well-defined and relatively short.

To bring the same conveniences to UUCP, the UUCP MAPPING PROJECT was created. This group publishes regularly updated maps of data that are sent to many UUCP computers. The mail routing software on these computers can use this data to decide the best path to take between any two points. This allows you to send mail to a UUCP address simply by specifying its location. You do not need to use a complete bang path.

Some of the addresses that you will encounter will look like Internet addresses, but really contain the names of computers that have UUCP connections. For example, if you see the address:

```
mail ron@sigstar.com
```

it may well be that the machine **sigstar** is actually on the Internet or connects to an Internet computer regularly. However, it may also be that **sigstar** is really a UUCP computer that is several hops away from an Internet machine.

When you send mail to **sigstar**, the routing software will decide the best path to take. It will all be invisible to you.

In practice, such a message will probably be sent to a machine near to **sigstar**, say, the closest Internet computer. Once this computer receives the message, its routing software will figure out the best way to pass the message to **sigstar**.

Occasionally, you will see addresses that use a top-level domain of **uucp**. For example:

```
rick@tsi.uucp
```

The name **uucp** is not an Internet sub-domain. Rather, it is a signal to the mail routing software to look up the computer name in the UUCP mapping data and construct the best possible address.

Mailing to Other Networks

From the Internet, there are gateways (connections) to many other networks. If you know the right address, you can send mail through a gateway to anyone on these networks. What is nice is that, even if the recipient uses a commercial system that charges for mail, you, as an Internet user, can send and receive for free.

There are numerous networks that have gateways to the Internet. In this section, we will discuss the most popular ones.

First, there are the commercial mail systems, Compuserve and MCI Mail. To send mail to users on these systems, just use one of the following domains:

```
compuserve.com
mcimail.com
```

Instead of a userid, specify the recipient's account number. (Note: Compuserve account numbers contain a comma. Simply change the comma to a period.)

Here are some examples. To send mail to the Compuserve user with account number "12345,678", use:

```
mail 12345.678@compuserve.com
```

To send mail to the MCI Mail user with account number "1234567", use:

```
mail 1234567@mcimail.com
```

Aside from the commercial networks, you may encounter an address from FidoNet, a large network of personal computers that connect via dial-up telephone lines. (Conceptually, FidoNet is similar to UUCP.) There are several FidoNet sites that act as gateways to the Internet. You can reach these sites by sending mail to **fidonet.org**. (Be forewarned: because of the nature of the connections, FidoNet mail often moves slowly.)

FidoNet addresses consist of three parts: a zone number, a net number and a node number. Here is a typical FidoNet address: 1:123/456. To send mail to FidoNet, you encode the three-part address, in reverse order, as follows:

```
fnode.nnet.zzone.fidonet.org
```

FidoNet uses full names for recipients. Just separate each name by a period. Thus, to send a message to Ben Dover at address 1:123/456, use:

```
mail Ben.Dover@f456.n123.z1.fidonet.org
```

Finally, the last gateway we will mention is the one that goes to BITNET, a collection of different networks based in Europe, Canada, the United States and Mexico. To mail to a BITNET user, simply use a top-level domain of **bitnet**. The sub-domain to the left will be the name of the BITNET host computer.

For example, to send mail to a user with a BITNET name of **jmeoff**, at the BITNET host **cunyvm**, use:

```
mail jmeoff@cunyvm.bitnet
```

Note: Many BITNET host names end in "vm" because they are IBM mainframes running the Virtual Machine operating system.

Mail

Mail is one of the most important services provided by Unix. In this chapter, we will discuss the standard Unix mail program. You will learn everything you need to know to send and receive messages.

As you will see, the mail program offers many facilities and is quite complex. Although we will be explaining a lot of details, you really only need to memorize the few parts that are necessary for everyday work. What is important is that you develop an appreciation of what the mail program can do for you. You can always look up the technical points as you need them.

In Chapter 13, we discussed the mail system in general terms, as well as the Internet and electronic addressing. If you have not yet read Chapter 13, it would be a good idea to at least skim it before you read this chapter.

The Unix Mail Programs: `mail`, Elm, MH, Mush, Zmail, RMAIL

As we explained in Chapter 13, Unix comes with a built-in mail system. The most important part of this system is the user interface, the program that you use to send and read messages. The most common such program is named **mail**.

In this chapter, we will show you how to use **mail** effectively. Even if you decide to use a different program, it is a good idea to be familiar with **mail**. It is the basic Unix mail program, and you will find it, in one form or another, on all Unix systems.

On some systems, you will have an alternative to the **mail** program. Although we won't be able to go into the details of such programs, you might find it useful to take a quick look at what else may be available on your computer.

WHAT'S IN A NAME?

mail   Originally, there was a simple program called **mail**. This program was adequate, but limited.

Years ago, **mail** was replaced by more powerful programs. System V Unix had a program named **mailx** ("extended mail"), while Berkeley Unix had **Mail** (with an uppercase "M").

Both **mailx** and **Mail** are upwards compatible with **mail** and are actually quite similar to one another. When these programs first came out, users had to use the **mailx** or **Mail** commands. This, of course, was not as simple as using a command named "**mail**". Moreover, if someone forgot the new name and did type "**mail**", he or she would end up with the clunky, old mail program.

These days, just about all systems are set up to automatically execute the newer program when you type "**mail**". In other words, the name **mail** will point to either **mailx** or **Mail**, whichever is appropriate. If you really want the old mail program, there is usually a way to get at it, but it is rarely used.

The evolution of **mail** illustrates one of the Unix traditions: when a program is replaced by a brand new one, the old one is not thrown away. Even if the new program eventually usurps the old name, the old program is still kept around (possibly under a different name) for the sake of continuity.

This is one of the reasons why Unix grows ever larger.

Aside from the basic **mail** program, the most popular programs that you may encounter are Elm, MH, Mush, Zmail and RMAIL. One thing that all of these systems have in common is that they greatly extend the functionality of **mail**, offering many extra features.

 HINT   Many advanced mail programs depend on using the full screen. If you are accessing a Unix computer via a slow phone line, you may find it faster and easier to use the standard line-oriented **mail** program.

If one of these other programs is available on your system and you get serious about mail (or if you start to receive a lot of messages), it is certainly worth your time to learn how to use an advanced mail program. All of them are complete mail handling systems with many capabilities. If you become a mail fanatic, some of these systems even allow you to write mail-handling programs!

Elm is a popular, menu-driven program that is easy and quick. If you have ever used a mail program, you may be able to start using Elm without even reading the documentation.

The MH system is actually a large set of commands. Rather than working within one main program, you enter separate commands for whatever you want to do. This means that you can intersperse handling your mail with doing other work. If you receive a great deal of mail and you like memorizing new commands, you will love MH.

Mush (the "mail user's shell") is a program with two faces. It can be used with a line-oriented interface (like **mail**) or with a screen-oriented interface (like Elm).

Zmail is a commercial product, based on Mush. It has many extensions, including support for X Window, using either the Motif or Open Look window managers. (X Window is discussed in Chapter 5.)

RMAIL is the name of the mail facility that is built into some versions of Emacs. (Emacs is a complete working environment that is based on a particularly powerful text editor.) If you are an Emacs user, you will find it useful to learn how to use RMAIL. Although you can use the standard **mail** program, RMAIL is more convenient as it is integrated into Emacs. (We discuss Emacs briefly in Chapter 19.)

Orientation to the **mail** Program

Although your Unix system may have more than one mail program, you can count on it having the standard program **mail**. Even if you are going to use another program, there are two good reasons why you should at least become familiar with **mail**. First, it is the only mail program that you can count on seeing in every Unix system. Second, the ideas that you will learn with **mail** are basic to all mail programs.

 HINT   Learn how to use the standard Unix **mail** program. Once you understand **mail**, other mail programs will be variations on a familiar theme.

Using **mail** is actually like using two different programs: one for sending mail and one for receiving mail. We will discuss each task in turn. Along the way, we will explain a number of ancillary topics that you will need to understand in order to work efficiently.

Before we start, here is a quick summary of how you send and receive messages. This summary leaves out the details and the power of **mail** (which we will get to presently).

To send mail, enter the **mail** command followed by the address of the recipient. For example:

```
mail harley@nipper.ucsb.edu
```

Type your message, one line at a time. Press **^D** (the **eof** key) when you are finished. The message will be sent automatically.

While composing a message, you can edit and review it. You can also include text from a file or from another message.

To read your mail, enter:

```
mail
```

You will see a summary of your messages. Using the various commands, you read and dispose of each message in turn. When you are finished, you enter the command to quit. The program terminates, leaving you back at the shell prompt.

Sending Mail

To send mail, use the **mail** command with the following syntax:

```
mail [-v] [-s subject] address...
```

The most common way to send mail is to specify only the address of the recipient. (Chapter 13 explains the various types of addresses.) If the recipient is on your system, you need only specify the userid. For example:

```
mail addie
```

If the recipient is on a different system, you must specify the full address. For example:

```
mail melissa@misty.acme.com
```

If the recipient is within your campus network, you can often leave out part of the address. For example, say that your address is **myname@alpha.ucal.edu** and you are mailing to a friend who uses a different computer on the network. His address is **friend@beta.ucal.edu**. You are usually safe in leaving off the part of the address that you both have in common: that is, the part of the address that describes your campus. So, in this case, you could use:

```
mail friend@beta
```

The mail software should be able to figure out that this is a local address and deliver the message properly. If you have a problem, you may have to use the full address.

Every system should have a userid named **postmaster** to whom you can send queries. For example, say that you have trouble finding out the address of someone who uses a computer named **misty.acme.com**. You can send a message asking for the person's mail address to:

postmaster@misty.acme.com

In Chapter 25, we will discuss a number of ways that you can find out another person's mail address.

☑ **HINT**   If you have a problem with mail not reaching its destination:
1. Check the spelling of the address.
2. Make sure you have specified the full address.
3. When all else fails, send a query to the **postmaster** userid.

When you want to send the same message to more than one person, simply specify more than one userid:

```
mail curly larry moe melissa@misty.acme.com
```

Each recipient will get a copy of the message. If you want to receive a copy yourself, put your userid in the list.

Once you enter the **mail** command, you will be able to compose your message. (We describe the details below.) However, there will be times when you have a message stored in a file, all ready to go, and there is no need to go through the process of typing and editing. If so, you can send your message directly by telling **mail** where to find the file.

At the end of the **mail** command, type a **<** (less than) character, followed by the name of the file. (The **<** character tells **mail** to redirect the "standard input" from the keyboard to a file. We will explain such techniques in Chapter 15.)

For example, to send a message contained in a file named **notice** to three userids named **curly**, **larry** and **moe**, enter:

```
mail curly larry moe < notice
```

mail will send the message and return you to the shell prompt immediately. Note: Be careful to use the **<** (less than) character, not the **>** (greater then) character.

In Chapter 13, we explained that some addresses use the **!** character. However, when you are using the C-Shell, the **!** is used for history substitution to specify an event (see Chapter 11). Thus, you must make sure that the **!** characters in an address are not interpreted by the shell.

To do so, you must put a \ (backslash) character in front of each **!** character. For example, to send mail to **alpha!beta!murray** you would enter:

```
mail alpha\!beta\!murray
```

A backslash tells the shell to take the next character literally.

If you forget to use the ****, the shell will try to interpret the **!** characters, and you will see a message like:

```
beta!murray: Event not found.
```

Re-enter the command and put in the **** characters.

 HINT   If you are using the C-Shell, don't forget to put a backslash in front of each **!** character that appears in an address. For example:

```
mail alpha\!beta\!murray
```

Specifying the Subject of the Message

All messages have a few lines of information at the beginning of the message. One of these lines shows the subject of the message.

When you check your mail, the first thing you will see is a summary of all the messages that are waiting. This summary shows the userid who sent the message, the time it was received, the size of the message, and the subject.

Thus, it is always a good idea to specify the subject when you send a message. This allows the recipient to see the topic of the message without having to read it. If you are sending mail to a person who receives many messages a day (such as a system manager), he or she will scan the summaries before reading the messages. If you have left out the subject, the person may take a long time to get around to reading your message. (It is not unusual for busy people to get over a hundred messages a day.)

When you enter the **mail** command, you can specify the subject directly by using the **-s** option. For example:

```
mail -s Hello addie
```

In this case, the subject is "Hello".

If your subject has space characters or punctuation, you must enclose it in single quotes. Otherwise, the shell will interpret the spaces and punctuation in a way that will be incorrect. Using single quotes tells the shell to pass the character string to **mail** exactly as you typed it. For example:

```
mail -s 'Do you want free money?' addie
```

If we had left out the single quotes:

```
mail -s Do you want free money? addie
```

the command would have been interpreted as a message with subject "Do", that should be sent to five different userids. Moreover, the shell would have interpreted the **?** character in a special way (which we will explain in Chapter 21).

☑ **HINT** When you send mail, keep the subject line short (less than 35 characters is a good rule of thumb). Excess characters may be truncated when the recipient looks at a summary of messages.

If you do not specify a subject, **mail** will prompt you to enter one by displaying:

Subject:

Since **mail** is now reading your input directly, you do not need to use single quotes.

☑ **HINT** If your **mail** program does not prompt you for a subject, you can force it to do so by including a **set ask** command in your **.mailrc** initialization file (explained later in the chapter).

Having entered the **mail** command along with the subject, you are now ready to enter your message.

Entering Your Message

Entering a message is simple. Type the message, one line at a time. At the end of each line, press the <Return> key. After you press <Return> for the last line, press **^D** (the **eof** key that we discussed in Chapter 6). This tells **mail** that there is no more data. Mail will display **EOT** (end of transmission) and send off your message. You will then return to the shell prompt.

As you type, you can use the special keys that we discussed in Chapter 6. These are shown in Figure 14-1.

Here is a typical session with **mail**. The **%** characters indicate a shell prompt.

```
% mail -s 'Do you want free money?' addie harley
They will be giving free money away today at 3PM.
Do you want some?
-- Harley
EOT
%
```

Code	Usual Key to Use	Purpose
erase	**^H** or <Backspace>	erase the last character typed
werase	**^W**	erase the last word typed
kill	**^U** (sometimes **^X**)	erase the entire line

Figure 14-1
Keyboard Keys to Use While Composing a Message

In this example, we have entered the **mail** command with two recipient userids. The first indicates the person to whom we are sending the message (**addie**); the second is our own userid (**harley**), so that we will receive a copy of the message.

The message consists of three lines. After typing the third line, we pressed <Return>, and then pressed **^D**. **mail** responded by displaying **EOT**, sending the message, and returning us to the shell.

If, while entering a message, you decide that the whole thing was a mistake, press the **intr** key (usually **^C**, see Chapter 6). **mail** will display:

```
(Interrupt - one more to kill letter)
```

This means that **mail** has recognized that you pressed the **intr** key. However, it might have been by accident. **mail** is asking you to confirm that you really want to kill the message.

If so, press the **intr** key once more. **mail** will save the message in a file named **dead.letter** and then return you to the shell prompt.

If you really did press the **intr** key by accident, just keep typing.

Watching Your Message Being Delivered: the -v Option

Sometimes, you may want to ensure that the message is actually delivered. One idea is to send yourself a copy, as we did in our previous example. If you receive your copy, you might infer that the other person received his.

Of course, such an inference is not always correct. For example, say that you enter a message correctly, but that you make a mistake in the other person's address. You will receive your copy, but the other person will not receive his.

If you want to watch your message being delivered, just use the **-v** (verbose) option when you enter the **mail** command:

```
mail -v -s 'New time for the meeting'
melissa@misty.acme.com
```

This option tells **mail** to show you the details as the message is being delivered.

If the message is being sent to a computer on the Internet, you will be able to see the connection being made. If the address is wrong, it should be obvious.

If the message is being sent to a non-Internet computer, you will not be able to see all the connections. If you have made a mistake in the address, it will not be immediately obvious.

In any event, if a message cannot be delivered, it will be mailed back to you. When you read it, there will be notes from the various computers that handled it along the way. You should be able to read these notes and figure out what went wrong.

For your interest, here is a sample session with **mail** using the **-v** option. We start by entering the command:

```
mail -v -s 'Mail Test' navarra@madsci.nwu.edu
```

Next, we enter a short but meaningless message. At the end of the message, we press **^D** (the **eof** key). **mail** displays "**EOT**" (End of Transmission):

```
This is a test.
EOT
```

Now the mail delivery program (**sendmail**) sends the mail on its way. (**sendmail** is a type of program called a daemon. A daemon executes in the background and provides a service of general interest. See Chapter 18.)

As we watch, we see our computer (**nipper**) issue the appropriate commands (**HELO**, **VERB** and so on) to send the message. The actual message is being sent following the **DATA** command. Finally, we are told that the message has been sent.

```
navarra@madsci.nwu.edu... Connecting to hub.tcplocal...
220 hub.ucsb.edu Sendmail ready at Sat, 12 Sep 92 11:53:39 PDT
>>> HELO nipper
250 hub.ucsb.edu Hello nipper.ucsb.edu, pleased to meet you
>>> VERB
200 Verbose mode
>>> ONEX
200 Only one transaction
>>> MAIL From:<harley@nipper>
250 <harley@nipper>... Sender ok
>>> RCPT To:<navarra@madsci.nwu.edu>
250 <navarra@madsci.nwu.edu>... Recipient ok
>>> DATA
354 Enter mail, end with "." on a line by itself
>>> .
250 Mail accepted
>>> QUIT
221 hub.ucsb.edu delivering mail
navarra@madsci.nwu.edu... Sent
```

Depending on how your system is configured, you may or may not see this much detail. Some systems are configured so that you will see an interesting remark (like "pleased to meet you"), as each command is processed. You may see some strange things.

Note: You may be able to check that someone has received their mail by using the **finger** command. See Chapter 12 for the details and the caveats.

The Tilde Escapes

As you type a message, there are commands that you can send to the **mail** program. However, it is important that **mail** be able to distinguish between commands and text. Thus, the commands have a special format: they all start with a ~ (tilde) at the beginning of the line.

Here is an example. You are typing a message and, after pressing <Return>, you enter:

~p

This tells **mail** to display (print out) what you have typed so far.

When used in this way, the tilde is called an ESCAPE CHARACTER. An escape character tells a program that what follows is to be treated in a special way. That is, it tells the program to "escape" from its standard way of interpreting data. For this reason, these commands are called the TILDE ESCAPES.

The table in Figure 14-2 contains a list of the tilde escapes. The most important is **~?**. This is the command that will display a summary of all the tilde escapes. If you forget the commands, you can always enter **~?**.

You might ask, what do you do if you really want to enter a line that begins with a tilde? Just use two tildes at the beginning of the line. For example:

~~This line starts with a tilde.

The first tilde tells **mail** that the second tilde is just a regular character. In your message, there will be only one tilde.

We will describe each tilde escape in turn. But first, we must talk about the two parts of a message: the header and the body.

The Parts of a Message: Header and Body

Each message has two parts. The HEADER consists of a number of lines of information at the beginning of the message. The BODY consists of the text of the message. Here is a typical message:

```
To: addie
Subject: 'Do you want free money?'
Cc: melissa randolph
Bcc: murray

They will be giving free money away today at 3 PM.
Do you want some?
-- Harley
```

Command	Description
~?	help: display summary of tilde escapes
~b *address...*	add addresses to "Blind copy" line
~c *address...*	add addresses to "Copy" line
~d	read in contents of **dead.letter** file
~e	invoke text editor
~f *messages*	read in old messages
~h	edit header lines
~m *messages*	read in old messages
~p	display (print) current message
~q	quit (same as pressing **intr** key twice)
~r *file*	read in contents of a file
~s *subject*	change "Subject" line
~t *address...*	add new addresses to the "To" line
~v	invoke visual editor (usually same as ~e)
~w *file*	write current message to a file
~! *command*	execute shell command
~| *command*	pipe current message through a filter

Note: Tilde escapes must start at the beginning of a line and must be the only thing on the line.

Figure 14-2

Summary of Tilde Escapes to Use with **mail**

In this example, the header consists of the first four lines. The body consists of the last three lines.

There are four basic lines in the header. The first is the "To" line. This is the only header line that is required; the others are optional. The "To" line shows the recipients of the message. In this case, there is only one recipient, **addie**.

Next is the "Subject" line. We explained above how to specify the subject. If you want to change it as you are typing the message, use the ~s tilde escape. For example, you can enter:

~s Do you want extra free money?

The next line of the header is the "Copy" line. This line begins with **Cc** and indicates who should receive a copy of the message.

There is no important difference between putting an address in the "To" line or the "Cc" line. However, for political reasons, you may find it better to list certain people as receiving a "copy" of a message. Moreover, when you send someone a copy, there is an assumption that the message is being sent only for that person's information and he or she should not feel obligated to reply.

To add one or more addresses to the "Copy" line, use the **~c** tilde escape. For example:

`~c marilyn`

If you want to replace the "Copy" line completely, use the **~h** tilde escape (described below).

The final part of the header is the "Blind Copy" line. This functions like the "Copy" line, but will not be sent as part of the message. In our original example, the message will contain the lines:

```
To: addie
Subject: 'Do you want free money?'
Cc: melissa randolph
```

However, the line:

```
Bcc: murray
```

will not be included. Thus, no one else knows that **murray** was sent a copy of the message.

To add one or more addresses to the "Blind Copy" line, use the **~b** tilde escape. For example:

`~b mitch`

The most convenient way to replace all four lines of the header is to use the **~h** tilde escape. This will prompt you for each line in turn. After you change the header, you may want to check the new header by using the **~p** tilde escape to display the message.

Using a Text Editor to Compose Messages

You enter a message one line at a time. While you are typing, you can use the special keyboard codes (**erase**, **werase** and **kill**) to make corrections. However, if you are composing a long message it is usually more convenient to use a text editor. You can do this by using either the **~e** or **~v** tilde escape.

Why are there two tilde escapes to start the same program? Originally, **~e** invoked a standard text editor that was provided by **mail**, while **~v** started the **vi** ("visual") screen-oriented editor. (We will discuss **vi** in Chapter 19.) These days, only **vi** is used, so both commands are essentially the same.

When you enter a **~e** or **~v** tilde escape, **mail** starts **vi** with a copy of your message in the editing buffer. When you finish editing, quit **vi** in the usual way. You will be back in **mail**. As always, press **^D** (the **eof** key) to send your message.

After you learn how to use **vi**, you should make a point of memorizing one of these two tilde escapes. Using a text editor makes typing messages a lot easier.

Reading Data Into Your Current Message

There will be times when you want to copy existing text into the body of your message. There are several ways to do this.

First, you can use the **~d** tilde escape to copy the contents of the **dead.letter** file. (As we explained earlier, this is the file into which a message is placed when you abort the **mail** command.) Using **~d** is a convenient way to recall the old, unsent message.

Similarly, you can copy the contents of any file into your message by using the **~r** (read) tilde escape. For example, to read in a file named **announcement**, use:

~r announcement

If you are responding to a message that you have just read, you can use the **~f** and **~m** tilde escapes to place a copy of that message into the current message. (We will explain how this works later in the chapter.)

Finally, you can save the message you are composing to a file by using the **~w** (write) tilde escape. For example, the command:

~w safekeeping

will save the message you are typing to a file named **safekeeping**.

Executing Shell Commands While Composing a Message: fmt

There are two ways for you to execute regular shell commands as you type a message. First, you can use the **~!** tilde escape, followed by the name of the command you want to execute. For example, if you want to find out the time and date, you can enter:

~! date

When the command is finished, you will be returned to **mail** automatically.

If you want to enter more than one command, you can start a brand new shell. Just enter the name of your shell as a command. For instance, to start a C-Shell, use:

~! csh

You can now enter as many commands as you want. When you are finished, end the shell by pressing **^D** (the **eof** key). You will be returned to **mail**.

The second way you can use a regular shell command is as a filter through which you can pipe the contents of the current message.

(Informally, a filter is a program that reads data, modifies it in some way, and outputs the result. When we send data to such a program, we say that we "pipe" the data through the filter. For example, if you need to sort some data, you can pipe it through the **sort** filter. We will discuss filters and pipes in Chapter 16.)

To pipe the current message through a filter, use the ~| tilde escape (the |, vertical bar character, is used in Unix as the "pipe" symbol). The data that comprises the message will be replaced by the output of the filter. For example, if for some reason you wanted to sort the contents of the current message, you could enter:

```
~| sort
```

After you have used the ~| command, you may want to use **~p** to see what the new, filtered message looks like.

If the filter command fails, **mail** will make sure that the original message is not changed. This protects you against, say, misspelling the name of the command.

The most useful filter for processing a message is the **fmt** command. This command was designed specifically to format messages prior to mailing (although it is also useful for other simple tasks).

What **fmt** does is read the input and, using the same text, generates lines that are as close as possible to 72 characters long. **fmt** will preserve spaces at the beginning of lines, spaces between words and blank lines. In other words, **fmt** will make your message look nice without changing the paragraph breaks.

For example, say that you are in the middle of entering a message, line by line. To check what it looks like, you enter the **~p** command and you see:

```
Ron,
    Be sure to visit me when you come to the
university next Thursday.
    I will be glad to
show you around and introduce
you to all the people in the Computer Science department.
We can see the movie you wanted to see,
as it is playing at the campus theater.
    -- Harley
```

Now you format the message by piping it through the **fmt** filter:

```
~| fmt
```

To check the output, you use **~p** to display the formatted message:

```
Ron,
    Be sure to visit me when you come to the university
next Thursday.
    I will be glad to show you around and introduce you
to all the people in the Computer Science department.
We can see the movie you wanted to see, as it is playing
at the campus theater.
    -- Harley
```

If the message now meets with your approval, you can press **^D** to send it on its way.

☑ **HINT**   To make your messages easy for people to read, use:

~| fmt

to format them before they are mailed.

Sending Mail to a File or to a Program

Most people do not know it, but you can send messages to files (for storage) or to programs (for special processing).

To send a message to a file, specify an address that is the name of the file. If the file already exists, **mail** will add the message to the end of the file.

How does **mail** know if a recipient is a file name? It will assume this to be the case if the address contains a **/** (slash) character. If you want to specify the name of a file in your current directory, use **./**, for example, **./message**. (File names and directories are explained in Chapter 21.)

Here is an example. You regularly send notes to three userids named **curly**, **larry** and **moe**. However, you would like to keep a copy of all these notes. Use the command:

```
mail curly larry moe ./stooges
```

This will send a copy of the message to a file named **stooges** in your current directory.

As strange as it sounds, you can send messages not only to a userid or to a file, but to a program as well. The program will receive the message and do whatever it does with input. For instance, you might have a program named **broadcast** that sends out a copy of its input to a large number of people. Thus, you could send a message in this manner by mailing it to **broadcast**.

To mail to a program, use an address that consists of a **|** (vertical bar), followed by the name of the program. Because the **|** character has a special meaning to the shell, you must enclose the whole thing within single quotes. For example, to mail a message to a program named **broadcast**, use:

```
mail '|broadcast'
```

(The **|** is called a "pipe" symbol. It tells Unix to take the output of one program and use it as the input for another program. We will discuss pipes in Chapter 15.)

Here is an easy way for you to test this facility. In Chapter 16, we will see that the **wc** program counts the number of lines, words and characters in its input. Try sending a message to **wc**:

```
mail '|wc'
```

mail is picky about how you specify the program name: it can be only a single argument. Thus, you must be careful not to put any spaces within the quotes.

You will run into trouble if you try to mail to a command that consists of more then one argument. For example, the command **lpr -p** will format and print a file. However, you can't send mail directly to **'|lpr -p'**. The solution is to use a mail alias in your **.mailrc** file (described later in the chapter). This allows you to use a single word to refer to a complex name. For example, you might define the mail alias:

```
alias lprp '|lpr -p'
```

You can now specify the "address" **lprp** whenever you want to print a copy of a message. For example, the command:

```
mail harley lprp
```

will send a message to userid **harley** and to the printing command **lpr -p**.

Hints for Practicing Safe Mail

If you are new to electronic mail, it may take you a while to appreciate the subtleties. Here are some hints to save you trouble.

First, assume that there is no privacy. Do not send messages that, within the bounds of reason, you would not want everyone to see. It is a good idea to avoid intimate love letters, temperamental tirades, mean-spirited insults, and so on.

As we will see later in the chapter, it is easy to copy an existing message, which you can then forward to another person. Some people love to forward mail, just as some people like to gossip. Don't assume that, just because you send a message to only one person, the message is private.

Moreover, don't assume that when you delete a message it cannot be restored. More than likely, your system manager does regular backups of the file system. If you delete a sensitive message on Tuesday, chances are it was preserved as part of the regular Monday night backup. Unix does not have a paper shredder.

Second, develop an appreciation for the fact that electronic messages do not carry the body language or voice inflection of regular conversation. It is all too easy to be insulting when you mean to be funny.

Thus, whenever you write something that has a chance of being misinterpreted, use a smiley. (We talked about this in detail in Chapter 12, at the end of the discussion on the **talk** command.)

A smiley looks like this:

`:-)`

(Turn your head sideways to the left and you will see the smile.)

Use a smiley to indicate irony that is so subtle that your correspondent might miss it. For example:

Are you always such a jerk? :-)

The next hint is to be careful what you promise. It is the nature of electronic mail that people tend to take messages they receive more seriously than messages they send. Moreover, it is easy to save messages – as we will see later in the chapter – and some people keep their mail forever.

Don't let yourself get in the position where someone can say to you: "What do you mean that you are too busy to help me paint my house? I have a message right here from four years ago in which you told me that if I ever needed any help I should just ask."

Finally, make a point to be polite and to keep your temper. If someone sends you a message that really bothers you, wait a day before you respond. This is especially true with people whom you have not met in person and whose motivations may not be clear.

How Do You Know that Mail Has Arrived? `from`, `biff`

How do you know when mail has arrived? To read mail, you enter the **mail** command with no arguments:

`mail`

If there are no messages, you will be told that there is no mail for your userid. For instance, if your userid is **harley**, you will see:

No mail for harley

If you do have mail, you will see a summary of the messages. For example:

```
Mail version SMI 4.0 Sat 10/13/90  Type ? for help.
"/usr/spool/mail/harley": 2 messages 2 new
>N  1 addie  Sun Aug 30 12:12  15/385  I would like some free
 N  2 melissa@misty.acme.com  Sun Aug 30 12:12  15/367  No th
```

However, there are three ways for you to know that you have mail waiting without having to actually start the **mail** program.

First, whenever you log in, Unix will check to see if there is mail for you. If so, you will see:

`You have new mail.`

Second, from the shell prompt, you can use the **from** command:

`from`

This will display a quick summary of all the mail that you have waiting. For example:

```
From addie Sun Aug 30 12:12 1992
From melissa@misty.acme.com Sun Aug 30 12:12 1992
```

The **from** command is handy when new mail arrives. Using **from**, you can quickly scan your mailbox without having to start the **mail** program.

Many people put a **from** command in their `.login` file so that they will automatically see what mail is waiting each time they log in. (The `.login` file is discussed in Chapter 11.)

The third way to check for mail is to use the **biff** command. This tells Unix whether or not you want a special announcement whenever a new message arrives. If you want such an announcement, enter:

`biff y`

Whenever a new message arrives, you will see a notice, followed by a summary of the message. For example:

```
New mail for harley@nipper has arrived:
—Date: Sun, 30 Aug 92 14:41:54 -0500
From: addie
To: harley
Subject: Re:  I would like some free money.
Harley,
I would like some free money.
...more...
```

The last line, ...**more**..., shows us that there is more to the message than we see. If you do not want to be bothered with such announcements, use:

`biff n`

If you want to see the current **biff** setting, enter the command with no arguments:

`biff`

Many people execute **biff y** in their `.login` file to make sure that Unix always tells them when mail arrives.

If you are an X Window user (see Chapter 5), there is an X client named **xbiff** that you can use. Typically, **xbiff** displays a small picture of a mailbox. When mail arrives, **xbiff** will beep and raise the flag on the mailbox.

WHAT'S IN A NAME?

`biff`   You might think that the name `biff` stands for something like "Be notified if mail arrives and show who it is from". Actually, `biff` is named after a dog.

Biff the dog belonged to Heidi Stettner, who, in the summer of 1980, was about to become a Computer Science graduate student at the University of California at Berkeley (see Figure 14-3). She spent that summer working for a professor in Evans Hall, where the latest version of Berkeley Unix was being developed. (This was the version that introduced virtual memory to Unix.)

There is an apocryphal story that the `biff` command – which tells you when new mail has arrived – was named after Biff the dog because he always barked when the mailman came.

Here is the real story: Biff the dog was a universal favorite at Evans Hall. He was one of the first dogs who regularly visited the Computer Science department, and he had a sociable, friendly disposition. People liked to come to Heidi's office to visit Biff and play with him by throwing a ball down the long hallway. Biff even had his photo on the bulletin board that showed pictures of all the Computer Science graduate students. (Biff was described as studying for his Ph.Dog degree.)

Heidi remembers: "Biff used to come to classes with me. In one instance, a compiler class, he even got a grade. The teacher gave Biff a B, which was higher than some of the students."

One day, John K. Foderero, one of the grad students who was working on Berkeley Unix, decided to create a command named after Biff. He came up with the idea of writing a program to check for mail. In Heidi's words: "I had no idea that the `biff` command was in the works until after it was done. The hardest thing was for someone to think of what the name could mean. Bill Joy and John were the ones who racked their brains to come up with a long name that `biff` could stand for."

[Note: John Foderero wrote the compiler for Berkeley's version of Lisp (a programming language) which was called Franz Lisp. Bill Joy wrote much of Berkeley Unix, including the C-Shell and the `vi` editor. He later went on to found Sun Microsystems.]

Today, Heidi Stettner is an accomplished Unix programmer, while Biff – who at the time this book was written was 14 and a half years old – is enjoying a well-deserved retirement.

Figure 14-3
Heidi Stettner and Biff, circa 1980

How Mail Is Stored

Before we talk about the details of reading your mail, let's take a moment to discuss how mail is stored.

All mail is kept by the system in a set of files, one for each userid. Typically, mail is kept in a directory named **/usr/spool/mail**. Thus, if your userid is **harley**, your mail will be kept in a file named **/usr/spool/mail/harley**. (We will discuss directories and file names in Chapter 21.) This file is called your SYSTEM MAILBOX.

When you enter the **mail** command with no arguments:

```
mail
```

the **mail** program checks your system mailbox, looking for messages.

All your messages are stored together, as one long file. **mail** can tell where one message ends and another begins by looking for the distinctive lines that lie within the header of each message.

To read your mail, you examine each message. After reading a message, you can save it to a file of your own. If the file already exists, **mail** will append the new message to the end of the file.

After you are finished with a message, you delete it, which removes it from your system mailbox. If you do not delete a message, it will be saved for you automatically in a file called **mbox** in your home directory. (We discuss the home directory in Chapter 21.)

It is a good idea to read and dispose of your messages in a timely fashion so they do not accumulate in the system mailbox. On some systems, you will receive automatic warnings (by mail) when your mailbox becomes too large. If your mailbox grows past a certain point, it may be moved to your **mbox** file (where, presumably, the disk space is charged to your personal account).

The nice thing about saving messages is that they are stored in the same format as incoming mail. Thus, you can use the **mail** program itself to examine and manipulate old messages. If you want to examine such a file, start **mail** using the **-f** option, followed by the name of the file. For instance, if you enter the command:

```
mail -f personal
```

mail will look in the file named **personal**, rather than in your system mailbox. By default, **mail** will read from a file named **mbox** when you use the **-f** option without a file name. Thus, the following two commands are equivalent:

```
mail -f mbox
mail -f
```

Either one will read the messages that have been stored in your **mbox** file.

Starting to Read Your Mail

Once you start the **mail** program (with or without the **-f** option), you will see a summary of all the messages that are waiting for you. Here is a typical summary.

```
Mail version SMI 4.0 Sat 10/13/90  Type ? for help.
"/usr/spool/mail/harley": 2 messages 2 new
>N  1 addie  Sun Aug 30 12:12  15/385  I would like some free
 N  2 melissa@misty.acme.com  Sun Aug 30 12:12  15/367  No th
```

The first line shows the version of the **mail** program (the date refers to the **mail** program itself) followed by the suggestion that we can use the **?** command to display help. The next line shows us what file we are reading. In this case, it is our system mailbox. We have two messages, both of which are new.

The last two lines show a summary of these messages. Each one-line summary shows the userid who sent the message, the time and date it was received, the size of the message (lines/characters), and as much of the subject as will fit on the rest of the line. We can see that the first message is 15 lines long and has a subject that starts with "I would like some free".

Once the summary is displayed, **mail** will display an **&** (ampersand) character. This is a prompt, to tell you that you can now enter a command.

At this point, you have some 60-75 different commands that you can use to read and process your messages.

Fortunately, there are only a few crucial commands that you need to remember. These commands are summarized in Figures 14-4 and 14-5. You can use either the full name or the abbreviation. Most people use abbreviations exclusively.

At any time, you can display a summary of the most important commands by entering **?** (a question mark). You can also display a list of all the commands – without a description – by entering the **l** (list) command.

Displaying Header Information

When you start **mail**, the first thing you will see is a summary of your messages. This summary is taken from the information in the message headers. At any time, you can redisplay the summary by entering the **h** (header) command. This is a convenient way to remind yourself what messages remain to be read.

If you have a lot of messages, the summary will not list all of them. To see the next group, enter **z**. If you have many messages, you can move through the list by entering one **z** command after another.

To display the summary for the previous group of messages (that is, to move backwards) enter **z-**.

Abbreviation	Full Name	Description
?	—	display summary of important commands
!	—	execute a single shell command
+	—	display the next message
-	—	display the previous message
<Return>	—	display the next message
number	—	display message #*number*
d	`delete`	delete messages
dp	—	delete current message, display next message
e	`edit`	use text editor on messages
h	`headers`	display header summaries
l	`list`	list names of all available commands
m	`mail`	send new message to specified userid
n	`next`	display the next message
p	`print`	display (print) messages
pre	`preserve`	keep messages in system mailbox
q	`quit`	quit `mail`
r	`reply`	reply to sender and all other recipients
R	`Reply`	reply to sender only
s	`save`	save messages to specified file
sh	`shell`	pause `mail`, start a new shell
to	`top`	display top few lines of messages
u	`undelete`	undelete previously-deleted messages
w	`write`	same as **s**, only do not save header
x	`exit`	quit `mail`, neglect any changes
z	—	show next set of header summaries
z-	—	show previous set of header summaries

Note: On some systems, the sense of **r** and **R** is reversed.

Figure 14-4
Summary of Important `mail` *Commands: Alphabetic Order*

Abbreviation	Full Name	Description
Stopping `mail`		
q	`quit`	quit `mail`
x	`exit`	quit `mail`, neglect any changes
Help		
?	—	display summary of important commands
l	`list`	list names of all available commands
Headers		
h	`headers`	display header summaries
z	—	show next set of header summaries
z-	—	show previous set of header summaries
Displaying Messages		
+	—	display the next message
-	—	display the previous message
<Return>	—	display the next message
number	—	display message #*number*
n	`next`	display the next message
p	`print`	display (print) messages
to	`top`	display top few lines of messages
Replying and Mailing		
m	`mail`	send new message to specified userid
r	`reply`	reply to sender & all other recipients
R	`Reply`	reply to sender only
Processing a Message		
d	`delete`	delete messages
dp	—	delete current msg, display next msg
e	`edit`	use text editor on messages
pre	`preserve`	keep messages in system mailbox
s	`save`	save messages to specified file
u	`undelete`	undelete previously-deleted messages
w	`write`	same as **s**, only do not save header
Shell Commands		
!	—	execute a single shell command
sh	`shell`	pause `mail`, start a new shell

Note: On some systems, the sense of **r** and **R** is reversed.

Figure 14-5
Summary of Important `mail` *Commands: Grouped by Function*

Displaying a Message

At all times, **mail** recognizes one of your messages as being the CURRENT MESSAGE. By default, **mail** commands are interpreted relative to the current message. When you display the message summary, the current message is marked with a **>** character. In the following example, the current message is #1.

```
Mail version SMI 4.0 Sat 10/13/90  Type ? for help.
"/usr/spool/mail/harley": 2 messages 2 new
>N  1 addie   Sun Aug 30 12:12  15/385  I would like some free
 N  2 melissa@misty.acme.com  Sun Aug 30 12:12  15/367  No th
```

You can display the current message by entering the **p** (print) command. To display the next message, simply press <Return> (with no command). Thus, you can display all your messages, one at a time, by pressing <Return> repeatedly. (**mail** knows to start with message #1.)

As an alternative, you can also display the next message by entering either the **n** (next) or **+** (plus) commands.

To display the previous message, enter the **–** (minus) command.

To display a specific message, simply enter its number. For example, if you have 20 messages and you only want to see message #15, enter:

15

Finally, if you only want a preview of a message, enter the **to** (top) command. This will display the first few lines of a message.

☑ **HINT**

In Chapter 17, we will explain how to use the paging programs: **more**, **pg** and **less**. These programs can be used to display a long message one screenful at a time so that the data does not scroll off the top of your screen.

Once you learn how to use one of the paging programs, set the **PAGER** environment variable. This will tell **mail** which program you want to use. (All of this is explained in Chapter 17.)

Saving a Message

After you display a message, you have to decide what to do with it. There are several choices.

First, you can write the body of a message to a file by using the **w** (write) command. Enter the command, followed by the name of the file. For example, to write a message to a file named **personal**, enter:

w personal

As an alternative, the **s** (save) command will write the entire message, including the header. For example:

```
s personal
```
If you save messages to a file using this command, you can later read the file using **mail** with the **-f** option.

Another way to process a message is to edit it. If you enter the **e** (edit) command, **mail** will start the text editor using the message as data. (The editor will probably be **vi**, which we will discuss in Chapter 19.) Within the editor, you can make any changes you want and save your work using the editor's commands. When you quit the editor, you will be returned to **mail**.

Replying to a Message

You can reply to a message by using the **R** command. After entering this command, you type your message in the regular manner, one line at a time, just as we described earlier in the chapter. When you are finished, press **^D** (the **eof** key). Your reply will be sent automatically to the userid who sent you the original message.

While you are typing the message, you can use all the regular tilde escape commands. In particular, you can use **~p** to display (print) the new message and **~e** (edit) to start the text editor. Remember that you can change all or part of the header by using the **~s, ~t, ~c, ~b** or **~h** tilde escapes. (Don't forget that tilde escapes must start at the beginning of a line and must be the only thing on the line.)

If you are replying to a message that was sent to more than one recipient, you can send your reply to all the recipients, and not just the sender of the message, by using the **r** (lowercase "r") command.

☑ **HINT**

Before you reply to a message, check to see if there were other recipients. If so, make sure to use the **R** command (not **r**) unless you really want everybody to see your reply.

On some systems, the sense of **r** and **R** is reversed. You will have to test these commands for yourself. If you don't like the default, you can change it by setting the **Replyall** option, discussed later in the chapter.

When you are replying to a message, there are several other tilde escapes that are particularly useful. You can copy the old message into the new message by using the **~f** tilde escape. This is handy if you want to incorporate all or part of the old message into your reply.

A similar tilde escape is **~m**. This also copies the old message into the new one. However, each line of the old message is indented by a single tab.

Finally, you can include text from a file into the new message by using the **~r** (read) tilde escape. For example, to include the text from a file named **info**, enter:

```
~r info
```

A common technique is to use **~m**, followed by **~e**, to set yourself up to reply to a message. The **~m** copies the old message; the **~e** starts the editor.

Within the editor, it is a simple task to delete the lines you don't want. You can then reply to various portions of the original message by placing your replies directly under the appropriate lines. For example, if someone sends you a message that contains several questions, you can frame a reply in which you type each answer directly under the original question.

☑ **HINT**   When you are using the **vi** editor to reply to a message that you have copied by using the **~m** tilde escape, change the tab at the beginning of each line to ">> ". To do this, enter the command:

:%s/<Tab>**/>> /**

(The <Tab> after the first **/** means to press the <Tab> key.)
This will preface each line of the original message with ">> ", which looks nicer than a plain indentation.

Originating a New Message

There may be times when, as you read your mail, you decide to send a brand new message. Of course, you could quit reading and enter a new **mail** command, but this is a lot of bother.

Instead, you can use the **m** (mail) command. Enter the command followed by the recipient addresses. For example, say that you are reading your mail and you suddenly decide to send a new message to a person whose userid is **harley**. At the **&** prompt, enter the command:

m harley

You can now compose a message in the usual manner.

When you are finished, press **^D** (the **eof** key) to send the message. You will be returned to the **&** prompt.

You can now continue reading your mail.

Deleting a Message

Once you have displayed and (possibly) saved or replied to a message, you should delete it by using the **d** command. If you display a message, but do not delete or save it before you quit, **mail** will automatically save it to a file named **mbox**.

If you make a mistake, you can undelete a message by using the **u** command.

As a convenience, you can enter the **dp** (delete/print) command. This will delete the current message and display the next one.

Finally, if you have read a message and you are not ready to delete or save it, you can use the **pre** (preserve) command. This tells **mail** to retain this message when you quit. The message will be preserved as if it were new; it will not be saved to the **mbox** file.

Note: When you preserve a message, Unix may incorrectly tell you that you have just received new mail.

Message Lists

By default, almost all commands will act upon the current message. However, wherever it makes sense, you can specify a MESSAGE LIST to specify one or more messages. The command will act on all the messages.

For example, to delete messages 3 through 5, you can enter:

d 3-5

To display all the messages from userid **root**, use:

p root

Figure 14-6 contains a summary of the different ways to specify a message list. Figure 14-7 shows examples, using the **p** (print) command.

Note: In general, **mail** assumes that you do not want to refer to deleted messages unless it makes sense to do so. Thus, where **d *** will delete all messages that have not yet been deleted, **u *** will undelete all messages that have already been deleted.

Specification	Meaning
. [a period]	the current message
n	message number *n*
n-m	all messages from *n* to *m* inclusive
^ [a circumflex]	the first message
\$ [a dollar sign]	the last message
* [an asterisk]	all messages
userid	all messages from specified userid
/*pattern*	all messages containing pattern in subject
:n	all new messages
:o	all old messages
:r	all messages that have been read
:u	all messages that are still unread

Figure 14-6
Summary of Ways to Specify a Message List

Command	Meaning
p .	display the current message
p 3	display message 3
p 3-5	display messages 3 though 5 inclusive
p ^	display the first message
p $	display the last message
p *	display all messages
p harley	display messages from userid **harley**
p /hello	display messages with "hello" in subject
p :n	display new messages
p :o	display old messages
p :r	display messages that have been read
p :u	display messages that are still unread

Figure 14-7
Examples of Specifying a Message List

Stopping the `mail` Program

When you are finished reading your messages, you stop the **mail** program by entering the **q** (quit) command.

When you quit, **mail** will remove all the messages that you have saved or deleted. If there were any messages that you read but did not save or delete, **mail** will save them in a file named **mbox**. Later, you can read these messages by using the command:

```
mail -f mbox
```

When you use the **pre** command to preserve a file, it will be treated as a new message. When you quit, it will not be saved to **mbox**.

If you quit using the **x** (exit) command instead of **q**, **mail** will leave your mailbox completely unchanged. This is handy when you make a mess of your mailbox by deleting the wrong messages. Using **x** puts everything back the way it was.

Hints for Managing Your Mail

Once you build up a correspondence, it doesn't take long before you have more messages than you have time to deal with. Many people routinely ignore (or preserve) messages, with the result that their mailboxes become clogged past the point of no return.

As we mentioned at the beginning of this chapter, there are other mail programs, besides `mail`, that have more sophisticated features. Some of these features are designed to make it easy to handle large amounts of mail.

However, the secret of maintaining control over your mailbox is not really what program you use. The secret is your approach to managing your mail. All you need to do is use the following guidelines:

- Look at each message only once.
- Reply or save immediately.
- Before you move on to the next message, delete the one you have just read.

Finally, the most important rule of all:

- When in doubt, throw it out.

Thus, a typical session of reading mail should look like this:

```
To start, enter the mail command.
Press <Return> to read the first message.
Save or reply to the message as you wish.
Enter dp to delete the message and display the next one.
Repeat steps (3) and (4) until all your messages have
been read.
Enter q to quit.
```

Customizing `mail`: the `.mailrc` File

Each time `mail` starts, it looks for a file named `.mailrc` in your home directory. (The home directory is discussed in Chapter 21.) If `mail` finds such a file, it reads it and executes all the commands that it finds.

Thus, you can initialize `mail` to your liking by creating a `.mailrc` file to hold certain commands. To create such a file, you will have to use a text editor like **vi** (which is discussed in Chapter 19).

There are four commands that are especially useful within `.mailrc` files.

First, any lines that begin with a **#** (pound sign) are assumed to be comments and are ignored. Blank lines are also ignored.

Second, you can use the **alias** command to define an abbreviation for one or more addresses. The syntax is:

```
alias name address...
```

Here are two examples:

```
alias melissa melissa@misty.acme.com
alias workgroup al bill carol dave emily melissa
```

Once an alias is defined, you can use the name as an address and **mail** will make the substitution for you automatically.

Using the first alias, we can mail to **melissa** instead of trying to remember the full address each time. Using the second alias, we can send a message to six different userids simply by using the address **workgroup**. Notice that once we define an alias (in this case, **melissa**) we can use it in subsequent alias definitions.

Aliases are also useful for defining a name that stands for a command. For example, the command **lpr -p** will format and print data. Say that you define the alias:

```
alias lprp '|lpr -p'
```

You can now format and print a message by mailing it to **lprp**. (This technique is explained earlier in the chapter.)

The last two commands that are useful within a **.mailrc** file are **set** and **unset**. These commands allow you to modify a number of built-in options.

Most of the options are esoteric and can be ignored. However, there are a few that you might want to use. These are shown in Figure 14-8. If you want to see all the available options and the defaults for your system, look at the manual page for the **mail** command (use the **man mail** command).

The **ask** and **askcc** options tell **mail** to ask you to specify the "Subject" line and "Copy" line every time you create a new message.

The **autoprint** option tells **mail** that each time you delete a message, you want to automatically display the next message. In other words, the **d** command should act like the **dp** command.

The **verbose** option tells **mail** to show you the details each time a message is delivered. This is the same as invoking **mail** with the **-v** option that we explained earlier in the chapter.

The **Replyall** option reverses the meaning of the **r** and **R** commands. One of these commands sends a reply to everyone who received a copy of a message; the other command replies only to the person who sent the message. Not all systems are the same. You will have to experiment on your system to see which command does what. If you don't like the default, set the **Replyall** option.

Option	Meaning
ask	prompt for the "Subject" line of each message
askcc	prompt for the "Copy" line of each message
autoprint	after deleting, display the next message
verbose	show details of mail delivery (same as **-v** option)
Replyall	reverse the sense of the **r** and **R** commands

Figure 14-8

Useful Options for the **.mailrc** *Files*

The **set** and **unset** commands turn an option on or off respectively. Thus, to have **mail** prompt you for a "Subject" line but not for a "Copy" line, use:

```
set ask
unset askcc
```

Figure 14-9 shows a sample `.mailrc` file.

```
# .mailrc file for Harley Hahn

# OPTIONS ---------------------set ask
unset askcc
set autoprint
unset verbose

# ALIASES --------------------# Melissa the Expert
alias melissa melissa@misty.acme.com
# The Anaconda Research Society
alias workgroup melissa al bill carol dave emily
# format and print a message
alias lprp '|lpr -p'
```

Figure 14-9
A Sample `.mailrc` *File*

Redirection and Pipes

From the beginning, Unix has always had a certain something that makes it different from other operating systems. That "something" is the Unix toolbox: the large variety of programs that are a part of every Unix system, and the simple, elegant ways in which we can use them.

In this chapter, we will explain the philosophy behind the Unix toolbox. We will then show you how to combine basic building blocks into powerful tools of your own. In Chapter 16, we will survey the most important of these programs, so that you will have a good feel for what resources are available for your day-to-day work.

The Unix Philosophy

In Chapter 1, we explained how the original developers of Unix had worked previously on an operating system called Multics. One of the problems with Multics was that it was too unwieldy. The Multics design team had tried to make their product do too many things to please too many people.

When Unix was designed – at first, by only two people – the developers felt strongly that it was important to avoid the complexity of Multics and other such operating systems.

Thus, they developed a spartan attitude in which economy of expression was paramount. Each program, they reasoned, should be a single tool with, perhaps, a few basic options. A program should do only one thing, but should do it well. When you need to perform a complex task, you should do so by combining existing tools, not by writing a new program.

Here is a common example: Virtually all programs generate some type of output. When you display a large amount of output, the data may come so fast that all but the last part will scroll off the screen before you can read it.

One solution is for each program to be able to control its output. Whenever output is to be displayed on the screen, the program can present it one screenful at a time. This is just the type of solution that the original Unix developers wanted to avoid. Why should each program need to incorporate the same functionality?

Moreover, why should each program need to know where its output is going? Sometimes you may want to look at data on the screen; other times you may want to send it to a file; you may even want to send output to another program for more processing.

So, the Unix designers built a single tool whose job was to display data, one screenful at a time. Whenever you used a program that generated a lot of output, you could specify that the output was to be sent to the screen display tool. Thus, no matter how many different programs you used, you needed only one tool to display output on the screen.

This approach has three important advantages. First, when you design a new program, you can keep it simple. You do not have to give it every possible capability. For example, you do not have to endow your new program with the ability to display data one screenful at a time: there is already a tool to do that.

The second advantage is that, since each tool only does one thing, you can concentrate your effort. When you are designing, say, a screen display program, you can make it the best possible screen display program; when you are designing a sorting program, you can make it the best possible sorting program; and so on.

The third advantage is ease of use. As a user, once you learn the commands to control the standard screen display program, you know how to control the output for *any* program.

Thus, in two sentences, we can summarize the Unix philosophy:

- Each program or command should be a tool that does only one thing and does it well.

- When you need a new tool, you should combine existing tools, not write new ones.

Some people describe this philosophy as: "Small is beautiful."

Since Unix is well into its second decade as an operating system, it makes sense to ask if the Unix philosophy has been successful. The answer is, yes and no.

To some extent, the original philosophy is still intact. As you will see in Chapter 16, there are a great many single-purpose tools, and Unix makes it easy to combine them as the need arises.

However, the original philosophy has proved inadequate in two important ways. First, too many people could not resist creating alternative versions of the basic tools. This means that you must sometimes learn how to use more than one tool in a single category.

For example, there are three screen display programs in common use: **more**, **pg** and **less**. Although you may decide to use, say, **more**, you should probably also have some familiarity with **pg**. One day you will log in to a system that employs **pg** to display screenfuls of output when you look at the online manual (see Chapter 8). If you know only **more**, you will be confused.

On the other hand, many systems do use **more** as a default and you cannot get by knowing only **pg**. Finally, many people have a personal preference for **less** (which is not available on all systems). Such people need to make sure that they have at least a passing acquaintance with **more** and **pg**.

Second, the idea that small is beautiful has a lot of appeal. But, as users grew more sophisticated and their needs grew more demanding, it became clear that simple tools were often not enough.

For instance, the original mail program had only a few commands. It was simple to use and could be learned in a short time. However, as electronic mail grew in size and importance, the original mail program became seriously inadequate.

The result is that, as we described in Chapter 14, a wide variety of mail programs have been developed. Moreover, the original Unix mail program has been replaced with an enhanced program that has many, many commands. (Although you may think that Chapter 14 – the mail chapter – is long, we covered less than half the available commands and settings.)

What this means is that you must approach the learning of Unix carefully. In 1980, the original design of Unix was still intact, and you could learn just about everything about all the common commands. Today, there is so much more to learn that you can't possibly know it all. This means that you should be selective about which programs you want to learn, and, within each program, you should be selective about which options and commands you want to remember.

As you read this chapter, make an effort to understand the basic ideas. By all means, work in front of your terminal as you read, and enter commands to test them out as you learn.

However, don't try to memorize the details of each program. Just remember what is available and where to look for help when you need it.

HINT When you learn how to use a new program, do not try to memorize every detail. Learn:

1. what the program can do for you
2. the basic details
3. where to look for help when you need it

Standard Input and Standard Output

If there is one single idea that is central to using Unix effectively, it is the concept of standard input and output. Understand this one idea, and you are a long way towards becoming a competent Unix user.

The basic idea is a simple one: Every program should be able to accept input from any source and write output to any target.

For instance, say that you have a program that sorts lines of data. You should have your choice of typing the data at the keyboard, reading it from an existing file, or even accepting data that is the output from another program. Similarly, the sorting program should be able to display its data on your screen, write it to an output file, or send it to another program for more processing.

Such a system has two wonderful advantages. First, as a user, you have enormous flexibility. You can define the input and output for a program as you see fit. Moreover, you need to learn how to use only one program for each task. The same program that displays sorted data on your screen will also send its output to a disk file.

The second advantage is that designing and writing programs becomes a lot easier. When you write a program, you don't need to worry about all the variations of input and output. You can concentrate on the details of your program and depend on Unix to handle the standard resources for you.

The crucial idea is that the source of input and the target of output are not specified by the programmer. Rather, he or she writes the program to read and write in a general way. Later, *at the time you run the program*, the shell will connect the appropriate source to the input and the appropriate target to the output.

To implement this idea, the developers of Unix designed a general way to read data called STANDARD INPUT and a general way to write data called STANDARD OUTPUT. We refer to these ideas together as STANDARD I/O.

In practice, we often speak of these terms informally as if they were actual objects. Thus, we might say, "To save the output of a program, send the standard output to a file." What we really mean is, "To save the output of a program, tell the shell to set the output target to be a file." It is a good idea to remember that standard input and output are really ideas, not actual repositories of data.

Redirecting Standard Output

When you log in, the shell automatically sets standard input to be your keyboard and standard output to be your screen. This means that, by default, most programs will read from your keyboard and write to your screen.

However – and here's where the power of Unix comes in – every time you enter a command, you can tell the shell to reset the standard input or output, just for the duration of that command.

Thus, you might tell the shell: "I want to run the **sort** command and save the output to a file named **names**. Thus, for this command only, I want you to send the standard output to that file. After the command is over, I want you to reset the standard output back to my screen."

Here is how it works: If you want the output of a command to go to your screen, you don't have to do anything. This is automatic.

If you want the output of a command to go to a file, type a **>** (greater-than sign) followed by the name of the file, at the end of the command. For example, the command:

```
sort > names
```

will send its output to a file named **names**. The **>** character is nice because it looks like an arrow showing the path of the output.

If the file does not exist, Unix will create it. If the file already exists, its contents will be replaced. (So be careful.)

If you use two **>>** characters in a row, Unix will append data to the end of an existing file. Thus, consider the command:

```
sort >> names
```

If the file **names** does not exist, Unix will create it. If it does exist, the new data will be appended to the end of the file.

When we send the standard output to a file, we say that we REDIRECT it. Thus, both of these **sort** commands redirect their output to the **names** file.

When you redirect output, it is up to you to decide whether to use **>** (and replace data) or **>>** (and append data). When the file does not yet exist, there is no difference.

Protecting Files from Being Replaced by Redirection

In the previous section, we explained that when you use the **>** character to redirect standard output to a file, any data that already exists in the file will be replaced. We also explained that when you use **>>** to append output to a file, the file will be created if it does not already exist.

There may be times when you do not want Unix to make such assumptions on your behalf. For example, say that you have a file called **names** that contains 5,000 lines of data. You want to append the output of a **sort** command to the end of this file. In other words, you want to enter the command:

```
sort >> names
```

However, you make a mistake and accidentally enter:

```
sort > names
```

What happens? All of your original data is wiped out.

To prevent such catastrophes, the C-Shell lets you set a variable named **noclobber**. (We explained C-Shell variables and how to use them in Chapter 11.) When **noclobber** is set, the shell will not replace an existing file when you use **>** to redirect output. Likewise, the shell will not create a new file when you use **>>** to append data. In other words, when you set **noclobber**, the shell does exactly what you ask, but no more.

To set this variable, use:

```
set noclobber
```

To unset this variable, use:

```
unset noclobber.
```

(Note: There is no built-in C-Shell variable named **clobber**. Thus, entering **set clobber** will not do anything. You must set and unset **noclobber**.)

Once **noclobber** is set, you have built-in protection. For example, if the file **names** already exists and you enter:

```
sort > names
```

you will see:

```
names: File exists.
```

If you really want to replace the file, type an **!** (exclamation mark) after the **>** character:

```
sort >! names
```

This will override the automatic check.

Similarly, if you try to append data to a file that does not exist, for example:

```
sort >> notfile
```

You will see a message like:

```
notfile: No such file or directory
```

If you really want to create a file, type an **!** after the **>>** characters:

```
sort >>! notfile
```

This will override the automatic check.

When you use an **!** character in this way, you can think of it as meaning "Do what I tell you!"

☑ **HINT** There are four common uses for the ! (exclamation mark) character in Unix. Do not be confused.

1. The ! is used to indicate event information when you use the C-Shell history mechanism. (See Chapter 11.) For example, when you enter ! ! the C-Shell will re-execute your previous command.

   Note: When you use ! as part of a command and you do not want it to be interpreted as an event indicator, you must preface it with a \ (backslash) character. This tells the C-Shell to take the ! literally.

2. The ! is used to delimit the parts of a UUCP bang path address. (See Chapter 13.) For example:

   ```
   mail tinker\!evers\!chance
   ```

3. The ! is used within some interactive programs to execute a single shell command.

   For example, when you are using **mail** to read your mail, you can display the time and date by entering:

   ```
   !date
   ```

   When the **date** command is finished, you will be returned to the original program.

   When the ! is used in this way, it is sometimes called the SHELL ESCAPE CHARACTER.

4. The ! character is sometimes used to override an automatic check.

   For instance, if you are using the C-Shell with the **noclobber** variable set, the shell will not replace an existing file when you use > to redirect the standard output. To override this automatic check, you can use >!. For example:

   ```
   sort >! notfile
   ```

Pipelines

If you want the output of a command to go to another program for further processing, type a | (vertical bar) followed by the name of the program. For example, to send the output of the **sort** program to the **lpr** command (which will print the data), use:

```
sort | lpr
```

When we send the standard output to another program, we say that we PIPE the output. Thus, the **sort** program pipes its output to the **lpr** program.

Once you know how to pipe output, you can build a command in which output is passed from one program to another in sequence. For example, the following command sends the output of the **cat** program to **grep**, the output of **grep** to **sort**, and finally, the output of **sort** to **lpr**:

```
cat newnames oldnames | grep Harley | sort | lpr
```

You don't need to worry about the details for now.

(Okay, we can worry about a few of the details. The **cat** program combines files; **grep** extracts all the lines of data that contain a specified string of characters, in this case, the letters "Harley"; **sort** sorts the data; and **lpr** prints the data. Thus, we end up with a printed, sorted list of all the lines in the files **newnames** and **oldnames** that contain the characters "Harley".)

When we combine commands in this manner, we call it a PIPELINE. The image of a pipeline, in which data is sent in at one end and emerges at the other end, is a clear one. However, you would be better off thinking of it as an assembly line in which each program performs a different function on the data. The raw data goes in one end of the assembly line and comes out the other end in finished form.

✅ **HINT** The art of using Unix well is in knowing when and how to solve a problem by combining programs into a pipeline.

Redirecting Standard Input

By default, the standard input is set to your keyboard. This means that when you enter a command that needs to read data, Unix expects you to enter the data by typing it, one line at a time. When you are finished entering data, you press **^D** (the **eof** key that we discussed in Chapter 6). Pressing this key indicates that there is no more data.

Here is an example that you can try for yourself. Enter:

```
sort
```

The **sort** command is now waiting for you to enter data from the standard input (the keyboard). Type as many lines as you want. For example, you might enter:

```
Harley
Addie
Melissa
Randolph
```

After you have pressed <Return> on the last line, press **^D** to indicate that there is no more data. The **sort** program will now sort all the data alphabetically and write it to the standard output (which, by default, is the screen).

With the data in our example, you would see the output:

```
Addie
Harley
```

```
Melissa
Randolph
```

There will be many times when you want to redirect the standard input to a file. In other words, you will want the shell to tell a program to read its data from a file, not from the keyboard. Simply type a **<** (less-than sign), followed by the name of the file, at the end of the command.

For example, to sort the data contained in a file named **temp**, use the command:

```
sort < temp
```

As you can see, the **<** character is a good choice as it looks like an arrow showing the path of the input.

Here is an example you can try for yourself. As we mentioned in Chapter 12, the system information about each userid is usually contained in the file **/etc/passwd**. You can display a sorted version of this file by entering the command:

```
sort < /etc/passwd
```

Here is a common use for redirecting standard input. When you have prepared a message that you want to mail, you can tell the mail program to read its input from a file. (The Unix mail program is discussed in Chapter 14.)

For example, say that you have a file, named **notice**, that contains a message that you want to mail to three userids, **curly, larry** and **moe**. You can use the command:

```
mail curly larry moe < notice
```

As you might imagine, it is possible to redirect both the standard input and the standard output at the same time. For example, the command:

```
sort < rawdata > names
```

reads data from a file named **rawdata**, sorts it, and writes the output to a file called **names**.

☑ **HINT**

When you enter a command that redirects or pipes standard I/O, it is not necessary to put spaces around the <, > or | characters. However, it is a good idea to use such spaces.

For example, instead of:

```
cat newnames oldnames|grep Harley|sort|lpr
sort <rawdata >names
```

it is better to use:

```
cat newnames oldnames | grep Harley | sort | lpr
sort < rawdata > names
```

This makes your commands easier for you to understand and minimizes the chances of a typing error.

Splitting a Pipeline with Tees: `tee`

There may be times when you want the output of a program to go to two places at the same time. For example, you may want to save the output to a file, but you may also want to send the output to another program for more processing.

Take a look at this example:

```
cat newnames oldnames | grep Harley | sort | lpr
```

This command uses **cat** to combine the two files **newnames** and **oldnames**. It then sends the output to **grep**, which extracts all the lines of data that contain the characters "Harley". Next, the output of **grep** is sent to **sort** to be sorted.

Now, let us say that, at this point, you want to save the sorted output to a file named **save**. However, you also want to send the sorted data to **lpr** (to be printed). The solution is to use what is called a TEE. This is a mechanism that sends a copy of its input to a file as well as to the standard output.

To create a tee, use the **tee** command. The syntax is:

```
tee [-a] file...
```

Normally, you use the command with a single file name. For example:

```
cat newnames oldnames | grep Harley | sort | tee save | lpr
```

In this case, the output of the **sort** program will be saved in the file **save**. At the same time, the output will also be sent to the **lpr** program for further processing.

The syntax of the **tee** command allows you to create duplicate copies of the output by specifying more than one file name. For example, the **tee** command in the following pipeline copies the output to two files, **c1** and **c2**.

```
cat newnames oldnames | grep Harley | sort | tee c1 c2 | lpr
```

If a file you name in a **tee** command does not exist, **tee** will create it for you. However, if a file already exists, **tee** will overwrite it and the original contents will be lost. If you want to have **tee** add data to the end of an existing file instead of replacing it, use the **-a** (append option). For example:

```
cat newnames oldnames | grep Harley | sort | tee -a save | lpr
```

This command will save the output of the **sort** command in a file named **save**. If this file already exists, the output will be appended to the end of the file.

Filters

In Chapter 15, we explained how the Unix philosophy led to the development of many programs, each of which can be used as a tool to perform a single function. We showed how to use redirection to control the source and target of input/output, and we showed how to build pipes to create assembly lines in which data is passed from one program to the next.

In this chapter, we will discuss a number of the most useful Unix tools. Using these programs, and the techniques from Chapter 15, you will be able to build flexible, customized tools to solve a wide variety of problems.

At the end of this chapter, we will explain two important Unix facilities: command substitution and regular expressions.

Filters

In Chapter 15, we saw how a series of programs could be joined using a pipeline. For example, the following command passes data through four programs in sequence: **cat**, **grep**, **sort** and **lpr**.

```
cat newnames oldnames | grep Harley | sort | lpr
```

By now, you should be able to appreciate how useful a program can be if it is designed to be part of a pipeline. Such a program will read data, perform some operation on the data, and then write out the results.

We call such programs FILTERS. Strictly speaking, a filter is any program that reads from standard input and writes to standard output. Informally, we also expect that a filter will do only one task and will do it well.

☑ **HINT** If you use filters to develop a pipeline that you use a lot, define it as an alias and place it in your `.cshrc` file. This will allow you to use the pipeline without having to type the whole thing every time. (Aliases and the `.cshrc` file are discussed in Chapter 11.)

If you are a programmer, it is not hard to create your own filters. You can use a programming language (like C) or the built-in language that comes with the shell. All you need to do is make sure that your program reads and writes using the standard I/O and your program will be a filter. In other words, if your program or shell script reads from standard input and writes to standard output, it can be part of a pipeline.

Interestingly enough, the first and last programs in a pipeline do not have to act like filters. In our last example, for instance, the **lpr** program is used to print the output of the **sort** program. Clearly, the output of **lpr** is not going to the standard output, it is going to the printer. (More precisely, the output is going to a system file where it will wait to be printed.)

Similarly, the first command in the pipeline, **cat** (which combines files), does not read from the standard input. In this case, it reads from two files, **newnames** and **oldnames**.

The Simplest Possible Filter: `cat`

A filter reads from standard input, does something, and then writes the results to standard output.

What would be the simplest possible filter? The one that does nothing at all. Its name is **cat** (we will see why in a moment). All **cat** does is copy data from standard input to standard output.

Here is a simple example that you can perform for yourself. Enter the command:

```
cat
```

The system is now waiting for data from the standard input. That is, **cat** is waiting for you to type something. (Remember, by default, the standard input is the keyboard.)

When you press the <Return> key at the end of each line, the line will be sent to **cat**, which will copy it to the standard output (the screen). The result is that each line you type is displayed twice. For example:

```
this is line 1
this is line 1
this is line 2
this is line 2
```

When you are finished, press **^D** (the **eof** key). This tells Unix that there is no more input. The **cat** command will end, and you will be returned to a shell prompt.

You might ask, what use is a filter that does nothing? Of course, there is no need to use **cat** within a pipeline. However, you can take advantage of the mechanics of standard I/O to use **cat** as a quick way to create short files. Consider the following command:

```
cat > data
```

In this command, the standard input is still the keyboard, but the standard output has been redirected to a file named **data**. Each line that you type is copied to this file. If the file does not already exist, Unix will create it for you. If the file does exist, its contents will be replaced.

You can type as many lines as you want and end by pressing **^D**. Thus, using **cat** with redirected output is an easy way to create a file that contains a small amount of data. (Unfortunately, if you notice a mistake after you have pressed <Return> at the end of a line, you have to re-enter the command and start typing all over again.)

If you want to append data to the end of an existing file, use **>>** to redirect the standard output:

```
cat >> data
```

(As we explained in Chapter 15, when you redirect output with **>>**, the shell will append the output, rather than replace an existing file.)

You can also use **cat** to display a short file. Simply redirect the standard input to the file you want to display. For example:

```
cat < data
```

By default, the standard output will go to your screen.

Finally, you can use **cat** to make a copy of a file by redirecting both the standard input and output. For example, to copy the file **data** to another file named **newdata**, enter:

```
cat < data > newdata
```

Now, for day-to-day work, there are better ways to perform these functions. Normally, you would use a paging program (like **more** or **pg**) to display a file, a text editor (like **vi** or **emacs**) to create a file, and the copy command (**cp**) to copy a file.

However, it is important that you read and understand these examples. They will help you appreciate the power of standard I/O and filters. Look how much we can do with a filter that does nothing!

Putting **cat** through its paces provides us with a good example of the elegance of Unix. What seems like a simple concept – that data should flow from standard input to standard output – turns out to bear fruit in so many unexpected ways.

☑ **HINT** Part of the charm of Unix is, all of a sudden, having a great insight and saying to yourself, "So THAT'S why they did it that way."

Increasing the Power of Filters

By making one significant change to a filter, it is possible to increase its usefulness enormously. That enhancement is to allow you to specify the names of input files.

As you know, the strict definition of a filter requires it to read its data from the standard input. If you want to read data from a file, you must redirect the standard input to that file.

However, what if we also had the option of reading from a file whose name we would specify as a parameter. For example, instead of having to enter:

```
cat < data
```

we could enter:

```
cat data
```

At first, such a small change seems insignificant. True, we make the command line slightly simpler, but at a price. The **cat** program itself must be more complex. It not only has to be able to read from the standard input, it also has to be able to read from any file. Moreover, by extending the power of **cat**, we have lost a little of the beauty and simplicity of a pure filter.

However, many filters are extended in just this way. The reason is not because it makes it easier to read from one file, but because it makes it possible to read from multiple files.

Here is an abbreviated version of the syntax for the **cat** command:

```
cat file...
```

where *file* is the name of a file from which **cat** will read.

Notice the three dots after the *file* parameter. This means that we can specify more than one file name. (Command syntax is explained in Chapter 9.)

Thus – and this point is important – in extending the power of **cat** to read from a file, we have also allowed it to read from more than one file. This means that we can specify multiple files, and **cat** will read from each of them in turn and then write all the data to the standard output.

In other words, we can use **cat** to combine the data from multiple files.

Take a look at the following examples:

```
cat name address phone
cat name address phone > info
cat name address phone | sort
```

The first example combines the data from three files (**name**, **address** and **phone**) and writes it to the screen. The second example combines the data from three files and writes it to a fourth file (**info**). The third example combines the data from three files and pipes it to another program (**sort**).

We have already mentioned that other filters, and not only **cat**, can also read input from multiple files. Technically, this is not necessary. If we want to operate on data from more than one file, we can collect the data with **cat** and then pipe it to whatever filter we want. For example:

```
cat name address phone | sort
```

This is appealing in one sense. By extending **cat** to read from files, and not only the standard input, we have lost some of the elegance of the overall design. However, by using **cat** to feed other filters, we can at least retain the purity of the other filters.

However, as in many aspects of life, utility has won out over beauty and purity. It is just too much trouble to combine files with **cat** every time we want to send such data to a filter. Thus, most filters allow us to specify multiple file names as parameters.

For example, the following commands will sort the data in more than one file:

```
sort name address phone
sort name address phone > info
sort name address phone | grep Harley
```

The first command displays the output on the screen. The second command saves the output to a file. The third command pipes the output to another command for further processing.

To summarize, let us ask the following esoteric techno-nerd question: Strictly speaking, a filter reads its data from the standard input. Does this mean that a program is not really a filter if it reads its input from a file?

There are two answers. First, we can decide that when a program like **cat** or **sort** reads from standard input it is a filter, but when it reads from a file it is not a filter. Or we can broaden the definition of a filter to allow it to read from either the standard input or from one or more files.

Talk about controversy!

A List of Useful Filters

Having explained the basics of using filters, we will spend the rest of the chapter discussing the most important of these programs. Figure 16-1 shows a list of useful filters. We will discuss all of these in this chapter except for **fmt** (Chapter 14), **head**, **less**, **more**, **pg** and **tail** (Chapter 17), and **nl** and **pr** (Chapter 18).

Filter	Purpose
cat	combine files; copy standard input to standard output
colrm	remove specified columns from each line of data
crypt	encode or decode data using a specified key
cut	extract selected portions (columns) of each line
fmt	format text to fit a 72-character line
grep	extract lines that contain a specified pattern
head	display the first few lines of data
less	display data, one screenful at a time
look	extract lines beginning with a specified pattern
more	display data, one screenful at a time
nl	create line numbers
paste	combine columns of data
pg	display data, one screenful at a time
pr	format data, suitable for printing
rev	reverse order of characters in each line of data
sort	sort or merge data
spell	check data for spelling errors
tail	display the last few lines of data
tr	translate or delete selected characters
uniq	look for repeated lines
wc	count number of lines, words or characters

Figure 16-1
A List of Useful Filters

As we discuss each filter, bear in mind that we will cover only the most important material. If you want to learn all the details, including the more esoteric options, use the **man** command to check the online manual. (The online manual is explained in Chapter 8.)

In addition, you may find that not all of these programs are available on your system. If you have any doubts, check the online manual or use the **whatis** command (Chapter 8).

Note: If you decide to skim through the rest of this chapter, be sure to read the last two sections on command substitution and regular expressions.

Combining Files: cat

The **cat** program copies data, unchanged, to the standard output. The data can come from the standard input or from one or more files. The syntax is:

```
cat [-bns] file...
```

where *file* is the name of a file.

You can use **cat** to combine files, for example:

```
cat name address phone
cat name address phone > info
cat name address phone | sort
```

You can also use **cat** to display one or more files:

```
cat name
cat name address phone
```

to create a file:

```
cat > newfile
```

to append data to an existing file:

```
cat >> oldfile
```

and to copy a file:

```
cat < data > newdata
```

There is one common mistake that you must be sure to avoid: Do not redirect output to one of the input files. For example, say that you want to append the contents of **address** and **phone** to the file **name**. You cannot use:

```
cat name address phone > name
```

This is because Unix sets up the output file before starting the **cat** program. Thus, the file **name** is already cleared out *before* **cat** reads and combines its input. By the time **cat** looks in **name**, it is already empty.

If you enter a command like the one above, you will see a message like:

```
cat: input name is output
```

However, it is too late. The original contents of **name** have been lost.

The safe way to append the contents of **address** and **phone** to the file **name** is to use:

```
cat address phone >> name
```

The options for **cat** are as follows. The **-n** (number) option will place a line number in front of each line. The **-b** (blank) option is used with **-n** and tells **cat** not to number blank lines. The **-s** (squeeze) option changes more than one consecutive blank line to a single blank line.

HINT Although you can display a file with `cat`, it is best to get in the habit of using a paging program, such as `more` (see Chapter 17), which will display data one screenful at a time.

People like to use `cat` because the name is cute and easy to type. However, unless the file is short, most of the data will scroll off the top of the screen before you can read it.

WHAT'S IN A NAME?

`cat`   Many people believe that the name `cat` stands for "concatenate". Not really.

The name `cat` actually comes from the archaic word "catenate" which means "to join in a chain". (As all classically educated computer scientists know, "catena" is the Latin word for chain.)

Removing Columns of Data: `colrm`

The `colrm` command reads from the standard input, removes specified columns of data, and then writes the remaining data to the standard output. The syntax of the `colrm` command is:

`colrm [`*startcol* `[`*endcol*`]]`

where *startcol* and *endcol* specify the starting and ending range of the columns to be removed. Numbering starts with column 1.

Here is an example: You are a tenured professor at a university in California and you have to print a list of grades for all the students in your PE 201 class ("Intermediate Surfing"). This list should not show the students' names.

You have a master data file, named **students**, that contains one line of information about each student. Each line has a student number, a name, the final exam score and the course grade:

```
012-34-5678   Ambercrombie, Al    95%   A
123-45-6789   Barton, Barbara     65%   C
234-56-7890   Canby, Charles      77%   B
345-67-8901   Danfield, Deann     82%   B
```

To construct the list of grades, you need to remove the names, which are in columns 14 through 28 inclusive. Use the command:

`colrm 14 28 < students`

The output is:

```
012-34-5678        95%   A
123-45-6789        65%   C
234-56-7890        77%   B
345-67-8901        82%   B
```

To print this list, all you need to do is pipe the output to the **lpr** program:

```
colrm 14 28 < students | lpr
```

(Using **lpr** to print files is explained in Chapter 18.)

If you specify only a starting column, **colrm** will remove all the columns from that point to the end of the line. For example:

```
colrm 14 < students
```

displays:

```
012-34-5678
123-45-6789
234-56-7890
345-67-8901
```

If you specify neither a starting nor ending column, **colrm** will delete nothing.

Extract Selected Columns of Each Line: cut

The **cut** command extracts columns of data. This command has a great deal of flexibility. You can extract either specific columns or delimited portions of each line (called fields). If you are a database expert, you can consider **cut** as implementing the projection of a relation. (If you are not a database expert, don't worry. Nobody really understands that stuff anyway.)

In this section, we will concentrate on the basic features of **cut**; we will not deal with fields. If you want more details, check the online manual (described in Chapter 8) by using the **man cut** command.

The syntax of the **cut** command is:

```
cut -clist [file...]
```

where *list* is a list of columns to extract, and *file* is the name of an input file.

You use the list to tell **cut** which columns of data you want to extract. Specify one or more column numbers, separated by commas. For example, to extract column 10 only, use **10**. To extract columns 1, 8 and 10, use **1,8,10**.

You can also specify a range of column numbers by joining the beginning and end of the range with a hyphen. For example, to extract columns 10 through 15, use **10-15**. To extract columns 1, 8, and 10 through 15, use **1,8,10-15**.

Here is an example of how to use **cut**. Say that you have a file named **info** that contains information about a group of people. Each line contains data pertaining to one person. In particular, columns 14-30 contain a name and columns 42-49 contain a phone number. Here is some sample data:

```
012-34-5678   Ambercrombie, Al   01/01/72   555-1111
123-45-6789   Barton, Barbara    02/02/73   555-2222
234-56-7890   Canby, Charles     03/03/74   555-3333
345-67-8901   Danfield, Deann    04/04/75   555-4444
```

To display the names only, use:

```
cut -c14-30 info
```

You will see:

```
Ambercrombie, Al
Barton, Barbara
Canby, Charles
Danfield, Deann
```

To display the names and phone numbers, use:

```
cut -c14-30,42-49 info
```

You will see:

```
Ambercrombie, Al 555-1111
Barton, Barbara  555-2222
Canby, Charles   555-3333
Danfield, Deann  555-4444
```

To save this information, you can redirect the standard output to a file. For example:

```
cut -c14-30,42-49 info > phonelist
```

If you want to rearrange the columns of a table, you can use **cut** with the **paste** command (explained later in this chapter.)

The **cut** command is handy to use in a pipeline. Here is an example. You want to make a list of the userids that are currently logged in to the system. Since some userids may be logged in more than once, you want to show how many times each userid is logged in.

Start with the **who** command that we described in Chapter 12. This command will generate a report with one line for each userid that is logged in. Here is a sample:

```
addie     console Jul  8 10:30
harley    ttyp1   Jul 12 17:46
tln       ttyp4   Jul 12 21:22    (feline)
addie     ttyp0   Jul 12 16:45
kim       ttyp3   Jul 12 17:41    (tintin.ucsb.edu)
```

As you can see, the userid is displayed in columns 1 through 8. Thus, we can extract the userids by using:

```
cut -c1-8
```

Next, we sort the list of userids using **sort**, and count the number of duplications using **uniq -c**. (Both the **sort** and **uniq** commands are explained later in the chapter.)

Putting the whole thing together, we have:

```
who | cut -c1-8 | sort | uniq -c
```

(As you can see, there is no problem using options within a pipeline).

If the output of the **who** command was the same as our example above, the result of this pipeline would be:

```
2 addie
1 harley
1 kim
1 tln
```

An interesting variation is to solve the problem, how can you display the names of all userids who are logged in twice? The solution is to search the output of **uniq** for all the lines that begin with "2". You can do so using the **grep** command (explained later in the chapter):

```
who | cut -c1-8 | sort | uniq -c | grep 2
```

The output is:

```
2 addie
```

Encoding and Decoding Data: `crypt`

The **crypt** command encodes data. To use **crypt**, you specify a password called a KEY. **crypt** uses the key to create an encoded version of the data. The encoded data itself looks like nonsense. However, if you know the key, you can use **crypt** to decode the data and recover the original message.

The **crypt** command is useful to protect sensitive data such as student grades, a completed homework assignment, or the questions for an upcoming examination. Although Unix does provide for specific file permissions (see Chapter 22), it is possible that someone might find a way to read your files. Thus, if you have top secret data lying around, you may wish to encode it.

For cryptography buffs: The **crypt** command implements a one-rotor machine similar to the German Enigma used during World War II. The main difference is that **crypt** uses a 256-element rotor.

Note: This command is not available on all systems. In particular, for reasons of national security, this command is not supposed to be available on systems that are shipped outside of the United States. (This may seem silly, but we in America do sleep more soundly at night.)

The syntax of the **crypt** command is:

`crypt [key]`

where *key* is the password to be used to encode the data.

To use **crypt**, enter the name of the command, with or without a key. If you do not specify a key, **crypt** will ask you for one. **crypt** will read from the standard input, encode what it reads, and write the result to the standard output.

Here is an example. You want to create a quick message in code and save it in a file named **message**. Enter:

`crypt > message`

You will be asked for a key:

`Enter key:`

Enter whatever key you want and press <Return>. For secrecy, the key will not be echoed as you type, just like when you type your login password.

You can now type your message, as many lines as you want. After you have pressed <Return> for the last line, press **^D** (the **eof** key) to tell **crypt** that there is no more data from the standard input. **crypt** will encode your message and write it to the file you specified.

To view the coded message, enter:

`crypt < message`

Once again, **crypt** will ask you for the key. After you enter it, **crypt** will decode the message and display the output on your screen (the default standard output).

Here is another example: You have a file named **bigsecrets** that you want to protect from prying eyes. You decide to encode it, using the key "duckface", and save the encoded data in a file named **notimportant**. Enter the command:

`crypt duckface < bigsecrets > notimportant`

Now you can remove the original file by using the **rm** command (explained in Chapter 22):

`rm bigsecrets`

When you want to recover the original data, you can display it on your screen by using:

`crypt duckface < notimportant`

You can restore it to a file (in this case **bigsecrets**) by using:

`crypt duckface < notimportant > bigsecrets`

☑ **HINT for paranoids**

> To be extra careful, do not enter the key as part of your command. The person who is spying on you can use the **w** or **ps** commands to see your entire command line and read your key.

If you encrypt files, make sure to keep your keys secret. Anyone who can access the files will be able to read them if they know your key. Without a key, even the system manager cannot read an encrypted file.

However, make sure that you do not forget the key. If you do, there is no way to recover the original data.

Extracting Lines that Contain a Specified Pattern: grep

(Note: After you read about **grep**, be sure to look at the section on regular expressions, at the end of this chapter. Regular expressions allow you to specify search patterns that can be used with **grep**.)

The **grep** command will search for all the lines in a collection of data that contain a specified pattern and write these lines to the standard output. For example, you can search a file for all the lines that contain the word **Harley**.

The **grep** command is actually part of a family. The other members are **fgrep** and **egrep**. At the time that **grep** was first developed, computer speed and memory were limited. Three separate programs were developed, each with trade-offs.

grep was designed to be the general purpose program. It can search for patterns that are exact characters (such as "Harley"), or for patterns that match a more general specification. For example, the specification "H[a-z]*y" will match the letter "H", followed by any number of lowercase letters, followed by the letter "y". (We will explain what the name **grep** means at the end of the chapter.)

fgrep was designed to be a faster searching program. However, it can only search for exact characters, not for general specifications. The name **fgrep** stands for "fixed character **grep**". (The name does not stand for "fast **grep**".)

egrep was designed to be the most powerful program. It can search for more complex patterns than **grep**, and it is usually the fastest of the three programs. However, the method that **egrep** uses sometimes requires more memory than **grep** or **fgrep**. The name **egrep** stands for "extended **grep**".

These days, computers are faster and memory is more plentiful. There is rarely any need to use **fgrep**. In fact, some people say that the best idea is to use **egrep** almost all the time.

However, most people still use **grep** for two reasons: First, **grep** is well-known among Unix people, who, like all of us, do preserve a certain amount of tradition; second, the name **grep** is cuter and easier to type than the name **egrep**.

Thus, we suggest that, as a rule, you use **grep** unless you need the extended features of **egrep**. You can forget about **fgrep**.

The **grep** family provides a wide range of text searching capabilities. In this section, we will discuss only the most useful features of the basic **grep** program. If you want more details, or if you want to learn about **egrep**, check the online manual (described in Chapter 8) by using the **man grep** command.

The syntax of the **grep** command is:

```
grep [-cilnvw] pattern [file...]
```

where *pattern* is the pattern to search for, and *file* is the name of an input file.

grep reads all the input data and selects those lines that contain the specified pattern. Here is an example.

In Chapter 12, we explained that most Unix systems keep general login information in the file named **/etc/passwd**. Each userid has one line of information in this file. You can display the information about your userid by using **grep** to search the file for that pattern. For example, if your userid is **harley**, use the command:

```
grep harley /etc/passwd
```

If **grep** does not find any lines that match the specified pattern, there will be no output or warning message. Like most Unix commands, **grep** is terse. When there is nothing to say, **grep** says nothing.

When you specify a pattern that contains punctuation or special characters, you should place them in single quotes so the shell will interpret the command properly. For example, to search a file named **info** for all the lines that contain a colon followed by a space, use the command:

```
grep ': ' info
```

Much of the flexibility of **grep** comes from the fact that you can specify not only exact characters, but a more general search pattern. To do this, you use what are called "regular expressions".

Regular expressions are extremely important in Unix, so we will describe them in a separate section at the end of the chapter. In that section, we will give examples using **grep**.

As useful as **grep** is for searching files, it really comes into its own in a pipeline. What makes **grep** so handy is that it can reduce a large amount of raw data to a small amount of useful information. Here are some examples.

The **w** command (discussed in Chapter 12) displays information about all the users and what they are doing. Here is some sample output:

```
8:44pm up 9 days, 7:02, 5 users, load average: 0.11, 0.02, 0.00
User     tty        login@  idle    JCPU    PCPU   what
addie    console    Wed10am 4days   42:41   37:56  -csh
addie    ttyp0       4:45pm          1:40    0:36  vi existential
harley   ttyp1       5:47pm         15:11           w
tln      ttyp4       9:22am  1:40      20       1  -rn rec.pets.cats
kim      ttyp3       5:41pm    10    2:16      13  -csh
```

Say that you want to display all the users who logged in during the afternoon or evening. You can search for lines of output that contain the pattern "pm". Use the pipeline:

```
w -h | grep pm
```

(Notice that we use **w** with the **-h** option to suppress the header information: the first two lines.) Using the above data, the output of the previous command would be:

```
addie    ttyp0       4:45pm          1:40    0:36  vi existential
harley   ttyp1       5:47pm         15:11           w
kim      ttyp3       5:41pm    10    2:16      13  -csh
```

Suppose we just want to display the userids and not all the other information. We can pipe the output of **grep** to the **cut** command and extract the first 8 columns of data:

```
w -h | grep pm | cut -c1-8
```

The output is:

```
addie
harley
kim
```

The **grep** command has several options that you can use. The **-c** (count) option will display the number of lines that have been extracted, rather than the lines themselves. For example, to count the number of users who logged in during the afternoon or evening, use:

```
w -h | grep -c pm
```

The **-i** option ignores the difference between upper- and lowercase letters when making a comparison. (Note that, with the **look** and **sort** commands, discussed later in the chapter, the same option is named **-f**.)

The **-n** option writes a relative line number in front of each line of output. Your data does not have to actually contain line numbers; **grep** will count lines as it processes the input. The **-n** option is useful when you are searching a large file. If you need to, say, use a text editor to change the lines that **grep** finds for you, the line numbers will help you locate the data quickly.

The **-l** (listfile) option is useful when you want to search a number of files for a particular pattern. This option will output not the lines that contain the pattern, but the names of files in which such lines were found.

For example, say that you have three files, **names**, **oldnames** and **newnames**. You want to see which files, if any, contain the pattern "Harley". Use:

```
grep -l Harley names oldnames newnames
```

The **-w** option specifies that you want to search only for complete words. For example, say that you have a file named **memo** that contains the following lines:

```
We must, of course, make sure that all the
data is now correct before we publish it.
I thought you would know this.
```

You want to display all the lines that contain the word "now". If you enter:

```
grep now memo
```

you will see:

```
data is now correct before we publish it.
I thought you would know this.
```

grep did not distinguish between "now" and "know" because they both contain the specified pattern. However, if you enter:

```
grep -w now memo
```

you will see only the output you want:

```
data is now correct before we publish it.
```

Finally, the **-v** (reverse) option will select all the lines that do *not* contain the specified pattern. For example, say that you have a file, named **homework**, to keep track of your assignments. This file contains one line for each assignment. Once you have finished an assignment, you mark it "DONE". For example:

```
Math: problems 12:10-33, due Monday
Basket Weaving: make a 6-inch basket, DONE
Psychology: essay on Animal Existentialism, due end of term
Surfing: catch at least 10 waves, DONE
```

To list all the assignments that are not yet finished, enter:

```
grep -v DONE homework
```

If you want to see the number of assignments that are not finished, you can use:

```
grep -cv DONE homework
```

Extracting Lines Beginning with a Specified Pattern: look

The **look** command will search data that is in alphabetical order and will find all the lines that begin with a specified pattern. The syntax of the **look** command is:

look [**-df**] *pattern* [*file*]

where *pattern* is the pattern to search for, and *file* is the name of a file.

There are two ways to use **look**. First, you can use sorted data from one or more files. For example, say that the file **evaluations** contains data regarding student evaluations of professors. The data consists of a ranking (A, B, C, D or F) followed by the name of the professor. For example:

```
A    William Wisenheimer
C    Peter Pedant
F    Norman Knowitall
```

You want to display the names of all the professors who received an A rating. Use **look** to search for all the lines of the file that begin with **A**:

```
look A evaluations
```

If you want to prepare data to use with **look**, you should be aware that it cannot read from the standard input. (Thus, **look** is not really a filter and cannot be used within a pipeline.) This is because **look** uses a search method – called a "binary search" – that needs to access all the data at once. With standard input, a program can read only one line at a time.

However, all you need to do is prepare your data and save it in a file, then use the **look** command. For example, say that the four files **frosh**, **soph**, **junior** and **senior** all contain evaluations. To search all of them for professors who received an A, use the **sort** command to sort and combine the files. Then use **look** to find the information you want:

```
sort -dfu frosh soph junior senior > evaluations
look A evaluations
```

(The **sort** command is explained later in the chapter.)

When you use **look** to select lines, there are two options that will control the comparisons. The **-d** (dictionary) option tells **look** to consider only upper- and lowercase letters, numerals, tabs and spaces.

The **-f** (fold) option tells **look** to treat uppercase the same as lowercase.

The second way to use **look** is to specify only a search pattern but not a source of input. In this case, **look** will examine the file **/usr/dict/words**, using both the **-d** and **-f** options.

The name **/usr/dict/words** refers to the file **words**, which lies within the **/usr/dict** directory. (Such names are explained in Chapter 21.) **/usr/dict/words** is a master file of correctly spelled words and is used by the **spell** command (which is discussed later in the chapter).

Since the master word file is sorted, **look** can search it successfully. You can display all the words that start with a particular pattern by using:

look -df *pattern* **/usr/dict/words**

However, as we mentioned, the **-d** and **-f** options and the file name **/usr/dict/words** are defaults. Thus, you can simplify the command to:

look *pattern*

Using **look** in this way is handy when you are not sure how to spell a word. For example, say that you want to use the word "simultaneous", but you are not sure how to spell it. Enter:

look simu

You will see the list:

```
simulate
simulcast
simultaneity
simultaneous
```

You can now pick the correct word.

☑ **HINT** If you are working with the **vi** text editor (see Chapter 19), you can display words by using **:r!** to issue a quick **look** command. For example:

:r !look simu

will insert all the words that begin with "simu" into your editing buffer. You can now delete all but the word that you want.

Combining Columns of Data: **paste**

The **paste** command combines columns of data. This command has a great deal of flexibility. You can combine several files – each of which has a single column of data – into one large table. You can also combine consecutive lines of data to build multiple columns.

In this section, we will concentrate on the basic feature of **paste**: combining separate files. If you want more details, check the online manual (described in Chapter 8) by using the **man paste** command.

The syntax of the **paste** command is:

paste [**-d** *char*] *file*...

where *char* is a character to be used as a separator, and *file* is the name of an input file.

You use **paste** to combine columns of data into one large table. For example, say that you have four files named **idnumber**, **name**, **birthday** and **phone**. These files contain the following data:

```
idnumber
   012-34-5678
   123-45-6789
   234-56-7890
   345-67-8901
name
   Ambercrombie, Al
   Barton, Barbara
   Canby, Charles
   Danfield, Deann
birthday
   01/01/72
   02/02/73
   03/03/74
   04/04/75
phone
   555-1111
   555-2222
   555-3333
   555-4444
```

You want to build one large file named **info** that combines all this data into a single table. Use:

```
paste idnumber name birthday phone > info
```

If you display the data in **info**, it will look like this:

```
012-34-5678    Ambercrombie, Al    01/01/72    555-1111
123-45-6789    Barton, Barbara     02/02/73    555-2222
234-56-7890    Canby, Charles      03/03/74    555-3333
345-67-8901    Danfield, Deann     04/04/75    555-4444
```

☑ **HINT** Think of **cat** as combining data vertically and **paste** as combining data horizontally.

The reason for the spacing of the output in our last example is that, by default, **paste** puts a tab character between each column entry. As we explained in Chapter 6, Unix assumes that tabs are set every 8 positions, starting with position 1. In other words, Unix assumes that tabs are set at positions 1, 9, 17, 25 and so on.

If you would like **paste** to use a different character between columns, use the **-d** (delimiter) option followed by an alternative character in single quotes. For example, to create the same table with a space between columns, use:

```
paste -d' ' idnumber name birthday phone > info
```

Now your output looks like this:

```
012-34-5678 Ambercrombie, Al 01/01/60 555-1111
123-45-6789 Barton, Barbara  02/02/61 555-2222
234-56-7890 Canby, Charles   03/03/62 555-3333
345-67-8901 Danfield, Deann  04/04/63 555-4444
```

Note: **paste** will allow you to specify more complex delimiters than what we have shown here. For more details, check the online manual (**man paste**).

Using **cut** and **paste** in sequence, you can change the order of columns in a table. For example, say that you have a file named **pizza** with the following columns of data:

```
mushrooms regular sausage
olives    thin    pepperoni
onions    thick   meatball
tomato    pan     liver
```

You want to change the order of the first and second columns.

First, save each column to a separate file:

```
cut -c1-9 pizza > vegetables
cut -c11-17 pizza > crust
cut -c19-27 pizza > meat
```

Now combine the three columns into a single table, specifying the order that you want:

```
paste -d' ' crust vegetables meat > pizza
```

To display this file, use the **more** command (see Chapter 17):

```
more pizza
```

The data now looks like this:

```
regular mushrooms sausage
thin    olives    pepperoni
thick   onions    meatball
pan     tomato    liver
```

Finally, use the **rm** command (see Chapter 22) to remove the three temporary files:

```
rm crust vegetables meat
```

Reversing the Order of Characters: rev

The **rev** command reverses the order of characters in each line of input. The data may come from the standard input or from one or more files. The syntax of the **rev** command is:

```
rev [file...]
```

where *file* is the name of a file.

The output of **rev** is written to the standard output. **rev** does not change the original file.

Here is an example. You have a file named **data** that contains:

```
12345
abcde
AxAxA
```

You enter:

```
rev data
```

The output is:

```
54321
edcba
AxAxA
```

Later in the chapter, we will show you an example of how using **rev** (with command substitution) might save your life.

Sorting and Merging Data: sort, the Ascii Code

The **sort** command performs two main tasks. First, as you would expect, it sorts data. You will find that **sort** is highly useful for sorting files of data and for sorting data within a pipeline. Second, **sort** will read files that contain previously sorted data and merge them into one large, sorted file.

sort has a great deal of flexibility. You can compare entire lines or selected portions of each line (called fields). In this section, we will concentrate on the basic features of **sort**; we will not deal with fields. If you want more details, check the online manual (described in Chapter 8) by using the **man sort** command.

The syntax for using **sort** to sort data is:

```
sort [-dfnru] [-o outfile] [infile...]
```

where *outfile* is the name of a file to hold the output, and *infile* is the name of a file that contains input.

The syntax for using **sort** to merge data is:

```
sort -m [-o outfile] sortedfile...
```

where *outfile* is the name of a file to hold the output, and *sortedfile* is the name of a file that contains sorted data.

The simplest way to use **sort** is to sort a single file and display the results on your screen. Say that you have a file called **names** that contains:

```
Barbara
Al
Deann
Cathy
```

To sort this data and display the results, enter:

```
sort names
```

You will see:

```
Al
Barbara
Cathy
Deann
```

To save the sorted data to a file named **masterfile**, you can redirect the standard output:

```
sort names > masterfile
```

This last example saves the sorted data in a new file. There will be times when you want to save the data in the same file. That is, you will want to replace a file with the same data in sorted order.

Unfortunately, you cannot use a command that redirects the output to the input file:

```
sort names > names
```

As we explained earlier (in the discussion about the **cat** command), when you redirect the standard output, Unix sets up the output file before starting the command. This means that by the time **sort** is ready to read from **names**, it will be empty. Thus, the result of your entering this command would be to wipe out all your data.

sort provides a special option just for this situation. You can use **-o** (output) followed by the name of the file you want to use for output. If the output file is the same as one of your input files, **sort** will make sure to protect your data.

Thus, to sort a file and save the output in the same file, use a command like:

```
sort -o names names
```

In this case, the original data in **names** will be replaced by the sorted data.

If you need to sort the combined data from more than one file, just specify more than one file name. For example, to sort the data from the files **names**, **oldnames** and **extranames**, and save the output in the file **masterfile**, use:

```
sort names oldnames extranames > masterfile
```

To sort the same files but save the output in **names** (one of the input files), use:

```
sort -o names names oldnames extranames
```

The **sort** command is often used as part of a pipeline to process data that has been produced by another program. The following example combines two files, extracts only those lines that contain the characters "Harley", sorts those lines, and then sends the results to be printed.

```
cat newnames oldnames | grep Harley | sort | lpr
```

By default, data is sorted in ascending order according to a specification called the ASCII CODE. The ASCII code is a description of the entire set of 128 different characters that was adopted by Unix. This set includes lower-case letters, uppercase letters, numerals, punctuation and miscellaneous symbols. It also contains the space, the tab, and the control characters (which, as we described in Chapter 6, are used for special purposes). For reference, we have included a copy of the ASCII code in Appendix D.

What is important here is that the ASCII code is like our regular alphabet in that the characters are in a certain order, and it is this order that **sort** uses for comparisons.

The order of characters in the ASCII code is as follows:

- control characters (including the tab)
- the space character
- (symbols) **! " # $ % & ' ( ) * + , - . /**
- (the numerals) **0 1 2 3 4 5 6 7 8 9**
- (more symbols) **: ; < = > ? @**
- (uppercase letters) **A B C ... Z**
- (more symbols) **[\ ] ^ _ `**
- (lowercase letters) **a b c ... z**
- (more symbols) **{ | } ~**

☑ **HINT** As a rule of thumb, all you need to remember about the ASCII code is: space, numerals, uppercase letters, lowercase letters, in that order. Think of "SNUL".

Thus, if you use **sort** to sort the following data (in which the third line starts with a space):

```
hello
Hello
 hello
1hello
:hello
```

The output will be:

```
 hello
1hello
:hello
Hello
hello
```

The **sort** command has several options that you can use to affect the sorting order:

The **-d** (dictionary) option considers only letters, numerals and spaces, and ignores other characters.

The **-f** (fold) option treats uppercase letters as if they were lowercase.

The **-n** (numeric) option will recognize numbers at the beginning of a line and sort them numerically. Such numbers may include leading spaces, negative signs and decimal points.

The **-r** (reverse) option sorts the data in reverse order.

Finally, the **-u** (unique) option will look for identical lines and suppress all but one. For example, if you use the command:

```
sort -u
```

to sort the following data:

```
Barbara
Al
Barbara
Barbara
Deann
```

the output will be:

```
Al
Barbara
Deann
```

Aside from sorting data, **sort** will also merge multiple files that contain sorted data. To use **sort** in this way, specify the **-m** (merge) option.

For example, say that you have three files, **names**, **oldnames** and **extranames**, that contain the following data:

names	*oldnames*	*extranames*
Al	Barbara	Deann
Barbara	Cathy	Fred
Edward	Edward	

The following command will merge all the data into a single file named **masterfile**:

```
sort -m names oldnames extranames > masterfile
```

If you want to merge the three files, and save the output to **names** (replacing the original data), use the **-o** (output):

```
sort -m -o names names oldnames extranames
```

Check Data for Spelling Errors: `spell`

The **spell** command will read data and generate a list of all the words that look as if they are misspelled. This command has a number of esoteric options and capabilities. In this section, we will cover only the basic functions. For more details, check the online manual (see Chapter 8) by using the **man spell** command.

The syntax of the **spell** command is:

spell [**-b**] [*file...*]

where *file* is the name of an input file.

Using **spell** is straightforward. For example, say that you have a file named **document**. To display a list of misspelled words, one word per line, use:

spell document

Each word is listed only once, even if it appears in several places.

To count the number of different misspelled words, pipe the data to the **wc** filter (discussed later in the chapter) using the **-l** (line count) option:

spell document | wc -l

Aside from specifying an input file, you can pipe data to **spell**. For example, to look for spelling mistakes in the **spell** manual page, enter:

man spell | spell

By default, **spell** uses American spelling. If you would like **spell** to use British/Canadian spelling, use the **-b** option. For example, the word "colour" will be used instead of "color".

The **spell** command is actually one of a family of programs that uses a master file of sorted words to provide a spell-checking service. This file is **/usr/dict/words**. You can look at all the words by entering:

more /usr/dict/words

(The **more** program displays one screenful of data at a time. See Chapter 17. When you use **more**, press the <Space> bar to display the next screenful; press the **q** key to quit.)

Since the master word file is sorted, you can search it with the **look** command. (See the description of **look** for more details.)

Translate or Delete Selected Characters: **tr**

The **tr** (translate) command will read data and replace specified characters with other characters. It will also delete specified characters. For example, you might change all uppercase letters to lowercase. Or you might delete all the left and right parentheses.

The syntax of the **tr** command is:

tr [**-cds**] [*set1* [*set2*]]

where *set1* and *set2* are sets of characters.

The idea is that `tr` reads data from the standard input and looks for any characters from *set1*. Whenever `tr` finds such a character, it replaces the character with the corresponding character from *set2*.

For example, say that you have stored information in a file named **olddata**. You want to replace all the **a** characters with **A** and store the translated output in a file named **newdata**. Use the command:

```
tr a A < olddata > newdata
```

By defining longer sets of characters, you can replace more than one different character. The following command looks for and makes three different replacements: **a** is replaced by **A**, **b** is replaced by **B**, and **c** is replaced by **C**:

```
tr abc ABC < olddata > newdata
```

If the second set of characters is shorter than the first, the last character in the second set is duplicated. Thus, the following two commands are equivalent:

```
tr abcde Az < olddata > newdata
tr abcde Azzzz < olddata > newdata
```

They both replace **a** with **A**, and the other four characters with **z**.

If you want to specify characters that have a special meaning to the shell, you must place these characters within single quotes. This tells the shell to treat these characters literally. For example, say that you want to change all the colons, semicolons and question marks to periods. Use:

```
tr ':;?' '.' < olddata > newdata
```

When you specify a set of characters, you can define a range by using a hyphen. For example, you can use **a-z** to stand for all the lowercase letters, from "a" to "z". Thus, the following command will change all uppercase letters to lowercase:

```
tr A-Z a-z < olddata > newdata
```

If you want to use a character that cannot be typed easily, you can look it up in the ASCII code and use its three-digit numeric value. (We discussed the ASCII code in the section describing the **sort** command.)

Each character within the ASCII code corresponds to a three-digit number. This number is actually the position within the code, expressed as an octal value (base 8). If this doesn't mean anything to you, just use the number and forget about it. Base 8 is not all that important.

To use such a value, simply type a \ backslash, followed by the three digits. Place the entire expression within single quotes. Here is a list of the few values that you are likely to need:

Name	Octal Value
backspace	010
tab	011
newline	012

(The **newline** character marks the end of each line. See Chapter 6 for details.)

Thus, to translate all the tabs in a file to spaces, use:

```
tr '\011' ' ' < olddata > newdata
```

The **tr** command has three options that let you affect the processing of data. The **-d** option deletes all the characters that you specify. When you use **-d**, you only define one set of characters. For example, to delete all the left and right parentheses, use:

```
tr -d '()' < olddata > newdata
```

The **-s** (squeeze) option changes all repeated characters that match the specified set into a single such character. For example, the following command replaces any occurrence of more than one consecutive space by a single space.

```
tr -s ' ' ' ' < olddata > newdata
```

What we are doing is replacing one space by another space, while squeezing out repeated characters.

Finally, the **-c** option tells **tr** to match all the characters that are not in the first set. For example, to replace all the characters that are not upper- or lowercase letters with a period, use:

```
tr -c A-Za-z '.' < olddata > newdata
```

The **-c** stands for "complement". In mathematics, the complement of a set is all the elements that are not part of the set. (Notice that you do not put a comma or a space between **A-Z** and **a-z**, as they define one single set of characters.)

Here is an interesting example that combines two options and shows the power of **tr**. You have two files named **document** and **essay**. You want to know how many different words are used in the files.

The best plan is to use a pipeline. First, use **cat** to combine the two files.

Next, use **tr** to place each word on a separate line by replacing each non-alphabetic character with a **newline**. Use the **-c** option to define all characters that are not upper- or lowercase letters, and the **-s** option to squeeze out all such repeated characters. Finally, use numeric code 012 to stand for **newline**. The **tr** command is:

```
tr -cs A-Za-z '\012'
```

Now, after isolating each word on its own line, use the **sort** filter with the **-u** (unique) option to sort the data and eliminate the repeated lines.

Finally, use the **wc** filter with the **-1** (line) option to count the number of lines. (The **wc** command is explained later in the chapter.)

The completed pipeline looks like this:

```
cat document essay | tr -cs A-Za-z '\012' | sort -u | wc -1
```

Thus, you have a single Unix command line that will tell you how many different words are contained in a collection of input files.

Look for Repeated Lines: `uniq`

The **uniq** command will examine data, line by line, looking for consecutive, duplicate lines. **uniq** can perform four different tasks: retain only duplicate lines, retain only unique lines, eliminate duplicate lines, or count how many times lines are duplicated.

In making its comparisons, **uniq** can work with parts of each line rather the entire line. However, in this section we deal with whole line comparisons only. If you want more details, check the online manual (described in Chapter 8) by using the **man uniq** command.

The syntax of the **uniq** command is:

```
uniq [-cdu] [infile [outfile]]
```

where *infile* is the name of an input file, and *outfile* is the name of an output file.

The **-d** option will retain one copy of all lines that are duplicated. Remember, though, the duplicate lines must be consecutive. For example, say that the file **data** contains:

```
Barbara
Al
Al
Cathy
Barbara
```

The command:

```
uniq -d data
```

produces:

```
Al
```

The **-u** (unique) option retains only those lines that are not duplicated. For example, the command:

```
uniq -u data
```

produces:

```
Barbara
Cathy
Barbara
```

With no options, **uniq** behaves as if both **-d** and **-u** are specified. This effectively eliminates all duplicate lines. Thus, the command:

```
uniq data
```

produces:

```
Barbara
Al
Cathy
Barbara
```

Finally, the **-c** option counts how many times each line is found. The command:

```
uniq -c data
```

produces:

```
1 Barbara
2 Al
1 Cathy
1 Barbara
```

So far, we have used simple examples. The real power of **uniq** is when you use it with sorted data in a pipeline. When data is sorted, it guarantees that all duplicate lines will be consecutive.

For example, say that you have two files that contain the names of students enrolled in two different courses, **math100** and **math150**. To show which students are taking both courses, use:

```
sort math100 math150 | uniq -d
```

To show which students are taking one course only, use:

```
sort math100 math150 | uniq -u
```

To show all the students, with no duplications, use:

```
sort math100 math150 | uniq
```

(You could also use **sort -u math100 math150**.)

Finally, to list each student, showing how many courses he or she is taking, use:

```
sort math100 math150 | uniq -c
```

Counting Lines, Words and Characters: wc

The **wc** (word count) command counts lines, words and characters. The data may come from the standard input or from one or more files. The syntax of the **wc** command is:

```
wc [-lwc] [file...]
```

where *file* is the name of a file.

This command is straightforward. Its output is three numbers: the number of lines, words and characters in the data. If you specify the name of a file, **wc** will write the name after the three numbers. If you specify more than one file, **wc** will also give you total statistics.

Note: **wc** considers a "word" to be an unbroken sequence of characters, delimited by spaces, tabs or **newline** characters. (The **newline** character marks the end of a line; see Chapter 6.)

Here is an example. You have a file named **poem** that contains the following:

There was a young man from Nantucket,
Whose girlfriend had told him to

The command:

wc poem

displays the following output:

```
   2        13        71 poem
```

In this case your file has 2 lines, 13 words and 71 characters. If you forget which number is which, just remember that there will usually be more words than lines, and more characters than words.

When **wc** counts characters, it also includes characters that are usually hidden from you, such as the **newline** at the end of each line. (The **newline** character is explained in Chapter 6.)

If you specify more than one file at a time, you will also see total statistics. For example:

wc poem message story

might write output like this:

```
   2        13        71 poem
   1         4        17 message
  31       178      1200 story
  34       195      1288 total
```

If you do not want all three numbers, you can use the options: **-l** counts lines, **-w** counts words, and **-c** counts characters. For example, to see how many lines are in the file named **story**, use:

wc -l story

To see how many words and characters are in the file named **message**, use:

wc -wc message

There are two important uses for **wc**. First, there are times when you need a quick measure of the size of a file. For example, say that you send a file to someone over a network. The file is important, and you want to double-check that it arrived intact. Run the **wc** command on the original file. Then tell the recipient to run **wc** on the other file. If the two sets of results do not match, you know that some data was lost (or that some spurious data was included).

The second use for **wc** is far more important. You can pipe the output of another command to **wc** and check how many lines were generated. Many commands will generate one item of information per line. By counting the lines, you know how much information was generated. Here are two examples.

The **ls** command (see Chapter 21) lists the names of files in a directory. If you enter:

```
ls /etc
```

you will see the names of all the files in the **/etc** directory. (Directories are explained in Chapter 21).

The **ls** command has many options. However, there is no option for counting the number of files. To do so, simply pipe the output of **ls** to **wc**. Thus, to count the number of files in the **/etc** directory, enter:

```
ls /etc | wc -l
```

This example demonstrates an important principle: When you learn about **ls**, you will see that, normally, it displays its output in columns, with more than one name per line. However, when **ls** knows that its output is going to a file or pipeline, it will write only one name per line.

In other words, when **ls** thinks that you might want to process the data further, it will be cooperative and write its data in a form that is easy to process.

✅ **HINT** Many Unix commands (especially filters) generate output in which each piece of information is on a separate line. This makes it convenient to pipe the data to another program.

Here is one final example. In Chapter 12, we showed how to use the **who** command to find out which userids are logged in to your system. We can use the pipeline:

```
who | wc -l
```

to count the number of userids that are currently logged in.

Command Substitution: tset

Command substitution allows you to use the output of one command as part of another command.

In order to show an example, we would first like to introduce the **echo** command. This command simply displays the values of its parameters. For example, if you enter:

echo Hello there

you will see:

Hello there

The **echo** command is usually used within a shell script (a program written in the shell's programming language).

Now, to use command substitution, you place part of a command within ` (backquote) characters. The shell will evaluate the part within backquotes as a command on its own. Then the shell will substitute the output of this command into the larger command.

Here is an example. If you enter:

echo The time is date.

you see:

The time is date.

If you enter:

echo The time is `date`.

you will see something like this:

The time is Sun Sep 6 23:32:39 PDT 1992.

The shell has executed the **date** command, substituted its output into the **echo** command, and then executed the newly constituted **echo** command.

In Chapter 21, we will explain how the **pwd** command displays the name of your working directory. Try the following example:

echo My working directory is `pwd`.

Be sure not to confuse the backquote with the single quote.

There is one common situation in which you might use command substitution. As we explained in Chapter 11, your **.login** file contains commands that are to be executed each time you log in. One of these commands should use **setenv** to set the global variable **TERM** to the type of terminal you are using. For example:

setenv TERM vt100

You can use command substitution to help you set this variable correctly.

There is a command named **tset** (terminal setup) that can be used to help choose the type of terminal you are using and to initialize the terminal.

Using **tset** is complicated and the details are beyond the scope of this book. However, the following is a typical example.

Say that most of the time you use a terminal at school that is directly connected to the Unix host computer. However, you sometimes use your personal computer at home to emulate a VT-100 terminal and connect over the telephone line. (These concepts are explained in Chapter 3.)

The following **tset** command writes the name of the appropriate terminal to the standard output:

```
tset - -m:dialup:vt100
```

In your **.login** file, you can use the command:

```
setenv TERM `tset - -m:dialup:vt100`
```

to set the value of **TERM** to the output of the **tset** command. Thus, **TERM** will be set correctly no matter which terminal you happen to use to log in.

A Real-life Example of Command Substitution

Here is an example of how using the **rev** filter with command substitution might save your life.

You are an international spy and you need to send a secret message. You want to use **crypt** to encode the message and save it as a file. You can leave the file for your partner to decode and read.

Unfortunately, the system manager for your computer is a spy for a rival country. You know that he can easily access the file with the encoded message. However, unless he knows the key you used with **crypt**, he will not be able to decode the message. So he arranges that one of his grad students should accidentally walk by your terminal just as you are typing the key.

For good luck, you decide to use a key of "harley". Normally, you would enter the command:

```
crypt > message
```

and let **crypt** prompt you for the key. After you enter **harley**, you would enter your message. Once you press **^D** (the **eof** key), **crypt** would encode the message and save it in a file named **message**.

However, without letting anyone see, you actually enter the command:

```
crypt `rev` > message
```

At this point, the grad student (who knows you are about to enter the key) watches your fingers as you type. You enter:

```
harley
```

The grad student hurries away to report to the system manager. What he doesn't know is that **rev** has effectively reversed the key to **yelrah**.

Meanwhile, you press **^D** (to end the **rev** command) and enter your message:

```
Secret meeting tonight. Midnight, at abandoned warehouse.
The system manager is a spy.  Take care.
```

Again, you press **^D**, this time to end the message.

You now have an encoded file named **message** which you can leave for your partner. He enters the command:

```
crypt < message
```

and, using the key **yelrah**, decodes your message.

The system manager, on the other hand, sneaks a copy of your file, but works in vain for hours, trying to decode it with a key of **harley**.

Regular Expressions

A REGULAR EXPRESSION is a compact way of specifying a general pattern of characters. There are many places in Unix where you can use a regular expression instead of an exact pattern. For example, you might want to use **grep** to search for all the lines in a file that contain the letter "H", followed by any number of lowercase letters, followed by the letter "y".

You can use regular expressions with many commands, including the text editors (such as **vi**, Chapter 19), and the paging programs (such as **more**, Chapter 17).

Unfortunately, the details of what regular expressions are acceptable may vary slightly from program to program. For example, the **egrep** (extended **grep**) program will recognize more complex regular expressions than will **grep**.

However, regular expressions are an integral part of Unix and you *must* learn how to use them. In this section, we will discuss the regular expressions that you can use with **grep**. The rules you learn in this section are typical of regular expressions in general. Remember these rules, and you will need to learn only a few variations as the need arises.

The name "regular expression" comes from Computer Science and refers to a set of rules for specifying patterns. Within a regular expression, certain symbols have special meanings. These symbols are summarized in Figure 16-2.

Here are some examples that will show you how this all works. Each of these examples uses the **grep** command to search a file named **data**.

First, within a regular expression, any character that does not have a special meaning stands for itself. For example, to search for lines that contain "Harley", use:

```
grep Harley data
```

(This is nothing new.)

Symbol	Meaning
.	match any single character except **newline**
*	match zero or more of the preceding characters
^	match the beginning of a line
$	match the end of a line
\<	match the beginning of a word
\>	match the end of a word
[ ]	match one of the enclosed characters
[^]	match any character that is not enclosed
\	take the following symbol literally

Figure 16-2

Summary of Symbols Used in Regular Expressions

To indicate that you want to match only patterns at the beginning of a line, use ^ (the circumflex). For example, to search for lines that start with "Harley", use:

```
grep '^Harley' data
```

Notice that we placed the pattern within single quotes. Be sure to do this whenever you use special characters. Otherwise, some of them may be interpreted incorrectly by the shell. Using the single quotes tells the shell to leave these characters alone and pass them on to the program (in this case, **grep**).

The $ (dollar sign) indicates that you want to match patterns at the end of a line. For example, to search for lines that end with "Harley", use:

```
grep 'Harley$' data
```

You can combine ^ and $ in the same regular expression as long as what you are doing makes sense. For example, to search for all the lines that contain only "Harley", use:

```
grep '^Harley$' data
```

Another way of thinking about this is that you are telling **grep** to search for all lines that consist entirely of "Harley".

You can also specify that a pattern must occur at the beginning or at the end of a word. You indicate the beginning of a word by using \<. For example, to find the pattern "kn", but only if it occurs at the beginning of a word, use:

```
grep '\<kn' data
```

To find the pattern "ow", but only at the end of a word, use:

```
grep 'ow\>' data
```

To search for complete words, use both \< and \>. For example, to search for "know", but only as a complete word, use:

`grep '\<know\>' data`

This would find the line:

`I know who you are, and I saw what you did.`

but not the line:

`Who knows what evil lurks in the minds of men?`

Using **grep** with \< and \> gives the same results as the **-w** (word) option. (See the section on **grep**.)

The . (period) symbol will match any single character except **newline**. (As we explained in Chapter 6, the **newline** character marks the end of a line.) For example, to search for all lines that contain the letters "Har" followed by any two characters, followed by the letter "y", use:

`grep 'Har..y' data`

This command will find lines that contain patterns like:

`Harley    Harxxy    Harlly`

To match a character from a set, you can enclose the set in square brackets. For example, to search for all lines that contain the letter "H", followed by either of the letters "a" or "A", use:

`grep 'H[aA]' data`

If you want to specify a range of characters, use a hyphen to separate the beginning and end of the range. For example, to search for all the lines that contain the letter "H", followed by any single lowercase letter (from "a" through "z"), use:

`grep 'H[a-z]' data`

When you specify a range, the order must be the same as in the ASCII code (discussed earlier in this chapter).

You can use more than one range of characters in the same pattern. For example, to search for all the lines that contain the letter "H", followed by any single lowercase or uppercase letter, use:

`grep 'H[A-Za-z]' data`

Remember, a range stands for only one character. Thus, the previous regular expression stands for two characters.

You can use the * (asterisk) to match multiple characters. The * symbol stands for zero or more occurrences of the preceding character. (We discussed the idea of "zero or more" in Chapter 9.) For example, to search for all the lines that contain the letter "H", followed by zero or more lowercase letters, use:

`grep 'H[a-z]*' data`

This command will find patterns like:

H   Harley   Halloween   Hint   Hundred

Sometimes, you may want to search for one or more occurrences of a character. Simply specify the character, followed by zero or more occurrences of that character. For example, to search for all the lines that contain the letter "H", followed by one or more lowercase characters, use:

```
grep 'H[a-z][a-z]*' data
```

Literally, you are asking for the letter "H", followed by a single lowercase character, followed by zero or more lowercase characters.

It is often convenient to combine the . (period) with the * (asterisk). For example, to search for all the lines that contain a colon, followed by zero or more occurrences of any other characters, followed by another colon, use:

```
grep ':.*:' data
```

The final rule you need to remember is that if you want to include one of the special symbols as part of a regular expression, precede it by a backslash. This indicates that the following symbol is to be taken literally. For example, to search for all the lines that contain a dollar sign, use:

```
grep '\$' data
```

If you want to search for a backslash character itself, use two of them. For example, to find all the lines that contain the characters *****, followed by any characters, followed by **$**, use:

```
grep '\\\*.*\$' data
```

We can break this down as follows:

\\	a single backslash
*	a single asterisk
.*	any number of other characters
\$	a single dollar sign

Next, here are two examples that search the file **/usr/dict/words**. This file contains the master word list used by the **spell** program (discussed earlier in the chapter).

The first example finds all words that begin with "qu" and end with "y":

```
grep '^qu[a-z]*y$' /usr/dict/words
```

The second example solves an old riddle: Can you name an English word that contains the letters "a", "e", "i", "o" and "u", in that order? The letters do not have to be adjacent, but they must be in order.

To solve this problem, we must search for the letter "a", followed by zero or more other letters, followed by "e", followed by zero or more other letters, and so on. The full command is:

```
grep 'a[a-z]*e[a-z]*i[a-z]*o[a-z]*u' /usr/dict/words
```

To avoid suspense, we will tell you that this command found three such words:

```
adventitious
facetious
sacrilegious
```

Finally, here is a command to search the Unix system itself for historical artifacts. In the olden days, many Unix commands were two letters long. The text editor was **ed**, the copy program was **cp**, and so on. Let us find all such commands.

The older Unix programs are contained in the **/bin** directory. To list all the files in this directory, we can use the command:

```
ls /bin
```

(The **ls** command is discussed in Chapter 21.)

To analyze the output of **ls**, we can pipe it to the **grep** filter. **ls** will automatically place each name on a separate line because the output is going to a filter. With **grep**, we can search for lines that consist of only two lowercase letters. The full pipeline is:

```
ls /bin | grep '^[a-z][a-z]$'
```

This will display all the basic Unix commands whose names consist of only two characters. If you want to see how many such commands there are, use **grep** with the **-c** (count) option:

```
ls /bin | grep -c '^[a-z][a-z]$'
```

WHAT'S IN A NAME?

grep

The name **grep** is a strange one. It is actually an acronym for the expression "global regular expression print".

- "global" reminds us that **grep** searches all of the input data
- "print" is traditionally used in Unix to mean "display"

Thus, the name tells us that this command will search all of its input for a regular expression, and then display the results.

Within the old **ed** text editor, the command to perform such a search was **g/**, followed by the regular expression, followed by **/p**. In other words, the **ed** command was:

g/_re_**/p**

where _re_ stands for a regular expression. It is this serendipitous abbreviation that first suggested the name **grep**.

It is the custom among Unix people to use the word "grep" as a verb. Thus, you might say to someone, "If you want to find all the words that end with a particular pattern, you can grep the **/usr/dict/words** file."

Displaying Files

With all the time we spend using the computer, it is interesting to realize that the main product of all our effort is some type of output, either displayed on our screen or printed on paper. Unix has a number of important commands that you can use to control the displaying and printing of data.

In this chapter, we will discuss the commands that provide the service of displaying data in a manageable fashion. We will start by showing you how to display the beginning or end of a file. Next, we discuss the commands that let you page though an entire file, one screenful at a time.

In Chapter 18, we will complement what we cover in this chapter by showing you how to print files.

Note: When we refer to "files", we assume the intuitive idea that a file has a name and contains information. For example, you might have a file named **memo** that contains the text of a memorandum. In Chapter 20, we will discuss the Unix file system in detail, at which time we will give a strict definition for a file.

Displaying the Beginning of a File: head

To display the beginning of a file, use the **head** command. The syntax is:

```
head [-count] [file...]
```

where `count` is the number of lines you want to display, and `file` is the name of a file.

By default, **head** will display the first 10 lines of a file. This is useful when you want to get a quick look at a file to check its contents. For example, to display the first 10 lines of a file named **memo**, use:

```
head memo
```

If you want to display a different number of lines, specify that number as an option. For example, to display the first 20 lines of the same file, use:

`head -20 memo`

The **head** command is useful at the end of a pipeline. Here is an example that combines three operations. The **cat** command combines the two specified files. The **grep** command extracts all the lines that contain the specified pattern. The **sort** command sorts the result.

`cat newnames oldnames | grep Harley | sort`

If you enter this command line, you will see the entire output of the **sort** command. If you only want to see the first five lines, pipe the output to the **head** command:

`cat newnames oldnames | grep Harley | sort | head -5`

(Pipelines are discussed in Chapter 15. The **cat**, **grep** and **sort** commands are discussed in Chapter 16.)

Displaying the End of a File: `tail`

To display the end of a file, use the **tail** command. There are two forms of this command:

`tail [+`*startfr*`] [`*file*`]`
`tail [-`*startfr*`] [`*file*`]`

where *start* is the line number at which you want to start, and *file* is the name of a file.

By default, **tail** will display the last 10 lines of a file. For example, to display the last 10 lines of a file named **memo**, use:

`tail memo`

To start displaying at a particular line, you can use either **+** or **-**, followed by a number. If you use **+**, **tail** counts from the beginning of the file. If you use **-**, **tail** counts from the end of the file.

For example, to display the last 20 lines of the file, use:

`tail -20 memo`

To display from line 35 to the end of the file, use:

`tail +35 memo.`

(As you can see, **tail** is one of the few Unix commands that has an option that does not start with a - character.)

Like the **head** command, **tail** is useful at the end of a pipeline. For example:

`cat newnames oldnames | grep Harley | sort | tail -5`

This **tail** command displays the last 5 lines of output from **sort**.

The **-r** option displays the output in reverse order. By default, **-r** displays all the lines in the file, not just 10 lines. For example, to display the entire file named **memo** in reverse order, use:

```
tail -r memo
```

To display the last 10 lines of the file, in reverse order, use:

```
tail -10r memo
```

To display from line 35 to the end of the file, in reverse order, use:

```
tail +35r memo
```

 HINT   To reverse the order of all the lines in a file, use **tail -r**.

The final option, **-f**, is useful when you are waiting for data to be written to a file. This option tells **tail** not to quit when it reaches the end of the file. Rather, **tail** will wait and display more output as the file grows.

For example, say that over the next few minutes, a particular program will be adding output to the end of a file named **results**. You want to follow the progress of this program. Enter:

```
tail -f results
```

tail will start by displaying the last 10 lines of the file. As new lines are added, **tail** will display them as well. When you get tired of watching, you stop the command by pressing **^C** (the **intr** key, see Chapter 6). The command will not stop by itself.

The Paging Programs

In the next few sections, we will discuss three programs that you can use to display a file. They are named **more**, **pg** and **less**.

The distinguishing feature of these programs is that they display an entire file, one screenful at a time. These programs are sometimes called PAGING PROGRAMS, or PAGERS, because you can page through a file at your own speed. As you read, there are a multitude of commands to use. For example, you can enter a command to search for a particular pattern.

WHAT'S IN A NAME?

`pg`, `more`, `less`

The three paging programs have strange names. Here is how they originated:

`pg`: An abbreviation for "pager".

`more`: After displaying a screenful of data, this program displays the prompt `--More--`, to show that there is more to come. The program is named after this prompt.

`less`: This program was developed as a replacement for `more` and `pg`. The name `less` was chosen as a funny name that insiders with a sense of irony would understand. Although the name is `less`, the program actually offers a lot more than `more`.

All three of the paging programs have a variety of options and many internal commands that you can use as you are displaying a file. It may take a while to learn all the nuances.

Generally speaking, you only need to learn the details of one paging program. However, you do need at least a passing acquaintance with both `more` and `pg`. The reason is that both these programs are standards and are used as defaults under various circumstances.

For example, when you use the `man` command to display a page from the online Unix manual (see Chapter 8), the output is piped to a paging program to be displayed. On most systems, this program will be either `more` or `pg` and, on some systems, you may not have a choice. So you need to know the basics of both programs because you never know which one you will run into, especially if you use more than one Unix system.

The basics, however, are not much. You just need to understand how to move from one screenful to the next, how to search for a pattern, and how to stop the program. Ten minutes of practice should do it.

☑ **HINT**   Pick one of the paging programs - `more`, `pg` or `less` - and learn it well.

The `less` program has an important advantage in that it allows you to move backward and forward through a file easily. With the other programs, it is more awkward to move backward.

If you are not sure which pager to choose, use `more`.

Whichever pager you choose, you should learn the basics of both `more` and `pg`.

Should You Use `cat` to Display Files?

Aside from the paging programs, the **cat** command will also display a file. Why? The job of **cat** is to combine files and write the result to standard output. By default, the standard output is the screen of your terminal. Thus, a command like:

`cat memo`

will write the contents of **memo** to your screen. (Standard output is explained in Chapter 15. **cat** is explained in Chapter 16.)

The problem is that, much of the time, the files you display will be longer than the size of your screen. With **cat**, all the output is written without interruption. Unless the file is a short one, most of the output will scroll by so fast that you won't be able to read it.

The best idea is to pick one pager - either **more**, **pg** or **less** - as your favorite. Get in the habit of using that program when you need to display a file. Even when the file is short enough to fit completely on the screen, there is no real advantage to using **cat**.

 HINT   Using the **cat** program to display files is a bad habit. Instead, pick one of **more**, **pg** or **less** to use exclusively.

Displaying a File Using `more`

The **more** program is a pager that you can use to display data one screenful at a time. The syntax is:

`more [-cs] [+`*startline*`] [+/`*pattern*`] [`*file...*`]`

where:

> *startline*: number of the line at which you want to start
> *pattern*: an initial pattern to search for
> *file*: the name of a file

In this section, we will describe the basic options and features of the **more** program. For more information, look at the manual page by using **man more**. (The online Unix manual is described in Chapter 8.)

The **more** program displays the contents of the files you specify. The data is displayed one screenful at a time. After each screen is written, you will see a prompt at the bottom left corner of the screen. The prompt looks like this:

`--More--(40%)`

(You can see where the name **more** comes from.)

At the end of the prompt is a number in parentheses. This shows you how much of the data has been displayed. In our example, the prompt shows that you are 40% of the way through the file.

The simplest way to use **more** is to specify a single file name. For example:

```
more memo
```

If the data fits on a single screen, it will be displayed all at once. Otherwise, the data will be displayed one screenful at a time, with the prompt at the bottom.

Once you see the prompt, you can enter a command. The most common command is simply to press the <Space> bar. This will page to the next screen. You can press <Space> repeatedly to page through the entire file. After displaying the last screenful of data, **more** will stop automatically.

One of the most common uses of **more** is to display the output of a pipeline, one screenful at a time. Here are two examples:

```
cat newnames oldnames | grep Harley | sort | more
ls -l | more
```

(Pipelines are explained in Chapter 15. Filters, the programs that are used within a pipeline, are explained in Chapter 16.)

When you use **more** in a pipeline, the prompt will not show the percentage:

```
--More--
```

This is because **more** displays the data as it arrives and has no idea how much there will be.

When **more** pauses, there are many commands that you can use. For most commands, you do not have to press <Return>, just type the name. The most important command is **h** (help). This will display a summary of all the possible commands.

Figure 17-1 contains a summary of the most useful **more** commands. The best way to learn about **more** is to type the **h** command, see what is available, and experiment.

When you use the **/** command to search for a pattern, you can use the same type of regular expression that we described at the end of Chapter 16. When **more** finds the pattern you want, it will display two lines before that location so you can see the line in context.

There are a number of options that you can use when you start **more**. The two most useful are **-s** and **-c**. The **-s** (squeeze) option replaces multiple blank lines with a single blank line. This is useful for condensing output in which multiple blank lines are not meaningful. Of course, this does not affect the original file.

The **-c** (clear) option tells **more** to display each new screenful of data from the top down. Each line is cleared before it is replaced. Without **-c**, new lines scroll up from the bottom line of the screen. Some people find that long files are easier to read with **-c**. You will have to try it for yourself.

Basic Commands

Command	Description
h	display help information
\<Space\>	display the next screenful
q	quit the program

More Advanced Commands

Command	Description
\<Return\>	go forward one line
n\<Return\>	go forward *n* lines
d	go forward (down) a half screenful
*n*f	go forward *n* screenfuls
b	go backward one screenful
*n*b	go backward *n* screenfuls
v	start the **vi** editor using file you are displaying
/*pattern*	search forward for the specified pattern
n	repeat the previous search command
!*command*	execute the specified shell command
=	display the current line number
.	repeat the previous command

Do not press \<Return\> after a command except with **/** and **!**.

Figure 17-1
Summary of the Most Useful **more** *Commands*

Two other options allow you to control the line at which **more** starts to display data. You can use a **+** (plus sign) followed by a number to tell **more** to start at that line number. For example, to display the contents of the file **memo** starting at line 37, use:

```
more +37 memo
```

Second, you can use **+/** (plus, slash) followed by a pattern, and **more** will search for that pattern before it starts displaying data. For example, to display the same file, starting with a search for the word **Harley**, use:

```
more +/Harley memo
```

Note: You cannot use both the **+** and **+/** options at the same time.

☑ **HINT** If you are used to using **pg**, there are two basic differences with **more**:

1. You do not press <Return> after each command.
2. You press <Space>, not <Return>, to display the next screenful of data.

Displaying a File Using pg

The **pg** program is a pager that you can use to display data one screenful at a time. The syntax is:

pg [**-cn**] [**+***startline*] [**+/***pattern*] [*file...*]

where:

startline: number of the line at which you want to start
pattern: an initial pattern to search for
file: the name of a file

In this section, we will describe the basic options and features of the **pg** program. For more information, look at the manual page by using **man pg**. (The online Unix manual is described in Chapter 8.)

The **pg** program displays the contents of the files you specify. The data is displayed one screenful at a time. After each screen is written, you will see a prompt at the bottom left corner of the screen. The prompt will be a colon:

:

The simplest way to use **pg** is to specify a single file name. For example:

pg memo

If the data fits on a single screen, it will be displayed all at once. Otherwise, the data will be displayed one screenful at a time, with the prompt at the bottom.

Once you see the prompt, you can enter a command. The most common command is simply to press <Return>. This will page to the next screen. You can press <Return> repeatedly to page through the entire file.

After displaying the last screenful of data, **pg** will not stop automatically. You will see the following prompt (which stands for "End of File"):

(EOF):

To quit, press <Return>.

One of the most common uses of **pg** is to display the output of a pipeline, one screenful at a time. Here are two examples:

cat newnames oldnames | grep Harley | sort | pg
ls -l | pg

(Pipelines are explained in Chapter 15. Filters, the programs that are used within a pipeline, are explained in Chapter 16.)

When **pg** pauses, there are many commands that you can use. After each command, you must press <Return> (unless you use the **-n** option which we will discuss below). The most important command is **h** (help). This will display a summary of all the possible commands.

Figure 17-2 contains a summary of the most useful **pg** commands. The best way to learn about **pg** is to enter the **h** command, see what is available, and experiment.

When you use the **/** or **?** commands to search for a pattern, you can use the same type of regular expressions that we described at the end of Chapter 16.

There are a number of options that you can use when you start **pg**. The two most useful are **-n** and **-c**. The **-n** (newline) option tells **pg** to execute the single letter commands without your having to press <Return> (just like the **more** program).

Basic Commands

Command	Description
h	display help information
<Return>	display the next screenful
q	quit the program

More Advanced Commands

Command	Description
*n***l**	go to line *n*
l	go to the next line
+*n***l**	go forward *n* lines
−*n***l**	go backward *n* lines
d	go forward (down) a half screenful
-d	go backward (up) a half screenful
1	go to the first line
$	go to the last line
/*pattern*	search forward for the specified pattern
?*pattern*	search backward for the specified pattern
!*command*	execute the specified shell command

You must press <Return> to enter a command unless you start **pg** with the **-n** option.

Figure 17-2

Summary of the Most Useful **pg** *Commands*

The `-c` (clear) option tells **more** to display each new screenful of data from the top down. Before new data is written, the entire screen is cleared. Without `-c`, new lines scroll up from the bottom line of the screen. Some people find that long files are easier to read with `-c`. You will have to try it for yourself.

☑ **HINT** When you use the `-c` option, **pg** clears the entire screen at once before displaying new data. When you use `-c` with **more**, it clears one line at a time. Compare the two programs and see which one you like better.

Two other options allow you to control the line at which **pg** starts to display data. You can use a `+` (plus sign) followed by a number to tell **pg** to start at that line number. For example, to display the contents of the file **memo** starting at line 37, use:

`pg +37 memo`

Second, you can use `+/` (plus, slash) followed by a pattern, and **pg** will search for that pattern before it starts displaying data. For example, to display the same file, starting with a search for the word **Harley**, use:

`pg +/Harley memo`

Note: You cannot use both the `+` and `+/` options at the same time.

☑ **HINT** If you are used to using **more**, there are two basic differences with **pg**:
1. You must press <Return> after each command.
2. You press <Return>, not <Space>, to display the next screenful of data.

Displaying a File Using `less`

The **less** program is a pager that you can use to display data one screenful at a time. The syntax is:

less `[-cmsCM]` `[-x`*tab*`]` `[+`*command*`]` `[`*file...*`]`

where:

command: a command to be executed automatically
file: the name of a file
tab: the tab spacing you want to use

Like **more** and **pg**, **less** is a paging program. It is designed as a replacement for both of these programs. However, it is not a standard part of Unix and may not be on your system.

For basic work, **less** acts much like the other two programs. However, for advanced users, **less** is a lot more sophisticated. It has many commands and allows a great deal of customization. One of the major advantages of **less** is that it is easy to move backward and forward through a file.

The commands in **less** are based on those found in **more** and in the **vi** editor (Chapter 19). They make it particularly easy to move around in the file. If you are a serious Unix user, it is worth your while to master **less**.

In this section, we will describe the basic options and features of the **less** program. For more information, look at the manual page by using **man less**. (The online Unix manual is described in Chapter 8.)

The **less** program displays the contents of the files you specify. The data is displayed one screenful at a time. After each screen is written, you will see a prompt at the bottom left corner of the screen. The first prompt will show you the name of your file. Each subsequent prompt will be a colon:

```
:
```

If you use the **-m** option, **less** will display a prompt that is similar to that of the **more** command by showing you how far you are through the file. For example:

```
40%
```

In this example, the prompt shows that you are 40% of the way through the file.

☑ **HINT**   For ambitious fanatics with a lot of time, **less** offers more flexibility for customizing your prompt than any paging program in the history of the world.

The simplest way to use **less** is to specify a single file name. For example:

```
less memo
```

If the data fits on a single screen, it will be displayed all at once. Otherwise, the data will be displayed one screenful at a time, with the prompt at the bottom.

Once you see the prompt, you can enter a command. The most common command is simply to press the <Space> bar. This will page to the next screen. You can press <Space> repeatedly to page through the entire file.

After displaying the last screenful of data, **pg** will not stop automatically. You will see the following prompt:

```
(END)
```

To quit, press **q**.

One of the most common uses of **less** is to display the output of a pipeline, one screenful at a time. Here are two examples:

```
cat newnames oldnames | grep Harley | sort | less
ls -l | less
```

(Pipelines are explained in Chapter 15. Filters, the programs that are used within a pipeline, are explained in Chapter 16.)

When **less** pauses, there are many commands that you can use. For most commands, you do not have to press <Return>; just type the name. The most important command is **h** (help). This will display a summary of all the possible commands.

Figure 17-3 contains a summary of the most useful **less** commands. The best way to learn about **less** is to type the **h** command, see what is available, and experiment. There are many **less** commands. In particular, **less** uses many of the same screen control commands as the **vi** editor (Chapter 19).

Some of the commands have more than one name. In Figure 17-3, we show the simplest name. For more information, use the **h** (help) command. If you don't like the command names, you can make your own by using the **lesskey** command. (Enter **man lesskey** for the details.)

When you use the **/** command to search for a pattern, you can use the same type of regular expressions that we described at the end of Chapter 16.

There are a large number of options that you can use when you start **less**. The two most useful are **-s** and **-c**. The **-s** (squeeze) option replaces multiple blank lines with a single blank line. This is useful for condensing output in which multiple blank lines are not meaningful. Of course, this does not affect the original file.

The **-c** (clear) option tells **less** to display each new screenful of data from the top down. Without **-c**, new lines scroll up from the bottom line of the screen. Some people find that long files are easier to read with **-c**. The **-C** (uppercase "C") option is like **-c** except that the entire screen is cleared before new data is written. You will have to try these options for yourself and see what you prefer.

The **-m** option, which we mentioned earlier, makes the prompt look like the **more** prompt by showing the percentage of the file that has been displayed. The **-M** (uppercase "M") option makes the prompt show even more information: the name of the file, the line number, and the percentage that has been displayed. For example, say that you start **less** to view a file named **memo** by using:

```
less -M memo
```

A typical prompt would look like this:

```
memo line 48/75 93%
```

Basic Commands

Command	Description
h	display help information
<Space>	go forward one screenful
q	quit the program

More Advanced Commands

Command	Description
<Return>	go forward one line
n<Return>	go forward *n* lines
b	go backward one screenful
y	go backward one line
*n*y	go backward *n* lines
d	go forward (down) a half screenful
u	go backward (up) a half screenful
g	go to the first line
*n*g	go to line *n*
G	go to the last line
*n*p	go to the line that is *n*% through the file
v	start the **vi** editor using file you are displaying
/*pattern*	search forward for the specified pattern
?*pattern*	search backward for the specified pattern
n	repeat the previous search command
!*command*	execute the specified shell command
=	display the current line number and name of file
−*option*	change an option
_*option*	display the current value of an option

Do not press <Return> after a command except with /, ? and !.

Figure 17-3

Summary of the Most Useful **less** *Commands*

Note: The line number refers to the top line on the screen, while the percentage includes all the lines on the screen. In our example, line 48 (of 75) is at the top of the screen. However, once you have read all the lines on the screen, you are 93% of the way through the file.

The **+** (plus sign) option allows you to control the line at which **less** starts to display data. Whatever appears after the **+** will be executed as an initial command. For example, to display the file **memo**, with the initial position at the end of the file, use:

```
less +G memo
```

To display the same file, starting with a search for the word **Harley**, use:

```
less +/Harley memo
```

As a special case, a number after the **+** tells **less** to start at that line. For example, to start at line 37, use:

```
less +37 memo
```

This is really an abbreviation for:

```
less +37g memo
```

Finally, the **-x** option followed by a number tells **less** to set the tabs at the specified regular interval. This controls the spacing for data that contains tab characters.

For example, to set the tabs to every 5 spaces, use:

```
less -x5 memo
```

The default value is to set the tabs to every 8 spaces. (This is the case for most Unix programs.)

If you want to change an option while you are viewing a file, use the **-** (hyphen) command at the prompt. Type **-** followed by the new option. For example, to change the prompt to the **-M** version, type:

```
-M
```

To display the current value of an option, use an **_** (underscore) followed by the option. For example, to check how the prompt is set, use:

```
_m
```

☑ **HINT**   To learn **less**, use the **-** (change option) and **_** (display option) commands to experiment with the various options. This is especially useful if you want to use the **-P** option (which we did not discuss) to change the prompt.

Using Environment Variables to Customize Your Paging Program

As we explained in Chapter 15, the Unix philosophy is that each program should do only one thing and should do it well. The paging programs are examples of this philosophy: they are designed specifically to display data.

The paging programs are available to any other program that wants to display data. For example, the **man** command will automatically call upon a paging program to display data from the online Unix manual. Other programs, such as **mail**, also use a paging program when necessary.

Once you decide what paging program you like best, you can make sure that other programs use it by setting the **PAGER** environmental variable to the name of the pager you want to use. When other programs need to display data, they will look at this variable and use the paging program you specify.

(Environment variables, sometimes called global variables, are explained in Chapter 11. You usually define environment variables in your **.login** initialization file. This makes the variables available to every program that you use.)

The following command (in your **.login** file) specifies that you want to use the **more** program for your pager:

```
setenv PAGER more
```

Similarly, you might choose to use one of the following commands instead:

```
setenv PAGER pg
setenv PAGER less
```

The **more** and **less** programs offer an added degree of customization. You can define an environment variable named **MORE** (or **LESS**) that contains the options you want to use each time you start the program.

For example, say that you always use **more** with the **-c** and **-s** options. You can define:

```
setenv MORE '-cs'
```

From now on, whenever you start **more**, it will automatically use these options without your having to specify them. If you always use **less** with the **-s**, **-C** and **-M** options, you can define:

```
setenv LESS '-sCM'
```

Unfortunately, the **pg** program does not support this type of customization.

The above examples, using **setenv**, are for shells in the C-Shell family. If you use a shell in the Bourne shell family (the Bourne shell, the Korn shell, Bash, or the Zsh), you will use different commands. For example:

```
PAGER=more; export PAGER
MORE='-cs'; export MORE
```

These commands will go in your **.profile** initialization file. (The various shells are discussed in Chapter 10.)

Printing Files

In Chapter 17, we explained how to display data at your terminal. In this chapter, we finish the discussion of processing output by showing you how to print data.

We start by explaining how Unix offers the service of printing and what happens when you start a print job.

From there, we will move on to the commands. First, we will explain how to format a file before you print it. Next, you will see how to print a file, how to check which files are waiting to be printed, and how to cancel a print job. Finally, we will show you how to print pages from the online Unix manual that we discussed in Chapter 8, and how to print large signs.

Note: When we refer to "files", we assume the intuitive idea that a file has a name and contains information. For example, you might have a file named **memo** that contains the text of a memorandum. In Chapter 20, we will discuss the Unix file system in detail, at which time we will give a strict definition for a file.

Orientation to Printing

In principle, printing a file is similar to displaying a file. They both involve copying data to an output device. However, there are some important differences. Printing has its own special considerations, its own commands, and its own terminology.

Perhaps the biggest difference between printing and displaying is that printing is slow. If every file you printed was finished within a few seconds, you wouldn't mind waiting for it. Of course, this is rarely the case. Even with modern printers, it can take a while for your output to be ready. Moreover, you may not have a printer of your own. Your file may have to wait its turn if someone else is using the community printer.

The Unix system was designed to assume that all printing requests may have to wait. When you enter the command to print a file, Unix generates a PRINT JOB. Most systems will display an identification number called the JOB NUMBER that you can use to keep track of the job. (If your system does not display the job number automatically, you can use the **lpq** command to display the number.)

To print a file and to control the print job, you use certain commands. Unfortunately, Berkeley Unix has different commands from System V Unix. (See Chapter 2 for a discussion of the different types of Unix.) In this chapter, we will explain the Berkeley commands. Many Unixes, including the modern version of System V, contain the Berkeley commands, so you shouldn't have a problem. If your system has only the older System V commands, you can use the **man** command to look them up in the online Unix manual (see Chapter 8).

For reference, Figure 18-1 compares the commands for each system. For the most part, they perform the same functions, although they do have different options.

WHAT'S IN A NAME?

lp

You will notice that all but one of the print commands start with the letters **lp**. What does this mean?

As we described in Chapter 6, the earliest Unix terminals printed output on paper. For this reason, it became traditional to refer to the output of a terminal as being "printed". For example, the command to display the name of your working directory (Chapter 19) is **pwd**: print working directory.

To refer to the actual printer, Unix uses the term "line printer". (This describes the type of printer that was used by the first developers of Unix.) Thus, whenever you see a command or system name that begins with **lp**, it refers to real printing.

Berkeley Unix	System V	Description
`lpr`	`lp`	send a file to be printed
`lpq`	`lpstat`	show what print jobs are waiting
`lprm`	`cancel`	cancel a print job

Figure 18-1
The Printing Commands

What Happens When You Print a File: Spooling

At all times, Unix maintains a list of all the print jobs that are waiting to be processed. This list is called the PRINT QUEUE. When you use the **lpr** command to print a file, Unix makes a temporary copy of the file and saves it in a special directory. It then adds your job to the print queue and displays the job number.

As soon as the printer becomes available, Unix starts printing the next job in the queue. At any time, you can use the **lpq** command to check what is in the print queue or the **lprm** command to remove a job from the queue.

When your print job finishes, Unix removes the temporary file and goes on to the next job. By using the **-m** option with **lpr**, you can have Unix send you a mail message to tell you when a print job is completed.

The most important idea about this entire process is that Unix does not print a file the moment you enter the **lpr** command. Rather, Unix saves a copy of the file and prints it at an appropriate time. This arrangement is called SPOOLING.

The word "spool" is a flexible one. It can be used:

- as an adjective: The temporary file is called a SPOOL FILE.

- as a noun: The program that handles all the details is called the PRINT SPOOLER or, sometimes, just the SPOOLER.

- even as a verb: "The system SPOOLED my job six hours ago and it still hasn't printed."

 HINT   "Spool" is a cool word.

WHAT'S IN A NAME?

Spool   The term "spool" dates from the olden days of mainframes (the early 1960s). In those days, the main processor was expensive and, by our standards, slow. When output needed to be sent to a peripheral device, such as a printer, the processing time involved in sending the data was considerable.

On the larger computers, a system was used where the output was kept in a temporary storage area. Another processor, perhaps a smaller, cheaper computer, would take over the job of sending the output to the peripheral device. This freed the main processor for more important tasks, thus making the whole system more efficient.

This type of organization was called spooling, which stood for "simultaneous peripheral operations offline". (In case you haven't guessed, this term was invented at IBM.)

Daemons and Dragons

The print spooler is an example of a DAEMON, a program that executes in the background and provides a service of general interest. Unix has a number of such programs. Some daemons are started automatically when the system is initialized and are always available. Other daemons sleep most of the time, waking up at predefined intervals or in response to some event.

Daemons perform all kinds of functions to keep the system running smoothly: managing memory, overseeing print jobs, sending and receiving mail, executing commands at specific times, responding to remote finger requests (see Chapter 12), and so on.

The print spooling daemon is called `lpd` (line printer daemon). The finger daemon is called `fingerd`. The most common mail daemon is `sendmail`. The most well-known daemon is `cron`. Its purpose is to execute jobs at predefined times.

WHAT'S IN A NAME?

Daemons and Dragons

Although the name is pronounced "dee-mon", it is correctly spelled "daemon". Nobody knows if the name used to be an acronym or why we use a British variation of the spelling. (In Celtic mythology, a daemon is usually good or neutral, merely a spirit or inspiration. A demon, however, is always an evil entity.)

You may occasionally read that the name stands for "Disk and Executing Monitor", a term from the old DEC 10 and 20 computers. However, this explanation was made up after the fact.

The name "daemon" was first used by MIT programmers who worked on CTSS (the Compatible Time-sharing System), developed in 1963. They coined the name to refer to what were called DRAGONS by other programmers who worked on ITS (the Incompatible Time-sharing System).

(CTSS and ITS were both ancestors of Unix. ITS was an important, but strange, operating system that developed a cult following at MIT. To this day, ITS is still revered among aging east-coast hackers.)

Strictly speaking, a dragon is a daemon that is not invoked explicitly but is always there, waiting in the background to perform some task. The `cron` daemon, for example, might be called a dragon. Although many Unix users have heard of daemons, very few people know about dragons. (But now you do.)

Formatting a File for Printing: `pr`, `nl`

Before we get down to the business of printing a file, let's take a moment and discuss two filters that are used to format data before you print it: **pr** and **nl**.

(Filters are discussed in Chapter 16. Basically, they are programs that read from the standard input and write to the standard output. As such, filters can be combined with other programs into a pipeline in which each program reads data, does something to it, and passes it on the the next program. Pipelines are discussed in Chapter 15.)

The **pr** command reads from the standard input or from a text file and produces output which is paginated and labeled. **pr** can also arrange text into columns. The intention is that you will use **pr** to prepare data before you print it.

The **pr** command does not change the original file. Like all filters, **pr** writes to the standard output. Thus, if you do not redirect the output, it will be displayed on your terminal.

The syntax for the **pr** command is:

```
pr [-h title] [-lpagelength] [file...]
```

where:

> `title`: what you want to print in the header
> `pagelength`: the number of lines per page
> `file`: the name of a file

Unless you specify otherwise, **pr** will format and paginate according to certain defaults. It assumes that the length of a page is 66 lines (the number of lines that normally print on an 11-inch piece of paper). Of these lines, the first 5 are used as a header, the last 5 are used as a trailer. Thus, **pr** will use 56 lines per page for your output.

The header consists of 2 blank lines, 1 line of text, and another 2 blank lines. The line of text will show the date, the name of the file, and the page number. The trailer is just 5 blank lines.

Normally, you pipe the output of **pr** to the **lpr** program (discussed later in the chapter) which will print the file. For example, to format and print a file named **memo**, you can use:

```
pr memo | lpr
```

A common way to use **pr** is to send its output from a pipeline. For example, the following command uses **cat** (Chapter 16) to combine three files, and then formats and prints the result.

```
cat names extra.names old.names | pr | lpr
```

The next command formats and prints a long directory listing of the **/bin** and **/usr/bin** directories:

```
ls -l /bin /usr/bin | pr | lpr
```

(We discuss pipelines in Chapter 15, and directories and the **ls** command in Chapter 19.)

There are several options that you can use to change the default formatting values. We will explain only the most important ones. For more information, including a description of how to format text into columns, look at the manual page for **pr** by using the command **man pr**. (The online Unix manual is discussed in Chapter 8.)

The **-l** (length) option changes the number of lines on a page. Use **-l** followed by the number, but do not put a space after the **-l**. For example, to format and print the **memo** file using 50 lines per page, use:

```
pr -l50 memo | lpr
```

The length that you specify includes both the header and the trailer.

✓ **HINT** You normally print the output of **pr** by piping it to the **lpr** program. If you are testing various options, first send the output to a paging program (such as **more**, see Chapter 17), so you can preview it at your terminal. For example:

```
pr -l50 memo | more
```

Once you are happy with what you see, you can send the same output to **lpr**:

```
pr -l50 memo | lpr
```

The **-h** (header) option allows you to specify a title for the header instead of the name of the file. Use **-h** followed by whatever you want to print. If you want to use more than a single word or if you want to use special characters, enclose your specification in single quotes.

For example, to print "Important Memo" within the header of each page, use:

```
pr -h 'Important Memo' memo | lpr
```

Note: The **-h** option replaces only the file name. You will still get the date and the page number.

✓ **HINT** When you format data from a pipeline, there will be no file name for the header. In such cases, it is a good idea to use **-h** to specify a title for the printout. For example:

```
ls -l /bin /usr/bin | pr -h 'Directory List' | lpr
```

The second filter that you can use to format data before printing is **nl**, a program to create line numbers. The input can be from the standard input or from a file.

(Note: Not all Unix systems have this program.)

There are many options that give you exquisite control over how the line numbers are generated and formatted. However, most of the time you will ignore the options and use the defaults, so we will not discuss the details. If you want more information, see the manual page for **nl**. (Use the command **man nl**).

Ignoring the options, the syntax for **nl** is simple:

nl [*file...*]

Here are several examples. Say that you want to number each non-blank line of the file **memo**, starting from line number 1 (these are the defaults). You want to format and then print the output. Use:

nl memo | pr | lpr

The next example combines three files, numbers each non-blank line, formats the output and then prints the result:

cat names extra.names old.names | nl | pr | lpr

A second use for **nl** is to create a file with actual line numbers. For example, say that you have a file named **raw.data** that you want to have line numbers. You want the numbered text to be stored in a file named **master.data**. Use:

nl raw.data > master.data

(We explain how to use **>** to redirect output to a file in Chapter 15.)

Printing a File: **lpr**

To print a file, use the **lpr** (line printer) command. The syntax is:

lpr [*-mprh*] [*-#num*] [*-J name*] [*-P printer*] [*-T title*] [*file...*]

where:

num: the number of copies you want
name: the name of the job
printer: the name of a printer
title: the title that you want to print in the header
file: the name of a file

The **lpr** command has many options. In this section, we will discuss only the most important ones. If you want to find out more about **lpr**, look at the manual page by using the command **man lpr**. (The online Unix manual is covered in Chapter 8.) In particular, there are special options that you can use if you are printing output from a text formatter such as **troff**, **ditroff** or TeX.

The basic way to use **lpr** is to specify the names of one or more files to be printed. For example, to print a file named **memo**, use:

```
lpr memo
```

You can also use **lpr** at the end of a pipeline to print the output. For example, the following command line uses **cat** to combine three files. The output of **cat** is sent to **nl** to be numbered and then to **pr** to be formatted. The result is piped to **lpr** to be printed:

```
cat names extra.names old.names | nl | pr | lpr
```

When you use **lpr**, most systems will display a job number that identifies your print request. You can use this job number with the **lpq** command to check on the progress of the job and with the **lprm** command to remove the job from the print queue. If your system does not display a job number automatically, you can use the **lpq** command to display the number.

As a convenience, **lpr** can send you mail to tell you that the job is finished printing. Just use the **−m** option:

```
lpr -m memo
```

To print more than one copy, use **−#** followed by the number of copies. Do not put a space before the number. For example, to print 5 copies of the file **memo**, use:

```
lpr -#5 memo
```

If you have created a file only to hold data for printing, you may want to remove it once the print job has finished. The **−r** (remove) option will do this for you. For example, to print and then remove a file named **raw.data**, use:

```
lpr -r raw.data
```

(The idea of removing a file is discussed in detail in Chapter 20.)

Many systems have more than one printer. If this is the case with your system, each printer will have a name. To send your output to a specific printer, use the **−P** (uppercase "P") option followed by the name of the printer. For example, to print the file **memo** on the printer named **laser2**, use:

```
lpr -P laser2 mem
```

If you do not use the **−P** option, **lpr** will use whatever printer is the default for your system. If you want to specify your own default printer, you can set the **PRINTER** environment variable. For example, say that you want **lpr** to consider the printer named **laser1** to be the default printer. Use the following command in your **.login** file:

```
setenv PRINTER laser1
```

(Environment variables and the **.login** initialization file are discussed in Chapter 11.)

HINT   Ask around and find out what printers are available on your system and which is the default printer. Otherwise, you may find yourself waiting for output at the wrong printer.

At the beginning of each printout, **lpr** will print an extra page that contains identification information, including a job name and a job classification. The page is called a BURST PAGE.

WHAT'S IN A NAME?

Burst Page   When you print on continuous fan-fold paper, the burst page indicates where to separate one printout from the next. The word "burst" refers to the act of tearing apart the pages of a printout.

Normally, the job name on the burst page is the name of the file that you are printing. You can change this name by using the **-J** option followed by a different name. If the name is more than one word or if it contains special characters, enclose it in single quotes.

For example, to print the file **memo** with a job name of "Privileged Information", use:

```
lpr -J 'Privileged Information' memo
```

If you are printing a document on your own printer, you will probably want to dispense with the burst page entirely. You can do so by using the **-h** (header) option. For example:

```
lpr -h memo
```

In the previous section, we explained how you can use the **pr** filter to format data before printing. For example, the following command line formats and prints a file named **memo**:

```
pr memo | lpr
```

An alternative to using a pipeline is to use the **-p** option. This tells **lpr** to use **pr** to format the data before printing it. For example, the following command is equivalent to the previous one:

```
lpr -p memo
```

If you invoke **pr** in this way, you can use the **-T** (uppercase "T") option to tell **pr** what title to use in the page headers. Use **-T** followed by the title. For example, the following two commands are equivalent:

```
pr -h 'Important Memo' memo | lpr
lpr -p -T 'Important Memo' memo
```

If you want to use other formatting options, you will have to invoke **pr** directly and pipe the output to **lpr**.

Checking the Status of Print Jobs: `lpq`

To check on the status of a print job, use the **lpq** (line printer queue) command. The syntax is:

`lpq` `[-l]` `[job...]` `[-P` `printer]`

where *job* is a job number, and *printer* is the name of a printer.

If you enter the command with no options, it will show you information about all the jobs in the print queue for the default printer. (If you have set the **PRINTER** environment variable, **lpq** will use that as the default.) Here is some sample output:

```
lp is ready and printing
Rank    Owner        Job  Files        Total Size
active harley        773  memo         25646 bytes
```

Of course, with a busy system, the print queue will often be long and you may have to wait a while for your printout.

Normally, **lpq** will display only a small amount of information to ensure that the description of each print job fits on a single line. If you want to see more information, you can use the **-l** (long listing) option:

`lpq -l`

To display information about the print queue of a particular printer, use the **-P** (uppercase "P") option followed by the name of the printer. For example, to look at the print queue for a printer named **laser2**, use:

`lpq -P laser2`

Finally, if you specify one or more job numbers, **lpq** will display information about those jobs only. For example:

`lpq 773`

The **lpq** command has other, less important options which we do not cover here. For more information, display the manual page by using the command **man** **lpq**. (The online Unix manual is discussed in Chapter 8.)

 HINT   Some systems operate the print queues on a first-come first-served basis. Other systems look at the file to be printed and give priority to small jobs.

Cancelling a Print Job: `lprm`

To cancel a print job, use the **`lprm`** (line printer remove) command. This command will remove an entry from the print queue. The syntax is:

`lprm` `[-]` `[job...]` `[-P printer]`

where `job` is a job number, and `printer` is the name of a printer.

If you use the command with no options:

`lprm`

it will cancel the job that is currently active (as long as it is one of your jobs).

To cancel a specific job, specify the job number. For example:

`lprm 773`

To cancel all your print jobs, use the – option:

`lprm -`

 HINT The **`lprm`** command will remove only jobs that were sent by your userid. Don't waste your time trying to remove other people's jobs to make yours print faster.

Normally, **`lprm`** will cancel jobs for the default printer. (If you have set the **PRINTER** environment variable, **`lpq`** will use that as the default.) If you want to cancel jobs from a particular printer, use the **`-P`** (uppercase "P") option followed by the name of the printer. For example, to cancel all your jobs for a printer named **laser2**, use:

`lprm - -P laser2`

When **`lprm`** cancels a print job, you will see some type of message. Here is a typical example:

`dfA773nipper dequeued`
`cfA773nipper dequeued`

This message indicates that two files have been removed from the print spool directory.

The first file, **`dfA773nipper`**, contains the data to be printed. The other file, **`cfA773nipper`**, contains the control information. The spool files were named using a suffix of **`nipper`** because that is the name of the computer.

If **`lprm`** does not cancel anything, there will be no message.

Interesting Things to Print: Manual Pages and Signs

There are two interesting things that you might like to print. First, it can be handy to print selected pages from the online Unix manual (see Chapter 8). When you use the **man** command, it automatically formats the output for printing. Thus, all you need to do is pipe the output of **man** to the **lpr** command.

For example, to print a copy of the manual page for the **who** command on the default printer, use:

```
man who | lpr
```

If for some reason your **man** command does not format the data, you can always pipe it through **pr**. Either of the following commands will do the job:

```
man who | pr | lpr
man who | lpr -p
```

The second interesting thing to print is a sign made up of large letters. You can generate such a sign by using the **banner** command that we described in Chapter 7. To print a sign, all you have to do is pipe the output of **banner** to **lpr**. For example:

```
banner 'This sign is silly.' | lpr
```

Note: The **banner** program is in the **/usr/games** directory. If this directory is not in your search path, you will see an error message when you try to run the program because Unix will not be able to find the program:

```
banner: Command not found.
```

If so, you will have to preface the command with the name of the directory that contains the **banner** program. Use:

```
/usr/games/banner 'This sign is silly.' | lpr
```

This is explained in Chapter 7. Directories are explained in Chapter 19.

☑ **HINT**   When you use **banner** to generate a sign, print the output on continuous paper. If you use separate sheets of paper, you will have to tape them together.

The vi Editor

An EDITOR, or TEXT EDITOR, is a program that you use to create and modify files. TEXT is data that consists of letters, numbers, punctuation and so on.

This chapter covers one of the most important topics in Unix: the **vi** editor. It is important to learn **vi** or, at least, some editor program. Even if you don't want to create documents or programs, there are many times when you will need to use an editor.

For example, if you want to mail someone a message, you can type it directly, line by line. (This is all explained in Chapter 14.) But without an editor, there is no way to make changes in the message. Moreover, you cannot prepare a message in advance.

Similarly, once you start reading the Usenet news (see Chapter 24), you may want to post an article of your own. Unless you can use an editor, you will have no way to create the article. In fact, any time you need to manipulate textual data directly, you need an editor.

A number of Unix programs have built-in commands to start an editor should you need one. Usually this editor will be **vi** and you must know how to use it.

In this chapter, we will explain the basics of using **vi**. Although we will not be able to explain everything – that would take at least several chapters – we will show you most of what you need to know.

> ☑ **HINT** If you use a non-Unix computer to access Unix – say, a Macintosh or a PC – it is possible to create a file on that computer and send it to Unix. However, in many cases, you are better off doing the work on the Unix computer.
>
> Thus, no matter how you access Unix, you do need to learn to use a Unix editor. If you know how to use `vi`, you can edit files on any Unix system that you may encounter.

Emacs: An Alternative to `vi`

As a Unix user, you need to learn how to use an editor. The two main choices are `vi` and Emacs. If you were to ask experienced Unix people what editor they use – and all experienced Unix people use *some* editor – you would find their loyalties divided.

In this chapter, we will show you how to use `vi`. This is because `vi` is available on every Unix system and will do just fine. Moreover, `vi` is a standard tool. It has not changed in years, nor will it change in the future. Emacs will also suffice, but it is not always available. It is our opinion that you should learn `vi` first. You can always learn Emacs later.

We don't have room to teach Emacs in detail. However, Emacs comes with a built-in tutorial that is easy to follow. In the next section, we will talk a bit about Emacs and show you how to get started, should you decide to try it. The bulk of this chapter, however, will be about `vi`. If you are not interested in Emacs, you can skip right to `vi`.

WHAT'S IN A NAME?

Emacs, GNU, Free Software Foundation

The first Emacs was actually a set of editing macros written in 1975 at MIT by Richard Stallman. Hence, the name "Emacs" for "editing macros".

The original Emacs worked under the auspices of an editor named TECO. (The early TECO stood for "Tape Editor and Corrector"; later TECO became "Text Editor and Corrector".) TECO was used by many people, but was complex to the point of dementia. The purpose of Emacs was to make TECO easier to use.

Since then, Emacs has been re-written as a separate program and greatly improved. It is available in a number of versions, the most popular being GNU Emacs, a product of the Free Software Foundation (FSF). This is the version of Emacs that you are most likely to encounter on a Unix system.

continued

The FSF was founded by Stallman in 1985. The philosophy of the FSF is that high-quality software should be freely available without the usual commercial restrictions. One of the FSF's principal goals is to create an unrestricted version of Unix. The general name of this project is "GNU", which is a recursive acronym meaning "GNU's not Unix".

GNU is pronounced "Ga-New" (it rhymes with the sound you make when you sneeze).

Getting Started with Emacs

If your system has Emacs, you can start it by entering the command:

`emacs`

On some systems, you may have to enter:

`gmacs`

Before you start Emacs, you should understand how it uses the keyboard. As we discussed in Chapter 6, you use the <Ctrl> key by holding it down and pressing another key, for instance, <Ctrl-C>. In Unix, we often indicate this by using a ^ (circumflex) character. For example, instead of writing "press the <Ctrl-C> key", we would write "press `^C`".

Emacs uses two such keys: the standard <Ctrl> key and the not-so-standard <Meta> key. Moreover, Emacs has its own way of writing key names. The abbreviation "C-" stands for Ctrl; the abbreviation "M-" stands for Meta. In addition, the names of the alphabetic keys are written in lowercase.

Thus, instead of referring to a key as <Ctrl-C> or `^C`, Emacs will use C-c. This means hold down the <Ctrl> key and press <C>. Similarly, when you see a key named M-x, it means hold down the <Meta> key and press <X>.

By now, you are probably saying: What <Meta> key? Ain't no stinkin' <Meta> key on my keyboard.

Indeed, most keyboards do not have a such a key. Instead, you use the <Esc> (escape) key. However, you don't hold it down like <Ctrl>. You press <Esc>, let it go, and then press the next key. For example, if you need to use M-x, you would press <Esc>, let it go, and then press the <X> key.

To begin Life With Emacs, all you need to know is how to start the built-in tutorial. Start Emacs by entering the appropriate command (either **emacs** or **gmacs**). Then, press:

`C-h t`

In other words, press <Ctrl-H>, then press the letter <T>.

To quit Emacs, use the command:

`C-x C-c`

<Ctrl-X> followed by <Ctrl-C>.

Emacs is popular because it is a lot more than an editor: it is a total working environment. You can enter regular shell commands, send and read mail, write and debug programs, and a lot more. (GNU Emacs contains the RMAIL facility that we mentioned in Chapter 14.) Emacs can even act like the **vi** editor.

Some people do all of their work within Emacs. Moreover, if you are ambitious, you can customize and extend any part of the system to your liking. Emacs is a favorite of hackers and crackers. (Such people are discussed in Chapter 4.)

☑ **HINT**   Emacs is not just an editor: Emacs is a way of life.

☑ **HINT**   If you are learning **vi** and you become temporarily discouraged, take a break and try a little Emacs. Emacs will seem so complex and impossible that you will feel a lot better about using **vi**.

(Interestingly enough, this advice works both ways. If you are learning Emacs and you become discouraged, try **vi** for a few minutes. **vi** will seem so complex and impossible that you will feel a lot better about using Emacs.)

What is **vi**?

In Chapter 6, we explained that the early Unix developers used teletype-like terminals that printed on paper. Later they used rudimentary display terminals that were, by today's standards, slow and awkward.

The first Unix editor (**ed**), was a LINE-ORIENTED EDITOR or LINE EDITOR. This means that the lines of text were numbered and you would enter commands based on these numbers. For example, you might enter a command to print lines 10 though 20, or delete line 17. Such an approach was necessary because of the slowness of the terminals. (It is from these early terminals, by the way, that the Unix tradition developed of using the word "print" to mean "to display data".)

Later, at U.C. Berkeley, Bill Joy developed a more powerful line editor that he named **ex** (extended editor). **ex** was far more comprehensive and powerful than **ed**. (Bill Joy also wrote much of Berkeley Unix, including the C-Shell. He later founded Sun Microsystems.)

Line editors display data, line by line, at the bottom of the screen. As each new line is displayed, the others scroll up. With the availability of fast, flexible terminals, there arose a need for SCREEN EDITORS that would take advantage of the increased functionality. Such editors allow you to enter and display data anywhere on the screen, much like a modern word processing program.

Joy wrote a screen-oriented interface for **ex** which he called **vi** (visual editor). **vi** supports all of the **ex** commands, but it has its own special commands and conventions that make use of the full screen. **vi** became the standard Unix editor and, as we mentioned earlier, is included as part of all Unix systems.

Interestingly enough, **vi** and **ex** are really the same program. If you start the program with the **ex** command, it uses a line-oriented interface. If you start the program with the **vi** command, it uses the screen-oriented "visual" interface. Consequently, as you are using **vi**, all the **ex** commands are still available. Indeed, as you will see, it is often more effective to use an **ex** command than a **vi** command.

WHAT'S IN A NAME?

ed, ex, vi   In the early days of Unix, many commands were given short, two-letter names. The convention is to pronounce these names as two separate letters. For example, "ee-dee" (**ed**), "ee-ex" (**ex**) and "vee-eye" (**vi**). It is incorrect to pronounce **vi** as a single syllable rhyming with "my".

The choice of small names had a practical reason. The old terminals were agonizingly slow, and it was convenient to use terse commands that were easy to type correctly.

This limitation also gave rise to one of Unix's distinguishing characteristics: its terseness. When a program has nothing to say, it says nothing. For example, if you enter a command to search for data and it finds none, it does not display a message. It simply returns you to the shell prompt. Similarly, error messages are short and to the point.

Like the two-letter command names, the tradition of brevity was the product of smart, quick people who were forced to work with slow equipment. Today, the esthetic of "small is beautiful" is still an important (though vanishing) part of the Unix culture.

If you are interested in seeing what two-letter command names are still in use, look in Chapter 16 at the end of the section on regular expressions. In that section, we show how to use the **grep** command to find these names on your own system. If you have a few moments, you might look up these commands in the online manual. You will find some forgotten gems.

How to Start **vi**

To start **vi**, you enter the **vi** command. The basic syntax is:

vi *file*

where *file* is the name of a file you want to edit. (There are also two useful options which we will cover later.)

In Chapter 20, we will discuss the concept of a file in detail. For now, it is enough to assume the intuitive idea that a file is a repository of data, usually stored on a disk, that you can access by using a name.

Thus, if you want to edit a file named **memo**, you can enter:

vi memo

If the file does not already exist, **vi** will create it for you.

It is okay to start **vi** without a file name. **vi** will let you specify a name when it comes time to save the data.

Command Mode and Input Mode

When you work with **vi**, all the data is kept in what is called the EDITING BUFFER. This means that when you use **vi** to edit an existing file, you are not working with the actual file. **vi** copies the contents of the file to the editing buffer. It is not until you tell **vi** to save your data that the contents of the editing buffer are copied to the file. Thus, if you accidentally mess up the data in the editing buffer, you can still recover the original file.

vi works in two distinct ways, called INPUT MODE and COMMAND MODE. When **vi** is in input mode, everything you type is inserted into the editing buffer. When **vi** is in command mode, the characters you type are interpreted as commands. There are many different commands that you can issue: delete certain lines, move from place to place in the file, search for a pattern, make changes, and so on.

If you have ever used a word processor program, you know that it allows you to move to any place in the file and start typing. With a personal computer, you would move around the file by using special keys like PageUp, PageDown, Home and End, as well as the cursor control (arrow) keys. You might also use a mouse. When **vi** was developed, terminals did not have special keys or a mouse. There were only the regular keyboard and the <Ctrl> key.

Thus, **vi** was designed to use two different modes. The effect of what you type depends on what mode **vi** is in at the time. For example, if **vi** is in command mode and you press "D", it acts as a delete command. If **vi** is in input mode, pressing "D" will actually insert the character "D" into the editing buffer. In this way, you do not need any special keys and **vi** will work on any type of terminal.

Here is what it feels like when you work with **vi**. Say that you want to add some data to the middle of a file. When you start **vi**, you are automatically in command mode. The cursor shows your current position in the editing buffer. Using appropriate commands, you move the cursor to the place where you want to add the data. You type a command to change to input mode and start typing. Everything you type is inserted into the editing buffer. When you are finished, you change back to command mode.

Although it is **vi** that changes from one mode to another, we usually talk as if you, the user, are making the change. For example, we might say, "There are many commands that you can use when you are in command mode."

As you working with **vi**, you frequently change back and forth between command mode and insert mode. In command mode, there are a number of commands to change to input mode. Each of these commands is a single letter. For example, the **I** command allows you to start inserting data at the beginning of the current line. The **A** (append) command allows you to start inserting data at the end of the current line. We will explain all these commands in due time.

When you are in insert mode (typing data), there is only one way to change to command mode: you press the <Esc> key. (If you are in command mode and you press the <Esc> key, **vi** will beep at you.) At first, it will seem strange to have to change to a special mode just to start typing data. Moreover, there is no way to tell from looking at the screen what mode you are in.

If you are not sure what mode you are in, you can always press <Esc> twice. This is guaranteed to leave you in command mode and to beep. Why? If you are in insert mode, the first <Esc> will change to command mode, and the second <Esc> will beep. If you are already in command mode, both <Esc>s will beep.

☑ **HINT**   When using **vi**: If you are not sure what mode you are in, press <Esc> twice. You will be in command mode, and you will hear a beep.

You might ask, why doesn't **vi** do something to show you what mode you are in? Actually, once you get used to **vi**, you will know what you are doing, and you will always just know what mode you are in. It's not really that much of a problem.

vi was designed extremely well. At first, many things may seem awkward. However, once you become experienced, everything will make sense, and **vi** will seem natural and easy to use. This suggests the following hint which, in Chapter 1, we applied to Unix in general:

☑ **HINT**   vi is easy to use, but difficult to learn.

If you are a touch typist, you will find that **vi** is particularly easy to use once you have memorized the basic commands. You will be able to do anything you want without taking your hands off the keyboard. The only special keys you need to use are <Ctrl> and <Esc>. As you may know, this is not the case with word processors that use keys like PageUp or PageDown, or that use a mouse.

Starting vi as a Read-only Editor: The -R Option, view

There may be times when you want to use **vi** to look at an important file that should not be changed. There are two ways to do so. First, you can start **vi** with the **-R** (read-only) option. This tells **vi** that you do not want to save data back into the original file. Second, you can start the editor by using the **view** command.

There is really no difference between **vi -R** and **view**. You can use whichever is easier to remember. Thus, the following two commands are equivalent:

```
vi -R importantfile
view importantfile
```

They both start **vi**, using a file named **importantfile** for reading only. Using **vi** in this way protects you from accidentally replacing important data.

Recovering Data After a System Failure: The -r Option

From time to time, it may happen that the system will go down while you are working with **vi**. If so, **vi** will usually make it possible for you to recover all or most of your data. Remember, when you use **vi** to edit a file, you are not editing the actual file. **vi** copies the data to the editing buffer. This buffer is usually preserved, even when the system goes down unexpectedly.

Once the system is restarted, a daemon (see Chapter 18) will mail you a message similar to this one:

```
You were editing the file "memo"
at <Sat Sep 19 11:00> on the machine ``nipper''
when the editor was killed.

You can retrieve most of your changes to this file
using the "recover" command of the editor.
An easy way to do this is to give the command "vi -r memo".
This method also works using "ex" and "edit".
```

As the message implies, you can recover your data by starting **vi** with the **-r** (recover) option. First, enter:

```
vi -r
```

and **vi** will show you all the files that you may recover. If the file you want is available, enter the same command, but this time specify the name of the file. For example:

```
vi -r memo
```

This will start **vi** and, hopefully, leave you where you were when the system went down.

Note: Be careful not to confuse the **-r** (recover) option with the **-R** (read-only) option.

How to Stop **vi**

There are two situations that you may find yourself in when you are ready to stop **vi**. Usually, you will want to save the contents of the editing buffer to a file and then stop. Occasionally, you may decide to quit without saving your work.

In either case, you must be in command mode to enter the command to quit. If you are in input mode, press <Esc> to change to command mode.

To save your work and then stop, the command is:

```
ZZ                      or use    :wq
```

That is, hold down the <Shift> key and press <Z> twice. You do not need to press <Enter>.

WHAT'S IN A NAME?

ZZ This command, used to stop **vi**, certainly has a strange name, but there is a reason. The name **ZZ** was chosen because it is difficult to type by accident. If you are in command mode, but for some reason, you think you are in input mode, it is unlikely that you would type **ZZ** as input. If **vi** used a simple command like **s** (for stop), it would be easy to type it accidentally.

To quit without saving your work, the command is:

```
:q!
```

After you type this command, you do need to press the <Return> key. In the section after next, we will explain why the command starts with a colon and why you need to press <Return>. Rest assured, it all makes sense.

Be careful: When you use **ZZ** to stop **vi**, it will check if you have saved your data. If not, **vi** will save it for you. However, when you use the **:q!** command, **vi** will not save your data.

In Unix, the **!** character is often used to indicate that you want to override some type of automatic check. In the case of **:q!**, the **!** tells **vi** not to check if you have saved your data. (For a summary of how the **!** character is used in Unix, see Chapter 15.)

How vi Uses the Screen

As we explained in Chapter 6, many Unix programs look at the global variable **TERM** to see what type of terminal you are using. Whenever you start **vi**, it uses the **TERM** variable to make sure that it sends the correct commands to control your terminal. In particular, **vi** will try to use as many lines as your terminal can display.

☑ **HINT**   If you ever find that **vi** is displaying data strangely, make sure that your **TERM** variable is set correctly.

Inn Chapter 11, we explained how to set this variable; in Chapter 16 we showed how the **tset** command can help with this initialization.

The bottom line of your screen is called the COMMAND LINE. As we will see in a moment, **vi** uses this line to display certain commands as you type them. All of the other lines are used to display data. **vi** will show as much of the editing buffer as will fit on your screen at one time.

When you have a small amount of data, there may not be enough lines to fill up the screen. For example, say that your terminal has 25 lines. The bottom line is the command line, leaving 24 lines to display data. Now, say that the editing buffer contains only 10 lines. It would be confusing if **vi** displayed the empty 14 lines as being blank. After all, you might actually have blank lines as part of your data.

Instead, **vi** marks the beginning of each empty line with a ~ (tilde) character. As you add new lines, they will take up more and more of the screen, and the tildes will disappear.

If, at any time, your screen becomes garbled – for instance, if someone sends you a message – you can tell **vi** to redisplay everything by pressing **^L**. Some people set **mesg** to **n** before they use an editor so their work won't be interrupted by a message. (The **mesg** command is explained in Chapter 12.)

Most of the time, your data will consist of regular characters, letters, numbers, punctuation and so on. However, if the need arises, you can enter control characters (see Chapter 6) into your editing buffer. To do so, press

^ = control

^V followed by the control character you want to enter. For example, if you want to type a **^C**, press **^V^C**. If, for some strange reason, you actually want to enter a **^V**, type **^V^V**.

When **vi** displays control characters, you will see the ^ character followed by a letter, for example, **^C**. Remember that this is really only a single character, even though it takes up two spaces on your screen.

As we explained in Chapter 6, the tab character is **^I**. **vi**, like Unix in general, assumes that tabs are set for every 8 positions. (You can change the positioning, but most people don't bother.) When you enter a tab in the editing buffer, **vi** does not display **^I**. Rather, **vi** displays as many spaces as necessary to make it look as if your data is aligned according to the tab.

This is just for your convenience. Don't forget that these extra spaces do not really exist. The editing buffer contains only a single tab character.

Using **vi** and **ex** Commands

We explained earlier that **vi** and **ex** are really different faces of the same program. This means that when you use **vi**, you have access to both **vi** and **ex** commands.

Most **vi** commands are one or two letters. For example, to move the cursor forward one word, you use the **w** command. (Just type "w".) To delete the current line, you use the **dd** command. (Just type "dd".) Since **vi** commands are so short, they are not echoed as you type.

For most **vi** commands, you do not press <Return>. For example, as soon as you type "w", the cursor moves forward one word. As soon as you type "dd", the current line disappears.

If you make a mistake and type a bad **vi** command, you will hear a beep. There will not be an error message.

ex commands are longer and more complex than **vi** commands. For this reason, they are echoed on the command line as you type. All **ex** commands start with : (colon). For example, the command:

`:1,5d`

deletes lines 1 through 5. The command:

`:%s/harley/Harley/g`

changes all occurrences of "harley" to "Harley".

As soon as you type the initial colon, **vi** will move the cursor down to the command line (the bottom line of your screen). As you type the command, each character will be echoed. When you are finished typing the command, you must press <Return>.

If you make a mistake before you press <Return>, you have two choices. First, you can press <Esc>. This will cancel the command completely. Second, you can correct the command using the special keys that we discussed in Chapter 6. These are shown in Figure 19-1. You can use these same keys when you are in input mode to make corrections as you type.

When you make a correction, the cursor will move backwards. However – and this is important – **vi** will not erase the characters from the screen. Logically, they will be gone, but physically, they will still be on the screen.

For example, say that you enter:

```
:1,5del
```

Before you press <Return>, you realize that you did not need to type "el" at the end of the command. So, you press <Backspace> twice and the cursor will move back two positions. However, the "e" and "l" – even though they are not really there any longer – will not be erased from the screen. Just ignore them. You can now press <Return>.

A Strategy for Learning **vi** Commands

As you know, the cursor shows your position on the screen. When you want to add data into the editing buffer, you must follow these steps:

1. Move the cursor to the place at which you want to add data.
2. Type a command to change to input mode.
3. Enter the data.
4. Press <Esc> to change back to command mode.

Once your editing buffer has data, there are various commands that you can use to make changes. So, there are three main types of commands that you need to learn:

- commands to move the cursor
- commands to enter input mode
- commands to make changes

We will describe each family of commands in turn.

One thing that may surprise you is the large number of commands in **vi**. For example, there are 12 different commands that you can use to enter input mode. And there are 40 different commands just to move the cursor. (These

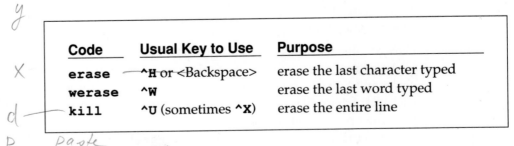

Code	Usual Key to Use	Purpose
erase	^H or <Backspace>	erase the last character typed
werase	^W	erase the last word typed
kill	^U (sometimes ^X)	erase the entire line

Figure 19-1
Keyboard Codes to Use While Using **vi**

are just the *simple* cursor commands.)

As you might guess, you don't really need to know 40 different ways to move the cursor. However, it is useful to know as many commands as possible. What makes **vi** so easy to use – once you are experienced – is that there are so many different ways to perform the same task.

For example, say that you want to move from the top left of the screen to a word halfway down and to the right. You could move the cursor one position at a time, which would be slow and awkward. But if you knew all 40 cursor movement commands, you could quickly choose the best ones to use and, by typing three or four keys, quickly jump to where you want.

 HINT

The art of using **vi** well is in being familiar with so many of the commands that, in any situation, you know the best way to do what you want quickly.

In this chapter, we will be able to cover only the basic commands. For reference, Appendix C contains a summary of **vi**. Every now and then, take a moment and teach yourself a new command. They are all useful.

As you read the rest of the chapter, work in front of your terminal and follow along. As you learn about each new command, try it out. If you need a file of data to practice with, use either of the following commands:

```
cp /etc/passwd temp
man vi > temp
```

The first command copies the system password file to a file named **temp**. The second command copies the manual page for **vi** to a file named **temp**. (The **cp** command is explained in Chapter 22; the password file in Chapter 12; the online manual in Chapter 8; and the redirection of standard output using **>** in Chapter 15.)

Either of these commands will leave you with a file named **temp** that you can use for practice. Once you have such a file, you can edit it by entering the command:

```
vi temp
```

When you are finished, you can remove the file by using:

```
rm temp
```

(The **rm** command is explained in Chapter 22.)

Moving the Cursor

A good strategy for using **vi** is to teach yourself a variety of ways to move the cursor. Each time you want to jump to a different part of the editing buffer, take a moment and think about which sequence of commands will work best. After a while, choosing the right commands will become second nature.

In some cases, there are several ways to make the exact same cursor movement. For example, as you will see in a moment, there are three different commands that will move the cursor one position to the left. There is no need to learn all of them. Pick the commands you like the best and practice those.

To move the cursor a single position, you have a lot of choices. The best commands to use are **h**, **j**, **k** and **l**. They work as follows:

h	move cursor one position left
j	move cursor one position down
k	move cursor one position up
l	move cursor one position right

Why such an odd choice of keys? When you type using the proper finger positions, these four keys are easy to press with your right hand. (Take a look at your keyboard.)

If you are not a touch typist, there are alternatives that are easier to remember. If your terminal has cursor control keys (arrow keys), you can use those. (We will call them <Left>, <Down>, <Up> and <Right>.) You can also use <Backspace> to move left and the <Space> bar to move right.

<Left>	move cursor one position left
<Down>	move cursor one position down
<Up>	move cursor one position up
<Right>	move cursor one position right
<Backspace>	move cursor one position left
<Space>	move cursor one position right

Another way to move up and down is to use the − and + commands. Pressing − moves to the beginning of the previous line; pressing + moves to the beginning of the next line. As an alternative, pressing <Return> also moves to the beginning of the next line.

−	move cursor to beginning of previous line
+	move cursor to beginning of next line
<Return>	move cursor to beginning of next line

These keys are handy if you have a PC-type keyboard with a numeric keypad. The rightmost keys will be <->, <+> and <Enter>. (<Enter> is the same as <Return>.)

Within the current line, the **0** (number zero) command moves to the beginning of the line. The **$** (dollar sign) command moves to the end of the line. If the current line is indented, you can use the ^ (circumflex) to move to the first character in the line that is not a space or tab.

0	move cursor to beginning of current line
$	move cursor to end of current line
^	move cursor to first non-space/tab in current line

Aside from moving by character or line, there are several commands you can use to move from word to word. To move forward, use the **w** or **e** commands. **w** moves to the first character of the next word; **e** moves to the last character (end) of the next word. By using either **w** or **e**, you can move exactly where you want and save keystrokes.

To move backward, use **b** to move to the first character in the previous word.

w	move cursor forward to first character of next word
e	move cursor forward to last character of next word
b	move cursor backward to first character of previous word

One thing about the **w**, **e** and **b** commands is that they stop at each punctuation character. This is okay if your data does not contain many such characters. However, if your data does contain much punctuation, **w**, **e** and **b** can be rather slow. Instead, use the **W**, **E** and **B** commands. These work the same way except they recognize only spaces and **newlines** as ending a word.

W	same as **w**; ignore punctuation
E	same as **e**; ignore punctuation
B	same as **b**; ignore punctuation

For example, say that the cursor is at the beginning of the following line:

```
this is an (important) test; okay
```

If you press **w** several times, you will stop at each parenthesis and at the semicolon, as well as at the beginning of each word. That is, you will have to press **w** eight times to reach the last word of the line. If you use **W**, you will stop only after each space. You will have to press **W** only five times to reach the last word of the line. Try it for yourself.

If you are editing a document, you can use the parentheses commands to jump from sentence to sentence, and the brace bracket commands to jump from paragraph to paragraph.

)	move forward to next sentence beginning
(	move backward to previous sentence beginning
}	move forward to next paragraph beginning
{	move backward to previous paragraph beginning

Again, these are commands that you should try for yourself to make sure you understand exactly how they work.

There will be times when you want to make a large move from one part of your screen to another. To start such a move, you can use the **H**, **M** or **L** commands. They jump to the top, middle or bottom of the lines that are currently on your screen.

H	move cursor to top line
M	move cursor to middle line
L	move cursor to last line

The art of moving the cursor is to get where you want in as few keystrokes as possible. Here is an example. Say that the cursor is on the top line of the screen. The last line of data on the screen contains:

today if you can. Otherwise give me a call.

You want to move to the "c" in call so you can insert the word "phone".

You could press <Down> many times to move to the line you want, and then press <Right> many times to move to the word you want. However, you can do the whole thing in three keystrokes:

L$b

This means: **L** (last line), **$** (end of line), **b** (back up one word).

Wherever it makes sense, you can have **vi** automatically repeat a cursor movement command by typing a number – called a "repeat count" – before the command. For example, to move forward 10 words, type:

10w

Notice that you do not put a space after the number.

Here are two more examples. To move down 50 lines, type any of the following commands:

50j
50<Down>
50+
50<Return>

To move back three paragraphs, type:

3{

As a general rule, you can repeat any **vi** command – not just cursor commands – by typing a number in front of it, as long as doing so makes sense.

☑ **HINT**   Whenever you need to move from one place to another, challenge yourself to do it in as few keystrokes as possible.

(This may help you work your way through college. You can go into bars and bet that you can move the **vi** cursor faster than anyone. At first, use a lot of short movement commands like <Up> and <Down>. After you have lost a few bets and the odds increase, you can use **H**, **M** and **L**, followed by repeated sentence and word commands, and clean up.)

Moving Through the Editing Buffer

vi will display as much of the editing buffer as will fit on your screen. To display different parts of the editing buffer, there are several commands you can use.

First, you can use the **^F** (forward) command to move down one screenful. (Remember, **^F** refers to <Ctrl-F>.) The opposite command is **^B** (backward), which moves up one screenful. There are also two variations: **^D** moves down a half screenful, and **^U** moves up a half screenful.

^F	move down one screenful
^B	move up one screenful
^D	move down a half screenful
^U	move up a half screenful

If you type a number in front of **^F** or **^B**, it acts, as you would expect, as a repeat factor. For example, to move down 6 screenfuls, type:

6^F

Since you can use **^F** and **^B** to jump over many lines in this manner, you do not need to be able to repeat **^D** and **^U** commands. Thus, when you type a number in front of **^D** or **^U**, it is used for something different: it sets the number of lines that either of these commands should jump.

For example, if you type:

10^D

(or **10^U**), it not only jumps 10 lines, it tells **vi** that all subsequent **^D** and **^U** commands should also jump 10 lines (until you reset it). You can also set number of lines to a large amount. For example, if you would like to be able to jump 100 lines at a time, use **100^D** (or **100^U**). Until you reset this number, all **^D** and **^U** commands will jump 100 lines.

Searching for a Pattern

Another way to move around the editing buffer is to jump to a line that contains a particular pattern. To do so, use the **/** and **?** commands.

When you type **/**, **vi** will display a **/** on the command line (at the bottom of the screen). Now type any pattern you want and press <Return>. **vi** will search for the next occurrence of that pattern. If you want to search again for the same pattern, just type **/** again and press <Return>.

Here is an example. You are editing a list of people to whom you want to send money, and you wish to find the next occurrence of the pattern "Harley". Type:

/Harley

and press <Return>. **vi** will jump to the next line that contains the pattern. To repeat the search and jump once more, type:

/

and press <Return>. Since you did not specify a new pattern, **vi** will assume that you want the same one as the previous **/** command.

When **vi** looks for a pattern, it starts from the cursor position and searches forward. When it gets to the end of the editing buffer, **vi** wraps around to the beginning. Thus, **vi** will search the entire editing buffer.

If you want to search backwards, use the **?** command. For example:

?Harley

This works the same as **/** except that **vi** searches in the opposite direction. Once you use **?** to specify a pattern, you can search backwards for the same pattern by using **?** by itself:

?

If **vi** gets to the beginning of the editing buffer, it will wrap around to the end and continue to search backwards.

Once you have specified a pattern with a **/** or **?** command, there are two convenient commands to continue searching for the same pattern. The **n** (lowercase "n") command searches in the same direction as the original command. (Think of **n** as standing for "next".) The **N** (uppercase "N") command searches in the opposite direction.

For example, say that you have already entered the command:

/Harley

You now want to find the next occurrence of the same pattern. All you have to do is press **n**. (Do not press <Return>.) This is the same as if you had entered the **/** command with no pattern.

To search repeatedly for the same pattern, press **n** as many times as you want. If you press **N**, **vi** will make the same search backwards.

Now, say that you have entered the command:

?Harley

Pressing **n** will search backwards (the same direction) for the next occurrence. Pressing **N** will search forwards (the opposite direction).

For flexibility, you can use a regular expression to specify a pattern. (A regular expression is a compact way of specifying a general pattern of characters.) We discussed regular expressions in detail at the end of Chapter 16; you can look there for a lot of examples. **vi** uses the same type of regular expressions, so everything from Chapter 16 will work here.

For reference, Figure 19-2 shows the various symbols that have special meanings within a regular expression.

Symbol	Meaning
.	match any single character except **newline**
*	match zero or more of the preceding characters
^	match the beginning of a line
$	match the end of a line
\<	match the beginning of a word
\>	match the end of a word
[ ]	match one of the enclosed characters
[^]	match any character that is not enclosed
\	interpret the following symbol literally

Figure 19-2
Summary of Symbols Used in Regular Expressions

Here are a few examples. To search for the next occurrence of an "H", followed by any two characters, use:

/H..

To search for an "H" followed by any two lowercase characters, use:

/H[a-z][a-z]

To search for an "H", followed by zero or more lowercase characters, followed by "y", use:

/H[a-z]*y

To search for the next line that begins with "Harley", use:

/^Harley

As you can see, regular expressions are particularly useful. For more examples and a longer discussion, see Chapter 16.

To summarize:

/rexp	search forward for specified regular expression
/	repeat forward search for previous pattern
?rexp	search backward for specified regular expression
?	repeat backward search for previous pattern
n	repeat last **/** or **?** command, same direction
N	repeat last **/** or **?** command, opposite direction

Using Line Numbers

Internally, **vi** keeps track of each line in the editing buffer by assigning it a line number. If you would like to see these numbers, enter the command:

`:set number`

For example, say that you are using **vi** to write your Applied Philosophy dissertation. The editing buffer contains:

```
I have a little shadow that goes
in and out with me,
And what can be the use of him
is more than I can see.
```

If you enter the `:set number` command, you will see:

```
1   I have a little shadow that goes
2   in and out with me,
3   And what can be the use of him
4   is more than I can see.
```

It is important to realize that the numbers are not really part of your data. They are only there for your convenience. If you want to get rid of the numbers, enter:

`:set nonumber`

There are two important uses for line numbers. First, as we will see later, you can use them with many of the **ex** commands. Second, you can use the **G** (goto) command to jump to a specific line. Simply type the number of the line, followed by **G**. Do not type a space or press <Return>.

For example, to jump to line 100, type:

`100G`

To jump to the beginning of the editing buffer, type:

`1G`

If you want to jump to the end of the editing buffer, type **G** by itself:

`G`

To summarize:

*n***G**	jump to line number *n*
1G	jump to first line in editing buffer
G	jump to last line in editing buffer

Most of the time, you will use only **G** and **1G**.

Inserting Data into the Editing Buffer

With a word processor, you move the cursor to where you want to insert data and you start typing. With **vi**, you must type a command to change to input mode before you can enter your data. When you are finished entering data, you must press <Esc> to leave input mode and return to command mode.

(When you press <Esc> in command mode, **vi** will beep. If you are not sure what mode you are in, press <Esc> twice. When you hear the beep, you will know you are in command mode.)

There are twelve commands to change to insert mode. Half of these commands are for entering new data; the other half are for replacing existing data.

Of course, you will ask, why do I need so many different commands just to change to input mode? The answer is that each command opens the editing buffer in a different place. Here are the commands for entering new data:

i	change to insert mode: insert before cursor position
a	change to insert mode: insert after cursor position
I	change to insert mode: insert at start of current line
A	change to insert mode: insert at end of current line
o	change to insert mode: open below current line
O	change to insert mode: open above current line

To see how this all works, let's say that you are editing a term paper for your Advanced Classical Music class. The current line is:

For a dime you can see Kankakee or Paree

The cursor is under the letter "K" and you are in command mode.

If you type **i**, you will change to ~~command~~ *insert* mode. As you type, the data will be inserted before the "K". The letters to the right will be moved over to make room.

For example, say that you type:

iAAA<Esc>

(The <Esc> returns you to command mode.) The current line would look like:

For a dime you can see AAAKankakee or Paree

Now, instead, suppose you type **a** to change to insert mode. As you type, the data will be inserted after the "K". If you start with the original line and type:

aBBB<Esc>

the current line would look like:

For a dime you can see KBBBankakee or Paree

 HINT   To remember the difference between the **i** and **a** commands, think of **i**=insert, **a**=append.

By using the **I** (uppercase "I") and **A** (uppercase "A") commands, you can insert data at the beginning or end of the current line, respectively. For example, if you start with the original line and type:

ICCC<Esc>

the current line would look like:

CCCFor a dime you can see Kankakee or Paree

If the current line is indented using spaces or tabs, **vi** will do the intelligent thing and start inserting after the indentation.

If you start with the original line and type:

ADDD<Esc>

the data you type is appended to the end of the line. The current line would now look like:

For a dime you can see Kankakee or PareeDDD

Finally, to insert below the current line, use the **o** (lowercase letter "o") command. To insert above the current line, use the **O** (uppercase "O") command. In either case, **vi** will open a brand new line for you.

☑ **HINT**   To remember the difference between the o and O commands, think of the command name as being a balloon filled with helium. The larger balloon, O, floats higher, above the current line. The small balloon, o, floats lower, below the current line.

As we explained earlier, there are many commands to move the cursor. In particular, the **^** (circumflex) command moves to the beginning of the current line (after any indentation); the **$** (dollar sign) command moves to the end of the current line.

Thus, if you want to insert data at the beginning of the current line, you can type **^** followed by **i**, instead of **I**. Similarly, you can insert at the end of the line by using **$a** instead of **A**.

Here, in a nutshell, is an illustration of the beauty of the design of **vi**. By learning a couple of extra commands, you can often type one character (**I** or **A**) instead of two (**^i** or **$A**). If you are a beginner, this may not seem like much. But after just a few days with **vi**, you will see that anything that saves keystrokes for common operations is a real convenience. Of course, you do have to learn the extra commands. This is why we say that **vi** is easy to use, but difficult to learn.

If you are used to using a mouse with your editor, do not scoff at **vi**'s older, command-oriented design. Take some time to learn all the important **vi** commands. Once you do, you will be pleased at how easy it is to edit data without having to take your hands away from the keyboard to move a mouse or to press special keys. Moreover, you will find that using **vi**'s powerful cursor movement commands is a lot easier and a lot faster than using a mouse to click on a scroll bar.

☑ HINT   Tools that are simple enough to use the first day are often a real pain after the first month.

As you work in input mode, remember:

- You can use the keys listed in Figure 19-1 to correct mistakes. For example, if you mistype a word, you can erase with by pressing **^W** without having to leave insert mode.

- You can enter a control character by prefacing it with **^V**; for example, to enter a backspace, type **^V^H**. On the screen it will look like the two characters **^H**, even though it is really a single character.

Making Changes to the Editing Buffer

In the last section, we looked at the commands that change to input mode so you can insert new data into the editing buffer. In this section, we will examine how to change data that is already in the editing buffer.

First, we will discuss seven **vi** commands. All but one of these replace data by changing to insert mode. Let's start with the one command that does not change to insert mode.

To replace a single character by another character, type **r** followed by the new character. For example, let's say that you are writing one of your professors a letter explaining why you were not able to finish your term paper. You are in command mode, and the current line is as follows:

would mean missing The Simpsons. I gm sure you

You notice that the word "gm" is wrong. Move the cursor to the "g" and type:

ra

The current line now looks like:

would mean missing The Simpsons. I am sure you

Since you changed only one character, there was no need to enter insert mode.

Suppose you want to replace more than one character by overwriting. Move to where you want to start the replacement and type **R** (uppercase "R"). Now each character that you type will replace one character on the current line. When you are finished, press <Esc> to return to command mode.

Here is an example. The current line is as you left it above. You move the cursor to the "T" character and type:

RMa's funeral<Esc>

The current line is now:

would mean missing Ma's funeral. I am sure you

Sometimes, you will want to replace one or more characters with data that is not exactly the same size. There are a number of commands you can use. The **s** (substitute) command allows you to replace a single character with many characters. In our example, move the cursor to the "a" in "Ma" and type:

s

vi will change the "a" to a "$" and put you in insert mode. You will see:

would mean missing M$'s funeral. I am sure you

The "$" shows you which character is being replaced. Type as much as you want and press <Esc> when you are done. Say that you type:

other<Esc>

The current line would be:

would mean missing Mother's funeral. I am sure you

The **C** (uppercase "C") command is a variation of this type of change. It allows you to replace all the characters from the cursor to the end of the line. In our example, say that you move to "I" and type:

C

vi will put you in insert mode and mark the last character to be replaced with a "$". You will see:

would mean missing Mother's funeral. I am sure yo$

Now type whatever you want and press <Esc>. If you type:

We all hoped that<Esc>

The current line is now:

would mean missing Mother's funeral. We all hoped that

Sometimes the easiest thing to do is replace an entire line. There are two commands that will do the job: **S** or **cc**. Just move to the line you want to replace and type either of these commands. You will be in insert mode. When you press <Esc>, whatever you typed will replace the entire line.

Why are there two identical commands whose names look so different? If you were to look at all the **vi** commands, you would see that the names follow a pattern (most of the time). There are names with one lowercase letter, two lowercase letters, or one uppercase letter. According to this pattern, both **S** and **cc** should be the command to replace an entire line.

Thus, you can use whichever one makes more sense. (If you can't see the pattern right now, don't worry about it. Wait until you learn some more commands.)

The final **vi** command to replace data is extremely useful. This command is **c** followed by one of the **vi** commands that move the cursor. Once again, you will be put into insert mode. This time, whatever you type will replace everything from the cursor up to the position indicated by the move command.

This can be a tad confusing, so here are a few examples. Say that the current line is:

would mean missing Mother's funeral. We all hoped that

The cursor is at the "M". You want to replace the entire word "Mother" with "my dog". Type:

cw

vi will put you in insert mode and mark the last character to be replaced with a "$". You will see:

would mean missing Mothe$'s funeral. We all hoped that

Now you type:

my dog<Esc>

The current line is now:

would mean missing my dog's funeral. We all hoped that

In other words, **cw** allows you to change one word.

You can use **c** with any of the cursor movement commands that are single characters, possibly with a repeat count. For example, if you use **c4b**, it will replace from the current position back 4 words. If you use **c (**, it replaces back to the beginning of the sentence. If you use **c}**, it replaces to the end of the paragraph. To replace 6 paragraphs, move to the beginning of the first paragraph and type **c6}**.

The following summary shows the **vi** replacement commands:

r	replace exactly 1 character (does not enter input mode)
R	replace by typing over
s	replace 1 character by insertion
C	replace from cursor to end of line by insertion
cc	replace entire current line by insertion
S	replace entire current line by insertion
c*move*	replace from cursor to *move* by insertion

Replacing a Pattern

If you want to replace a particular pattern with something else, you can use the **ex** command named **:s** (substitute). To make a substitution on the current line, use:

:s/pattern**/**replace**/**

where pattern is the pattern you want to replace, and replace is the replacement text.

For example, to replace "UNIX" with "Unix" on the current line, use:

:s/UNIX/Unix/

Using **:s** by itself will replace the first occurrence of the pattern. If you want to replace all occurrences, put **g** (global) at the end of the command. For instance, to change all occurrences of "UNIX" to "Unix" on the current line, use:

:s/UNIX/Unix/g

If you want **vi** to ask your permission before making the change, you can add **c** (confirm) to the end of the command:

:s/UNIX/Unix/c

At the bottom of the screen, **vi** will display the line that contains the pattern, point out the location of the pattern and wait for your decision. If you want to make the replacement, type **y** (for yes). Otherwise, type **n** (for no). Of course, you can combine both **g** and **c**:

:s/UNIX/Unix/cg

If you want to remove a pattern, just replace it with nothing. For example, to remove all the occurrences of "UNIX" on the current line, use:

:s/UNIX//g

For convenience, if you do not use a **c** or a **g** at the end of the command, you can omit the final **/** character. As an example, the following two commands are equivalent:

:s/UNIX/Unix/
:s/UNIX/Unix

There are two important variations of the **:s** command. First, you can specify a particular line number after the colon. **vi** will make the substitution on that line. For example, to change the first occurrence of "Unix" to "UNIX" on line 57, use:

:57s/UNIX/Unix/

Remember, as we explained earlier, you can tell **vi** to display line numbers by entering the command:

:set number

You can tell **vi** to stop displaying line numbers by entering:

:set nonumber

Instead of a single line number, you can indicate a range by separating two line numbers with a comma. For example, to make the same replacement on lines 57 through 60, use:

:57,60s/UNIX/Unix/

Most of the time, you won't use specific line numbers. However, there are two special symbols that really make this command useful: a **.** (period) stands for the current line, and a **$** (dollar sign) stands for the last line in the editing buffer.

The following command replaces all occurrences of "UNIX" with "Unix", from the current line to the end of the editing buffer:

:.,$s/UNIX/Unix/g

To make the same change from the beginning of the editing buffer (line 1) to the current line, use:

:1,.s/UNIX/Unix/g

lines in the editing buffer. Thus, to change every occurrence of "UNIX" to "Unix" in the entire editing buffer, use:

:%s/UNIX/Unix/g

This is the same as making the substitution from line 1 to line **$** (the end of the editing buffer):

:1,$/UNIX/Unix/g

Obviously, using **%** is a lot more convenient. If you want to make such a change and have **vi** ask for confirmation before each substitution, use:

:%s/UNIX/Unix/gc

If you use such a command, and you want to stop it part way through, press **^C** (the **intr** key). The aborts the entire command, not just the current substitution.

Here is a summary of the **:s** command. To replace the first occurrence of a pattern on each line:

:s/*pattern***/***replace***/**	substitute, current line
:*lines***/***pattern***/***replace***/**	substitute, specified line
:*line***,***lines***/***pattern***/***replace***/**	substitute, specified range
:%s/*pattern***/***replace***/**	substitute, all lines

At the end of the command, you can use **c** to tell **vi** to ask for confirmation, and **g** (global) to replace all occurrences on each line. For line numbers, you can use an actual number or **.** (period) for the current line, and **$** (dollar sign) for the last line in the editing buffer.

To finish this section, here is a particularly useful substitution. Say that you want to save a copy of the manual page of a particular command. (The online manual is explained in Chapter 8.) You enter:

man vi > vipage

This command saves a copy of the **vi** manual page in the file named **vipage**. Now, take a look at the file using **vi**:

`vi vipage`

You will probably see a lot of instances of:

`_^H`

For example:

`_^Hv_^Hi is a display-oriented text editor based on`
`_^He_^Hx.`

Although **^H** takes up two spaces on your screen, it is really a single character. In fact (as we explained in Chapter 6) **^H** is the backspace character. So, `_^H` is just an underscore followed by a backspace. This means that when this line is printed (and the online manual is formatted for printing), each character following a `_^H` will be underlined.

This is fine for paper, but on your screen the `_^H` characters just get in the way. The best thing to do is to get rid of them all by replacing them with nothing. Here is the command:

`:%s/_^H//g`

Since **^H** is a control character, you can't enter it directly. You must first press **^V** and then **^H**. Of course, you do not type four separate characters **^ V ^ H**. You type the two characters <Ctrl-V> and <Ctrl-H>:

`:%s/_<Ctrl-V><Ctrl-H>//g`

You type **^V** only to tell **vi** to take the next character literally; only the **^H** will be displayed. If you were to enter this command, our example would become:

`vi is a display-oriented text editor based on ex.`

After entering this command, there may still be some **^H** characters left in the editing buffer. If so, you can get rid of them all by using:

`:%s/^H//g`

The reason that you couldn't just use this command straight off is that it would not remove the underscores that precede **^H** characters.

Undoing or Repeating a Change

Once you start making substitutions, it becomes important to be able to undo such changes. For instance, say that you wanted to change all the occurrences of the word "advertisement" to "ad". So you decide to enter:

`:%s/advertisement/ad/g`

However, you make a typing mistake and accidentally leave out the second "d":

`:%s/advertisement/a/g`

You have replaced all occurrences of "advertisement" with the letter "a".
You can't just change "a" to "ad" because there are "a"s all over the place.
You could use the :**q**! and quit without saving your work – if you were
working with an existing file – but then you would lose all your changes for
that editing session.

vihas two commands for just such emergencies. They are:

u   undo last command that modified the editing buffer
U   restore current line

The **u** (lowercase "u") command will undo the last command that
changed the editing buffer: an insertion, a substitution, a change or a
deletion. In our example above, all you would have to do is type **u** and your
substitution would be nullified.

If, after pressing **u**, you decide that you really did want the change, simply
press **u** again. The **u** command can undo itself.

The **U** (uppercase "U") command will undo all the changes that you made
to the current line since you last moved to it. For example, let's say you move
to a line and start doing a lot of editing. You make a big mess of it. Finally,
you decide that all you want is for the line to be just as it was when you last
moved to it. Simply type **U**. If you type the **U** command, but you don't like
the results, you can undo them with a **u** command.

The **U** command will undo as many changes as necessary. Remember,
though, **U** will only work as long as you stay on the line with the changes.
As soon as you move to a new line, the **U** command will apply to that line.

Aside from **u**, there is another important command that involves the
previous change to the editing buffer. It is the **.** (period) command:

.   repeat last command that modified the editing buffer

The **.** command will repeat the last insertion, substitution, change or
deletion. Here is an example of how you might use it.

Say that you want to insert the name "Mxyzptlk" at several different
places in the editing buffer. This is a difficult name to spell, and it is a bother
to have to type it more than once.

Here's what to do: Move to the place where you want to make the first
insertion and type:

iMxyzptlk<Esc>

Now, move to the place where you want to make the next insertion and type:

.

The insertion will be repeated for you.

You can use the **.** command as many times as you want. Be careful
though: as soon as you make another change, even a tiny one-character
deletion, the effect of the **.** command will change as well.

Changing the Case of Letters

It may happen that you will need to change letters from lowercase to uppercase, or from uppercase to lowercase. To do so, you can use the ~ (tilde) command:

~   change the case of a letter

Simply move to the letter you want to change and press:

~

vi will change the case of the letter and advance the cursor one position. For example, say that the current line contains:

`"By Jove," he said, "that's a CAPITAL idea."`

The cursor is at the "C". You press:

~

The current line will look like:

`"By Jove," he said, "that's a cAPITAL idea."`

The cursor is now at the "A".

Since, ~ moves the cursor one position to the right, you can type ~ repeatedly to change a sequence of letters. In our example, you can change the rest of the word to lowercase by typing:

~~~~~~

(six tildes).

If you type ~ when the cursor is at a character that is not a letter, such as a punctuation symbol, **vi** will advance the cursor, but will not make a change. Thus, it is safe to "tilde" your way across a vast distance. **vi** will simply skip over the non-alphabetic characters.

It would be useful if you could put a repeat count in front of this command. For example, to change the case of a 7-letter word, it would be nice to be able to type **7~**. Some versions of **vi** will allow this, but many will not. You will have to check your system to see if it works.

Controlling the Length of Lines

When you type a document, you will have to break the text into lines. One way to do this is to press <Return> at the end of each line. Pressing <Return> will insert a **newline** character and – as we explained in Chapter 6 – a **newline** marks the end of a line.

Of course, as you edit, there will be times when you need to break long lines into two. For example, say that you have the following line:

`This line is much too long and must be broken into two.`

You want to break it after the word "and". The easiest way is to move the cursor to the space following "and" and type:

r<Return>

Using the **r** command replaces a single character with another character. In this case, the **r** command replaces the space with a **newline**, effectively breaking the line.

If you need to join two lines, you can use the **J** command:

J   join lines

All you need to do is move to the first line and type **J**. **vi** will join that line and the next line into one large line.

When **vi** joins lines, it automatically inserts spaces in appropriate places. For example, **vi** will put a single space between words. If the end of the first line was the end of a sentence, **vi** will insert two spaces.

If you want to join more than one line, you can put a repeat count before the **J** command. Here is an example. Your editing buffer contains the following lines:

```
This sentence
is short.
This sentence is also short.
```

You move the cursor to the first line and type:

3J

The result is:

```
This sentence is short.   This sentence is also short.
```

The **r** and **J** commands are handy when it comes to small adjustments. But when you are typing large amounts of text, it is a lot easier to let **vi** break your lines for you. To do this, use the **:set wm** command:

:set wm=n auto line break within n positions of right margin

This command affects only input mode. The command tells **vi** to break a line into two when it gets within n characters of the right margin.

For example, to have **vi** break your lines automatically when they get within 6 characters of the right margin, use:

:set wm=6

The name **wm** is an abbreviation for "wrap margin". If you wish, you can spell it out (with no space):

:set wrapmargin=6

Use whatever you find easier to remember.

If you want the longest possible lines, you can use:

:set wm=1

However, it is usually a good idea to leave room for small changes.

☑ **HINT** When setting the automatic margin control, leave enough room for small changes by setting **wm** to between 6 and 10.

To turn off the automatic margin control, set **wm** to **0**:

`:set wm=0`

If you make changes to existing text and you want to re-format it, you can use the **fmt** command as described later in this chapter.

Deleting Data from the Editing Buffer

There are several ways to delete data from the editing buffer. There are five **vi** commands:

x	delete character at cursor
X	delete character to left of cursor
D	delete from cursor to end of line
d*move*	delete from cursor to *move*
dd	delete the entire current line

and two variations of an **ex** command:

:*line***d**	delete specified line
:*line*,*line***d**	delete specified range

No matter what command you use, you can undo any deletion by using the **u** command.

The simplest delete command is **x** (lowercase "x"). It deletes the character at the current cursor position. For example, say that you are writing a letter to your parents telling them all about life at school. The current line of the editing buffer contains:

`I often go to heiQnous paWrties and avoid the library as a rule`

You notice that there is a mistake in the fifth word. You move the cursor to the "Q" and type:

`x`

The current line is now:

`I often go to heinous paWrties and avoid the library as a rule`

The **X** (uppercase "X") command also deletes a single character. The difference is that **X** deletes the character to the left of the cursor. For example, you notice that there is another mistake in the sixth word. You move to the "r" and press:

`X`

The current line is now:

`I often go to heinous parties and avoid the library as a rule`

The **D** (uppercase "D") command deletes from the cursor to the end of the line. For example, say that you move to the space following the word "library" and type:

D

The current line becomes:

`I often go to heinous parties and avoid the library`

The next **vi** deletion command is **d** (lowercase "d") followed by a cursor movement command. **vi** will delete from the cursor up to the position indicated by the move command. This is similar to the **c** (change) command we discussed earlier. Here are some examples:

dw	delete 1 word
d10w	delete 10 words
d10w	delete 10 words (ignore punctuation)
db	delete backwards, 1 word
d2)	delete 2 sentences
d5}	delete 5 paragraphs

☑ **HINT**   Two of the most useful **d** commands are:

dG	delete from cursor to the end of the editing buffer
d1G	delete from cursor to the beginning of the editing buffer

---

To continue our example, say that you move to the beginning of the word "heinous" and type:

d4w

The current line becomes:

`I often go to the library`

The final **vi** deletion command is **dd**. This deletes the entire current line. If you want to delete more than one line, you can put a repeat count in front of the command. For example, to delete 10 lines, use:

10dd

There will be times when it is more convenient to delete using line numbers. At such times, you can use the **ex** command **:d**.

Remember, as we explained earlier, you can tell **vi** to display line numbers by entering the command:

:set number

You can tell **vi** to stop displaying line numbers by entering:

:set nonumber

To use the **:d** command, you can specify either a single line number or a range (two numbers separated by a comma). For example, to delete line 50, use:

:50d

To delete lines 50 through 60, use:

:50,60d

As with the other **ex** commands, the symbol **.** (period) stands for the current line and **$** (dollar sign) stands for the last line in the editing buffer. For example, to delete from the beginning of the editing buffer to the current line, use:

:1,.d

To delete from the current line to the end of the editing buffer, use:

:.,$d

To delete the entire editing buffer, use either of the following commands:

:1,$d
:%d

(Remember, as we explained earlier, **%** stands for all the lines in the editing buffer.)

Copying the Last Deletion

At all times, **vi** keeps a copy of the last thing that you deleted. You can copy this deletion to any place in the editing buffer by using the **p** and **P** (put) commands.

The **p** (lowercase "p") command inserts the last deletion after the current position of the cursor. For example, say that the current line contains:

This good is a sentence.

You move to the "g" and delete one word by typing:

dw

The current line now looks like:

This is a sentence.

Now you move to the space between "a" and "sentence", and type:

p   (lowercase "p")

The deleted word is inserted to the right of the cursor. The current line is now:

This is a good sentence.

Here is an example that uses the **P** command. Say that the current line contains:

This is right now.

You move to the space before the word "right" and type:

de

This erases up to the end of the word and leaves you with:

This is now.

Now move to the period and type:

P   (uppercase "P")

The deletion is inserted to the left of the cursor. The current line becomes:

This is now right.

Consider now the combination **xp**. The **x** command deletes the character at the current cursor position. The **p** command inserts the deletion to the right of the cursor. The net result is to transpose two characters.

For example, say that the current line is:

I ma never mixed up.

You move to the first "m" and type:

xp

The current line is now:

I am never mixed up.

Another important combination is **deep**. Here is an example. Say that the current line contains:

I am mixed never up.

Move to the space before the word "mixed". (Take care to move to the space before the word, not the first letter of the word.) Now type:

deep

The **de** deletes the space and the following word, after which the current line looks like:

I am never up.

The **e** moves forward to the end of the next word. The **p** inserts the deletion after the cursor. The net result is:

I am never mixed up.

Thus, the effect of **deep** is to transpose two words.

When you delete whole lines, **p** and **P** will insert whole lines. **p** will insert below the current line; **P** will insert above the current line.

Consider, then, what happens when you type **ddp**. The **dd** command deletes the current line. The next line becomes the new current line. The **p** inserts the deletion below the new current line. The net result is to transpose two lines.

 HINT   Remember the following **vi** command combinations:

      xp
      deep
      ddp

To summarize:

p   copy last deletion; insert after/below cursor
P   copy last deletion; insert before/above cursor

As we explained earlier, using a repeat count in front of the **dd** command will delete multiple lines. One way to move lines is to use **dd** to delete them, and then use **p** or **P** to insert the lines in their new location.

For instance, say that you want to move 10 lines. Position the cursor on the first line and type:

10dd

This deletes the 10 lines. Now position the cursor at the line below which you want to make the insertion. Type:

p

The 10 deleted lines will be inserted. You can even move to another part of the editing buffer and use the **p** command to insert the same lines once again.

Copying and Moving Lines

There will be times when it is convenient to copy or move lines while referring to them by number. For these operations, you can use the **ex** commands **:co** (copy) and **:m** (move).

Remember, as we explained earlier, you can tell **vi** to display line numbers by entering the command:

:set number

You can tell **vi** to stop displaying line numbers by entering:

:set nonumber

The **:co** and **:m** commands use the same format. The only difference is that **:m** deletes the original lines, while **:co** makes a copy.

To use these commands, you specify a single line number, or a range of line numbers, before the command name. After the command name, you specify the target line number. The new lines will be inserted below the target line. Here are some examples:

:5co10	copy line 5, insert below line 10
:4,8co20	copy lines 4 through 8, insert below line 20
:5m10	move line 5, insert below line 10
:4,8m20	move lines 4 through 8, insert below line 20

As with other **ex** commands, you can use a . (period) to refer to the current line and a $ (dollar sign) to refer to the last line in the editing buffer. For example:

:1,.m$	move lines 1 through current line, to bottom

You can also use line 0 (zero) to refer to the beginning of the editing buffer:

    : . , $m0   move current line through last line, to top

These last two commands are interesting. They both swap the top and bottom parts of the editing buffer. However, there is a subtle difference. With the first command, the current line ends up at the bottom of the editing buffer. With the second command, the current line ends up on top.

To summarize, the **ex** copy and move commands are:

: *line***co***target*	copy specified *line*; insert below *target*
: *line* , *line***co***target*	copy specified range; insert below *target*
: *line***m***target*	move specified *line*; insert below *target*
: *line* , *line***m***target*	move specified range; insert below *target*

Entering Shell Commands

There are several ways to enter regular shell commands from within **vi**. First, you can issue a command by typing : ! followed by the command. **vi** will send the command to the shell to be executed.

For example, to display the time and date, enter:

: !**date**

After the command is finished, **vi** will display:

[**Hit return to continue**]

Press <Return> and you will be back in **vi**.

To repeat the most recent shell command – regardless of long it has been since you entered it – use:

: ! !

For example, if the last shell command you entered was **date**, you can display the time and date once again by using : ! !.

If you would like to enter a number of shell commands, you can start a new shell. There are two ways to do this. First, you can use the : **sh** command:

: **sh**

This will pause **vi** and start a new copy of whatever shell you use. You can now enter as many commands as you want. When you are finished with the shell, stop it – by pressing ^D or by entering the **exit** command – and you will be returned to **vi**.

If, for some reason, this doesn't work on your system, you can run a new copy of the shell as an actual command. For example, to start a new C-Shell, run the **csh** program:

: !**csh**

(The names of the various shells are discussed in Chapter 10.) When you end the shell, you will be returned to **vi**.

Here is a summary:

`:!`*command*	pause **vi**, execute specified shell command
`:!!`	pause **vi**, execute previous shell command
`:sh`	pause **vi**, start a shell
`:!csh`	pause **vi**, start a new C-Shell

If you want to insert the output of a shell command directly into the editing buffer, you can use the `:re !` command, described in the next section.

Reading Data into the Editing Buffer

To read data from an existing file into the editing buffer, use the `:r` command. Here is an example:

`:10r info`

Before the command name, you specify the line number where you want to insert the new data. **vi** will insert the data *after* the specified line. After the command name, leave a space and specify the name of the input file. Our example inserts the contents of the file **info** into the editing buffer after line 10.

If you want to refer to the beginning of the editing buffer, use line 0 (zero). For example, to insert the contents of **info** at the beginning of the editing buffer, use:

`:0r info`

To refer to the end of the editing buffer, use `$`:

`:$r info`

If you omit the line number, **vi** will insert after the current line. This is probably the most useful form of the `:r` command. For example, to insert the contents of the file **info** into the editing buffer, move to where you want the data and enter:

`:r info`

There is a variation of the `:r` command that is especially useful. If, instead of a file name, you type an `!` (exclamation mark) followed by a regular shell command, **vi** will execute that command and insert its output into the editing buffer.

Here is an example. In Chapter 21, you will learn how the **ls** command displays a list of your files. If you are editing and you want to insert such a list after the current line, enter:

`:r !ls`

If you want to insert the time and date at the end of the editing buffer, use:

`:$r !date`

Here is a wonderful time-saving idea. In Chapter 16, we showed you how to use the **look** command to help you find out how to spell a word. For example, say that you want to use the word "simultaneous", but you are not sure how to spell it. You can use the command:

```
look simu
```

In this case, the output is:

```
simulate
simulcast
simultaneity
simultaneous
```

When you are using **vi**, you can use **:r** to insert the output of such a command directly into the editing buffer. So, let's say that you are typing and you want to use the word "simultaneous", but you are not sure how to spell it. Press <Esc> to change to command mode and enter:

```
:r !look simu
```

The output of the **look** command will be inserted after the current line (which is the line you were last typing).

Now delete all but the word you want. (If you don't want any of the words, use the **u** command to undo the change.)

Once you have deleted all but the correct word, move up to the last line you typed and type:

```
J
```

This will join the new word onto the end of the line. Finally, to return to insert mode at the end of the line, type:

```
A
```

(Remember, the **A** command allows you to append data to the end of the current line.)

This sequence of commands may seem a bit complex, but it is actually quite simple. Try it. It's way cool.

Here is a summary of the **:r** command:

*:line***r** *file*	insert contents of *file* after specified *line*
:r *file*	insert contents of *file* after current line
*:line***r** *!command*	insert output of *command* after specified *line*
:r *!command*	insert output of *command* after current line

 HINT   If you don't like the result of a **:r** or **:r!** command, you can reverse it with the **u** (undo) command.

Using a Shell Command to Process Data

Using the ! and ! ! (exclamation mark) commands, you can send lines from the editing buffer to a regular shell command. The output of the command will replace the original lines. For example, you can replace some lines with the same data in sorted order.

To do this, move to the line where you want to start. Type the number of lines you want to process, followed by ! !, followed by the shell command, followed by <Return>.

For example, say that you have five lines that contain the following data:

```
entertain
balloon
anaconda
dairy
coin
```

Move to the first line and enter:

```
5!!sort
```

(The **sort** command is discussed in Chapter 16.)

Once you type the second !, **vi** will move the cursor to the command line and display an !. You can now type your shell command directly on the command line. If necessary, you can back up and make corrections before you press <Return>.

In our example, the original 5 lines will be replaced by:

```
anaconda
balloon
coin
dairy
entertain
```

 HINT   If you use ! or !! to process data in the editing buffer with a shell command and you don't like the results, you can undo the change by using the **u** command.

Here is another example that is especially useful. In Chapter 14, we described the **fmt** (format) command. This command reads its input and, using the same text, generates lines that are as close as possible to 72 characters long. **fmt** will preserve spaces at the beginning of lines, spaces between words and blank lines. In other words, **fmt** will make your message look nice without changing the paragraph breaks.

fmt is useful for formatting all or part of your editing buffer when you are creating documents. If you use **fmt**, you don't have to worry so much about line breaks as you are entering and editing your data.

The following command will format 10 lines, starting from the current line:

10!!fmt

The **!** command works much the same as the **!!** command, except that you have more flexibility in specifying the range of input lines. Type **!** followed by a command that moves the cursor, followed by the shell command. For example:

!}fmt

This command sends all the data from the current line, up to and including the line specified by the cursor move, to be processed by the **fmt** command. In this example, we will process all the lines to the end of the paragraph (because the **}** command moves to the end of the paragraph).

Once you type the **!**, **vi** will move to the command line and display **!**, just as with the **!!** command.

Here is an easy way to format the entire editing buffer. Move to the first line of the editing buffer by typing:

1G

Then enter:

!Gfmt

(Remember, the **G** command moves to the end of the editing buffer.) Similarly, you could sort the entire editing buffer by using:

!Gsort

To summarize:

n!!*command*	execute *command* on *n* lines
! *move command*	execute *command* from cursor to *move*

Writing Data to a File

When you stop **vi** using the **ZZ** command, it automatically saves your data. However, there are several commands that you can use to write data to a file whenever you want.

:w	write data to original file
:w *file*	write data to specified *file*
:w>> *file*	append data to specified *file*

The **:w** command will write the contents of the editing buffer back to the original file. For example, say that you started **vi** by entering the command:

vi memo

The contents of the file **memo** are copied to the editing buffer. No matter how many changes you make to the editing buffer, the original file, **memo**, is not changed. This arrangement is important as it allows you to quit without changing your file (by using the :**q!** command).

However, at any time, you can enter:

:**w**

This will copy the editing buffer back to the file. Normally, you don't need to do this unless you are going to use the :**e** command to start editing a new file (see below). However, if you have made a lot of changes, you might want to take a moment and save them back to the original file. This will protect you against losing your work if something goes wrong.

If you specify the name of a file after the :**w** command, **vi** will write the data to that file. For example, to save the contents of the editing buffer to a file named **extra**, enter:

:**w extra**

If the file does not already exist, **vi** will create it. If the file does exist, **vi** will replace its contents.

Remember this: if you use :**w** to write to a file that exists, the old contents will be lost. If you want to append the new data to the end of an existing file, type **>>** (two greater-than signs) after the command name. For example:

:**w>> memo**

Using **>>** will preserve the old data. (Note: The **>>** notation is also used to redirect the standard output of a command to an existing file. See Chapter 15.)

If you want to write only certain lines of the editing buffer, you can specify them in the usual manner. For example, to write line 10 to a file named **save**, enter:

:**10w save**

To append lines 10 through 20 to a file named **save**, use:

:**10,20w>> save**

Changing the File You Are Editing

When you start **vi**, you usually specify the name of the file you want to edit. For example, to edit a file named **memo**, you enter:

vi memo

If you are within **vi** and you decide that you want to edit a different file, you do not have to quit and restart the program. Instead, you can use the :**e** and :**e!** commands:

    :**e** *file*   edit the specified file
    :**e!** *file*   edit the specified file, omit automatic check

To change to a new file, use the `:e` command, followed by the name of the file. For example, to begin editing a file named **document**, enter:

`:e document`

When you start editing a new file, the old contents of the editing buffer are lost. Thus, make sure to use the `:w` command first and save your data. When you use the `:e` command, **vi** will check to see if you have saved your data. If there is unsaved data, **vi** will not let you change to a new file.

If you would like to override this protection, use the `:e!` command. For example, say that you start **vi** using the command:

`vi memo`

The contents of **memo** are copied to the editing buffer. As it happens, you make so many mistakes that you would rather just start over. The last thing you want to do is save the contents of the editing buffer back to the original file. Enter:

`:e! memo`

You are now editing a copy of the original file. The previous changes have been thrown away.

Using Abbreviations

By using the `:ab` command, you can create abbreviations for frequently used words or expressions. For example, say that you are working on a resume for a summer job. You would find it tiresome to type "exceptionally gifted" over and over. Instead, you can establish an abbreviation of, say, "eg".

Type `:ab`, followed by the short form, followed by the long form. For example,

`:ab eg exceptionally gifted`

From now on, whenever you type "eg" as a separate word (in input mode), **vi** will automatically replace it by "exceptionally gifted". **vi** is smart enough not to replace "eg" within a word, such as "eggplant".

If you want to see a list of all the current abbreviations, enter the command name by itself:

`:ab`

If you want to remove an abbreviation, use the `:una` (un-abbreviate) command. Type `:una` followed by the name of the short form you wish to remove. For example:

`:una eg`

To summarize:

`:ab` *short long*	set *short* as an abbreviation for *long*
`:ab`	display current abbreviations
`:una` *short*	cancel abbreviation *short*

Using the `.exrc` File to Initialize `vi`

When `vi` starts, it looks for a file named `.exrc` in your home directory. If such a file exists, `vi` will read and execute any `ex` commands that it finds. This allows you to initialize your working environment automatically.

(We discuss the home directory in Chapter 21. We discuss initialization files in Chapter 11. The name `.exrc` stands for "`ex` run commands".)

An `.exrc` file is a great place to put `:set` and `:ab` commands that you use all the time. You can also put in regular shell commands by using the `:!` command.

Before we continue, we want to take a moment to describe one more `ex` command (`:map`) that is especially useful within an `.exrc` file.

You use the `:map` command to define what is called a "macro": a one-character abbreviation for a command. Macros are not used all that often, and we won't go into the details. However, there is one particular macro that is handy and should always be defined. It lets you use the letter `g` as a synonym for `1G`. The command to create this macro is:

`:map g 1G`

Once you define this macro, you can move to the beginning of the editing buffer by typing `g` (lowercase "g"), and to the end of the editing buffer by typing `G` (uppercase "G"). (Of course, you must be in command mode.)

Now, to continue, `vi` will ignore any lines within the `.exrc` file that begin with `"` (a double quote). You can use such lines to hold descriptive comments. In addition, `vi` will ignore space and tab characters at the beginning of a command. This allows you to indent commands to make them easier to read. Finally, within an `.exrc` file, you do not need to start any of the commands with a colon.

Here is a sample `.exrc` file:

```
" set the options
    set wrapmargin=6
" set abbreviations
    ab eg exceptionally gifted
" define the g macro
    map g 1G
" display the time and date and pause for 2 seconds
    !date; sleep 2
```

(Note: The `sleep` command tells Unix to pause for the specified number of seconds.)

If your `.exrc` file contains a bad command, `vi` will quit executing the file at that command. Although `vi` will start properly, the rest of the commands in the `.exrc` file will not be processed. `vi` will usually display some type of error message, but it will probably go by so fast that you will have trouble reading it. Make sure that you test each command carefully before you place it in your `.exrc` file.

The Unix File System

The most important part of any computer system is its data: the information that is stored and manipulated by the programs. Unix has a FILE SYSTEM whose job it is to maintain all the data that is stored in the computer. This includes programs, documents, databases, text files and so on.

Most of the time, the Unix file system runs automatically. The file system does need some care and feeding occasionally, but this is the responsibility of your system manager. All you need to understand are the basic concepts and how to use a few of the commands.

In this chapter, we will orient you to the Unix file system. In Chapters 21 and 22, you will learn how to use the file system commands that will help you in your day-to-day work.

What Is a File?

In everyday life, the idea of a file is straightforward: a collection of papers, such as you might keep in a folder in your desk. If you have used a computer, you may know a more specific meaning for the word "file". On most computer systems, a file is a collection of data, stored on a disk or tape. A computer file might contain a document, a program, a spreadsheet, a picture, a message or whatever. Each file has a name by which you can reference it.

Within Unix, the definition of a file is much broader. A FILE is any source from which data can be read, or any target to which data can be written. Thus, the term "file" refers not only to a repository of data like a disk file, but to any physical device. In particular, the keyboard (a source of input) is a file, the display (an output target) is a file, and each printer (also an output target) is a file.

In this chapter, you will learn that all files are named in a standard way. In fact, it is just as easy to send input to one of your disk files as to, say, the screen of the terminal that your friend is using in the next room.

To put this in perspective, remember that the disk is inside the host computer which may be, say, in the office of the system administrator on the other side of the building (or across the campus). (See Chapter 3.)

This generality is of enormous importance: it means that Unix programs are much more flexible than programs in other computer systems. Any program that reads and writes using standard input/output (see Chapters 15 and 16) can use any input source and any output target. Moreover, you will find that the Unix file system has a compelling beauty: everything makes sense.

 HINT   In Unix, the term "file" refers to any source of input or target of output, not only to a repository of data.

The Three Types of Unix Files

Unix has three types of files: ordinary files, directories and special files.

An ORDINARY FILE is what most people think of when they use the word "file". Ordinary files contain data and are stored on disk or, less often, on tape. These are the files that you will work with most of the time. For example, when you use a text editor program to modify a document, both the document and the editor program itself are stored in ordinary files. Sometimes, these types of files are called REGULAR FILES.

The next type of file is a DIRECTORY. A directory is stored on disk and contains information that is used to organize and access other files. Conceptually, a directory "contains" other files. For example, you might have a directory named **homework** within which you keep all the files having to do with your assignments.

You yourself do not create the directory, nor do you put files in it or maintain it. You use commands to tell Unix to do the work for you. For example, if you want to see what is in a directory, you don't actually look inside. You use a command to tell Unix to look inside, figure out what it means, and display a summary for you. (This is the **ls** [list] command.)

If you did look inside a directory, all you would see is gibberish. A directory does not really contain files, it contains the information that Unix needs to access the files. The best way to understand a directory is to think of it as pointing to a number of files.

A directory can also point to other directories. This allows you to organize your files into a hierarchical system using whatever design suits your needs.

Philosophical difference, Directories are in fact files that specify how to access other files

As we will see later, the whole Unix file system is organized as one large hierarchy with directories inside of directories inside of directories. Whenever you want, you can tell Unix to make or remove directories. Thus, you can change your organization as your needs change.

The last type of file, a SPECIAL FILE or DEVICE FILE, is an internal representation of a physical device. For example, your keyboard, your display screen, a printer, the disk drive – all the devices on your system can be accessed as files. To send data to the screen on someone else's terminal, all you have to do is write the data to the file that represents that device.

WHAT'S IN A NAME?

File

There are three types of Unix files: ordinary files, directories and special files. However, the word "file" is often used, informally, to refer to just ordinary files.

When you see or hear the word "file", you must decide, by context, what it means. Sometimes it means any type of file, sometimes it means just ordinary files.

For example, say that you read the sentence: "The `ls` command lists the names of all the files in a directory." In this case, the word "file" refers to any type of file: an ordinary file, a special file or a directory. All three types of files can be stored in a directory and, hence, listed with the `ls` command.

But what if you read, "You can use the `vi` editor to modify your text files." In this sentence, the word "file" refers only to ordinary files – files that contain data – because they are the only type of files that it makes sense to edit.

Thus, the word "file" is used in two ways: to mean any type of Unix file, and to mean the plain vanilla ordinary files that we work with from minute to minute. Most of the time, the difference is clear by context.

Text Files and Binary Files, Bits and Bytes

Special files represent physical devices; directories organize other files. It is the ordinary files that contain actual data (including programs).

There are as many types of ordinary files as there are types of data. However, broadly speaking, we can categorize ordinary files into two groups: text files and binary files.

TEXT FILES are ordinary files that contain only ASCII characters: the type of data that you can generate by typing at a keyboard. In fact, the term ASCII FILE is often used as a synonym for text file.

(The ASCII character set is explained in Chapter 16. Briefly, it is a set of 128 different codes that represent the different characters that we use for textual data: upper- and lowercase letters, numerals, the space, the tab, punctuation, as well as the control characters.)

Text files are used to hold documents, memos, shell scripts and so on. You can edit a text file with a text editor, such as **vi** or **emacs** (see Chapter 19). When you display a text file on your screen, it is composed of normal, everyday characters, and it makes sense when you look at it.

BINARY FILES are ordinary files that contain non-textual data. If you try to display or edit a binary file, the output will look like gibberish. Binary files contain data that only makes sense when processed by a program. For example, say that you use a program that maintains a database. Chances are that the data will be stored in a binary file, using a format that makes sense only to the database program.

Here is a more common example involving binary files: You are writing a computer program, say, in the C programming language. You create the program by editing a text file that contains instructions in the C language. However, the computer cannot execute instructions in the C language. They must first be translated into so-called machine instructions that the computer can understand.

To do so, there are two special programs that you use – a compiler and a linker – to make the translation. We won't go into the details here. The main idea is that the C program you write is stored in a text file that you can edit and understand. The compiler and linker use this text file and generate a binary file that contains the equivalent machine language program.

The original C program – the one that you create with a text editor – is called the SOURCE PROGRAM or, more simply, the SOURCE. The machine language program, the binary file that you can execute, is called the EXECUTABLE PROGRAM. Thus, when you program, you create a text file, but the computer executes a binary file.

The distinction between text files and binary files becomes important when you transfer data from one computer to another. In many cases, you have to use different commands to transfer the two types of data. Thus, you need to be aware of what type of file you are using.

☑ **HINT**   As a rule of thumb: If an ordinary file contains data that you can display or edit, it is a text file. Otherwise, it is a binary file.

Technical Differences Between Text Files and Binary Files

If you have followed the discussion carefully, you may have felt dissatisfied. So far, we have not really defined the difference between text files and binary files, we have only given examples and appealed to your intuition.

The difference between these two types of files is highly technical. We will explain it briefly, but if you don't understand it at first, don't worry.

Within a computer, data is stored as a long series of BITS. A bit consists of a single binary digit: that is, a single element that is either a 0 or a 1. In other words, computers store data as long strings of 0s and 1s.

A string of bits is divided into groups of 8, each group being known as a BYTE. Thus, we can consider computer data as being stored in bytes, each of which contains 8 bits, each of which consists of a 0 or a 1.

Data is represented using codes of 0s and 1s. The ASCII code contains the rules for representing textual data. You can look at the ASCII code (see Appendix D) and see the bit pattern for each character. For example, the uppercase letter "A" is represented by the bits 01000000. The lowercase letter "a" – a completely different character – is represented by the bits 01100001.

Using the ASCII code, a text file stores one character per byte. Thus, a file that contains 1000 characters will be 1000 bytes long.

Strictly speaking, the ASCII code uses only 7 bits per character. The 8th bit – the leftmost one – is always set to 0. Thus, when a text file (which contains ASCII data) is transferred to another computer, the transferring programs need only pay attention to the rightmost 7 bits in each character. The 8th bit is ignored, or is used for other purposes (which we won't go into).

Binary files also store data in bytes. However, the data in binary files does not necessarily use the ASCII code. Each binary file contains data that was stored in the way that makes sense to the program that created the file.

The important idea is that, where text files only use 7 bits out of each byte, binary files use all 8 bits. That means that when you transfer a binary file, the transferring programs need to make sure that all 8 bits are accounted for. This is why you must tell the transferring program whether you are using text files or binary files.

To summarize: A text file contains ASCII characters that use 7 bits per byte. A binary file contains data that uses the full 8 bits per byte.

Directories and Subdirectories

We use directories to organize files into a hierarchical system. To do so, we collect files together into groups and keep each group in its own directory. Since directories are themselves files, a directory can contain other directories. This is what creates the hierarchy.

Here is an example. Say that you are taking three classes for which you have to write essays: History, Literature and Surfing. You use the **vi** editor (Chapter 19) to write the essays, of which there are several for each class.

To organize all this work, you make a directory called **essays** (don't worry about the details for now). Within this directory, you make three more directories: **history**, **literature** and **surfing**. Within each of these directories, you keep your essays. Each essay is stored in a text file that has a descriptive name. Figure 20-1 shows a diagram of what it all looks like.

PARENT DIRECTORY A PARENT DIRECTORY is one that contains other directories. A *SUBDIRECTORY* SUBDIRECTORY is a directory that lies within another directory. In Figure 20-1, **essays** is a parent directory that contains three subdirectories: **history**, **literature** and **surfing**. Sometimes a subdirectory is called a CHILD DIRECTORY.

It is common to talk about directories as if they contain other files. For example, we might say that **essays** contains three subdirectories. Or we might say that **literature** contains four text files.

Thus, you might imagine that if we looked inside the **literature** directory we would actually see the four files. Actually, Unix stores all files as distinct items. If we were to look inside **literature** (and we can't really), we would see, not four text files, but the information that Unix needs to access these files.

However, there is really no reason to care about the technical details. Unix maintains the whole file system for us automatically. All we need to do is use the appropriate command, and Unix will do whatever we want: make a directory, remove a directory, move a file from one directory to another and so on. From our point of view, everything just works, and we can, indeed, think of directories as containing other files.

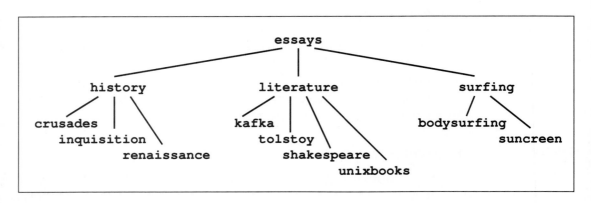

Figure 20-1
An Example of Organizing with Directories

The Tree-Structured File System

Unix systems contain many, many files that are organized using directories and subdirectories. The Unix file system is based upon a single main directory called the ROOT DIRECTORY. (The name will make sense in a moment.) The root directory is the parent or ancestor of every directory in the system.

Figure 20-2 shows the outline of the Unix file system. You can see the root directory at the top. This figure shows the directories that are used with systems based on Berkeley Unix. If your system is based on System V (see Chapter 2) or another variation of Unix, your file system may be somewhat different.

What you see in Figure 20-2 is the bare skeleton. All Unix systems will have other directories created by the system manager. It is not really important to memorize the name of each directory. All you need is a general idea of how the file system is organized. (We will take a quick look at these directories in a moment.)

As you can see, the outline of the Unix file system is like an upside-down tree. The name "root" was chosen to indicate the main trunk of the tree. (Only a weenie would have called it the "trunk" directory.)

Since the root directory is so important, its name must often be specified as part of a command. It would be tiresome to always have to type the letters "root". Instead, the root directory is indicated by a single **/** (slash).

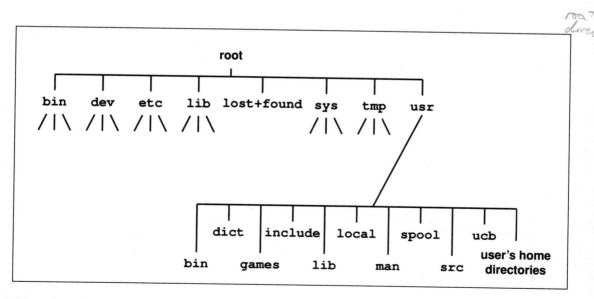

Figure 20-2
The Unix File System

For example, the `ls` command will list the names of all the files in a specific directory. To list all the files in the root directory, you use:

`ls /`

When you specify the name of a directory or a file that lies within the root directory, you write a **/** followed by the name. For example, the formal name of the **etc** directory is **/etc**. To list all the files in this directory, use:

`ls /etc`

Formally, this means "the directory named **etc** that lies within the **/** (root) directory".

To indicate a directory or file within another directory, separate the names with a **/**. For example, within the **/etc** directory is a file named **passwd**. The formal name of this file is **/etc/passwd**. Similarly, within the **/usr** directory is another directory named **dict**. Within this directory is a file named **words**. The formal name of this file is **/usr/dict/words**.

 HINT   The / character has two different meanings. At the beginning of a file name, / stands for the root directory. Within a file name, / acts as a delimiter.

Once you understand the tree in Figure 20-2, you can see that all directories, except the root directory, lie within another directory. Thus, all directories, except the root directory, are actually subdirectories. In day-to-day speech, we use the term "subdirectory" only when we want to emphasize that a particular directory lies within another directory. Mostly, we just say "directory".

A Tour of the Root Directory

The root directory is the base of the entire file system. Mostly, it contains only other directories. However, the root directory does contain at least one important file: the program that is the heart of Unix (called the "kernel"). On Berkeley Unix systems, this program is in a file named **vmunix**. (The name stands for "virtual memory Unix". Virtual memory is a technique for using disk space to simulate large amounts of memory.)

Vmunix

The **/bin** directory contains basic programs that are part of Unix. This is where many of the Unix commands are stored. The name "bin" refers to the fact that many of these programs are binary files. However, we like to think of this directory as a storage bin for programs.

/bin

The **/dev** directory contains the special files that represent the physical devices. You usually won't need to use these files, but, if you do, here they are.

/dev

The **/etc** directory is mostly for the system administrator. Here lie the programs and files that are used for managing the system. Perhaps the most well-known file is **passwd**, the system password file (see Chapter 12). Another well-known file is **termcap**, a database that contains technical descriptions of all the terminals that Unix can use. (Some Unix systems use a different database called **terminfo**.)

/etc

The **/lib** directory contains libraries of programs used by programmers.

The **/lost+found** directory is used by a special program that checks the Unix file system. Whenever this program finds a file that does not seem to belong anywhere (accidents do happen), it will put it in the **/lost+found** directory. The system manager can then look at the file and dispose of it appropriately.

The **/sys** directory contains what are called system source files. These are of interest only to the system manager and to programmers.

The **/tmp** directory is used for temporary storage. Anybody is allowed to store files in this directory, and, from time to time, all the files in this directory are removed automatically. Typically, a program will use the **/tmp** directory to store files that are needed for only a short time.

For example, when you use **vi** editor (Chapter 19), it makes a copy of the file you want to edit. This copy is stored in the **/tmp** directory. Thus, you are always working with a temporary copy and not with the original file. (This temporary file is the editing buffer that we discussed in Chapter 19.)

The **/usr** directory contains a number of important subdirectories of its own, which we will discuss later in the chapter.

Using the Special Files in the /dev Directory: tty

We have already explained how special files are used to represent physical devices. All the special files are kept in the **/dev** directory. To display the names of the special files on your system, use the command:

`ls /dev`

You will see many names. You will rarely have a need to use most of these special files. For the most part, they are for system programs. However, there are a few special files that are interesting to know about.

All the files that begin with the letters "tty" represent terminals. For example, terminal **tty01** is represented by the special file **/dev/tty01**. If you send output to this file, it is just like sending output to the screen of that terminal.

For example, say that you have a file named **scary** that displays a short, scary message. You use the **who** command (Chapter 12) and find out that one of your friends is logged in to terminal **tty01**. You can use the **cp** (copy) command (see Chapter 22) to copy the contents of the scary file directly to your friend's terminal screen:

`cp scary /dev/tty01`

The message will appear from nowhere, thus scaring him into an early decline. On some systems, this command will work even if your friend has set **mesg** to **n** (see Chapter 12).

(Disclaimer: The above command is given only as an example. Only a bored, immature person would actually play such a trick.)

If you want to display the name of the special file that represents your terminal, use the command:

tty

For example, you might see the output:

/dev/tty02

This means that you are logged in to terminal **tty02**.

As a convenience, you can always use the file **/dev/tty** as a synonym to represent your terminal. Thus, you could display data on your screen by copying it to **/dev/tty**. If you ever use a program that must write its output to a file, you can display the output by telling the program to write to **/dev/tty**.

The most useful file in the **/dev** directory is named **null**. This file represents an non-existent, empty device. When you read from **/dev/null** you get nothing; when you write to **/dev/null** the output disappears.

The **null** file is handy when you have a program that writes spurious output that you want to ignore. If you send the output to **/dev/null**, it will disappear forever.

For example, say that you have a program that updates data in certain files. The program is named **updatefiles**. The usual way to run the program would be to enter its name as a command:

updatefiles

However, as the program runs, it generates lines of output that are displayed on your terminal: output that you would just as soon not have to look at. Using the **>** symbol, you can redirect the output to the **/dev/null** file:

updatefiles > /dev/null

Essentially, this runs the program, but throws away the output. (Redirection is explained in Chapter 15.)

When you read the Usenet discussion groups (Chapter 23), you will sometimes see a remark like: "If you don't like my comments, send your criticisms to **/dev/null**." This is a not-so-subtle way of telling people who disagree to go pound sand.

A Tour of the /usr Directory

The **/usr** directory is one of the most important subdirectories in the root directory. The **/usr** directory holds a number of subdirectories of its own. (As you will see, the name "usr" indicates that some of these subdirectories are given to users to hold their personal files.)

The **/usr/bin** directory, like its namesake in the root directory, is used to hold executable programs.

The **/usr/dict** directory contains files used by the Unix dictionary (actually a word list). For more details, see the discussion of the **look** command in Chapter 16.

The **/usr/games** directory contains the Unix games and diversions (see Chapter 7).

The **/usr/include** directory contains the so-called "include" files that are used by programmers. These hold predefined instructions that are included in many different programs.

The **/usr/lib** directory, like its counterpart **/lib**, contains libraries of programs and data used by programmers.

The **/usr/local** directory is used for the convenience of the system manager. He or she can use this directory to store local programs and documentation.

The **/usr/man** directory contains the directories and files used by the online Unix manual (explained in Chapter 8).

The **/usr/spool** directory acts as a way station. It is used to hold data that is waiting to be sent somewhere. For example, when you print a file (see Chapter 18), a copy of the file, along with some system information, is kept in this directory. The file waits here until it can be printed. Similarly, when you send mail (see Chapters 13 and 14), it is kept in this directory until it can be delivered. As we explained in Chapter 18, the word "spool" is an old acronym, originally meaning "simultaneous peripheral operations of-fline".

The **/usr/src** directory holds source programs. If your site has the right type of Unix license (software is licensed, not sold), this directory may contain the actual programs that make up Unix itself. If so, you can look at them to your heart's content. If you can read the C programming language, reading the Unix programs can be a fascinating (and time-consuming) venture into the unknown.

The **/usr/ucb** directory contains programs that were developed at the Computer Science department of the University of California at Berkeley. If you want to see the principal commands that were added to standard System V Unix by the developers of Berkeley Unix, you can list the files in this directory. Use the command:

```
ls /usr/ucb
```

This directory is found in all modern systems, since, these days, virtually all Unix systems contain the Berkeley programs. (For a discussion of the different types of Unix, see Chapter 2.)

Home Directories

With so many system directories chock-full of important files, it is clear that we need an orderly system for users to store their personal files. Of course, people like you and me wouldn't make a mess of things if we were allowed to, say, store our own programs in the **/bin** directory. But, for the most part, we can't have people putting their files, willy-nilly, wherever they want.

The solution is to give each user a HOME DIRECTORY. This is a directory, associated with a particular userid, which is completely under the auspices of that userid. When your system manager registers you with the system, he or she assigns you a home directory. The name of your home directory is kept in the system password file (see Chapter 12). When you log in, the system automatically places you in this directory. (The idea of being "in" a directory will make more sense after you have read Chapter 21.)

Within this home directory, you can do whatever you want. You can store files and create other subdirectories as you see fit. Many people have large elaborate tree structures of their own, all under their personal home directory.

The traditional place for the system manager to create home directories is under the **/usr** directory. The name of the home directory is the name of the userid. For example, if your userid is **harley**, your home directory would be **/usr/harley**. Many system managers place home directories elsewhere. On some systems, home directories are within a directory named **u**; on other systems, they are within a directory named **users**; still others use parent directories that categorize users into groups, such as **undergrad**, **grad**, **profs** and **staff**.

When you log in, the environment variable **$HOME** is set to the name of your home directory. (Environment variables are discussed in Chapter 11.) Thus, one way to display the name of your home directory is to enter:

```
echo $HOME
```

(The **echo** command simply displays the values of its arguments.)

If you use the C-Shell, the symbol ~ (tilde) can be used as an abbreviation for your home directory. For example, you can display the name of this directory by using:

```
echo ~
```

Whatever its name, the important thing about your home directory is that it is yours to use as you see fit. (However, there will probably be a quota that limits the total amount of disk space that you can use.) One thing that many people do is create a **bin** subdirectory to store their own programs. You can put the name of this directory – for example, **/usr/harley/bin** – in your search path.

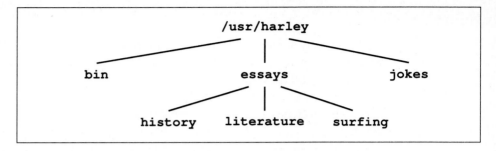

Figure 20-3
A Typical Home Dirctory-Based Tree Structure

(The search path is explained in Chapter 11. Basically, your search path is a list of directories. This list is stored in the shell variable named **path**. Whenever you enter the name of a command that is not built into the shell, Unix looks in the directories specified in your search path to find the appropriate program to execute.)

Figure 20-3 shows a typical directory structure based on the home directory of **/usr/harley**. This home directory has three subdirectories: **bin**, **essays** and **jokes**. The **essays** directory has three subdirectories of its own: **history**, **literature** and **surfing**. All of these directories contain files (which are not shown in the diagram). As you will see in Chapter 21, making and removing subdirectories is easy. Thus, it is a simple matter to enlarge or prune your directory tree as you see fit.

Working with Directories

*finally! A bit
late in the book,
eh?*

*This is
Chapt.
1
mater*

In Chapter 20, we described how the Unix file system is organized as a hierarchy of directories and subdirectories. We explained how each user is assigned a home directory to organize as he or she sees fit.

In this chapter, you will learn the commands and techniques you need to organize your directories. You will also learn how to move from one directory to another as you work. Finally, you will learn how to use **ls**, one of the most important Unix commands, to display the contents of a directory.

Pathnames and Your Working Directory

In Chapter 20, we saw how to write the full name for a file. Start with a **/** (slash), which stands for the root directory. Then write the names of all the directories you have to pass through to get to the file. Separate each name with a **/** character. Finally, write the name of the file.

Here is an example:

/usr/dict/words

In this case, the file **words** lies in the **dict** directory, which lies in the **usr** directory, which lies in the root directory.

When we write the name of a file in this manner, we call it a PATHNAME, because it shows the path through the directory tree from the root directory to the file in question.

Let's say that your userid is **harley** and your home directory (see Chapter 20) is **/usr/harley**. You have a file named **memo** that you want to edit using the **vi** editor (Chapter 19). You enter:

vi /usr/harley/memo

Later, you want to edit another file, named **document**. You enter:

vi /usr/harley/document

As you can see, it is a lot of bother to have to specify the full pathname every time you want to use a file. To make life easier, Unix allows you to designate one directory at a time as your WORKING DIRECTORY (also known as your CURRENT DIRECTORY). When you want to use a file that is in your working directory, you do not need to specify the whole path: you only need to type the file name.

For example, if you tell Unix that you will be working in the directory **/usr/harley**, you can enter the commands:

vi memo
vi document

Another way of expressing this idea is that if a file name does not start with a **/**, Unix will assume that the file is in your working directory.

The best way to understand how all this works is to remember that the Unix file system can be understood as a large tree. The trunk of the tree is the root directory. Think of the various directories as being branches of the tree. For example, if a directory has three subdirectories, you can think of that branch as having three sub-branches. (If you want a more visual picture, look at the figures in Chapter 20.)

Now, imagine that you are sitting on some branch of the tree. The branch you are sitting on is your working directory. If you want to change your working directory, you must move to a different branch of the tree.

When you log in, Unix automatically sets your working directory to be your home directory. In other words, as soon as you log in, you instantly find yourself sitting on the branch of the tree that represents your home directory.

Absolute and Relative Path Names

There are two main ways to specify file names. You can choose whichever method is most convenient at the time.

In order to show you how it all works, we will use the sample directory tree in Figure 21-1. This tree shows several subdirectories based on a home directory of **/usr/harley**.

Under the home directory, we have two subdirectories, **bin** and **essays**. In keeping with the Unix tradition, the files in the **bin** directory contain our personal programs. There are two such programs, **funky** and **spacewar**. The **essays** subdirectory contains two subdirectories of its own, **history** and **literature**. Each of these directories contains two files.

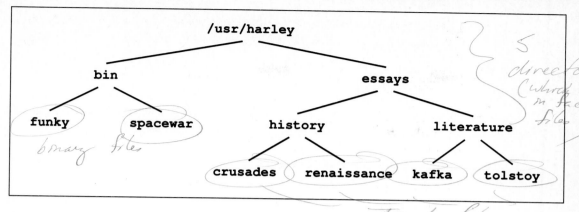

Figure 21-1
A Sample Directory Tree

(To recall the terminology of Chapter 20, we have eleven files: five directories and six ordinary files. Of the ordinary files, the two programs are binary files and the four essays are text files.)

Let us say that we have just logged in. Our working directory is automatically set to be the home directory, **/usr/harley**. Now let's take a look at how we might specify the names of the various files.

Say that we want to use a command in which we need to refer to the **bin** directory. Of course, we can call it **/usr/harley/bin**, which is the pathname. However, an easier way is to take advantage of the current setting of our working directory.

Unix assumes that any file name that begins with a **/** shows the full path to the file, starting from the root directory. However, if a file name does not begin with a **/**, Unix assumes that it describes a path starting from the working directory.

In this case, the working directory is **/usr/harley**. Thus, you do not have to type the long name **/usr/harley/bin**. All you need to type is **bin**.

Here is another example using the same working directory. You want to enter a command for which you need to specify the name of the **tolstoy** file in the **literature** directory. The full name – the pathname – of this file is:

/usr/harley/essays/literature/tolstoy

However, since the working directory is **/usr/harley**, you can refer to the file as:

essays/literature/tolstoy

Here is one final example. Say that you want to do a lot of work with the files **kafka** and **tolstoy**. It is inconvenient to refer to these files using the full pathnames:

```
/usr/harley/essays/literature/kafka
/usr/harley/essays/literature/tolstoy
```

Moreover, it is only slightly more convenient to use names relative to the working directory:

```
essays/literature/kafka
essays/literature/tolstoy
```

The best thing to do is to change the working directory to be:

```
/usr/harley/essays/literature
```

(We will show you how to do this in a moment.) Having changed the working directory, you can refer to the files more simply, as **kafka** and **tolstoy**.

The idea is to choose your working directory so as to make file names easy to type. Think of the working directory as a base of operations that you can change whenever you want. When you log in, you start out in your home directory, but you can change to any directory you want, whenever you want.

To distinguish between the two ways of specifying file names, we sometimes call a pathname – a name that starts with a **/** – an ABSOLUTE PATHNAME. When we use a name that does not start with a **/**, we call it a RELATIVE PATHNAME.

In other words, an absolute pathname starts from the root directory. A relative pathname starts from the working directory. The idea is to set your working directory so that you can use short, relative pathnames whenever possible.

When we show sample commands in this book, such as:

```
vi document
```

we are actually using relative pathnames. In this case, the command will start the **vi** editor using the file named **document**. We assume that **document** resides in the working directory.

Three Handy Pathname Abbreviations: . . . ~

Unix provides three handy pathname abbreviations. The first is two periods in a row:

```
. .
```

which is often called "dot-dot". When you use **. .** in a pathname it refers to the parent directory.

To illustrate how this works, let us use the sample directory tree from Figure 21-1. Within our home directory **/usr/harley**, we have two subdirectories, **bin** and **essays**. The **bin** directory contains two files. The **essays** subdirectory contains two subdirectories of its own, **history** and **literature**. Each of these directories contains two files.

Say that we set the working directory to be:

/usr/harley/essays/literature

We can now refer to the two files in this directory as **kafka** and **tolstoy** (using relative pathnames).

From this working directory, the specification .. refers to the parent directory. From within our current working directory, .. means the same as:

/usr/harley/essays

So, let's say we wanted to use the file **crusades** within the **history** directory. One way is to use the absolute pathname:

/usr/harley/essays/history/crusades

An easier way is to use .. to stand for the parent directory:

../history/crusades

Unix will replace the .. with the name of the parent directory.

Now, say that we want to refer to the **bin** directory. We could use the absolute pathname:

/usr/harley/bin

Alternatively, we can use the .. abbreviation twice:

../../bin

assuming we're now at

The first parent directory is:

/usr/harley/essays

/usr/harley/essays/literature

The second parent directory is:

/usr/harley

Here is another example. Let's say that we want to refer to the **funky** file within the **bin** directory. The absolute pathname is:

/usr/harley/bin/funky *which is ----?*

But, starting from our working directory, we can use:

../../bin/funky

Finally, here is one last extreme example. From our working directory:

/usr/harley/essays/literature

we can refer to the root directory as:

../../../..

And we can refer to the **/etc** directory as:

../../../../etc

Of course, you would probably never use these examples, as it is a lot easier to type **/** and **/etc**. The .. abbreviation is most useful when you want to refer to directories near your working directory, without having to actually change your working directory.

The second pathname abbreviation is a single period:

.

This is usually called "dot". A single . refers to the working directory itself. For example, if the working directory is:

```
/usr/harley/essays/literature
```

the following three specifications all refer to the same file:

```
/usr/harley/essays/literature/kafka
./kafka
kafka
```

Certainly, it is a lot easier to type . than the full name of the working directory. But, as you can see, you don't really need to specify any directory name. As long as a file name does not begin with a **/**, Unix will assume that the name is relative to your working directory.

rarely use

You might ask, why would you ever need to use a single . abbreviation? The answer is, you rarely do. However, there are certain situations in which you must specify an absolute pathname. In such cases, you can use the . abbreviation and Unix will replace it with the name of your working directory.

The idea is to avoid typing a long pathname, but not only out of laziness (although that is a good idea). Using the . makes it much less likely that you will make a spelling mistake. And, as you probably know by now, it is far too easy to make spelling mistakes when you are typing Unix commands.

Here is a quick example. Let's say that you have written a program called **plugh**. (We leave it to your imagination as to what this program might do.) The program is in the directory **/usr/harley/adventure**, which is your working directory.

Normally, you run a program by entering its name:

```
plugh
```

However, Unix can only run a program when it lies in one of the directories in your search path (see Chapter 11). In this case, it happens that the directory that contains the program is not in your search path.

As an alternative, Unix will find any program if you specify the absolute pathname of the file. In this case, you can run the program by typing:

```
/usr/harley/adventure/plugh
```

An easier way is to use . to stand for your working directory:

```
./plugh
```

As this example illustrates, when you start a file name with `..` or `.` you are really specifying an absolute pathname. The `..` and `.` are abbreviations that Unix replaces appropriately.

The third pathname abbreviation is the `~` (tilde). You can use this symbol at the beginning of a file name to stand for your home directory. For example, to use the **ls** command to list the names of all the files in your home directory, you can use:

```
ls ~
```

To refer to the subdirectory **bin** that lies within your home directory, you can use:

```
~/bin
```

Note: You cannot use the `~` abbreviation with the Bourne shell, although you can use it with the C-Shell, the Korn shell, Bash, the Tcsh and the Zsh. (The various shells are discussed in Chapter 10.)

Moving Around the Directory Tree: cd, pwd

To change your working directory, use the **cd** (change directory) command. The syntax is:

```
cd [directory]
```

where *directory* is the name of the directory to which you want to change. If you enter the command without a directory name, **cd** will, by default, change to your home directory.

To display the name of your working directory, use the **pwd** (print working directory) command. The syntax is easy:

```
pwd
```

pwd is one of the most useful Unix commands. You will find yourself using it a lot.

WHAT'S IN A NAME?

pwd　　In Chapter 6, we explained how the early Unix developers used teletype terminals that printed output on paper. Over the years, Unix has retained the convention of using the word "print" to mean "to display information".

Thus, the name **pwd** stands for "print working directory", even though it has been a long time since anyone actually printed the name of their working directory.

continued

If you are using the C-Shell, it is a simple matter to create an alias for the **pwd** command (say **dwd**, for "display working directory"):

alias dwd pwd

However, nobody really bothers. **pwd** is kind of a cute name, even if it is anachronistic.

(Using aliases with the C-Shell is explained in Chapter 11.)

☑ **HINT**

When we talk about **cd**, it is common to talk as if the user were really the one changing directories. For example, we might say, "You can use the **cd** command to change to the **/usr/harley/essays** directory," as if you yourself were doing the changing.

Sometimes, we use the name of the command as a verb: "You can **cd** to the **/usr/harley/essays** directory and check for the file you want."

This convention recalls our earlier metaphor in which you imagine yourself sitting on a branch of the directory tree. Wherever you are sitting is your working directory. Using the **cd** command moves you from branch to branch.

Here are some examples of how to use the **cd** command. You may want to practice using similar examples on your own terminal. If so, use the **pwd** command from time to time to check where you are.

To change your working directory to **/usr/harley/essays**, use:

cd /usr/harley/essays

To change to **/bin**, use:

cd /bin

To change to **/** (the root directory) use:

cd /

The **cd** command is especially convenient when you use relative path-names or abbreviations. For example, say that your working directory is **/usr/harley**. Within this directory, you have two subdirectories, **bin** and **essays**. To change to **bin** (which is really **/usr/harley/bin**), enter:

cd bin

Because the directory name (**bin**) does not start with a **/**, Unix assumes it is a relative pathname, based on the current value of the working directory.

Here is another example. Your working directory is **/usr/harley**. This time you want to change to:

/usr/harley/essays/history

Using a relative pathname, you can enter:

cd essays/history

As we mentioned above, entering the **cd** command without a directory name:

cd

will change to your home directory, no matter where you are in the tree. Thus, you never really need to know the full pathname of your home directory.

☑ **HINT**   Whenever you get lost in the directory tree, just enter:

cd

to return to your home directory. (Using the **cd** command in this way is equivalent to clicking your heels together and repeating "There's no place like home...")

Using the **cd** command in this way is convenient when you are exploring in some distant branch of the file system and you want to work with your own files. For example, say that your working directory happens to be **/etc/local/programs**. You want to move to the **bin** directory within your home directory. Just enter:

cd
cd bin

To make it more convenient, recall that you can enter more than one command on the same line as long as you separate the commands with a semicolon. (See Chapter 9.) Thus, no matter where you are in the tree, you can move to your own personal **bin** directory by entering:

cd; cd bin

The first command changes to your home directory. The second command changes to the **bin** directory within your home directory.

You can also use the standard pathname abbreviations that we discussed earlier. As you remember, . . stands for the parent directory. For example, say that your working directory is:

/usr/harley/essays/history

To change to **/usr/harley/essays** directory, you can use:

cd ..

You could change to **/usr/harley/ essays/literature** from the same working directory by using:

cd ../literature

As with other commands, you can use the `. .` abbreviation more than once. For example, from the same working directory, you can change to `/usr/harley/bin` by using:

```
cd ../../bin
```

Question: What happens if you are in the root directory and you enter:

```
cd ..
```

Answer: The root directory does not have a parent directory. Nothing happens.

The other useful abbreviation is `~` (tilde), which stands for the name of your home directory. (Remember, you cannot use this abbreviation with the Bourne shell.) Thus, the following two command lines are equivalent:

```
cd ~/bin
cd; cd bin
```

Both will change to the `bin` directory within your home directory.

☑ **HINT** To make it easy to remember where you are in the directory tree, create an alias that displays the name of your working directory every time you use a `cd` command:

```
alias cd 'cd \!*; echo $cwd'
```

This alias replaces the `cd` command with two commands: a `cd` command followed by an `echo` command. The `echo` command displays the value of the built-in shell variable `cwd` (which contains the name of your current working directory).

For example, if your home directory is `/usr/harley` and you enter:

```
cd ~/bin
```

you will see:

```
/usr/harley/bin
```

If you like what this alias does, place it in your `.cshrc` file to make it a permanent part of your personal toolbox.

The details of this alias are discussed in Chapter 11, as is the `.cshrc` file.

Making a New Directory: `mkdir`

To make a directory, use the `mkdir` command. The syntax is:

```
mkdir [directory]...
```

where `directory` is the name of a directory you want to make.

Using this command is straightforward. You can name a new directory anything you want as long as you follow a few simple rules. We will go over the rules in Chapter 22 when we talk about naming files. (Remember, as we explained in Chapter 20, directories are really files.) Basically, you can use letters, numbers, and those punctuation symbols that do not have a special meaning.

☑ **HINT**   When you name directories, life will be easier if you stick to lowercase letters only.

For example, to make a directory named **extra**, within your working directory, use:

```
mkdir extra
```

When you specify a directory name, you can use either an absolute or relative pathname, as well as the standard abbreviations.

As an example, let's say that you want to create the directory tree in Figure 21-2. (These are the directories that we used as examples earlier in the chapter.) Within your home directory, you want to make two subdirectories, **bin** and **essays**. Within the **essays** directory, you want to make two more subdirectories, **history** and **literature**.

To start, make sure that you are in your home directory:

```
cd
```

Now, make the first two subdirectories:

```
mkdir bin essays
```

Next, change to the **essays** directory:

```
cd essays
```

and make the final two subdirectories:

```
mkdir history literature
```

To illustrate the various ways to specify pathnames, let's take a look at two more ways to create the same directories. First, you could have done the whole thing without leaving the home directory:

```
cd
mkdir bin essays essays/history essays/literature
```

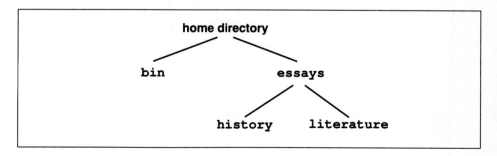

Figure 21-2
Making a Sample Directory Tree

The first command changes to the home directory. The second command specifies all four names, relative to the new working directory.

In the following example, we don't even bother changing to the home directory:

```
mkdir ~/bin ~/essays ~/essays/history ~/essays/literature
```

Remember, the ~ (tilde) character is an abbreviation for your home directory.

There are times when it is handy to use the `..` abbreviation to indicate a parent directory. For example, say that you have changed to the **essays** directory:

```
cd ~/essays
```

You now decide to create a subdirectory named **extra** within the **bin** directory. The **bin** directory and the **essays** directory have the same parent (the home directory). You can use:

```
mkdir ../bin/extra
```

When you create a directory, Unix makes you follow two sensible rules. First, within a single parent directory, you cannot make two directories with the same pathname. For example, you cannot have two directories named `~/essays/history`. (How would you tell them apart?)

However, you can have two directories with the same name if they are in different parent directories. For example:

```
~/essays/history
~/homework/history
```

The second rule is that you cannot make a subdirectory if its parent directory does not exist. For example, you cannot make a directory named `~/homework/history` unless you have already made `~/homework`.

When you specify more than one directory within a single **mkdir** command, Unix will make the directories in the order that you specify. Thus, the command:

```
mkdir ~/homework ~/homework/history
```

will work, because the **homework** directory is made before Unix tries to make the **history** directory. However, the command:

```
mkdir ~/homework/history ~/homework
```

will not work.

Recall for a moment our analogy comparing the file system to a tree. The main trunk is the root directory, and each branch is a subdirectory. The two rules merely say that (1) you cannot make two identical branches, and (2) you cannot make a new branch that has nowhere to attach to the tree.

Removing a Directory: `rmdir`

To remove a directory, use the **rmdir** command. The syntax is straightforward:

```
rmdir directory...
```

where *directory* is the directory that you want to remove.

For example, to remove the directory **extra** from within the working directory, use:

```
rmdir extra
```

When you use **rmdir**, you can specify one or more directory names using absolute or relative pathnames. You can also use the standard abbreviations: `..` for the parent directory, and ~ (tilde) for the home directory.

Let's take a look at some examples using the sample directory tree that we built in the previous section. Within the home directory, we have two subdirectories, **bin** and **essays**. Within the **essays** directory, we have two more subdirectories, **history** and **literature**. Figure 21-2 shows this tree.

Say that you want to delete all of these directories. There are several ways to do the job. First, move to the **essays** directory:

```
cd ~/essays
```

From here, you can delete the two subdirectories:

```
rmdir history literature
```

Next, move to the parent directory (the home directory):

```
cd ..
```

Remove the two main subdirectories:

```
rmdir bin essays
```

An alternate method would be to move to the home directory and remove all four subdirectories in one command:

```
cd
rmdir essays/history essays/literature essays bin
```

As a final example, you could do all the work without moving to the home directory:

```
rmdir ~/essays/history ~/essays/literature ~/essays ~/bin
```

When you remove a directory, Unix makes you follow two sensible rules. First, you cannot remove a directory unless it is empty. This is a safeguard. (A directory is not empty if it contains a subdirectory.)

For example, say that you have two directories, **data** and **olddata**. The **data** directory contains 100 important files. The **olddata** directory is empty.

You decide to remove the **olddata** directory. However, just as you enter the command, a meteorite smashes through the window hitting the nerd sitting at the next terminal. In the confusion, you accidentally type:

`rmdir data`

Fortunately, Unix is prepared for just such an eventuality. You see the message:

`rmdir: data: Directory not empty`

Your **data** directory is left untouched.

There may be occasions when you really do want to remove a directory that is not empty. For this operation, you can use the **rm** command with the **-r** option. Using **rm -r** will also remove all subdirectories and their contents. This command is explained in Chapter 22. Obviously, this is a command to use carefully.

The second rule for removing directories is that you cannot remove any directory that lies between your working directory and the root directory.

For example, say that your working directory is:

`/usr/harley/essays/literature`

You cannot remove the **essays** directory, because it lies between you and the root directory. However, you can remove the directory:

`/usr/harley/essays/history`

by using:

`rmdir ../history`

After all, the **history** directory does not lie between you and the root directory.

If you want to remove **essays**, you must first move closer to the root directory, say to **/usr/harley**. Now you can remove the directory:

`cd /usr/harley`
`rmdir essays/history essays/literature essays`

(This example assumes that you have already removed all the files from the three directories. To remove files, use the **rm** command which we will discuss in Chapter 22.)

Question: Your working directory is **/etc**. Can you remove a subdirectory that lies within your home directory? The answer is yes, because your working directory (**/etc**) does not lie between the root directory and the directory you want to remove.

To remember this rule, just recall our analogy to a real tree. The trunk is the root directory. Each branch is a subdirectory. At any time, you are sitting on some branch that is your working directory. You can think of removing a directory as sawing off a branch of the tree.

The restriction on removing directories simply states that you cannot saw off a branch that is holding up the one you are sitting on.

☑ **HINT**   It is possible to remove your working directory. This is like cutting off the branch of the tree that you are sitting on. Probably Unix shouldn't let you do this, but it does.

Removing your working directory will only cause you problems. Don't do it.

Moving or Renaming a Directory: mv

To move or rename a directory, use the **mv** command. The syntax is:

mv *directory target*

where *directory* is the name of the directory you want to move or rename, and *target* is the name of the target.

The **mv** command will perform either a move or rename operation, whichever is appropriate. (Note: The **mv** command can be used to move or rename any type of file, not just a directory. In Chapter 22, we will use **mv** with ordinary files.)

Here is an example. Say that you have a directory named **data** in your working directory. You want to change the name of this directory to **extra**. Assuming that a directory named **extra** does not already exist (in your working directory), you can use the command:

mv data extra

As you can see, renaming a directory is essentially the same as "moving" it to a different name. Thus, the **mv** command performs both these operations.

If the target directory already exists, **mv** will move the original directory into the target. For example, say that the following two directories already exist:

/usr/harley/data
/usr/harley/storage

You want to move the **data** directory to lie within the **storage** directory. Use:

mv /usr/harley/data /usr/harley/storage

The pathname of the **data** directory is now:

/usr/harley/storage/data

Of course, if your working directory is **/usr/harley**, you can simplify the command:

mv data storage

When **mv** moves a directory, it also moves all the files and subdirectories that lie within that directory. For example, say that, before the move, you had a file named **document** within the **data** directory. Its absolute pathname was:

`/usr/harley/data/document`

After the move, the absolute pathname becomes:

`/usr/harley/storage/data/document`

If you had subdirectories – perhaps even a whole sub-tree – under **data**, they are moved as well.

Thus, you can use the **mv** command for three purposes:

1. Rename a directory.
2. Move a directory.
3. Move an entire sub-tree.

Listing the Contents of a Directory: `ls -rCFR1`

To display information about the contents of a directory, use the **ls** (list) command. You will find that **ls** is one of the most frequently used Unix commands. As such, it has many options to control its output. The standard Berkeley Unix **ls** command has 18 options. Most commercial versions of Unix have even more options.

In our discussion of **ls**, we will show you the most important options. If you would like more details, see the **ls** manual page for your system. (Use the command **man ls**. The online Unix manual is explained in Chapter 8.)

In this section, we will introduce the **ls** command and discuss the simple options. In the following sections, we will talk about the advanced features of **ls** and discuss the more complex options.

The syntax for the **ls** command is:

`ls [-adglrsCFR1] [name...]`

where *name* is the name of a directory or an ordinary file.

Notice that **ls** has a **-l** (lowercase "l") option and a **-1** (the number "1") option. Do not confuse them. (Actually, the **-l** option is used a lot. The **-1** option is used rarely.)

The basic function of **ls** is to display an alphabetical list of names of files in a directory. For example, to list the files in the **/bin** directory, use:

`ls /bin`

To list the files in both the **/bin** and **/etc** directories, use:

`ls /bin /etc`

It is useful to use the **. .** abbreviation with the **ls**. For example, to list the files in the directory that contains your working directory, use:

ls . .

To list the files in the directory that contains the parent directory, use:

ls . ./. .

The most common way to use **ls** is without parameters:

ls

By default, **ls** will display the names of all the files in your working directory.

 HINT

To list the names of the files in your working directory, use the **ls** command with no parameters:

ls

This is possibly the single most frequently used Unix command (after **mail harley**).

When **ls** sends its output to your terminal (which is usually the case), the output will be organized into columns. For example, here are the first five lines of output of a directory listing of the **/bin** directory. (On this particular system, the actual output was 23 lines.)

[	e	li	nice	sh5
ar	echo	line	nm	shutdown
as	ed	ll	od	size
awk	expr	ln	pagesize	strip
cat	false	login	passwd	stty
.	.	.	.	.
.	.	.	.	.
.	.	.	.	.

Notice that the file names are arranged alphabetically by column. That is, you read down, not across. As we explained in Chapter 20, the **/bin** directory contains many of the Unix commands, so some of the names in this directory will look familiar.

(Yes, in answer to your question, there really is a command with the odd name of **[**. It is used in writing Bourne shell scripts, but we will not go into the details.)

When you redirect the output of **ls** to a file or to a pipeline, **ls** will write only one file name per line. This makes it easy to process the output of **ls** with another program. (Redirection and pipelines are explained in Chapter 15. Filters – programs that are used in pipelines – are explained in Chapter 16.)

A common example is:

```
ls | wc -l
```

The **wc -l** command counts the number of lines of input it receives. Thus, this combination of **ls** and **wc** tells you how many files you have in your working directory.

If you want to force **ls** to write columns to a file or pipeline, use the **-C** option (uppercase "C"):

```
ls -C
```

If you want to force **ls** to write one line per file name to your terminal, use the **1** option (the number "1"):

```
ls -1
```

By default, **ls** displays file names in alphabetical order. (More precisely, **ls** uses the order of the characters in the ASCII code. See Chapter 16.) If you want to display the names in reverse order, use the **-r** (lowercase "r") option:

```
ls -r
```

You will often find yourself in the position of wanting to find out what types of files a directory contains. In such cases, you can use the **-F** (flag) option. This option flags certain file names with an identification character. Names of directories are followed by a **/** (slash). Names of ordinary files that contain executable programs are followed by an ***** (asterisk). Other types of ordinary files are not marked.

For example, say that your working directory contains a directory named **documents**, a text file named **memo**, and a binary file named **spacewar** that contains a program. The command:

```
ls -F
```

will display:

```
documents/    memo    spacewar*
```

The last **ls** option that we will discuss in this section is **-R** (uppercase "R"), which stands for "recursive". This option can be used when you specify a directory name. The option tells **ls** to list information about all the subdirectories and files that lie within the directory you name. In other words, **ls -R** displays information about an entire sub-tree.

For example, to list all the files and subdirectories that are descendents of your home directory, use:

```
ls -R ~
```

(Remember, ~ is an abbreviation for your home directory.) Be careful not to confuse the **-r** and **-R** options when you enter a command.

WHAT'S IN A NAME?

Recursive   There are several file and directory commands that have either a **-R** or **-r** option to process an entire sub-tree. When you use such an option, it tells the command to process all the subdirectories and files that are descendents of the directory you specify.

The letters "R" or "r" stand for the word "recursive", which is actually a technical term with several meanings. In computer science, a recursive program is one that can put itself on hold and start a new copy of itself. (Yes, this can make sense as long as the programmer ensures that everything works properly.)

It is hard to see how this has anything to do with processing a directory tree. The only real connection is that it is possible to write recursive programs to work with tree structures. However, this really doesn't apply to Unix commands.

So, don't worry if the name makes no sense to you. Just remember that, with Unix file commands, "recursive" (**-R** or **-r**) means "process the entire sub-tree".

Keeping Track of Your Disk Space Usage: `ls -s, du, quota`

One use for the **ls** command is to see how much storage space your files use on the disk. It is possible that your userid has some type of quota restricting you to a maximum amount of disk space. So, from time to time, it is a good idea to see how much storage you are using.

Disk storage is measured in kilobytes, megabytes and gigabytes. One KILOBYTE is 1,024 (2^{10}) bytes; one MEGABYTE is 1,048,576 (2^{20}) bytes; one GIGABYTE is 1,073,741,824 (2^{30}) bytes. Within a text file, one byte holds one character. For example, 100 characters requires 100 bytes of disk storage. Most of your files will be measured in kilobytes.

If you want to find out how much disk space a directory or file uses, you can use the **ls** command with the **-s** (size) option. **ls** will preface each file name with its size in kilobytes. If you specify a directory name, **ls** will also show a total for the entire directory.

For example, here are the first six lines of output of a directory listing of the **/bin** directory using the **-s** option. (On this particular system, the actual output was 38 lines.)

```
total 4055
  12 [              40 init             1 pr
   1 ar            96 init.old        168 ps
   1 as            24 kill            24 pwd
   1 awk            1 ksh             24 radisk
  28 cat           128 l              168 rdump
   .                .                  .
   .                .                  .
   .                .                  .
```

On the top line, you can see that the total space used by all the files in the directory is 4,055 kilobytes. The other lines show how much space the various files require. The **cat** file, for example, uses 28 kilobytes.

Another command you can use is **du** (disk usage). The syntax is:

`du [-as] [name...]`

where *name* is the name of a directory or file.

When you specify the name of one or more directories, **du** will show you the number of kilobytes used by those directories and all the subdirectories that come under them. If you do not specify a name, **du** will assume you mean your working directory.

If you use the **-s** (sum) option, **du** will display only the grand total. If you use the **-a** (all) option, **du** will break down the total and show the size of each directory and file that it counted. To see a nice display of all your file usage:

`du -a ~`

(Remember, ~ is an abbreviation for your home directory.) This command will show you each of your files and directories and how much space they use. The last line of the output will show your home directory and the grand total.

When you specify the name of one or more files, you must use the **-a** option. For example:

`du -a /bin/cat /bin/echo`

When you use **du** in this way, you will see how much space is used by each of the files you specify.

Many systems impose a quota on how much disk space each userid is allowed to use. If your system has such a quota, you can use the **quota** command to check on your usage and limits:

`quota`

To display extra information, use the **-v** (verbose) option:

`quota -v`

Note: The three commands **ls -s**, **du** and **quota** estimate storage usage in different ways, so don't be surprised if the numbers vary somewhat.

> ☑ **HINT**
>
> It is important to remember that you are sharing your file system, usually with many other people. Disk space is often at a premium, and you should make sure that you don't use more than you really need.
>
> From time to time, check how much space you are using. If you have files that you do not need, especially large files, be considerate and remove them.
>
> Don't think of it as being forced to live within your quota. Think of it as being a good neighbor.

Wildcards, Filename Substitution, Globbing

When you use directory and file commands, you can employ special characters called WILDCARDS to specify a pattern of file names.

For example, say that you want to list the names of all the files in your working directory that start with "h". You can use:

```
ls h*
```

Using wildcards is a lot like using the regular expressions that we described in Chapter 16 (filters) and Chapter 19 (the **vi** editor). In fact, you can think of wildcards as being a limited type of regular expression. However, there are important differences. Figure 21-3 shows the basic wildcards and how they are used to specify file names. You might find it interesting to compare this table with the ones that describe the standard regular expressions. (Figures 16-2 and 19-2.)

When you use wildcards, the shell interprets the pattern and replaces it with the appropriate file names. For example, when you enter:

```
ls h*
```

Symbol	Meaning
*	match any sequence of zero or more characters
?	match any single character
[ ]	match one of the enclosed characters

Note: You must specify a / (slash) character explicitly. You cannot match it with a wildcard.

Figure 21-3

Summary of Wildcards Used to Specify File Names

the shell replaces the **h*** with all the file names that begin with the letter **h**. For instance, if your working directory contains six files: **a, b, h, h1, h2** and **z**, the previous command is changed to:

ls h h1 h2

This concept is known formally by different names, depending on what shell you are using. With the C-Shell and Tcsh, it is called FILENAME SUBSTITUTION. With the Bourne shell, the Korn shell and the Zsh, it is called FILENAME GENERATION. With Bash, it is called PATHNAME EXPANSION. You get the idea.

The actual operation of substituting file names for a wildcard pattern is called GLOBBING. Sometimes, the word GLOB is used as a verb, as in, "Unless you set the **noglob** variable, the C-Shell globs automatically."

What happens if you specify a wildcard pattern that does not match any files? The shell will display an appropriate message and abort the command. The message you see depends on what shell you are using. Shells in the C-Shell family (C-Shell, Tcsh) display a message like:

No match

Shells in the Bourne shell family (Bourne shell, Korn shell, Bash, Zsh) display your pattern followed by:

not found

(The various shells are discussed in Chapter 10.)

Here are some examples so you can see how it all works. The first character with a special meaning is ***** (the asterisk). This stands for zero or more of any character except a **/** (which, as you know, has a special meaning within a pathname). For example, the following wildcard specifications match patterns as indicated:

Ha*   names that begin with **Ha**
Ha*y   names that begin with **Ha** and end with **y**
Ha*l*y names that begin with **Ha**, contain an **l**, and end with **y**

The **?** (question mark) stands for any single character. For example, to match file names that start with **d**, followed by a single character, use **d?**. To match file names that start with any character and end with **y**, use **?*y**. To find all the 2-character file names, use **??**.

To specify characters from a set, use **[** and **]** (square brackets) to enclose the set. This represents a single instance of any of the specified characters. For example, to match file names that begin with either an **H** or an **h**, use **[Hh]***. To match the file names **spacewar.c** or **spacewar.o**, use **spacewar.[co]**.

To specify a range of characters within square brackets, you can use a **-** (hyphen). For example, the wildcard pattern **[a-z]** represents all the lowercase letters. The pattern **[a-zA-Z]** represents all the lowercase and uppercase letters.

Thus, to match all the file names that begin with a lowercase letter, use **[a-z]***. To match all the file names that begin with a lowercase or uppercase letter and end with a numeral, use **[a-zA-Z]*[0-9]**.

Here is an example. You want to display the name and size of the files that hold the oldest Unix commands. Most of these command names consist of two lowercase letters, like **ls**. The best place to look for old commands is in the **/bin** and **/usr/bin** directories (see Chapter 20). Thus, we can use the **ls** command with the **-s** (size) option to examine these directories:

```
ls -s /bin/[a-z][a-z] /usr/bin/[a-z][a-z]
```

Try it on your system and see what you find.

If you use the C-Shell, Tsch or Bash, there are two types of abbreviations that you can use in addition to the wildcard symbols. These are shown in Figure 21-4.

First, as we explained earlier, you can use a ~ (tilde) at the beginning of a file name to stand for the name of your home directory.

Second, you can use **{** and **}** (the brace brackets) to enclose a list of patterns, separated by commas. For example:

```
{harley,addie}
```

The shell will form a separate file name using each pattern in turn. Note: Do not put spaces before or after the commas.

For example, say that you want to list the names of all the files in the directories **/usr/harley**, **/usr/addie** and **/usr/tln**. You could specify all the names:

```
ls /usr/harley /usr/addie /usr/tln
```

Or you can use brace brackets to abbreviate:

```
ls /usr/{harley,addie,tln}
```

Here is another example. You want to combine the contents of the files **olddata1**, **olddata2**, **olddata3**, **newdata1**, **newdata2** and **newdata3**. You want to store the result in a brand new file named **master**. Use the command:

Symbol	Meaning
~	the name of your home directory
{ }	use separate instances of specified patterns

Figure 21-4

Abbreviations Used to Specify File Names (C-Shell)

```
cat {old,new}data{1,2,3} > master
```

(The **cat** command, which combines files, is discussed in Chapter 16. The > symbol, which redirects the standard output, is discussed in Chapter 15.)

Dotfiles (Hidden Files): `ls -a`

Any file whose name begins with a . (period) is called a DOTFILE or a HIDDEN FILE. The names of hidden files, such as **.login**, are not listed when you use the **ls** command unless you use the **-a** (all) option.

You would probably not use a dotfile to hold your own personal data. However, there are standard dotfiles which are normally found in each user's home directory. By convention, these files are used by programs to hold startup or configuration information.

If you want to see all your dotfiles, change to your home directory and enter:

```
ls -a
```

Figure 21-5 lists the names of the standard dotfiles that you may one day want to modify. There may be other dotfiles in your home directory, but unless you really know what you are doing, you should leave them alone.

☑ **HINT** Many of the dotfiles are crucial. Before you edit a dotfile, make a backup copy. For example:

```
cp .login .login.bak
```

(The **cp** command is explained in Chapter 22.) If you accidentally ruin the file, you will be able to restore it.

Long Directory Listings: `ls -dgl`

To display the most information about a directory or file, use the **ls** command with the **-l** (long) option. The output consists of a disk storage summary followed by one line per file. Here is an example. You enter:

```
ls -l
```

and you see:

```
total 7
-rw-rw-r—  1 harley        2255 Oct  3 21:52 article
drwxrwxr-x  2 harley         512 Oct  1 11:40 bin
drwxrwxr-x  2 harley         512 Oct  1 11:41 essays
-rw-rw-r—  1 harley        1825 Sep 26 20:03 memo
```

The first line tells us that the files in this directory use approximately 7 kilobytes of disk storage. The rest of the lines show us information about the files.

File Name	Used by	To Contain
`.bash_logout`	Bash	logout commands
`.bash_profile`	Bash	login initialization commands
`.bashrc`	Bash	initialization commands
`.cshrc`	C-Shell	initialization commands
`.emacs`	Emacs editor	initialization commands
`.exrc`	**vi** editor	initialization commands
`.forward`	mail delivery	address for forwarding mail
`.inputrc`	Bash	changes to default key bindings
`.login`	C-Shell	login initialization commands
`.logout`	C-Shell	logout commands
`.netrc`	**ftp**	auto-login information
`.newsrc`	news programs	info about newsgroups that you read
`.mailrc`	**mail**	initialization commands
`.plan`	**finger**	info displayed when fingered
`.project`	**finger**	more info displayed when fingered
`.profile`	Bourne shell	initialization commands
`.profile`	Korn shell	initialization commands
`.signature`	news programs	signature for when you post articles
`.tcshrc`	Tcsh shell	initialization commands
`.xsession`	X Window	auto-startup initialization commands
`.xinitrc`	X Window	other startup initialization commands
`.zshenv`	Zsh	initialization commands
`.zshrc`	Zsh	initialization commands
`.zlogin`	Zsh	login initialization commands
`.zlogout`	Zsh	logout commands
`.zprofile`	Zsh	login initialization commands

Figure 21-5

Dotfiles (Hidden Files) That You Might Want to Change

At the far left, the first character of each line shows you the type of file. There are several possibilities, but the only ones you need care about are **d**, which means a directory, and **–**, which means an ordinary file. In this listing, we have two directories and two ordinary files. (You may also see the letter **l**, which indicates a symbolic link. This is explained in Chapter 22.)

Let's look at the rest of the information from left to right. At the far right are the file names. Next, we see the time and date that the file was last modified. For example, the file named `article` was last modified on October 3 at 9:52 PM. (Remember, Unix uses a 24-hour clock.)

To the left of the date is the size of the file in bytes. With a text file, one byte holds one character of data.

To the left of the size is the userid of the owner of the file. All of these files are owned by `harley`. To the left of the owner's userid is a number that shows how many links there are to this file. Finally, the string of nine characters at the far left (just to the right of the initial character) show the file permissions.

We will discuss file ownership, links and permissions in Chapter 22, at which time we will look at the output of the `ls -l` command in more detail.

For completeness, we will mention that some types of Unix display the name of the group just to the right of the owner's userid. (Groups are also discussed in Chapter 22.) Berkeley Unix does not display this information unless you use the `-g` (group) option.

The information displayed by the `-l` option can be used in many imaginative ways by piping the output to a filter (see Chapters 15 and 16). For example, to list the names of all the files that were last modified in September, you can use:

```
ls -l | grep Sep
```

To count how many files were last modified in September, use:

```
ls -l | grep Sep | wc -l
```

When you specify the name of a directory, `ls` lists information about the files in that directory. For example, to display a long listing about all the files in the `/bin` directory, you would use:

```
ls -l /bin
```

If you want information about the directory itself, use the `-d` (directory) option. Thus, to display information about the `/bin` directory as a file in its own right, use:

```
ls -dl /bin
```

Useful Aliases for Using `ls`

The `ls` command is used a lot. For this reason, it is common to define certain aliases to make it easy to use `ls` with the most useful options. (Defining aliases with the C-Shell is explained in Chapter 11.)

The most common aliases are:

```
alias ll  'ls -l'
alias la  'ls -a'
alias lla 'ls -la'
```

These aliases make it easy to display a long listing (**ll**), a listing of all files (**la**), and a long listing of all files (**lla**).

For example, once you have defined the **ll** alias, you can display a long listing of the **/bin** directory by using:

```
ll /bin
```

To display a long listing of your working directory, use:

```
ll
```

Two other common aliases are:

```
alias ls  'ls -F'
alias ls  'ls -lF'
```

These aliases make **ls**, by default, always display the flag that marks the file type (**/** for directories, ***** for executable files). The second alias makes **ls**, by default, display a long listing as well. (Of course, you would define only one of these aliases.)

It may be that your system manager has already set up some of these aliases in your **.cshrc** file (see Chapter 11). To check what aliases you have, enter the command:

```
alias
```

If you don't like your aliases, you can change or remove them by editing your **.cshrc** file. (If you decide to edit this file, be sure to make a copy first.)

Working with Files

In Chapter 20, we discussed the Unix file system. We explained that there are three types of files: directories, special files and ordinary files. In Chapter 21, we discussed directories and covered the commands that you use to work with directories.

With this chapter, we finish our discussion of the file system by showing the commands that you use with ordinary files. You will learn how to create and manipulate files. You will also learn how to control the permissions that let Unix users share files with one another. Finally, we will explain what goes on behind the scenes and how manipulating files really means working with links.

Note: The commands we discuss in this chapter work with ordinary files. Thus, in this chapter, when we say "file" we are referring to an ordinary file. When we need to refer to directories we do so explicitly.

Creating a File: `touch`

How do you create a file? Strangely enough, you don't. Unix will create files for you as the need arises. You never really need to create a new file for yourself.

There are three common situations in which a file will be created for you automatically. First, many programs will create a file on your behalf. For example, let's say you start the **vi** editor (Chapter 19) by using the command:

```
vi memo
```

This command specifies that you want to edit a file named **memo**. If **memo** does not exist, **vi** will create it for you.

Second, when you redirect output to a file (Chapter 15), Unix will create the file if it does not already exist. For example, say that you want to save the output of the **ls** command to a file named **listing**. You enter:

```
ls > listing
```

If **listing** does not exist, Unix will create it for you.

Third, when you make a copy of a file, Unix will create the new file automatically. For example, say that you want to copy the file **data** to a file named **extra**. You enter the following command:

```
cp data extra
```

Unix will create the file **extra** for you. (The **cp** command is explained later in the chapter.)

In Chapter 21, we explained that you use the **mkdir** command to make a new directory. Is there an analogous command that will make an ordinary file? The answer is no, but there is a command that has the side effect of creating an empty file. This command is **touch**. Here is how it works.

When we discussed the **ls** command in Chapter 21, we explained that the **-l** (long listing) option displays the time and date that a file was last modified. The job of the **touch** command is to change this modification time to the current time and date.

For example, say that a file named **memo** was last modified on July 8 at 2:30 PM. You enter:

```
ls -l memo
```

and you see:

```
-rw-------  1 harley       4883 Jul  8 14:30 memo
```

It is now 10:30 AM, December 21. You enter:

```
touch memo
```

Now when you enter the same **ls** command you see:

```
-rw-------  1 harley       4883 Dec 21 10:30 memo
```

By the way, **touch** works by reading a character from the file and writing it back. On some systems, **touch** will let you specify the exact time and date you want. For information on how **touch** works on your system, see the online manual (Chapter 8). Use the command **man touch**.

For most people, the **touch** command is of limited usefulness. (Although it does come in handy when you want to make people think that you have updated a memo.) However, **touch** has one important side effect: if the file that you specify does not exist, **touch** will create it. Thus, you can use **touch** to create a brand new, empty file.

For example, to create a file named **newfile**, use:

```
touch newfile
```

The modification time will be the current time and date.

Normally, though, there is no need to use **touch**. As we explained above, new files are usually created for you automatically as the need arises.

 HINT The **touch** command is handy for creating a group of temporary files in order to experiment with the Unix file commands.

Choosing a File Name

Unix is liberal with respect to naming files. There are only two basic rules:

1. File names can be up to 255 characters long. (Some older System V Unix systems allow only 14 characters.)
2. A file name can contain any character except **/** (which, as we explained in Chapter 21, has a special meaning within a pathname).

 HINT Create file names that are meaningful to you. When you have not used a file for a while, it is helpful when the name reminds you of what the file contains.

The rules allow you to create a file name that contains all sorts of weird characters: control characters, backspaces, punctuation, even space characters. Obviously, such filenames will cause trouble.

For example, what if you use the **ls -l** command to list information about a file named **info;date**:

```
ls -l info;date
```

Unix would interpret the semicolon as separating two commands:

```
ls -l info
date
```

Here is another example. Say that you have a file named **-info**. It would be a lot of trouble using the name in a command, for example:

```
ls -info
```

Unix would interpret the **-** (hyphen) character as indicating an option.

Generally speaking, you will run into trouble with any name that contains a character with a special meaning (**<**, **>**, **|**, **!** and so on). The best idea is to confine yourself to characters that cannot be misinterpreted. These are shown in Figure 22-1.

As we explained in Chapter 21, files whose names begin with a **.** (period) are called dotfiles or hidden files. When you use **ls**, such files are listed only if you specify the **-a** (all) option. By convention, such names are used to

a, b, c...	(lowercase letters)
A, B, C...	(uppercase letters)
0, 1, 2...	(numbers)
.	(period)
_	(underscore)

Figure 22-1

Characters That Are Safe to Use in File Names

indicate files that initialize or support a particular program. Figure 21-5 contains a list of the common dotfiles.

Remember that Unix distinguishes between upper- and lowercase. Thus, the names **info**, **Info** and **INFO** are considered to be completely different.

There is a convention that names that begin with uppercase letters are reserved for files that are important in some special way. For example, you might see a file named **README**.

Because uppercase comes before lowercase in the ASCII code (Chapter 16), such names will come first in the directory listing and will stand out.

 HINT When you name files or directories, it is a good idea to stick to lowercase letters.

Some programs expect to use files whose names end in a period followed by one or more specific letters. For example, the C compiler expects C programs to be stored in files that end in **.c**, such as **myprog.c**. The **uncompress** command expects input files that end in **.Z** (uppercase "Z"), such as **data.Z**.

In such cases, the suffix is sometimes referred to as an EXTENSION. For example, we might say files that hold C programs should have an extension of **.c**.

Such extensions are convenient as they allow you to use wildcard specifications to refer to a group of files. For example, you can list the names of all the C programs in a directory by using:

```
ls *.c
```

(Wildcards are explained in Chapter 21.)

Copying a File: cp

To make a copy of a file, use the **cp** command. The syntax is:

cp [**-ip**] *file1* *file2*

where *file1* is the name of an existing file, and *file2* is the name of the destination.

Using this command is straightforward. For example, if you have a file named **data** and you want to make a copy named **extra**, use:

cp data extra

Here is another example. You want to make a copy of the system password file (see Chapter 12). The copy should be called **pword** and should be in your home directory. Use:

cp /etc/passwd ~/pword

(As we explained in Chapter 21, the ~ character is an abbreviation for the pathname of your home directory.)

If the destination file does not exist, **cp** will create it. If the destination file already exists, **cp** will replace it. Consider the first example:

cp data extra

If the file **extra** does not exist, it will be created. But if the file **extra** does exist, it will be replaced. All the data in the original **extra** file will be lost and there is no way to get it back.

☑ **HINT** If you want to append data to the end of a file, use the **cat** command and redirect the output. (See Chapter 16.) For example, the command:

cat data >> extra

appends the contents of **data** to the end of **extra**. The original contents of **extra** are preserved.

If you want to be cautious about replacing data, use the **-i** (interactive) option. For example:

cp -i data extra

This tells **cp** to ask your permission before replacing a file that already exists. If you type an answer that begins with the letter **y** or **Y** (for "yes"), **cp** will replace the file. If you type any other answer, **cp** will not make the replacement.

The second option is **-p** (preserve). This option makes the destination file have the same modification times and permissions as the source file. (Permissions are explained later in the chapter.)

Copying Files to a Different Directory: cp

The **cp** command will also copy one or more files to a different directory. The syntax is:

```
cp [-ip] file... directory
```

where *file* is the name of an existing file, and *directory* is the name of an existing directory. The **-i** and **-p** options work as described above.

Here is an example. To copy the file **data** to a directory named **backups**, use:

```
cp data backups
```

To copy the three files **data1**, **data2** and **data3** to the **backups** directory, use:

```
cp data1 data2 data3 backups
```

 HINT You may be able to use wildcards to specify more than one file name (see Chapter 21.) For example, to copy the three files **data1**, **data2** and **data3** to the **backups** directory, you can use:

```
cp data[123] backups
```

If there are no other files whose names begin with **data**, you can use:

```
cp data* backups
```

If there are no other files whose names begin with **d**, you can use:

```
cp d* backups
```

Copying a Directory to Another Directory: cp -r

You can use **cp** to copy a directory and all of its files to another directory by using the **-r** option. The syntax is:

```
cp -r [-ip] directory1... directory2
```

The **-i** and **-p** options work as described above. The **-r** (recursive) option tells **cp** to copy an entire sub-tree.

Here is an example. Say that, within your working directory, you have two subdirectories: **essays** and **backups**. Within the **essays** directory, you have many files and subdirectories. You enter:

```
cp -r essays backups
```

A copy of **essays**, including all its files and subdirectories, is now in **backups**. The **cp** command will create the new directories automatically.

For instance, say that **essays** contains a subdirectory named **literature** that contains a file named **kafka**:

```
essays/literature/kafka
```

The copy of this file is:

backups/essays/literature/kafka

☑ **HINT** To copy all the files in a directory, and only the files, use **cp** with an ***** wildcard (see Chapter 21). To copy the directory itself (as well as its contents), use **cp** with the **-r** option.

For example, to copy the files in a directory named **documents** to another directory named **backups**, use:

cp documents/* backups

To copy the directory **documents** itself to the directory **backups**, use:

cp -r documents backups

Moving a File: mv

To move a file to a different directory, use the **mv** (move) command. The syntax is:

mv [**-if**] *file*... *directory*

where *file* is the name of an existing file, and *directory* is the name of the target directory.

The **mv** command will move one or more files to an existing directory. (You can make a directory using the **mkdir** command, explained in Chapter 21.)

Here are two examples. The first moves a file named **data** to a directory named **archive**:

mv data archive

(If a directory named **archive** does not exist, **mv** will think that you want to rename the file. See below.)

The next example moves three files, **data1**, **data2** and **data3**, to the **archive** directory:

mv data1 data2 data3 archive

As with most file commands, you can use a wildcard specification. For example, the last command can be abbreviated to:

mv data[123] archive

If the target to which you move a file already exists, **mv** will replace the file. All the data in the original file will be lost, and there is no way to get it back (so be careful).

If you want to be cautious about losing data, use the **-i** (interactive) option. For example:

mv -i data archive

This tells **mv** to ask your permission before replacing a file that already exists. If you type an answer that begins with the letter **y** or **Y** (for "yes"), **mv** will replace the file. If you type any other answer, **mv** will not make the replacement.

In this case, **mv** would ask your permission before replacing a file named **archive/data**.

The second option is **-f** (force). This forces **mv** to replace a file. The **-f** option will override the **-i** option as well as restrictions imposed by file permissions (explained later in the chapter). Use **-f** with care and only when you know exactly what you are doing.

Renaming a File or Directory: mv

To rename a file or directory, use the **mv** (move) command. The syntax is:

mv [**-if**] *oldname newname*

where *oldname* is the name of an existing file or directory, and *newname* is the new name. The **-i** and **-f** options work as described above.

Renaming a file or directory is straightforward. For example, to rename a file from **memo** to **important**, use:

mv memo important

If the target (in this case, **important**) already exists, it will be replaced. All the data in the original target will be lost, and there is no way to get it back (so be careful). You can use the **-i** and **-f** options, described above, to control the replacement.

As you might expect, you can use **mv** to rename and move at the same time. For example, say that **memo** is a file and **archive** is a directory. Consider the command:

mv memo archive/important

This command moves a file named **memo** to the directory named **archive** (which must already exist). As part of the move, the file will be renamed to **important**.

Removing a File: rm

To remove (delete) a file, use the **rm** command. The syntax is:

rm [**-fir**] *file*...

where *file* is the name of a file you want to remove.

WHAT'S IN A NAME?

Remove   (Note: The following explanation will be easy to understand after you have learned about links, which are discussed later in this chapter.)

In Unix, we do not talk about deleting or erasing a file. We talk about "removing" the file.

When Unix creates a file, it establishes a link between the file name and the actual file that the name represents. When we use the **rm** or **rmdir** commands, Unix removes this link.

Removing a link is not really the same as deleting. There may be more than one link to the file, and Unix will not delete the actual file until the last link is removed.

In almost all cases, there is only one link to a file, so removing this link deletes the file. This is why, most of the time, **rm** and **rmdir** act as delete commands.

To remove a file, just specify its name. Here are some examples:

```
rm data
rm ~/memo
rm bin/spacewar
```

The first command removes a file named **data** in the working directory. The second command removes a file named **memo** in your home directory. The next command removes a file named **spacewar** in the directory named **bin**, which lies in the working directory.

As with all file commands, you can use wildcard specifications (see Chapter 21). Here are two examples:

```
rm data[123]
rm *
```

The first command removes the files **data1**, **data2** and **data3** in the working directory. The second command is a powerful one: it removes all the files in your working directory.

Once you remove a file, it is gone for good. There is no way to get back an erased file, so be careful.

☑ **HINT**   If you are using **rm** with a wildcard specification, it is a good idea to test it first with an **ls** command (Chapter 21) to see what files are matched.

Say that you want to delete the files named **data.backup, data.old** and **data.extra**. You are thinking about using the wildcard specification

data* which would match all files whose names begin with **data**. However, to be prudent, you check this specification by entering:

`ls data*`

The output is:

`data.backup    data.extra    data.important    data.old`

You see that you had forgotten the file **data.important**. If you had used **rm** with **data*** you would have lost this file. Instead, you can use:

`rm data.[beo]*`

This will match only those files that you really want to remove.

How to Keep from Removing the Wrong Files: `rm -if`

As we mentioned in the previous section, it is a good idea to to check a file specification with **ls** before you use it with a **rm** command. However, even if you check the specification with **ls**, you might still type it incorrectly when you enter the **rm** command.

The following is an alias that you can put in your **.cshrc** file to prevent such an occurrence.

`alias del 'rm \!ls:*'`

(This alias is discussed in detail in Chapter 11.)

Here is how to use the alias, which is named **del**. First, enter an **ls** command with the wildcard specification that describes the files you want to remove. For example:

`ls data.[beo]*`

Take a look at the list of files. If they are really the ones you want to remove, enter:

`del`

This will execute the **rm** command using the file names from the previous **ls** command.

A handy alternative is to use the **-i** (interactive) option. This tells **rm** to ask your permission before removing each file. For example, you can enter:

`rm -i data*`

rm will display a message for each file, asking your permission to proceed. For example:

`rm: remove data.backup?`

If you type a response that begins with **y** or **Y** (for "yes"), **rm** will remove the file. If you type anything else (including simply pressing <Return>), **rm** will leave the file alone.

It is common for people to create an alias that automatically inserts the **-i** option every time they use the **rm** command:

```
alias rm 'rm -i'
```

Some system managers even put this alias in everybody's `.cshrc` file, thinking they are doing their users a favor.

This practice is to be deplored for two reasons. First, Unix was designed to be terse and exact. Having to type **y** each time you want to remove a file slows down your thought processes. Using an automatic **-i** option makes for sloppy thinking because users come to depend on it.

(If you feel like arguing the point, think about this: It is true that, during the first week, a new user may accidentally remove one or two files. However, it won't be long before he or she will learn to use the commands well. In the long run, developing your skills is always the better alternative to being coddled.)

The second reason for not automatically using the **-i** option is that, eventually, everyone uses more than one Unix system. When people become used to a slow, clunky, ask-me-before-you-remove-each-file **rm** command, they forget that most Unix systems do not work in this way. Because they never learn how to use **ls** and **rm** properly, it is easy to make a catastrophic mistake when they move to a new system.

For this reason, if you really must create an alias for **rm -i**, give it a different name, for example:

```
alias erase 'rm -i'
```

Later in the chapter, we will discuss file permissions. At that time, you will see that there are three types of permissions: read, write and execute. We won't go into the details now. All we want to say is that, without write permission, you are not allowed to remove a file.

If you try to remove a file for which you do not have write permission, **rm** will ask your permission to override the protection mechanism.

For example, say that the file **data.important** has file permissions of 400. (The "400" will make sense later. Basically, it means that you have read permission, but not write or execute permission.) You enter:

```
rm data.important
```

You will see the question:

```
rm: override protection 400 for data.important?
```

To remove the file, type a response that starts with **y** or **Y**. If you type anything else, **rm** will leave the file alone.

The **-f** (force) option tells **rm** to remove all the files you specify regardless of file permissions. For example:

```
rm -f data.important
```

This option will also override the **-i** option. Use **-f** only when you are one hundred percent sure of what you are doing.

Removing an Entire Sub-tree: `rm -r`

To remove an entire sub-tree, use the **rm** command with the **-r** (recursive) option and specify the name of a directory. **rm** will remove not only the directory, but all the files and subdirectories that lie within the directory. This, in effect, removes an entire sub-tree.

For example, say that you have a directory named **extra**. Within this directory are a number of files and subdirectories. Within each subdirectory are still more files and subdirectories. To remove everything, enter:

```
rm -r extra
```

Here is another example: deceptively simple, yet powerful. To remove everything under your working directory, use:

```
rm -r *
```

Obviously, **rm -r** can be a dangerous command. If you are not sure what you are doing, **-r** is a good option to forget about. At the very least, use the **-i** option if you have the least doubt as to what files you want to remove. For example, you might enter:

```
rm -ir extra
```

rm will ask permission before removing each file and directory.

If you want to remove an entire sub-tree quickly and quietly, you can use the **-f** option. For example:

```
rm -fr extra
```

rm will not ask your permission for anything. (Remember, **-f** will override the **-i** option, so there is no point in using them together.)

 HINT Before using **rm -r** to delete files, use the **pwd** command to display your working directory. If you are in the wrong directory, you will remove the wrong files.

To conclude the discussion of the **rm** command, let's take a quick look at how easy it is to wipe out all your files. Say that your home directory contains many subdirectories, the result of months of hard work. You want to remove all the files and directories under the **extra** directory.

As it happens, you are not in your home directory. What you should do is change to your home directory and then enter the **rm** command:

```
cd
rm -fr extra
```

However, you think to yourself, "There is no point in typing two commands. I can do the whole thing in a single command." You intend to enter:

```
rm -fr ~/extra
```

(Remember, as we explained in Chapter 21, the ~ (tilde) character is an abbreviation for the pathname of your home directory.)

But, being in a hurry, you accidentally type a space before the slash:

```
rm -fr ~ /extra
```

In effect, you have entered a command to remove all the files in two sub-trees: ~ (your home directory) and **/extra**.

Once you press <Return>, don't even bother trying to hit **^C** (the **intr** key) to abort the command. The computer is a lot faster than you: there is no way to catch a runaway **rm** command. All your files are gone, including your dotfiles. (Note: We tested this command so you don't have to. Just believe us.)

In Chapter 4, we explained that there is a special userid named **root** that offers superuser privileges. When your system manager logs in as **root**, he or she can do just about anything, including remove any file or directory in the system.

For extra credit: What would happen if someone logged in as superuser and entered the command:

```
rm -fr /
```

(Makes you wonder if Man is really Nature's last word...)

Is It Possible to Restore a File that Has Been Removed?

No.

File Permissions

In order to control access within the file system, Unix maintains a set of FILE PERMISSIONS (often called PERMISSIONS) for each file. These permissions control who can access the file and in what way.

There are three types of permissions, each independent of one another: READ PERMISSION, WRITE PERMISSION and EXECUTE PERMISSION. With respect to a particular file, you either have a permission or you don't. For example, you might have read and write permission, but not execute permission.

When applied to an ordinary file, the meaning of a permission is straightforward: Read permission means that you are allowed to read the file. Write permission means that you are allowed to write to the file. Execute permission means that you are allowed to execute the file.

Of course, it makes no sense to try to execute a file unless it is executable. In practice, a file is executable if it is a program or a script of some type. (A shell script, for example, contains commands to be executed by the shell.)

The three types of permissions are distinct, but they do work together. For example, in order to change a file, you need both read and write permission. In order to execute a shell script, you need both read and execute permission.

As you will see later in the chapter, you are able to set and change the permissions for your own files. You do so for two reasons:

- To restrict access by other users
- To guard against your own errors

If you want to protect a file from being deleted accidentally, you can make sure that there is no write permission for the file. Many commands that replace or delete data will ask for confirmation before changing a file that does not have write permission.

With directories, the permissions are analogous, but have somewhat different meanings. Read permission means that you can read the names in the directory. Write permission means that you can make changes to the directory (create, move, copy, remove). Execute permission means that you can search the directory.

If you have read permission only, you can list the names in a directory, but that is all. Unless you have execute permission, you cannot, for example, check the size of a file, look in a subdirectory, or use **cd** to change to the directory.

Although it is an unlikely combination, what would it mean if you had write and execute permission for a directory, but not read permission? You would be able to access and modify the directory without being able to read it. Thus, you could not list the contents, but, if you knew the name of a file, you could remove it.

☑ **HINT** When you first learn about the directory permissions, they may seem a bit confusing. Later in this chapter, you will learn that a directory entry contains only a file name and a pointer to the file, not the actual file itself.

Once you understand this, the directory permissions make sense. Read permission means you can read directory entries. Write permission means you can change directory entries. Execute permission means you can use directory entries.

For reference, Figure 22-2 contains a summary of file permissions as they apply to ordinary files and directories.

Ordinary File

Read:	you can read from the file
Write:	you can write to the file
Execute:	you can execute the file

Directory

Read:	you can read the directory
Write:	you can create, move, copy or remove entries
Execute:	you can search the directory

Figure 22-2
Summary of File Permissions

How Unix Maintains File Permissions: `id`

The programmers at Bell Labs who created the first Unix system (see Chapter 1) organized file permissions in a way that is still in use today. At the time Unix was developed, people at Bell Labs worked in small groups that needed to share programs and documents. From the point of view of a single user, the programmers divided the entire world into three parts: the user, the user's group, and everybody else.

Thus, for each file, Unix keeps three sets of permissions: one for the userid, one for the userids in the group, and one for all the userids on the system. This means that, for each file and directory, you can assign separate read, write and execute permissions for yourself, for the people in your group, and for everybody else. Figure 22-3 shows the possibilities.

Here is an example. The people in your group maintain a particular program. The file that contains this program resides in one of your personal directories. Set up the file so that you and your group have read, write and execute permission, while all the other users on the system have only read and execute permission. This means that, while anyone can execute the program, only you or members of your group can change it.

You:	read, write, execute
Your group:	read, write, execute
Everybody:	read, write, execute

Figure 22-3
The Possible File Permissions

Here is another example. You have a document that you don't want anyone else to see. Give yourself read and write permission. Give no permissions to your group or to everybody else.

When your system manager created an account for you, he or she also assigned you to a group. Just as each user has a name called a userid, each group has a name called a GROUPID (pronounced "group-eye-dee"). The list of all the groupids in your system is kept in the file **/etc/group**, which you are free to examine.

If you want to see the name of your group, use the command:

```
id
```

This will show you your userid and your groupid.

Although groups sound like a good idea, in practice they are ignored most of the time. System managers generally don't find it worthwhile to maintain groups that are small enough to be useful. For example, if you are an undergraduate, your userid is probably part of a large group (such as all social science students) with whom sharing would be a meaningless experience.

 HINT Ignore your group by giving it the same permissions that you give to everybody.

Displaying File Permissions: `ls -l`

To display the file permissions for a file, use the **ls** command with the **-l** (long listing) option. The permissions are shown on the left-hand side of the output. If you want to display permissions for a specific directory itself, you can use the **-d** option along with **-l**. (The **ls** command, along with these options, is explained in Chapter 21.)

Here is an example. You enter the following command to look at the files in your working directory:

```
ls -l
```

The output is:

```
total 109
-rwxrwxrwx  1 harley       28672 Oct 11 16:37 program.everybody
-rwxrwx---  1 harley       36864 Oct 11 16:38 program.group
-rwx------  1 harley       24576 Oct 11 16:32 program.user
-rw-rw-rw-  1 harley        7376 Oct 11 16:34 text.everybody
-rw-rw----  1 harley        5532 Oct 11 16:34 text.group
-rw-------  1 harley        6454 Oct 11 16:34 text.user
```

We discussed most of this output in Chapter 21. Briefly, the file name is on the far right. Moving to the left, we see the time and date of last modification, the size (in bytes), and the userid of the owner. To the left of the owner is the number of links (which we will discuss later in this chapter).

At the far left, the first character of each line shows us the type of file. An ordinary file is marked by -, a hyphen; a directory (there are none in this example) is marked by a **d**.

If you want to display the name of the group as well as the owner, you can use **ls** with the **-g** (group) option. On some systems, this is the default.

What we want to focus on here are the 9 characters to the right of the file type character. Their meaning is as follows:

r   <-- read permission
w   <-- write permission
x   <-- execute permission
-   <-- permission not granted

To analyze the permissions for a file, divide the 9 characters into three sets of 3. From left to right, these sets show the permissions for the owner of the file, the owner's group, and for everybody else. (The owner is the userid that created the file.)

```
owner    group    everybody
rwx      rwx       rwx
```

Let's do this for all the files in the example:

```
owner    group    everybody
rwx      rwx       rwx         <--    program.everybody
rwx      rwx       ---         <--    program.group
rwx      ---       ---         <--    program.user
rw-      rw-       rw-         <--    text.everybody
rw-      rw-       ---         <--    text.group
rw-      ---       ---         <--    text.user
```

We can now see exactly how each permission is assigned. For instance, the file **text.user** has read and write permissions for the owner, and no permissions for the group or for everybody else.

File Modes

Unix uses a compact, three-number code to represent the full set of file permissions. This code is called a FILE MODE or, more simply, a MODE. For example, we will see that the mode for the **text.user** file in the last example is **600**.

Within a mode, each number stands for one set of permissions. The first number represents the owner's permissions. The second number represents the group's permissions. The third number represents everybody else's permissions. Using the example we just mentioned, we get:

```
6    <-- permissions for owner
0    <-- permissions for group
0    <-- permissions for everybody
```

Here's how the code works. We start with the following numeric values for the various permissions:

```
   read permission = 4
  write permission = 2
execute permission = 1
     no permission = 0
```

Now, for each set of permissions, we add the appropriate numbers. For example, to indicate read and write permission, we add 4 and 2. Figure 22-4 shows each possible combination along with its numeric value.

Let's do an example. What is the mode for a file in which:

- the owner has read, write and execute permissions?
- the group has read and write permissions?
- everyone else has read permission only?

```
  Owner: read + write + execute  =  4+2+1  =  7
  Group: read + write            =  4+2+0  =  6
Everyone: read                   =  4+0+0  =  4
```

Thus, the mode is 764.

Let's look at the examples from the previous section:

owner		group		everybody				mode
rwx	7	rwx	7	rwx	7	<--	program.everybody	777
rwx	7	rwx	7	---	0	<--	program.group	770
rwx	7	---	0	---	0	<--	program.user	700
rw-	6	rw-	6	rw-	6	<--	text.everybody	666
rw-	6	rw-	6	---	0	<--	text.group	660
rw-	6	---	0	---	0	<--	text.user	600

Now, let's do an example going backwards. What does a file mode of **540** mean? Using Figure 22-4, we see:

```
  Owner: 5   -->   read, execute
  Group: 4   -->   read
Everyone: 0   -->   nothing
```

Thus, the owner can read and execute the file. The group can only read the file. Everybody else has no permissions.

read	write	execute	VALUE	read		write		execute
-	-	-	0	0	+	0	+	0
-	-	yes	1	0	+	0	+	1
-	yes	-	2	0	+	2	+	0
-	yes	yes	3	0	+	2	+	1
yes	-	-	4	4	+	0	+	0
yes	-	yes	5	4	+	0	+	1
yes	yes	-	6	4	+	2	+	0
yes	yes	yes	7	4	+	2	+	1

Figure 22-4

Numeric Values for File Permission Combinations

Changing File Permissions: chmod

To change the permissions for a file, use the **chmod** (change mode) command. The syntax is:

chmod `mode file`...

where `mode` is the new file mode, and `file` is the name of a file or directory. Only the owner or the superuser can change the file mode for a file. Unix automatically makes you the owner of each file you create.

Here are some examples. The first command changes the mode for the specified files to give read and write permission to the owner, and read permission to the group and to everyone else. These permissions are suitable for a file that you want to let anyone read, but not modify.

chmod 644 memo1 memo2 document

The next command gives the owner read, write and execute permissions, with read and execute permissions for the group and for everyone else. These permissions are suitable for a file that contains a program that you want to let other people execute but not modify.

chmod 755 spacewar

In most cases, it is best to restrict permissions unless you have a reason to do otherwise. The following commands set permissions only for the owner. First, read and write permissions:

chmod 600 homework.text

Next, read, write and execute permissions:

chmod 700 homework.program

When you create a script using a text editor (see Chapter 19), it will have only read and write permissions by default. In order to execute the script, you will have to add execute permission. Use **chmod 700** (or **chmod 755** if you want to share).

☑ **HINT**   To avoid problems, do not give execute permission to a file that is not executable.

How Unix Assigns Permissions to a New File: umask

When Unix creates a new file, it starts with a file mode of:

666:   for non-executable ordinary files
777:   for executable ordinary files
777:   for directories

From this initial mode, Unix subtracts the value of the USER MASK. The user mask is a mode, set by you, showing which permissions you want to restrict.

To set the user mask, use the **umask** command. The syntax is:

umask [*mode*]

where *mode* specifies which permissions you want to restrict. It is a good idea to put a **umask** command in your **.login** file (see Chapter 11) so that your user mask will be set automatically each time you log in.

Here is an example. You want write permission to be withheld from your group and from everybody else. Use a mode of **022**:

umask 022

This user mask shares your files without letting anyone change them.

To be as private as possible, you can withhold all permissions – read, write and execute – from your group and from everybody else. Use a mode of **077**:

umask 077

☑ **HINT**   Unless you have reason to do otherwise, make your files completely private by using **umask 077** in your **.login** file. If you want to share, you can do so on a file-by-file basis by using the **chmod** command.

To check the current value of your user mask, enter the **umask** command without a parameter:

umask

Note: With some shells, the **umask** command will not display leading zeros. Thus, if your user mask is **022**, you may see:

22

If your user mask is **002**, you may see:

2

If this is the case with your shell, just pretend that the zeros are there.

The Idea of a Link

The rest of the material in this chapter is supplementary. It is useful and interesting, but not as important as what we have covered so far. If you have the time, do take a few minutes to read through the next few sections. They will help you understand a lot more about the Unix file system, and show you how everything actually makes sense.

When Unix creates a file, it does two things. First, it sets aside space on a disk to store whatever data is in the file. Second, it creates a structure called an INODE or INDEX NODE to hold the basic information about the file. (The word "inode" is pronounced "eye-node".)

The inode contains all the information that Unix needs to make use of the file. As a user, you don't really need to know what is in an inode, but, in case you are interested, Figure 22-5 will show you.

Unix keeps all the inodes in a large table. Within this table, each inode is known by a number called the INUMBER or INDEX NUMBER. For example, say that a particular file is described by inode #24. We say that the file has an inumber of 24.

When we work with directories, we talk as if they actually contain files. For example, you might hear someone say that his **bin** directory contains a file named **spacewar**.

- the name of the userid that owns the file
- the type of the file (ordinary, directory, special...)
- the size of the file
- where the data is stored
- file permissions
- the last time the file was modified
- the last time the file was accessed
- the last time the inode was modified
- the number of links to the file

Figure 22-5

The Contents of an Inode (Index Node)

However, the directory does not really contain the file. All the directory contains is the name of the file and its inumber. Thus, the contents of a directory are actually quite small. They consist of a list of names and, for each name, an inumber.

Let's look at an example. What happens when you create a file named **spacewar** in your **bin** directory? First, Unix sets aside storage space on the disk to hold the file. Next, Unix looks in the inode table and finds a free inode. Let's say that it is inode #24. Unix fills in the information in the inode that pertains to the new file. Finally, Unix places an entry in the **bin** directory. This entry contains the name **spacewar** along with an inumber of 24.

When Unix needs to use the file, it is a simple matter to look up the name in the directory, use the corresponding inumber to find the inode, and then use the information in the inode to access the file.

The connection between a file name and its inode is called a LINK. Conceptually, a link connects a file name with the file itself.

Multiple Links to the Same File

One of the most elegant features of the Unix file system is that it allows multiple links to the same file. In other words, the same file can be known by more than one name.

Remember, the unique identifier of a file is its inumber, not its name. There is no reason why more than one name cannot reference the same inumber.

Here is an example. Let's say that your home directory is **/usr/harley**. Within your home directory, you have a subdirectory called **bin**. You have created a file in the **bin** directory by the name of **spacewar**. It happens that this file has an inumber of 24.

Using the **ln** command (described later in the chapter), you create another file, in the same directory, named **funky**, so that it has the same inumber as **spacewar**. Since both **spacewar** and **funky** have the same inumber, they are, essentially, different names for the same file.

Now you move to your home directory and create another file named **extra**, also with the same inumber. Then you move to the home directory of a friend, **/usr/addie**, and create a fourth file named **myfile**, also with the same inumber.

At this point, you still have only one file – the one identified by inumber 24 – but it has four different names:

```
/usr/harley/bin/spacewar
/usr/harley/bin/funky
/usr/harley/extra
/usr/addie/myfile
```

Would you ever want to do this? Probably not. (Although, it can be handy to have various people access the same file by different names.)

But it is important to understand how links work, because they underlie the operation of the basic file commands: **cp** (copy), **mv** (move), **rm** (remove) and **ln** (link). If you just memorize how to use the commands, you will never really understand what is happening, and the rules for using the file system will not make sense.

You might ask, which of these names is the most important one? Does the original name have any special significance?

The answer is that Unix treats all links as being equal. It doesn't matter what the original name of the file was. A new link is considered to be just as important as the old one. Files are not controlled by their names or locations. Files are controlled by ownership and permissions.

Creating a New Link: ln

To create a new link to an ordinary file, use the **ln** command. There are two forms of this command. To make a new link to a single file, use the syntax:

ln *file newname*

where *file* is the name of an existing ordinary file, and *newname* is the name that you want to give the link.

For example, say that you have a file named **spacewar**. To make a new link with the name **funky**, use:

ln spacewar funky

You will end up with two file names, each of which refers to the same file (that is, to the same inumber). Once a new link is created, it is indistinguishable from the original directory entry.

You can also use **ln** to make new links for one or more ordinary files and place them in a specified directory. The syntax is:

ln *file... directory*

where *file* the name of an existing ordinary file, and *directory* is the name of the directory in which you want to place the new links.

Here is an example. Your home directory is **/usr/harley**. In this directory, you have two files, **data1** and **data2**. Your friend has a home directory of **/usr/addie**. In this directory, she has a subdirectory named **work**. You want to create new links to the two files and place then in your friend's **work** directory. Use the command:

ln /usr/harley/data1 /usr/harley/data2 /usr/addie/work

Of course, you can use a wildcard specification (see Chapter 21):

ln /usr/harley/data[12] /usr/addie/work

Another way to simplify this command is to change to your home directory before entering the **ln** command:

```
cd
ln data[12] /usr/addie/work
```

Once you have created these links, the two files reside simultaneously in both directories: **/usr/harley** and **/usr/addie/work**.

How the Basic File Commands Work

All of the basic file commands can be understood in terms of changing file names and links. There are four basic operations:

1. COPY [the **cp** command]
   When you copy a file, Unix creates a brand new file with its own inumber. (Remember, the inumber – inode number – is what really identifies a file.) You end up with two files. The old file name points to the old inumber; the new file name points to the new inumber.

2. RENAME or MOVE [the **mv** command]
   When you rename or move a file, Unix changes the file name, but keeps the same inumber. You end up with one file. The new file name points to the old inumber.

3. CREATE A LINK [the **ln** command]
   When you create a new link, Unix makes a new directory entry using the file name you specify. You end up with one file and two file names. Both file names point to the same inumber.

4. REMOVE [the **rm** and **rmdir** commands]
   When you remove a file, Unix deletes the link between the file name and the inumber by removing the directory entry. If this happens to be the only link to the file, Unix also deletes the file. This means that the actual file is not deleted until the last link is removed.

Here is an example. You have a file named **spacewar**. You decide to make a new link to this file and call it **funky**:

```
ln spacewar funky
```

Now you remove **spacewar**:

```
rm spacewar
```

Even though the original file name is gone, the file still exists. The file itself will not be deleted until the last link (**funky**) is removed. This is why Unix has a remove command and not a "delete" or "erase" command.

☑ **HINT**

If you want to see how many links a file has, use the `ls -l` command. The number of links is displayed between the permissions and the name of the owner. For example, say that you enter:

`ls -l data spacewar`

The output is:

```
-rw-------   1 harley      4070 Oct 14 09:50 data
-rwx------   2 harley     81920 Oct 14 09:49 spacewar
```

You can see that **data** has only one link, while **spacewar** has two links.

Symbolic Links: `ln -s`

The links that we described in the previous two sections allow you to have more than one name refer to the same file. However, such links have two limitations.

First, you cannot create a link to a directory. Second, you cannot create a link to a file in a different file system.

(On many systems, parts of the directory tree are stored separately, perhaps on different devices, perhaps in different "partitions" on the same disk. Each of these parts is called a FILE SYSTEM. Unix combines all the file systems into a single integrated tree structure. To you, it looks like one big file system. To Unix, it is really several file systems joined together.)

To create a link to a directory or to a file in a different file system, you need to use `ln` with the `-s` option. Such a link does not contain the inumber of the original file. Rather, it contains the pathname of the original file. Thus, it is called a SYMBOLIC LINK. When you access a symbolic link, Unix uses the pathname to find and access the original file.

It is unlikely that you would ever need to create a symbolic link (or, for that matter, a regular link). We only mention such links because you may encounter them if you explore your system.

When you use `ls -l` to display the long listing for a file that is a symbolic link, you will notice two things. First, the leftmost character of the output line will be the letter `l`. Second, the actual symbolic link is shown at the right side of the line.

Here is an example from a system where there is a symbolic link from **/bin/csh** to **/usr/bin/csh**. You enter:

`ls -l /bin/csh`

The output is:

`lrwxr-xr-x 1 root      14 Sep 25 14:17 /bin/csh -> ../usr/bin/csh`

As you can see, this "file" is only 14 bytes long: just long enough to hold the pathname of the real file.

To see the long listing for the real file, you enter:

`ls -l /usr/bin/csh`

The output is:

`-rwxr-xr-x 1 root   249856 Mar 19  1991 /usr/bin/csh`

This file has 249,586 bytes. As you might have guessed from the name, this file holds the C-Shell program.

(Note: Some Unix systems show you the size of the actual file when you display information about the symbolic link.)

To distinguish between the two types of links, a regular link is called a HARD LINK, while a symbolic link is called a SOFT LINK. When we use the word "link" by itself, we mean a hard link.

 HINT When you use the `ls -l` command, you see the number of hard links. There is no easy way to see how many soft links there are to a file.

Usenet: The Worldwide Users' Network

To many people, Usenet is the best part of the Unix community. It is a medium by which hundreds of thousands of people around the world share information and discuss virtually every topic that you can imagine.

In this chapter, we will explain Usenet: what it is and what it offers. By the time you finish reading, you will have an appreciation for just how much is waiting for you.

In Chapter 24, we will continue the discussion and show you how to access this wonderful resource.

What Is Usenet?

Usenet is a vast, decentralized association of computer systems that allow people around the world to share information. This information is in the form of discussion groups, each with its own topic. Worldwide, there are well over 4,000 such groups. Many of these groups are primarily of local or regional interest. However, about half of them are of general interest and are transported globally.

Usenet started in 1979 as an experiment to share information between Unix systems in North Carolina. At first, there were only two sites: the University of North Carolina and Duke University. Through the years, Usenet has grown beyond comprehension. Suffice it to say that there are now tens of thousands of sites worldwide.

Usenet is a descriptive name, not the name of an actual network. There are many networks whose members participate in Usenet. The largest of these networks is the Internet (which we discussed in Chapter 13).

The character of Usenet is difficult to capture until you start to participate. Some people describe it as a large BBS (electronic bulletin board system), but it is really much more.

The distinctiveness of Usenet comes from its size. There is literally nothing else in the world that involves so many people from so many places. It is not at all unusual for, say, a person in California to send a message and, the next day, to receive a response from someone in England.

It is impossible to generalize about what types of people participate in Usenet. Although many of these people use Unix, you will find all kinds of individuals using virtually every type of computer system. Usenet sites include universities and colleges, high schools, small and large businesses, government agencies, and all types of personal computers.

Put simply, Usenet is the largest information utility in existence.

Basic Terminology

In the early days, Usenet was conceived as a means for passing news items from one system to another. Before long, Usenet evolved into a set of discussion groups. However, the original metaphor was retained, and you will find that much of the Usenet terminology is "news" oriented, even though there is relatively little actual news.

In general, the information carried within Usenet is called THE NEWS or NETNEWS. The discussion groups are referred to as NEWSGROUPS or, more simply, GROUPS. Within each newsgroup, the messages are called ARTICLES or POSTINGS. When you send an article, we say that you POST the article.

For example, here is a dull, but illustrative conversation between two students:

Student 1: Did you read the news today?
Student 2: Yes, I saw your article in the `rec.humor` newsgroup.

Usenet itself is often referred to as THE NET:

(some time later...)

Student 1: Where did you get that fabulous recipe for groatcakes?
Student 2: I got it on the net, from the `rec.food.recipes` group.

When you start to read a news group, we say that you SUBSCRIBE to the group. The term is a metaphor; there is no subscription fee, nor is there any formal process that you need to follow. All you need to do is tell your newsreader program that you want to read a certain group. At any time, you can stop reading a newsgroup by telling your newsreader that you want to UNSUBSCRIBE.

Because there are so many Usenet postings (millions of bytes a day), articles are kept only for a specified time and then discarded automatically. When this happens, we say that such articles have EXPIRED. The length of time that news is kept on your system is determined by your system manager. Typically, you can expect news articles to be retained for one to three weeks.

 HINT   You can divide the world of computer people into two categories. Those who have access to the net and those who don't.

What Is It Like to Use Usenet?

Using Usenet means reading the articles in the various news groups. To do so, you use a program called a NEWSREADER. The newsreader allows you to choose which groups you want to read. Within each group, the newsreader helps you read the individual articles.

There are a number of different newsreader programs. You can choose the one you like best from whatever is available on your system. In Chapter 24, we will show you how to use two of the most popular newsreaders, **rn** and **nn**.

The minute-to-minute experience of reading the news depends a great deal on what newsreader you use. Each of the newsreaders presents the articles in its own way. For example, the **rn** program shows you the beginning of each article. You can decide if you want to read the rest of the article or skip to the next one. The **nn** program shows you a list of subjects that describe the articles. Based on these one-line descriptions, you choose the articles you want to read.

When you use Usenet, you spend most of your time reading. From time to time, you press a key to display the next screen of an article or to move to the next article. At any time, you can change to another newsgroup or stop reading altogether.

In order to display an article, the newsreader calls upon a paging program to display the text of the article, one screenful at a time. (Paging programs are discussed in Chapter 17.) As you read, there are many commands that you can enter.

The most common choices are to display the next part of the article or skip to another article. You can also save the article to a file, mark the article as unread (so you can read it again later), or tell the newsreader that you do not want to read any more articles on the same subject.

On occasion, you may decide to respond to an article. There are two ways to do so. First, you can send a private mail message to the author of the article. Second, you can post a new article in response to the one you have just read. Your article will be dispatched by your system and, eventually, your response will be sent to everyone else who reads the same newsgroup.

Once you gain a little experience, you will want to post brand new articles of your own.

How Does the News Get from Place to Place?

In order to provide access to the news, at least one computer on your network must be set up to store the Usenet articles. This computer is called a NEWS SERVER. Every day, your news server receives a large number of new articles. This is called a NEWS FEED. When you read the news, your newsreader program connects to the news server and requests the articles that you want to read.

Usenet is a distributed system in which each news server communicates with a small number of other computers, perhaps only a single computer. Whenever a news server connects to another computer, it passes on all its new articles. In this way, articles move from computer to computer. Eventually, a new article is propagated throughout the world.

As we mentioned earlier, Usenet contains over 4,000 different newsgroups, most of which are of local or regional interest. It is up to the system manager of your news server to decide which groups he or she wants to carry.

For example, say that you are using a computer in New York City. Your system manager will probably decide to carry the newsgroups for your region. Other regional newsgroups, for instance, those for the San Francisco Bay area, may not be carried.

Whenever you post an article, you are asked to specify what distribution you want. As an example, here are some of the choices you have at the University of California at San Diego:

`local:`	local to the site
`ucsd:`	local to the UCSD campus
`uc:`	all the University of California campuses
`sdnet:`	local to San Diego County
`ca:`	everywhere in California
`usa:`	everywhere in the USA
`na:`	everywhere in North America
`world:`	everywhere in the world

Here is another example from a system at the Vienna Technical University in Austria:

`inst182:`	local to department #182 (Institut #182)
`tuwien:`	local to the university (Technische Universitaet Wien)
`at:`	everywhere in Austria
`europe:`	everywhere in Europe
`world:`	everywhere in the world

By using various distributions, Usenet allows you to post articles to a specific area. For example, if you want to sell a car in San Diego, you can post a notice to the local newsgroup **sdnet.forsale** using a distribution of **sdnet**.

When you make a distribution choice, it does not actually control where the article will go. Rather, it provides information to news servers so they can accept or reject the article. As we mentioned earlier, the system manager controls what articles a news server will accept. Some news servers are configured to accept all articles, which can make for interesting reading.

For instance, you might post an article in Austria with a distribution of **europe** (all of Europe) and two days later receive a reply from someone in New York. Why? Because, for some reason, one of the news servers in New York is configured to accept articles from European newsgroups.

Who Runs Usenet?

Usenet has no central authority. It is run by volunteers throughout the world. Each Usenet site donates the time of its system administrator and the cost of maintaining a news server. This cost includes the computer itself as well as the disk space needed to hold megabytes (millions of characters) of news articles. Each local system does whatever is necessary to make the news available to its users.

In order for Usenet to run smoothly, there are a number of guidelines that people follow voluntarily. For example, if you want to respond to an article in a personal manner, it is considered good etiquette to mail a message to the author of the article rather than to the entire newsgroup. There are many such guidelines that you will learn in time.

Since Usenet is not a formal network, the telecommunication links are not managed by a central authority. Much of the Usenet data is sent over large networks (like the Internet) that are maintained for non-Usenet purposes. Other Usenet data is sent from computer to computer using the UUCP system (see Chapter 13). The Usenet communication facilities are paid for by governments, private companies, universities and other organizations.

In an environment in which the news server is connected to the Internet – as is the case at most universities – new articles arrive all the time, often only hours after being posted from the other side of the world.

You might ask: If no one person or organization is in charge, how is order maintained? Usenet is run by the countless system managers who administer the many thousands of news servers around the world. On the whole, these people tend to be knowledgeable and responsible. Using the facilities of Usenet itself, the system managers discuss various issues and reach a consensus as to how operations should be managed. (There are newsgroups devoted to discussing the operation of Usenet.) However, no system manager has any real power over any news server except the one that he or she administers.

So the real answer to the question is that order is maintained through cooperation.

The Usenet Hierarchies

We mentioned earlier that there are a large number of newsgroups. To make life manageable, the newsgroups are divided into HIERARCHIES. The most important hierarchies are shown in Figure 23-1. The newsgroups in these hierarchies are distributed all over the world.

Each newsgroup is given a name that shows the hierarchy to which it belongs. For example, the main discussion group for asking Unix questions is called `comp.unix.questions`.

The Usenet hierarchies are divided into two categories referred to as MAINSTREAM and ALTERNATE. By agreement, the mainstream hierarchies are carried on all Usenet news servers. For this reason, they are sometimes referred to as the WORLD hierarchies. The alternate hierarchies are considered to be optional.

On each news server, the system manager decides what newsgroups to carry. Your news server will probably offer all the mainstream hierarchies and most of the alternative hierarchies. However, you may not have all the newsgroups.

Within a hierarchy, the system manager decides which groups to carry. Since the alternate hierarchies are considered less important, system managers often drop some of the less relevant newsgroups or even an entire hierarchy. For example, a system manager who is short of disk space might decide that the `alt.sex.wanted` newsgroup is less important than `comp.unix.questions`.

Before a newsgroup can be started in one of the mainstream hierarchies, certain procedures must be followed. We won't go into the details, but, briefly, there must be a period of discussion, a Usenet-wide vote, and the cooperation of a lot of people.

Name	Topic
`alt`	alternative newsgroups, many different topics
`bionet`	biology
`bit`	discussion groups from the Bitnet network: all topics
`biz`	business, marketing, advertisements
`comp`	computers
`ddn`	Defense Data Network
`gnu`	Free Software Foundation and its GNU project
`ieee`	Institute of Electrical and Electronics Engineers
`k12`	kindergarten through high school
`misc`	anything that doesn't fit into another category
`news`	Usenet itself
`rec`	recreation, hobbies, the arts
`sci`	science of all types
`soc`	social issues
`talk`	debate on controversial topics
`u3b`	AT&T 3B computers
`vmsnet`	DEC VAX/VMS and DECNET computer systems

Figure 23-1

The Most Important Usenet Newsgroup Hierarchies

The procedure for starting a newsgroup in most of the alternate hierarchies is much more relaxed. In particular, the **alt** hierarchy is the repository for all kinds of bizarre newsgroups, some of which are short-lived. This is a good place to look when you are searching for something strange to read.

The mainstream and alternate hierarchies are shown in Figures 23-2 and 23-3. In these tables, we have indicated how many newsgroups were in each hierarchy at the time we wrote this chapter. As you might imagine, such numbers change frequently, especially in the **alt** hierarchy.

You will notice that some types of newsgroups are in more than one category. For example, although most of the **comp** (computer) newsgroups are mainstream and are carried by all news servers, a smaller number are considered to be alternate newsgroups, carried only by some news servers.

Note: The distinction between mainstream and alternate hierarchies is made only for purposes of organization. There is no real difference when you read the articles. The main consideration is that your particular news server will probably not carry all the alternate newsgroups.

Name	Number of Newsgroups
comp	356
misc	35
news	23
rec	240
sci	60
soc	77
talk	18

Figure 23-2
The Mainstream Usenet Newsgroup Hierarchies

Aside from the general hierarchies that we have already discussed, there are other hierarchies that contain newsgroups of local or regional interest. For example, users in Santa Barbara, California, have three such hierarchies:

ucsb the Santa Barbara campus of the University of California
uc all the campuses of the University of California
ca the state of California

There are a great many regional and local hierarchies. Some, like **ucsb**, serve a relatively small community. Others cover a larger area. For example, **eunet** is a hierarchy for all of Europe. Two other well-known hierarchies are **de**, for discussions in German (Deutsch), and **fj**, for discussions in Japanese.

When you start to read the news, you will be able to see just what newsgroups are available on your system. Some regional newsgroups have become so popular that they are carried far beyond their area. Thus, you may find newsgroups from faraway places on your news server.

How Many Newsgroups Are There?

Let's take a moment to discuss a few statistics.

At the time we wrote this chapter, there were 809 mainstream newsgroups and 734 alternate newsgroups, for a total of 1,542 worldwide groups. In addition, we found 2,650 local and regional newsgroups that are carried outside their area, for a grand total of 4,193.

Bear in mind that this number is actually a low estimate. Most, perhaps half, of all newsgroups are not distributed beyond their immediate area and are not counted in our figures.

Name	Number of Newsgroups
alt	359
bionet	32
bit	168
biz	23
comp	52
ddn	2
gnu	28
ieee	12
k12	21
news	1
rec	2
sci	3
soc	1
u3b	5
vmsnet	24

Figure 23-3

The Alternate Usenet Newsgroup Hierarchies

The best way to appreciate the vastness and the variety of Usenet is to take a look at Appendix F. This contains the names of all the worldwide (mainstream and alternate) newsgroups. A quick look at this appendix will convince you that Usenet is well beyond the comprehension of a single person.

One survey of the Usenet readership estimates that there are about 60,000 Usenet sites and 1,565,000 people who read the news: about 26% of the users at those sites. Another set of statistics indicates that the average number of new articles is about 20,000 per day (excluding purely local postings).

As our contribution to the Usenet culture, we performed a complex and time-consuming mathematical analysis (using Bessel functions) and came up with some illuminating results. Of the 1,543 worldwide newsgroups, the following popular areas of human interest are represented as follows:

computers:	613
sex:	28
jokes:	3
Star Trek:	7

Of the 613 computer newsgroups, 45 pertain directly to some aspect of Unix.

Understanding Newsgroup Names

In this section, we will discuss the conventions for naming the various Usenet newsgroups. To use as examples, Figures 23-4 and 23-5 list two important collections of newsgroups. Figure 23-4 shows the newsgroups that contain jokes and humor. Figure 23-5 shows the newsgroups that are, in some way, related to sex.

The first thing to notice is that newsgroup names reflect the overall Usenet organization. The name of the hierarchy is followed by one or more specific names, each of which is separated by a period. For example, the names of the **alt** groups all begin with **alt.**, the **soc** groups all begin with **soc.**, and so on. (You might notice some similarity to the pathnames that we use in the Unix file system.)

By looking at the names of related groups, you can often tell what they have in common and how they differ. For example:

```
alt.binaries.pictures.erotica.female
alt.binaries.pictures.erotica.male
```

The first part of a newsgroup name, the hierarchy, tells you something about the group's overall focus. For example, you can expect **soc.women** to be devoted to social issues, while **talk.abortion** would be more of a debate. On the other hand, it is fair to assume that **alt.sex.bestiality**, being in the **alt** hierarchy, would be somewhat removed from mainstream culture. (Notice that, of the 28 sex-related groups, only the 6 most pedestrian are in mainstream hierarchies.)

The next point to notice is some newsgroup names end in **.d**. This indicates that the newsgroup is devoted to a discussion of contents of another newsgroup. For example, consider:

```
alt.binaries.pictures.erotica
alt.binaries.pictures.erotica.d
```

The first newsgroup contains erotic pictures and only erotic pictures. The second newsgroup is for any discussion about these pictures. For instance,

---

Name of Newsgroup

```
alt.tasteless.jokes
rec.humor
rec.humor.funny (moderated)
```

Figure 23-4
Newsgroups that Contain Jokes

```
Name of Newsgroup

alt.binaries.pictures.erotica
alt.binaries.pictures.erotica.d
alt.binaries.pictures.erotica.female
alt.binaries.pictures.erotica.male
alt.binaries.pictures.tasteless
alt.binaries.sounds.erotica
alt.personals
alt.personals.ads
alt.personals.bondage
alt.personals.misc
alt.personals.poly
alt.sex
alt.sex.bestiality
alt.sex.bondage
alt.sex.homosexual
alt.sex.masturbation
alt.sex.motss
alt.sex.movies
alt.sex.stories
alt.sex.wanted
alt.sex.wizards
alt.sex.woody-allen
rec.arts.erotica (moderated)
soc.bi
soc.men
soc.motss
soc.women
talk.abortion
```

Figure 23-5

Newsgroups Related to Some Aspect of Sex

if you have a problem displaying a particular picture on your computer, you can post a question to the **.d** newsgroup.

Here is a more important example. In Figure 23-4, you can see that there is a newsgroup named **rec.humor**. Anyone can post a joke or funny story to this group. However, if you want to discuss a joke, you are expected to post to a different newsgroup, named **rec.humor.d**. That way, people who only want to read the jokes are not bothered by arguments and discussions. (The reason we did not list **rec.humor.d** in Figure 23-4 is because it does not contain jokes. It contains articles *about* jokes.)

☑ **HINT** It is a convention within **rec.humor** that you should not post an article unless it contains a joke. Occasionally, someone feels an uncontrollable urge to offer an opinion about something or other. In such cases, the person will often include a joke, called an OBLIGATORY JOKE (abbreviated as OBJOKE). This is considered good manners.

In general, it is a good idea to stay within the bounds of a newsgroup when you post an article.

For the most part, newsgroup names are chosen to be descriptive. In most cases, you should have no problem guessing what a particular group is for. Some names, of course, are esoteric. However, if the group is within your area of expertise, the name will usually be meaningful. For example, a biologist will certainly recognize that **bionet.molbio.proteins** refers to proteins within the realm of molecular biology.

However, there are a few standard abbreviations that you will encounter. These are shown in Figure 23-6. (By the way, in case the entry **alt.sex.motss** in Figure 23-5 puzzled you, **motss** stands for "members of the same sex".)

Moderated News Groups

Take another look at Figures 23-4 and 23-5. You will notice that two of the newsgroups – **rec.humor.funny** and **rec.arts.erotica** – are designated as being MODERATED.

Abbreviation	Description	Example
binaries	binary files	comp.binaries.ibm.pc
fan	fans of...	alt.fan.monty-python
pictures	pictures to display	alt.fractals.pictures
sources	computer source programs	comp.sources.games
std	technical standards	comp.std.unix

Figure 23-6
Common Abbreviations Used in Usenet Newsgroup Names

This means that you cannot post freely to these groups. Rather, all articles are automatically sent to one person, called a MODERATOR. The moderator decides which submissions should be posted. He or she may also do some editing.

The idea behind moderated groups is to cut down on the amount of low-quality postings. The job of the moderator is to guide the discussion without excessive interference.

For example, the **rec.humor** group is one of the most popular in all of Usenet. Everybody likes to read a joke, and anyone can post jokes to **rec.humor**.

Of course, as we all know, many jokes are not all that funny. And when you read, for the hundredth time, the same collection of light bulb jokes, they do begin to lose their charm.

The moderated group **rec.humor.funny** contains only those jokes that someone has already judged to be funny. The moderator of **rec.humor.funny** receives a large number of submissions. It is up to her to choose what she feels are the best jokes, omitting the ones that most people have probably already heard.

The result is that **rec.humor.funny** is more widely read than **rec.humor**. Many busy people just don't have the time to read through all of **rec.humor** looking for the funny stuff.

Some moderated newsgroups offer a regular posting, called a DIGEST, that collects questions, answers and discussions. A digest is actually an informal electronic magazine.

For example, the newsgroup **comp.sys.ibm.pc.digest** is devoted to the world of IBM PC compatible computers. Each posting has its own volume and issue number and offers a collection of moderated submissions. At the beginning of the posting is a table of contents, so you can decide which items you want to read.

The idea of a moderated group is to collect articles that are interesting and appropriate. The nice thing about such a group is that the junk has already been eliminated by someone else. On the other hand, if you want to post an article to a moderated group, you must play by the moderator's rules. (For example, **rec.humor.funny** is rather heavy-handed and has a lot of rules.)

In a way, this system is a form of censorship because the moderator has absolute power over what appears in the newsgroup. However, there are always plenty of non-moderated groups, so you need never feel deprived.

Clarinet: A Real News Service

Although we refer to newsgroups and talk about "the news", Usenet does not really contain actual news. There is, however, a real news service, named Clarinet, that you can access just like Usenet.

Clarinet is run by a private company and is a service for which organizations must pay. Many universities, schools and companies subscribe to Clarinet. If your site pays for Clarinet, you can access it in the same manner as Usenet. (There is no cost to you.) Clarinet news is continually updated and comes from many sources, including a live UPI newswire.

Like Usenet, Clarinet is organized into newsgroups. There are groups for many different topics, including sports, politics, business and computers, as well as the columns from popular writers. There are also many local and regional newsgroups that contain news for a specific area.

☑ **HINT**   Until you start reading Clarinet, you cannot fully appreciate how much news there really is in the world.

Figure 23-7 shows a few of the Clarinet newsgroups so you can get the idea. At the time we wrote this chapter, there were 217 different newsgroups. As you can see, all Clarinet newsgroups start with the name **clari**.

If your news server offers Clarinet, you can read the newsgroups in the same manner as the Usenet newsgroups. Just tell your newsreader program which newsgroup you want to read.

Even if your school or organization does not subscribe to Clarinet, there is a Usenet newsgroup that you can read called **biz.clarinet.sample**. Clarinet regularly sends interesting articles to this newsgroup as free samples.

```
clari.biz.economy
clari.canada
clari.feature.dave_barry
clari.feature.miss_manners
clari.local.massachusetts
clari.net.announce
clari.net.newusers
clari.news.arts
clari.news.headlines
clari.news.sex
clari.sports.basketball.college
```

Figure 23-7
A Few of the Clarinet Newsgroups

Frequently Asked Questions: FAQ

An interesting aspect of human nature is that most beginners tend to ask the same questions. When you start to learn Unix, for example, you will wonder about many of the same things that everyone else wondered about when they learned Unix.

(For instance, one of the most common Unix questions asked by beginners is: "Can I get back a file that I erased accidentally?" The answer to this question, by the way, is in Chapter 22.)

The phenomenon of perpetual curiosity is nowhere more prevalent than on Usenet. Every newsgroup of substance has posed and answered the same basic questions repeatedly. Although such questions are interesting to beginners, you will find them a nuisance once you have followed the newsgroup for a while.

For instance, has there ever been a new reader of **alt.atheism** who has not asked, "Isn't it impossible to prove the non-existence of something?"

Similarly, you can imagine that the readers of **rec.arts.movies** have been asked many times if anyone has a full list of all the James Bond movies.

To satisfy such predictable queries, experienced newsgroup readers collect and publish lists of FREQUENTLY ASKED QUESTIONS or FAQs. At regular intervals, many newsgroups will carry a FAQ article for the benefit of newcomers. Each such newsgroup has a volunteer who maintains the FAQ and updates it as necessary.

It is expected that, before you enter into the discussion of a newsgroup, you will look for and read the appropriate FAQ. As a convenience, the group **news.answers** is a collection of all the FAQs as well as related material. Every time a FAQ is posted, it is also sent to **news.answers**.

Another newsgroup, **news.newusers.questions** is devoted to the concerns of people who are just starting to use Usenet. This group has articles to assist you in reading the news. In particular, look for a regularly posted article entitled "What is Usenet?"

Finally, **news.announce.newusers** has many helpful articles written specifically to help a new user. When you have a spare moment, this newsgroup well repays inspection.

☑ **HINT**　When you start reading a newsgroup for the first time, look for and read the FAQ article before you submit any articles of your own.

Mailing Lists

An alternative to discussing a topic in a Usenet newsgroup is to exchange messages with people on a MAILING LIST. A mailing list contains the addresses of a group of people, all of whom are interested in a single topic. When you mail a message to a designated address, it goes to everyone on the list. Some mailing lists are moderated, in which case the message goes to the moderator.

Using a mailing list to share ideas and information is a lot like using a Usenet newsgroup. In fact, many newsgroups are also distributed as mailing lists.

The main differences are logistical. With Usenet, a message is broadcast as part of a newsgroup. You read the message by using a newsreader program. With a mailing list, a message is sent by electronic mail and arrives in your personal mailbox. You read the message by using a mail program. (The Unix mail system is discussed in Chapters 13 and 14.)

There are a large number of public mailing lists to which you can subscribe. To see a description of these lists, look in the newsgroup named **news.answers** for an article called "Publicly Accessible Mailing Lists".

Earlier in the chapter, we mentioned that one of the alternate hierarchies is named **bit** (see Figure 23-1). We described this hierarchy as containing discussion groups from a network called Bitnet. Bitnet serves many thousands of users of IBM mainframe computers.

(The name "Bitnet" is a silly acronym that stands for "Because-It's-Time Network". Go figure.)

Within Bitnet, there are many discussion groups implemented as mailing lists. The Usenet **bit** hierarchy implements some of these mailing lists as newsgroups. For a description of the Bitnet mailing lists, look in the newsgroup **news.answers** for an article called "Mailing Lists Available in Usenet".

To send an article to a mailing list, you use a mail address in the standard form that we described in Chapter 13:

name@*domain*

For example, one of the more popular mailing lists is named:

risks@csl.sri.com.

(This mailing list, which is also available as the newsgroup **comp.risks,** deals with the risks and consequences of using computers.)

To join (or withdraw from) a mailing list, you must mail a request to a different, administrative address. By convention, the administrative address for many of the mailing lists is the same as the main address with **-request** appended to the first part of the name:

name-**request**@*domain*

For example, to subscribe to the list we just mentioned, you would send a request to:

`risks-request@csl.sri.com`

You can use this same pattern for most of the mailing lists you encounter.

Some private mailing lists are administered in a different manner. In such cases, you must follow exact instructions from the moderator. For example, Jeff Knodel at Ohio State University maintains a mailing list, called Netwit, that will regularly mail you a small number of jokes. To get on this list, you must send a message to:

`knodel@cis.ohio-state.edu`

For the subject of the message, use the word **ADD**, followed by your mail address. For example:

`ADD harley@nipper.ucsb.edu`

Although many mailing lists correspond to newsgroups, others, like Netwit, are more private and are available only by mail at the discretion of the moderator.

Reading the Usenet News

In Chapter 23, we described Usenet: the large, worldwide collection of newsgroups. In this chapter, we will show you how to participate in Usenet.

We will start by discussing what you can expect: what a news article looks like, the terminology that you will encounter, and so on. We will also discuss what approach you should take to participating in Usenet. We will then show you how to use the two most popular newsreader programs, **rn** and **nn**.

If you have not already read Chapter 23, you should at least skim through it before continuing with this chapter. In particular, you should be familiar with the technical terms that we defined.

What a News Article Looks Like

For the most part, using Usenet means reading news articles, so let's take a look at what you can expect to see.

A news article consists of three parts: a HEADER, a BODY and an optional SIGNATURE (often called a SIG). Like the mail messages that we discussed in Chapter 14, the header contains identification and system information, most of which is generated automatically. The body is the text of the article.

The signature is a short coda, usually four lines or less, that is created in advance by a user. To have a signature, use an editor such as **vi** (Chapter 19) to create a file named **.signature** in your home directory. Whatever is in this file will be appended automatically to each article that you post. The intention is that your signature should show your name, mail address and any other standard information that you feel to be important. As you will see, many people use their signature as a chance to demonstrate creativity and wit.

Figure 24-1 shows a typical news article. Let's take a line-by-line look. Before we start, you should know that the makeup of the header may differ somewhat on your system. The exact header lines depend on what program the author used to post the article and what program you use to read the news. You can also control the appearance of the article you read by setting options in your newsreader program. For Figure 24-1, we used the **rn** newsreader.

The top line is not part of the article. Rather, this line is displayed by the newsreader to show us the number of the article and how many unread articles remain in this newsgroup.

Each article has an identification number assigned to it when it arrives at your news server. The news server maintains separate numbering for each newsgroup. Your newsreader program uses these numbers to keep track of which articles you have already read. The actual number assigned to an article depends on when it arrives at your news server. If you were to read the same news at a different location, the numbers would be different.

```
Article 37268 (9 more) in rec.humor:
From: mich@vmars.tuwien.ac.at (Michael Schuster)
Newsgroups: rec.humor
Subject: Riddle about programmers
Summary: a light bulb joke about programmers
Keywords: programming, light bulb
Message-ID: <1992Nov4.082938.707@email.tuwien.ac.at>
Date: Wed, 4 Nov 1992 08:29:38 GMT
Distribution: world
Sender: news@email.tuwien.ac.at
Organization: Tech Univ Vienna, Dept of Realtime Systems, AUSTRIA
Lines: 11


Here is a riddle:
How many programmers does it take to change a light bulb?


The Answer:
None. It's a hardware problem.


--Michael Schuster        | Place the quote: author, characters...
TU Vienna, Austria        | "Coincidence was his father and luck
mich@vmars.tuwien.ac.at   |         his inheritance"
+43/1/12345               | Replies will be rewarded a cookie.
```

Figure 24-1
A Typical Usenet Article

The first group of lines is the HEADER. Like the header on a mail message (see Chapter 14), each line contains one specific item of information. The headers that you see will vary. Here is what each line means in our example.

From: This line shows us the address and name of the person who sent the article. In this case, we see that it is Michael Schuster (a well-known programmer and humorist from Vienna, Austria).

Newsgroups: Here we see the names of the newsgroups to which the article was posted. In this case, the article was sent to a single newsgroup, **rec.humor**. You will also see articles that have been sent to more than one newsgroup. In such cases, we say that an article has been CROSSPOSTED.

Subject: Several words describing the topic of the posting. The subject is important because some newsreaders, such as **nn**, show you a list of subjects and ask you to decide which articles you want to read. In addition, you can ask your newsreader to search for articles with a particular subject.

Summary: The summary provides extra information to help you decide if you want to read a long article.

Keywords: This is another line that helps you decide if you want to read an entire article. This line is also useful when you want to search for articles that pertain to a specific topic.

Message-ID: As mentioned above, the article number is assigned by your newsreader when the article arrives. Thus, it is a local number that varies from site to site. The Message-ID is a unique number that is generated by the program that posted the article. You can ignore this line; it is used by the software.

Date: Here are the time and the date that the article was posted. For most articles, the time will be in Greenwich Mean Time, the standard time used by Unix.

Distribution: This shows the distribution specified by the person who posted the article. This value is used by news servers to decide whether or not to accept the article (see Chapter 23). A distribution of "world", as we see in this example, means that the article should be propagated throughout Usenet. However, you should remember that most news servers do not carry every newsgroup. The choice is up to the system manager.

Sender: The address of the userid that actually submitted the article to Usenet. Each system will have a standard userid that posts articles for that system. The actual work is done by a daemon (see Chapter 18). In our example, the article was handled by a userid named **news**, from a machine named **email.tuwien.ac.at**. This is the machine that handles much of the communication with the outside world at the Technical University of Vienna.

Organization: The name of the organization to which the author of the article belongs. This name is inserted automatically by the news posting program, but it can be changed by the author.

Lines: The size of the article, not including the header, but including blank lines.

After the header comes the body of the article. In this case, this is a short article and there are only six lines of text. Most articles, though, are much longer.

Finally, the last part of the article is the signature. If you have a dotfile named `.signature` in your home directory, the news posting program will automatically append the contents of this file to the end of every article that you write. Whatever you put into this file becomes your signature. (We discuss dotfiles in Chapter 21, and home directories in Chapter 20.)

The basic purpose of the signature is to allow the author to identify him- or herself. The custom is to put your name, mail address and, possibly, your organization or department.

You will find, though, that the signature is also used to demonstrate creativity. Aside from the standard information, you will also see quotations, jokes, observations, announcements, pictures and so on. The whole idea is to see how witty and creative you can be in such a short space.

In Figure 24-1, you can see that the author uses his signature to pose a question. He is asking people to identify a quotation and promises a cookie to those people who respond.

☑ **HINT**   It is considered good manners to restrict your signature to four lines or less. (Some news posting programs will enforce this rule.)

When someone sends a posting in response to another posting, we call it a FOLLOWUP ARTICLE. As you will see later in the chapter, your news-reader program makes it easy for you to create a followup article. The program will automatically set things up and start your editor program. When you have finished editing the followup article, the newsreader program will post it for you.

When you create a followup article, you can have the newsreader insert the body of the original article into the editing buffer for you. (The editing buffer, as we explained in Chapter 19, holds the text you are editing.) Each line of the original article will be prefaced by a special character, usually >. This makes it easy for you to quote all or part of the original article within your response.

Figure 24-2 shows a typical followup article. Notice how, in this case, the body of the original article is short. If the original article were long, it would be a good idea to edit it to include only those passages that are relevant. In our example, the original signature was edited out of the followup article.

☑ **HINT** When you are editing a followup article that contains the original article, take a moment to delete anything that is not relevant.

It is irritating to read articles filled with junk because the author could not be bothered to do some editing.

The format of a followup article is pretty much the same as an original article. However, there will be an extra line in the header, **References:**, that identifies the original article.

```
Article 37293 (9 more) in rec.humor
From: harley@nipper.ucsb.edu (Harley Hahn)
Newsgroups: rec.humor
Subject: Re: Riddle about programmers
Summary: Riddle about light bulbs and Unix programmers
Keywords: Unix programming, light bulb
Message-ID: <6548@ucsbcsl.ucsb.edu>
Date: 6 Nov 92 04:37:23 GMT
References: <1992Nov3.184303.1@vax1.mankato.msus.edu>
Sender: news@ucsbcsl.ucsb.edu
Distribution: world
Organization: Harley Hahn Consultants
Lines: 19

In article <1992Nov4.082938.707@email.tuwien.ac.at>
mich@vmars.tuwien.ac.at (Michael Schuster) writes

>Here is a riddle:
>How many programmers does it take to change a light bulb?
>
>The Answer:
>None. It's a hardware problem.

How many Unix programmers does it take to change a light bulb?
Four.

One to change the bulb.
One to write the manual page.
One to describe what all the options are for.
One to explain why it is better to change light bulbs with
Unix than with DOS.

--Harley Hahn, writer of Unix books
```

Figure 24-2

A Typical Followup Article

Usenet Acronyms

As you read news articles, you will encounter a large number of slang words and acronyms. Most of these will become familiar as you gain experience. In the next few sections, we'll take a look at the most common Usenet terms and conventions.

Certain acronyms are used frequently. These are shown in Figure 24-3.

Note: MUD refers to a computer program that creates a virtual-reality world to which users can connect, explore, role-play and so on.

☑ **HINT for students**

MUD is time-consuming and addictive. Don't start playing if you want to graduate.

Acronym	Meaning
BTW	by the way
FAQ	frequently asked questions
FAQL	frequently asked question list
FOAF	friend of a friend
FYI	for your information
IMHO	in my humble opinion
IMO	in my opinion
MOTAS	member of the appropriate sex
MOTOS	member of the opposite sex
MOTSS	member of the same sex
MUD	multiple user dimension
Ob-	(as a prefix) obligatory
Objoke	obligatory joke
OS	operating system
PD	public domain
SO	significant other
ROTFL	rolling on the floor laughing
RTFM	read the fuckin' manual
WRT	with respect to

Figure 24-3
Common Usenet Acronyms

Usenet Slang

Aside from the acronyms that we discussed in the last section, you will also encounter a large number of slang expressions and words. In this section, we will start you off with a few of the most important terms.

First, the prefix "net" is often used to refer to a concept as it applies to Usenet. For example, the guidelines to follow when you post articles are sometimes referred to as NETIQUETTE. Sometimes a period is inserted after "net" to mimic the format of a newsgroup name. For example you may see a well-known Usenet person referred to as a NET.ENTITY. Or the general Usenet user might be called a NET.CITIZEN.

Perhaps the most common Usenet term is FLAME. This refers to a posting in which someone criticizes someone else. The same word is also used as a verb, as in "I asked a dumb question and people all over the net flamed me." Some flames will be posted to the newsgroup in which the discussion occurred; others are sent as private messages to the user's mail address.

From time to time, a FLAME WAR arises, in which people send a large number of argumentative postings and mail messages excoriating one another. Although flame wars do have their interesting moments, most of the postings seem to boil down to the fundamental argument: "I know you are, but what am I?"

In Chapter 20, we explained that the special file **/dev/null** is used as a target for output that should be discarded. In other words, any data that is sent to **/dev/null** is ignored. Within an argumentative news article, you will sometimes see a comment like "Send all flames to **/dev/null**." This means, "Don't bother flaming me. Your flames will be ignored."

Another term that you will encounter is THREAD. This refers to a series of postings on the same subject. For example, say that someone posts an article to the **comp.unix.questions** newsgroup asking the question "Is Unix Dead?" (In other words, is the future of Unix limited owing to new, more modern operating systems?)

A question like this is bound to start a thread. Someone responds with an opinion. Someone else responds to that opinion, and so on. Eventually, the thread will die out, more because people get bored than because an actual consensus was reached. As you read the news, you can follow a thread by telling your newsreader to skip to the next article with the same subject. You can also JUNK or KILL a thread by telling your newsreader to ignore all articles with that subject.

Experienced users will sometimes refer to the Usenet computing and telecommunication resources as BANDWIDTH. This term is often used by nerds who will point out that people who ask dumb questions are "wasting bandwidth". In other words, such neophytes are wasting precious Usenet resources.

Another such term, SIGNAL/NOISE RATIO, is used to describe the proportion of useful to useless information. For example, a large posting, in which the author has included very little of value, might be said to have a low signal/noise ratio.

Finally, the term SPOILER refers to information about a movie or book that other people might not yet have seen or read. For example, if you are posting an article that gives away the ending for a mystery movie, you should put the word "spoiler" in the subject. This tells people who intend to see the movie that they should skip your article.

Foo and Bar

One of the most interesting Usenet (and Unix) idiosyncrasies is the use of the words FOOBAR, FOO and BAR as generic identifiers. For example, you might read a posting in the `comp.unix.questions` newsgroup in which an expert is describing how to combine files: "Say that you have a file named `foo` and a file named `bar`, and you want to combine them..."

Or you might read a question: "I want to send a message to another computer. I tried mailing it to an address like `foobar.edu`, but the message bounced..."

You will see these words used repeatedly: in the Usenet newsgroups, in Unix books, in the Unix online manual, even in person when Unix experts gather. In fact, one day you will find yourself explaining a technical point to someone by using `foo` and `bar`. On that day, you will have the revelation that you are finally a Unix person!

WHAT'S IN A NAME?

Foobar   It is easy to understand how words such as foo, bar and foobar might be used widely. After all, there are many times when we need to give an example of a generic name in order to illustrate an idea. The question is, where did these names come from?

The word foobar derives from the acronym FUBAR, coined during World War II, meaning "Fucked Up Beyond All Recognition". The word foo, however, seems to have a more complicated history. No doubt it owes some of its popularity to foobar, but it seems to have existed on its own even earlier. For example, in a 1938 cartoon, Daffy Duck holds up a sign that reads "SILENCE IS FOO!" Some authorities speculate that the word foo may have roots in the Yiddish "feh" and the English "phoo".

Whatever the origin, nobody knows how the words were adopted by the Unix and Usenet communities.

RTFM

One of the most important Unix ideas is that expressed by the word RTFM. Originally, this was an acronym meaning "Read the fuckin' manual". The idea was to tell someone, categorically, that he or she should look up a particular item in the online Unix manual (Chapter 8) and not bother everyone else.

Through the years, the term RTFM has come to stand for the more reasonable idea of trying to help yourself before you ask for assistance. For example, it is expected that before you ask a question in one of the Usenet computer newsgroups, you will try to find the answer for yourself. At the very least, you should look in the online manual. When someone posts the answer to a question that is covered in the manual, he or she will gently remind the person to RTFM.

Today, RTFM is a word in its own right in spite of its earthy origins. It is not really an acronym any longer. (Otherwise, how could we use it in a family book?)

The word RTFM is used as a verb, both in the imperative and active voices and as an infinitive. For example, you might tell someone, "RTFM and, if you still can't find what you want, I will check it out for you."

Or you might see the question: "Does anyone know how to use the foo command? I RTFM'ed, but I couldn't find it anywhere."

In other words, to ask is human, to RTFM is divine.

☑ **HINT**

Now that you know what RTFM means, take a moment and re-read the story at the end of Chapter 6.

Smileys

When you talk with someone – in person or over the telephone – you use the inflections in your voice and the timing of your words to ensure that your listener understands the emotional overtones. However, when you communicate on Usenet, such techniques are impossible and shades of meaning are easily lost.

We talked about this idea in Chapter 12, when we discussed the `talk` command (used to carry on a real-time conversation with another person). At the time, we explained that the convention is to use a SMILEY FACE (often called a SMILEY) to indicate irony. The basic smiley looks like this:

`:-)`

Turn your head sideways to the left and you will see the smiling face.

We use a smiley to make sure that someone is not accidentally offended by an ambiguous remark. For example, say that you are posting a followup article in which you are arguing the question, where is the best place in the world to live? You write:

```
... So my philosophy is, if God did not want us to
live in California, why did he make us smarter than
everyone else? :-)
```

Putting the smiley at the end of the sentence is the same as saying "only kidding" (at least somewhat).

Through the years, people have developed many different smileys. For example, look sideways at the following characters:

```
8-)
```

This is a cool, California surfer-dude smiley with sunglasses.

The basic `:-)` smiley is almost always the one to use. For your enjoyment, Figure 24-4 shows a few more such concoctions. There are literally hundreds.

Smiley as Typed	Smiley Sideways	Meaning
:-)		smiling
:-D		laughing
;-)		winking
:-(		frowning
:-I		indifferent
:-#		smiley with braces
:-{)		smiley with a mustache
{:-)		smiley with a toupee
:-X		my lips are sealed
=:-)		punk-rocker
=:-(		real punk rockers don't smile

Figure 24-4
Smileys

Guidelines for Posting Articles

From the point of view of other Usenet users, reading the news is a passive activity. You can read all day long, and nobody else will care. However, as soon as you start to post articles, people will expect you to respect the culture.

Over the years, Usenet has developed many rules. Since the whole system runs on cooperation, it behooves you to follow the rules, at least in spirit. Before you start to post, it is a good idea to read the introductory articles in **news.answers** and **news.newusers.questions** (see Chapter 23).

Unfortunately, as soon as you read these articles, you may be put off by how much other people are telling you what to do. Much of the advice given to new users seems to be "Don't do this, don't do this, don't do that..." Of course, people mean well. It's just that, at the beginning, you may not understand why we need to have so many rules.

The irony of the whole thing is that there is no real way for anyone to make anyone else do what they want. There are no net.police to enforce the law. If a person does something *really* obnoxious, other people might complain to his system manager who might throw the person off the system. However, this is unusual.

We suggest that you gain a little experience reading Usenet before you start posting. In particular:

- It is a good idea to read Usenet for at least two weeks before you post your first article. (Patience is a virtue.)

- Before you post to a particular newsgroup, read it for at least a week.

- Before you ask a question, read the FAQ list for the newsgroup.

 HINT To practice sending an article, or to check your signature, post to one of the test groups and use a local distribution. Two of the test groups are **misc.test** and **alt.test**.

As you know, the Usenet resources cost somebody money, and the system is run by cooperation. For this reason, some people feel that whenever you post anything unnecessary, you are wasting real money which is, somehow, a bad thing to do.

A typical example is some nerd in a computer newsgroup chastising another person for posting a dumb article. On such occasions, the rallying cry is "Don't waste bandwidth". Such people are more than glad to point out that, even though we do not pay real money out of our pockets, Usenet is not really free. Somebody somewhere is paying for the computers, communication lines and so on, not to mention the time of all the system managers. "Usenet is a privilege, not a right," goes the refrain. "If we overload the system with unnecessary traffic, they may take it away."

All of this, in fact, is silly. When such people (perhaps with the best of intentions) complain about the wasted bandwidth of a particular computer question, we politely point them to `rec.pets.cats` where people regularly post immense articles describing all the cute things their kitten has done.

Look, no one is going to take away Usenet. It's there for you to use, so use it. However, there are rules to follow. You must cooperate, and you must use common sense. To make life simple, we have summarized all of the rules into the three simple guidelines you see in Figure 24-5.

---

1. Be considerate.

2. If you can't be considerate, at least don't be a jerk.

3. Don't let yourself be bothered by people who do not follow rules 1 and 2.

Figure 24-5
Rules for Posting to Usenet

Choosing a Newsreader

To read the news, you use a newsreader program. This program connects to your news server and displays the articles that you choose to read.

Your newsreader also performs a variety of other functions. You use it to subscribe and unsubscribe to newsgroups. As you read, you can search for specific articles, follow a thread, or junk articles you don't want to read. Your newsreader will also help you post a followup article or send a mail message to the author of an article.

Newsreaders are highly complex programs with many options and commands. In this chapter, we will discuss two of the more popular newsreaders, **rn** and **nn**. One of these programs should be available on your system (although there are other choices). If both programs are available, you should choose one and learn it well.

A newsreader is your window into Usenet. Your experience in reading the news is very much influenced by your choice of newsreader. Both **rn** and **nn** have their advantages and disadvantages.

With both newsreaders, you start by specifying what newsgroup you want to read. **rn** will display each article, one at a time. You look at the first screenful and decide if you want to read the rest of the article.

nn does not start by displaying an article. Rather, it shows you a list of the subjects of each article in the newsgroup. Based on this list, you mark only those articles you want to read. **nn** will then display the selected articles, one after another.

Which is better? It depends on how your mind works. The advantage of **rn** is that you get to see at least one screenful of all the articles. If you can only look at the subject lines before you decide what to read, you will miss out on a lot of postings that were more interesting than they looked. (Many people are not good at writing subject lines.)

The advantage of **nn** is that it allows you to process a lot of articles quickly. It is fast and easy to scan a list of subjects and choose what you want to read. You do not have to spend so much time looking at every article. **nn** was developed specifically to help people read the news quickly.

Actually, the names of the programs reflect the overall design. The name **rn** stands for "read news". The name **nn** stands for "no news is good news".

Rot-13

To start using Usenet, look at the remainder of this chapter and read the portions that discuss the newsreader that you plan to use (either **rn** or **nn**). To practice reading, we suggest that you start with one of the newsgroups that contains jokes (see Chapter 23). Choose from one of the following:

```
alt.tasteless.jokes
rec.humor
rec.humor.funny
```

Warning: The jokes in **alt.tasteless.jokes** really are tasteless. If you are offended, there is no one to whom you can complain.

In the **rec.humor** and **rec.humor.funny** newsgroups, you will occasionally see a joke that is so offensive that it must be encoded. The coding scheme is called ROT-13 (explained in a moment). When you encounter such an article, the subject line will include **(rot-13)** and the body of the article will look like gibberish.

You can read a rot-13 article by using a special command within your newsreader. You must enter this command deliberately, so it is impossible to read a rot-13 article by accident. Thus, no one has the right to complain about being offended. If a person feels that the subject of the article is offensive, he or she can skip the article completely. The articles in **alt.tasteless.jokes** are rarely encoded, as they are expected to be offensive.

The scheme for encoding potentially offensive articles is a simple replacement cipher in which each letter is rotated 13 positions within the alphabet. The actual substitutions are shown in Figure 24-6.

The rot-13 scheme can be implemented using the `tr` command that we explained in Chapter 16. The actual command is:

```
tr '[a-m][n-z][A-M][N-Z]' '[n-z][a-m][N-Z][A-M]'
```

If you want to practice decoding, use this `tr` command on the following rot-13 encoded text:

```
Uryyb sevraqf. V'z lbhe Ivgnzrngnirtnzva tvey.
```

The `.newsrc` File

You might wonder, how does a newsreader keep track of newsgroups and articles? From one session to the next, your newsreader needs to know which newsgroups you have subscribed to and which articles you have read.

The answer is that all newsreaders maintain a file named `.newsrc` in your home directory. Within this file, your newsreader keeps information about the status of each newsgroup. (Files like `.newsrc`, whose names begin with a period, are called dotfiles. They are discussed in Chapter 21. Newsreaders also maintain other dotfiles, but we won't cover them here.)

a → n	n → a	A → N	N → A
b → o	o → b	B → O	O → B
c → p	p → c	C → P	P → C
d → q	q → d	D → Q	Q → D
e → r	r → e	E → R	R → E
f → s	s → f	F → S	S → F
g → t	t → g	G → T	T → G
h → u	u → h	H → U	U → H
i → v	v → i	I → V	V → I
j → w	w → j	J → W	W → J
k → x	x → k	K → X	X → K
l → y	y → l	L → Y	Y → L
m → z	z → m	M → Z	Z → M

Figure 24-6
The Substitutions Used to Implement the Rot-13 Code

The format of a `.newsrc` file is simple. There is one line for each newsgroup. This line contains:

- the name of the newsgroup
- a colon (`:`) or an exclamation mark (`!`)
- a set of numbers

If there is a colon after the newsgroup name, it means that you are currently subscribed to that group. An exclamation mark means that you are unsubscribed. The range of numbers indicate which articles you have already read. (You will remember that each article is given an identification number as it arrives at the news server.)

Here are a few lines from a `.newsrc` file:

```
comp.unix.questions: 1-15253
rec.humor.funny: 1-1224
rec.humor: 1-37293,37298,37300
sci.space.shuttle! 1-1669
misc.books.technical!
```

You can see that the first three newsgroups are subscribed and the last two are unsubscribed. Within each newsgroup, you can also see which articles have been read. For example, in the `rec.humor` group, articles 1 through 37,293, plus articles 37,298 and 37,300 have been read. Finally, notice that, although `sci.space.shuttle` is unsubscribed, it was subscribed at one time. You can tell because articles 1 through 1,669 have been read.

We mention all this in detail because you can use `vi` or another editor (see Chapter 19) to edit your own `.newsrc` file. There are two reasons why you would want to do so. First, you will probably want to change the order of the newsgroups. When you start your newsreader, it will look at the newsgroups in the order it finds them. By editing your `.newsrc` file, you can put the more interesting groups first. You can use your newsreader to make such changes, but it is usually a lot easier to edit the `.newsrc` file and do it yourself.

The second reason to edit your `.newsrc` file is to make changes to your newsgroup subscriptions – that is, to specify exactly which newsgroups you want to read. Again, this is something that you can do with your newsreader, but if you want to make a lot of changes, editing the file is faster.

☑ **HINT**

Before you edit your `.newsrc` file, make a backup copy. That way, if you ruin the original, you can restore it from the copy. This is good advice for editing any important file.

Preparing Your `.newsrc` File: `newsetup`

When you start to read the news, you will not be subscribed to any news-groups. You will not even have a `.newsrc` file. The first time you use **rn** or **nn**, they will detect that you do not have such a file and will create one in your home directory. (The home directory is discussed in Chapter 20.)

This file will contain the name of every newsgroup carried by your news server, and they will all be marked as subscribed. You can, if you want, start reading right away. However, you will immediately encounter a vast number of newsgroups, most of which will not be of interest to you. You can use your newsreader to unsubscribe to the bulk of the newsgroups, but this will be time consuming.

The best idea is to prepare your `.newsrc` by hand *before* you start reading the news for the first time. To do so, you will need to use an editor such as **vi** (see Chapter 19). Here is the plan:

Start by using a single editing command to mark all newsgroups as unsubscribed. In other words, change all the colons to exclamation marks. Then go through the entire list, changing the few newsgroups that you do want back to being subscribed. Finally, move these groups up to the top of the list and put them in the order you want to read them.

Here are exact instructions. Before you start, make sure you are in your home directory. You can change to this directory by entering the command:

`cd`

(See Chapter 21.)

The first step is to create a `.newsrc` file. If you are using **rn**, the easiest way is to enter the command:

`newsetup`

This is a program that comes with **rn**. The purpose of **newsetup** is to create a new `.newsrc` file from the master list of newsgroups. If you use **rn** before you have a `.newsrc` file, **rn** will run **newsetup** for you.

 HINT At any time, you can run **newsetup** to create a brand new `.newsrc` file with all the newsgroups subscribed. If you already have an existing `.newsrc` file, **newsetup** will save it under the name `.oldnewsrc`.

If you are using **nn**, you can create a full `.newsrc` file by starting **nn** and quitting right away. Do the following. Enter the command:

`nn`

When **nn** starts, you may see a welcoming message. If so, press the <Space> bar to move on to the next screen. You may see a prompt, asking you if you want to read a particular newsgroup. If so, press <Space>. Eventually, you will see a list of articles. Type **Q** (uppercase "Q") to quit. You should now have a brand new **.newsrc** file.

Now that you have a **.newsrc** file, you need to edit it. Here is how to do the job using **vi**. Start **vi** as follows:

vi .newsrc

Enter the following **:s** command to replace all the colons with exclamation marks:

:%s/:/!/

You are now unsubscribed to every newsgroup.

Next, move to each of the newsgroups you want to read and change the exclamation mark to a colon. There are many ways to do this, but here is an easy method. Read all the instructions before you start.

- Type **1G** to move to the top of the file.
- Type **$** to move to the end of the line.

Your cursor should be on the exclamation mark.

- Move the cursor down, one line at a time. Use the **j** command or press the <Down> arrow key. As you move down, the cursor will stay at the end of the current line, on the exclamation mark. If you want to move up, use **k** or the <Up> key.

Each time you come to a newsgroup you want, change the exclamation mark to a colon.

- The first time, you should use the command **r:**

This will replace a single character (an exclamation mark) with a colon.

- From then on, all you have to do to make the same change is type **.** (a period).

(As you may remember from Chapter 19, typing **.** repeats the last command that changed the editing buffer. In this case, the last such command was **r:**, the command to replace the current character with a colon.)

☑ **HINT**   Remember, when you are using **vi**, you can undo the last change by typing **u**.

When you get to the bottom of the list, you will have selected all the newsgroups you want to read. The next step is to move all such newsgroups to the top of the file. Enter the following command:

:g/:/m0

(Here is how it works. The first **:** indicates an **ex** command. The **g/:/** means to perform the following command on all lines that contain a colon.

m0 is the command to move a specified line to line 0, the beginning of the file. Thus, you move all lines that contain a colon to the beginning of the file.)

You can now arrange the subscribed newsgroups – the lines that end with a colon – in the order you want. Here is an easy way to move a line. Move the cursor to that line. Type **dd** to delete the line. Move the cursor to the destination line. Type **P** to insert the deleted line.

That's it. You now have a personalized **.newsrc** file ready to go. Save your work and quit **vi** by typing **ZZ**.

> **NOTE:** From this point on, we will be discussing how to use **rn** and **nn**. We will start with **rn**. If you will be using **nn**, you can skip over the **rn** sections.

Overview of the rn Newsreader

The **rn** program has many options and commands that offer far more functionality than you will ever need. The best strategy is to learn the basics and practice for a while. Once you have some experience, you can look at the **rn** manual page and experiment with whatever looks interesting. (The online Unix manual is discussed in Chapter 8.)

To start **rn**, enter the command:

```
rn
```

Although there are many options, we will discuss only the most important ones, later in this section.

The first thing **rn** will do is look at your **.newsrc** file to see which newsgroups you have subscribed to. The program will then check which of these groups have unread articles. It will display the names of the first few such groups to give you an idea of what news is waiting for you. For example:

```
Unread news in rec.humor                      75 articles
Unread news in comp.unix.questions            83 articles
Unread news in rec.humor.funny                 2 articles
Unread news in biz.clarinet.sample             1 article
Unread news in alt.tasteless.jokes           202 articles
etc.
```

 HINT   If all you want to do is check for unread news but not read it right away, you can start **rn** with the **-c** (check) option:

```
rn -c
```

The program will report if there is any news and then exit. This is a good command to put in your **.login** file to check for news every time you log in. (The **.login** file is discussed in Chapter 11.)

Once **rn** has reported on unread news, it will look at the master list of newsgroups to see if there are any that are not in your **.newsrc** file. If so, **rn** will display each name and ask you if you want to subscribe. For example:

```
Newsgroup alt.comedy.british not in .newsrc--subscribe? [ynYN]
```

You must now make a choice. Press **y** for yes or **n** for no. If you want to accept or reject all the new groups, you can press **Y** or **N**, respectively. If you press **y**, you will be asked where you want to place the new newsgroup within your **.newsrc** file. Press **h** (help) to see your choices and pick the one you want.

If you decide that checking for new groups each time you start **rn** is too time-consuming, you can bypass it by starting **rn** with the **-q** (quiet) option:

```
rn -q
```

Once **rn** has finished the preliminaries, you are ready to look at articles. **rn** will present the first newsgroup with unread articles and ask you if you want to read it. For example:

```
******** 75 unread articles in rec.humor--read now? [ynq]
```

Type **y** to read this newsgroup. Type **n** to go on to the next newsgroup.

Within **rn**, you will spend most of your time responding to a prompt of some kind. There are four general rules that you need to remember.

1. Most commands and choices are a single letter. In such cases, you need only type the letter and the program will react immediately. You do not need to press <Return>. When a program reads input in this way, we say that it is in CBREAK MODE.

2. At any time, you can press **h** (help) to see a list of choices. In almost every case, there will be more choices than you know what to do with.

3. Pressing **q** (quit) will stop whatever you are doing. If you press **q** enough times, you will end up leaving **rn**.

4. At each prompt, **rn** will display a short list of the most common choices. The first choice is the default, and you can always select it by pressing the <Space> bar.

Consider the example above where **rn** is asking if you want to read the **rec.humor** newsgroup. The line ends with:

```
[ynq]
```

In this case, the most common choices are yes, no and quit. If you press <Space> it is the same as pressing **y**. If you press **q**, you will stop the program. If you press **h**, you will see a help list. The **h** choice is never displayed, but it is always there. It is by far the most useful command, so don't forget it.

☑ **HINT**   At all times, pressing the <Space> bar will choose the default. **rn** was carefully designed so that you can read news all day long just by pressing the <Space> bar.

The **rn** Commands

Once you get started, you will always be within one of three environments: selecting a newsgroup, selecting an article, or paging through a long article. Each environment has its own list of commands. Whatever you are doing, you can display a command summary by pressing **h**. To stop a command that is in progress, press **^C** (the **intr** key).

Our advice is to learn how to use **rn** by practicing. Whenever you are not sure how to something, press **h** and find the command that does what you want. For reference, Figures 24-7, 24-8 and 24-9 show the most useful commands for each of the three environments. For the most part, all the commands are straightforward. However, a few do have their nuances, so we will offer some pointers.

Pointers for Selecting a Newsgroup

1. To go to a specific group, use the **g** command followed by the name of the group. For example:

   g rec.bicycles

2. To search for a group whose name contains a specific pattern, use the **/** command followed by the pattern. For example:

   /archa

   Here is a typical result from such a search:

   Searching...
   ******** 100 unread articles in sci.archaeology--read now? [ynq]

   To repeat a search for the same pattern, simply enter the **/** command without a pattern.

3. To list the names of unsubscribed groups that contain a pattern, use the **l** command followed by the pattern. For example:

   l unix

   This command will find all the unsubscribed groups whose name contains **unix**.

4. To use a shell command, type **!** followed by the command. For example:

   ! date

This command will display the time and date and then return to **rn**. If you want to enter a series of shell commands, enter **!** by itself:

!

This will pause **rn** and start a new shell. You can now enter as many commands as you want. To return to **rn**, stop the shell in the regular manner, either by pressing **^D** or by using the **exit** command.

rn: Useful Commands When Selecting a Newsgroup

Basic Commands

h	display help information
q	quit **rn**
<Space>	choose the default (**y** = read newsgroup)
y	read the newsgroup
=	same as **y**, but start by showing list of subjects
u	unsubscribe to the newsgroup
c	catch up: mark all articles in newsgroup as read

Control Newsgroups

n	go to next newsgroup with unread articles
p	go to previous newsgroup with unread articles
^	go to first newsgroup with unread articles
$	go to the end of the list of newsgroups
g *newsgroup*	go to specified newsgroup
/ *pattern*	scan forward for newsgroup that matches *pattern*
? *pattern*	scan backward for newsgroup that matches *pattern*
/	scan forward for previous pattern
?	scan backward for previous pattern
l *pattern*	list unsubscribed newsgroups containing *pattern*
L	list current state of newsgroups in **.newsrc** file

Enter a Shell Command

! *command*	execute the specified shell command
!	pause **rn** and start a shell

Figure 24-7

rn: Useful Commands When Selecting Articles

Basic Commands

h	display help information
q	quit this newsgroup, go to newsgroup selection
\<Space\>	choose the default (will be either **n** or **^N**)
n	forward: to next unread article
^N	forward: to next unread article on same subject
k	(kill) mark as read articles with same subject
=	display list of all the unread articles
u	unsubscribe to newsgroup
c	catch up: mark all articles in newsgroup as read

Re-display the Current Article

^R	re-display the current article
v	(verbose) re-display current article with header
^X	decode current article using rot-13
b	go back one page

Move to Another Article

-	re-display the last article that was displayed
number	go to article with the specified number
N	forward: to next article, whether read or unread
$	forward: to end of the last article
p	backward: to previous article
^P	backward: to previous article with same subject
P	backward: to next article, read or unread
^	backward: to first unread article

Search for an Article

/ *pattern*	forward: look for subject containing *pattern*
/	forward: repeat search using previous pattern
? *pattern*	backward: look for subject containing *pattern*
?	backward: repeat search using previous pattern

continued

Figure 24-8

rn: Useful Commands When Selecting Articles *(continued)*

Respond to an Article

r	(reply) send mail message to author of article
R	same as **r**, include original message
f	start **Pnews** program to create a followup article
F	same as **f**, include original message

Save an Article

s *file*	save entire article to specified file
w *file*	(write) same as **s**, but do not save the header

Enter a Shell Command

! *command*	execute the specified shell command
!	pause **rn** and start a shell

Figure 24-8

Pointers for Selecting an Article

1. As we explained, a thread is a set of articles that have the same subject. To follow a thread, press **^N** to go to the next article with the same subject. Once you start to follow a thread, the default command will become **^N**.

2. To junk a thread, use the **k** (kill) command. This will junk all the articles with the same subject.

3. To see a quick list of all the articles, press **=** (the equal sign). This will display a summary showing the subject of each unread article, along with its number. You can make a note of the number for each article that looks interesting. To display a particular article, simply enter its number. For example, to display article number 12143, enter:

   12143

4. When you happen upon an article encoded using rot-13, press **^X** to decode the article. (This is a FAQ.)

5. To save a copy of an article, use the **s** or **w** commands. The **w** command will not save the header. For example, to save the current article to a file named **ideas**, use:

   s ideas

By default, **rn** will save the file in a directory named **News** in your home directory. If the file already exists, **rn** will append the article to the end of the file.

Before **rn** saves an article into a new file, it will ask you if you want to save it in "mailbox format". If you answer yes, it will be saved in the format of a mail message. Later, you can read such files using the **mail** program. Specify the **-f** option followed by the name of the file. For example:

```
mail -f ~/News/ideas
```

The **-f** option tells **mail** to read from a specified file rather than from your regular mailbox. (We discuss **mail** in detail in Chapter 14.)

rn: Extra Commands to Use When Paging Through Articles

As you are paging through an article, you can use all the commands in Figure 24-8 as well as the extra commands in this table.

Page Through an Article

h	display help information
q	go to the end of the article
\<Space>	display the next page
d	display half a page more
b	go back one page
j	(junk) mark article as read and go to end
g *pattern*	forward: search for specified *pattern*
G	forward: repeat search using previous pattern
^G	while reading a digest: go to next subject
\<Tab>	followup articles: skip text from older article

Figure 24-9

Pointers for Paging Through an Article

1. If an article is too long to be displayed all at once, **rn** will act as a paging program. Its behavior will be a lot like the **more** program we discussed in Chapter 17.

2. As you are paging through an article, you can use all the regular selection commands, as well as extra commands that control the paging.

3. The only tricky command is **g**. You might expect to use **/** to search for a pattern within the article (as is the case with **more** and **vi**). However, you must remember that **/** is an article selection command. It will search for the next article whose subject contains the specified pattern. To search *within* an article, use **g** (go to). For example:

g computer

This will search the current article for the next occurrence of the pattern **computer**. When **rn** makes such a search, it does not distinguish between upper- and lowercase letters.

Using **rn** to Post Articles: **Pnews**

The program that comes with **rn** for posting news articles is called **Pnews**. There are three ways to start it. First, you can enter the **Pnews** command. The syntax is:

Pnews [*newsgroup* [*subject*]]

where *newsgroup* is the newsgroup to which you want to post, and *subject* is the subject of the message. If the subject is more than a single word or if it contains punctuation, you should place it in single quotes.
Here is a typical **Pnews** command:

Pnews rec.food.cooking 'Choosing a turkey'

If you don't specify the subject, **Pnews** will ask you for it. If you don't specify the newsgroup or the subject, **Pnews** will ask you for both of them. Thus, you can start **Pnews** with no parameters:

Pnews

The program will talk you through the process of posting, prompting you for everything it needs.

 HINT If you want to practice posting an article, send it to the **misc.test** or **alt.test** newsgroups and use a local distribution.

The second way to post an article is as a followup while you are reading the news with **rn**. When you are within a newsgroup, you can type the **f** command to respond to the current article. This command will automatically start **Pnews** for you. If you want to include the original article in your response, use the **F** command. The original article will be indented and a **>** character will be placed at the beginning of each line. It is a good idea to delete all the unnecessary lines before you post the final article.

Finally, there is one more way to start **Pnews**. Say that you are reading a newsgroup and you decide to post an article on a brand new subject. You could stop **rn**, enter a **Pnews** command, post the article, and then restart **rn** to continue reading. However, here is an easier way. Type **$** to move to the end of the newsgroup. Now type the **f** command. Since you are past the last article, **Pnews** will assume that you are not posting a followup article and will ask you to specify a new subject.

Once **Pnews** starts, it will lead you through the process of posting an article. All you have to do is answer the questions. When **Pnews** is ready for you to create the article, it will automatically start the editor program, which will probably be **vi** (see Chapter 19).

As we mentioned earlier in the chapter, you can create a file named **.signature** in your home directory to hold a signature. If such a file exists, **Pnews** will append its contents to the end of all your postings.

☑ **HINT**　　When you read an article to which you want to respond, ask yourself if your response will be interesting to everybody or just to the author. In many cases, you are better off using the **r** or **R** commands to respond directly to the author by mail, rather than posting a followup that will go all over the world.

An Overview of the nn Newsreader

The **nn** newsreader is fast, easy to learn and very powerful. On the other hand, **nn** is a complex program. There are a vast number of commands, options and settings, far more than you will ever need. In this section, we will show you how to get started with **nn**. Once you gain some experience, you can read the **nn** entry in the online Unix manual (see Chapter 8) and experiment with whatever looks interesting.

nn was designed to solve the problem of too much news and too little time. In the past few years, the size of Usenet has grown enormously, to the point where some news servers carry over 4,000 different newsgroups (see Chapter 13). Even sites with restricted access to Usenet will routinely carry several hundred newsgroups.

nn makes it easy to choose the newsgroups you want to follow and, within each newsgroup, the articles you want to read. A typical session with **nn** runs as follows:

You enter the **nn** command to start the program. **nn** displays a list of articles for your first newsgroup. Each article has a short, one-line description showing the subject. You mark only those articles that you want to read. After marking all such articles, you type the command that tells **nn** to start displaying articles.

As you read, there are a number of actions you can take: you can save the article to a file, send mail to the author, create a followup article, junk all articles with the same subject, decode the article using rot-13, and so on. At any time, you can move to another article or to another newsgroup. After finishing with one newsgroup, you move on to the next one. When you get tired of reading, you quit **nn**.

When you use **nn**, you spend most of your time doing one of two things. You are either selecting articles to read, or you are reading articles. As you move from one newsgroup to the next, you change back and forth between selecting and reading.

One of the nice things about **nn** is that help is always available in three ways. First, when you are reading or selecting, you can type **?** to get a summary of the most important commands. Second, you can use the **:help** command to display information about selected topics. Finally, you can use the **:man** command to display selections from the **nn** manual page (which is, in reality, a large manual in itself).

Most **nn** commands are one or two letters. As soon as you type them, **nn** responds. For example, as soon as you press the **?** key, you will see the help screen. You do not have to press <Return>. When a program acts in this way, we say that it is in CBREAK MODE. A few of the commands are longer and you do have to press <Return>. Such commands will be obvious by context. An example is the **:help** command that we just mentioned.

Occasionally you will enter a command that requests some type of input. You must type the input and then press <Return>. If you change your mind before you press <Return>, you can press **^G** to cancel the command.

The best strategy for understanding **nn** is to learn the basics and then practice. At any time, you can press **?** to see a list of possible commands. It is a good idea to display this list from time to time and try out something new.

The nn Selection Screen

The **nn** command has many options, of which we will discuss the most important. However, most of the time you will start the program with no options:

nn

The program begins in one of two ways. In some cases, **nn** will ask if you want to read a particular newsgroup. Alternatively, **nn** may jump right into a newsgroup. Once you get started with a newsgroup, **nn** will show you a selection of unread articles. Figure 24-10 shows a typical screen.

This screen contains a lot of information. The top line shows you the name of the newsgroup (in this case, **misc.forsale**). To the right, we see the number of unread articles (354), the total number of articles (817) and the number of articles that have arrived since you last read this newsgroup (4).

```
Newsgroup: misc.forsale                    Articles: 354 of 817/4 NEW

a*T. L. Nipper         5   Dish with separate water compartment
b.Frederick Bean      39   used PC 486 + poetry collection
c.Samuel Jackson      33   >> Cowboy Hat... cheap
d.Judge Wiley         29   men's bicycle
e M. Wiggins          11   >
f Sniffy Wilson        4   Perfume Samples
g.William Bean         8   Electric Beard Warmer
h Frederick Bean      10   Wanted: Sherlock Holmes on CD-ROM
i Orestes Boomsch     16   Circus Tickets
j C. Jimpson Camp     15   various camping equipment
k*Henry Anderson      30   real estate: suitable for lake-side hotel
l*Herb Garble         12   >
m*Uncle Wesley        28   >
n*J.J. Pomeroy        13   >
o Old Whibley         19   books
p Bannister           14   -
q Henrietta           53   Children's toys
r Charles             31   full set of Henhouse Magazine
s Jimmy Witherspo     17   baseball glove

-- 15:49 -- SELECT -- help:? -----Top 5%-----
```

Figure 24-10

A Typical **nn** *Selection Screen*

The bottom line shows the time (remember, Unix uses a 24-hour clock) and reminds you that you are selecting articles and that you can ask for help by pressing **?** (question mark). To the right, we see that we are at the top of the list of articles. We also see that the last article displayed is 5% of the way through the list.

The number of articles listed depends on how many lines your terminal can display. Each article has an ARTICLE ID, a single character to the left of the line. **nn** uses the letters of the alphabet, **a** through **z**, as article ids. If your screen holds more than 26 articles, **nn** will use the digits **0** through **9**. In this case, there are 19 articles, marked **a** through **s**.

To the right of the article id is the name of the author, the number of lines and the subject. For convenience, **nn** collects all articles with the same subject (that is, an entire thread).

nn has five different patterns for displaying the author and subject. If you type type **"** (double quote character), **nn** will use a different pattern. You can press " repeatedly and cycle through the various patterns to see which one you like best.

As we saw earlier in the chapter, the subject line of a followup article has the characters **re:** inserted before the original subject. For example, say that an article has a subject of:

```
men's bicycle
```

A followup article will have a subject of:

```
re: men's bicycle.
```

When **nn** groups the articles in a thread, the followup articles are indicated by a **>** character. In our example, articles **d** and **e** form a short thread. Articles **k** though **n** also form a thread. If an article is a followup to a followup, you will see two **>>** characters. This is the case for article **c**.

If more than one article has the same subject, but without the **re:**, **nn** indicates it with a **-** character. This is the case with articles **o** and **p**. This may mean that the articles happen to have the same subject but are not related to one another.

To the right of the article id is a single character called the ARTICLE ATTRIBUTE that indicates the status of the article. There are a number of possible attributes of which two are the most common. A period indicates that the article has already been read. In our example, this is the case with articles **b**, **c**, **d** and **g**. A space means that the article has not yet been read.

When you select articles to read (we will show you how in a moment), **nn** marks them for you. If your terminal can highlight text, **nn** will mark your selections in this manner. Otherwise, the line will be marked with an asterisk attribute. In our example, you can see that articles **a**, **k**, **l**, **m** and **n** are selected. Most terminals, though, support some type of highlighting. For example, a selected article may be displayed in reverse colors.

The nn Commands

Once you get started, you will always be within one of two environments: selecting articles or reading articles. Each environment has its own list of commands which you can display by pressing **?**.

Our advice is to learn how to use **nn** by practicing. Whenever you are not sure how to do something, press **?** and find the command that does what you want. For reference, Figures 24-11, 24-12 and 24-13 show the most useful commands. Figure 24-11 shows commands that are always available, Figure 24-12 shows commands for selecting articles, while Figure 24-13 shows commands for reading articles. For the most part, all the commands are straightforward. However, a few do have their nuances, so we will offer some pointers.

nn: Commands that Are Always Available

Basic Commands

\<Space\>	do the most reasonable thing/accept default
Q	quit **nn**
^G	cancel a command that is waiting for input
:post	post a new article

Display Help

?	display summary of available commands
:help	show extra sources of help
:man	read the **nn** entries in the online manual

Control Newsgroups

G	(go to) jump to a newsgroup out of sequence
U	unsubscribe/subscribe to the current newsgroup
Y	show overview of newsgroups with unread articles

Enter a Shell Command

! *command*	execute the specified shell command
!	pause **nn** and start a shell

Figure 24-11

Pointers for General Commands

1. In general, pressing the \<Space\> bar will do whatever is the most reasonable thing to do in your current situation. When you are selecting articles, pressing \<Space\> takes you to the next part of the list. At the end of the list, \<Space\> will tell **nn** to start reading. As you are reading, \<Space\> will page through an article, go to the next article, and ultimately return you to selecting. When you enter a command that asks for input, \<Space\> will usually give you the default choice.

2. You can read the online manual pages for all the **nn** commands – there is actually a family of commands – by entering :**man**. You access the manual pages the same way you read news articles. Select the subjects you want, then read.

3. As a rule, **nn** reads the newsgroups in the order they are listed in your .**newsrc** file. (It is possible to change this. See the manual.) If you

want to jump to a newsgroup out of sequence, you can use the **G** (go to) command. This is a complex command with all kinds of options. Here is how to use it in its most basic form. Type:

G

You will see:

`Group or Folder (+./~ %=sneN)`

Ignoring the strange choices, simply type the name of a newsgroup and press <Return>. For example:

`rec.humor` <Return>

You will see:

`Number of articles (uasne)    (a)`

Press <Space> to get the default. You will now jump to the specified newsgroup.

4. To unsubscribe to the current newsgroup, use the **U** command. To resubscribe to a newsgroup, use **G** to jump to the newsgroup and then type **U**. When you are already unsubscribed, the **U** command resubscribes you. (This is a FAQ.)

Pointers for Selecting Articles

1. When you type an article id (a letter or number), the article is selected. If you type the same article id again, the article is unselected. Thus, typing an article id acts as an on/off toggle.

2. To specify a range of articles, use two article ids separated by a hyphen. For example, to select articles **k**, **l**, **m** and **n**, type **k-n**.

3. To select an entire thread, type the article id marking the beginning of the thread followed by an asterisk. For example, to select all the articles that have the same subject as article **k**, type **k***.

4. You can move up and down by using the cursor control keys. However, it is much more convenient to use **,** (comma), **.** (period) and **/** (slash). Look at the bottom right-hand corner of your keyboard. Notice how these three keys are next to one another. By keeping the first middle three fingers of your right hand on these keys and your thumb on the <Space> bar, you can zip through the list, selecting and unselecting like nobody's business. (Now, if we only had a convenient system for left-handed people...)

 HINT You can change the default key for an **nn** command to be any key you want. See the manual page for details. Look at the section on key mappings.

---

nn: Useful Commands When Selecting Articles

(id represents an article id: **a...z, 0...9**)

Select and Unselect Articles

id	select/unselect specified article
id-id	select/unselect specified range of articles
id*	select/unselect articles with same subject as *id*
,	move down one line
.	select/unselect current article, then move down
/	move up one line
*	select/unselect same subject as current article
@	reverse selections on current page
=.<Return>	select all articles in the newsgroup
~~	unselect all articles in the newsgroup

Display the Selection List

<Space>	go to next page, unselected articles become read
>	go to next page
<	go to previous page
^	go to first page
$	go to last page
"	change the layout

Start Reading

<Space>	start reading (when on last page)
z	start reading; return to newsgroup when done
x	start reading; go to next newsgroup when done

Figure 24-12

nn: Useful Commands When Reading Articles

Move Within an Article

\<Space\>	forward: one page
d	forward: one half page (down)
\<Return\>	forward: one line
$	forward: to last page
\<Backspace\>	backward: one page
u	backward: one half page (up)
^	backward: to first page
g*line*	go to specified line
/ *pattern*	forward: search for specified pattern
.	repeat previous search
\<Tab\>	followup articles: skip text from older article

Display an Article

h	display with full header
D	decode using rot-13
c	(compress) omit multiple spaces and tabs

Move to Another Article

\<Space\>	go to next article (if on last page)
n	go to the next selected article
P	go to the previous selected article
k	(kill) mark as read articles with same subject
*	go to next article with same subject

Return to Selecting

\<Space\>	return to selecting (when on last article)
=	return to selecting current newsgroup
N	go to next newsgroup
X	go to next newsgroup, mark all articles as read

Respond to an Article

r	(reply) send mail message to author of article
f	create a followup article
m	mail a copy of the article to someone

Figure 24-13

Pointers for Reading Articles

1. You can read all the news you want with just two keys. Use <Space> to page through the selected articles. If an article is boring, use **k** to junk the rest of the articles in the thread.

2. When you happen upon an article encoded using rot-13, press **D** to decode the article. (This is a FAQ.)

3. If you are not sure if you want to read an entire thread, select only the first article. After you read it, you can press ***** to select and read the followup articles.

Using nn to Post Articles

There are three ways to post an article using **nn**. No matter how you do it, posting is easy. **nn** will lead you through the process by asking you questions. All you have to do is supply reasonable answers and **nn** will do most of the work.

When **nn** is ready for you to create the article, it will automatically start the editor program, which will probably be **vi** (see Chapter 19).

 HINT   If you want to practice posting an article, send it to the **misc.test** or **alt.test** newsgroups and use a local distribution.

While you are reading the news, you can post a followup to an article by using the **F** command. **nn** will ask you if you want to include the original article in your followup. If you answer yes, the original article will be indented and a **>** character will be placed at the beginning of each line. It is a good idea to delete all the unnecessary lines before you post the final article.

You can also post a brand new article whenever you want by entering the **:post** command. **nn** will ask you for all the relevant information: newsgroup, subject and so on.

Finally, you can post an article while you are not reading news by using the **nnpost** program (which comes as part of the **nn** package). Enter the command:

```
nnpost
```

The program will behave just as if you entered **:post** within **nn**.

The easiest way to use **nnpost** is without options. The program will ask you everything it needs to know. However, you can specify all or part of the information that the program needs by using options. You can even automate the process of posting an article. See the **nnpost** manual page for details. (Use the command **man nnpost**, or, from within **nn**, use **:man**.)

As we mentioned earlier in the chapter, you can create a file named `.signature` in your home directory to hold a signature. If such a file exists, **nn** will append its contents to the end of all your postings.

☑ **HINT**   When you read an article to which you want to respond, ask yourself if your response will be interesting to everybody or just to the author. In many cases, you are better off using the **R** command to respond directly to the author by mail, rather than posting a followup that will go all over the world.

Various Ways to Start nn

There are many options and parameters that you can use when you start **nn**. In this section, we will show you the most useful of these. For more details, see the **nn** page in the online manual.

If you specify the names of one or more newsgroups, **nn** will read only those newsgroups. For example:

```
nn rec.humor comp.unix.questions
```

When you are finished with those newsgroups, **nn** will quit automatically.

The **-g** (go to) option tells **nn** to start by asking you which newsgroup you want to read:

```
nn -g
```

You can specify whatever you want. After you are finished with that newsgroup, **nn** will quit automatically.

You can have **nn** ask for one newsgroup after another by combining **-g** with the **-r** (repeat) option:

```
nn -gr
```

This is like **-g** except that **nn** will not quit after the first newsgroup. Rather, it will keep on asking you for a newsgroup name.

Finally, there are four options that can be combined in a particularly useful manner. They are:

-m	merge all articles into an artificial "meta" group
-x	scan all articles: read and unread
-X	look at all newsgroups: subscribed and unsubscribed
-s*word*	show only articles whose subject contains specified word

Use these options together to tell **nn** to search every newsgroup for all the articles on a particular topic. The results will be presented together as a meta group. For example, to find all the articles that have the word "unix" in the subject, you can use:

```
nn -mxX -sunix
```

During our tests, **nn** took 85 seconds to search 107,781 articles in 2,502 newsgroups. It found 458 articles that fit our specification.

To cut down on the number of newsgroups to search, you can specify names as parameters. The special name **all** refers to all the newsgroups in a family. For example:

```
nn -mxX -sunix comp.all
```

This command searches all the newsgroups in the **comp** (computer) hierarchy.

The nn Family of Commands

The **nn** program is actually one of a family of commands. The entire family is shown in Figure 24-14.

Command	Purpose
nn	read the news
nncheck	check for unread articles
nngoback	mark specified days' articles as unread
nngrab	find all articles whose subject contains a pattern
nngrep	display all newsgroup names that contain a pattern
nnpost	post news articles
nntidy	clean and adjust your .newsrc file
nnusage	display statistics showing who has been using nn

Figure 24-14
The **nn** *Family of Commands*

We have already discussed the **nnpost** command and, of course, the **nn** command. We won't cover the other programs here. However, we do recommend that after you gain some experience, you check out these commands in the online manual. In particular, **nngrab** is a fast alternative to the combination of options we used in the previous section to search all the newsgroups for a specific topic.

 HINT   Put an **nncheck** command in your .login file. Whenever you log in, you will see how much news is waiting for you. (The .login file is discussed in Chapter 11.) If there are no new articles, you will see the message:

```
No News (is good news)
```

(This may also mean that the news server is down.)

Internet Services

In Chapter 13, we discussed the Internet, the global network that connects hundreds of thousands of computers. The Internet provides important functions to a vast number of people around the world. We can catagorize these functions in four ways:

1. Mail
2. Usenet news
3. File transfer
4. Remote login

We discussed mail in Chapters 13 and 14, and Usenet in Chapters 23 and 24. (Although Usenet is supported by a collection of networks, the Internet does carry a large share of the traffic.)

In this chapter, we will cover file transfer and remote login. We will then discuss the many important INTERNET SERVICES that are based on these functions. The variety of these services is so vast as to be almost beyond comprehension. If we were to tell you, right now, everything that is available over the Internet, you would have difficulty believing us.

In this chapter alone, we will show you examples of:

- Finding the Unidentified Flying Object program.

- Getting copies of an electronic magazine containing collections of weird stuff.

- Connecting to a computer in Switzerland to find obscure song lyrics.

- Searching for the name of a person who, at some time in the past, sent an article to Usenet.

We will show you how to do all this and much, much more. Along the way, we will meet some of the most fascinating and useful tools that you have ever seen, including **archie** and **veronica**, the **gopher**, **wais** and the World-Wide Web.

Basic Terminology

We first discussed the Internet in Chapter 13. At the time, we explained that the Internet is supported by a family of programs and protocols (communication standards) called TCP/IP. In this chapter, we will be using two of the most important TCP/IP programs, **ftp** and **telnet**.

The **ftp** program allows you to transfer files from one computer to another. The name "**ftp**" comes from File Transfer Protocol, the underlying protocol that supports this program. The **telnet** program allows you to log in to remote computers.

It is common to use the words "**ftp**" and "**telnet**" not only as the names of programs, but as verbs to describe using these programs. For example, someone might tell you, "You can get a copy of the Usenet FAQ (frequently asked question) lists by **ftp**'ing to **pit-manager.mit.edu**." Or you might read, "If you want to find someone who uses an Internet computer, you can **telnet** to **bruno.cs.colorado.edu** and use a special search program." Notice also, that we routinely refer to Internet computers by their addresses. (For a basic discussion of Internet addresses, see Chapter 13.)

Much of what we do on the Internet involves transferring files from one computer to another. When we get a file from another computer, we say that we DOWNLOAD the file. When we send a file to another computer, we say that we UPLOAD the file. One way to remember these terms is to imagine the other computer floating above you in the sky. You send data up, the other computer sends data down.

More About Internet Addresses: host

In Chapter 13, we discussed Internet addresses and explained how they are used. Basically, an Internet address has the form:

userid@domain

For example:

harley@nipper.ucsb.edu

In this case, the userid is **harley** and the domain is **nipper.ucsb.edu**. Each part of the address is a sub-domain. The rightmost part (**edu**) is the top-level domain.

When you use an address that is local to your network, you do not have to specify the common part of the domain. For example, if you are using a computer on the same network, as in our example (**ucsb.edu**), you can use the simplified address:

harley@nipper

In most cases, though, you will be using addresses that are not on your local network, so you do have to specify the full domain (as in our first example). Such a specification is called a FULLY QUALIFIED DOMAIN NAME, sometimes abbreviated to FQDN. A fully qualified domain name spells out everything that the system needs to find another computer.

The Internet is vast. It has over 500,000 connected sites, each of which must have its own unique fully qualified domain name. Inside the United States and Canada, many sites use an old-style, descriptive top-level domain. These are shown in Figure 25-1. Virtually all other sites use a top-level domain that consists of a two-letter country abbreviation. Some of these are shown in Figure 25-2. For reference, Appendix E contains a list of the abbreviations for all the countries connected to the Internet.

Domain	Meaning
com	commercial organization
edu	educational institution
gov	government
int	international organization
mil	military
net	networking organization
org	non-profit organizations

Figure 25-1
Top-Level Domains for United States and Canada

When you enter a command that uses a fully qualified domain name, your system must have a way to find out exactly where that computer is. This is done by a service called DOMAIN NAME SYSTEM or DNS.

As you know, the addresses that we use consist of names. However, the official Internet addresses are actually numbers. One of the jobs of DNS is to convert the domain address to the official numeric address.

For example, later in this chapter we will show how to use a program called **ftp** to connect to other computers and transfer files. You will see an example in which we connect to a computer named **pit-manager.mit.edu**. We use the command **ftp** followed by the name of the computer. As it

Domain	Meaning
`at`	Austria
`au`	Australia
`ca`	Canada
`ch`	Switzerland ("Cantons of Helvetia")
`de`	Germany ("Deutschland")
`dk`	Denmark
`es`	Spain ("España")
`fr`	France
`gr`	Greece
`ie`	Republic of Ireland
`jp`	Japan
`nz`	New Zealand
`uk`	United Kingdom (England, Scotland, Wales, N. Ireland)
`us`	United States

Figure 25-2
Some of the International Top-Level Domains

happens, the official numeric address of this computer is **18.172.1.27**. Thus, the following two commands are equivalent:

```
ftp pit-manager.mit.edu
ftp 18.172.1.27
```

In Chapter 13, we explained that the part of the networking system that moves packets of data is called IP (Internet Protocol). Thus, the numeric version of an address is called the IP ADDRESS. For example, we can say that the IP address of **pit-manager.mit.edu** is **18.172.1.27**.

Normally, you do not have to use IP addresses. You use the regular domain address, and DNS does the translation for you behind the scenes. Occasionally, though, you may run across a computer whose domain name is not registered with DNS. In such cases, you will have to use the IP address (which always works). When you see reference material that contains Internet addresses, you may see the addresses listed in both forms. The intention is that if the domain name doesn't work from where you are, the IP address will.

If you would like to test the DNS system, you can use the **host** command. (If the **host** comand is not available on your system, you may be able to use the **nslookup** command). Enter the command, followed by a domain name. For example:

`host pit-manager.mit.edu`

The **host** will use DNS to look up the name and will display the IP address:

`pit-manager.mit.edu has address 18.172.1.27`

You can also specify an IP address if you want **host** to find the domain name. For example:

`host 18.172.1.27`

The output of this command is:

```
Name: PIT-MANAGER.MIT.EDU
Address: 18.172.1.27
```

For more information, display the manual pages for **host** or **nslookup**. (You can use the commands **man host** and **man nslookup**. The online Unix manual is discussed in Chapter 8).

Transferring Files from a Remote Computer: `ftp`

To transfer files from another computer over the Internet, you use the **ftp** program. This is an interactive program that you start by using the following command:

`ftp [-i] [host-computer]`

where *host-computer* is the name of the computer to which you want to connect. There are a number of options, of which we will discuss only **-i** in the next section. For more information, see the **ftp** manual page. (You can use the command **man ftp**. The online Unix manual is discussed in Chapter 8.)

The idea is that your **ftp** program connects to another computer and communicates with an **ftp** program there. (The remote **ftp** program is a daemon. We discuss daemons in Chapter 18.) Once the connection is made, the two programs communicate to carry out whatever commands you enter. For example, you might enter a command to display a directory of the other computer. You might then enter a command to copy a file from that directory to your own computer.

Once you make the connection, your computer is called the LOCAL computer, while the other computer is called the REMOTE computer. Whenever you enter a command, your local **ftp** program decides if it can handle the request itself. If not, it passes it to the remote computer.

To start an **ftp** session, enter the **ftp** command with the name of the remote computer. For example, say that you want to transfer files from the computer named **pit-manager.mit.edu**. Start the **ftp** session by entering:

`ftp pit-manager.mit.edu`

This starts your **ftp** program and tells it to make the specified connection. When the connection is made, the remote computer will ask you to log in. You will see messages similar to the following:

```
Connected to pit-manager.mit.edu.
220 pit-manager.MIT.EDU FTP server
   (Version 4.179 Tue Jul 7 18:37:28 EDT 1992) ready.
Name (pit-manager.mit.edu:harley):
```

Notice that one of the lines has a number in front of it. All the messages that come from the remote computer will have such numbers, which you can ignore.

At this point, the **ftp** program is asking for the userid that you want to use on the remote computer. The program displays the name of the computer followed by the userid you used to log in to the local system. (In this case, we are logged in with a userid of **harley**.) You now have two choices. You can enter a different userid for the remote system, or you can simply press <Return> and use the local userid. For example, if you are **ftp**'ing to a computer on which you have an account under the same name, you can just press <Return>.

Once you enter a userid, you will be asked for a password:

```
Password (pit-manager.mit.edu):
```

Enter the password that you use on the remote system. The characters will not be echoed as you type, just like when you log in to any Unix computer.

Once you are successfully logged in, your **ftp** program will display the following prompt:

```
ftp>
```

You can now enter **ftp** commands (which we will discuss in the next section).

To close the connection and end the **ftp** program, enter the **quit** command. You can also press **^D**, the **eof** key (see Chapter 6). To close the connection without ending the **ftp** program, enter the **close** command.

It is possible to start the **ftp** program without specifying the name of a computer:

```
ftp
```

In this case, the program will immediately display a prompt. You must now use the **open** command to establish a connection. The syntax is:

open [*host* [*port*]]

here *host* is the name of the remote computer to which you want to connect, and *port* is an optional port number. If you don't know what a port number is, ignore it. To connect to the computer we used above, you would enter:

```
open pit-manager.mit.edu
```

Why, you might ask, is it important to know the **open** command? After all, you can specify the name of the remote computer when you enter the **ftp** command. When would you ever use **open**?

There are two answers. First, if you enter an **ftp** command where the computer name is spelled wrong, the **ftp** program will start, but no connection will be made. In that case, you will have to use an **open** command (with the correct name) to make the connection. (Of course, you could always quit and start over, but that's a bother.)

Second, you may want to transfer files from more than one remote computer. When you are finished with the first one, you can use **close** to terminate the connection and **open** to establish a new connection, all without leaving the **ftp** program.

If you connect successfully, but there is something wrong with your userid or password, you will not lose your connection. However, you will not be able to do anything until you specify a valid userid and password. To do so, enter the **user** command. The syntax is:

user [*name* [*password*]]

For example:

user harley 34%Aqw

If you do not specify the password, you will be asked for it. Many people do not specify the password as part of the command in case someone is reading over their shoulder. When the command is typed separately, it is not echoed.

ftp Commands

Once you are connected to a remote computer, you will see the prompt:

ftp>

You can now enter any **ftp** command that you want. There are many such commands. For reference, we have summarized the most important ones in Figure 25-3. In the next section, we will talk about something called "anonymous **ftp**". The commands in Figure 25-3 are the ones you will need to use **ftp** in this way. If you want to read about the other commands, see the **ftp** entry in the online manual. (Enter **man ftp** at the shell prompt.)

In general, if a command requires a parameter and you do not specify it, you will be prompted for it. For example, say that you enter the **open** command (discussed in the previous section) without specifying the name of the remote computer:

open

Basic Commands

quit	close connection to remote, stop **ftp** program
help	display a list of all **ftp** commands
help *command*	display help for the specified command
?	display a list of all **ftp** commands
? *command*	display help for the specified command
!	local: pause **ftp** and start a shell
! *command*	local: execute specified shell command

Connecting

close	close the connection to remote, stay in **ftp**
open [*host* [*port*]]	establish connection to specified computer
user [*name* [*password*]]	set user name

Directories

cd [*directory*]	remote: change to specified directory
cdup	remote: change to parent directory
dir [*directory* [*local-file*]]	remote: display a long directory listing
lcd [*directory*]	local: change directory
ls [*directory* [*local-file*]]	remote: display a short directory listing
pwd	remote: display name of current directory

Transferring Files

get [*remote-file* [*local-file*]]	download one file
mget [*remote-file*...]	download multiple files

Setting Options

ascii	(default) set file type to ASCII text file
binary	set file type to binary file
hash	yes/no: show **#** for each data block transferred
prompt	yes/no: prompt for multiple file transfers
status	display current status of options

Figure 25-3
Useful **ftp** *Commands*

The **ftp** program will ask you to enter the computer name. Thus, you can always enter a command name by itself and let the program ask you for what it needs.

Most of the commands are straightforward. To display a short description of a command, enter **help** or **?** followed by the name of the command. For example:

```
help open
```

To display a list of commands, enter **help** or **?** by itself:

```
help
```

If you want to send a regular command to your local computer, preface it with an **!** character. For example, to display the time and date, you can use:

```
!date
```

If you want to enter a number of local commands, use:

```
!
```

This will pause the **ftp** program and start a local shell. You can now enter as many local commands as you want. When you are finished, terminate the shell in the regular manner (using **^D** or the **exit** command), and you will return to **ftp**.

Most of the time, you will be using **ftp** to download files from a remote computer. In such cases, the best idea is to change to the remote directory you want and then transfer the files. To change directories, you use the **cd** command, which works much like the regular Unix **cd** command (see Chapter 21). The main difference is that you cannot use wildcards. That is, you cannot use characters like ***** and **?** to specify a name.

For example, to change to the remote directory named **pub**, use:

```
cd pub
```

To change to the remote parent directory, you can use a special command:

```
cdup
```

(In other words, this command changes to the remote directory that is one level higher in the directory tree.) **cdup** has the same effect as entering:

```
cd ..
```

To display the name of the remote current (working) directory, use **pwd**.

To change your local current directory, use the **lcd** command. This allows you to control where a downloaded file will be stored. For example:

```
lcd documents
```

The **lcd** command will display a message confirming your new local current directory.

There are two commands that you can use to display the names of remote files. The **ls** command displays only the names of the files. The **dir** command displays a long listing, similar to the Unix **ls** **-l** command. You will find that the **dir** command is usually more useful because it shows the length of each file. To interrupt a long directory listing, press **^C** (the **intr** key).

When you use these commands, you can specify the name of a directory or file, just like the regular Unix **ls** command. For example, to display the contents of the **pub** directory, use:

```
dir pub
```

You can also specify the name of a local file at the end of the command. If you do, the **ftp** program will save the directory listing in this file instead of displaying the information on your terminal. Here are two examples:

```
dir pub pub-files
dir . list
```

The first example saves a directory listing of the remote directory **pub** in the local file named **pub-files**. The second command saves a directory listing of the remote current directory in the local file **list**. (You may remember that in Chapter 21, we explained that a single period is an abbreviation for the current directory.)

Once you have found the files you want to download, there are two commands you can use to make the transfer. The **get** command downloads one file at a time. You cannot use a wildcard specification, but you can specify a different name to use on the local computer. For example, to download the remote file **index**, use:

```
get index
```

This command stores the file under the same name on your local computer. If you want to use a different name, say, **master-index**, you can specify it as follows:

```
get index master-index
```

If you specify a local file name of – (a hyphen), **ftp** will send the data to the standard output on your local computer. In other words, it will display the data on your screen instead of saving it to a file. For example, to display the contents of the remote file named **index**, use:

```
get index -
```

The **mget** (multiple **get**) command has two advantages: you can specify more than one file name, and you can use wildcards. However, you cannot specify new names for the files. Here is an example. You want to download five files from the remote current directory. The files are named **part1**, **part2** and so on, up to **part5**. You can use either of the commands:

```
mget part1 part2 part3 part4 part5
mget part[1-5]
```

If there are no other files that begin with **part**, you can use:

`mget part*`

When you use **mget**, the **ftp** program will prompt you for confirmation before starting to transfer each file. (You can answer **y** or **n**.) That way, you can use a general specification and decide, one by one, which files you want to download. If you know in advance that you want all the files, you can turn off the prompting by entering:

`prompt`

To turn it back on, simply enter the command again. It acts as an off/on toggle switch. If you want to see the current value of this switch, enter:

`status`

You will also see the status of other options. If you decide that you would like **prompt** turned off as a default, you can start the **ftp** program using the **-i** (interactive) option.

 HINT　　You can stop a file transfer by pressing ^C (the **intr** key).

Aside from **prompt**, there are three other useful commands that affect settings. The **hash** command tells the **ftp** program to display a # (hash mark) character every time one disk block is transferred. This allows you to watch the progress when you are downloading a large file. The **hash** command is also an off/on toggle switch. Each time you enter the command, it reverses the switch.

The last two commands are **binary** and **ascii**. These commands set the REPRESENTATION TYPE for the files you are about to transfer. The **binary** command says that you will be transferring a binary file. The **ascii** command says that you will transferring a text file. (We discussed these types of files in Chapter 20. Basically, a text file holds ordinary characters, a binary file holds data in some other format.)

When you start the **ftp** program, the default will be **ascii**. You may find that you can transfer binary files successfully without changing the default. But if you do have trouble, try using the **binary** command before downloading.

 HINT　　As we will discuss later, files prepared for downloading are often stored in one of two common formats. Compressed files have names that end in **.z** Tar files have names that end in **.tar** Be aware that such files are binary files. The same goes for any files that contain pictures.

Anonymous `ftp`

Using the `ftp` program we described in the last section, you can connect to virtually any computer on the Internet. However, without a valid userid and password for that computer, you will not be able to do anything.

ANONYMOUS `ftp` is a system that allows people to download files from a computer without having to be registered as a user. The system manager sets up a special userid named **anonymous**. Anyone, anywhere, is allowed to `ftp` to that machine and connect using this userid. In most cases, you can enter whatever password you want. However, the custom is to use your mail address so the keepers of the system can know who is accessing their files.

At first, anonymous `ftp` sounds okay, but not really all that special. So anyone can access files on another computer, what's the big deal? The big deal is that the world of anonymous `ftp` is huge. Many people around the world have generously donated disk space and computing facilities to make virtually every type of information available for free, to anybody, whenever they want it.

How important is this? Although what we are about to say may sound like an exaggeration, we solemnly assure you that it is not. Anonymous `ftp` is one of the most significant inventions in the history of mankind. We don't blame you if you think that such a statement sounds a bit silly. All we can say is, spend some time investigating what is available and make up your own mind.

How does anonymous `ftp` work? All you have to do is find out what computer contains an item you need, `ftp` to that machine, connect using the **anonymous** userid and download what you want. The trick is, of course, to be able to find out where interesting items are located. We will show you various ways to do this throughout the rest of the chapter. Here, though, is an example so you can see what anonymous `ftp` looks like. In this example, we will omit the lines that contain extraneous messages.

A friend tells you that some of the Usenet newsgroups have postings that contain pictures. He is not sure which newsgroups they are or what software you need to display the pictures, so you decide to track them down. The only clue you have is that there is a FAQ (frequently asked question) list explaining how this all works.

You remember (because you read it earlier in this chapter) that the computer **pit-manager.mit.edu** offers Usenet archives via anonymous `ftp`. You enter the following command:

```
ftp pit-manager.mit.edu
```

Your `ftp` program starts and you see the following:

```
Connected to pit-manager.mit.edu.
220 pit-manager.MIT.EDU FTP server
   (Version 4.179 Tue Jul 7 18:37:28 EDT 1992) ready.
Name (pit-manager.mit.edu:harley):
```

You have connected successfully, and you are being asked for a userid. Your **ftp** program suggests your personal userid (in this case, **harley**). Instead, you enter:

```
anonymous
```

The remote computer responds:

```
Password (pit-manager.mit.edu:anonymous):
```

It is asking you for a password. Following the Internet convention, you enter your mail address. You now see the following messages. (Remember, you can ignore the numbers).

```
331 Guest login ok, send ident as password.
230 Guest login ok, access restrictions apply.
```

The first line tells you that you have logged in as a guest and reminds you to use your mail address as a password. The second line tells you that, with a userid of **anonymous**, there are restrictions as to what you can access. The next thing you see is the **ftp** prompt:

```
ftp>
```

To track down the FAQ list you want, you display the current directory by entering:

```
dir
```

You see:

```
total 3
drwxrwxr-x    2 root      wheel       512 Nov 21  1990 bin
drwxrwxr-x    2 root      wheel       512 Nov 21  1990 etc
drwxrwxr-x   15 root      wheel      1024 Oct 21 15:05 pub
```

You are in the root directory and there are three subdirectories. The one that you want is **pub**. This is the most common name for a directory that holds public information. You change to this directory and display its contents:

```
cd pub
dir
```

You now see a long directory listing. We won't list the whole thing, but one of the lines is:

```
drwxrwxr-x 414 jik       wheel     11264 Nov 12 02:59 usenet
```

You realize that the Usenet information is kept in the **usenet** directory within the **pub** directory. You change to the **usenet** directory and display its contents:

```
cd usenet
dir
```

This time you see an even longer directory listing. There are many subdirectories (over 400, actually), each of which have the name of a Usenet newsgroup. One of the subdirectories is:

```
drwxrwxr-x 112 jik       wheel      6656 Nov 14 01:31 news.answers
```

This is the directory that contains the archives for the **news.answers** newsgroup. Such a directory must contain many entries, so it would be a good idea to think of a way to find what you want without having to display a huge directory listing. You decide to ask for such a listing, but to save it to a file named **temp** on your local computer. You enter:

```
dir news.answers temp
```

You see:

```
output to local-file: temp?
```

You respond **y** (yes), and the command is executed. Now you need to search the file **temp**, on your computer, for something that has to do with pictures. To do so, use the **grep** command (see Chapter 16) to find all the lines that contain the word "picture":

```
!grep picture temp
```

Since you preface this command with an **!** character, it is executed as a regular command on your local computer. The output is:

```
drwxrwxr-x  2 jik       wheel       512 Nov  2 18:45
pictures-faq
```

This looks like what you want: a subdirectory of **news.answers** that holds FAQ lists about pictures. You change to this directory and display the contents:

```
cd news.answers/pictures-faq
dir
```

The output is:

```
-rw-rw-r--  7 root       wheel     40668 Nov  2 18:45 part1
-rw-rw-r--  7 root       wheel     51870 Nov  2 18:45 part2
```

Now you have it! There are two files, **part1** and **part2**, that contain FAQ lists explaining pictures. All you have to do is download the files. To prepare, you enter the command to tell the **ftp** program not to prompt you before each file transfer:

```
prompt
```

To transfer the files, you use the **mget** command:

```
mget part1 part2
```

After the transfer is complete, you stop the **ftp** program:

```
quit
```

You are now back at the shell prompt on your local computer. You clean up by removing the temporary file and then display the two FAQ files:

```
rm temp
more part1 part2
```

A Sample `ftp` Session

For reference, Figure 25-4 contains a full listing of an **ftp** session. In this session, we connected to **pit-manager.mit.edu** and changed to the **pictures-faq** directory. We then downloaded the two files that we mentioned in the previous section. The boldface shows the commands that we entered.

One of the more important Usenet archive computers is **pit-manager** at MIT, run by Jonathan Kamens (who is somewhat of a net.entity). The full name of the computer is **pit-manager.mit.edu**. The facilities are gra-

```
% ftp pit-manager.mit.edu

Connected to pit-manager.mit.edu.
220 pit-manager.MIT.EDU FTP server
    (Version 4.179 Tue Jul 7 18:37:28 EDT 1992) ready.

Name (pit-manager.mit.edu:): anonymous
Password (pit-manager.mit.edu:anonymous):
331 Guest login ok, send ident as password.
230 Guest login ok, access restrictions apply.

ftp> cd /pub/usenet/news.answers/pictures-faq
250 CWD command successful.

ftp> prompt
Interactive mode off.

ftp> mget part1 part2
200 PORT command successful.
150 Opening ASCII mode data connection for part1 (40668 bytes).
226 Transfer complete.
local: part1 remote: part1
41411 bytes received in 2.5 seconds (16 Kbytes/s)
200 PORT command successful.
150 Opening ASCII mode data connection for part2 (51870 bytes).
226 Transfer complete.
local: part2 remote: part2
53092 bytes received in 4.9 seconds (11 Kbytes/s)

ftp> quit
221 Goodbye.
```

Figure 25-4
A Sample **ftp** *Session*

ciously donated by MIT to serve as a repository of various types of information and software. In particular, Kamens maintains an archive of important Usenet postings.

In Chapter 23, we explained that the newsgroup **news.answers** contains copies of the FAQ (frequently asked questions) lists for all the other newsgroups. The current postings to **news.answers** are archived on **pit-manager**.

WHAT'S IN A NAME?

pit-manager

The **pit-manager** computer at MIT is one of the important Usenet archive sites. It is administered by Jonathan Kamens and contains a collection of Usenet FAQ lists. You will often see this computer mentioned as a source for anonymous **ftp** files. **pit-manager** also serves as a mail server (sending out requested files by mail) and as a Usenet name finder (which we will describe later in the chapter).

You might wonder, where does the name **pit-manager** come from? Is it an acronym of some kind, or does it have something to do with prunes?

The real story starts when Kamens was an undergraduate student at MIT. For a time, he was the office manager for the MIT Student Information Processing Board. As such, he demonstrated organizational methods that involved a certain amount of artistic license and free expression. So much so that, eventually, the office area became known as "The Pit". Sometime later, when he was given a computer for his job at MIT, he decided to name it after himself, the Pit Manager.

To satisfy what, by now, must be an immense amount of curiosity on your part, we have included a photograph of Kamens and **pit-manager** in Figure 25-5. (**pit-manager** is the one on the right.)

Hints for Using Anonymous ftp

Whenever you connect to a new computer via anonymous **ftp**, start by looking for certain directories and files. First, look for a directory named **pub** or **public**. Most **ftp** sites use such a directory to hold all the public files and subdirectories.

Second, look for one or more of the following files:

README
index
ls-lR.Z
ls-ltR.Z

Figure 25-5
Jonathan Kamens and `pit-manager`

If any of these files exist, download and read them before you use the system.

The **README** will hold general information about the system. The **index** will show you what is available. The files `ls-1R.Z` and `ls-1tR.Z` will contain directory listings for all the public files. The names reflect the information within these listings.

As we explained in Chapter 21, the `ls` command has many options. The **-l** (long) option displays a detailed listing, the **-R** (recursive) option displays the contents of all subdirectories, and the **-t** (time) option sorts the output, showing the most recently modified files first.

The file `ls-1R.Z` contains the output of the command:

```
ls -1R
```

In other words, this file has a full listing of all the public files and subdirectories. The file `ls-1tR.Z` contains the output of the command:

```
ls -ltR
```

This is a full listing, sorted by modification time, of all the public files and subdirectories.

The file extension .**Z** indicates that this file is compressed. Once you download it, you must uncompress it before you can read it. This is explained in the next section. Notice that the file names, unlike the commands, do not contain any spaces.

Using Compressed (.Z) Files: `compress, uncompress, zcat`

In order to make downloading fast and simple, there are two widely used systems that are used to compress and combine files. You should understand how these systems work, because you will find that many of the files you download via anonymous **ftp** will be in these formats. In this section, we will explain how files are compressed. In the next section, we will explain how files are combined.

There are a number of different compression schemes. The most common one is provided by the **compress** command. This command reads a file and compresses it, significantly reducing its size. This is important for two reasons. First, a compressed file requires less space to store on a disk. Second, downloading a compressed file is faster than downloading the original file. Once such a file is downloaded, you can restore it by using the **uncompress** command.

The syntax for the **compress** command is:

```
compress [-cv] [file...]
```

where *file* is the name of a file to be compressed. There are other options, but you will probably not need them. **compress** is a filter, so you can use it in a pipeline (see Chapters 15 and 16).

When **compress** processes a file, it replaces it with the compressed file. This new file has the same name with an extension of .**Z** (uppercase "Z"). For example, say that you have a file named **info** that you want to compress. Enter:

```
compress info
```

The result will be that **info** will be replaced by a compressed file named **info.Z**.

The -**c** option tells **compress** to write the compressed data to standard output (Chapter 15) without replacing the original file. For example:

```
compress -c info > extra.Z
```

In this case, the compressed data is stored in **extra.Z**. The file **info** is left unchanged.

The **-v** (verbose) option displays the percentage of reduction for each file that was compressed and will tell you the name of the new file. Here is a typical message:

```
info: Compression: 46.61% -- replaced with info.Z
```

The **uncompress** command has the following syntax:

```
uncompress [-cv] [file...]
```

where *file* is the name of a file to be restored. As with **compress**, there are other options, but you will probably not need them. The **-c** and **-v** options are used in the same way. Also like **compress**, **uncompress** is a filter, so you can use it in a pipeline.

uncompress expects the file names you specify to end in **.Z**. You do not have to actually type the **.Z**. For example, the following two commands are equivalent:

```
uncompress info.Z
uncompress info
```

They both replace the file **info.Z** with the restored file named **info**.

There may be a time when you want to access contents of a compressed file without restoring it. To do this, you can use the **zcat** command. The syntax is:

```
zcat [file...]
```

where *file* is the name of a compressed file. The **zcat** command is the same as **uncompress -c**. Thus, the following two commands are equivalent:

```
zcat info | more
uncompress -c info | more
```

They display the restored contents of **info.Z** by piping the data to **more** (see Chapter 17). The file **info.Z** is left unchanged.

As a user of anonymous **ftp**, all you will usually need is **uncompress**, to restore files that you have downloaded.

 HINT   If you have large files, you can use **compress** to compress them and save disk space. Whenever you want, you can use **uncompress** or **zcat** to restore the original data. Many people use this technique when their disk space is limited by a quota.

Using Archived (`.tar`) Files: `tar`

It is common to download a whole set of files. For example, a piece of software or a long document may consist of a number of parts, each of which is stored in a separate file. It would be time-consuming and bothersome to have to download each file separately. Instead, the files are prepared ahead of time by packaging them into one large file called an ARCHIVE. The program that does the work is named **tar**. (The original version of this program was developed to save files on magnetic tape. Hence the name, "tape archiver".)

The **tar** program has many options and variations. In this section, we will describe what you need to know to access archives that you download. For more information, display the **tar** manual page for your system. (You can use the command **man tar**. The online Unix manual is discussed in Chapter 8.)

When you download a file whose name ends with an extension of `.tar`, it means that the file is a **tar** archive. For example:

document.tar

To restore the original files, you use the **tar** command. There are two important forms of this command:

tar -xvf *file*
tar -tvf *file*

where *file* is the name of a **tar** archive.

The **-f** option means that the following argument is the name of the file that contains the archive. The **-x** option extracts the files from an archive, while the **-t** (table of contents) option lists the contents of the archive.

When **tar** extracts or lists files, each file name is displayed as it is processed. If you use the **-v** (verbose) option, **tar** will display file information in a long format such as you see when you use the **ls -l** command (see Chapter 21).

Here are two examples. To list the files contained in an archive named **document.tar**, use:

tar -tvf document.tar

To extract these files, use:

tar -xvf document.tar

If you omit the **-v** option, the list of file names will be simpler.

A **tar** archive can contain not only ordinary files, but directories. Thus, when you extract files from an archive you sometimes end up with a whole system of subdirectories.

 HINT   After you have extracted files from an archive, don't forget to remove the original `.tar` file. Unlike **compress**, **tar** does not remove the original file.

The **tar** command is unusual in that the options do not need to be preceded by a hyphen. Thus, the following two commands are equivalent:

```
tar -xvf document.tar
tar xvf document.tar
```

You will often see **tar** commands written this way, so don't be confused.

Using Compressed and Archived (.tar.z) Files

A common way to prepare files for anonymous **ftp** is to combine them into an archive and then compress the archive. The result is a single, compressed file that may contain many files and directories. You can recognize such files as they will have names that end with the extension **.tar.Z**.

To use such a file, all you have to remember is to look at the extension and undo each operation from right to left. For example, say that you have downloaded a file named **unixbook.tar.Z**. This compressed archive contains a number of chapters of a book. Each chapter has its own subdirectory. Within each subdirectory are separate files for the various sections. The whole thing has been combined using **tar** and then compressed using **compress**.

Here is how you can extract the information. We will assume that **unixbook.tar.Z** is in your current directory. Since a file like this will expand into a set of directories, it is a good idea to isolate it in its own directory. Let's start by making a new directory named **unixbook**:

```
mkdir unixbook
```

(Making a directory is explained in Chapter 21.) Next, move the compressed archive to this directory and make it your current directory:

```
mv unixbook.tar.Z unixbook
cd unixbook
```

Now uncompress the archive:

```
uncompress unixbook.tar.Z
```

The compressed file has now been replaced by **unixbook.tar**. Extract all the files and directories from this archive:

```
tar -xvf unixbook.tar
```

Finally, remove the archive file:

```
rm unixbook.tar
```

 HINT

If you are going to download an archive, plan ahead of time. Create a directory first and download the archive directly to this directory. In this way, you can uncompress and extract without having to move the file.

For reference, Figure 25-6 shows the steps used to process the various combinations of compressed files and archives.

Uncompressing a file:

```
uncompress file.Z
```

Extracting files from an archive:

```
tar -xvf archive.tar
rm archive.tar
```

Uncompressing and extracting a compressed archive:

```
uncompress archive.tar.Z
tar -xvf archive.tar
rm archive.tar
```

Figure 25-6
Examples of Processing Compressed Files and Archives

Logging in to a Remote Computer: `telnet`

To log in to a remote computer, use the **telnet** command. The syntax is:

telnet [*host-computer* [*port*]]

where *host-computer* is the name of the computer to which you want to connect, and *port* is the number of a port on that computer (explained below).

The most common way to use **telnet** is to specify the name of a computer as part of the command. This computer can be on your campus network or anywhere on the Internet. If you **telnet** to a local computer, you only need to specify the local name. If you **telnet** to a distant computer, you must specify the full Internet name. Here are two examples:

```
telnet alishaw
telnet consultant.micro.umn.edu
```

The first command connects to a local computer. The second command connects to a distant computer. (However, for the purposes of our discussion, they are both "remote" computers.) If, for some reason, **telnet** cannot use the name you specify, you can try the IP address (discussed earlier in the chapter).

There are two ways to run a **telnet** session. When you specify a computer name, but not a port number (explained in a moment), you will see a standard **login:** prompt. You can now log in in the usual manner by entering a userid and password. When you log out, the **telnet** program will terminate automatically.

Some computers offer special services by running a program that waits for a user to connect at a particular PORT. This is an identification number that tells the computer which program should be connected to the terminal session. When you read about Internet services to which you can **telnet**, you will often see that you must specify a port number.

For example, the University of Michigan has a computer to which you can **telnet** in order to display weather reports. The name of the computer is:

`downwind.sprl.umich.edu`

When you **telnet** to this computer, you must specify port number **3000** to connect to the weather report program. The command you would use is:

`telnet downwind.sprl.umich.edu 3000`

When you **telnet** with a port number, the remote computer will usually start a program automatically without asking you to log in. In this way, system managers can allow anyone on the Internet to run a restricted program. As an example, when you **telnet** to the computer we specified above, the weather report program will start automatically.

telnet supports a special escape character that allows you to pause the terminal session and interact with **telnet** itself. This character is **^]** (Ctrl-Right Bracket). When you press this key combination, you will see the prompt:

`telnet>`

At this point, there are a number of **telnet** commands you can enter. If you simply press <Return>, you will be returned to your terminal session on the remote computer.

Most of the time, you will not need to use **telnet** commands, so we will not go into them in detail. However, there are several that we will mention briefly. They are summarized in Figure 25-7.

Basic Commands

`quit`	close connection to remote, stop **telnet**
`?`	display a list of all **telnet** commands
`?` *command*	display help for the specified command

Connecting

`close`	close connection to remote, stay in **telnet**
`open` [*host* [*port*]]	establish connection to specified computer

---

Figure 25-7
Useful **telnet** *Commands*

To close the connection to the remote computer and stop **telnet**, use **quit**. To close the connection without stopping **telnet**, use **close**. Once you close a connection, you can use **open** to connect to another computer.

It is possible to start **telnet** without specifying a computer name:

```
telnet
```

At the **telnet** prompt, you can enter an **open** command to connect to a computer. Similarly, if you specify an invalid computer name:

```
telnet bad-computer-name
```

you will see an error message and the **telnet** prompt:

```
bad-computer-name: unknown host
telnet>
```

This will happen, for example, if you make a spelling mistake. Since you are at the **telnet** prompt, you can use an **open** command to connect to the remote computer. You do not have to quit the program.

`archie` Servers: Searching for Anonymous `ftp` Resources

We said earlier that anonymous **ftp** is one of the most significant inventions in the history of mankind. The variety of information and software that is accessible via anonymous **ftp** is literally too vast to comprehend. It is estimated, for example, that there are well over two million available files. This makes anonymous **ftp** the largest distributed library system in the history of the world. Moreover, it is a library that is constantly changing.

The most important problem in using anonymous **ftp** is finding the files that you want. Imagine a library with over two million books and no card catalog. This is where **archie** comes in.

archie is the name of a service that searches the anonymous **ftp** file list and finds what you want. Once **archie** has told you the location of a file, it is a simple matter to **ftp** to that site and retrieve whatever it is you want.

A computer that provides this service is called an **archie** SERVER. The first **archie** server was developed as a project by students and volunteer staff at the McGill University School of Computer Science in Montreal, Canada. The software was written by Alan Emtage and Bill Heelan with help from Peter Deutsch. It didn't take long for the Internet community to recognize **archie** as a significant service. In fact, at the time we wrote this chapter, there were eleven **archie** servers on the Internet (see Figure 25-8). At first, **archie** compiled lists only of anonymous **ftp** files. Since then, **archie** has been expanded to search on-line directories and other Internet resources.

The idea behind **archie** is conceptually simple. An **archie** server maintains a list of all anonymous **ftp** sites. On a regular basis, a special

Location	Internet Address	IP Address
Australia	`archie.au`	`139.130.4.6`
Canada	`archie.mcgill.ca`	`132.206.2.3`
England	`archie.doc.ic.ac.uk`	`146.169.11.3`
Finland	`archie.funet.fi`	`128.214.6.100`
Israel	`archie.cs.huji.ac.il`	`132.65.6.15`
Japan	`archie.wide.ad.jp`	`133.4.3.6`
Taiwan	`archie.ncu.edu.tw`	`140.115.19.24`
USA: Maryland	`archie.sura.net`	`128.167.254.179`
USA: Nebraska	`archie.unl.edu`	`129.93.1.14`
USA: New Jersey	`archie.rutgers.edu`	`128.6.18.15`
USA: New York	`archie.ans.net`	`147.225.1.2`

Log in using a userid of **archie**.

Figure 25-8
archie *Servers*

program connects to each site and retrieves a full list of all the public files. The schedule is arranged so that each site is contacted about once a month. The file lists are stored in a large database that can be searched quickly. At the time we wrote this chapter, **archie** servers were keeping track of over 1,000 different Internet sites.

There are three ways to access an **archie** server. First, you can **telnet** to one of the **archie** servers and log in as **archie**. This starts the **archie** program. You enter commands specifying what you want. **archie** searches the database and displays the results.

Second, you can send commands to an **archie** server in a mail message. **archie** will read the message, carry out your commands, and mail the results back to you.

Finally, you can run a program, called an **archie** CLIENT, on your own computer. When you run this program, you specify what you are looking for. The **archie** client automatically connects to an **archie** server, gets the information, and displays it for you. You can redirect the output to a file (see Chapter 15) and use Unix commands like **grep** (Chapter 16) to find what you need.

Aside from searching for files, **archie** servers provide a WHATIS service. **archie** maintains a second database that contains short descriptions of thousands of programs, data files and documents. You specify a name and **archie** will display the description. This service is similar to the Unix **whatis** command that you can use to display a description of a command from the online manual (see Chapter 8).

To use **archie**, all you need to do is **telnet** to an **archie** server and log in using a userid of **archie**. Figure 25-8 shows a list of **archie** servers. To help minimize network traffic, it is a good idea to use one of the **archie** servers that is geographically close to you. Of course, we expect the list in Figure 25-8 to change. Most **archie** servers display a list of other servers whenever you log in, so it is not hard to keep up to date.

Setting `archie` Variables

Once you **telnet** to an **archie** server and log in with a userid of **archie**, you will see the following prompt:

`archie>`

The **archie** program is ready for your commands. In a moment, we will give you a general strategy for conducting an **archie** search. First, though, we will discuss the basic ideas.

archie maintains a number of variables that allow you to specify certain preferences. Some of these variables contain numbers, some contain strings of characters, and others are yes/no toggle switches. The full list of variables is shown in Figure 25-9.

You can see that two of the variables are of type "boolean". This is a programming term that describes a variable that acts as a yes/no toggle switch. (The term is named after the nineteenth century English mathematician George Boole.) To turn on a boolean variable, use **set**. To turn it off, use **unset**.

Name	Type	Description
`autologout`	numeric	length of idle time until automatic logout
`mailto`	string	address to which output should be mailed
`maxhits`	numeric	stop **prog** search after this many matches
`pager`	boolean	yes/no, display output using a pager
`search`	string	specify how **prog** is to match patterns
`sortby`	string	specify how **prog** should sort output
`status`	boolean	yes/no, **prog** displays status during search
`term`	string	the type of terminal you are using

Figure 25-9
`archie` *Variables*

```
archie> show
# 'autologout' (type numeric) has the value '15'.
# 'mailto' (type string) is not set.
# 'maxhits' (type numeric) has the value '1000'.
# 'pager' (type boolean) is not set.
# 'search' (type string) has the value 'regex'.
# 'sortby' (type string) has the value 'none'.
# 'status' (type boolean) is set.
# 'term' (type string) has the value 'dumb 24 80'.
```

Figure 25-10

Typical `archie` *Output for the* **show** *Command*

To see the current setting of the variables, use the **show** command. To set a variable, use the **set** command. Figure 25-10 shows typical output from the **show** command. We will discuss each variable in turn.

`autologout`:

This variable controls how long **archie** will wait before logging out an idle connection. In the example, **archie** will wait for 15 minutes.

`mailto`:

If you would like the results of your searches mailed to you, you can set this variable to your address. That way, you won't have to specify it each time you use the **mail** command (explained below).

`maxhits`:

The database that **archie** searches is so large that it is not at all unusual to find hundreds of matches to a specific pattern. Since you usually only need one such match, it is a good idea to set a limit. This variable sets a maximum on the number of matches that **archie** will find. Once this number is reached, **archie** will stop. If the results were not adequate, you can always set **maxhits** higher and try again. We suggest starting with a value of 10.

`pager`:

This is a boolean variable that tells **archie** whether or not you want it to display its output using a pager program (see Chapter 17).

`search`:

To control how **prog** matches the pattern you specify you can set this variable to one of several choices:

```
set search sub
set search subcase
```

```
set search exact
set search regex
```

The **sub** specification tells **archie** to match your pattern as a substring. For example, if you search for **pc**, it would match an entry that contains **IBM-pc**. The characters **pc** do not have to appear as a separate word.

The **subcase** specification is the same as **sub** except that **archie** distinguishes between upper and lower case. For example, **pc** would match **IBM-pc** but not **IBM-PC**.

The **exact** specification tells **archie** to match your pattern exactly, including case. To match **IBM-PC**, you have to specify **IBM-PC**. These types of searches are the fastest and, when you know exactly what you want, yield the best results.

The **regex** specification allows you to use a regular expression to specify a pattern. We discussed the rules for regular expressions in Chapter 16.

If you would like more information about these search specifications, you can enter the **archie** command **help set search**.

sortby:

This variable tells **archie** how to sort the results of your search. There are several choices:

`set sortby hostname`	alphabetical by name of computer
`set sortby time`	newest to oldest
`set sortby size`	largest to smallest
`set sortby filename`	alphabetical by name of file
`set sortby none`	not sorted

You can tell **archie** to sort in reverse order by placing an **r** in front of the sort specification:

`set sortby rhostname`	reverse by name of computer
`set sortby rtime`	oldest to newest
`set sortby rsize`	smallest to largest
`set sortby rfilename`	reverse by name of file

☑ **HINT**   To prepare for an **archie** search, use **set sortby time** and keep the value of **maxhits** small. This will usually find what you need quickly and manageably.

---

status:

This is a boolean variable that tells **archie** whether or not to display a status line that reports on the progress of the search as it is taking place.

term:

This variable tells **archie** what type of terminal you are using. After the name of the terminal, you can optionally specify the number of rows, or the number of rows and columns. Here are three common examples:

```
set term vt100
set term xterm 60
set term xterm 24 100
```

As we explained in Chapter 3, the VT-100 is the terminal that is most commonly emulated by a communications program. The other two examples refer to X terminals that are used with the X Window system that we discussed in Chapter 5.

Using **archie** Commands

When **archie** is ready to accept commands, it will display the prompt:

archie>

You can now enter one command after another. When you are finished, enter the **quit** command to log off and close the **telnet** connection.

Like other interactive programs, **archie** has a built-in help system. To start the system, enter:

help

You will see a list of all possible commands followed by the prompt:

Help topic?

Either press <Return> to return to the main prompt or enter the name of a command.

At the main prompt, you can ask for help on a specific command by typing its name as part of the **help** command. For example:

help prog

There are a number of **archie** commands that you can use. We will discuss only the most important ones. For reference, Figure 25-11 contains a summary.

The main command is **prog**. (The original **archie** was used to search for computer programs.) This tells **archie** to start a search of the database, looking for the pattern that you specify. The pattern is interpreted according to the value of the **search** variable that we discussed in the previous section.

Here is an example. To search for a file named **internet-cmc** use:

prog internet-cmc

To interrupt a search in progress, press **^C** (the **intr** key).

After **archie** has finished a search, it displays the results. It is usually convenient to tell **archie** to use a pager by using the **set pager** command. We discussed the three main pagers – **more**, **pg** and **less** – in Chapter 17.

Basic Commands

quit	log off and close the **telnet** connection
help	display general information
help *command*	display help for the specified command
set *variable* [*value*]	set a variable
show	display current settings of all variables
unset *variable*	unset a variable

Searching Commands

list [*pattern*]	display a list of sites
mail [*address...*]	mail the results of your last search
prog *pattern*	find files whose names contain *pattern*
site [*site*]	display list of files at specified site
whatis *pattern*	search **whatis** database for *pattern*

Figure 25-11
Useful **archie** *Commands*

Most **archie** servers use **less**, although some of them use **more**. As you may remember, we suggested in Chapter 17 that, no matter which pager is your favorite, it is a good idea to learn the basic commands for all three pagers. When you use an **archie** server, you do not have a choice as to which pager will be used.

After you see the results of a search, you may want **archie** to mail you the list of files so you can look at it on your own computer. To do this, use the **mail** command. Simply specify your mail address, for example:

```
mail harley@nipper.ucsb.edu
```

archie will mail you the results of the last search.

If you plan on doing several searches, it is more convenient to set the **mailto** variable. For example:

```
set mailto harley@nipper.ucsb.edu
```

Now you can request a copy of a search without having to specify your address. All you have to enter is:

```
mail
```

The last command we will discuss is **whatis**. This searches the special **whatis** database that we described earlier, looking for descriptions that contain the pattern you specify. The entries in the **whatis** database must be created by hand. Typically, a person who offers a program or data file by anonymous **ftp** will create a short description and send it to the **archie** administrators to be included in the database.

When you can find a useful entry in the **whatis** database, it is especially helpful as it will show you the exact name of the file you need to search for. However, most files are not cataloged in this way, so it is common to draw a blank.

Here is an example of how to use the **whatis** command. A friend has told you that there is a radical program that you can use to display a flying object on your X terminal. (The X Window system is discussed in Chapter 5.) Unfortunately, your friend can't remember the name of the program.

Not to worry, **archie** will find it. Telnet to the most convenient **archie** server, log in and enter the command:

```
whatis fly
```

You see the results:

```
ufo         Fly objects around one or more displays (X11)
xufo        Unidentified Flying Object for X11
```

Evidently, there are two such programs, **ufo** and **xufo**. You can now find the anonymous **ftp** sites that carry these programs by entering the commands:

```
set search exact
prog ufo
prog xufo
```

Since you know the name of the program you want, you can do an **exact** search, which is a lot faster than a **sub** search.

A Sample archie Session

It was a dark and stormy night.

We sat at our desk, feet up, dreaming of a certain Southern California beauty with the voice of an angel and a set of curves that looked like a Mongolian railway map.

Suddenly, a shot rang out.

Stopping only long enough to pick up the Old Persuader and a shot of tequila, we jerked open the front door to see a long black limousine pulling away from the curb. At the wheel was a dwarf in a dark red uniform.

At our feet lay a mysterious foreigner. He was a short, fat man, dressed in a turban and caftan. Except for a sign around his neck that said "His most esteemed Highness, Abd al-Halim Hafiz", there was absolutely no clue to his identity. In his left hand was an envelope marked "The Secret".

Thinking quickly, we ripped the envelope from his hand, carried the body to the recycling bin, and hightailed it back to our desk. Call it a hunch, call it intuition, but something here was strange.

Gingerly, we opened the envelope. At first, it looked empty, but closer examination revealed a small piece of embossed manuscript paper. On the paper was written the single word:

UNPLASTIC

Unplastic, unplastic....What could this possibly mean? There was only one way to find out. We logged in to the nearest **archie** server and searched for the pattern **unplastic**. (The session is shown in Figure 25-12. The boldface shows the commands that we entered.)

In less time than it would take to shake down a politician caught with his pants down, we found a match: a directory named **Unplastic_News** at the computer **ftp.eff.org**. It was the work of a moment to **ftp** to this computer, change to the directory and download the files.

What we uncovered was an electronic magazine called *The Unplastic News*. Subsequent investigation revealed this to be a publication devoted to the aberrant, bizarre and preposterous. Weird, humorous quotes, floating around the electronic underground. By twisting a few arms, we discovered that *The Unplastic News* is edited by Thaloneous Platypus and B. Hathrume Duk (a.k.a. Todd Christopher Tibbetts and Andrew Moss).

Over the next few hours, we were able to penetrate this organization. The details were gruesome, and there was more than one joker who had to be quietly eliminated. What we found was not for children. This so-called magazine was not only accessible by **ftp**, but any Jill or Jack could subscribe just by sending a request to **tibbetts@hsi.hsi.com**.

Moreover, the whole thing was supported by a much larger organization known as the EFF (Electronic Frontier Foundation). According to secret copies of their memos (don't even ask), this group is "dedicated to the pursuit of policies and activities that will advance freedom and openness in computer-based communications".

It was as we were reading these memos that the phone rang. We picked up the receiver just in time to hear a single piercing scream. Then a cackling voice, that sounded like a mutant albino with a squint, said, "The old mill" and hung up.

The boys at the EFF would have to wait. We logged off, grabbed the keys to the black Jaguar and dashed out the door.

It was still a dark and stormy night.

```
% telnet archie.sura.net
Trying...
Connected to nic.sura.net.
Escape character is '^]'.

SunOS UNIX (nic.sura.net)
login: archie

Last login: Mon Nov 16 02:04:41 from cash.UCSC.EDU
SunOS Release 4.1.2 (ARCHIE) #3: Sat Feb 15 15:09:08 EST 1992
               Welcome to the ARCHIE server at SURAnet
```

...welcoming messages deleted ...

```
archie> set pager
archie> set maxhits 10
archie> set sortby hostname
archie> prog unplastic
# matches / % database searched:   10 / 60%
Sorting by hostname
```

...some responses deleted ...

```
Host kragar.eff.org    (192.88.144.4)
Last updated 02:14 13 Nov 1992

Location: /pub/journals/Unplastic_News
    FILE      rw-r--r--      30823  Oct 15  1991    unplasticnews.3
    FILE      rw-r--r--      50897  Aug 26  1991    unplasticnews.2
    FILE      rw-r--r--      15625  Nov  5 16:09    unplasticnews.4
    FILE      rw-r--r--      29811  Jul 22  1991    unplasticnews.1

archie> quit
```

Figure 25-12

*A Sample **archie** Session*

The gopher

The **gopher** is a powerful system that, at first, seems deceptively simple. The **gopher** consists of a collection of menus from which you make selections. From these selections, you can access virtually every type of information from all over the Internet. You can also access other Internet services like **ftp**, **archie**, **wais** and the World-Wide Web.

Once you start the **gopher** (we will show you how in a moment), you will see the first menu. Each time you make a selection, the **gopher** gives you whatever that menu item represents. Some choices are menus in themselves. Choosing one of these will display a new menu. Figure 25-13 contains an example of a **gopher** menu.

The power of the **gopher** lies in the fact that the resources listed in the menu may lie anywhere on the Internet. When you select a menu item, the **gopher** gets whatever information you requested no matter where it is. For example, item #9 in our example allows you to read the Usenet news. In order to carry out this selection, the **gopher** may have to connect to a different computer. The **gopher** will do whatever it needs to do, but it will all be transparent to you. All you will notice is that you have a new menu.

Notice item #6 in our example. This allows you to access other **gopher** programs at other locations. The nice thing about using a **gopher** is that the menu interface remains the same. You may switch from one computer to another and never even know it.

What this all means is that the **gopher** is nothing less than a global information delivery service, distributed across the Internet. Every item on

```
          Internet Gopher Information Client

 -- >  1.   Introduction to the Gopher.
        2.   Fun and Games/
        3.   Internet File Server (ftp) sites/
        4.   Library of Congress Catalog <TEL>
        5.   News of the Day.
        6.   Other Gopher and Information Servers/
        7.   Search Gopherspace using Veronica/
        8.   Phone Books <CSO>
        9.   Usenet News/
       10.   Search Literature Databases  <?>
       11.   Class Schedules/
```

Figure 25-13
An Example of a **gopher** *Menu*

every **gopher** in the world is available to you by using a simple, consistent menu system. As you might imagine, local **gopher** administrators are always adding new items to their menus. Thus, the features of the **gopher** world are always changing.

The first **gopher** was developed at the University of Minnesota in April of 1991. The work was done by Bob Alberti, Farhad Anklesaria, Paul Lindner, Mark McCahill and Daniel Torrey of the Department of Computer and Information Systems. Their idea was to create a distributed campus information service in which each department could control the information that it offered. Within a short time, the **gopher** was enthusiastically embraced by people all over the world. Today, there are hundreds of interconnected **gopher** systems.

WHAT'S IN A NAME?

gopher   The name **gopher** has a double origin. First, the slang word "go-fer" is often used to describe a person whose job it is to run miscellaneous errands. Such a person is told to "go for" this and "go for" that.

Second, the sports teams at the Twin Cities campus of the University of Minnesota are called the Golden Gophers. As you no doubt already know, Minnesota is sometimes referred to as the Gopher State.

The name **gopher** is an apt one. What could be more appealing than the image of a cute, computerized rodent, burrowing through the Internet looking for whatever you need.

Although we talk as if there are many different **gopher** facilities, we really have one large, interconnected global **gopher** with many parts, each part being administered by a different organization. Anyone on the Internet can start their own **gopher** and link it into the system.

For this reason, the global **gopher** system is sometimes called the INTERNET **gopher**. The set of all possible resources through which the **gopher** can burrow on our behalf is called GOPHERSPACE.

Understanding a gopher Menu

Take another look at the sample **gopher** menu in Figure 25-13. You will notice that each of the items ends with a special code. This code tells you what type of item you are looking at.

An item that ends in a period (.) is a text file. If you select such an item, the **gopher** will display the text file. A selection that ends in a slash (/) is another menu. If you select this type of item, the **gopher** will display the new menu.

For example, if you were to select item #1, the **gopher** would display the text file that has information entitled "Introduction to the Gopher". If you were to select item #2, the **gopher** would display a new menu called "Fun and Games". Most of the time, you will either be displaying text or moving to a new menu.

Aside from text files and menus, there are other types of menu items that you may see. We will discuss the most common ones. First, the **<TEL>** code indicates a **telnet** session. If you select a **<TEL>** item (such as #4 in our example), the **gopher** will start a **telnet** session for you with the appropriate host computer. When you end the session, you will be back in the **gopher**.

The **<CSO>** code indicates a CSO NAME SERVER. This is a program that helps you search for someone's address and phone number at a particular location. For example, some universities have CSO name servers that you can use to find someone at that university. (The name CSO stands for the Computing Services Office at the University of Illinois, Urbana, where the software was first developed.) A CSO server is an example of a type of service referred to as a WHITE PAGES DIRECTORY: a program that helps you find basic information about a person, much like a computerized telephone book. We will talk about other such services later in the chapter.

The last common **gopher** code is **<?>**. This indicates a database of some kind that the **gopher** can search by keyword. You enter one or more keywords, and the **gopher** will display all the items in the database that contain those words. To perform such a search, the **gopher** calls on another program. It may be an **archie** server (discussed earlier in the chapter), or a **wais** server (discussed later in the chapter), or some other search program.

☑ **HINT**   Although you can use a **gopher** to access a **wais** server, **wais** works better when you access it directly. The setup of the **gopher** command line does not let you use all the capabilities of **wais**.

For reference, Figure 25-14 summarizes the most common types of items that you will find in a **gopher** menu.

Using a gopher

The **gopher** system involves two main programs. The program with which you interact is called a **gopher** CLIENT. The **gopher** client is responsible for displaying the menus and interpreting your commands. The program that actually provides the services is called a **gopher** SERVER.

Implementing a **gopher** is not necessarily an expensive undertaking. For example, at the University of Minnesota, there is a computer that handles

Code	Meaning
.	text file
/	another menu
`<CSO>`	CSO name server
`<TEL>`	`telnet` session
`<?>`	a database to search by keyword

Figure 25-14

The Most Common Types of Items in **gopher** *Menus*

requests from **gopher** clients from all over the world. At the time we wrote this chapter, that computer was a Macintosh IIci (a small personal computer) running Apple's version of Unix.

To use the **gopher**, all you have to do is find a **gopher** client. When you start the client, it connects to a **gopher** server and fetches the initial menu. The **gopher** client then waits for you to make a selection. Whatever you select, the **gopher** client will get it for you.

There are two ways to run a **gopher** client. First, your school or organization may have a **gopher** client already installed. Finding out is easy. Just enter the command:

`gopher`

If a **gopher** client exists, it will start. Otherwise you will see a message like:

`gopher: Command not found.`

If your system does not have a **gopher** client, you can **telnet** to one of the public ones. These are shown in Figure 25-15. This list was current when we wrote this chapter, but, no doubt, there are more public **gopher** clients by the time you read this.

When you **telnet** to one of these computers, log in using the userid that is shown. For example, if you **telnet** to **panda.uiowa.edu**, log in using a userid of **panda**. The **gopher** client will usually ask for your terminal type and then start automatically.

Once the **gopher** client starts, you are free to make your selections and explore gopherspace. To make your choices and control your session, there are a number of **gopher** commands. These are summarized in Figure 25-16.

Like the **rn** and **nn** newsreader programs that we discussed in Chapter 24, the **gopher** runs in cbreak mode. This means that, for single-character commands, you do not have to press <Return>. Simply typing the character is enough.

Location	Internet Address	IP Address	Log in as...
Australia	info.anu.edu.au	150.203.84.20	info
Chile	tolten.puc.cl	146.155.1.16	gopher
Ecuador	ecnet.ec	157.100.45.2	gopher
Japan	gan.ncc.go.jp	160.190.10.1	gopher
Sweden	gopher.chalmers.se	129.16.221.40	gopher
Sweden	gopher.sunet.se	192.36.125.2	gopher
USA: Illinois	gopher.uiuc.edu	128.174.33.160	gopher
USA: Iowa	panda.uiowa.edu	128.255.40.201	panda
USA: Minnesota	consultant.micro.umn.edu	134.84.132.4	gopher

Figure 25-15

Public **gopher** *Clients to Which You Can* **telnet**

There are a few basic commands. Enter **Q** or **q** to quit. If you use **q**, you will be asked to confirm that you really want to quit. To display a summary of **gopher** commands, enter **?** (question mark).

Negotiating gopherspace is simple. You can do virtually everything with six keys: the four cursor control keys, the <Space> bar and the **b** key. Use <Up> and <Down> to move the pointer up and down within a menu. Use <Right> to select (move into) a menu item and <Left> to move back to the previous menu. If a menu has so many items that they cannot be displayed at once, press <Space> to display the next part of the menu. Press **b** to move back to the previous part of a menu.

To jump directly to a particular item, just enter its number. For example, to move to item #8, enter:

8

To jump to a menu item that contains a particular pattern, type a **/** (slash) followed by that pattern. For example, to search for the next menu item that contains the word "humor", enter:

/humor

To repeat the search with the same pattern, use the **n** (next) command. Finally, to jump to the main menu, use **m**.

For convenience, there are alternative commands that you can use to move the pointer and to move from one menu to another. These are shown in Figure 25-16.

Basic Commands

Q	quit the **gopher** immediately
q	quit the **gopher** with a prompt
?	display a help summary
=	display technical information about an item
o	examine and change **gopher** options

Fundamental Commands to Move Through Gopherspace

\<Right\>	select the current item
\<Left\>	back up one level to the previous menu
\<Up\>	move pointer up one item
\<Down\>	move pointer down one item
\<Space\>	move to next page of the menu
b	move back to previous page of the menu
number	move pointer to specified item
/*pattern*	search for next menu item containing *pattern*
n	search for next menu item using same pattern
m	jump to the main menu

Alternate Commands for Moving the Pointer

\<Return\>	select the current item
u	back up one level to the previous menu
k	move pointer up one item
j	move pointer down one item
^P	move pointer up one item (previous)
^N	move pointer down one item (next)
>	move to next page of the menu
<	move to previous page of the menu
+	move to next page of the menu
−	move to previous page of the menu

Using Bookmarks

a	add current item to the bookmark list
A	add current menu/search to bookmark list
d	delete a bookmark
v	display the bookmark list (view)

Figure 25-16
gopher *Commands*

Many **gopher** text items are long. When the **gopher** displays text, it looks for an environment variable named **PAGER**. If this is set, the **gopher** will use the specified paging program to display data. (This variable, as well as the Unix pagers, is discussed in Chapter 17.)

After the **gopher** displays a text item, you will see the following prompt:

`Press <RETURN> to continue, <m> to mail, <s> to save, or <p> to print:`

If you want to save a copy of whatever was displayed, press **s**. If you want to print a copy, press **p**. When you **telnet** to a public **gopher** client, you will not be able to save or print a file on that machine. In that case, you can press **m** and mail it to yourself.

The hardest part about using the **gopher** is knowing just where everything is. As you explore, you will certainly find interesting places to which you will want to return. To make it easy to find such places whenever you want, the **gopher** allows you to build your own custom menu. You can use this menu to hold selections from any **gopher** that you happen to use. Over a period of time, you can build up a menu of your favorite locations in gopherspace. Aside from exploring gopherspace on your own, you can also use **veronica** (see next section) to help you find what you want.

Once you find an item that you want to remember, you can save it as a BOOKMARK. The gopher will maintain a BOOKMARK LIST for you in the form of a customized menu. To add a menu item to your bookmark list, use the **a** (lowercase "a") command. Whatever item you are pointing to will be saved. If you use the **A** (uppercase "A") command, the gopher will save your current menu.

The **A** command also has another use. After you have searched a keyword database (marked by **<?>**), entering **A** will save the search using the exact keywords you specified. Here is an example of how this can come in handy.

Say that your local **gopher** can access the Clarinet newsgroups that we discussed in Chapter 23. You will have a menu item to search the database of news articles. Let's say that, every morning, you want to find out if anything interesting has happened in the world of computers. Select the search item from the appropriate menu and specify a keyword of "computer". Then save the search by using the **A** command. You now have a bookmark on your customized menu that will carry out this exact search whenever you want.

To begin your **gopher** session using your personal bookmark list, start the **gopher** by using the command:

`gopher -b`

The **gopher** saves your bookmark list in a file named `.gopherrc` in your home directory. (This is an example of a dotfile. See Chapter 21.) Thus, you can only save this information if you are using a **gopher** client on your own computer. If you **telnet** to a public **gopher** client, there is no way to save your personal **.gopherrc** file.

At any time, you can jump to your bookmark list by using the **v** (view) command. To return to the previous menu, move up one level (by pressing <Left>, for example).

Another command that can help you remember the location of an interesting resource is **=** (equal sign). This command will display technical information about the current item. In particular, you will see what computer holds that item.

The final **gopher** command is **O** (uppercase "O"). This command will display certain options which you can change (although you will probably not want to).

veronica Servers: Searching Gopherspace

A **veronica** SERVER is a resource that helps you search gopherspace to find specific menu items. Using **veronica**, you can quickly check all the known **gopher** servers looking for menu items that contain specified keywords. **veronica** will create a customized menu listing of all the items in gopherspace that meet your requirements. You can examine each item in turn, saving the ones you like in your bookmark list.

You access **veronica** via the **gopher**. All you have to do is find a menu item that will connect to a **veronica** server. Once you do, you will see the **veronica** menu. Start by displaying the item that explains how it all works. **veronica** searching is easy and straightforward.

veronica has some similarities to **archie** (which we discussed earlier in the chapter), although the details are much different. **veronica** connects to all the known **gopher** servers on a regular basis and takes an inventory of what is available. When you initiate a search, **veronica** needs only check her database to find whatever it is you want.

The result of a **veronica** search is a menu that you can use immediately. You need never know the actual details as to which **gopher** servers are involved. If you do want to know where a particular item was found, you can move to it and use the **=** (equal sign) command.

The first **veronica** server was developed in November, 1992, by Steven Foster and Fred Barrie of the University of Nevada at Reno, System Computing Services department.

WHAT'S IN A NAME?

veronica   You might hear that the name **veronica** stands for Very Easy Rodent-Oriented Netwide Index to Computerized Archives. Actually, this explanation was invented after **veronica** was already named.

The **veronica** server was envisioned by Steven Foster as doing for gopherspace what the **archie** server does for anonymous **ftp**. The name **veronica** comes from the comic book series based on the Archie Andrews character. In this comic, Archie's girlfriend is named Veronica Lodge. Knowledgeable readers will keep an eye out for new Internet services named after Archie's other friends, Betty, Jughead and Reggie.

Using wais to Find Data on a Wide Area Network: swais, xswais

The **wais** system is another service that offers a way to find data that is spread throughout the Internet. The name **wais** – pronounced "wayz" – stands for "Wide Area Information Service". This is the name of a project started in 1989 by Thinking Machines, Apple and MIT.

The purpose of **wais** is to answer your questions by searching databases. Although **wais** can search any type of data, it is usually used with text files. **wais** does not understand the meaning of your questions. Rather, it searches multiple databases, looking for the actual words that you typed. Based on what it finds, **wais** makes a guess at which files are most likely to contain the information you are looking for.

All this is useful, of course, but not earth shattering. What gives **wais** its power are two important capabilities. First, **wais** can search many databases, called SOURCES, scattered throughout the Internet. Second, **wais** searches the entire text of the article, not just predefined keywords.

The **wais** system uses two types of programs: **wais** SERVERS and **wais** CLIENTS. A **wais** server is a program that maintains a particular database for searching. There are hundreds of **wais** servers throughout the Internet, providing data on a large variety of topics. A **wais** client is the program that you use to access the servers. The client reads and processes your commands. Based on your requests, the client accesses the appropriate databases and retrieves the relevant information.

There are **wais** client programs available for different types of computers. For Unix, there are two **wais** clients that you might encounter: a character-based client named **swais** (simple **wais**), and an X Window client named **xswais**. (X Window is discussed in Chapter 5.) We won't go into all the details of using these **wais** clients. If one or the other exists on your system, there will be documentation available.

Location	Internet Address	IP Address
USA: California	`quake.think.com`	`192.31.181.1`
USA: Massachusetts	`nnsc.nsf.net`	`128.89.1.178`
Finland	`wais.funet.fi`	`128.214.6.100`

Log in using a userid of **wais**.

Figure 25-17
Public **wais** *Clients*

If your system does not have a **wais** client, you can **telnet** to one of the public **swais** facilities listed in Figure 25-17. After you connect, log in with a userid of **wais**.

The general idea when you are using **swais** is to find what you need by a two-step process. First, select which sources you want **swais** to access. (You will have a lot to choose from.) Next, specify the words for which you want to search. When the search is complete, **swais** will show you a list of the documents it has found. The ones that **swais** thinks are the most promising will be at the top. One by one, you select which ones you would like to look at and **swais** will retrieve them for you.

To get started, log in and press **?** (question mark) to display a help summary. If you decide that you would like to use **wais** as a permanent tool, you can use **archie** to find a **wais** client to install on your system.

☑ **HINT**   It is easy to be overwhelmed by the number of sources. However, you can use **swais** to tell you what sources to select.

There is one source that contains a master list. It is listed under the name **directory-of-servers**. Select this source and search it using the words that describe your general area of interest. The result will be a list of the sources that you should tell **swais** to search.

When **swais** displays the results, be sure to write down the names. There is no way to tell **swais** to use the results of a search as a source list for further searching.

The World-Wide Web: WWW

The World-Wide Web – also referred to as WWW and W3 – is a hypertext-based service that allows you to retrieve and find data based on keyword searches.

HYPERTEXT is data that contains links to other data. When you encounter a link, you can choose to follow it no matter where it leads. For example, say that you are reading a document that contains links to other documents. If you decide to follow one of the links, the Web will figure out what document the link points to, retrieve that document, and display it for you. The new document, of course, may have links of its own. You can spend all day following one link after another. The Web will do all the work for you while hiding the technical details.

In principle, hypertext can be any type of data: sound, images, video and so on. When mixed data like this is linked, it is sometimes referred to as HYPERMEDIA. In practice, you will find that most hypertext is regular text that you display on your terminal.

The main problem with hypertext is that it is so time consuming to create. Someone has to decide where each link should go and where it should point to. However, there is already a considerable amount of hypertext data on the Internet that you can access using the Web. Moreover, you can start your own local Web by using certain tools to create hypertext out of your own data. (We won't go into the details here.) If you want, you can share this data with everyone else by letting the global Web know where it is. Even if you keep your data private, it can still contain links to data anywhere on the Internet.

To use the Web, you need a client program called a BROWSER to act as an interface. There are different types of browsers available. The two most common are the LineMode browser and Viola. The LineMode browser is used with regular character-based terminals. Viola is used with X terminals. (The X Window system is discussed in Chapter 5.)

There is also a combined browser/editor for Next computers, a "curses" browser (for character terminals) that manipulates the entire screen, and several other browsers for X Window, including one for Motif. Tools like this are always being developed, so keep an eye out for new ones.

☑ **HINT**   Browsers tend to be created as research projects, not as commercial products. You will find that some of them are still in development and, hence, are somewhat buggy.

Although the Web is itself a complex entity, using it is simple. At every point, there is online help. Moreover, the help itself is hypertext, so you can jump from one topic to another in a natural manner.

Location	Internet Address	IP Address
Finland	`info.funet.fi`	`128.214.6.100`
Israel	`vms.huji.ac.il`	`128.139.4.3`
Switzerland	`info.cern.ch`	`128.141.201.74`
USA (New Jersey)	`eies2.njit.edu`	`128.235.1.43`

If you are asked to log in, use a userid of **www**.

Figure 25-18
Public World-Wide Web Browsers

If you have a browser on your system (ask around), just start it and do whatever makes sense. You can't hurt anything by experimenting, and the best way to learn about the Web is to use it. If your system does not have a browser, you can **telnet** to one of the public browsers listed in Figure 25-18. Once you connect, the browser may start automatically, or you may be asked to log in. If you need to log in, use a userid of **www**.

If, after using the Web, you decide that you would like your own browser (or you can convince your system manager of the need), it is a simple matter to use the Web itself to find the anonymous **ftp** sites that contain the browser programs. Alternatively, you can use **archie** (explained earlier in the chapter). If you do, start with a **whatis** search for **www**.

A Sample Session with the Web

To show you what it is like to use the Web, let's take a look at a typical session. The purpose of this session is to search for the lyrics from a song that contain the words "Central Scrutinizer". Before we start, we do not know the name of the song, nor do we know the name of the artist or album.

As we use the Web, we will start by following general links. As the choices become more specific, we will move from one link to another until we find what we want. This is called NAVIGATING the Web.

To start our search, we **telnet** to a public LineMode browser:

```
telnet info.cern.ch
```

Once the connection is made, the browser starts automatically and we see the first screen:

```
                                              Overview of the Web
                        GENERAL OVERVIEW

There is no "top" to the World-Wide Web. You can look at it from
many points of view. If you have no other bias, here are some
places to start:

by Subject[1]    A classification by subject of interest.
                 Incomplete but easiest to use.

by Type[2]       Looking by type of service (access protocol,
                 etc) may allow you to find things if you know
                 what you are looking for.

About WWW[3]     About the World-Wide Web global information
                 sharing project.
```

The numbers in brackets indicate the hypertext links. We can follow a link
simply by entering its number. To start our search, we decide to follow link #1.
In response, the Web displays a long list of 42 subjects to choose from. Here
are a few of the more interesting ones.

```
Computing      Networking[6], Jargon[7], newsgroups[8],
               Software Technology[9], Languages[10],
               Algorithms[11]

Geography      CIA World Fact Book[12]

Law            US Copyright law[15]

Libraries      Few libraries currently have servers. You have
               to log on to them. But you can find out how with
               Art St.George's list of library systems[16],
               about "Library" in the internet resource
               guide[17], and the hytelnet index[18].
Literature     Project Gutenberg[19]: two classic books a month.
               See their explanations[20], the index and
               newsletter[21], books published in 1991[22],
               1992[23], and reserved for the USA[24].

Humanities     BMCR classical reviews[25], Poetry[26], SciFi
               reviews[27]. See also electronic journals[28].

Meteorology    US weather[30], state by state.

Music          MIDI interfacing[32], Song lyrics[33]

Reference      Roget's Thesaurus[37]. English dictionary[38].
```

Since we want to search for song lyrics, we select link [33]. We see the following:

```
                                          LYRICS index
                       LYRICS

Server created with WAIS release 8 b3.1 on Oct 27 03:43:27 1991.
Please send contributions to datta@cs.uwp.edu.
Selections from the following performers included:
```

After this comes a long list of 379 different musical artists and groups. To perform our search we use the **find** command. (You can enter **help** to teach yourself how to use the commands.)

find central scrutinizer

At this point, the Web searches the full database of lyrics looking for documents that contain the keywords we specified. Once the results have been compiled, the Web will analyze them and estimate which documents are the most relevant. Each document will be given a score. The most relevant document (in the Web's opinion) is always given a score of 1000. The other scores are relative to this. Here is the first part of our results:

```
              CENTRAL SCRUTINIZER

Index LYRICS contains the following 23 items relevant to
'central scrutinizer'.

joes.garage     /mas/el/u/uriw/lyrics/files/zappa.frank/[1]
                        Score: 1000, lines: 138

tonight    /mas/el/u/uriw/lyrics/files/bowie.david/[2]
                        Score:  409, lines: 321

all_rem_lyrics    /mas/el/u/uriw/lyrics/files/rem/[3]
                        Score:  364, lines:2505
```

Taking the Web's advice, we select #1 and hit pay dirt. Here, in part, is what we find:

```
This is the CENTRAL SCRUTINIZER.  It is my responsibility to
enforce all the laws that haven't been passed yet.  It is also
my responsibility to alert each and every one of you to the
potential consequences of various ordinary everyday activities
you might be performing which could eventually lead to The Death
Penalty (or affect your parents' credit rating).  Our criminal
institutions are full of little creeps like you who do wrong
things, and many of them were driven to these crimes by a
horrible force called MUSIC!
```

To finish our work with the Web, we enter the **quit** command. This stops the browser and logs out, which closes the **telnet** session.

How to Find Someone on the Internet: `whois`, `netfind`

One of the most frequently asked questions is, "How do I find someone on the Internet?" There is no central directory, but there are a number of places that you can look. Here's a few ideas to try when you need to track down someone.

We won't go into all the details – each of these systems works differently – but we will point you in the right direction. These systems are all examples of white pages directories: services that help you find a name or address.

The Usenet Address Server

A program on **pit-manager.mit.edu** automatically scans the vast bulk of Usenet articles looking for the **From** lines in the headers. (As we explained in Chapter 23, the **From** line shows the name and address of the person who posted the article.) The program sorts all these addresses and saves them in a database. If the person you are looking for has posted a Usenet article lately, there is a good chance that **pit-manager** will know about it.

To use this service, send a mail message (see Chapter 14) to:

mail-server@pit-manager.mit.edu

Leave the **Subject** line blank. In the body of the letter, type a line with the following format:

send usenet-addresses/*name*

where *name* describes the person you are looking for. **pit-manager** will send back all the lines in the database that contain the pattern you specify. As an example, we used this service to track down John Navarra, who calls himself "The MaD ScIenTIst". We sent the following message:

```
To: mail-server@pit-manager.mit.edu
Subject:
send usenet-addresses/navarra
```

In a short time, we received mail that contained the following:

```
navarra@casbah.acns.nwu.edu (John 'tms' Navarra)   (Oct 2 91)
```

whois *Servers*

A **whois** server keeps a database of names and addresses that you can query interactively. To reach the most general **whois** server, **telnet** to **nic.ddn.mil**. When you connect, you will be logged in automatically. Enter **help** to get started.

There are a large number of other **whois** servers on the Internet that provide information about a particular university or organization. You can use anonymous **ftp** to download a list of these servers. You can then look for one that is likely to help you.

To find these anonymous **ftp** sites, use **archie**. **telnet** to an **archie** server and use the following commands:

```
set search sub
prog whois-servers-list
```

The **gopher** is also good at accessing **whois** servers.

Finally, there may be a **whois** server on your system. To find out, enter the command:

```
whois
```

If there is a server, this command will start it.

netfind *Servers*

netfind is a program that will actively search through the Internet looking for a computer that knows about the person you are trying to find. **netfind** works well as long as you have some idea of where the person is.

If your system does not have **netfind**, you can **telnet** to one of the public **netfind** servers. They are shown in Figure 25-19. When you connect, log in with a userid of **netfind**. There will be a menu offering help to get you started.

The Knowbot

A KNOWBOT is an automated robot-like program that intelligently searches for information on your behalf. Although people have been talking about knowbots for some time, the idea has not yet been fully developed. However, there is one knowbot that you can **telnet** to and have it search a number of name and address databases (including the one for MCI Mail).

Location	Internet Address	IP Address
Australia	`archie.au`	`139.130.4.6`
Chile	`malloco.ing.puc.cl`	`146.155.1.43`
Czechslovakia	`sun.uakom.cs`	`192.108.131.11`
USA (Alabama)	`redmont.cis.uab.edu`	`138.26.64.4`
USA (Colorado)	`bruno.cs.colorado.edu`	`128.138.243.151`
USA (Minnesota)	`mudhoney.micro.umn.edu`	`134.84.132.7`
USA (Texas)	`netfind.oc.com`	`192.82.215.92`

Log in with a userid of `netfind`.

Figure 25-19
Public `netfind` *Servers*

To use this knowbot, `telnet` to `nri.reston.va.us` using port number 185:

`telnet nri.reston.va.us 185`

Once you connect, type **?** (question mark) for help to get started.

`fred` *and X.500 Directories*

The X.500 directory system was developed by the International Standards Organization (ISO) to keep track of vast amounts of names and addresses on a global scale. X.500 was designed to be the white pages directory of the future. Unfortunately, X.500 is complicated and not all that easy to use.

To make it simpler to access X.500 databases, an interface named **fred** was developed. To access a **fred** server that has access to a number of X.500 systems, `telnet` to either `wp.psi.com` or `wp2.psi.com` and log in as `fred`. Once you log in, enter **help** for a list of commands or **manual** for more detailed help.

Ask a Postmaster

If you know the mail address of someone, but not his userid, and you can't find him using any of the services we just described, send a message to the postmaster for his computer. Use a userid of **postmaster**.

For example, if you need to find the userid of someone who uses the computer named **nipper.ucsb.edu**, you can use:

`mail postmaster@nipper.ucsb.edu`

All Internet computers are supposed to have a **postmaster** userid which accepts appropriate queries from the outside world.

This is not an automated service. A real person has to read your message, look up what you want and send a reply. Try the automated services first.

The Four Best Lists of Internet Services

We have spent a lot of time in this chapter discussing Internet services. We have covered the main ones, but there are many more. The best way to keep abreast of this ever-changing universe is to download one of several lists that keep track of Internet services. Figure 25-20 (on the next page) shows where you can download the four best lists. Each of these lists contains the names of other lists, so one list can keep you busy for months.

For each list, we show the **ftp** information that was available at the time we wrote this chapter. If you have any problem locating these lists, you can always find them with **archie**. You can also check the Usenet newsgroup **alt.internet.services**.

 **HINT**   Unix is fun!

The Big Fun List

Official name	Big Fun in the Internet with Uncle Bert
Creator	Jeremy ☺ Smith
`ftp` site	`cerberus.cor.epa.gov`
directory	`/pub/bigfun`
file name	`bigfun.txt.Z`

The December List

Official name	Information Sources
Creator	John December
`ftp` site	`ftp.rpi.edu`
directory	`/pub/communications`
file name	`internet-cmc`

The Porter List

Official name	High Weirdness by Email
Creator	Mitchell Porter
`ftp` site	`ftp.uu.net`
directory	`/doc/political/umich-poli/Resources`
file name	`weirdness.Z`

(Also, check the Usenet newsgroups `alt.slack` and `talk.bizarre`.)

The Yanoff List

Official name	Internet Services List
Creator	Scott Yanoff
`ftp` site	`pit-manager.mit.edu`
directory	`/pub/usenet/news.answers`
file name	`internet-services`

Figure 25-20
The Four Best Internet Services Lists

Summary of Unix Commands Covered in this Book

!	repeat specified command (11)
!!	repeat previous command (11)
^^	repeat previous command with substitution (11)
adventure	the original text-based adventure game (7)
alias	assign a name to specified command list (11)
apropos	display command names based on keyword search (8)
archie	client program to use **archie**/anonymous **ftp** search (25)
arithmetic	program to help you practice simple computation (7)
backgammon	backgammon dice/board game (7)
banner	write large characters, suitable for printing (7)
bash	the Bash shell (10)
battlestar	an adventure game (7)
bc	an arbitrary-precision, easy-to-use calculator (7)
bcd	convert text to BCD cardpunch format (7)
biff	notify when mail arrives (14)
bj	blackjack card game (7)
boggle	Boggle word game (7)
btlgammon	backgammon dice/board game (7)

Chapter references are indicated by the numbers in parentheses.

`cal`	display a calendar (7)
`cancel`	System V version of **`lprm`** (18)
`canfield`	solitaire card game (7)
`cat`	combine, copy standard input to standard output (16)
`cd`	change the current (working) directory (21)
`chess`	chess game (7)
`chfn`	change your **`finger`** information (12)
`ching`	display advice from the Book of Changes (7)
`chmod`	change permissions (mode) of a file or directory (22)
`chsh`	change your default shell (10)
`colrm`	remove specified columns from each line of data (16)
`compress`	generate a compressed (`. z`) file (25)
`cp`	copy files (22)
`craps`	craps dice game (7)
`cribbage`	cribbage card game (7)
`crypt`	encode or decode text using a specified key (16)
`csh`	the C-shell (10)
`cut`	extract selected portions (columns) of each line (16)
`date`	display the time and date (7)
`du`	display disk storage usage statistics (21)
`echo`	write arguments to standard output (11)
`ed`	old, standard Unix line-oriented text editor (19)
`egrep`	like **`grep`**, searches for full regular expressions (16)
`emacs`	the Emacs editor (19)
`ex`	standard Unix line-oriented text editor (19)
`exit`	exit a shell (4)
`factor`	decompose a number into its prime factors (7)
`fgrep`	like **`grep`**, searches for fixed character string (16)
`finger`	display information about a specified userid (12)
`fish`	the Go Fish card game (7)
`fmt`	format text to fit a 72-character line (14)
`fortune`	display an interesting message (7)
`from`	show if mail is waiting (14)
`ftp`	transfer files to/from another computer (25)

Chapter references are indicated by the numbers in parentheses.

gmacs	the Emacs editor (19)
gopher	client program to use **gopher** information service (25)
grep	extract lines that contain a specified pattern (16)
hack	fantasy game (a replacement for **rogue**) (7)
hangman	hangman word game (7)
head	display the first part of a file (17)
history	display the history event list (11)
host	display domain/IP address of an Internet computer (25)
hostname	display the name of your system (7)
hunt	multi-player shooting game (7)
id	display userid and groupid (22)
ksh	the Korn shell (10)
leave	display reminder at specified time (7)
less	display data, one screenful at a time (17)
ln	make a link between two directory entries (22)
lock	temporarily lock your terminal (7)
login	terminate a login shell and initiate a new login (4)
logout	terminate a login shell (4)
look	extract lines beginning with a specified pattern (16)
lp	System V version of **lpr** (18)
lpq	show what print jobs are waiting (18)
lpr	send a file to be printed (18)
lprm	remove (cancel) a job from the print queue (18)
lpstat	System V version of **lpq** (18)
ls	display information about files (21)
mail	send or read mail (14)
Mail	Berkeley Unix version of **mail** (14)
mailx	System V version of **mail** (14)
man	display entries from online Unix reference manual (8)
mesg	allow or deny receiving messages at your terminal (12)
mille	Mille Bournes board game (7)
mkdir	make (create) a directory (21)
monop	Monopoly board game (7)

Chapter references are indicated by the numbers in parentheses.

moo	guessing game (7)
more	display data, one screenful at a time (17)
msgs	display local system messages (7)
mv	move or rename files (21, 22)
mwm	the Motif window manager (5)
netfind	client program to access **netfind** service (25)
news	display the local system news (7)
newsetup	set up a new `.newsrc` (24)
nl	add line numbers to text (18)
nn	read Usenet articles using **nn** newsreader (24)
nncheck	check for unread Usenet articles (24)
nngoback	mark specified Usenet articles as unread (24)
nngrab	find all Usenet articles with specified subject (24)
nngrep	display names of specified Usenet newsgroups (24)
nnpost	post Usenet article (24)
nntidy	clean and adjust Usenet newsreader `.newsrc` file (24)
nnusage	display statistics showing who has been using **nn** (24)
number	convert a number to English words (7)
olwm	the Open Look window manager (5)
passwd	change your login password (4)
paste	combine columns of data (16)
pg	display data, one screenful at a time (17)
ping	check if an Internet computer is responding (12)
Pnews	post Usenet article (24)
ppt	convert text to paper tape format (7)
pr	format text, suitable for printing (18)
primes	generate prime numbers larger than specific value (7)
printenv	display values of environment variables (11)
pwd	display pathname of current (working) directory (21)
quiz	question and answer game (7)
quota	display your system resource quotas (21)
rain	display animated raindrops (7)
rev	reverse order of characters in each line of data (16)

Chapter references are indicated by the numbers in parentheses.

rm	remove (delete) files or directories (22)
rmdir	remove empty directories (21)
rn	read Usenet articles using **rn** newsreader (24)
robots	shooting-at-robots game (7)
rogue	fantasy game, exploring the Dungeons of Doom (7)
ruptime	display how long local systems have been up (7)
rwho	display info about userids on local network (12)
sail	multi-player sailing game (7)
set	set or display the value of shell variables (11)
setenv	set or display value of environment variables (11)
sh	the Bourne shell (10)
snake	chase game (7)
sort	sort or merge data (16)
spell	check text for words that may be spelled wrong (16)
stty	set/display operating options for your terminal (6)
swais	client program to access **wais** service (25)
tail	display the last part of a file (17)
talk	send messages back and forth to another user (12)
tar	unpackage/create a collection (archive) of files (25)
tcsh	the Tcsh shell (10)
tee	copy standard input to a file and standard output (15)
telnet	connect to another computer (25)
touch	update access and modification times of a file (22)
tr	translate or delete selected characters (16)
traceroute	display Internet route to another computer (13)
trek	Star Trek-inspired game (7)
tset	initialize your terminal (1, 16)
tty	show special file that represents your terminal (20)
twm	the Tab window manager (5)
umask	set user (file mode) mask for file creation (22)
unalias	remove a name previously defined by **alias** (11)
uncompress	expand a (**.Z**) file created by **compress** (25)
uniq	remove adjacent repeated lines in a text file (16)
unset	remove a shell variable (11)

Chapter references are indicated by the numbers in parentheses.

uptime	display how long your system has been up (7)
users	display userids that are currently logged in (12)
vi	standard Unix screen-oriented (visual) editor (19)
view	same as **vi**, in read-only mode (19)
w	display info about userids and active processes (12)
wc	count number of lines, words or characters (16)
whatis	display one-line summary of specified command (8)
who	display info about currently logged in userids (12)
whoami	display the userid that is currently logged in (7)
whois	client program to access a **whois** server (25)
worm	worm-growing game (7)
worms	display worms on your terminal (7)
write	send messages back and forth to another local user (12)
wump	the game of hunt-the-wumpus (7)
xbiff	X Window version of **biff** (show if mail waiting) (14)
xcalc	X Window calculator (5)
xclock	X Window clock (5)
xhost	tell X server that you will use a remote computer (5)
xinit	start X Window (5)
xswais	X Window client program to access **wais** service (25)
xterm	start an X Window terminal session (5)
zcat	access a (**.Z**) file created by **compress** (25)
zsh	the Zsh shell (10)

Chapter references are indicated by the numbers in parentheses.

Summary of Unix Commands by Category

This appendix contains a summary of all the Unix commands covered in this book, organized by category. The categories are:

Editing

Entering a Command

Directories

Displaying Data

Diversions

Downloading Files

Files

Filters

Games

Information

Internet

Logging In and Out

(Online) Manual

Mail

Numbers

Printing

Shells

Terminal

Time and Dates

Usenet

Users

Variables

X Window

Editing

ed	old, standard Unix line-oriented text editor (19)
emacs	the Emacs editor (19)
ex	standard Unix line-oriented text editor (19)
fmt	format text to fit a 72-character line (14)
gmacs	the Emacs editor (19)
vi	standard Unix screen-oriented (visual) editor (19)
view	same as **vi**, in read-only mode (19)

Entering a Command

!	repeat specified command (11)
!!	repeat previous command (11)
^^	repeat previous command with substitution (11)
alias	assign a name to specified command list (11)
history	display the history event list (11)
unalias	remove a name previously defined by **alias** (11)

Directories

cd	change the current (working) directory (21)
chmod	change permissions (mode) of a file or directory (22)
ln	make a link between two directory entries (22)
ls	display information about files (21)
mkdir	make (create) a directory (21)
pwd	display pathname of current (working) directory (21)
rm	remove (delete) files or directories (22)
rmdir	remove empty directories (21)
umask	set user (file mode) mask for file creation (22)

Displaying Data

head	display the first part of a file (17)
less	display data, one screenful at a time (17)
more	display data, one screenful at a time (17)
pg	display data, one screenful at a time (17)
tail	display the last part of a file (17)

Chapter references are indicated by the numbers in parentheses.

Diversions

`arithmetic`	program to help you practice simple computation (7)
`banner`	write large characters, suitable for printing (7)
`bcd`	convert text to BCD cardpunch format (7)
`ching`	display advice from the Book of Changes (7)
`fortune`	display an interesting message (7)
`number`	convert a number to English words (7)
`ppt`	convert text to paper tape format (7)
`rain`	display animated raindrops (7)
`worms`	display worms on your terminal (7)

Downloading Files

`archie`	client program to use `archie`/anonymous `ftp` search (25)
`compress`	generate a compressed (`.Z`) file (25)
`ftp`	transfer files to/from another computer (25)
`tar`	unpackage/create a collection (archive) of files (25)
`uncompress`	expand a (`.Z`) file created by `compress` (25)
`zcat`	access a (`.Z`) file created by `compress` (25)

Files

`chmod`	change permissions (mode) of a file or directory (22)
`cp`	copy files (22)
`ln`	make a link between two directory entries (22)
`ls`	display information about files (21)
`mv`	move or rename files (21, 22)
`rm`	remove (delete) files or directories (22)
`touch`	update access and modification times of a file (22)
`umask`	set user (file mode) mask for file creation (22)

Chapter references are indicated by the numbers in parentheses.

Filters

fmt	format text to fit a 72-character line (14)
head	display the first part of a file (17)
less	display data, one screenful at a time (17)
cat	combine, copy standard input to standard output (16)
colrm	remove specified columns from each line of data (16)
crypt	encode or decode text using a specified key (16)
cut	extract selected portions (columns) of each line (16)
egrep	like **grep**, searches for full regular expressions (16)
fgrep	like **grep**, searches for fixed character string (16)
grep	extract lines that contain a specified pattern (16)
look	extract lines beginning with a specified pattern (16)
nl	add line numbers to text (18)
more	display data, one screenful at a time (17)
paste	combine columns of data (16)
pg	display data, one screenful at a time (17)
pr	format text, suitable for printing (18)
rev	reverse order of characters in each line of data (16)
sort	sort or merge data (16)
spell	check text for words that may be spelled wrong (16)
tail	display the last part of a file (17)
tee	copy standard input to a file and standard output (15)
tr	translate or delete selected characters (16)
uniq	remove adjacent repeated lines in a text file (16)
wc	count number of lines, words or characters (16)

Chapter references are indicated by the numbers in parentheses.

Games

adventure	the original text-based adventure game (7)
backgammon	backgammon dice/board game (7)
battlestar	an adventure game (7)
bj	blackjack card game (7)
boggle	Boggle word game (7)
btlgammon	backgammon dice/board game (7)
canfield	solitaire card game (7)
chess	chess game (7)
craps	craps dice game (7)
cribbage	cribbage card game (7)
fish	Go Fish card game (7)
hack	fantasy game (a replacement for **rogue**) (7)
hangman	hangman word game (7)
hostname	display the name of your system (7)
hunt	multi-player shooting game (7)
mille	Mille Bournes board game (7)
monop	Monopoly board game (7)
moo	guessing game (7)
quiz	question and answer game (7)
robots	shooting-at-robots game (7)
rogue	fantasy game, exploring the Dungeons of Doom (7)
sail	multi-player sailing game (7)
snake	chase game (7)
trek	Star Trek-inspired game (7)
worm	worm-growing game (7)
wump	the game of hunt-the-wumpus (7)

Information

du	display disk storage usage statistics (21)
msgs	display local system messages (7)
news	display the local system news (7)
quota	display your system resource quotas (21)
ruptime	display how long local systems have been up (7)
uptime	display how long your system has been up (7)

Chapter references are indicated by the numbers in parentheses.

Internet

`archie`	client program to use **`archie`**/anonymous **`ftp`** search (25)
`ftp`	transfer files to/from another computer (25)
`gopher`	client program to use **`gopher`** information service (25)
`host`	display domain/IP address of an Internet computer (25)
`netfind`	client program to access **`netfind`** service (25)
`ping`	check if an Internet computer is responding (12)
`swais`	client program to access **`wais`** service (25)
`telnet`	connect to another computer (25)
`traceroute`	display Internet route to another computer (13)
`whois`	client program to access a **`whois`** server (25)
`xswais`	X Window client program to access **`wais`** service (25)

Logging In and Out

`login`	terminate a login shell and initiate a new login (4)
`logout`	terminate a login shell (4)
`passwd`	change your login password (4)

(Online) Manual

`apropos`	display command names based on keyword search (8)
`man`	display entries from online Unix reference manual (8)
`whatis`	display one-line summary of specified command (8)

Mail

`biff`	notify when mail arrives (14)
`fmt`	format text to fit a 72-character line (14)
`from`	show if mail is waiting (14)
`mail`	send or read mail (14)
`Mail`	Berkeley Unix version of **`mail`** **(14)**
`mailx`	System V version of **`mail`** (14)

Numbers

`bc`	an arbitrary-precision, easy-to-use calculator (7)
`factor`	decompose a number into its prime factors (7)
`primes`	generate prime numbers larger than specific value (7)
`xcalc`	X Window calculator (5)

Chapter references are indicated by the numbers in parentheses.

Printing

`cancel`	System V version of **lprm** **(18)**
`lp`	System V version of **lpr** **(18)**
`lpq`	show what print jobs are waiting (18)
`lpr`	send a file to be printed (18)
`lprm`	remove (cancel) a job from the print queue (18)
`lpstat`	System V version of **lpq** **(18)**
`nl`	add line numbers to text (18)
`pr`	format text, suitable for printing (18)

Shells

`bash`	the Bash shell (10)
`chsh`	change your default shell (10)
`csh`	the C-Shell (10)
`exit`	exit a shell (4)
`ksh`	the Korn shell (10)
`sh`	the Bourne shell (10)
`tcsh`	the Tcsh shell (10)
`zsh`	the Zsh shell (10)

Terminal

`lock`	temporarily lock your terminal (7)
`mesg`	allow or deny receiving messages at your terminal (12)
`stty`	set/display operating options for your terminal (6)
`tset`	initialize your terminal (6, 16)
`tty`	show special file that represents your terminal (20)

Time and Dates

`cal`	display a calendar (7)
`date`	display the time and date (7)
`leave`	display reminder at specified time (7)
`xclock`	X Window clock (5)

Chapter references are indicated by the numbers in parentheses.

Usenet

`newsetup`	set up a new `.newsrc` (24)
`nn`	read Usenet articles using **nn** newsreader (24)
`nncheck`	check for unread Usenet articles (24)
`nngoback`	mark specified Usenet articles as unread (24)
`nngrab`	find all Usenet articles with specified subject (24)
`nngrep`	display names of specified Usenet newsgroups (24)
`nnpost`	post Usenet article (24)
`nntidy`	clean and adjust Usenet newsreader `.newsrc` file (24)
`nnusage`	display statistics showing who has been using **nn (24)**
`Pnews`	post Usenet article (24)
`rn`	read Usenet articles using **rn** newsreader (24)

Users

`chfn`	change your **finger** information (12)
`finger`	display information about a specified userid (12)
`id`	display userid and groupid (22)
`rwho`	display info about userids on local network (12)
`talk`	send messages back and forth to another user (12)
`users`	display userids that are currently logged in (12)
`w`	display info about userids and active processes (12)
`who`	display info about currently logged in userids (12)
`whoami`	display the userid that is currently logged in (7)
`write`	send messages back and forth to another local user (12)

Variables

`echo`	write arguments to standard output (11)
`printenv`	display values of environment variables (11)
`set`	set or display the value of shell variables (11)
`setenv`	set or display value of environment variables (11)
`unset`	remove a shell variable (11)

Chapter references are indicated by the numbers in parentheses.

X Window

Command	Description
`mwm`	the Motif window manager (5)
`olwm`	the Open Look window manager (5)
`twm`	the Tab window manager (5)
`xbiff`	X Window version of **biff** (show if mail waiting) (14)
`xcalc`	X Window calculator (5)
`xclock`	X Window clock (5)
`xhost`	tell X server that you will use a remote computer (5)
`xinit`	start X Window (5)
`xswais`	X Window client program to access **wais** service (25)
`xterm`	start an X Window terminal session (5)

Chapter references are indicated by the numbers in parentheses.

Summary of *vi* Commands

This appendix contains a summary of all the **vi** commands covered in this book. For more information, see Chapter 19 in which **vi** is discussed in detail.

Starting

vi *file*	start **vi**, edit specified file
vi -R *file*	start **vi** read-only, edit specified file
view *file*	start **vi** read-only, edit specified file

Stopping

zz	save data and stop
:q!	stop without saving data

Recovering After System Failure

vi -r	display names of files that can be recovered
vi -r *file*	start **vi**, recover specified file

Controlling the Display

`^L`	redisplay the current screen
`:set number`	display internal line numbers
`:set nonumber`	do not display internal line numbers

Moving the Cursor

`h`	move cursor one position left
`j`	move cursor one position down
`k`	move cursor one position up
`l`	move cursor one position right
`<Left>`	move cursor one position left
`<Down>`	move cursor one position down
`<Up>`	move cursor one position up
`<Right>`	move cursor one position right
`<Backspace>`	move cursor one position left
`<Space>`	move cursor one position right
`-`	move cursor to beginning of previous line
`+`	move cursor to beginning of next line
`<Return>`	move cursor to beginning of next line
`0`	move cursor to beginning of current line
`$`	move cursor to end of current line
`^`	move cursor to first non-space/tab in current line
`w`	move cursor forward to first character of next word
`e`	move cursor forward to last character of next word
`b`	move cursor backward to first character of prev. word
`W`	same as **w**; ignore punctuation
`E`	same as **e**; ignore punctuation
`B`	same as **b**; ignore punctuation
`)`	move forward to next sentence beginning
`(`	move backward to previous sentence beginning
`}`	move forward to next paragraph beginning
`{`	move backward to previous paragraph beginning
`H`	move cursor to top line
`M`	move cursor to middle line
`L`	move cursor to last line

Moving Through the Editing Buffer

^F	move down one screenful
^B	move up one screenful
*n***^F**	move down *n* screenfuls
*n***^B**	move up *n* screenfuls
^D	move down a half screenful
^U	move up a half screenful
*n***^D**	move down *n* lines
*n***^U**	move up *n* lines

Searching for a Pattern

/*rexp*	search forward for specified regular expression
/	repeat forward search for previous pattern
?*rexp*	search backward for specified regular expression
?	repeat backward search for previous pattern
n	repeat last **/** or **?** command, same direction
N	repeat last **/** or **?** command, opposite direction

Special Characters to Use in Regular Expressions

.	match any single character except **newline**
*	match zero or more of the preceding characters
^	match the beginning of a line
$	match the end of a line
\<	match the beginning of a word
\>	match the end of a word
[ ]	match one of the enclosed characters
[^]	match any character that is not enclosed
****	interpret the following symbol literally

Line Numbers

*n***G**	jump to line number *n*
1G	jump to first line in editing buffer
G	jump to last line in editing buffer
:map g 1G	define macro so **g** will be the same as **1G**

Inserting

`i`	change to insert mode: insert before cursor position
`a`	change to insert mode: insert after cursor position
`I`	change to insert mode: insert at start of current line
`A`	change to insert mode: insert at end of current line
`o`	change to insert mode: open below current line
`O`	change to insert mode: open above current line

Making Changes

`r`	replace exactly 1 character (do not enter input mode)
`R`	replace by typing over
`s`	replace 1 character by insertion
`C`	replace from cursor to end of line by insertion
`cc`	replace entire current line by insertion
`S`	replace entire current line by insertion
`c`*move*	replace from cursor to *move* by insertion
`~`	change the case of a letter

Replacing a Pattern

`:s/`*pattern*`/`*replace*`/`	substitute, current line
`:`*line*`s/`*pattern*`/`*replace*`/`	substitute, specified line
`:`*line*`,,`*line*`s/`*pattern*`/`*replace*`/`	substitute, specified range
`:%s/`*pattern*`/`*replace*`/`	substitute, all lines

Undoing or Repeating a Change

`u`	undo last command that modified the editing buffer
`U`	restore current line
`.`	repeat last command that modified the editing buffer

Controlling the Length of Lines

`r`<Return>	replace a character with a **newline**
`J`	join lines
`:set wm=`*n*	auto line break within *n* positions of right margin

Deleting

x	delete character at cursor
X	delete character to left of cursor
D	delete from cursor to end of line
dd	delete the entire current line
d*move*	delete from cursor to *move*
dG	delete from cursor to end of editing buffer
d1G	delete from cursor to beginning of editing buffer
:*line***d**	delete specified line
:*line,line***d**	delete specified range

Copying the Last Deletion

p	copy last deletion; insert after/below cursor
P	copy last deletion; insert before/above cursor
xp	transpose two characters
deep	transpose two words (start to the left of first word)
ddp	transpose two lines

Copying and Moving Lines

:*line***co***target*	copy specified line; insert below target
:*line,line***co***target*	copy specified range; insert below target
:*line***m***target*	move specified line; insert below target
:*line,line***m***target*	move specified range; insert below target

Executing Shell Commands

:!*command*	pause **vi**, execute specified shell command
:!!	pause **vi**, execute previous shell command
:sh	pause **vi**, start a shell
:!csh	pause **vi**, start a new C-Shell

Reading Data

:*line***r** *file*	insert contents of *file* after specified line
:r *file*	insert contents of *file* after current line
:*line***r** **!***command*	insert output of *command* after specified line
:r **!***command*	insert output of *command* after current line
:r **!look** *pattern*	insert words that begin with specified pattern

Using Shell Commands to Process Data

`n!!`*command*	execute *command* on *n* lines
`!`*move* *command*	execute *command* from cursor to *move*
`!`*move* **fmt**	format lines from cursor to *move*

Writing Data

`:w`	write data to original file
`:w` *file*	write data to specified file
`:w>>` *file*	append data to specified file

Changing the File While Editing

`:e` *file*	edit the specified file
`:e!` *file*	edit the specified file, omit automatic check

Abbreviations

`:ab` *short long*	set *short* as an abbreviation for *long*
`:ab`	display current abbreviations
`:una` *short*	cancel abbreviation *short*

The ASCII Code

Character	Decimal	Hex	Octal	Binary	
	0	00	000	0000 0000	
Ctrl-A	1	01	001	0000 0001	
Ctrl-B	2	02	002	0000 0010	
Ctrl-C	3	03	003	0000 0011	
Ctrl-D	4	04	004	0000 0100	
Ctrl-E	5	05	005	0000 0101	
Ctrl-F	6	06	006	0000 0110	
Ctrl-G	7	07	007	0000 0111	(beep)
Ctrl-H	8	08	010	0000 1000	(backspace)
Ctrl-I	9	09	011	0000 1001	(tab)
Ctrl-J	10	0A	012	0000 1010	(newline)
Ctrl-K	11	0B	013	0000 1011	
Ctrl-L	12	0C	014	0000 1100	
Ctrl-M	13	0D	015	0000 1101	(return)
Ctrl-N	14	0E	016	0000 1110	
Ctrl-O	15	0F	017	0000 1111	
Ctrl-P	16	10	020	0001 0000	
Ctrl-Q	17	11	021	0001 0001	
Ctrl-R	18	12	022	0001 0010	
Ctrl-S	19	13	023	0001 0011	
Ctrl-T	20	14	024	0001 0100	
Ctrl-U	21	15	025	0001 0101	
Ctrl-V	22	16	026	0001 0110	
Ctrl-W	23	17	027	0001 0111	
Ctrl-X	24	18	030	0001 1000	
Ctrl-Y	25	19	031	0001 1001	
Ctrl-Z	26	1A	032	0001 1010	
Ctrl-[	27	1B	033	0001 1011	(escape)
Ctrl-\	28	1C	034	0001 1100	
Ctrl-]	29	1D	035	0001 1101	
Ctrl-^	30	1E	036	0001 1110	
Ctrl-_	31	1F	037	0001 1111	

Character	Decimal	Hex	Octal	Binary	
(space)	32	20	040	0010 0000	
!	33	21	041	0010 0001	(exclamation mark)
"	34	22	042	0010 0010	(double quote)
#	35	23	043	0010 0011	(number sign)
$	36	24	044	0010 0100	(dollar sign)
%	37	25	045	0010 0101	(percent)
&	38	26	046	0010 0110	(ampersand)
'	39	27	047	0010 0111	(single quote)
(	40	28	050	0010 1000	(left parenthesis)
)	41	29	051	0010 1001	(right parenthesis)
*	42	2A	052	0010 1010	(asterisk)
+	43	2B	053	0010 1011	(plus)
,	44	2C	054	0010 1100	(comma)
−	45	2D	055	0010 1101	(minus/hyphen)
.	46	2E	056	0010 1110	(period)
/	47	2F	057	0010 1111	(slash)
0	48	30	060	0011 0000	
1	49	31	061	0011 0001	
2	50	32	062	0011 0010	
3	51	33	063	0011 0011	
4	52	34	064	0011 0100	
5	53	35	065	0011 0101	
6	54	36	066	0011 0110	
7	55	37	067	0011 0111	
8	56	38	070	0011 1000	
9	57	39	071	0011 1001	
:	58	3A	072	0011 1010	(colon)
;	59	3B	073	0011 1011	(semicolon)
<	60	3C	074	0011 1100	(less than)
=	61	3D	075	0011 1101	(equals)
>	62	3E	076	0011 1110	(greater than)
?	63	3F	077	0011 1111	(question mark)

Character	Decimal	Hex	Octal	Binary	
@	64	40	100	0100 0000	(at sign)
A	65	41	101	0100 0001	
B	66	42	102	0100 0010	
C	67	43	103	0100 0011	
D	68	44	104	0100 0100	
E	69	45	105	0100 0101	
F	70	46	106	0100 0110	
G	71	47	107	0100 0111	
H	72	48	110	0100 1000	
I	73	49	111	0100 1001	
J	74	4A	112	0100 1010	
K	75	4B	113	0100 1011	
L	76	4C	114	0100 1100	
M	77	4D	115	0100 1101	
N	78	4E	116	0100 1110	
O	79	4F	117	0100 1111	
P	80	50	120	0101 0000	
Q	81	51	121	0101 0001	
R	82	52	122	0101 0010	
S	83	53	123	0101 0011	
T	84	54	124	0101 0100	
U	85	55	125	0101 0101	
V	86	56	126	0101 0110	
W	87	57	127	0101 0111	
X	88	58	130	0101 1000	
Y	89	59	131	0101 1001	
Z	90	5A	132	0101 1010	
[	91	5B	133	0101 1011	(left square bracket)
\	92	5C	134	0101 1100	(backslash)
]	93	5D	135	0101 1101	(right square bracket)
^	94	5E	136	0101 1110	(circumflex)
_	95	5F	137	0101 1111	(underscore)

Character	Decimal	Hex	Octal	Binary	
`	96	60	140	0110 0000	(back quote)
a	97	61	141	0110 0001	
b	98	62	142	0110 0010	
c	99	63	143	0110 0011	
d	100	64	144	0110 0100	
e	101	65	145	0110 0101	
f	102	66	146	0110 0110	
g	103	67	147	0110 0111	
h	104	68	150	0110 1000	
i	105	69	151	0110 1001	
j	106	6A	152	0110 1010	
k	107	6B	153	0110 1011	
l	108	6C	154	0110 1100	
m	109	6D	155	0110 1101	
n	110	6E	156	0110 1110	
o	111	6F	157	0110 1111	
p	112	70	160	0111 0000	
q	113	71	161	0111 0001	
r	114	72	162	0111 0010	
s	115	73	163	0111 0011	
t	116	74	164	0111 0100	
u	117	75	165	0111 0101	
v	118	76	166	0111 0110	
w	119	77	167	0111 0111	
x	120	78	170	0111 1000	
y	121	79	171	0111 1001	
z	122	7A	172	0111 1010	
{	123	7B	173	0111 1011	(left brace bracket)
|	124	7C	174	0111 1100	(vertical bar)
}	125	7D	175	0111 1101	(right brace bracket)
~	126	7E	176	0111 1110	(tilde)
	127	7F	177	0111 1111	

List of Internet Top-Level Domains

This appendix shows the top-level domains that were current at the time we wrote the book. As new countries connect to the Internet, new domains will be created using the standard international country codes.

The only country that does not use the standard two-letter code is Great Britain. They use **uk** rather than **gb**. (Of course, they also speak English with an accent.)

Old-Style Top-Level Domains

Domain	Meaning
com	commercial organization
edu	educational institution
gov	government
int	international organization
mil	military
net	networking organization
org	non-commercial organization

International Top-Level Domains

Domain	Meaning
aq	Antartica
ar	Argentina
at	Austria
au	Australia
be	Belgium
br	Brazil
ca	Canada
ch	Switzerland ("Cantons of Helvetia")
cl	Chile
de	Germany ("Deutschland")
dk	Denmark
ec	Ecuador
ee	Estonia
es	Spain ("España")
fi	Finland
fr	France
gr	Greece
hk	Hong Kong
hu	Hungary
ie	Ireland
il	Israel
in	India
is	Iceland
it	Italy
jp	Japan
kr	Korea (South)
mx	Mexico
nl	Netherlands
no	Norway
nz	New Zealand
pl	Poland
pt	Portugal
re	Reunion (French)
se	Sweden
sg	Singapore
su	Soviet Union

Domain	Meaning
th	Thailand
tn	Tunisia
tw	Taiwan
uk	United Kingdom (England, Scotland, Wales, N. Ireland)
us	United States
yu	Yugoslavia
za	South Africa

List of Usenet Newsgroups

This appendix contains a listing of all the nonlocal Usenet newgroups as of November 1992. They are divided in three categories: mainstream, alternative and Clarinet.

New groups are constantly being created and removed. However, most of the newsgroups, at least in the mainstream hierarchies, will not change. The alternative hierarchies are always adding new groups, and any master list will always be incomplete.

The master list of current newsgroups is posted regularly to **news.lists**. For a discussion of how to create a **.newsrc** file that contains all the newgroups carried by your news server, see Chapter 24.

Mainstream Hierarchies

`comp.admin.policy`	Discussions of site administration policies
`comp.ai`	Artificial intelligence discussions
`comp.ai.neural-nets`	All aspects of neural networks
`comp.ai.nlang-know-rep`	Natural language/knowledge representation (moderated)
`comp.ai.philosophy`	Philosophical aspects of artificial intelligence
`comp.ai.shells`	Artificial intelligence applied to shells
`comp.apps.spreadsheets`	Spreadsheets on various platforms
`comp.arch`	Computer architecture
`comp.arch.storage`	Storage system issues, both hardware and software
`comp.archives`	Descriptions of public access archives (moderated)
`comp.archives.admin`	Issues relating to computer archive administration
`comp.bbs.misc`	All aspects of computer bulletin board systems
`comp.bbs.waffle`	The Waffle BBS and Usenet system on all platforms
`comp.benchmarks`	Discussion of benchmarking techniques and results
`comp.binaries.acorn`	Binary-only postings for Acorn machines (moderated)
`comp.binaries.amiga`	Encoded public domain programs in binary (moderated)
`comp.binaries.apple2`	Binary-only postings for the Apple II computer
`comp.binaries.atari.st`	Binary-only postings for the Atari ST (moderated)
`comp.binaries.ibm.pc`	Binary-only postings for IBM PC/MS-DOS (moderated)
`comp.binaries.ibm.pc.archives`	Announcements related to IBM PC archive sites
`comp.binaries.ibm.pc.d`	Discussions about IBM/PC binary postings
`comp.binaries.ibm.pc.wanted`	Requests for IBM PC and compatible programs
`comp.binaries.mac`	Encoded Macintosh programs in binary (moderated)
`comp.binaries.os2`	Binaries for use under the OS/2 ABI (moderated)
`comp.bugs.2bsd`	Reports of Unix version 2BSD related bugs
`comp.bugs.4bsd`	Reports of Unix version 4BSD related bugs
`comp.bugs.4bsd.ucb-fixes`	Bug reports/fixes for BSD Unix (moderated)
`comp.bugs.misc`	General Unix bug reports and fixes (incl. V7, uucp)
`comp.bugs.sys5`	Reports of USG (System III, V, etc.) bugs
`comp.cad.cadence`	Users of Cadence Design Systems products
`comp.client-server`	Topics relating to client/server technology
`comp.cog-eng`	Cognitive engineering
`comp.compilers`	Compiler construction, theory, etc. (moderated)
`comp.compression`	Data compression algorithms and theory
`comp.compression.research`	Discussions about data compression research
`comp.databases`	Database and data management issues and theory
`comp.databases.informix`	Informix database management software discussions
`comp.databases.ingres`	Issues relating to INGRES products
`comp.databases.oracle`	The SQL database products of the Oracle Corporation
`comp.databases.sybase`	Implementations of the SQL Server
`comp.databases.theory`	Discussing advances in database technology
`comp.dcom.cell-relay`	Forum for discussion of Cell Relay-based products
`comp.dcom.fax`	Fax hardware, software and protocols
`comp.dcom.isdn`	The Integrated Services Digital Network (ISDN)
`comp.dcom.lans.ethernet`	Discussions of the Ethernet/IEEE 802.3 protocols
`comp.dcom.lans.fddi`	Discussions of the FDDI protocol suite
`comp.dcom.lans.misc`	Local area network hardware and software
`comp.dcom.modems`	Data communications hardware and software

`comp.dcom.servers`	Selecting and operating data communications servers
`comp.dcom.sys.cisco`	Info on Cisco routers and bridges
`comp.dcom.telecom`	Telecommunications digest (moderated)
`comp.doc`	Archived public-domain documentation (moderated)
`comp.doc.techreports`	Lists of technical reports (moderated)
`comp.dsp`	Digital Signal Processing using computers
`comp.edu`	Computer science education
`comp.emacs`	EMACS editors of different flavors
`comp.fonts`	Typefonts – design, conversion, use, etc.
`comp.graphics`	Computer graphics, art, animation, image processing
`comp.graphics.animation`	Technical aspects of computer animation
`comp.graphics.avs`	The Application Visualization System
`comp.graphics.explorer`	The Explorer Modular Visualization Environment (MVE)
`comp.graphics.gnuplot`	The GNUPLOT interactive function plotter
`comp.graphics.opengl`	The OpenGL 3D application programming interface
`comp.graphics.research`	Technical computer graphics discussion (moderated)
`comp.graphics.visualization`	Info on scientific visualization
`comp.groupware`	Software/hardware for shared interactive environments
`comp.human-factors`	Issues related to human-computer interaction (HCI)
`comp.infosystems`	Any discussion about information systems
`comp.infosystems.gis`	All aspects of Geographic Information Systems
`comp.infosystems.gopher`	Discussion of the gopher information service
`comp.infosystems.wais`	The Z39.50-based WAIS full-text search system
`comp.internet.library`	Discussing electronic libraries (moderated)
`comp.ivideodisc`	Interactive videodiscs – uses, potential, etc.
`comp.lang.ada`	Discussion about Ada
`comp.lang.apl`	Discussion about APL
`comp.lang.c`	Discussion about C
`comp.lang.c++`	The object-oriented C++ language
`comp.lang.clos`	Common Lisp Object System discussions
`comp.lang.eiffel`	The object-oriented Eiffel language
`comp.lang.forth`	Discussion about Forth
`comp.lang.fortran`	Discussion about FORTRAN
`comp.lang.functional`	Discussion about functional languages
`comp.lang.hermes`	The Hermes language for distributed applications
`comp.lang.idl-pvwave`	IDL and PV-Wave language discussions
`comp.lang.lisp`	Discussion about LISP
`comp.lang.lisp.mcl`	Discussing Apple's Macintosh Common Lisp
`comp.lang.logo`	The Logo teaching and learning language
`comp.lang.misc`	Different computer languages not specifically listed
`comp.lang.modula2`	Discussion about Modula-2
`comp.lang.modula3`	Discussion about the Modula-3 language
`comp.lang.objective-c`	The Objective-C language and environment
`comp.lang.pascal`	Discussion about Pascal
`comp.lang.perl`	Discussion of Larry Wall's Perl system
`comp.lang.postscript`	The PostScript Page Description Language
`comp.lang.prolog`	Discussion about PROLOG
`comp.lang.scheme`	The Scheme Programming language
`comp.lang.sigplan`	Info from ACM SIGPLAN (moderated)
`comp.lang.smalltalk`	Discussion about Smalltalk 80

`comp.lang.tcl`	The Tcl programming language and related tools
`comp.lang.verilog`	Discussing Verilog and PLI
`comp.lang.vhdl`	VHSIC Hardware Description Language, IEEE 1076/87
`comp.laser-printers`	Laser printers, hardware and software (moderated)
`comp.lsi`	Large scale integrated circuits
`comp.lsi.testing`	Testing of electronic circuits
`comp.mail.elm`	Discussion and fixes for ELM mail system
`comp.mail.headers`	Gatewayed from the Internet header-people list
`comp.mail.maps`	Various maps, including UUCP maps (moderated)
`comp.mail.mh`	The UCI version of the Rand Message Handling system
`comp.mail.misc`	General discussions about computer mail
`comp.mail.mush`	The Mail User's Shell (MUSH)
`comp.mail.sendmail`	Configuring and using the BSD sendmail agent
`comp.mail.uucp`	Mail in the UUCP network environment
`comp.misc`	General topics about computers not covered elsewhere
`comp.multimedia`	Interactive multimedia technologies of all kinds
`comp.newprod`	Announcements of new products of interest (moderated)
`comp.object`	Object-oriented programming and languages
`comp.org.acm`	Topics about the Association for Computing Machinery
`comp.org.decus`	Digital Equipment Computer Users' Society newsgroup
`comp.org.eff.news`	News from Electronic Frontiers Foundation (moderated)
`comp.org.eff.talk`	Discussion of EFF goals, strategies, etc.
`comp.org.fidonet`	FidoNews digest, news of FidoNet Assoc (moderated)
`comp.org.ieee`	Issues and announcements about the IEEE
`comp.org.issnnet`	The International Student Society for Neural Networks
`comp.org.sug`	Talk about/for the Sun User's Group
`comp.org.usenix`	USENIX Association events and announcements
`comp.org.usenix.roomshare`	Finding lodging during USENIX conferences
`comp.os.coherent`	Discussion and support of the Coherent operating system
`comp.os.cpm`	Discussion about the CP/M operating system
`comp.os.linux`	The free Unix clone for the 386/486, LINUX
`comp.os.mach`	The MACH OS from CMU and other places
`comp.os.minix`	Discussion of Tanenbaum's MINIX system
`comp.os.misc`	General OS-oriented discussion not carried elsewhere
`comp.os.ms-windows.advocacy`	Speculation and debate about Microsoft Windows
`comp.os.ms-windows.announce`	Announcements relating to Windows (moderated)
`comp.os.ms-windows.apps`	Applications in the Windows environment
`comp.os.ms-windows.misc`	General discussions about Windows issues
`comp.os.ms-windows.programmer.misc`	Programming Microsoft Windows
`comp.os.ms-windows.programmer.tools`	Development tools in Windows
`comp.os.ms-windows.programmer.win32`	32-bit Windows programming interfaces
`comp.os.ms-windows.setup`	Installing and configuring Microsoft Windows
`comp.os.msdos.apps`	Discussion of applications that run under MS-DOS
`comp.os.msdos.desqview`	QuarterDeck's Desqview and related products
`comp.os.msdos.misc`	Miscellaneous topics about MS-DOS machines
`comp.os.msdos.pcgeos`	GeoWorks PC/GEOS and PC/GEOS-based packages
`comp.os.msdos.programmer`	Programming MS-DOS machines
`comp.os.os2.advocacy`	Supporting and flaming OS/2
`comp.os.os2.apps`	Discussions of applications under OS/2
`comp.os.os2.misc`	Miscellaneous topics about the OS/2 system

`comp.os.os2.networking`	Networking in OS/2 environments
`comp.os.os2.programmer`	Programming OS/2 machines
`comp.os.os9`	Discussions about the OS/9 operating system
`comp.os.research`	Operating systems and related areas (moderated)
`comp.os.vms`	DEC's VAX line of computers and VMS
`comp.os.vxworks`	The VxWorks real-time operating system
`comp.os.xinu`	The XINU operating system from Purdue (D. Comer)
`comp.parallel`	Massively parallel hardware/software (moderated)
`comp.patents`	Discussing patents of computer technology (moderated)
`comp.periphs`	Peripheral devices
`comp.periphs.scsi`	Discussion of SCSI-based peripheral devices
`comp.programming`	Programming issues that transcend languages and OSs
`comp.protocols.appletalk`	Applebus hardware and software
`comp.protocols.ibm`	Networking with IBM mainframes
`comp.protocols.iso`	The ISO protocol stack
`comp.protocols.kerberos`	The Kerberos authentication server
`comp.protocols.kermit`	Info about the Kermit package (moderated)
`comp.protocols.misc`	Various forms and types of FTP protocol
`comp.protocols.nfs`	Discussion about the Network File System protocol
`comp.protocols.ppp`	Discussion of the Internet Point to Point Protocol
`comp.protocols.tcp-ip`	TCP and IP network protocols
`comp.protocols.tcp-ip.ibmpc`	TCP/IP for IBM(-like) personal computers
`comp.realtime`	Issues related to real-time computing
`comp.research.japan`	The nature of research in Japan (moderated)
`comp.risks`	Risks to the public from computers and users (moderated)
`comp.robotics`	All aspects of robots and their applications
`comp.security.misc`	Security issues of computers and networks
`comp.simulation`	Simulation methods, problems, uses (moderated)
`comp.society`	The impact of technology on society (moderated)
`comp.society.cu-digest`	The Computer Underground Digest (moderated)
`comp.society.development`	Computer technology in developing countries
`comp.society.folklore`	Computer folklore and culture, past and present (moderated)
`comp.society.futures`	Events in technology affecting future computing
`comp.society.privacy`	Effects of technology on privacy (moderated)
`comp.soft-sys.khoros`	The Khoros X11 visualization system
`comp.software-eng`	Software engineering and related topics
`comp.software.licensing`	Software licensing technology
`comp.sources.3b1`	Source code-only postings for the AT&T 3b1 (moderated)
`comp.sources.acorn`	Source code-only postings for the Acorn (moderated)
`comp.sources.amiga`	Source code-only postings for the Amiga (moderated)
`comp.sources.apple2`	Source code and discussion for the Apple2 (moderated)
`comp.sources.atari.st`	Source code-only postings for the Atari ST (moderated)
`comp.sources.bugs`	Bug reports, fixes, discussion for posted sources
`comp.sources.d`	For any discussion of source postings
`comp.sources.games`	Postings of recreational software (moderated)
`comp.sources.games.bugs`	Bug reports and fixes for posted game software
`comp.sources.hp48`	Programs for the HP48, HP28 calculators (moderated)
`comp.sources.mac`	Software for the Apple Macintosh (moderated)
`comp.sources.misc`	Posting of software (moderated)
`comp.sources.reviewed`	Source code evaluated by peer review (moderated)

`comp.sources.sun`	Software for Sun workstations (moderated)
`comp.sources.testers`	Finding people to test software
`comp.sources.unix`	Postings of complete, Unix-oriented sources (moderated)
`comp.sources.wanted`	Requests for software and fixes
`comp.sources.x`	Software for the X Window system (moderated)
`comp.specification`	Languages and methodologies for formal specification
`comp.specification.z`	Discussion about the formal specification notation Z
`comp.speech`	Research and applications in speech science and technology
`comp.std.c`	Discussion about C language standards
`comp.std.c++`	Discussion about C++ language, library, standards
`comp.std.internat`	Discussion about international standards
`comp.std.misc`	Discussion about various standards
`comp.std.mumps`	Discussion for X11.1 committee on Mumps (moderated)
`comp.std.unix`	Discussion for P1003 committee on Unix (moderated)
`comp.sw.components`	Software components and related technology
`comp.sys.3b1`	Discussion and support of AT&T 7300/3B1/UnixPC
`comp.sys.acorn`	Discussion on Acorn and ARM-based computers
`comp.sys.acorn.advocacy`	Why Acorn computers and programs are better
`comp.sys.acorn.announce`	Announcements for Acorn and ARM users (moderated)
`comp.sys.acorn.tech`	Software/hardware aspects of Acorn and ARM products
`comp.sys.alliant`	Info and discussion about Alliant computers
`comp.sys.amiga.advocacy`	Why an Amiga is better than XYZ
`comp.sys.amiga.announce`	Announcements about the Amiga (moderated)
`comp.sys.amiga.applications`	Miscellaneous Amiga applications
`comp.sys.amiga.audio`	Music, MIDI, speech synthesis, other sounds
`comp.sys.amiga.datacomm`	Methods of getting bytes in and out
`comp.sys.amiga.emulations`	Various hardware and software emulators
`comp.sys.amiga.games`	Discussion of games for the Amiga
`comp.sys.amiga.graphics`	Charts, graphs, pictures, etc.
`comp.sys.amiga.hardware`	Amiga computer hardware, Q&A, reviews, etc.
`comp.sys.amiga.introduction`	Group for newcomers to Amigas
`comp.sys.amiga.marketplace`	Where to find Amigas, prices, etc.
`comp.sys.amiga.misc`	Discussions not falling in another Amiga group
`comp.sys.amiga.multimedia`	Animations, video and multimedia
`comp.sys.amiga.programmer`	Developers and hobbyists discuss code
`comp.sys.amiga.reviews`	Reviews of Amiga software, hardware (moderated)
`comp.sys.apollo`	Apollo computer systems
`comp.sys.apple2`	Discussion about Apple II micros
`comp.sys.apple2.gno`	The AppleIIgs GNO multitasking environment
`comp.sys.atari.8bit`	Discussion about 8 bit Atari micros
`comp.sys.atari.st`	Discussion about 16 bit Atari micros
`comp.sys.atari.st.tech`	Technical discussions of Atari ST hard/software
`comp.sys.att`	Discussions about AT&T microcomputers
`comp.sys.cbm`	Discussion about Commodore micros
`comp.sys.concurrent`	Concurrent/Masscomp line of computers (moderated)
`comp.sys.dec`	Discussions about DEC computer systems
`comp.sys.dec.micro`	DEC Micros (Rainbow, Professional 350/380)
`comp.sys.encore`	Encore's MultiMax computers
`comp.sys.hp`	Discussion about Hewlett-Packard equipment
`comp.sys.hp48`	Hewlett-Packard's HP48 and HP28 calculators

`comp.sys.ibm.pc.digest`	The IBM PC, PC-XT and PC-AT (moderated)
`comp.sys.ibm.pc.games`	Games for IBM PCs and compatibles
`comp.sys.ibm.pc.hardware`	XT/AT/EISA hardware, any vendor
`comp.sys.ibm.pc.misc`	Discussion about IBM personal computers
`comp.sys.ibm.pc.rt`	Topics related to IBM's RT computer
`comp.sys.ibm.pc.soundcard`	Hardware and software aspects of PC sound cards
`comp.sys.ibm.ps2.hardware`	Microchannel hardware, any vendor
`comp.sys.intel`	Discussions about Intel systems and parts
`comp.sys.isis`	The ISIS distributed system from Cornell
`comp.sys.laptops`	Laptop (portable) computers
`comp.sys.m6809`	Discussion about 6809s
`comp.sys.m68k`	Discussion about 68k's
`comp.sys.m68k.pc`	Discussion about 68k-based PCs (moderated)
`comp.sys.m88k`	Discussion about 88k-based computers
`comp.sys.mac.advocacy`	The Macintosh computer family compared to others
`comp.sys.mac.announce`	Important notices for Macintosh users (moderated)
`comp.sys.mac.apps`	Discussions of Macintosh applications
`comp.sys.mac.comm`	Discussion of Macintosh communications
`comp.sys.mac.databases`	Database systems for the Apple Macintosh
`comp.sys.mac.digest`	Macintosh: info and uses, but no programs (moderated)
`comp.sys.mac.games`	Discussions of games on the Macintosh
`comp.sys.mac.hardware`	Macintosh hardware issues and discussions
`comp.sys.mac.hypercard`	The Macintosh Hypercard: info and uses
`comp.sys.mac.misc`	General discussions about the Apple Macintosh
`comp.sys.mac.programmer`	Discussion by people programming the Apple Macintosh
`comp.sys.mac.system`	Discussions of Macintosh system software
`comp.sys.mac.wanted`	Postings of "I want XYZ for my Mac."
`comp.sys.mentor`	Mentor Graphics products and Silicon Compiler System
`comp.sys.mips`	Systems based on MIPS chips
`comp.sys.misc`	Discussion about computers of all kinds
`comp.sys.ncr`	Discussion about NCR computers
`comp.sys.next.advocacy`	The NeXT religion
`comp.sys.next.announce`	Announcements related to NeXT (moderated)
`comp.sys.next.hardware`	Discussing the physical aspects of NeXT computers
`comp.sys.next.marketplace`	NeXT hardware, software and jobs
`comp.sys.next.misc`	General discussion about the NeXT computer system
`comp.sys.next.programmer`	NeXT related programming issues
`comp.sys.next.software`	Function, use and availability of NeXT programs
`comp.sys.next.sysadmin`	Discussions related to NeXT system administration
`comp.sys.novell`	Discussion of Novell Netware products
`comp.sys.nsc.32k`	National Semiconductor 32000 series chips
`comp.sys.palmtops`	Super-powered calculators in the palm of your hand
`comp.sys.pen`	Interacting with computers through pen gestures
`comp.sys.prime`	Prime Computer products
`comp.sys.proteon`	Proteon gateway products
`comp.sys.pyramid`	Pyramid 90x computers
`comp.sys.ridge`	Ridge 32 computers and ROS
`comp.sys.sequent`	Sequent systems (Balance and Symmetry)
`comp.sys.sgi`	Silicon Graphics's Iris workstations and software
`comp.sys.stratus`	Stratus products, incl. System/88, CPS-32, VOS and FTX

`comp.sys.sun.admin`	Sun system administration issues and questions
`comp.sys.sun.announce`	Sun announcements and Sunergy mailings (moderated)
`comp.sys.sun.apps`	Software applications for Sun computer systems
`comp.sys.sun.hardware`	Sun Microsystems hardware
`comp.sys.sun.misc`	Miscellaneous discussions about Sun products
`comp.sys.sun.wanted`	People looking for Sun products and support
`comp.sys.tahoe`	CCI 6/32, Harris HCX/7 and Sperry 7000 computers
`comp.sys.tandy`	Discussion about Tandy computers: new and old
`comp.sys.ti`	Discussion about Texas Instruments
`comp.sys.transputer`	The Transputer computer and OCCAM language
`comp.sys.unisys`	Sperry, Burroughs, Convergent and Unisys systems
`comp.sys.xerox`	Xerox 1100 workstations and protocols
`comp.sys.zenith.z100`	The Zenith Z-100 (Heath H-100) family of computers
`comp.terminals`	All sorts of terminals
`comp.text`	Text processing issues and methods
`comp.text.desktop`	Technology and techniques of desktop publishing
`comp.text.frame`	Desktop publishing with FrameMaker
`comp.text.interleaf`	Applications and use of Interleaf software
`comp.text.sgml`	ISO 8879 SGML, structured documents, markup lang.
`comp.text.tex`	Discussion about the TeX and LaTeX systems and macros
`comp.theory.info-retrieval`	Information retrieval topics (moderated)
`comp.unix.admin`	Administering a Unix-based system
`comp.unix.aix`	IBM's version of Unix
`comp.unix.amiga`	Minix, SYSV4 and other Unix on Amiga
`comp.unix.aux`	The version of Unix for Apple Macintosh II computers
`comp.unix.bsd`	Discussion of Berkeley Software Distribution Unix
`comp.unix.dos-under-unix`	MS-DOS running under Unix by whatever means
`comp.unix.internals`	Discussions on hacking Unix internals
`comp.unix.large`	Unix on mainframes and in large networks
`comp.unix.misc`	Various topics that don't fit other groups
`comp.unix.msdos`	MS-DOS running under Unix by whatever means
`comp.unix.osf.misc`	Various aspects of Open Software Foundation products
`comp.unix.osf.osf1`	The Open Software Foundation's OSF/1
`comp.unix.pc-clone.16bit`	Unix on 286 architectures
`comp.unix.pc-clone.32bit`	Unix on 386 and 486 architectures
`comp.unix.programmer`	Q&A for people programming under Unix
`comp.unix.questions`	Unix neophytes group
`comp.unix.shell`	Using and programming the Unix shell
`comp.unix.sys3`	System III Unix discussions
`comp.unix.sys5.misc`	Versions of System V which predate Release 3
`comp.unix.sys5.r3`	Discussing System V Release 3
`comp.unix.sys5.r4`	Discussing System V Release 4
`comp.unix.sysv286`	Unix System V (not Xenix) on the 286
`comp.unix.sysv386`	Versions of System V (not Xenix) on 386-based boxes
`comp.unix.ultrix`	Discussions about DEC's Ultrix
`comp.unix.wizards`	Questions for only true Unix wizards
`comp.unix.xenix.misc`	General discussions regarding Xenix (except SCO)
`comp.unix.xenix.sco`	Xenix versions from the Santa Cruz Operation
`comp.virus`	Computer viruses and security (moderated)
`comp.windows.garnet`	The Garnet user interface development environment

`comp.windows.interviews`	The InterViews object-oriented windowing system
`comp.windows.misc`	Various issues about windowing systems
`comp.windows.news`	Sun Microsystems' NeWS window system
`comp.windows.open-look`	Discussion about the Open Look GUI
`comp.windows.x`	Discussion about the X Window System
`comp.windows.x.apps`	Getting and using, not programming, applications for X
`comp.windows.x.intrinsics`	Discussion of the X toolkit
`comp.windows.x.pex`	The PHIGS extension of the X Window System
`misc.activism.progressive`	Information for progressive activists (moderated)
`misc.books.technical`	Discussion of books about technical topics
`misc.consumers`	Consumer interests, product reviews, etc.
`misc.consumers.house`	Discussion about owning and maintaining a house
`misc.education`	Discussion of the educational system
`misc.emerg-services`	Forum for paramedics and other first responders
`misc.entrepreneurs`	Discussion on operating a business
`misc.fitness`	Physical fitness, exercise, etc.
`misc.forsale`	Short, tasteful postings about items for sale
`misc.forsale.computers`	Computers and computer equipment for sale
`misc.forsale.computers.d`	Discussion of misc.forsale.computers
`misc.forsale.computers.mac`	Apple Macintosh related computer items
`misc.forsale.computers.other`	Selling miscellaneous computer stuff
`misc.forsale.computers.pc-clone`	IBM-PC related computer items
`misc.forsale.computers.workstation`	Workstation related computer items
`misc.handicap`	Items of interest for/about the handicapped (moderated)
`misc.headlines`	Current interest: drug testing, terrorism, etc.
`misc.int-property`	Discussion of intellectual property rights
`misc.invest`	Investments and the handling of money
`misc.invest.real-estate`	Property investments
`misc.jobs.contract`	Discussions about contract labor
`misc.jobs.misc`	Discussion about employment, workplaces, careers
`misc.jobs.offered`	Announcements of positions available
`misc.jobs.offered.entry`	Job listings only for entry-level positions
`misc.jobs.resumes`	Postings of resumes and "situation wanted" articles
`misc.kids`	Children, their behavior and activities
`misc.legal`	Legalities and the ethics of law
`misc.legal.computing`	Discussing the legal climate of the computing world
`misc.misc`	Various discussions not fitting in any other group
`misc.news.southasia`	News from Bangladesh, India, Nepal, etc. (moderated)
`misc.rural`	Devoted to issues concerning rural living
`misc.taxes`	Tax laws and advice
`misc.test`	For testing of network software. Very boring
`misc.wanted`	Requests for things that are needed (NOT software)
`misc.writing`	Discussion of writing in all of its forms
`news.admin`	Comments directed to news administrators
`news.admin.misc`	General topics of network news administration
`news.admin.policy`	Policy issues of USENET
`news.admin.technical`	Tech aspects of maintaining network news (moderated)
`news.announce.conferences`	Calls for papers/conference announcements (moderated)
`news.announce.important`	General announcements of interest to all (moderated)

`news.announce.newgroups`	Announcements for new groups (moderated)
`news.announce.newusers`	Explanatory postings for new users (moderated)
`news.answers`	Repository for periodic Usenet articles (moderated)
`news.config`	Postings of system down times and interruptions
`news.future`	The future technology of network news systems
`news.groups`	Discussions and lists of newsgroups
`news.lists`	News-related statistics and lists (moderated)
`news.lists.ps-maps`	Maps relating to Usenet traffic flows (moderated)
`news.misc`	Discussions of Usenet itself
`news.newsites`	Postings of new site announcements
`news.newusers.questions`	Q and A for users new to the Usenet
`news.software.anu-news`	VMS B-news software from Australian National Univ.
`news.software.b`	Discussion about B-news-compatible software
`news.software.nn`	Discussion about the **nn** news reader package
`news.software.notes`	Notesfile software from the Univ. of Illinois
`news.software.readers`	Discussion of software used to read network news
`news.sysadmin`	Comments directed to system administrators
`rec.antiques`	Discussing antiques and vintage items
`rec.aquaria`	Keeping fish and aquaria as a hobby
`rec.arts.animation`	Discussion of various kinds of animation
`rec.arts.anime`	Japanese animation fan discussion
`rec.arts.bodyart`	Tattoos and body decoration discussion
`rec.arts.books`	Books of all genres and the publishing industry
`rec.arts.cinema`	Discussion of the art of cinema (moderated)
`rec.arts.comics.info`	Reviews, conventions and comics news (moderated)
`rec.arts.comics.marketplace`	The exchange of comics and comic related items
`rec.arts.comics.misc`	Comic books, graphic novels, sequential art
`rec.arts.comics.strips`	Discussion of short-form comics
`rec.arts.comics.xbooks`	The Mutant Universe of Marvel Comics
`rec.arts.dance`	Any aspects of dance not covered in another newsgroup
`rec.arts.disney`	Discussion of any Disney-related subjects
`rec.arts.drwho`	Discussion about Dr. Who
`rec.arts.erotica`	Erotic fiction and verse (moderated)
`rec.arts.fine`	Fine arts and artists
`rec.arts.int-fiction`	Discussions about interactive fiction
`rec.arts.manga`	All aspects of the Japanese storytelling art form
`rec.arts.misc`	Discussions about the arts not in other groups
`rec.arts.movies`	Discussions of movies and movie making
`rec.arts.movies.reviews`	Reviews of movies (moderated)
`rec.arts.poems`	For the posting of poems
`rec.arts.sf.announce`	Major announcements of the SciFi world (moderated)
`rec.arts.sf.fandom`	Discussions of SciFi fan activities
`rec.arts.sf.marketplace`	Personal for sale notices of SciFi materials
`rec.arts.sf.misc`	Science fiction lovers' newsgroup
`rec.arts.sf.movies`	Discussing SciFi motion pictures
`rec.arts.sf.reviews`	Reviews of science fiction/fantasy/horror (moderated)
`rec.arts.sf.science`	Real and speculative aspects of SciFi science
`rec.arts.sf.starwars`	Discussion of the Star Wars universe
`rec.arts.sf.tv`	Discussing general television SciFi

`rec.arts.sf.written`	Discussion of written science fiction and fantasy
`rec.arts.startrek.current`	New Star Trek shows, movies and books
`rec.arts.startrek.fandom`	Star Trek conventions and memorabilia
`rec.arts.startrek.info`	Information about the universe of Star Trek (moderated)
`rec.arts.startrek.misc`	General discussions of Star Trek
`rec.arts.startrek.tech`	Star Trek's depiction of future technologies
`rec.arts.theatre`	Discussion of all aspects of stage work and theatre
`rec.arts.tv`	The boob tube, its history and past and current shows
`rec.arts.tv.soaps`	Postings about soap operas
`rec.arts.tv.uk`	Discussions of telly shows from the UK
`rec.arts.wobegon`	"A Prairie Home Companion" radio show discussion
`rec.audio`	High fidelity audio
`rec.audio.car`	Discussions of automobile audio systems
`rec.audio.high-end`	High-end audio systems (moderated)
`rec.audio.pro`	Professional audio recording and studio engineering
`rec.autos`	Automobiles, automotive products and laws
`rec.autos.driving`	Driving automobiles
`rec.autos.sport`	Discussion of organized, legal auto competitions
`rec.autos.tech`	Technical aspects of automobiles, et al
`rec.autos.vw`	Issues pertaining to Volkswagen products
`rec.aviation.announce`	Events of interest to aviation community (moderated)
`rec.aviation.answers`	Frequently asked questions about aviation (moderated)
`rec.aviation.homebuilt`	Selecting, designing, building and restoring aircraft
`rec.aviation.ifr`	Flying under Instrument Flight Rules
`rec.aviation.military`	Military aircraft of the past, present and future
`rec.aviation.misc`	Miscellaneous topics in aviation
`rec.aviation.owning`	Information on owning airplanes
`rec.aviation.piloting`	General discussion for aviators
`rec.aviation.products`	Reviews and discussion of products useful to pilots
`rec.aviation.simulators`	Flight simulation on all levels
`rec.aviation.soaring`	All aspects of sailplanes and hang-gliders
`rec.aviation.stories`	Anecdotes of flight experiences (moderated)
`rec.aviation.student`	Learning to fly
`rec.backcountry`	Activities in the great outdoors
`rec.bicycles`	Bicycles, related products and laws
`rec.bicycles.marketplace`	Buying, selling and reviewing items for cycling
`rec.bicycles.misc`	General discussion of bicycling
`rec.bicycles.racing`	Bicycle racing techniques, rules and results
`rec.bicycles.rides`	Discussions of tours and training or commuting routes
`rec.bicycles.soc`	Societal issues of bicycling
`rec.bicycles.tech`	Cycling product design, construction, maintenance, etc.
`rec.birds`	Hobbyists interested in bird watching
`rec.boats`	Hobbyists interested in boating
`rec.boats.paddle`	Talk about any boats with oars, paddles, etc.
`rec.climbing`	Climbing techniques, competition announcements, etc.
`rec.collecting`	Discussion among collectors of many things
`rec.crafts.brewing`	The art of making beers and meads
`rec.crafts.misc`	Handiwork arts not covered elsewhere
`rec.crafts.textiles`	Sewing, weaving, knitting and other fiber arts
`rec.equestrian`	Discussion of things equestrian

`rec.folk-dancing`	Folk dances, dancers and dancing
`rec.food.cooking`	Food, cooking, cookbooks and recipes
`rec.food.drink`	Wines and spirits
`rec.food.historic`	The history of food-making arts
`rec.food.recipes`	Recipes for interesting food and drink (moderated)
`rec.food.restaurants`	Discussion of dining out
`rec.food.sourdough`	Making and baking with sourdough
`rec.food.veg`	Vegetarians
`rec.gambling`	Articles on games of chance and betting
`rec.games.backgammon`	Discussion of the game of backgammon
`rec.games.board`	Discussion and hints on board games
`rec.games.board.ce`	The Cosmic Encounter board game
`rec.games.bridge`	Hobbyists interested in bridge
`rec.games.chess`	Chess and computer chess
`rec.games.corewar`	The Core War computer challenge
`rec.games.cyber`	Discussions of cyberpunk related games (moderated)
`rec.games.design`	Discussion of game design related issues
`rec.games.empire`	Discussion and hints about Empire
`rec.games.frp.advocacy`	Flames and rebuttals about various role-playing systems
`rec.games.frp.announce`	Role-playing world announcements (moderated)
`rec.games.frp.archives`	Archivable fantasy stories and other projects (moderated)
`rec.games.frp.dnd`	Fantasy role-playing with TSR's Dungeons and Dragons
`rec.games.frp.marketplace`	Role-playing game materials wanted and for sale
`rec.games.frp.misc`	General discussions of role-playing games
`rec.games.go`	Discussion about Go
`rec.games.hack`	Discussion, hints, etc., about the Hack game
`rec.games.int-fiction`	All aspects of interactive fiction games
`rec.games.misc`	Games and computer games
`rec.games.moria`	Comments, hints and info about the Moria game
`rec.games.mud.admin`	Administrative issues of multiuser dungeons
`rec.games.mud.announce`	Announcements about multiuser dungeons (moderated)
`rec.games.mud.diku`	All about DikuMuds
`rec.games.mud.lp`	Discussions of the LPMUD computer role playing game
`rec.games.mud.misc`	Various aspects of multiuser computer games
`rec.games.mud.tiny`	Discussion about Tiny muds, like MUSH, MUSE, MOO
`rec.games.netrek`	Discussion of X window system game Netrek (XtrekII)
`rec.games.pbm`	Discussion about Play by Mail games
`rec.games.pinball`	Discussing pinball-related issues
`rec.games.programmer`	Discussion of adventure game programming
`rec.games.rogue`	Discussion and hints about Rogue
`rec.games.trivia`	Discussion about trivia
`rec.games.video`	Discussion about video games
`rec.games.video.arcade`	Discussions about coin-operated video games
`rec.games.xtank.play`	Strategy and tactics for the distributed game Xtank
`rec.games.xtank.programmer`	Coding the Xtank game and its robots
`rec.gardens`	Gardening, methods and results
`rec.guns`	Discussions about firearms (moderated)
`rec.heraldry`	Discussion of coats of arms
`rec.humor`	Jokes and the like. May be somewhat offensive
`rec.humor.d`	Discussions on the content of rec.humor articles

`rec.humor.funny`	Jokes the moderator thinks are funny (moderated)
`rec.humor.oracle`	Sagacious advice from the Usenet Oracle (moderated)
`rec.humor.oracle.d`	Comments about the Usenet Oracle's comments
`rec.hunting`	Discussions about hunting (moderated)
`rec.juggling`	Juggling techniques, equipment and events
`rec.kites`	Talk about kites and kiting
`rec.mag`	Magazine summaries, tables of contents, etc.
`rec.martial-arts`	Discussion of the various martial art forms
`rec.misc`	General topics about recreational/participant sports
`rec.models.railroad`	Model railroads of all scales
`rec.models.rc`	Radio-controlled models for hobbyists
`rec.models.rockets`	Model rockets for hobbyists
`rec.models.scale`	Construction of models
`rec.motorcycles`	Motorcycles and related products and laws
`rec.motorcycles.dirt`	Riding motorcycles and ATVs off-road
`rec.motorcycles.harley`	All aspects of Harley-Davidson motorcycles
`rec.motorcycles.racing`	Discussion of all aspects of racing motorcycles
`rec.music.afro-latin`	Music with African and Latin influences
`rec.music.beatles`	Postings about the Fab Four and their music
`rec.music.bluenote`	Discussion of jazz, blues and related types of music
`rec.music.cd`	CDs: availability and other discussions
`rec.music.christian`	Christian music, both contemporary and traditional
`rec.music.classical`	Discussion about classical music
`rec.music.compose`	Creating musical and lyrical works
`rec.music.country.western`	C&W music, performers, performances, etc.
`rec.music.dementia`	Discussion of comedy and novelty music
`rec.music.dylan`	Discussion of Bob's works and music
`rec.music.early`	Discussion of pre-classical European music
`rec.music.folk`	Folks discussing folk music of various sorts
`rec.music.funky`	Funk, rap, hip-hop, house, soul, R&B and related
`rec.music.gaffa`	Discussion of alternative music (moderated)
`rec.music.gdead`	A group for (Grateful) Deadheads
`rec.music.indian.classical`	Hindustani and Carnatic Indian classical music
`rec.music.indian.misc`	Discussing Indian music in general
`rec.music.industrial`	Discussion of all industrial-related music styles
`rec.music.info`	News/announcements on musical topics (moderated)
`rec.music.makers`	For performers and their discussions
`rec.music.marketplace`	Records, tapes and CDs: wanted, for sale, etc.
`rec.music.misc`	Music lovers' group
`rec.music.newage`	"New Age" music discussions
`rec.music.phish`	Discussing the musical group Phish
`rec.music.reviews`	Reviews of music of all genres (moderated)
`rec.music.synth`	Synthesizers and computer music
`rec.music.video`	Discussion of music videos and music video software
`rec.nude`	Hobbyists interested in naturist/nudist activities
`rec.org.mensa`	Talking with members of the high IQ society Mensa
`rec.org.sca`	Society for Creative Anachronism
`rec.outdoors.fishing`	All aspects of sport and commercial fishing
`rec.pets`	Pets, pet care and household animals in general
`rec.pets.birds`	The culture and care of indoor birds

`rec.pets.cats`	Discussion about domestic cats
`rec.pets.dogs`	Any and all subjects relating to dogs as pets
`rec.pets.herp`	Reptiles, amphibians and other exotic vivarium pets
`rec.photo`	Hobbyists interested in photography
`rec.puzzles`	Puzzles, problems and quizzes
`rec.puzzles.crosswords`	Making and playing gridded word puzzles
`rec.pyrotechnics`	Fireworks, rocketry, safety and other topics
`rec.radio.amateur.misc`	Amateur radio practices, contests, events, rules, etc.
`rec.radio.amateur.packet`	Discussion about packet radio setups
`rec.radio.amateur.policy`	Radio use and regulation policy
`rec.radio.broadcasting`	Local area broadcast radio (moderated)
`rec.radio.cb`	Citizen band radio
`rec.radio.noncomm`	Topics relating to noncommercial radio
`rec.radio.shortwave`	Shortwave radio enthusiasts
`rec.radio.swap`	Offers to trade and swap radio equipment
`rec.railroad`	Real and model train fans' newsgroup
`rec.roller-coaster`	Roller coasters and other amusement park rides
`rec.running`	Running for enjoyment, sport, exercise, etc.
`rec.scouting`	Scouting youth organizations worldwide
`rec.scuba`	Hobbyists interested in SCUBA diving
`rec.skate`	Ice skating and roller skating
`rec.skiing`	Hobbyists interested in snow skiing
`rec.skydiving`	Hobbyists interested in skydiving
`rec.sport.baseball`	Discussion about baseball
`rec.sport.baseball.college`	Baseball on the collegiate level
`rec.sport.baseball.fantasy`	Rotisserie (fantasy) baseball play
`rec.sport.basketball.college`	Hoops on the collegiate level
`rec.sport.basketball.misc`	Discussion about basketball
`rec.sport.basketball.pro`	Talk of professional basketball
`rec.sport.cricket`	Discussion about the sport of cricket
`rec.sport.cricket.scores`	Cricket scores from around the globe (moderated)
`rec.sport.disc`	Discussion of flying disc based sports
`rec.sport.football.australian`	Discussion of Australian (Rules) Football
`rec.sport.football.college`	American-style college football
`rec.sport.football.misc`	Discussion about American-style football
`rec.sport.football.pro`	American-style professional football
`rec.sport.golf`	Discussion about all aspects of golfing
`rec.sport.hockey`	Discussion about ice hockey
`rec.sport.hockey.field`	Discussion of the sport of field hockey
`rec.sport.misc`	Spectator sports
`rec.sport.olympics`	All aspects of the Olympic Games
`rec.sport.paintball`	Discussing all aspects of the survival game paintball
`rec.sport.pro-wrestling`	Discussion about professional wrestling
`rec.sport.rugby`	Discussion about the game of rugby
`rec.sport.soccer`	Discussion about soccer (Association Football)
`rec.sport.swimming`	Training for and competing in swimming events
`rec.sport.tennis`	Things related to the sport of tennis
`rec.sport.triathlon`	Discussing all aspects of multi-event sports
`rec.sport.volleyball`	Discussion about volleyball
`rec.travel`	Traveling all over the world

`rec.travel.air`	Airline travel around the world
`rec.video`	Video and video components
`rec.video.cable-tv`	Technical and regulatory issues of cable television
`rec.video.production`	Making professional quality video productions
`rec.video.releases`	Prerecorded video releases on laserdisc and videotape
`rec.video.satellite`	Getting shows via satellite
`rec.windsurfing`	Riding the waves as a hobby
`rec.woodworking`	Hobbyists interested in woodworking
`sci.aeronautics`	The science of aeronautics and related technology
`sci.anthropology`	All aspects of studying humankind
`sci.aquaria`	Only scientifically oriented postings about aquaria
`sci.archaeology`	Studying antiquities of the world
`sci.astro`	Astronomy discussions and information
`sci.astro.fits`	Issues related to the Flexible Image Transport System
`sci.astro.hubble`	Processing Hubble Space Telescope data (moderated)
`sci.bio`	Biology and related sciences
`sci.chem`	Chemistry and related sciences
`sci.classics`	Studying classical history, languages, art and more
`sci.cognitive`	Perception, memory, judgement and reasoning
`sci.comp-aided`	The use of computers as tools in scientific research
`sci.cryonics`	Theory and practice of biostasis, suspended animation
`sci.crypt`	Different methods of data en/decryption
`sci.econ`	The science of economics
`sci.edu`	The science of education
`sci.electronics`	Circuits, theory, electrons and discussions
`sci.energy`	Discussions about energy, science and technology
`sci.engr`	Technical discussions about engineering tasks
`sci.engr.biomed`	Discussing the field of biomedical engineering
`sci.engr.chem`	All aspects of chemical engineering
`sci.engr.civil`	Topics related to civil engineering
`sci.engr.control`	The engineering of control systems
`sci.engr.mech`	The field of mechanical engineering
`sci.environment`	Discussions about the environment and ecology
`sci.fractals`	Objects of non-integral dimension and other chaos
`sci.geo.fluids`	Discussion of geophysical fluid dynamics
`sci.geo.geology`	Discussion of solid earth sciences
`sci.geo.meteorology`	Discussion of meteorology and related topics
`sci.image.processing`	Scientific image processing and analysis
`sci.lang`	Natural languages, communication, etc.
`sci.lang.japan`	The Japanese language, both spoken and written
`sci.logic`	Logic: math, philosophy and computational aspects
`sci.materials`	All aspects of materials engineering
`sci.math`	Mathematical discussions and pursuits
`sci.math.research`	Discussion of current mathematical research (moderated)
`sci.math.stat`	Statistics discussion
`sci.math.symbolic`	Symbolic algebra discussion
`sci.med`	Medicine and its related products and regulations
`sci.med.aids`	All aspects of AIDS (moderated)
`sci.med.nutrition`	Physiological impacts of diet

`sci.med.occupational`	Preventing, detecting and treating occupational injuries
`sci.med.physics`	Issues of physics in medical testing/care
`sci.military`	Discussion about science and the military (moderated)
`sci.misc`	Short-lived discussions on subjects in the sciences
`sci.nanotech`	Self-reproducing molecular-scale machines (moderated)
`sci.optics`	Discussion relating to the science of optics
`sci.philosophy.tech`	Technical philosophy: math, science, logic, etc.
`sci.physics`	Physical laws, properties, etc.
`sci.physics.fusion`	Info on fusion, esp. "cold" fusion
`sci.psychology`	Topics related to psychology
`sci.psychology.digest`	Psycoloquy: Refereed Psychology Journal (moderated)
`sci.research`	Research methods, funding, ethics and whatever
`sci.research.careers`	Issues relevant to careers in scientific research
`sci.skeptic`	Skeptics discussing pseudo-science
`sci.space`	Space, space programs, space-related research, etc.
`sci.space.news`	Announcements of space-related news (moderated)
`sci.space.shuttle`	The space shuttle and the STS program
`sci.systems`	The theory and application of systems science
`sci.virtual-worlds`	Modelling the universe (moderated)
`soc.bi`	Discussions of bisexuality
`soc.college`	College, college activities, campus life, etc.
`soc.college.grad`	General issues related to graduate schools
`soc.college.gradinfo`	Information about graduate schools
`soc.couples`	Discussions for couples (cf. soc.singles)
`soc.culture.afghanistan`	Discussion of the Afghan society
`soc.culture.african`	Discussions about Africa and things African
`soc.culture.african.american`	Discussions about African-American issues
`soc.culture.arabic`	Technological and cultural issues, NOT politics
`soc.culture.asean`	Countries of the Assoc. of SE Asian Nations
`soc.culture.asian.american`	Issues and discussion about Asian-Americans
`soc.culture.australian`	Australian culture and society
`soc.culture.bangladesh`	Issues and discussion about Bangladesh
`soc.culture.bosna-herzgvna`	The independent state of Bosnia and Herzegovina
`soc.culture.brazil`	Talking about the people and country of Brazil
`soc.culture.british`	Issues about Britain and those of British descent
`soc.culture.bulgaria`	Discussing Bulgarian society
`soc.culture.canada`	Discussions of Canada and its people
`soc.culture.caribbean`	Life in the Caribbean
`soc.culture.celtic`	Irish, Scottish, Breton, Cornish, Manx and Welsh
`soc.culture.china`	About China and Chinese culture
`soc.culture.czecho-slovak`	Bohemian, Slovak, Moravian and Silesian life
`soc.culture.europe`	Discussing all aspects of all-European society
`soc.culture.filipino`	Group about the Filipino culture
`soc.culture.french`	French culture, history and related discussions
`soc.culture.german`	Discussions about German culture and history
`soc.culture.greek`	Group about Greeks
`soc.culture.hongkong`	Discussions pertaining to Hong Kong
`soc.culture.indian`	Group for discussion about India and things Indian
`soc.culture.indian.telugu`	The culture of the Telugu people of India

`soc.culture.iranian`	Discussions about Iran and things Iranian/Persian
`soc.culture.italian`	The Italian people and their culture
`soc.culture.japan`	Everything Japanese, except the Japanese language
`soc.culture.jewish`	Jewish culture and religion. (cf. talk.politics.mideast)
`soc.culture.korean`	Discussions about Korean and things Korean
`soc.culture.latin-america`	Topics about Latin America
`soc.culture.lebanon`	Discussion about things Lebanese
`soc.culture.magyar`	The Hungarian people and their culture
`soc.culture.mexican`	Discussion of Mexico's society
`soc.culture.misc`	Group for discussion about other cultures
`soc.culture.nepal`	Discussion of people and things in and from Nepal
`soc.culture.netherlands`	People from the Netherlands and Belgium
`soc.culture.new-zealand`	Discussion of topics related to New Zealand
`soc.culture.nordic`	Discussion about culture up north
`soc.culture.pakistan`	Topics of discussion about Pakistan
`soc.culture.polish`	Polish culture, Polish past and Polish politics
`soc.culture.portuguese`	Discussion of the people of Portugal
`soc.culture.romanian`	Discussion of Romanian and Moldavian people
`soc.culture.soviet`	Topics relating to Russian or Soviet culture
`soc.culture.spain`	Discussion of culture on the Iberian peninsula
`soc.culture.sri-lanka`	Things and people from Sri Lanka
`soc.culture.taiwan`	Discussion about things Taiwanese
`soc.culture.tamil`	Tamil language, history and culture
`soc.culture.thai`	Thai people and their culture
`soc.culture.turkish`	Discussion about things Turkish
`soc.culture.usa`	The culture of the United States of America
`soc.culture.vietnamese`	Issues and discussions of Vietnamese culture
`soc.culture.yugoslavia`	Discussions of Yugoslavia and its people
`soc.feminism`	Discussion of feminism and feminist issues (moderated)
`soc.history`	Discussions of things historical
`soc.libraries.talk`	Discussing all aspects of libraries
`soc.men`	Issues related to men, their problems and relationships
`soc.misc`	Socially oriented topics not in other groups
`soc.motss`	Issues pertaining to homosexuality
`soc.net-people`	Announcements, requests, etc., about people on the net
`soc.penpals`	In search of net.friendships
`soc.politics`	Political problems, systems, solutions (moderated)
`soc.politics.arms-d`	Arms discussion digest (moderated)
`soc.religion.bahai`	Discussion of the Baha'i Faith (moderated)
`soc.religion.christian`	Christianity and related topics (moderated)
`soc.religion.eastern`	Discussions of Eastern religions (moderated)
`soc.religion.islam`	Discussions of the Islamic faith (moderated)
`soc.rights.human`	Human rights and activism (e.g., Amnesty International)
`soc.roots`	Genealogical matters
`soc.singles`	Newsgroup for single people, their activities, etc.
`soc.veterans`	Social issues relating to military veterans
`soc.women`	Issues related to women, their problems and relationships
`talk.abortion`	All sorts of discussions and arguments on abortion
`talk.bizarre`	The unusual, bizarre, curious and often stupid

`talk.environment`	Discussion the state of the environment and what to do
`talk.origins`	Evolution versus creationism (sometimes hot!)
`talk.philosophy.misc`	Philosophical musings on all topics
`talk.politics.animals`	The use and/or abuse of animals
`talk.politics.china`	Discussion of political issues related to China
`talk.politics.drugs`	The politics of drug issues
`talk.politics.guns`	The politics of firearm ownership and (mis)use
`talk.politics.mideast`	Discussion and debate over Middle Eastern events
`talk.politics.misc`	Political discussions and ravings of all kinds
`talk.politics.soviet`	Discussion of Soviet politics, domestic and foreign
`talk.politics.space`	Non-technical issues affecting space exploration
`talk.politics.theory`	Theory of politics and political systems
`talk.rape`	Discussions on stopping rape; not to be crossposted
`talk.religion.misc`	Religious, ethical and moral implications
`talk.religion.newage`	Esoteric and minority religions and philosophies
`talk.rumors`	For the posting of rumors

Alternative Hierarchies

`alt.3d`	Three-dimensional imaging
`alt.activism`	Activities for activists
`alt.activism.d`	A place to discuss issues in alt.activism
`alt.aeffle.und.pferdle`	German TV cartoon characters
`alt.alien.visitors`	Space Aliens on Earth! Abduction! Gov't Coverup!
`alt.amateur-comp`	The Amateur Computerist
`alt.angst`	Anxiety in the modern world
`alt.appalachian`	Appalachian regional issues discussion
`alt.archery`	Robin Hood had the right idea
`alt.artcom`	Artistic Community, arts and communication
`alt.astrology`	Twinkle, twinkle, little planet
`alt.atheism`	Godless heathens
`alt.atheism.moderated`	Focused Godless heathens (moderated)
`alt.autos.antique`	Discussion of all facets of older automobiles
`alt.bacchus`	The non-profit "BACCHUS" organization
`alt.backrubs`	Discussion of all aspects of backrubs
`alt.bass`	For bass guitarists, not fish
`alt.bbs`	Computer BBS systems and software
`alt.bbs.ads`	Ads for various computer BBSs
`alt.bbs.allsysop`	Discussions for sysops
`alt.bbs.internet`	BBS systems accessible via the Internet
`alt.bbs.lists`	Postings of regional BBS listings
`alt.bbs.lists.d`	Discussion about regional BBS listings
`alt.bbs.uupcb`	Discussions about UUPC BBSs
`alt.beer`	Good for what ales ya
`alt.best.of.internet`	All the best stuff on the Internet
`alt.binaries.multimedia`	Sound, text and graphics data rolled in one
`alt.binaries.pictures.d`	Discussions about picture postings
`alt.binaries.pictures.erotica`	Erotic pictures (only)
`alt.binaries.pictures.erotica.d`	Discussing erotic pictures
`alt.binaries.pictures.erotica.female`	Female erotic pictures (only)
`alt.binaries.pictures.erotica.male`	Male erotic pictures (only)
`alt.binaries.pictures.fine-art.d`	Discussion about fine art pictures (moderated)
`alt.binaries.pictures.fine-art.digitized`	Fine art pictures (moderated)
`alt.binaries.pictures.fine-art.graphics`	Graphics pictures (moderated)
`alt.binaries.pictures.fractals`	Fractal pictures
`alt.binaries.pictures.misc`	Miscellaneous pictures
`alt.binaries.pictures.tasteless`	Tasteless pictures
`alt.binaries.sounds.d`	Discussion of digitized sounds
`alt.binaries.sounds.erotica`	Erotic digitized sounds
`alt.binaries.sounds.misc`	Miscellaneous digitized sounds
`alt.birthright`	Birthright Party propaganda
`alt.bonsai`	The art of bonsai
`alt.boomerang`	Technology and use of the boomerang
`alt.business.multi-level`	Multi-level marketing businesses
`alt.cad`	Computer Aided Design
`alt.cad.autocad`	CAD as practiced by customers of Autodesk
`alt.california`	Discussions about California

`alt.callahans`	Callahan's bar for puns and fellowship
`alt.cascade`	Art or litter, you decide
`alt.cd-rom`	Discussions of optical storage media
`alt.censorship`	Discussion about restricting speech/press
`alt.child-support`	Raising children in a split family
`alt.chinese.text`	Postings in Chinese; Chinese language software
`alt.co-ops`	Discussion about cooperatives
`alt.cobol`	Relationship between programming and stone axes
`alt.colorguard`	Marching bands, etc.
`alt.comedy.british`	British humour
`alt.comics.buffalo-roam`	A postscript comic strip
`alt.comics.lnh`	Interactive net.madness in the superhero genre
`alt.comics.superman`	No one knows it is also alt.clark.kent
`alt.comp.acad-freedom.news`	Academic freedom related to computers (moderated)
`alt.comp.acad-freedom.talk`	Academic freedom related to computers
`alt.conference-ctr`	Conference center management issues
`alt.config`	Alternative subnet discussions and connectivity
`alt.consciousness`	Discussions on consciousness
`alt.conspiracy`	Be paranoid: they're out to get you
`alt.conspiracy.jfk`	The Kennedy assassination
`alt.cosuard`	Council of Sysops and Users Against Rate Discrimination
`alt.cult-movies`	Movies with a cult following (e.g., Rocky Horror PS)
`alt.culture.kerala`	People of Keralite origin and the malayalam language
`alt.culture.tamil`	Discussion of Tamil culture, history, etc.
`alt.culture.tuva`	Topics related to the Republic of Tannu Tuva
`alt.culture.usenet`	All about the Usenet culture
`alt.cyb-sys`	Cybernetics and Systems
`alt.cyberpunk`	High-tech low-life
`alt.cyberpunk.chatsubo`	Literary virtual reality in a cyberpunk hangout
`alt.cyberpunk.movement`	Cybernizing the Universe
`alt.cyberpunk.tech`	Cyberspace and Cyberpunk technology
`alt.cyberspace`	Cyberspace and how it should work
`alt.cybertoon`	Cyberpunk epic
`alt.dads-rights`	Rights of fathers trying to win custody in court
`alt.dcom.telecom`	Discussion of telecommunications technology
`alt.desert-storm`	The war against Iraq in Kuwait
`alt.desert-storm.facts`	For factual information on the Gulf War
`alt.desert-thekurds`	What's happening to the Kurds in Iraq
`alt.discrimination`	Quotas, affirmative action, bigotry, persecution
`alt.divination`	Divination techniques (e.g., I Ching, Tarot, runes)
`alt.dreams`	What do they mean?
`alt.drugs`	Recreational pharmaceuticals and related flames
`alt.drumcorps`	Drum and bugle corps discussion
`alt.education.disabled`	Learning experiences for the disabled
`alt.education.distance`	Learning over nets, etc.
`alt.elvis.sighting`	Mysterious sightings of famous dead people
`alt.emusic`	Ethnic, exotic, electronic, elaborate, etc., music
`alt.ernie-pook`	Lynda Barry and the Ernie Pook Comeek
`alt.evil`	Tales from the dark side
`alt.fan.BIFF`	COWABUNGA, D00D!!! MY BRO SEZ HES AWSUM

`alt.fan.brother-jed`	The born-again minister touring American campuses
`alt.fan.bugtown`	For fans of the works of Matt Howarth
`alt.fan.dan-quayle`	For discussion of the US Vice President
`alt.fan.dave_barry`	Electronic fan club for humorist Dave Barry
`alt.fan.dice-man`	Fans of Andrew Dice Clay
`alt.fan.disney.afternoon`	Disney Afternoon characters and shows
`alt.fan.don.no-soul.simmons`	From "Amazon Women On The Moon" fame
`alt.fan.douglas-adams`	Author of "The Meaning of Liff" and other fine works
`alt.fan.eddings`	The works of writer David Eddings
`alt.fan.frank-zappa`	All about bizarre musician Frank Zappa
`alt.fan.furry`	Fans of funny animals, ala Steve Gallacci's book
`alt.fan.gooley`	Fans of Markian Gooley and his followers
`alt.fan.goons`	Careful Neddy, it's that dastardly Moriarty again
`alt.fan.howard-stern`	Fans of the abrasive radio and TV personality
`alt.fan.itchy-n-scratchy`	Bart Simpson's favorite TV cartoon
`alt.fan.jimmy-buffett`	Country singer Jimmy Buffett
`alt.fan.john-palmer`	Tygra, tygra, burning blight..
`alt.fan.kevin-darcy`	For Kebbie
`alt.fan.letterman`	Electronic fan club for David Letterman
`alt.fan.mike-jittlov`	Electronic fan club for animator Mike Jittlov
`alt.fan.monty-python`	Electronic fan club for those wacky Brits
`alt.fan.mst3k`	Mystery Science Theatre 3000 tv show
`alt.fan.pern`	Anne McCaffery's science fiction oeuvre
`alt.fan.peter.hammill`	Fans of the avant-garde musician
`alt.fan.pratchett`	For fans of Terry Pratchett, science fiction humor writer
`alt.fan.q`	The Qmnipotent Qne holds court here
`alt.fan.shostakovich`	Classical music composer
`alt.fan.suicide-squid`	Breathtaking adventure stories
`alt.fan.tna`	For the college radio show "T n A"
`alt.fan.tom-robbins`	A novelist of quaint and affecting tales
`alt.fan.tom_peterson`	Portland, Oregon's favorite son
`alt.fan.warlord`	The War Lord of the West Preservation Fan Club
`alt.fandom.cons`	Announcements of conventions (SciFi and others)
`alt.fandom.misc`	Other topics for fans of various kinds
`alt.fashion`	All facets of the fashion industry discussed
`alt.fishing`	Fishing as a hobby and sport
`alt.flame`	Alternative, literate, pithy, succinct screaming
`alt.flame.psu`	Penn State gets its own
`alt.flame.spelling`	Fore andd abowt piple whoe kant spel
`alt.folklore.college`	Collegiate humor
`alt.folklore.computers`	Stories and anecdotes about computers (some true!)
`alt.folklore.ghost-stories`	Boo!
`alt.folklore.science`	The folklore of science, not the science of folklore
`alt.folklore.urban`	Urban legends, ala Jan Harold Brunvand
`alt.food`	Most folks like it
`alt.forgery`	One place for all forgeries, crossposting encouraged
`alt.fractals`	Fractals in math, graphics and art
`alt.freedom.of.information.act`	Discussion about Freedom of Information
`alt.galactic-guide`	Entries for the actual Hitchhiker's Guide to the Galaxy
`alt.games.gb`	The Galactic Bloodshed conquest game

`alt.games.lynx`	The Atari Lynx
`alt.games.mornington.crescent`	Discussion of and playing the Crescent game
`alt.games.omega`	The computer game Omega
`alt.games.sf2`	The video game Street Fighter 2
`alt.games.torg`	Gateway for TORG mailing list
`alt.games.xtrek`	All about a Star Trek game for X
`alt.gathering.rainbow`	For discussing the annual Rainbow Gathering
`alt.good.news`	A place for some news that's good news
`alt.gopher`	Discussion of the gopher information service
`alt.gothic`	The gothic movement: things mournful and dark
`alt.gourmand`	Recipes and cooking info (moderated)
`alt.graffiti`	Usenet spraypainters and their documenters
`alt.graphics`	Some prefer this to comp.graphics
`alt.graphics.pixutils`	Discussion of pixmap utilities
`alt.great-lakes`	Discussions of the Great Lakes and adjacent places
`alt.guitar`	Guitar enthusiasts
`alt.hackers`	Projects currently under development (moderated)
`alt.heraldry.sca`	Heraldry in the Society of Creative Anachronism
`alt.hindu`	The Hindu religion (moderated)
`alt.horror`	The horror genre
`alt.hotrod`	High speed automobiles (moderated)
`alt.hypertext`	Discussion of hypertext: uses, transport, etc.
`alt.individualism`	Philosophies where individual rights are paramount
`alt.industrial`	The Industrial Computing Society
`alt.irc`	Internet Relay Chat material
`alt.irc.corruption`	Is nowhere safe?
`alt.irc.recovery`	Kill your television... er, IRC client
`alt.karaoke`	Singing off-key with Karoke accompaniment
`alt.ketchup`	Whak* Whak* ...shake... Whak* Damn, all over my tie
`alt.kids-talk`	A place for the pre-college set on the net
`alt.lang.asm`	Assembly languages of various flavors
`alt.lang.basic`	The Language That Would Not Die
`alt.lang.cfutures`	Discussion of the future of the C programming language
`alt.lang.intercal`	A joke language with a real compiler
`alt.lang.ml`	The ML and SML symbolic languages
`alt.lang.teco`	The TECO editor language
`alt.locksmithing`	You locked your keys in *where*?
`alt.magic`	For discussion about stage magic
`alt.magick`	For discussion about supernatural arts
`alt.manga`	Discussion of non-Western comics
`alt.materials.simulaton`	Discussion of computer modeling of materials
`alt.mcdonalds`	Can I get fries with that?
`alt.meditation.transcendental`	Contemplation of states beyond the teeth
`alt.messianic`	Messianic traditions
`alt.mindcontrol`	You WILL read this group and ENJOY it!
`alt.missing-kids`	Locating missing children
`alt.models`	Model building, design, etc.
`alt.motd`	Messages of the day
`alt.motorcycles.harley`	All about Harley-Davidson motorcycles
`alt.mud.german`	For German-speaking MUD-ers

`alt.music.alternative`	Alternative music
`alt.music.enya`	Gaelic set to spacey music
`alt.music.filk`	SciFi/fantasy-related folk music
`alt.music.progressive`	Yes, Marillion, Asia, King Crimson, etc.
`alt.music.rush`	For Rushheads
`alt.music.the.police`	Don't stand so close
`alt.mythology`	Discussion of mythlogy
`alt.national.enquirer`	The National Enquirer newspaper
`alt.native`	Issues for and about indigenous peoples of the world
`alt.newbie`	Alt's answer to news.newusers
`alt.newgroup`	For people who don't like to rmgroup/newgroup things
`alt.news-media`	Discussions about the news media
`alt.out-of-body`	Discussion of out of body experiences
`alt.overlords`	Office of the Omnipotent Overlords of the Omniverse
`alt.pagan`	Discussions about paganism and religion
`alt.paranormal`	Phenomena that are not scientifically explicable
`alt.parents-teens`	Parent-teenager relationships
`alt.party`	Parties, celebration and general debauchery
`alt.peeves`	Discussion of peeves and related
`alt.personals`	General personal ads
`alt.personals.ads`	More personal ads
`alt.personals.bondage`	Personals: bondage
`alt.personals.misc`	Personals: miscellaneous
`alt.personals.poly`	Personals: multiple people
`alt.planning.urban`	Urban planning
`alt.politics.british`	British politics
`alt.politics.bush`	All about George Bush
`alt.politics.clinton`	All about Bill Clinton
`alt.politics.correct`	Politcal correctness
`alt.politics.democrats`	Politics: Democrats
`alt.politics.democrats.clinton`	Politics: Democrats and Bill Clinton
`alt.politics.democrats.d`	Politics: Democrats, discussion
`alt.politics.democrats.governors`	Politics: Democrats and governors
`alt.politics.democrats.house`	Politics: House of Representatives
`alt.politics.democrats.senate`	Politics: Senate
`alt.politics.elections`	Politics: elections
`alt.politics.homosexuality`	Politics and homosexuality
`alt.politics.perot`	Politics: Ross Perot
`alt.polyamory`	For those who maintain multiple love relationships
`alt.postmodern`	Postmodernism, semiotics, deconstruction and the like
`alt.privacy`	Privacy issues in cyberspace
`alt.prose`	Postings of original writings, fictional and otherwise
`alt.prose.d`	Discussions about postings in alt.prose
`alt.psychoactives`	Better living through chemistry
`alt.pub.dragons-inn`	A computer fantasy environment
`alt.pulp`	Paperback fiction, newsprint production, orange juice
`alt.radio.pirate`	Pirate radio stations
`alt.radio.scanner`	Discussion of scanning radio receivers
`alt.rap`	For fans of rap music
`alt.rap-gdead`	Fans of The Grateful Dead and Rap

`alt.rave`	Techno-culture: music, dancing, drugs, dancing
`alt.recovery`	For people in recovery programs (e.g., AA, ACA, GA)
`alt.religion.adm3a`	Flaming the merits of the Sigler-Lear ADM3A
`alt.religion.all-worlds`	Grokking the Church of All Worlds from Heinlein's book
`alt.religion.computers`	People who believe computing is "real life."
`alt.religion.emacs`	For those who love the Emacs computer environment
`alt.religion.kibology`	He's Fred, Jim
`alt.religion.scientology`	Scientology and dianetics
`alt.revisionism`	"It CAN'T be that way 'cause here's the FACTS"
`alt.rhode_island`	Discussion of the great little state
`alt.rissa`	Fans (and otherwise) of Patricia O'Tuama
`alt.rmgroup`	For the people who like to rmgroup/newgroup things
`alt.rock-n-roll`	Counterpart to alt.sex and alt.drugs
`alt.rock-n-roll.acdc`	AC/DC music group
`alt.rock-n-roll.hard`	Hard rock
`alt.rock-n-roll.metal`	For the headbangers on the net
`alt.rock-n-roll.metal.heavy`	Non-sissyboy metal bands
`alt.rock-n-roll.metal.metallica`	Metallica fans
`alt.rodney.king`	Rodney King related issues
`alt.romance`	Discussion about the romantic side of love
`alt.romance.chat`	Romantic talk
`alt.rush-limbaugh`	Fans of the conservative activist radio announcer
`alt.satanism`	Discussions about Satan
`alt.save.the.earth`	Environmentalist causes
`alt.sb.programmer`	Programming the Sound Blaster card for IBM PClones
`alt.sci.astro.aips`	Discussions of Astronomical Image Processing System
`alt.sci.physics.acoustics`	Sound advice
`alt.sci.physics.new-theories`	Scientific theories you won't find in journals
`alt.security.index`	Pointers to good stuff in {alt.misc}.security (moderated)
`alt.self-improve`	Self-improvement in less than 14 characters
`alt.sewing`	Working with needle and thread
`alt.sex`	All about sex
`alt.sex.bestiality`	Sex: Bestiality
`alt.sex.bondage`	Sex: Bondage
`alt.sex.homosexual`	Sex: Homosexuality
`alt.sex.masturbation`	Sex: Masturbation
`alt.sex.motss`	Sex: Members of the same sex
`alt.sex.movies`	Sex and movies
`alt.sex.stories`	Stories about sex
`alt.sex.wanted`	Requests for erotica, either literary or in the flesh
`alt.sex.wizards`	Questions for only true sex wizards
`alt.sex.woody-allen`	Sex and Woody Allen
`alt.sexual.abuse.recovery`	Helping others deal with traumatic experiences
`alt.skate-board`	Discussion of all apsects of skate-boarding
`alt.skinheads`	The skinhead culture/anti-culture
`alt.slack`	Posting relating to the Church of the Subgenius
`alt.snowmobiles`	All about snowmobiles
`alt.society.ati`	The Activist Times Digest (moderated)
`alt.society.civil-disob`	Civil disobedience
`alt.society.civil-liberties`	Individual rights

`alt.society.revolution`	Discussions on revolution(s)
`alt.society.sovereign`	Independantistes, unite!
`alt.sources`	Alternative source code, unmoderated. Caveat Emptor
`alt.sources.amiga`	Technically oriented Amiga PC sources
`alt.sources.d`	Discussion of posted sources
`alt.sources.index`	Pointers to source code in alt.sources (moderated)
`alt.sources.patches`	Reposted patches from non-bugs groups
`alt.sources.wanted`	Requests for source code
`alt.sport.bowling`	Bowling
`alt.sport.bungee`	Bungee cord jumping
`alt.sport.darts`	Darts
`alt.sport.lasertag`	Laser tag
`alt.stagecraft`	Technical theatre issues
`alt.startrek.creative`	Stories and parodies related to Star Trek
`alt.stupidity`	Discussion about stupid newsgroups
`alt.suburbs`	Sprawling on the fringes of the city
`alt.suicide.finals`	Talk of why suicides increase during finals
`alt.suicide.holiday`	Talk of why suicides increase at holidays
`alt.support`	Dealing with emotional situations and experiences
`alt.support.cancer`	Dealing with the Big C
`alt.support.diet`	Seeking enlightenment through weight loss
`alt.support.mult-sclerosis`	Discussion about living with multiple sclerosis
`alt.surfing`	Riding the ocean waves
`alt.sys.amiga.demos`	Code and talk to show off the Amiga
`alt.sys.amiga.uucp`	AmigaUUCP
`alt.sys.amiga.uucp.patches`	Patches for AmigaUUCP
`alt.sys.intergraph`	Support for Intergraph machines
`alt.tasteless`	Truly disgusting
`alt.test`	Alternative subnetwork testing
`alt.text.dwb`	Discussion of the AT&T Documenter's WorkBench
`alt.thrash`	Thrashlife
`alt.toolkits.xview`	The X windows XView toolkit
`alt.toon-pics`	Cartoon pictures
`alt.true.crime`	Discussion about real crime
`alt.tv.antagonists`	Fans of the new "The Antagonists" TV show
`alt.tv.dinosaurs`	Dinosaurs and TV
`alt.tv.la-law`	L.A. Law TV show
`alt.tv.northern-exp`	Northern Exposure TV show
`alt.tv.prisoner`	The Prisoner television series from years ago
`alt.tv.red-dwarf`	The British SciFi/comedy show
`alt.tv.ren-n-stimpy`	Ren and Stimpy TV show
`alt.tv.simpsons`	The Simpsons TV show
`alt.tv.tiny-toon`	Discussion about the "Tiny Toon Adventures" show
`alt.tv.twin-peaks`	Discussion about the popular (and unusual) TV show
`alt.usage.english`	English grammar, word usages and related topics
`alt.usenet.recovery`	Reupholster your news reader
`alt.uu.announce`	Announcements of Usenet University
`alt.uu.comp.misc`	Computer department of Usenet University
`alt.uu.future`	Planning the future of Usenet University
`alt.uu.lang.esperanto.misc`	Study of Esperanto in Usenet University

`alt.uu.lang.misc`	Language department of Usenet University
`alt.uu.math.misc`	Math department of Usenet University
`alt.uu.misc.misc`	Misc. department of Usenet University
`alt.uu.tools`	Tools for Usenet University and education
`alt.uu.virtual-worlds.misc`	Study of virtual worlds in Usenet University
`alt.vampyres`	Discussion of vampires and related writings, films, etc.
`alt.war`	Not just collateral damage
`alt.war.civil.usa`	The US Civil War
`alt.weemba`	Talk and flames about the one and only Weemba
`alt.whine`	Whining and complaining
`alt.zines`	Small magazines, mostly noncommercial
`bionet.agroforestry`	Discussion of agroforestry
`bionet.announce`	Announcements of interest to biologists (moderated)
`bionet.biology.computational`	Computer and mathematical applications (moderated)
`bionet.biology.tropical`	Discussions about tropical biology
`bionet.general`	General BIOSCI discussion
`bionet.genome.arabidopsis`	Information about the Arabidopsis project
`bionet.genome.chrom22`	Discussion of Chromosome 22
`bionet.immunology`	Discussions about research in immunology
`bionet.info-theory`	Discussions about biological information theory
`bionet.jobs`	Scientific job opportunities
`bionet.journals.contents`	Contents of biology journal publications
`bionet.molbio.ageing`	Discussions of cellular and organismal aging
`bionet.molbio.bio-matrix`	Computer applications to biological databases
`bionet.molbio.embldatabank`	Info about the EMBL nucleic acid database
`bionet.molbio.evolution`	How genes and proteins have evolved
`bionet.molbio.gdb`	Messages to and from the GDB database staff
`bionet.molbio.genbank`	Info about the GenBank nucleic acid database
`bionet.molbio.genbank.updates`	Hot off the presses! (moderated)
`bionet.molbio.gene-linkage`	Discussions about genetic linkage analysis
`bionet.molbio.genome-program`	Discussion of Human Genome Project issues
`bionet.molbio.hiv`	Discussions about the molecular biology of HIV
`bionet.molbio.methds-reagnts`	Requests for information and lab reagents
`bionet.molbio.proteins`	Research on proteins and protein databases
`bionet.neuroscience`	Research issues in the neurosciences
`bionet.plants`	Discussion about all aspects of plant biology
`bionet.population-bio`	Technical discussions about population biology
`bionet.sci-resources`	Information about funding agencies, etc.
`bionet.software`	Information about software for biology
`bionet.software.sources`	Software sources relating to biology (moderated)
`bionet.users.addresses`	Who's who in Biology
`bionet.women-in-bio`	Discussions about women in biology
`bionet.xtallography`	Discussions about protein crystallography
`bit.admin`	BITNET Newgroups Discussions
`bit.general`	Discussions Relating to BITNET/Usenet
`bit.listserv.9370-l`	IBM 9370 and VM/IS Specific Topics List
`bit.listserv.advanc-l`	Geac Advanced Integrated Library System Users
`bit.listserv.advise-l`	User Services List
`bit.listserv.aix-l`	IBM AIX Discussion List

`bit.listserv.allmusic`	Discussions on All Forms of Music
`bit.listserv.appc-l`	APPC Discussion List
`bit.listserv.apple2-l`	Apple II List
`bit.listserv.applicat`	Applications Under BITNET
`bit.listserv.ashe-l`	Higher Education Policy and Research
`bit.listserv.asm370`	IBM 370 Assembly Programming Discussions
`bit.listserv.autism`	Autism and Developmental Disability List
`bit.listserv.banyan-l`	Banyan Vines Network Software Discussions
`bit.listserv.big-lan`	Campus-Size LAN Discussion Group (moderated)
`bit.listserv.billing`	Chargeback of Computer Resources
`bit.listserv.biosph-l`	Biosphere, Ecology, Discussion List
`bit.listserv.bitnews`	BITNET News
`bit.listserv.buslib-l`	Business Libraries List
`bit.listserv.c+health`	Computer and Health Discussion List
`bit.listserv.c18-l`	18th Century Interdisciplinary Discussion
`bit.listserv.c370-l`	C/370 Discussion List
`bit.listserv.candle-l`	Candle Products Discussion List
`bit.listserv.cdromlan`	CD-ROM on Local Area Networks
`bit.listserv.christia`	Practical Christian Life
`bit.listserv.cics-l`	CICS Discussion List
`bit.listserv.cinema-l`	Discussions on All Forms of Cinema
`bit.listserv.circplus`	Circulation Reserve and Related Library Issues
`bit.listserv.cmspip-l`	VM/SP CMS Pipelines Discussion List
`bit.listserv.commed`	Communication Education
`bit.listserv.csg-l`	Control System Group Network
`bit.listserv.cumrec-l`	CUMREC-L Administrative Computer Use
`bit.listserv.cw-email`	Campus-Wide E-mail Discussion List
`bit.listserv.cwis-l`	Campus-Wide Information Systems
`bit.listserv.cyber-l`	CDC Computer Discussion
`bit.listserv.dasig`	Database Administration
`bit.listserv.db2-l`	DB2 Data Base Discussion List
`bit.listserv.dbase-l`	Discussion on the Use of the dBase IV
`bit.listserv.deaf-l`	Deaf List
`bit.listserv.decnews`	Digital Equipment Corporation News List
`bit.listserv.dectei-l`	DECUS Education Software Library Discussions
`bit.listserv.dipl-l`	Diplomacy Game Discussion List
`bit.listserv.disarm-l`	Disarmament Discussion List
`bit.listserv.domain-l`	Domains Discussion Group
`bit.listserv.earntech`	EARN Technical Group
`bit.listserv.edi-l`	Electronic Data Interchange Issues
`bit.listserv.edpolyan`	Professionals and Students Discuss Education
`bit.listserv.edstat-l`	Statistics Education Discussion List
`bit.listserv.edtech`	EDTECH: Educational Technology (moderated)
`bit.listserv.emusic-l`	Electronic Music Discussion List
`bit.listserv.envbeh-l`	Forum on Environment and Human Behavior
`bit.listserv.erl-l`	Educational Research List
`bit.listserv.ethics-l`	Discussion of Ethics in Computing
`bit.listserv.ethology`	Ethology List
`bit.listserv.euearn-l`	Eastern Europe List
`bit.listserv.film-l`	Film Making and Reviews List

`bit.listserv.fnord-l`	New Ways of Thinking List
`bit.listserv.frac-l`	FRACTAL Discussion List
`bit.listserv.games-l`	Computer Games List
`bit.listserv.gaynet`	GayNet Discussion List (moderated)
`bit.listserv.gddm-l`	The GDDM Discussion List
`bit.listserv.geodesic`	List for the Discussion of Buckminster Fuller
`bit.listserv.gguide`	BITNIC GGUIDE List
`bit.listserv.govdoc-l`	Discussion of Government Document Issues
`bit.listserv.gutnberg`	GUTNBERG Discussion List
`bit.listserv.hellas`	The Hellenic Discussion List (moderated)
`bit.listserv.history`	History List
`bit.listserv.i-amiga`	Info-Amiga List
`bit.listserv.ibm-hesc`	IBM Higher Education Consortium
`bit.listserv.ibm-main`	IBM Mainframe Discussion List
`bit.listserv.ibm-nets`	BITNIC IBM-NETS List
`bit.listserv.ibm7171`	Protocol Converter List
`bit.listserv.ibmtcp-l`	IBM TCP/IP List
`bit.listserv.info-gcg`	INFO-GCG: GCG Genetics Software Discussion
`bit.listserv.infonets`	Infonets Redistribution
`bit.listserv.ingrafx`	Information Graphics
`bit.listserv.innopac`	Innovative Interfaces Online Public Access
`bit.listserv.ioob-l`	Industrial Psychology
`bit.listserv.isn`	ISN Data Switch Technical Discussion Group
`bit.listserv.jes2-l`	JES2 Discussion Group
`bit.listserv.jnet-l`	BITNIC JNET-L List
`bit.listserv.l-hcap`	Handicap List (moderated)
`bit.listserv.l-vmctr`	VMCENTER Components Discussion List
`bit.listserv.lawsch-l`	Law School Discussion List
`bit.listserv.liaison`	BITNIC LIAISON
`bit.listserv.libref-l`	Library Reference Issues (moderated)
`bit.listserv.libres`	Library and Information Science Research
`bit.listserv.license`	Software Licensing List
`bit.listserv.linkfail`	Link Failure Announcements
`bit.listserv.literary`	Discussions About Literature
`bit.listserv.lstsrv-l`	Forum on LISTSERV
`bit.listserv.mail-l`	BITNIC MAIL-L List
`bit.listserv.mailbook`	MAIL/MAILBOOK Subscription List
`bit.listserv.mba-l`	MBA Student Curriculum Discussion
`bit.listserv.mbu-l`	Megabyte University: Computers and Writing
`bit.listserv.medlib-l`	Medical Libraries Discussion List
`bit.listserv.mednews`	MEDNEWS: Health Info-Com Network Newsletter
`bit.listserv.mideur-l`	Middle Europe Discussion List
`bit.listserv.netnws-l`	NETNWS-L Netnews List
`bit.listserv.new-list`	NEW-LIST: New List Announcements (moderated)
`bit.listserv.next-l`	NeXT Computer List
`bit.listserv.nodmgt-l`	Node Management
`bit.listserv.notabene`	Nota Bene List
`bit.listserv.notis-l`	NOTIS/DOBIS Discussion Group List
`bit.listserv.novell`	Novell LAN Interest Group
`bit.listserv.omrscan`	OMR Scanner Discussion

`bit.listserv.ozone`	OZONE Discussion List
`bit.listserv.pacs-l`	Public-Access Computer System Forum (moderated)
`bit.listserv.page-l`	IBM 3812/3820 Tips and Problems Discussion List
`bit.listserv.pagemakr`	PageMaker for Desktop Publishers
`bit.listserv.pmdf-l`	PMDF Distribution List
`bit.listserv.politics`	Forum for the Discussion of Politics
`bit.listserv.power-l`	IBM RS/6000 POWER Family
`bit.listserv.psycgrad`	Psychology Grad Student Discussions
`bit.listserv.qualrs-l`	Qualitative Research of the Human Sciences
`bit.listserv.relusr-l`	Relay Users Forum
`bit.listserv.rexxlist`	REXX Programming Discussion List
`bit.listserv.rhetoric`	Rhetoric, Social Movements, Persuasion
`bit.listserv.rscs-l`	VM/RSCS Mailing List
`bit.listserv.rscsmods`	The RSCS Modifications List
`bit.listserv.s-comput`	Supercomputers List
`bit.listserv.sas-l`	SAS Discussion
`bit.listserv.script-l`	IBM vs. Waterloo SCRIPT Discussion Group
`bit.listserv.scuba-l`	Scuba Diving Discussion List
`bit.listserv.seasia-l`	Southeast Asia Discussion List
`bit.listserv.sfs-l`	VM Shared File System Discussion List
`bit.listserv.sganet`	Student Government Global Mail Network
`bit.listserv.simula`	The SIMULA Language List
`bit.listserv.slart-l`	SLA Research and Teaching
`bit.listserv.slovak-l`	Slovak Discussion List
`bit.listserv.snamgt-l`	SNA Network Management Discussion
`bit.listserv.sos-data`	Social Science Data List
`bit.listserv.spires-l`	SPIRES Conference List
`bit.listserv.sportpsy`	Exercise and Sports Psychology
`bit.listserv.spssx-l`	SPSSX Discussion
`bit.listserv.sqlinfo`	Forum for SQL/DS and Related Topics
`bit.listserv.stat-l`	Statistical Consulting
`bit.listserv.tech-l`	BITNIC TECH-L List
`bit.listserv.test`	Test Newsgroup
`bit.listserv.tex-l`	The TeXnical Topics List
`bit.listserv.tn3270-l`	tn3270 Protocol Discussion List
`bit.listserv.trans-l`	BITNIC TRANS-L List
`bit.listserv.travel-l`	Tourism Discussions
`bit.listserv.ucp-l`	University Computing Project Mailing List
`bit.listserv.ug-l`	Usage Guidelines
`bit.listserv.uigis-l`	User Interface for Geographical Info Systems
`bit.listserv.urep-l`	UREP-L Mailing List
`bit.listserv.usrdir-l`	User Directory List
`bit.listserv.valert-l`	Virus Alert List (moderated)
`bit.listserv.vfort-l`	VS-Fortran Discussion List
`bit.listserv.vm-util`	VM Utilities Discussion List
`bit.listserv.vmesa-l`	VM/ESA Mailing List
`bit.listserv.vmslsv-l`	VAX/VMS LISTSERV Discussion List
`bit.listserv.vmxa-l`	VM/XA Discussion List
`bit.listserv.vnews-l`	VNEWS Discussion List
`bit.listserv.vpiej-l`	Electronic Publishing Discussion List

`bit.listserv.win3-l`	Microsoft Windows Version 3 Forum
`bit.listserv.words-l`	English Language Discussion Group
`bit.listserv.wpcorp-l`	WordPerfect Corporation Products Discussions
`bit.listserv.wpwin-l`	WordPerfect for Windows
`bit.listserv.x400-l`	x.400 Protocol List
`bit.listserv.xcult-l`	International Intercultural Newsletter
`bit.listserv.xedit-l`	VM System Editor List
`bit.listserv.xerox-l`	The Xerox Discussion List
`bit.listserv.xmailer`	Crosswell Mailer
`bit.listserv.xtropy-l`	Extopian List
`bit.mailserv.word-mac`	Word Processing on the Macintosh
`bit.mailserv.word-pc`	Word Processing on the IBM PC
`biz.books.technical`	A place to contact book sellers and buyers
`biz.clarinet`	Announcements about ClariNet
`biz.clarinet.sample`	Samples of ClariNet newsgroups for the outside world
`biz.comp.hardware`	Generic commercial hardware postings
`biz.comp.services`	Generic commercial service postings
`biz.comp.software`	Generic commercial software postings
`biz.comp.telebit`	Support of the Telebit modem
`biz.comp.telebit.netblazer`	The Telebit Netblazer
`biz.config`	Biz Usenet configuration and administration
`biz.control`	Control information and messages
`biz.dec`	DEC equipment and software
`biz.dec.ip`	IP networking on DEC machines
`biz.dec.workstations`	DEC workstation discussions and info
`biz.jobs.offered`	Position announcements
`biz.misc`	Miscellaneous postings of a commercial nature
`biz.sco.announce`	SCO and related product announcements (moderated)
`biz.sco.binaries`	Binary packages for SCO Xenix, Unix or ODT
`biz.sco.general`	Q&A, discussions and comments on SCO products
`biz.sco.opendesktop`	ODT environment and applications tech info, Q&A
`biz.sco.sources`	Source code ported to an SCO operating environment
`biz.stolen`	Postings about stolen merchandise
`biz.tadpole.sparcbook`	Discussions on the Sparcbook portable computer
`biz.test`	Biz newsgroup test messages
`comp.ai.edu`	Applications of artificial intelligence to education
`comp.ai.vision`	Artificial intelligence vision research (moderated)
`comp.dcom.lans.hyperchannel`	Hyperchannel networks within an IP network
`comp.editors`	Topics related to computerized text editing
`comp.edu.composition`	Writing instruction in computer-based classrooms
`comp.lang.asm370`	Programming in IBM System/370 assembly language
`comp.lang.clu`	The CLU language and related topics
`comp.lang.forth.mac`	The CSI MacForth programming environment
`comp.lang.icon`	Topics related to the ICON programming language
`comp.lang.idl`	IDL (Interface Description Language) related topics
`comp.lang.lisp.franz`	The Franz Lisp programming language
`comp.lang.lisp.x`	The XLISP language system
`comp.lang.rexx`	The REXX command language
`comp.lang.scheme.c`	The Scheme language environment

`comp.lang.visual`	Visual programming languages
`comp.lsi.cad`	Electrical computer aided design
`comp.mail.multi-media`	Multimedia mail
`comp.music`	Applications of computers in music research
`comp.os.aos`	Topics related to Data General's AOS/VS
`comp.os.cpm.amethyst`	Discussion of Amethyst, CP/M-80 software package
`comp.os.msdos.4dos`	The 4DOS command processor for MS-DOS
`comp.os.rsts`	Topics related to the PDP-11 RSTS/E operating system
`comp.os.v`	The V distributed operating system from Stanford
`comp.periphs.printers`	Information on printers
`comp.protocols.iso.dev-environ`	The ISO Development Environment
`comp.protocols.iso.x400`	X400 mail protocol discussions
`comp.protocols.iso.x400.gateway`	X400 mail gateway discussions (moderated)
`comp.protocols.pcnet`	Topics related to PCNET (a personal computer network)
`comp.protocols.snmp`	The Simple Network Management Protocol
`comp.protocols.tcp-ip.domains`	Topics related to Domain Style names
`comp.protocols.time.ntp`	The network time protocol
`comp.security.announce`	Announcements from CERT about security (moderated)
`comp.soft-sys.andrew`	The Andrew system from CMU
`comp.soft-sys.nextstep`	The NeXTstep computing environment
`comp.std.announce`	Announcements about standards activities (moderated)
`comp.sys.cdc`	Control Data Corporation computers (e.g., Cybers)
`comp.sys.handhelds`	Handheld computers and programmable calculators
`comp.sys.intel.ipsc310`	Anything related to the Intel 310
`comp.sys.northstar`	Northstar microcomputer users
`comp.sys.super`	Supercomputers
`comp.sys.ti.explorer`	The Texas Instruments Explorer
`comp.sys.zenith`	Heath terminals and related Zenith products
`comp.terminals.bitgraph`	The BB&N BitGraph terminal
`comp.terminals.tty5620`	AT&T dot mapped display terminals (5620 and BLIT)
`comp.theory`	Theoretical computer science
`comp.theory.cell-automata`	Discussion of all aspects of cellular automata
`comp.theory.dynamic-sys`	Ergodic theory and dynamical systems
`comp.theory.self-org-sys`	Topics related to self-organization
`comp.unix.cray`	Cray computers and their operating systems
`comp.unix.solaris`	Discussions about the Solaris operating system
`comp.windows.x.announce`	X Consortium announcements (moderated)
`comp.windows.x.motif`	The Motif GUI for the X Window system
`ddn.mgt-bulletin`	The DDN Management Bulletin (moderated)
`ddn.newsletter`	The DDN Newsletter from NIC.DDN.MIL (moderated)
`gnu.announce`	Status and announcements from the Project (moderated)
`gnu.bash.bug`	Bourne Again Shell bug reports and fixes (moderated)
`gnu.chess`	Announcements about the GNU Chess program
`gnu.emacs.announce`	Announcements about GNU Emacs (moderated)
`gnu.emacs.bug`	GNU Emacs bug reports and fixes (moderated)
`gnu.emacs.gnews`	News reading under Emacs using Weemba's Gnews
`gnu.emacs.gnus`	News reading under Emacs using GNUS (in English)
`gnu.emacs.help`	User queries and answers
`gnu.emacs.sources`	ONLY (please!) C and Lisp source code for GNU Emacs

`gnu.emacs.vm.bug`	Bug reports on the Emacs VM mail package
`gnu.emacs.vm.info`	Information about the Emacs VM mail package
`gnu.emacs.vms`	VMS port of GNU Emacs
`gnu.epoch.misc`	The Epoch X11 extensions to Emacs
`gnu.g++.announce`	Announcements about GNU C++ Compiler (moderated)
`gnu.g++.bug`	g++ bug reports and suggested fixes (moderated)
`gnu.g++.help`	GNU C++ compiler (G++) user queries and answers
`gnu.g++.lib.bug`	g++ library bug reports/suggested fixes (moderated)
`gnu.gcc.announce`	Announcements about the GNU C Compiler (moderated)
`gnu.gcc.bug`	GNU C Compiler bug reports/fixes (moderated)
`gnu.gcc.help`	GNU C Compiler (gcc) user queries and answers
`gnu.gdb.bug`	gcc/g++ DeBugger bugs and fixes (moderated)
`gnu.ghostscript.bug`	GNU Ghostscript interpreter bugs (moderated)
`gnu.gnusenet.config`	GNU's Not Usenet administration and configuration
`gnu.gnusenet.test`	GNU's Not Usenet alternative hierarchy testing
`gnu.groff.bug`	Bugs in the GNU roff programs (moderated)
`gnu.misc.discuss`	Serious discussion about GNU and freed software
`gnu.smalltalk.bug`	Bugs in GNU Smalltalk (moderated)
`gnu.utils.bug`	GNU utilities bugs (e.g., make, gawk. ls) (moderated)
`ieee.announce`	General Announcements for IEEE community
`ieee.config`	Postings about managing the IEEE groups
`ieee.general`	IEEE – general discussion
`ieee.pcnfs`	Discussion and tips on PC-NFS
`ieee.rab.announce`	Regional Activities Board - Announcements
`ieee.rab.general`	Regional Activities Board – general discussion
`ieee.region1`	Region 1 Announcements
`ieee.tab.announce`	Technical Activities Board - announcements
`ieee.tab.general`	Technical Activities Board – general discussion
`ieee.tcos`	The TCOS newsletter and discussion (moderated)
`ieee.usab.announce`	USAB – announcements
`ieee.usab.general`	USAB – general discussion
`k12.chat.elementary`	Informal discussion among students, grades K-5
`k12.chat.junior`	Informal discussion among students in grades 6-8
`k12.chat.senior`	Informal discussion among high school students
`k12.chat.teacher`	Informal discussion among teachers in grades K-12
`k12.ed.art`	Art curriculum in K-12 education
`k12.ed.business`	Business education curriculum in grades K-12
`k12.ed.comp.literacy`	Teaching computer literacy in grades K-12
`k12.ed.health-pe`	Health/Physical Education curriculum in grades K-12
`k12.ed.life-skills`	Home Economics and Career education in grades K-12
`k12.ed.math`	Mathematics curriculum in K-12 education
`k12.ed.music`	Music and Performing Arts curriculum in K-12 education
`k12.ed.science`	Science curriculum in K-12 education
`k12.ed.soc-studies`	Social Studies and History curriculum in K-12 education
`k12.ed.special`	K-12 education for students with special needs
`k12.ed.tag`	K-12 education for talented and gifted students
`k12.ed.tech`	Industrial Arts and vocational education in grades K-12
`k12.lang.art`	Language Arts curriculum in K-12 education
`k12.lang.deutsch-eng`	Bilingual German/English practice with native speakers

`k12.lang.esp-eng`	Bilingual Spanish/English practice with native speakers
`k12.lang.francais`	Bilingual French/English practice with native speakers
`k12.lang.russian`	Bilingual Russian/English practice with native speakers
`news.software.nntp`	The Network News Transfer Protocol
`rec.games.vectrex`	The Vectrex game system
`rec.mag.fsfnet`	A science fiction "fanzine" (moderated)
`sci.bio.technology`	Any topic relating to biotechnology
`sci.math.num-analysis`	Numerical analysis
`sci.philosophy.meta`	Discussions within the scope of "MetaPhilosophy"
`soc.culture.esperanto`	The neutral international language Esperanto
`u3b.config`	3B distribution configuration
`u3b.misc`	3B miscellaneous discussions
`u3b.sources`	Sources for AT&T 3B systems
`u3b.tech`	3B technical discussions
`u3b.test`	3B distribution testing
`vmsnet.admin`	Admin VMS internals gatewayed to MACRO32 list
`vmsnet.mail.misc`	Other electronic mail software
`vmsnet.mail.mx`	Mmail system from RPI, gatewayed to MX mailing list
`vmsnet.mail.pmdf`	Mail system, gatewayed to ipmdf mailing list
`vmsnet.misc`	General VMS topics not covered elsewhere
`vmsnet.networks.desktop.misc`	Other desktop integration software
`vmsnet.networks.desktop.pathworks`	DEC Pathworks desktop integration software
`vmsnet.networks.management.decmcc`	DECmcc and related software
`vmsnet.networks.management.misc`	Other network management solutions
`vmsnet.networks.misc`	General networking topics not covered elsewhere
`vmsnet.networks.tcp-ip.cmu-tek`	CMU-TEK TCP/IP package
`vmsnet.networks.tcp-ip.misc`	Other TCP/IP solutions for VMS
`vmsnet.networks.tcp-ip.multinet`	TGV's Multinet TCP/IP, gatewayed to info-multinet
`vmsnet.networks.tcp-ip.ucx`	DEC's VMS/Ultrix Connection (and TCP/IP)
`vmsnet.networks.tcp-ip.wintcp`	The Wollongong Group's WIN-TCP TCP/IP software
`vmsnet.pdp-11`	PDP-11 hardware and software, gatewayed to info-pdp11
`vmsnet.sources`	Source code postings ONLY (moderated)
`vmsnet.sources.d`	Discussion about or requests for sources
`vmsnet.sources.games`	Recreational software postings
`vmsnet.sysmgt`	VMS system management
`vmsnet.test`	Test messages
`vmsnet.tpu`	TPU language and applications, gatewayed to info-tpu
`vmsnet.uucp`	DECUS uucp software, gatewayed to vmsnet mailing list
`vmsnet.vms-posix`	Discussion about VMS POSIX

Clarinet Newsgroups

`clari.biz.commodity`	Commodity news and price reports (moderated)
`clari.biz.courts`	Lawsuits and business related legal matters (moderated)
`clari.biz.economy`	Economic news and indicators (moderated)
`clari.biz.economy.world`	Economy stories for non-US countries (moderated)
`clari.biz.features`	Business feature stories (moderated)
`clari.biz.finance`	Finance, currency, corporate finance (moderated)
`clari.biz.finance.earnings`	Earnings and dividend reports (moderated)
`clari.biz.finance.personal`	Personal investing and finance (moderated)
`clari.biz.finance.services`	Banks and financial industries (moderated)
`clari.biz.invest`	News for investors (moderated)
`clari.biz.labor`	Strikes, unions and labor relations (moderated)
`clari.biz.market`	General stock market news (moderated)
`clari.biz.market.amex`	American Stock Exchange reports and news (moderated)
`clari.biz.market.dow`	Dow Jones NYSE reports (moderated)
`clari.biz.market.ny`	NYSE reports (moderated)
`clari.biz.market.otc`	NASDAQ reports (moderated)
`clari.biz.market.report`	General market reports, S&P, etc. (moderated)
`clari.biz.mergers`	Mergers and acquisitions (moderated)
`clari.biz.misc`	Other business news (moderated)
`clari.biz.products`	Important new products and services (moderated)
`clari.biz.top`	Top business news (moderated)
`clari.biz.urgent`	Breaking business news (moderated)
`clari.canada.biz`	Canadian business summaries (moderated)
`clari.canada.features`	Alamanac, Ottawa Special, arts (moderated)
`clari.canada.general`	Short items on Canadian news stories (moderated)
`clari.canada.gov`	Government related news (all levels) (moderated)
`clari.canada.law`	Crimes, the courts and the law (moderated)
`clari.canada.newscast`	Regular newscast for Canadians (moderated)
`clari.canada.politics`	Political and election items (moderated)
`clari.canada.trouble`	Mishaps, accidents and serious problems (moderated)
`clari.feature.dave_barry`	Columns of humourist Dave Barry (moderated)
`clari.feature.kinsey`	Sex Q&A and advice from Kinsey Institute (moderated)
`clari.feature.mike_royko`	Chicago opinion columnist Mike Royko (moderated)
`clari.feature.miss_manners`	Judith Martin's humorous etiquette advice (moderated)
`clari.local.alberta.briefs`	Local news briefs (moderated)
`clari.local.arizona`	Local news (moderated)
`clari.local.arizona.briefs`	Local news briefs (moderated)
`clari.local.bc.briefs`	Local news briefs (moderated)
`clari.local.california`	Local news (moderated)
`clari.local.california.briefs`	Local news briefs (moderated)
`clari.local.chicago`	Local news (moderated)
`clari.local.chicago.briefs`	Local news briefs (moderated)
`clari.local.florida`	Local news (moderated)
`clari.local.florida.briefs`	Local news briefs (moderated)
`clari.local.georgia`	Local news (moderated)
`clari.local.georgia.briefs`	Local news briefs (moderated)
`clari.local.headlines`	Various local headline summaries (moderated)
`clari.local.illinois`	Local news (moderated)

`clari.local.illinois.briefs`	Local news briefs (moderated)
`clari.local.indiana`	Local news (moderated)
`clari.local.indiana.briefs`	Local news briefs (moderated)
`clari.local.iowa`	Local news (moderated)
`clari.local.iowa.briefs`	Local news briefs (moderated)
`clari.local.los_angeles`	Local news (moderated)
`clari.local.los_angeles.briefs`	Local news briefs (moderated)
`clari.local.louisiana`	Local news (moderated)
`clari.local.manitoba.briefs`	Local news briefs (moderated)
`clari.local.maritimes.briefs`	Local news briefs (moderated)
`clari.local.maryland`	Local news (moderated)
`clari.local.maryland.briefs`	Local news briefs (moderated)
`clari.local.massachusetts`	Local news (moderated)
`clari.local.massachusetts.briefs`	Local news briefs (moderated)
`clari.local.michigan`	Local news (moderated)
`clari.local.michigan.briefs`	Local news briefs (moderated)
`clari.local.minnesota`	Local news (moderated)
`clari.local.minnesota.briefs`	Local news briefs (moderated)
`clari.local.missouri`	Local news (moderated)
`clari.local.missouri.briefs`	Local news briefs (moderated)
`clari.local.nebraska`	Local news (moderated)
`clari.local.nebraska.briefs`	Local news briefs (moderated)
`clari.local.nevada`	Local news (moderated)
`clari.local.nevada.briefs`	Local news briefs (moderated)
`clari.local.new_england`	Local news (moderated)
`clari.local.new_hampshire`	Local news (moderated)
`clari.local.new_jersey`	Local news (moderated)
`clari.local.new_jersey.briefs`	Local news briefs (moderated)
`clari.local.new_york`	Local news (moderated)
`clari.local.new_york.briefs`	Local news briefs (moderated)
`clari.local.nyc`	Local news (New York City) (moderated)
`clari.local.nyc.briefs`	Local news briefs (moderated)
`clari.local.ohio`	Local news (moderated)
`clari.local.ohio.briefs`	Local news briefs (moderated)
`clari.local.ontario.briefs`	Local news briefs (moderated)
`clari.local.oregon`	Local news (moderated)
`clari.local.oregon.briefs`	Local news briefs (moderated)
`clari.local.pennsylvania`	Local news (moderated)
`clari.local.pennsylvania.briefs`	Local news briefs (moderated)
`clari.local.saskatchewan.briefs`	Local news briefs (moderated)
`clari.local.sfbay`	Stories datelined San Francisco Bay Area (moderated)
`clari.local.texas`	Local news (moderated)
`clari.local.texas.briefs`	Local news briefs (moderated)
`clari.local.utah`	Local news (moderated)
`clari.local.utah.briefs`	Local news briefs (moderated)
`clari.local.virginia+dc`	Local news (moderated)
`clari.local.virginia+dc.briefs`	Local news briefs (moderated)
`clari.local.washington`	Local news (moderated)
`clari.local.washington.briefs`	Local news briefs (moderated)
`clari.local.wisconsin`	Local news (moderated)

`clari.local.wisconsin.briefs`	Local news briefs (moderated)
`clari.nb.apple`	Newsbytes Apple/Macintosh news (moderated)
`clari.nb.business`	Newsbytes business and industry news (moderated)
`clari.nb.general`	Newsbytes general computer news (moderated)
`clari.nb.govt`	Newsbytes legal and gov't computer news (moderated)
`clari.nb.ibm`	Newsbytes IBM PC World coverage (moderated)
`clari.nb.review`	Newsbytes new product reviews (moderated)
`clari.nb.telecom`	Newsbytes telecom/online industry news (moderated)
`clari.nb.top`	Newsbytes top stories (crossposted) (moderated)
`clari.nb.trends`	Newsbytes new developments and trends (moderated)
`clari.nb.unix`	Newsbytes Unix news (moderated)
`clari.net.admin`	Announcements for news admins. (moderated)
`clari.net.announce`	Announcements for all Clarinet readers (moderated)
`clari.net.products`	New Clarinet products (moderated)
`clari.net.talk`	Discussion of Clarinet: only unmoderated group
`clari.news.almanac`	Daily almanac: "this date in history" (moderated)
`clari.news.arts`	Stage, drama and other fine arts (moderated)
`clari.news.aviation`	Aviation industry and mishaps (moderated)
`clari.news.books`	Books and publishing (moderated)
`clari.news.briefs`	Regular news summaries (moderated)
`clari.news.bulletin`	Major breaking stories of the week (moderated)
`clari.news.canada`	News related to Canada (moderated)
`clari.news.cast`	Regular U.S. news summary (moderated)
`clari.news.children`	Stories related to children and parenting (moderated)
`clari.news.consumer`	Consumer news, car reviews, etc. (moderated)
`clari.news.demonstration`	Demonstrations around the world (moderated)
`clari.news.disaster`	Major problems/ natural disasters (moderated)
`clari.news.economy`	General economic news (moderated)
`clari.news.election`	US and international elections (moderated)
`clari.news.entertain`	Entertainment industry news and features (moderated)
`clari.news.europe`	News related to Europe (moderated)
`clari.news.features`	Unclassified feature stories (moderated)
`clari.news.fighting`	Clashes around the world (moderated)
`clari.news.flash`	Ultra-important once-a-year news flashes (moderated)
`clari.news.goodnews`	Stories of success and survival (moderated)
`clari.news.gov`	General Government related stories (moderated)
`clari.news.gov.agency`	Government agencies, FBI, etc. (moderated)
`clari.news.gov.budget`	Budgets at all levels (moderated)
`clari.news.gov.corrupt`	Government corruption, kickbacks, etc. (moderated)
`clari.news.gov.international`	International government-related stories (moderated)
`clari.news.gov.officials`	Government officials and their problems (moderated)
`clari.news.gov.state`	State gov't news of national importance (moderated)
`clari.news.gov.taxes`	Tax laws, trials, etc. (moderated)
`clari.news.gov.usa`	US Federal government news (high volume) (moderated)
`clari.news.group`	Special interest groups (moderated)
`clari.news.group.blacks`	News of interest to Black people (moderated)
`clari.news.group.gays`	Homosexuality and gay rights (moderated)
`clari.news.group.jews`	Jews and Jewish interests (moderated)
`clari.news.group.women`	Women's issues and abortion (moderated)
`clari.news.headlines`	Hourly list of the top U.S./world headlines (moderated)

`clari.news.hot.east_europe`	News from Eastern Europe (moderated)
`clari.news.hot.iraq`	Persian Gulf Crisis news (moderated)
`clari.news.hot.rodney_king`	L.A. riot news (moderated)
`clari.news.hot.ussr`	News from the Soviet Union (moderated)
`clari.news.interest`	Human interest stories (moderated)
`clari.news.interest.animals`	Animals in the news (moderated)
`clari.news.interest.history`	Human interest/history in the making (moderated)
`clari.news.interest.people`	Famous people in the news (moderated)
`clari.news.interest.people.column`	Daily "People" column: tidbits on celebs (moderated)
`clari.news.interest.quirks`	Unusual or funny news stories (moderated)
`clari.news.issues`	Stories on major issues (moderated)
`clari.news.issues.civil_rights`	Freedom, racism, civil rights issues (moderated)
`clari.news.issues.conflict`	Conflict between groups around the world (moderated)
`clari.news.issues.family`	Family, child abuse, etc. (moderated)
`clari.news.labor`	Unions, strikes (moderated)
`clari.news.labor.strike`	Strikes (moderated)
`clari.news.law`	General group for law related issues (moderated)
`clari.news.law.civil`	Civil trials and litigation (moderated)
`clari.news.law.crime`	Major crimes (moderated)
`clari.news.law.crime.sex`	Sex crimes and trials (moderated)
`clari.news.law.crime.trial`	Trials for criminal actions (moderated)
`clari.news.law.crime.violent`	Violent crime and criminals (moderated)
`clari.news.law.drugs`	Drug related crimes and drug stories (moderated)
`clari.news.law.investigation`	Investigation of crimes (moderated)
`clari.news.law.police`	Police and law enforcement (moderated)
`clari.news.law.prison`	Prisons, prisoners and escapes (moderated)
`clari.news.law.profession`	Lawyers, judges, etc. (moderated)
`clari.news.law.supreme`	U.S. Supreme Court rulings and news (moderated)
`clari.news.lifestyle`	Fashion, leisure, etc. (moderated)
`clari.news.military`	Military equipment, people and issues (moderated)
`clari.news.movies`	Reviews, news and stories on movie stars. (moderated)
`clari.news.music`	Reviews and issues concerning music (moderated)
`clari.news.politics`	Politicians and politics (moderated)
`clari.news.politics.people`	Politicians and political personalities (moderated)
`clari.news.religion`	Religion, religious leaders, televangelists (moderated)
`clari.news.sex`	Sexual issues, sex-related political stories (moderated)
`clari.news.terrorism`	Terrorist actions around the world (moderated)
`clari.news.top`	Top US news stories (moderated)
`clari.news.top.world`	Top international news stories (moderated)
`clari.news.trends`	Surveys and trends (moderated)
`clari.news.trouble`	Less major accidents, problems and mishaps (moderated)
`clari.news.tv`	TV schedules, news, reviews and stars. (moderated)
`clari.news.urgent`	Major breaking stories of the day (moderated)
`clari.news.weather`	Weather and temperature reports (moderated)
`clari.sports.baseball`	Baseball scores, stories, games, stats (moderated)
`clari.sports.basketball`	Basketball coverage (moderated)
`clari.sports.features`	Sports feature stories (moderated)
`clari.sports.football`	Pro football coverage (moderated)
`clari.sports.hockey`	NHL coverage (moderated)
`clari.sports.misc`	Other sports, plus general sports news (moderated)

`clari.sports.motor`	Racing, motor sports (moderated)
`clari.sports.olympic`	The Olympic Games (moderated)
`clari.sports.tennis`	Tennis news and scores (moderated)
`clari.sports.top`	Top sports news (moderated)
`clari.streetprice`	Direct buyer prices for computer equipment (moderated)
`clari.tw.aerospace`	Aerospace industry and companies (moderated)
`clari.tw.computers`	Computer industry (moderated)
`clari.tw.defense`	Defense industry issues (moderated)
`clari.tw.education`	Stories involving universities and colleges (moderated)
`clari.tw.electronics`	Electronics makers and sellers (moderated)
`clari.tw.environment`	Environmental news, hazardous waste, etc. (moderated)
`clari.tw.health`	Disease, medicine, health care, sick celebs (moderated)
`clari.tw.health.aids`	AIDS stories, research, political issues (moderated)
`clari.tw.misc`	General technical industry stories (moderated)
`clari.tw.nuclear`	Nuclear power and waste (moderated)
`clari.tw.science`	General science stories (moderated)
`clari.tw.space`	NASA, astronomy and spaceflight (moderated)
`clari.tw.stocks`	Computer and technology stock prices (moderated)
`clari.tw.telecom`	Phones, satellites, media and general telecom (moderated)

Glossary

absolute pathname: A pathname in which the full name of every directory is specified, from the root directory to the actual file. (21)

account: An arrangement that allows someone to use a Unix system. An account keeps track of resources, such as disk space. Before you can use a Unix system, your system manager must set up an account for you and give you a userid. (4)

address: A formal description of the destination of a mail message. (13)

alias: 1. In the C-Shell, an alternate name given to a command or a list of commands. (11) 2. In the **mail** program, a name given to a list of addresses. (14)

alternate hierarchy: Within Usenet, one of several categories of newsgroups that are not carried on all news servers. Compare to **mainstream hierarchy**. (23)

anonymous ftp: An Internet service that allows you to download files from remote Internet computers without a special userid and password. To use anonymous **ftp**, you **telnet** to a remote computer that offers this service, and log in by specifying a userid of **anonymous**. (25)

archie: An Internet service that helps you find the names of anonymous **ftp** sites that carry a particular file. (25)

archie client: A program that allows you to access **archie**. (25)

archie server: A program that offers an **archie** resource. (25)

Chapter references are indicated by the numbers in parentheses.

archive: A collection of files that have been packed together into a single large file using the `tar` program. (25)

arguments: When you type a command, the items that follow the name of the command. The arguments for a commands are the options and the parameters. (9)

article: A message that has been posted to a Usenet newsgroup. (23)

article attribute: Within the **nn** newsreader, a marking within a list of news article subjects that indicates the status of an article. (24)

article id: Within the **nn** newsreader, a lowercase letter or a number that identifies a particular article within a list. (24)

ASCII code: A standardized system in which character data is represented as bits. Each character is stored in one byte (8 bits). Within a byte, the leftmost bit is ignored. The other 7 bits form a pattern of 0s and 1s that represents the particular character. The ASCII code contains 128 distinct bit patterns. The full ASCII code is shown in Appendix D. (16)

ASCII file: A file that contains data in the form of characters. Same as **text file.** (20)

backbone: A high-speed link connecting parts of a network. (3)

bandwidth: Within the Usenet community, slang for the resources used to transmit and store news articles. For example, someone might argue that people should be discouraged from sending frivolous or vacuous articles as they waste bandwidth. See also **signal/noise ratio**. (24)

bang path: An address, used with UUCP, consisting of a list of computer names and a userid, the names being separated by an ! character. For example, `tinker!evers!chance`. (The term "bang" is slang for the ! character.)

bar: A meaningless word, used to represent an unnamed item during a discussion or exposition. The word "bar" is usually used along with "foo" to refer to two unnamed items. The convention is to use "foo" for the first item and "bar" for the second item. For example, you might hear someone ask the question, "I have two files, `foo` and `bar`. How can I copy all the lines in `foo` that contain a particular pattern to end of `bar`?" See also **foo** and **foobar**. (24)

Bash: An upward compatible replacement for the Bourne shell developed by Free Software Foundation as part of the GNU project. (10)

Chapter references are indicated by the numbers in parentheses.

binary file: A file that contains data that makes sense only when read by a program. Binary files use a full 8 bits per byte to store data. Text files contain characters that use only 7 bits per byte. Compare to **text file**. (20)

bit: The basic element of data storage. A bit can hold a single element which is either in one state or another. The custom is to speak of a bit as containing either a 0 or a 1. A bit that contains a 0 is said to be "off". A bit that contains a 1 is said to be "on". The term **bit** is a contraction of "binary digit". (20)

body: 1. In a mail message, the main part of the message, the text. (14) 2. In a Usenet news article, the actual text of the article. (24) Compare to **header**.

bookmark: When using the **gopher**, a menu item that has been selected and retained for further reference. (25)

bookmark list: When using the **gopher**, a list of bookmarks chosen by the user. (25)

Bourne shell: The original Unix shell, named after its creator Steven Bourne. The Bourne shell has since been updated, although it lacks the advanced features of other shells. Many people consider the Bourne shell to be the best shell for executing scripts. However, as a primary interface, most users choose a shell that provides a more modern command processor. (10)

Bourne shell family: Collective name for the Bourne shell, Korn shell, Bash and the Zsh. (10)

browser: A client program used to access the World Wide Web. (25)

BSD: A multitasking, multiuser operating system developed at the University of California at Berkeley, originally based on Unix. The name stands for "Berkeley Software Distribution". (2)

BTW: Abbreviation for "by the way". (24)

byte: A unit of data storage, a collection of 8 consecutive bits. One byte can hold a single character. (20)

C: A programming language, originally developed by Ken Thompson and Dennis Ritchie. C has since been extended and standardized and is widely used throughout the world. (10)

C++: A programming language, developed by Bjarne Stroustrup. C++ is upward compatible with C and incorporates facilities for object-oriented programming. The name C++ is pronounced "see-plus-plus". (10)

Chapter references are indicated by the numbers in parentheses.

case sensitive: Describes a program or system that distinguishes between upper- and lowercase letters. (4)

cbreak mode: Describes a program that reads each character as it is typed. Such programs will interpret single-character commands as soon as the character is typed. Thus, it is not necessary to press <Return> after such commands. (24)

central scrutinizer: A futuristic, hybrid machine that carries out the job of enforcing all the laws that have not yet been passed. (25)

character terminal: A terminal that displays only characters: letters, numbers, punctuation and so on. (3)

child directory: A directory that lies within another directory. All directories, except the root directory, can be considered to be child directories. The directory that contains the child directory is called the parent directory. Same as **subdirectory**. (20)

Clarinet: A set of newsgroups, in the same format as Usenet newsgroups, that contain real news. Clarinet is a subscription service. Unlike Usenet, Clarinet is not free. (23)

click: To press a button on a pointing device (usually a mouse). (5)

client: A program that requests a resource from a server. (3)

client/server relationship: Describes the connection between a client (resource requester) and a server (resource provider). (3)

command line: 1. When you enter a Unix command, the entire line that you type before you press the <Return> key. (9) 2. When using the **vi** editor, the bottom line of the screen, upon which certain commands are echoed as they are typed. (19)

command mode: Within the **vi** editor, when the characters you type are interpreted as commands. Compare to **input mode**. (19)

command processor: A program that reads and interprets commands that you enter at your terminal. The shell is a command processor. (10)

command substitution: A feature of the shell in which the output of one command is inserted into another command which is then executed. (16)

command syntax: The formal description of how a command must be entered. (9)

console: The terminal (screen, keyboard, possibly a mouse) that is built into a host computer. (3)

Chapter references are indicated by the numbers in parentheses.

CPU: A synonym for processor, the main component of a computer. Originally, this term was an acronym standing for "Central Processing Unit". In Unix, the term simply refers to the processor. For example, the amount of processor time used by a program is called CPU time. (12)

cracker: A person who tries to break into computer systems for fun. (4)

crossposted: Within Usenet, designates an article that has been posted to more than one newsgroup. (24)

C-Shell: A shell developed by Bill Joy as the Berkeley Unix alternative to the Bourne shell. The programming language offered by this shell resembles the C language, hence the name C-Shell. The C-Shell is the default shell on many Unix systems, especially those derived from Berkeley Unix. The name C-Shell is pronounced "see-shell". (10)

C-Shell Family: Collective name for the C-Shell and the Tcsh. (10)

CSO name server: A program that acts as a white pages directory, searching for names and addresses associated with a particular institution. The name "CSO" refers to the Computing Services Office at the University of Illinois, Urbana, where the first CSO name server was developed. (25)

current directory: The designation for the directory that will be used, by default, when entering Unix commands. The current directory is set by using the **cd** (change directory) command and displayed by using the **pwd** (print working directory) command. Same as **working directory**. (21)

current message: Within the **mail** program, the default message upon which a command will act. Usually the last message that was read. (14)

cursor: A special character – often an underscore that blinks – that marks your current position on the screen of your terminal. (3)

daemon: A program that executes in the background, usually to provide a service of general interest. (18)

default: An assumed value that will be used when an particular item is not specified. (9)

demodulation: The conversion of telephone signals to computer signals. See also **modem**, **modulation**. (3)

device file: Same as **special file**. (20)

Chapter references are indicated by the numbers in parentheses.

digest: A type of Usenet posting that contains a collection of articles. (23)

directory: A type of file that, conceptually, contains other files, some of which might be other directories. Actually, a directory does not contain files, it contains the information that Unix needs to access the files. Directories are one of the three types of Unix files. Compare to **ordinary file, special file**. (20, 21)

display: In the X Window system, the screen, keyboard and pointing device (usually a mouse) associated with a particular terminal. (5)

display manager: An X Window program that handles the login procedure, automatically starting X Window and a window manager. (5)

display server: A program that takes care of the details of interacting with a graphical user interface on behalf of other programs. (5)

DNS: A system used within the Internet to convert domain addresses (using names) to IP addresses (using numbers). The name DNS is an abbreviation for "Domain Name System". (25)

domain: The part of a standard Internet address that indicates the complete name of the computer. For example, in the address **harley@nipper.ucsb.edu**, the domain is **nipper.ucsb.edu** (13)

domain address: An Internet address that uses names called domains. For example, **harley@nipper.ucsb.edu** is a domain address. Compare to **IP address**. (25)

Domain Name System: A system used within the Internet to convert domain addresses (using names) to IP addresses (using numbers). Abbreviated as "DNS". (25)

dotfile: A file whose name begins with a . (period) character. When listing file names with the **ls** command, dotfiles are not listed unless requested specifically. Same as **hidden file**. (21)

doubleclick: To press a button on a pointing device (usually a mouse) twice in rapid succession. (5)

download: To transfer data from a remote computer to your computer. (25)

drag: To use a pointing device (usually a mouse) to move a graphical object on the screen of your terminal. You point to the object, hold down a button, move the pointing device to indicate the new location, and then release the button.

Chapter references are indicated by the numbers in parentheses.

dragon: A type of daemon that is not invoked explicitly, but is always there, waiting in the background to perform some task. (18)

echo: To display a character on the screen that corresponds to a key pressed by a user. For example, when you press the <A> key, Unix echoes the letter "A". (3)

editing buffer: A working area, used by the **vi** editor, to hold the data you are editing. (19)

editor: A program used to create and modify text files. (19)

Emacs: An editor, originally developed by Richard Stallman and maintained by the Free Software Foundation. Emacs is a full working environment that is highly customizable. (19)

email: Same as **mail**. The term **email** is a contraction of "electronic mail". (13)

emulate: To run a program that causes a computer to act like a different device. For example, when you use a PC to connect to a Unix host computer, you run a program on the PC that emulates a terminal. (3)

entry: The documentation for a single topic within the online manual. Same as **page**. (8)

environment variable: Within the shell, an item, known by a name, that represents a value that is accessible to any program. (11)

escape character: A character that, when read by a program, tells the program that the data that follows is to be treated in a special way. (14)

event: Within the shell, a command that has been entered. (11)

event number: Within the shell, a number that identifies an event (a command that has been entered). (11)

executable program: A program that, having been translated into machine language and linked, is ready to be executed. (20)

execute: To follow the instructions contained in a program. Same as **run**. (2)

execute permission: A type of file permission that allows the execution of an ordinary file or the searching of a directory. (22)

expired: Describes a Usenet article that is deleted because its posting date is older than a specific threshold. Most system managers set up their news servers so that articles expire automatically within one to three weeks. (23)

Chapter references are indicated by the numbers in parentheses.

extension: The last part of a file name that follows a . (period) character. For example, the file name **foobar.c** has an extension of .c (22)

FAQ: A question that has been asked so many times that its answer has been written categorically and placed on a list of other such questions. Abbreviation for "frequently asked question". (23)

FAQL: Abbreviation for "frequently asked question list". (24)

file: Any source of input or target of output. There are three types of files: ordinary files, directories and special files. (20, 22)

file mode: A three-number value, for example, **755**, that describes three sets of file permissions: read, write and execute permissions. The first number describes the permissions for the userid that owns the file. The second number describes the permissions for the userid's group. The third number describes the permissions for everybody else. (22)

file permission: One of three types of authorizations (read, write and execute), that specifies how a file may be accessed. (22)

file server: A program or sometimes a computer that provides access to files over a network. (3)

filename generation: The term used with the Bourne shell, Korn shell and Zsh as a synonym for filename substitution. (21)

filename substitution: Within the C-Shell, replacing a pattern that is part of a command by all the file names that match the pattern. Within the pattern, certain characters named wildcards have special meanings. See also **globbing, wildcard**. (21)

filter: Any program that reads data from the standard input and writes data to the standard output. (16)

finger: To display information about a userid by entering the **finger** command. (12)

flame: Within Usenet, an angry or abusive response to a previous article. A flame may be sent as a followup article to the newsgroup in which the original article appeared, or it may be sent as a private communication via mail to the author of the original article. (24)

flame war: Within Usenet, a situation in which people post many flames on a specific topic. (24)

FOAF: Abbreviation for "friend of a friend". (24)

Chapter references are indicated by the numbers in parentheses.

focus: When using a graphical user interface, describes which window is active by being logically connected to the keyboard of your terminal. Once you focus on a window, whatever you type on the keyboard is used as input for the program running in that window. (5)

followup article: Within Usenet, an article in which the author responds to a previous article. (24)

foo: A meaningless word, used to represent an unnamed item during a discussion or exposition. When a second unnamed item must be discussed, it is often referred to as "bar". For example, you might hear someone ask the question, "I have two files, **foo** and **bar**. How can I copy all the lines in **foo** that contain a particular pattern to the end of **bar**?" See also **bar** and **foobar**. (24)

foobar: A meaningless word, used to represent an unnamed item during a discussion or exposition. "Foobar" is often used to represent some type of pattern. For example, you might see the following question posted to a Usenet newsgroup, "How do I remove a file named **foobar**?" See also **foo** and **bar**. (24)

FQDN: An Internet address that specifies all necessary domains. Abbreviation for "fully qualified domain name". (25)

frequently asked question: A question that has been asked so many times that its answer has been written categorically and placed on a list of other such questions. Abbreviated as **FAQ**. (23)

ftp: A program that allows you to transfer files between two computers. The name **ftp** stands for "file transfer protocol". (25)

fully qualified domain name: An Internet address that specifies all necessary domains. Abbreviated as **FQDN**. (25)

FYI: Abbreviation for "for your information". (24)

gateway: A computer that acts as a link between programs running on two different networks. (3)

GECOS field: Part of each entry in the password file. For each userid, the GECOS field contains the name and other information relating to the person using that userid. (12)

gigabyte: A unit of storage measurement, 2^{30} bytes. One gigabyte is 1,073,741,824 bytes. See also **kilobyte**, **megabyte**. (21)

Chapter references are indicated by the numbers in parentheses.

global variable: Same as **environment variable** (11)

globbing: Within a shell, the act of performing filename substitution. We say that a shell globs when it replaces a pattern in a command by all the file names that match the pattern. See also **filename substitution**, **wildcard**. (21)

GNU: A project of the Free Software Foundation dedicated to developing an entire Unix system independent of System V. The name GNU is a recursive acronym standing for "GNU's not Unix". (10)

gopher: An Internet service that allows you to use a simple, consistent menu to access a wide variety of distributed information and services. (25)

gopher client: A program that allows you to access the **gopher**. (25)

gopherspace: Describes all the information and services that, potentially, are accessible via the **gopher**. (25)

graphical user interface: A system in which the user interacts with the host computer by using a pointing device (usually a mouse) to manipulate windows, icons, menus and other graphical elements. (5)

graphics terminal: A terminal that displays not only characters, but anything that can be drawn on the screen using small dots. (3)

group: Within Usenet, a named collection of related articles. Same as **newsgroup**. (23)

groupid: The name of a group of userids. The groupid is used to allocate file permissions. (22)

GUI: Abbreviation for "graphical user interface." (5)

hack: To put forth a massive amount of nerd-like effort, usually by programming. (4)

hacker: A person who hacks. (4)

hard link: Synonym for **link**. (22)

hardware: The physical components of a computer: keyboard, display, mouse, disk, processor, memory, and so on. (2)

header: 1. In a mail message, a number of lines at the beginning of the message that contain descriptive information. (14)   2. In a Usenet news article, a number of lines at the beginning of the article that contain descriptive information. (24)

Chapter references are indicated by the numbers in parentheses.

hidden file: A file whose name begins with a . (period) character. When listing file names with the **ls** command, dotfiles are not listed unless requested specifically. Same as **dotfile**. (21)

hierarchy: Within Usenet, a collection of related newsgroups. (23)

history list: Within the shell, a list of commands that have been entered. (11)

history substitution: Within the shell, a facility that lets you edit and re-enter a previous command without having to re-type it. (11)

home directory: The directory that is designated to hold the files for a particular userid. Whenever you log in, your current directory is automatically set to be your home directory. (20)

hop: A single link in a chain of computers through which data must pass in order to reach a final destination. For example, say that a mail message must pass through three computers, **tinker** to **evers** to **chance**. We say that the mail takes two hops to reach its destination. Similarly, we might say that **chance** is two hops away from **tinker**. (13)

host: A computer that runs Unix. Users log in to the host to initiate a Unix work session. (3)

hypermedia: Describes hypertext in which various types of data can be stored – sound, images, video and so on – as well as regular text. (25)

hypertext: Describes text in which certain data items contain links to other items. (25)

icon: When using a graphical user interface, a small picture that represents a window. (5)

iconize: To change an open window into an icon. (5)

IMHO: Abbreviation for "in my humble opinion". (24)

IMO: Abbreviation for "in my opinion". (24)

index node: In the Unix file system, a structure that holds the basic information about a file. Same as **inode** (22)

index number: In the Unix file system, a number that identifies a particular index node (inode) within the table of index nodes. Same as **inumber**.

inode: In the Unix file system, a structure that holds the basic information about a file. Same as **index node** (22)

Chapter references are indicated by the numbers in parentheses.

input mode: Within the **vi** editor, when the characters you type are inserted into the editing buffer. Compare to **command mode**. (19)

Internet: The global wide area network that uses the IP protocol to communicate. The Internet connects countless computers around the world and provides many important services such as mail, file transfer and remote login. (3, 13)

Internet address: See **standard Internet address**. (13)

Internet service: A resource that is generally available to all users of the Internet. The basic categories of Internet services are mail, file transfer, remote login and support for Usenet. (25)

interpret: The action of an interpreter as it reads and executes a command. (11)

interpreter: A program that reads and executes a list of commands called a script. (11)

inumber: In the Unix file system, a number that identifies a particular index node (inode) within the table of index nodes. Same as **index number**.

IP: One of the TCP/IP protocols, the basic protocol of the Internet. IP is used to move packets of raw data from one computer to another. (13)

IP address: An Internet address that uses numbers rather than domains (names). For example, **18.172.1.27** is an IP address. Compare to **domain address**. (25)

job number: When printing a file, the number designated to identify the print job. (18)

junk: Within Usenet, to discard all the unread articles with the same subject. That is, to discard the rest of the thread. Same as **kill**. (24)

key: A password, used by the `crypt` program to encode data. (16)

kill: Within Usenet, to discard all the unread articles with the same subject. That is, to discard the rest of the thread. Same as **junk**. (24)

kilobyte: A unit of storage measurement, 2^{10} bytes. One kilobyte is 1,024 bytes. See also **gigabyte**, **megabyte**. (21)

knowbot: An automated, robot-like program that intelligently searches for information on your behalf. (25)

Korn shell: An upward compatible replacement for the Bourne shell, developed by David Korn. The Korn shell is the default shell on many Unix systems, especially those derived from System V. (10)

Chapter references are indicated by the numbers in parentheses.

LAN: Abbreviation for local area network. (3)

line editor: An editor that numbers lines of text and which uses commands based on these numbers. Same as **line-oriented editor**. Compare to **screen editor**. (19)

line-oriented editor: Same as **line editor**. (19)

link: Within the Unix file system, the connection between a file name and its inode. Same as **hard link**. See **inode**, **symbolic link**. (22)

local: With respect to a connection between two computers, describes your host computer. Compare to **remote**. For example, you can use `telnet` to log in to a remote computer from your local computer. (25)

local area network: A network in which the computers are connected directly by some type of cable. (3)

log in: To initiate a Unix work session. (4)

log out: To terminate a Unix work session. (4)

login: Describes the process of logging in. (4)

login shell: The shell that Unix starts automatically when you log in. (10)

logout: Describes the process of logging out. (4)

lowercase: Describes small letters, "a" to "z". (4)

mail: 1. A system in which messages, usually stored as files of text, are sent and received. For example, "You can use mail to send a message to someone else". 2. To send or receive such a message. For example, "Mail me the document that you want me to read." 3. The message itself. For example, "When I logged in, there was mail waiting for me." (13, 14)

mail server: A computer that acts as a way station for electronic mail. (3)

mailing list: A set of addresses that has a name. When you send a message to the name of the mailing list, a copy of the message is sent to each address on the list. (23)

main menu: When using X Window, the menu that appears when you move to an empty area of the screen and press a particular button on your pointing device. The main menu is used to start certain programs and to control your X Window session. (5)

Chapter references are indicated by the numbers in parentheses.

mainstream hierarchy: Within Usenet, one of several categories of newsgroups that are carried on all news servers. Compare to **alternate hierarchy**. (23)

manual: Same as the online manual. When Unix people refer to "the manual", they always mean the online manual. (8)

mask: Within the Unix file system, a three-number value that indicates which file permissions should be assigned by default to newly created files. (22)

maximize: To expand a window to its largest possible size. (5)

megabyte: A unit of storage measurement, 2^{20} bytes. One megabyte is 1,048,576 bytes. See also **kilobyte**, **gigabyte**. (21)

menu: A list of items from which you can make a selection. (5)

message of the day: A message, created by the system manager, that is displayed whenever someone logs in. (4)

message list: Within the `mail` program, the specification of one or more message numbers. (14)

minimize: Same as **iconize**. (5)

mode: Synonym for **file mode**. (22)

modem: A device – modulator/demodulator – that provides an interface between a computer and a telephone line. (3)

moderated newsgroup: Within Usenet, a newsgroup whose postings are controlled by a person called a moderator. All articles are sent to the moderator who then decides which ones should be posted to the newsgroup. (23)

moderator: A person who controls which articles are posted to a moderated newsgroup. (23)

modulation: The conversion of computer signals to telephone signals. (3)

MOTAS: Abbreviation for "member of the appropriate sex". (24)

MOTOS: Abbreviation for "member of the opposite sex". (24)

MOTSS: Abbreviation for "member of the same sex". (24)

Chapter references are indicated by the numbers in parentheses.

MUD: A computer program that creates a virtual-reality world to which users can connect, explore, role-play and so on. The name MUD is an abbreviation for "multiple user dimension". (24)

multitasking: Describes an operating system that can execute more than one program at the same time. (2)

multiuser: Describes an operating system that can support more than one user at the same time. (2)

navigate: When using the **gopher**, to make one's way through gopherspace. That is, to move from one menu item to another. (25)

net: A synonym for Usenet and, sometimes, for the Internet. Always referred to as "the net". (23)

netfind server: An program that helps you find someone's mail address by active searching. (25)

netiquette: Within Usenet, the generally accepted guidelines for good behavior. (24)

netnews: A synonym for Usenet. (23)

network: Two or more computers connected together in order to facilitate communication and to share resources. (3)

newline: The character, used in textual data, to indicate the end of a line. The **newline** character is **^J**.

news: 1. A collective name for the articles that are posted to the various Usenet discussion groups. For example, you might ask someone, "Have you read the news today?". You are asking if this person has read any Usenet articles. See **Usenet**. (23) 2. Announcements of local interest, displayed by using the **news** or **msgs** commands. (7)

news feed: A computer that provides a news server with a link to Usenet. (23)

newsgroup: Within Usenet, a named collection of related articles. Same as **group**. (23)

newsreader: A program that is used to read Usenet articles. (23)

news server: A computer that provides users on a network with access to the Usenet news. (3)

objoke: Synonym for **obligatory joke**. (23)

Chapter references are indicated by the numbers in parentheses.

obligatory joke: Within a humor newsgroup on Usenet, a joke that, by convention, must be included with an otherwise non-humorous posting. Same as **objoke**. (23)

one or more: Indicates that you must use at least one of something. For example, the syntax for a command might allow you to specify one or more file names. This means that you can specify more than one name, but you must use at least one name. Compare to **zero or more**. (9)

online manual: Information, available to all users at all times, that contains documentation about Unix commands and important system facilities. The online manual is divided into sections. Each section contains many entries (also called pages), each of which documents a single topic. To access the online manual, use the **man** command. With X Window, use the **xman** command. Users are encouraged to check the online manual before asking for help (see **RTFM**). (8)

operating system: A complex master control program whose principal function is to make efficient use of the hardware. The operating system acts as the primary interface to the hardware for both users and programs. (2)

options: An argument for a command, almost always prefaced with a – character, that specifies how you want the command to execute. For example, you might enter the command **ls -l**. This is the **ls** command with the **-l** option. In conversation, the – character is pronounced "minus" even though it has nothing to do with arithmetic. If you were to talk about the last example, you would say that you used the **ls** command with the "minus L" option. (9)

ordinary file: A file that contains data to be accessed by a person or a program. An ordinary file is what most people mean when they use the word "file". One of the three types of Unix files. Compare to **directory, special file**. (20)

page: The documentation for a single topic within the online manual. By tradition, the documentation for each topic is called a page even though it might be large enough to fill many printed pages. Same as **entry**. (8)

pager: A program that displays a text file or textual data, one screenful at a time. (17)

parameter: Within a command line, an argument that passes information to the program that will be executed. For example, a parameter might specify the name of a file. (9)

parent directory: A directory that contains another directory. The contained directory is called a subdirectory or child directory. (20)

Chapter references are indicated by the numbers in parentheses.

parse: The action of the shell as it analyzes the components of a command. (11)

password: A secret pattern of characters that must be typed as part of the login process to ensure that the user has proper authorization to use a particular userid. (4)

password file: A file, maintained by Unix, that contains information about all the userids in the system. On some systems, the password file also contains the passwords (encoded of course). On other systems, the passwords are kept separately in a shadow file. (12)

pathname: A description of a sequence of subdirectories. (21)

pathname expansion: The term used with Bash as a synonym for filename substitution. (21)

permission: Same as **file permission**. (22)

ping: To display information about the status of an Internet computer by entering the `ping` command. (12)

pipe: To pass data from one program to another so as to form a pipeline. (15)

pipeline: An arrangement in which two or more programs process data in sequence, the output of one program becoming the input to the next program. (15)

point and click: To use a pointing device (usually a mouse) to select a graphical object by moving to it and then clicking a button. (5)

pointing device: An instrument (usually a mouse) used to manipulate the elements of a graphical user interface. (5)

pop-up: When using a graphical user interface, describes a menu that appears from no apparent location as a result of some action you have taken. (5)

port: 1. The part of the host computer to which a terminal is connected. (6) 2. When using `telnet` to connect to another computer, a number that identifies a program that is to be automatically connected to the terminal session. (25)

post: To send an article to a Usenet newsgroup. (23)

posting: A Usenet article. (23)

print: 1. To display information on the terminal. For example, the command to display the name of your working (current) directory is named `pwd`, "print working directory". (6) 2. To print data on paper. (18)

Chapter references are indicated by the numbers in parentheses.

print job: Refers to a file that is printing or is waiting to be printed. (18)

print server: A program that coordinates the printing of data using various printers. (3)

program: A list of instructions that, when carried out by a computer, performs a task. (2)

protocol: A set of rules that allow different computers and programs to communicate with one another. (13)

pull-down: When using a graphical user interface, describes a menu which appears below a word once you use a pointing device (usually a mouse) to click on the word. (5)

queue: When printing, describes the list of files waiting to print. (18)

read permission: A type of file permission that allows the reading of an ordinary file or directory. (22)

real time: Describes a program or system that reacts instantly. (3)

recursive: For Unix file commands, describes options that process an entire sub-tree of directories. (21)

redirect: To send the output of a program to a designated destination. (15)

regular expression: A compact way of specifying a general pattern of characters. (16)

regular file: Synonym for **ordinary file**. (20)

relative pathname: A pathname that is interpreted as starting from the current directory. (21)

remote: With respect to a connection between two computers, describes the computer to which you are connected. Compare to **local**. For example, you can use **telnet** to log in to a remote computer from your local computer. (25)

remove: To erase a file by deleting its link. (22)

representation type: When using **ftp** to transfer files, describes the type of file – either text (ASCII) or binary – that will be transferred. (25)

root: The userid used by the system manager to become superuser. (4)

root directory: The main directory of the Unix file system. The root directory is, directly or indirectly, the parent directory of all the other directories. (20)

root menu: Same as **main menu**. (5)

Chapter references are indicated by the numbers in parentheses.

rot-13: Within Usenet, a scheme used to encode postings that are potentially offensive so they cannot be read by accident. (24)

router: A special-purpose computer that directs data from one network to another. (13)

RTFM: A reminder that someone should try to answer a question for him- or herself before asking someone else. The name RTFM is derived from the expression "read the fuckin' manual". (24)

run: To follow the instructions contained in a program. Same as **execute**. (2)

screen editor: An editor that allows you to enter and display data anywhere on the screen. Commands are not oriented toward line numbers. Compare to **line editor**. (19)

script: A list of commands to be executed by an interpreter such as a shell. (11)

scroll: To move lines on the screen of a terminal, usually up, to make room for new lines. (6)

search path: The names of the directories in which the shell looks to find a program. (11)

select: When using the **nn** newsreader, to mark an article that you want to read. (24)

server: A program or a computer that offers a resource, often over a network. A program that requests such a service is called a client. (3)

shadow file: A file that contains passwords (encoded, of course) as well as data relating to passwords, such as expiration dates. (12)

shell: A program that provides the primary interface to Unix by acting as a command processor and by interpreting scripts of commands. (10)

shell escape character: Within a program, the **!** character when used to indicate that the following command should be sent to the shell to be executed. (15)

shell prompt: One or more characters displayed by the shell to indicate that it is ready to accept a new command. (11)

shell script: A list of commands that can be executed by a shell. (11)

shell variable: An item, known by a name, that represents a value of some type within the shell. There are two types of shell variables: those that act as off/on switches and those that store a string of characters. (11)

sig: Same as **signature**. (24)

Chapter references are indicated by the numbers in parentheses.

signal: To send a control code to a program by pressing a special key. (6)

signal/noise ratio: With reference to a Usenet article, the ratio of worthwhile to non-worthwhile text. (24)

signature: Within Usenet, a short, predefined message that is appended automatically to each article that you post. A signature should contain your name and address, and should not be more than four lines. (24)

smiley: Several consecutive characters that, when viewed sideways, look like a small face. The basic smiley is :-) (Turn your head sideways to the left to see the face). A smiley is used in electronic communication to indicate a sense of irony or frivolity. In other words, the smiley replaces the charming smile that you would use in person to avoid the wrath of someone to whom you have just said something obnoxious or argumentative. (12,24)

smiley face: Same as **smiley**. (12, 24)

snail mail: Slang for regular postal office mail. In Unix, the unqualified term "mail" always refers to electronic mail. (13)

SO : Abbreviation for "significant other". That is, a wife, husband, girlfriend or boyfriend. See also **MOTAS, MOTOS, MOTSS**. (24)

soft link: Synonym for **symbolic link**. (22)

software: Computer programs of all types. (2)

source: 1. A program that has been written in a computer language. A synonym for **source program**. Before a source program can be executed, it must be translated into machine language. (20) 2. Within **wais**, a database that can be searched. (25)

source program: 1. A program that has been written in a computer language. Before a source program can be executed, it must be translated into machine language. Informally, a source program is referred to simply as **source**. (20)

special file: A file that represents a physical device. One of the three types of Unix files. Compare to **directory, ordinary file**. (20)

spoiler: In a Usenet article, a remark that gives away the ending to a movie or book. (24)

spool: To hold a file for further processing, such as printing, and to perform such processing at a convenient time. The name "spool" comes from an obsolete acronym meaning "simultaneous peripheral operations offline". (18)

Chapter references are indicated by the numbers in parentheses.

spool file: A temporary file that holds data for further processing at a convenient time, usually for printing. (18)

standard input: The technical designation for the default source of input for Unix programs. (15)

standard Internet address: An address in the form `userid@domain`. For example, `harley@nipper.ucsb.edu`. In this address, the userid is **harley**, and the domain is `nipper.ucsb.edu` (13)

standard output: The technical designation for the default target of output for Unix programs. (15)

subdirectory: A directory that lies within another directory. All directories, except the root directory, can be considered to be child directories. The directory that contains the child directory is called the parent directory. Same as **child directory**. (20)

sub-domain: In a standard Internet address, one part of the domain. For example, in the address **harley@nipper.ucsb.edu** there are three sub-domains, **nipper**, **ucsb** and **edu**. (13)

subscribe: When using a newsreader, to indicate that you want to read the articles in a particular Usenet newsgroup. (23)

superuser: A user, usually the system manager, who has logged in using the **root** userid (which affords special privileges). (4)

symbolic link: Within the Unix file system, a special type of link that is actually the pathname of another file. A symbolic link is sometimes called a **soft link** to distinguish it from a regular link. See **link**. (22)

syntax: Informally, the same as **command syntax**. The formal description of how a command must be entered. (9)

system administrator: The person who administers and manages a Unix system. Same as **system manager**. (4)

system mailbox: The file in which your mail is stored until you read it. (14)

system manager: The person who administers and manages a Unix system. Same as **system administrator**. (4)

Chapter references are indicated by the numbers in parentheses.

TCP: One of the TCP/IP protocols. TCP is used to coordinate the moving of data from one computer to another by breaking the data into packets. TCP stands for "transmission control protocol". (13)

TCP/IP: A collection of more than 100 different protocols used to connect computers within a network and to transmit data. TCP/IP is widely used, especially within the Internet. (13)

Tcsh: An upward compatible replacement for the C-Shell. The name Tcsh is pronounced "tee-see-shell". (10)

tee: A program, used within a pipeline, to save data in a specified file while, at the same time, sending the data to another program. (15)

teletype: An obsolete electro-mechanical communications device that printed its output on paper. Teletypes are the spiritual ancestors of modern Unix terminals. (6)

telnet: An Internet service that allows you to connect to and log in to a remote computer. (25)

termcap database: A collection of technical descriptions of all the different types of terminals. (6)

terminal: The hardware used by the someone to access a Unix system. A terminal has a keyboard, screen and possibly a mouse. (3)

terminal server: A special computer that acts as a switch, connecting terminals to host computers. (3)

text: Data that consists of ASCII characters: letters, numbers, punctuation and so on.

text editor: Synonym for **editor**. (19)

text file: A file that contains characters that can be displayed or printed. Text files use only 7 bits per byte because each character, as defined by the ASCII code, uses only 7 of the 8 bits. Same as **ASCII file**. Compare to **binary file**. (20)

thread: Within Usenet, a set of articles that have the same subject. (24)

tilde escape: Within the **mail** program, a command, prefaced by a ~ (tilde) character, that can be issued while you are typing a message. (14)

top-level domain: In a standard Internet address, the most general sub-domain. The top-level domain is the last sub-domain in the address. For example, in the address **harley@nipper.ucsb.edu**, the top-level domain is **edu**. (13)

Chapter references are indicated by the numbers in parentheses.

trap: For a program that is executing, to notice and react to a specific signal that otherwise might abort or affect the program. (6)

TTY: A terminal. (6)

Unix: 1. Any operating system that meets generally accepted "Unix-like" standards with respect to providing user and programming services. Modern Unix operating systems are both multitasking and multiuser and are usually derived, at least in spirit, from UNIX, BSD or both. 2. Describes a worldwide culture, based on the Unix operating system, involving interfaces, shells, programs, languages, conventions and standards. (2)

UNIX: The specific family of operating system products and associated software developed by AT&T/USL (Unix System Laboratories). (2)

unsubscribe: When using a newsreader program, to indicate that you do not want to read articles from a particular Usenet newsgroup. (23)

upload: To transfer data from your computer to a remote computer. (25)

uppercase: Describes capital letters, "A" to "Z". (4)

Usenet: A vast, decentralized association of computer systems that allows people around the world to share information. This information is in the form of articles sent to discussion groups, each with its own topic. Worldwide, there are well over 4,000 such groups, not including regional and local groups. Usenet articles are referred to as "news", even though they contain little real news. Usenet itself is sometimes referred to as "the net", "the news" or as "netnews". (23)

user: A person who uses a Unix system in some way. (4)

userid: The name, registered with a Unix system, that identifies an account. A userid usually represents a particular user. The word userid is pronounced "user-eye-dee". (4)

UUCP: A Unix-based networking system that allows any Unix computer to exchange files with any other Unix computer. (13)

UUCP address: An address, in the form of a bang path, used to send mail over the UUCP network. (13)

UUCP Mapping Project: A group that publishes regularly updated connection maps for the UUCP network. (13)

UUCP network: Same as **UUCP**. (13)

Chapter references are indicated by the numbers in parentheses.

veronica: An Internet service that allows you to search gopherspace for specific items. (25)

W3 : Synonym for the World Wide Web. (25)

wais: An Internet service that finds information for you by quickly searching one or more databases that may be stored anywhere on the Internet. The name **wais** stands for "wide area information service". (25)

wais client: A program that allows you to access **wais**. (25)

wais server: A program that offers a **wais** resource. (25)

WAN: Abbreviation for wide area network. (3)

whatis server: Within **archie**, a service that searches a database of file descriptions for a specified pattern. (25)

white pages directory: A program that provides the resource of searching for names and addresses. The name "white pages directory" was chosen to suggest the image of a computerized telephone directory. A white pages directory, however, typically contains information not found in a standard telephone directory, such as electronic mail addresses. (25)

whitespace: Consecutive space and tab characters that separate two items. (9)

whois server: A program that allows you to search a database for names and addresses. (25)

wide area network: A network connecting local area networks. (3)

wildcard: A character that has a special meaning when interpreted as part of a filename substitution pattern. See also **filename substitution, globbing**. (21)

window: A bounded region of the screen, manipulated by a graphical user interface. (5)

window manager: A program that, under the auspices of a graphical user interface, controls the appearance and characteristics of windows and other graphical elements. (5)

working directory: The designation for the directory that will be used, by default, when entering Unix commands. The working directory is set by using the **cd** (change directory) command and displayed by using the **pwd** (print working directory) command. Same as **current directory**. (21)

workstation: A Unix computer that is used by one person at a time. (3)

Chapter references are indicated by the numbers in parentheses.

World Wide Web: An Internet service that allows you to find information stored in a large number of hypertext-based databases by using a keyword search. (25)

write permission: A type of file permission that allows writing to an ordinary file or modifying the entries in a directory. (22)

WWW: Synonym for the World Wide Web. (25)

X client: An X Window program that calls upon an X server to act as its interface with the terminal. (5)

X server: An X Window display server. (5)

xterm: An X client that provides a virtual terminal within a window. (5)

X terminal: A graphics terminal designed to run X Window. (5)

X: Same as **X Window**. (5)

X Window: A widely used system designed to support graphical user interfaces. The correct usage of this term is singular, "X Window", not plural, "X Windows". The X Window system is often referred to simply as X. (5)

zero or more: Indicates that you can use one or more of something or that you can omit the item entirely. For example, the syntax for a command might allow you to specify zero or more file names. This means that you can specify one or more names, or omit the name entirely. Compare to **one or more**. (9)

Zsh: An replacement for the Bourne shell and C-Shell developed by Paul Falstad. The name Zsh is pronounced "zee-shell". (10)

Chapter references are indicated by the numbers in parentheses.

Reading List

Once you have read this book cover to cover several times, you will probably want to move onward and upward. In this section, we will thread our way through the serpentine streets and deadends of Unix-book land. We will thrust our hands into the oysters of literature and extract those pearls that are worth your time and your money. (Aren't you glad this book isn't fiction?)

We have organized our recommendations into the following categories:

Online Unix Book Lists
Publishers
Dictionaries
General Unix Books
Advanced Unix Books
The Shells
Perl
Editors: **vi** and Emacs
The Internet
Programming
X Window

Online Unix Book Lists

There are many, many Unix books. In this reading list, we describe the books that we particularly recommend. However, the best way to keep abreast of all that is current is to read one of the online book lists. These are maintained by volunteers and are accessible on the Internet via anonymous **ftp**. (We explain how to use anonymous **ftp** in Chapter 25.) You will also find book lists posted in certain Usenet newsgroups. *news.answers* and *misc.books.technical* are good places to look. (Usenet is explained in Chapter 23.)

      Name: *A Concise Guide to Unix Books*
      Editor: Samuel Ko
    `ftp` site: `pit-manager.mit.edu`
   Directory: `/pub/usenet/news.answers/books`
   File name: `unix.Z`
     Usenet: `news.answers, misc.books.technical`

      Name: *Yet Another Book List*
      Editor: Mitch Wright
    `ftp` site: `ftp.rahul.net`
   Directory: `/pub/mitch/YABL`
   File name: `yabl.Z`

You will notice that the names of the files end with a `.Z` extension. This means that they are stored in a compressed format. After transferring the file, you must use the **uncompress** command to access the data. (This is explained in Chapter 25.)

The *Concise Guide*, mentioned above, also contains the name of a few highly specialized Unix book lists. You can find other similar resources by looking at the lists of Internet services that are described at the end of Chapter 25.

Publishers

There are many publishers of Unix books. The two most important are:

O'Reilly & Associates
   (800) 998-9938
   (707) 829-0515
   (707) 829-0104 (fax)
   mail: **nuts@ora.com**

Prentice Hall
   (800) 922-0579 (customer service)
   (201) 767-4990 (customer service)
   (515) 284-6751 (to order a book)
   (515) 284-2607 (fax)

You can access the O'Reilly book catalog by anonymous **ftp** as follows:

Name: *O'Reilly & Associates Catalog*
ftp site: **ftp.ora.com**
Directory: **/pub**
File name: **book.catalog.Z**

(In the same directory, you will also find the examples from the O'Reilly books.) Alternatively, you can **telnet** to O'Reilly's **gopher** (see Chapter 25) at **gopher.ora.com**. Log in as **gopher**.

Dictionaries

If you liked the "What's in a Name?" vignettes throughout this book, you'll love *The New Hacker's Dictionary*: over 400 pages of words your mother wouldn't want you to know. You also get a marvelous essay on hacker folklore, as well as the largest list of acknowledgments east of the Mississippi.

Title: *The New Hacker's Dictionary*
Author: Eric Raymond
Publisher: MIT Press
ISBN: 0-262-68069-6

The material in this book is derived from the so-called "Jargon File" which is available by anonymous **ftp** from many different sites. To find an **ftp** site, you can use **archie** (see Chapter 25). First use **set search exact**, and then perform the search by using **prog jargon**. Here is one anonymous **ftp** site:

Name: The Jargon File
ftp site: **pit-manager.mit.edu**
Directory: **/pub/jargon**

You can also access the Jargon File via the World Wide Web (also discussed Chapter 25).

General Unix Books

The best general Unix book is, of course, this one. However, once you get into the Unix culture, *Life with Unix* will provide you with the inside scoop. This book has all kinds of stories and technical information that the "official" documentation and books never mention.

Title: *Life with Unix: A Guide for Everyone*
Authors: Don Libes and Sandy Ressler
Publisher: Prentice Hall
ISBN: 0-13-536657-7

For a technical reference, go for *Unix for the Impatient*. It is crammed full of material, covering every command and every option. This is not a book for reading. This is a book to have by your side late at night when nobody is around to answer your questions.

Title: *Unix for the Impatient*
Authors: Paul Abrahams and Bruce Larson
Publisher: Addison Wesley
ISBN: 0-201-55703-7

Of the many let's-all-learn-Unix books, there are four that we would like to mention. First, *Peter Norton's Guide to Unix* is well-written and has a spiffy picture on the front cover. (If the tiny picture on the back cover of this book left you feeling dissatisfied, the Norton book has a much larger picture of Harley Hahn.) More to the point, this book provides a good, all-around introduction to System V Unix and is especially useful if you are coming from a PC environment.

Title: *Peter Norton's Guide to Unix*
Authors: Peter Norton and Harley Hahn
Publisher: Bantam Books
ISBN: 0-553-35260-1

The next two books are from O'Reilly and are called *Unix in a Nutshell*. There are two versions, one for System V and one for Berkeley Unix. These books provide handy references to all the important commands as well as the basic Unix programs. Just the thing for a long bus ride or as a housewarming gift.

Title: *Unix in a Nutshell* (System V and Solaris 2.0)
Authors: Daniel Gilly and the O'Reilly staff
Publisher: O'Reilly & Associates
ISBN: 1-56592-001-5

Title: *Unix in a Nutshell* (Berkeley Unix)
Authors: Tim O'Reilly and the O'Reilly staff
Publisher: O'Reilly & Associates
ISBN: 0-937175-20-X

Finally, if you would like another approach to basic Unix, *The Unix Operating System* is a good alternative and goes into a few more advanced areas than this book. Some of the examples are a little goofy. (But who are we to talk?)

Overall, the author knows what he is doing and addresses the basic issues that are important for programmers.

    Title: *The Unix Operating System*
   Author: Kaare Christian
 Publisher: John Wiley & Sons
    ISBN: 0-471-84781-X

Advanced Unix Books

If you develop a curiosity about how things work on the inside, there are are three good books that explain the Unix internals. The ones by Bach and Andleigh explain System V; the one by Leffler explains Berkeley Unix.

    Title: *Unix System Architecture*
   Author: Prabhat Andleigh
 Publisher: Prentice Hall
    ISBN: 0-13-949843-5

    Title: *The Design of the Unix Operating System*
   Author: Maurice Bach
 Publisher: Prentice Hall
    ISBN: 0-13-201799-7

    Title: *The Design and Implementation of the 4.3 BSD Unix*
            Operating System
  Authors: Samuel Leffler et al
 Publisher: Addison-Wesley
    ISBN: 0-201-06196-1

The Shells

For advanced material on the Unix shells, we recommend three books. For the Korn shell, try *The KornShell Command and Programming Language*. This book is co-authored by Korn himself. As an alternative, many people prefer *Unix Desktop Guide to the Korn Shell* as being better for beginners. For the C-Shell, the clear choice is *The Unix C Shell Field Guide*. If you are interested enough in the shell to buy a book, don't even bother with the Bourne shell.

    Title: *The KornShell Command and Programming Language*
  Authors: Morris Bolsky and David Korn
 Publisher: Prentice Hall
    ISBN: 0-672-48513-3

Title: *Unix Desktop Guide to the Korn Shell*
Author: John Valley
Publisher: Sams
ISBN: 0-672-48513-3

Title: *The Unix C Shell Field Guide*
Authors: Gail Anderson and Paul Anderson
Publisher: Prentice Hall
ISBN: 0-13-937468-X

Perl

For system administration programming and just all-around general hacking, Perl is often the scripting language of choice. The definitive book is *Programming Perl*, by Perl's inventor (Larry Wall) and its most well-known proponent (Randal Schwartz).

Title: *Programming Perl*
Authors: Larry Wall and Randal Schwartz
Publisher: O'Reilly & Associates
ISBN: 0-937175--64-1

Editors: `vi` and Emacs

We covered the Unix editors in Chapter 19. Unfortunately we had room to do justice only to **vi**. To learn Emacs (aside from the built-in tutorial), try *Learning GNU Emacs*, yet another O'Reilly book. For reference, nothing could be finer than the *GNU Emacs Manual* from Mr. Emacs himself, Richard Stallman.

Title: *Learning GNU Emacs*
Authors: Debra Cameron and Bill Rosenblatt
Publisher: O'Reilly & Associates
ISBN: 0-937175-84-6

Title: *GNU Emacs Manual*
Author: Richard Stallman
Publisher: Free Software Foundation

For more on **vi** (if Chapter 19 of this book isn't enough), try *Learning the* **vi** *Editor* or *A Guide to* **vi**.

Title: *Learning the* **vi** *Editor*
Author: Linda Lamb
Publisher: O'Reilly and Associates
ISBN: 0-937175-67-6

Title: *A Guide to* **vi***: Visual Editing on the Unix System*
Author: Dan Sonnenschein
Publisher: Prentice Hall
ISBN: 0-13-371311-3

In spite of its wacky title (no doubt picked by a committee who never used **vi**), the Sonnenschein book is a good solid work: lots of examples, clear explanations and a good reference.

The Internet

We talked about the Internet in Chapters 13 and 25, but, as you can imagine, there is much, much more. There are many different Internet books, but only three worth mentioning.

By far, the best and most comprehensive Internet book is *The Internet Complete Reference* (written by Harley Hahn). This book explains everything you need to know to use the Internet and contains information that literally does not exist anywhere else. Moreover, the book contains a large catalog showing you how to access over 750 different Internet resources.

Title: *The Internet Complete Reference*
Author: Harley Hahn
Publisher: Osborne McGraw-Hill
ISBN: 0-07-881980-6

The grandfather of Important Internet Books was *The Whole Internet User's Guide Catalog*. Somewhat dated, but still popular, this is the book that introduced many users to the Internet.

Title: *The Whole Internet User's Guide Catalog*
Author: Ed Krol
Publisher: O'Reilly & Associates
ISBN: 1-56592-025-2

Finally, there is a reference covering mail addresses for the Internet and about a zillion other networks. The name is *!%@:: A Guide to Electronic Mail Addressing*. (Don't ask us how to pronounce it. We have trouble with easy words like Mxyzptlk and anitdisestablishmentarianism.)

Title: *!%@:: A Guide to Electronic Mail Addressing*
Authors: Donnalyn Frey and Rick Adams
Publisher: O'Reilly & Associates
ISBN: 0-937175-15-3-0

Programming

One of these days – either by choice or because someone forces you – you may decide to become a Unix programmer. Well, what better way to spend your short visit on planet Earth?

You will quickly find that the programming languages of choice are C and C++. (The meaning behind these names is explained in Chapter 10.) You will just as quickly find that there are more Introduction-to-C-programming books than you can shake several sticks at.

The classic, seminal book on the C language is *The C Programming Language* by Kernighan and Ritchie. Without this book on your shelf, your life as a C programmer is a meaningless sham. (Be sure to get the second edition.)

> Title: *The C Programming Language*
> Authors: Brian Kernighan and Dennis Ritchie
> Publisher: Prentice Hall
> ISBN: 0-13-110362-8

Not far behind in the list of programming books to be caught dead in a ditch with is *C: A Reference Manual*.

> Title: *C: A Reference Manual*
> Authors: Samuel Harbison and Guy Steel
> Publisher: Prentice Hall
> ISBN: 0-13-110933-2

For the object-oriented crowd, the soon-to-be classic, seminal book is by the father of C++, Bjarne Stroustrup (pronounced "Bjarne Stroustrup").

> Title: *The C++ Programming Language*
> Author: Bjarne Stroustrup
> Publisher: Addison-Wesley
> ISBN: 0-201-12078-X

Once you and C are acquainted with some intimacy, you will want to find all about C programming as it pertains to Unix. The following two books are categorical references:

> Title: *The Unix Programming Environment*
> Authors: Brian Kernighan and Rob Pike
> Publisher: Prentice Hall
> ISBN: 0-13-937681-X

Title: *Advanced Unix Programming*
Author: Marc Rochkind
Publisher: Prentice Hall
ISBN: 0-13-011818-4

(By now, you have probably figured out that, when it comes to Unix and programming, Prentice Hall is the big cheese.)

X Window

Our X Window discussion in Chapter 5 – please don't let us hear you say "X Windows" – was really a basic introduction. If you will be using X Window with any regularity, you might want to learn a little more about it, even if only to see what all the fuss is about. There are lots of X books, but the only one even partially fit for human consumption is from O'Reilly. There are two versions: Motif and Open Look. You pay your money and you take your choice.

Title: *X Window System Users' Guide*
Authors: Valerie Quercia and Tim O'Reilly
Publisher: O'Reilly & Associates
ISBN: 0-937175-61-7

Quick Index for the **vi** Editor

Topics

vi Commands

ex Commands

Special Characters

Keys

Index